KW-220-421

Answers for Every NT Question. . .

11. Ever wondered what Service Pack 3 changes in the registry? Chapter 14, "The Windows NT Service Pack 3," tells you what to look for.

12. To change icons on the desktop for Outlook, Exchange, Internet Explorer, and others, see Chapter 11, "The Windows NT's User Interface—Changing How It Looks."

13. Don't have a tape drive and want to back up the registry? See Chapter 2, "README.1st—Preventing Disaster!"

14. Registry data is stored in a number of standard data formats. These formats are described briefly in Chapter 1, "What Is a Registry. . . and Why?" and fully in Appendix B, "Registry Data Types."

15. The six main hives in the registry are first described in Chapter 1, "What Is a Registry. . . and Why?"

16. Want to change the desktop background, even before anyone logs on? See the section "Backgrounds and Wallpapers" in Chapter 11, "The Windows NT's User Interface—Changing How It Looks."

17. Chapter 13, "Microsoft Office," shows you how to customize Microsoft Office 97.

18. Need a quick list of all the world's telephone area and country codes? Check out the section "CurrentVersion\Telephony," in Chapter 18, "Introduction to HKEY_LOCAL_MACHINE\SOFTWARE," where such a list exists already.

19. Where is that Windows NT "Easter Egg?" Check out the "Easter Egg Hunt" section in Chapter 11, "The Windows NT's User Interface—Changing How It Looks."

20. Where is the registry? Chapter 2, "README.1st—Preventing Disaster!" tells you what files make up the registry, and where they are found.

Expert Guide™ to Windows NT® 4 Registry

Peter D. Hipson

SYBEX®

San Francisco • Paris • Düsseldorf •Soest

Associate Publisher: Gary Masters
Contracts and Licensing Manager: Kristine Plachy
Acquisitions & Developmental Editor: Peter Kuhns
Editor: Valerie Perry
Project Editor: Raquel Baker
Technical Editor: John Savill
Book Designer: Kris Warrenburg
Electronic Publishing Specialist: Kate Kaminski
Production Coordinator: Susan Berge
Indexer: Ted Laux
Cover Designer: Ingalls + Associates
Cover Illustrator/Photographer: Mark Johann

SYBEX is a registered trademark of SYBEX Inc.

Expert Guide is a trademark of SYBEX Inc.

TRADEMARKS: SYBEX has attempted throughout this book to distinguish proprietary trademarks from descriptive terms by following the capitalization style used by the manufacturer.

The author and publisher have made their best efforts to prepare this book, and the content is based upon final release software whenever possible. Portions of the manuscript may be based upon pre-release versions supplied by software manufacturer(s). The author and the publisher make no representation or warranties of any kind with regard to the completeness or accuracy of the contents herein and accept no liability of any kind including but not limited to performance, merchantability, fitness for any particular purpose, or any losses or damages of any kind caused or alleged to be caused directly or indirectly from this book.

Copyright ©1999 SYBEX Inc., 1151 Marina Village Parkway, Alameda, CA 94501. World rights reserved. No part of this publication may be stored in a retrieval system, transmitted, or reproduced in any way, including but not limited to photocopy, photograph, magnetic or other record, without the prior agreement and written permission of the publisher.

Library of Congress Card Number: 98-86866
ISBN: 0-7821-1983-2

Manufactured in the United States of America

10 9 8 7 6 5 4 3 2 1

This book is dedicated to those young people who have run away from home, but had the courage either to go back or call.

For a child to run away from home is to say that the fear of the known is greater than the fear of the unknown.

ACKNOWLEDGMENTS

An Acknowledgments section is always hard to write; there are just so many people who have helped. An author's greatest fear is forgetting someone. So, I always start off by saying thanks to everyone. If I didn't list you personally, please don't hate me!

Thanks go to Peter Kuhns, of course, who served as acquisitions and developmental editor for this book. Peter's help and advice were instrumental in making this a good book. (Of course, if you don't like this book, the blame falls on me and only me!)

Thanks to the Sybex editorial staff, especially Raquel Baker and Valerie Perry. Thanks also to Susan Berge, production coordinator, for her skillful proofreading and to Kate Kaminski, electronic publishing specialist, for her expert and speedy layout skills.

John Savill (SavillTech Ltd.) served well as our technical editor. It was John's job to make sure that I told no lies, made no mistakes. John also provided some of our tips from the experts, too. John's Web site at `http://www.ntfaq.com/` is a major stopping point for users of Windows NT; check it out.

Jerold Schulman (JSI, Inc.) maintains a Web page at `http://www.jsiinc.com/reghack.htm`. He provided a lot of expert hints for this book. If you need assistance with your Windows NT installation, check out Jerold's Web pages for his tips, tricks, and registry hacks.

Special thanks to Laura Belt at Adler & Robin Books. Laura is the person who makes this a business and not a hobby.

Thanks to Barry and Marcia Press for their input on the book's contents. Barry asked for a number of things to be covered, and I've tried to cover as many as I could.

Thanks to ClubWin, ClubIE (and my team members who put up with my slow responses), and everyone at Microsoft who helped too.

Of course, I would be remiss if I didn't thank my family, especially my wife, Nang, who gave up her vacation so I could finish this book on time. Imagine sitting at home for two weeks watching me work on this book! Thanks, Nang; we'll go shopping tomorrow.

CONTENTS AT A GLANCE

TABLE OF CONTENTS

PART III   Windows System Registry Entries

INTRODUCTION

The Windows NT registry has evoked emotions from terror to mystery. Few users of Windows NT ever think of the registry as their friend. After all, think of it: The registry is the heart and soul of the Windows NT operating system. The registry is everything—it is the brain of the operating system. Damage the registry, and Windows NT quickly develops brain damage and needs major surgery.

This is it—the only book on the Windows NT registry that you will need. Now, I won't kid you; there are a few other books on the Windows registry. However, most books try to cover both the Windows NT and Windows 95/98 registries together. This approach could be useful except that sufficient differences between the two operating systems make it difficult for one book to cover both well.

Will you need another book or tool besides this book? Maybe not. But I do recommend that you get Microsoft's Windows NT Resource Kit too; it has a lot of good utilities that you will find invaluable. The Windows NT Resource Kit also has a lot of good non-registry stuff too.

This book covers the Windows NT registry from A to Z. I've covered the standard stuff, from things that most of us should know to things that are not documented at all and probably only known by a very few first-rate system administrators.

Who Is This Book For?

This book is valuable to all Windows NT users. Even Windows 95/98 users may find good information in this book, though it is not oriented toward anything other than Windows NT 4.

This book is intended primarily for:

- General users who use Windows NT at their desks and are responsible for their own computer(s). Typically, these users don't have responsibility for other users' computers, though they may help their friends out from time to time.

- System administrators who are responsible for an organization's computers (and perhaps thousands of Windows NT installations). Administrators will be presented with virtually every conceivable problem over a given period of time. Whatever can go wrong will; Murphy's Law is applied double to system administrators.

- Help desk staff members don't usually administer the system, as such, but they do support users. Help desk staff members roam throughout the organization providing help and assistance as needed. All help desk people are going to find this book very useful.

If you are a user who wants to get the most out of your Windows NT installation (either Workstation or Server), this book is a very good starting point. Think of it this way: If you are a system administrator, this book is one of the tools that you will need to manage and administer your Windows NT network. Manning the help desk? If so, having this book close at hand can save you lots of time and effort.

Overview of the Contents

This book is made up of five major sections. Part I, Registry Basics, discusses ways to avoid problems, do backups, and restore the registry, and some of the tools that are used with the registry. The first chapter is called "What Is a Registry. . . and Why?" It introduces the registry. You'll learn about the registry's major sections, called hives. This chapter also tells you about the registry's history.

TIP
    The fastest way to access the registry is to use RegEdit.exe, which comes with Windows NT. To access RegEdit.exe, simply click the Start button, then Run. Type **RegEdit** in the dialog box and press Enter. The RegEdit window will appear.

Chapter 2 is called "README.1ST—Preventing Disaster!" It jumps right into one of the most important topics in this book: how to avoid getting into trouble. Most Windows NT disasters are registry related, and they are also preventable. Registry problems often arise because we don't have a good backup of the registry, and something comes along and damages it. Once damaged, the registry can be very difficult to recover.

Chapter 3, "Anatomy of the Registry—The Blood, Gore, and Guts," is an in-depth analysis of what's in the registry. Each major hive is covered in detail. The way in which the hives relate to each other is described, along with the principles of how Windows NT manages users in the registry.

Tools, tools, and more tools. Chapter 4, "Registry Tools and Tips—Getting the Work Done," takes a close look at the registry tools that are included with Windows NT. Registry editors are covered, as well as the RDisk utility and all the registry software that is included in the Windows NT Resource Kit. This chapter is long, but well organized; you can read what is important to you and skip everything else if you so desire.

Part II, Advanced Registry Stuff, covers OLE (object linking and embedding), some history of the WIN.INI and SYSTEM.INI files, removing excess baggage from the registry, registry programming interfaces, and the Performance Monitor entries. Getting into the advanced stuff, we jump right into the issues of OLE, associations, and such. Chapter 5 is called "Associations, Linkages, and OLE—Or How Confusing Can This Get?" It tries to clear the often muddy water that swirls about the OLE registry components. A major part of the registry is OLE related, with Windows NT using OLE to manage much of the user interface.

Even though the SYSTEM.INI and WIN.INI files have not been used for some time, we still have them. Chapter 6 is called "Why, Oh Why, Are There SYSTEM.INI and WIN.INI Files?" Here we delve into the issues of why these two files are still found under Windows NT, and what makes them necessary.

If you want to get rid of that memo from your boss telling you that your project is due, you toss it into the trash can. Something in the registry that is not needed can be more difficult to get rid of. Chapter 7, "Getting Rid of the Unwanted," introduces the problem of registry clutter and describes some very useful tools to clean up this excess.

The *Titanic* sank when it struck an iceberg. You can eliminate your registry icebergs by following the advice in Chapter 8, "Recovering from Disaster or Avoiding Icebergs." Here we try to make sure that disaster doesn't strike, but sometimes it just happens. Recovery, whether from backups or from manually cleaning the registry, is vital.

My name's Peter and I'm a programmer. Ah, there I said it, and I feel much better. I felt even better after writing Chapter 9, "Programming and the Registry—A Developer's Paradise?" This is where the programming interface to the registry is unveiled. Examples in C/C++ and a lot of information about Microsoft's MFC registry interface come to light in this chapter.

The Windows NT Performance Monitor allows analysis of the system's performance and the development of performance enhancement strategies. In Chapter 10, "The Performance Monitor Meets the Registry," we are able to understand how the Windows NT Performance Monitor interacts with the registry and how we can add performance monitoring technologies to our own applications.

Part III, Windows System Registry Entries, discusses the UI (user interface), networking, and internal Windows NT entries. What we see as users is all stored in the registry. Chapter 11, "The Windows NT User Interface—Changing How It Looks," delves into the various registry entries that control the look and feel of Windows NT. This chapter covers both the graphical desktop and the Windows command windows.

Under the hood of Windows NT are entries in the registry for both networking and other internal Windows NT components. Chapter 12, "Networking and Registry System Entries," digs into these less visible entries in the registry and explains them to you.

Part IV, More Common Registry Entries, covers the entries that are common to non-Windows NT items, such as Microsoft Office. Chapter 13, "Microsoft Office," covers changes that Microsoft Office has made to the registry. Sometimes Microsoft Office components are installed and then removed. Sadly, not all registry entries for these products are removed. Also, how do we create a configuration so those new users of Microsoft Office will get a predefined configuration? Care to program the registry using Visual Basic for Applications? It's easy, really. Check this chapter for the answers to these questions.

What would Windows NT be without the ever-present Service Packs? A *Service Pack* is a series of fixes and improvements to Windows NT that Microsoft releases from time to time. Sometimes, a Service Pack fixes one problem only to introduce a new one. Chapter 14, "The Windows NT Service Pack 3," covers the changes that Windows NT Service Pack 3 makes to the registry. Hopefully, this chapter will help you debug problems that the Service Pack might introduce.

Part V, The Registry Reference, is a reference to many of the registry entries arranged by hive. Program associations, OLE associations, and file type management are all part of HKEY_CLASSES_ROOT. Chapter 15, "Introduction to HKEY_CLASSES_ROOT," covers this hive's contents.

User information that is stored in HKEY_USERS and used in HKEY_CURRENT_USER is the subject of Chapter 16, "Introduction to HKEY_CURRENT_USER and HKEY_USERS." Windows NT keeps only the currently logged on user and the .DEFAULT user in HKEY_USERS; other users are saved in HKEY_LOCAL_MACHINE's SAM (Security Account Manager) sections.

HKEY_LOCAL_MACHINE is the hive that controls the system itself. This topic is so large that three chapters are dedicated to it. Chapter 17, "Introduction to HKEY_LOCAL_MACHINE," covers the major parts of HKEY_LOCAL_MACHINE. Information about installed software is found in Chapter 18, "Introduction to HKEY_LOCAL_MACHINE\SOFTWARE." Virtually every installed application or component is found in HKEY_LOCAL_MACHINE\Software. The system configuration is covered in Chapter 19, "Introduction to HKEY_LOCAL_MACHINE\SYSTEM and HKEY_CURRENT_CONFIG." System entries are critical to the health and welfare of Windows NT.

Typesetting Conventions

This book is typeset so that it is readable. Otherwise the pages would all be blank.

OK, seriously. This book uses various conventions to present information. Notes, Tips, and Warnings, shown here, appear throughout the text in order to call attention to special details.

NOTE   This is a note. Notes contain additional comments and information related to the discussion.

TIP   This is a tip. Tips highlight important information that you need to know when working with the registry.

WARNING   This is a warning. Warnings call attention to trouble spots and things to watch out for. Speaking of which, have you backed up your registry lately?

This book also takes advantage of different font styles. **Bold font** in the text indicates something that the user types. A `monospaced font` is used for program strings, entries, commands, and URLs.

Sybex Technical Support

If you have questions or comments for this book or other Sybex books, you can contact Sybex directly. The following contact information for Sybex is listed in order of preference from the most preferred method to contact Sybex (e-mail) to the least preferred method (snail mail).

For the Fastest Reply

E-mail us or visit the Sybex Web site! You can contact Sybex through the Web by visiting `http://www.sybex.com` and clicking Support. You may find the answer you're looking for on this site in the FAQ (Frequently Asked Questions) file. Check there too.

When you reach the support page, click `Support@sybex.com` to send Sybex an e-mail. You can also e-mail Sybex directly at `support@sybex.com`.

Make sure you include the following information in your e-mail:

> **Name**—The complete title of the book in question. For this book, it is *Expert Guide to Windows NT 4 Registry*.
>
> **ISBN number**—The ISBN that appears on the back cover of the book. This number appears at the bottom-right corner on the back cover and looks like this:
>
> 0-7821-1983-2
>
> **Printing**—The printing of the book. You can find this near the front of the book at the bottom of the copyright page. You should see a line of numbers as in the following:
>
> 10 9 8 7 6 5 4 3 2

For a Fast Reply

Call Sybex Tech Support and leave a message. Sybex guarantees they will call you back within 24 hours, excluding weekends and holidays.

Tech support can be reached at (510) 523-8233 ext. 563.

After you dial the extension, press 1 to leave a message. Sybex will call you back within 24 hours with a reply. Make sure you leave a phone number where you can be reached!

Other Ways To Reach Sybex

The slowest way to contact Sybex is through the mail. If you do not have access to the Net or a telephone, write Sybex a small note and send it to the following address:

SYBEX Inc.
Attention: Technical Support
1151 Marina Village Parkway
Alameda, CA 94501

Again, it's important that you include all the following information to expedite a reply:

Name—The complete title of the book in question.

ISBN number—The ISBN that appears on the back cover of the book. This number appears at the bottom right corner on the back cover and looks like this

0-7821-1983-2

Printing—The printing of the book. You can find this near the front of the book at the bottom of the copyright page. You should see a line of numbers as in the following:

10 9 8 7 6 5 4 3 2

Tell us what the lowest number is in the line of numbers. This is the printing of the book. The example here indicates that the book is the second printing.

NOTE   The ISBN number and printing are very important for technical support because it indicates the edition and reprint you have in your hands. Many changes occur between printings and editions. Don't forget to include this information!

Page number or file name—Include the page number where you have a problem or, if the problem is with the CD-ROM, please include the specific file name.

> **NOTE**   If you are having a problem with the CD for a book, make sure you read the README.TXT file on the CD before you contact Sybex. Chances are good that Sybex found a solution for any problems you might be having and put the information in the README.TXT file. You can find this file in the root directory of the CD.

PC details—Include the following information:

- Name of your PC (the manufacturer)
- Operating system being used
- The software you have installed that relates to the book (indicate the exact version number)
- Whether your machine has any unique characteristics

Your contact information—Please type your snail mail address or phone number in the letter you're sending.

Sybex technical support will try to answer your question quickly and accurately.

PART I

Registry Basics

CHAPTER

ONE

What Is a Registry...and Why?

- Organization

- How the registry is used

- Keys and hives

- Hints and kinks from the experts

Any sufficiently advanced technology is indistinguishable from magic.

Arthur C. Clarke

Some users of Windows NT know exactly what the registry is: A system designed to cause users and administrators to loose their hair. I know this is true because I can no longer feel the wind ruffling through my hair anymore. Oh, I feel the wind, I just don't feel the hair.

The registry, like so many things in Windows, was evolutionary. The registry started as a pair of flat text files, called WIN.INI and SYSTEM.INI. These two files live on even today in the latest copies of Windows NT.

The first registry to appear in Windows was created to solve two problems: performance (retrieving information from the original flat INI files was cumbersome) and maintenance (the flat INI files were organizationally impaired!)

Today, these INI files contain only a few entries used by legacy 16-bit applications. They are of no importance to us and we ignore them. Windows NT's registry is the most important system because it contains the heart and soul of Windows NT. Without the registry, Windows NT would be nothing more than a collection of programs, unable to perform even the basic tasks that we expect from an operating system.

Every bit of configuration information that Windows NT has is crammed into the registry. Information about the system's hardware, preferences, security, users—everything that can be set is set in the registry.

The registry has a limit in size, too. It's not infinitely large! A message telling you that you are low on registry quota indicates that the registry has grown too large for the current size allocation. Unless you change it, the registry size is set to 25 percent of the paged pool size. For most computers, the paged pool size is approximately equal to the amount of installed RAM, up to a maximum of 192MB.

The registry can be set to 80 percent of the paged pool size (80 percent of 192MB is just under 154MB, though good sense says to round down to 150MB).

By default, Windows NT automatically computes the maximum registry size. Windows NT will adjust this size based on the currently installed RAM. There are several registry entries affecting registry size, though most users will find that the defaults are acceptable for their use.

NOTE Microsoft has limited the size of any object that is stored in a registry data key to 1MB. This limit is basically only meaningful for REG_BINARY objects because strings and such are unlikely to become this large. If you find that you must store more than 1MB in a registry object, it will be necessary to store the information in a file and store a pointer to the file in the registry. Without this limitation, the registry could easily grow to be the largest file on your system.

Organization

The registry is organized into sections. Sections are called *hives*, which are analogous to directories on your hard drive. Inside a hive you may find both sub-hives (again, analogous to sub-directories on your hard disk) and data keys (analogous to files on your hard drive).

Both the Windows NT operating system and applications store data in the registry along with Windows NT. This is both good and bad! This is good because the registry makes an efficient, common storage location. Here's the bad part: as more and more applications and systems store information in the registry, it grows larger, and larger, and larger.

It is most unusual for the registry to get smaller—I'm unaware of any application that does a complete job of cleaning up all of its own registry entries when the application is uninstalled. Many applications leave tons of stuff in the registry when they are uninstalled, and not many applications clean up unused entries as a routine process. The end result is that the registry will grow, like Jack's magic beanstalk, as time goes on.

Hives and Sub-Hives

There are six main hives in the Windows NT registry:

- HKEY_CLASSES_ROOT
- HKEY_CURRENT_USER
- HKEY_LOCAL_MACHINE

- HKEY_USERS

- HKEY_CURRENT_CONFIG

- HKEY_DYN_DATA

Each main hive begins with the letters HKEY_. HKEY is an abbreviation for Hive Key, though the significance of this is not terribly important in understanding the registry. The H also signifies that the name is a handle for a program to interface with the registry. These handles are defined in the file winreg.h, included with the Windows NT SDK (Software Development Kit).

The registry contains duplication. For example, everything in HKEY_CURRENT_USER is actually also contained in the hive HKEY_USERS.

Microsoft found a need to make some parts of the registry appear to be in two places at one time. Microsoft didn't want to copy these sections because it could have created problems with keeping each section current. Instead, they wanted to create an *alias*, or another name, for some registry components. These aliases are created solely by Windows NT. You, as a user, can't create an alias no matter how hard you try!

The most common alias is the registry HKEY_CURRENT_USER. It is an alias to either the .DEFAULT user in HKEY_USERS, or the current user in HKEY_USERS. If you take a quick peek at HKEY_USERS, you will see two hives there: one is named .DEFAULT and the other is named with a long string of numbers and letters. These numbers and letters are SIDs (Security Identifiers). Windows NT uses them to identify users. We'll talk about SIDs in a later chapter to clear up what they are and how they are used.

There are also other aliases in the registry. For example, the registry hive HKEY_LOCAL_MACHINE\SYSTEM\CurrentControlSet is an alias to one of the other control sets—ControlSet001, ControlSet002, or sometimes ControlSet003. Again, this is that same magic; only one registry hive is there, it just has two names. Remember, in modifying a specific registry key or hive, don't be surprised when another registry key or hive seems to magically change also!

Data Keys

A data key may contain one, or in some instances, more than one data item. The only data key that contains more than one item is the REG_MULTI_SZ, which may contain zero, one, or more strings.

Data types for data keys include:

- REG_BINARY
- REG_DWORD
- REG_DWORD_BIG_ENDIAN
- REG_DWORD_LITTLE_ENDIAN
- REG_EXPAND_SZ
- REG_FULL_RESOURCE_DESCRIPTOR
- REG_LINK
- REG_MULTI_SZ
- REG_NONE
- REG_RESOURCE_LIST
- REG_RESOURCE_REQUIREMENTS_LIST
- REG_SZ
- REG_UNKNOWN

Applications may access each of these data types. Additionally, some applications store data in formats that only they understand. Actually, there is a provision in the registry that allows the storing application to assign a specific type to the registry data. Any application or component that doesn't understand the format would simply treat the data as a REG_UNKNOWN type and read the data as binary.

NOTE   Oops, did I say something special? Yes! Remember that applications also store data in the registry.

How the Registry Is Used

How does Windows NT use the registry? When is the registry first opened and used?

Every component of Windows NT uses the registry, without exception. There is a set of APIs (Application Program Interfaces) used to allow both Windows NT and other applications to access registry information easily and quickly.

Remember, the registry is a tree-based hierarchical system that offers quick access to data stored in almost any format. Actually, the registry is a rather flexible database.

Windows NT starts to use the registry at the very beginning stages of system boot-up. The Windows NT boot process is based on which file format is installed, though the important parts are identical in either case. The unimportant parts are the loading of the specific drivers to read the NTFS file system.

> **NOTE**   Throughout this book, unless I say otherwise, I refer to Windows NT installed on an Intel *x*86 platform. There are differences in the boot process on RISC-based systems (such as the Digital Alpha system), though these differences are not terribly significant when considering how the registry is used.

The Windows NT boot process consists of the following steps:

1. The system is powered up, the video is initialized, and the hardware self-tests are performed. The BIOS performs these tests, which are called POSTs (Power On Self Tests). Usually, the memory test is the most visible one. Its progress is shown on most computer screens.

2. After running POST, the system will initialize each adapter. If the adapter has its own built-in BIOS (Basic Input/Output System), the adapter's BIOS will be called to perform its own initialization. Some adapters, such as Adaptec's SCSI adapters, will display both messages and allow interaction by the user. Some adapters that don't have a BIOS won't get initialized until Windows NT loads their drivers much later in the boot-up process.

3. After all adapters that have a BIOS have been initialized, the system boot loader reads in the sector located at the very beginning of the first bootable disk drive and passes command to this code. This sector is called the *boot sector*, or the MBR (Master Boot Record), and is written by the operating system when the operating system is installed.

4. The code in the MBR then loads the file called NTLDR. (This file has no extension, though it is an executable file.) Once loaded, the MBR passes control to the code in NTLDR. When NTLDR is initialized, it displays on the

screen the message, "Windows NT Portable Boot Loader." Since our computers are so fast today, we never actually see this message—the screen is almost immediately cleared when NTLDR re-initializes the video system.

5. NTLDR then switches into 32-bit mode (remember an Intel *x*86 processor always boots into 16-bit real mode). It then loads a special copy of the necessary file system I/O files and reads in the file BOOT.INI.

6. The file BOOT.INI has information about each operating system that can be loaded. Remember, Windows NT supports multi-boot configurations. It is trivial to create a Windows NT installation that can boot both Windows NT and Windows 95/98, or even boot two different copies of Windows NT. NTLDR then processes the BOOT.INI file, displaying boot information to allow the user to select which operating system will be loaded. At this point, let's assume that Windows NT will be loaded.

7. When the user selects Windows NT to be loaded, NTLDR will load the file NTDETECT.COM. This program then collects information about the currently installed hardware and saves this information for the registry. Most of this information is stored in the HKEY_LOCAL_MACHINE hive.

8. Once NTDETECT has detected the hardware, control is passed back to NTLDR and the boot process continues. At this point, the registry has been substantially updated with the current hardware configuration and stored in HKEY_LOCAL_MACHINE\HARDWARE.

9. The prompt to select the configuration is then presented. This prompt, "Press spacebar now to invoke Hardware Profile/Last Known Good menu," allows the user to force Windows NT to use a specific configuration as stored in the registry hive HKEY_LOCAL_MACHINE.

10. Following the detection of NTDETECT, NTLDR will load and initialize the Windows NT kernel, load the services, and then start Windows.

11. When the kernel is loaded, the HAL (Hardware Abstraction Layer) is also loaded. (The HAL is used to manage hardware services.) Next, the registry system hive HKEY_LOCAL_MACHINE\SYSTEM is loaded into memory. Windows NT will scan the registry for all drivers with a start value of zero. This includes those drivers that should be loaded and initialized at boot time.

12. The user can notice the beginning of the next stage, kernel initialization. The screen will switch to a blue background and you will see a message about the Windows NT build number and the number of system processors.

Again, at this stage the system scans the registry and finds all drivers that must be started at the kernel initialization stage.

13.   From this point, Windows NT starts various components and systems. Each component and system reads the registry and performs various tasks and functions. The final stage is to start the program that manages the user logon, WinLogon. WinLogon allows the user to log on and use Windows NT.

Registry information comes from a number of sources:

- From installing Windows NT

- From booting Windows NT

- From applications, systems, and user interaction

Once Windows NT is booted, both the operating system and applications use the registry. The registry is dynamic, but usage of the registry may be dynamic or static. That is, some registry items are read one time and never reread until the system is restarted. Other items are reread every time they are referenced. There is no fixed rule as to what is reread each time it is needed and what is not, but to be on the safe side use this rule:

- Application-related data is probably read when the application starts. If changing application-based data, restart the application. In fact, this is the best path to follow: Do not change application-based data while the application is running.

- User interface data is sometimes dynamic, sometimes static. With user interface data, changing the data and waiting to see the results of the change is the way to go. If the change doesn't appear, try logging on again.

- System data is usually either static or otherwise buffered. Many system-related registry changes won't become effective until the system is restarted. Some system data is rewritten, precluding changes by users. Many of the items in HKEY_LOCAL_MACHINE may be reset at system boot time, especially those items that are hardware related.

Keys and Hives

The registry is comprised of hives, keys, sub-keys, values, and data keys. Well, actually, depending on the source, you may be faced with hives and data keys; or keys and items; or data keys; or who knows what else.

There is some indication that Microsoft wants to drop the original term for a registry section—the hive—and replace this term with the word, "key." In the Windows NT Resource Kit, Microsoft makes the following definition:

> The Registry is divided into parts called *hives*. A hive is a discrete body of keys, sub-keys, and values rooted at the top of the Registry hierarchy. Hives are distinguished from other groups of keys in that they are permanent components of the Registry; they are not created dynamically when the system starts and deleted when it stops. Thus, HKEY_LOCAL_MACHINE\ Hardware, which is built dynamically by the Hardware Recognizer when Windows NT starts, is not a hive.

This definition is absolute and states exactly what is a hive and what is not. However, in the real world, no one follows this exact definition. Many authors (such as myself) call holders of information a "hive" (or "sub-hive") and we call data objects "keys." Others never refer to hives at all, calling all holders "keys," or "sub-keys," and referring to data objects as "values."

Virtually every definition leaves something to be desired. To call the thing that holds data a "value" makes it awkward to refer to the contents. Consider these examples:

The value named asdf contains the value 1234.

The data value asdf contains data with a value of 1234.

The following example is much more readable:

The data key named asdf contains the value 1234.

Is there a need to distinguish between what Microsoft calls a hive (a top-level, permanent, registry component) and what Microsoft calls a key? When does a hive become a key, and is this important? I can't think of any context in which anything is gained by making this distinction. Referring to these holders as hives certainly frees up the term "key" to be used elsewhere!

Table 1.1 lists the terms used for both file systems (the disk drive) and the registry.

TABLE 1.1:   Registry Terminology Explained

Context	Collections	Sub-collections	Objects
Disks	Directories	Sub-directories	Files
Older registry terminology	Hives	Sub-hives	Data keys
Newer registry terminology	Keys	Sub-keys	ProgramObject

Hints and Kinks from the Experts

In each chapter we'll present a few hints and kinks from the experts. Our experts are a number of people who have a lot of experience in working with the registry. They have learned from their experiences and the experiences of others.

For example, every expert will tell you the same thing: the minute you start tinkering with the registry, you will create a mess that is so bad that only a clean reinstall (or restoration from backup) will fix it. To restore the backup, you would boot from the installation disks and choose repair, insert the ERD, and restore the registry—not restore a full backup. If you did restore a full backup, it would only work if the option Backup Local Registry were selected during the backup. That is the way it was with me the first time I had a serious registry problem—I'd change something and things would just get worse.

Some registry problems cannot be "hacked," or fixed manually. The only fix for these problems is to either reinstall or restore the system. However, this type of situation is unusual. My experience has been that these problems happen only when hardware (like the registry's drive) fails or an incredibly errant program totally trashes the registry. Neither of these happens very often at all.

Most users make minor tweaks or fixes in the registry. Most of the time, things go OK. Sometimes things go awry. Through it all, we toast the registry, and then it's back to the proverbial drawing board. Such is life.

CHAPTER

TWO

2

README.1ST— Preventing Disaster!

- Problems, problems, problems, or why is this so hard?

- Are two copies better than one?

- Backup techniques

- Restoring the registry

- Other backup and restore programs

- Hints and kinks from the experts

Preventing disaster is an important thing to do. No one wants a system failure, or to have to reinstall Windows NT.

You are reading this chapter for your own particular reason. Perhaps, as I am recommending, you are here because you want to prevent a disaster by making sure that you do everything possible to prevent problems with your Windows NT installation. Or, maybe you really, really want to recover from an existing disaster. If you are recovering from a problem, you may want to skip to the section later in this chapter titled "Restoring the Registry." For those of you who never do anything wrong, read on.

The registry has always been the one part of Windows that virtually every user has neither understood nor trusted. Just when things go well, the registry gets corrupted and it is time to reinstall everything.

The Windows NT operating system is quite robust. However, many things can cause problems. For example, a hard drive failure (even an innocuous small soft error on the system drive in the registry files), a controller failure, or a more complex memory bit that sometimes doesn't set correctly all can cause many problems with Windows NT and the registry.

WARNING   Windows NT is robust, but our hardware is not. Most Pentium systems do not have memory parity. Though earlier PC systems used memory parity, this feature disappeared quietly a few years back when memory prices skyrocketed and there was a serious effort to keep computer prices to a minimum. Most of the newest computers now do support parity for their memory; many of the systems still in use do not, and as a result routine memory errors won't be detected until it is much too late.

In this chapter we'll cover a number of potential problem areas:

Backup—You'll learn a number of ways to back up that pesky registry.

Restoration—What's difficult even under the best of conditions will be made simpler after you've perused these pages.

Recovery techniques—You'll discover ways to recover from a registry failure and retain as much of the existing installation of Windows NT as possible.

Hints and kinks from the experts—This is stuff from the Windows NT Resource Kit and a few ideas from some experts on how to keep things going well.

Problems, Problems, Problems, or Why Is This So Hard?

One of the biggest problems with the registry is Windows uses it constantly. The entire process of backing up and restoring the operating system is much more difficult because Windows keeps the registry files open as a restore is being done.

There are several ways to solve this problem. One solution is to use the Windows supplied tape backup program. Another would be to use an after-market backup program (which might back up to media other than tape, such as Zip disks). These backup programs would have to contain the code necessary to do registry backups and restores.

However, these techniques may not work well under your circumstances. You may already have had a registry failure and there may be no registry backup to rely on for recovery. Backing up and recovering the registry without a tape backup can be excruciatingly difficult using the Windows NT backup program.

Using the ERD (emergency repair diskette) is easy, but you cannot simply stick in a diskette, type restore registry, and expect it to work. In fact, the process of using the ERD to restore the registry requires the Windows NT installation program. It's not that bad; you don't have to reinstall Windows, but the installation program will restore the registry from the ERD, if necessary.

The menu that is presented when you boot up Windows NT also allows a user to restore parts of the registry based on copies of the registry saved from previous sessions.

NOTE   Always, always make sure that you back up the registry whenever you install new software or hardware, or you remove anything from your computer. If you do not back up the registry and you restore a previous copy from an old backup, the system will not work as expected!

Where Exactly *Is* the Registry?

One of the first questions we are asked is, where is the registry located? Sometimes the answer seems to involve magic because the standard registry editors don't tell us where the registry is; they simply load it automatically. However, many times we need to know where to find the registry files. This task isn't difficult; the registry's files are in the directory %SystemRoot%\System32\config.

Environment Variables

Every Windows NT installation automatically has some shortcut variables installed that are accessible to the user and the system. These variables are called *environment variables*. One environment variable, %SystemRoot%, contains the drive, path, and directory name for the directory that Windows NT was installed in.

Using these environment variables makes it easy to write batch files and to otherwise locate components of your current Windows NT installation. For example, you might type at a command prompt:

CD %SystemRoot%

This command would then change to the directory that Windows NT was installed in.

Using the environment variables can be very useful when writing software that must be run on a number of different Windows NT installations, especially where these installations are made to different drives or directories.

The %SystemRoot%\System32\config directory includes the following set of files:

SAM.*—The SAM (Security Account Manager) registry file

default.*—The default registry file

SECURITY.*—The security registry file

system.*—The system registry file

software.*—The application software registry file

In the registry, the most important files are those with no extension—these are the current registry files. There will also be a file called SYSTEM.ALT. This file is a duplicate of the 'system.' registry file.

The files in %SystemRoot%\System32\config directory that have extensions of LOG or SAV contain a history that may be viewed with the Event Viewer program. For example, files with the extension SAV were saved using the last known good booting process. Files with the extension of LOG are records of changes made to the registry, made when registry auditing is turned on.

Though both the LOG and the SAV files are not strictly necessary to having a working Windows NT installation, it is best to consider each of these files as a member of a complete set.

Also, be careful not to replace one file in the registry without replacing all the others; it is simply too easy to get one file out of sync with the remaining registry files and this would spell disaster.

Side Trip

Restoring a copy of Windows NT from a backup can be a difficult process. First, most backup programs require Windows NT to run. Without a working copy of Windows NT, you can't run the backup and restore programs. This makes it necessary to install a new copy of Windows NT to be able to run the restore program. This new copy of Windows NT is used to restore the original Windows NT system from the backup. Many times, users will reformat the drive, reinstall Windows NT into the same directory that the original Windows NT installation was made to, and restore on top of this new installation. There may be nothing wrong with doing this, except there can be a problem. If you installed any Windows NT service packs on your original installation, these service packs must also be installed on the new Windows NT installation being used to run the restoration program. Here's what happens if you don't install the service packs. When Windows NT restores system files from the original installation (with the service pack) on top of the new files (without the service pack), the files will be out of version sync with the existing operating system files and the registry. This will usually cause the restore to crash without much of a warning as to what happened.

To perform a full restore of Windows NT (and everything else on the drive) do the following:

1. Format the drive. Remember that you're doing a full restore here and nothing that was on the drive is considered valuable at this point.

2. Install Windows NT, using your original distribution CD-ROM.

3. Install the service packs that were installed with the version of Windows NT that is being restored. Remember that the service packs are cumulative so you need only reinstall the last service pack. For example, if service pack 3 was installed, it will not be necessary to install service packs 1 and 2. You only need to reinstall service pack 3.

4. Reinstall your backup/restore program and begin your restoration process.

Backup Copies

The registry is the heart and soul of the Windows NT operating system. It contains information critical to both the operation and security of Windows NT. There are many ways that someone could use your backup registry files to breach your system's security, perhaps costing you money or (gasp!) your job.

Danger, Will Robinson, Danger!

Throughout this chapter and this book we talk about backing up the registry, saving the registry to diskettes, other drives, and tapes. That's all well and good. However, you must remember that the registry contains sensitive information, especially if it is for a Windows NT Server.

Be absolutely sure you maintain the highest levels of security for any copies of the registry that you make. If saved to external media (diskettes, tapes, or Zip drives, for example) make sure these copies are securely locked up. Why? Someone could, with little effort, completely subvert system security and then use the backup copies of the registry to hide their actions.

I recommend a quality fireproof safe be used for storage or a strong box. Me, I use a fireproof, locked strong box inside a Federal Government rated Mosler safe and I don't think I'm being too overly protective, either.

Are Two Copies Better Than One?

Generally, two of anything is better than one. It's easier to ride a bicycle than a unicycle. However, it is even easier to drive a car you don't even have to keep balance. Where the registry is concerned, *at least* two copies of it is a good idea. However, I'd recommend that you keep at least four according to these guidelines:

- The special copy created by the RDisk utility, which is stored in the Windows NT directory %SystemRoot%\Repair. This copy of the registry can only be used by the Windows NT setup program to repair an existing copy of Windows NT.

- The copy created by the RDisk utility, which is stored on the Windows NT ERD. Again, this copy of the registry can only be used by the Windows NT setup program to repair an existing copy of Windows NT.

- One (or more) backup copies, created using a backup technique on a media that is compatible with the backup and restore program of choice. (See below for some backup methods to use.)

- A copy of the registry files contained in %SystemRoot%\System32\config stored on separate media, such as a different drive, diskettes, a Zip drive, or some other easily accessible, writable media. Avoid media requiring special drivers and such because these drivers may not work when you need to restore that pesky registry. This copy may only be made by dual-booting into another copy of Windows NT (or Windows 95/98 if the drive is FAT compatible).

As I mentioned above, be absolutely sure you keep these copies secure. Lock 'em up, stash 'em away. Oh, and by the way, that lock on your desk drawer is not good enough; use a fireproof safe or a good strong box.

Backup Techniques

Windows NT supports two different file systems. The first file system, called FAT (File Allocation Table), is identical to the file system used with both DOS and Windows 95/98. The FAT file system is not secure and offers no resistance to hackers and others who want to access files improperly.

NOTE　There are several flavors of FAT file systems: FAT-12, FAT-16, and FAT-32. Windows NT does not support FAT-32 except in a very limited, read-only manner. You cannot install Windows NT onto a FAT-32 drive. FAT-12 is antiquated and is unlikely to be found on Windows NT systems.

The second file system, NTFS (NT File System), is unique to Windows NT. Though it is possible to read a NTFS drive from DOS or Windows 95 using shareware utilities, it is generally not possible to write to an NTFS drive unless you are using the Windows NT operating system. However, System Internals (see their Internet site at `http://www.sysinternals.com.`) has two utilities that allow writing to an NTFS volume.

Back Up to Tape

The Windows NT backup program, NTBackup, is one of a whole slew of compatible backup programs that allow backing up the system registry to tape. The process is straightforward and can be done as part of a regular backup cycle, or whenever desired. Just check the Backup Local Registry option to back up using NTBackup.

Using NTBackup is simple if you are familiar with creating and restoring tape backups. However, there are a few difficulties in using tape backups of the registry.

First, to keep the registry backup easily accessible, it would be wise to place the registry backup on its own tape. If tapes are inexpensive this is a viable practice, but if you are paying an arm and a leg for tape media, this can be costly because each registry backup is relatively small.

Second, the registry backups must be kept secure; perhaps more secure than standard backups. Everyone's situation is different, just realize that unrestricted access to the registry could allow someone to have unrestricted, unaudited access to everything else as well.

Finally, tape backups are sometimes slow. Stick the tape in the drive and the first thing that happens is that the tape gets rewound (to re-tension it). This process alone can take some time—time that is not available when you are working on getting a server up and running.

Backup Using Copy or Xcopy

It is not possible to copy the registry while Windows NT is using it. Period. Therefore, to back up using either copy or xcopy, it is necessary to shut down Windows NT and start another operating system, such as DOS, Windows 95/98, or a second copy of Windows NT.

Which operating system is started depends on which file system is being used on the computer. If the file system is FAT, this means it is compatible with DOS or Windows 95/98. If the file system is NTFS, it is only compatible with a second copy of Windows NT.

Backing Up the FAT File System

Those Windows NT users who were using the FAT file system are able to simply boot a DOS diskette formatted with the /sys option. This will allow the user to read from and write to the hard drive quite easily.

To create a bootable disk, simply use the Windows 95/98 or DOS FORMAT command with the /sys system option. Then copy the xcopy command's files to the diskette, too. This disk may then be booted in the Windows NT computer allowing unrestricted accesses to all FAT drives that are installed on that computer.

When using Zip drives it may be necessary to add DOS drivers for these drives to your boot diskette.

NOTE If the system is already configured for dual booting, it is only necessary to boot a diskette to get into DOS. It probably won't matter which alternate OS is installed (DOS, Windows 95/98, or even Windows NT); all will work fine for the purpose of backing up the registry. There is no need for boot diskettes in this situation.

After booting into DOS it is a simple task to copy the registry files to a safe location, such as another hard drive or a set of diskettes (the registry won't fit on a single diskette).

NTFS

Users with NTFS are presented with a much more difficult problem. The NTFS file system is a secure file system that may not be easily accessed using other operating systems such as DOS or Windows 95/98.

Files on an NTFS drive may only be written by Windows NT and not by other operating systems. Sure, there are utilities that allow NTFS to be accessed from Windows 95/98. However, the mode of access is read-only; there is no chance of a restore that way.

To be able to access the registry files on an NTFS drive, it is necessary to install a second copy of Windows NT. Actually, this is not major problem because everyone should have at least two installations of Windows NT. Windows NT supports multiple book configurations quite effectively. To create a multiple boot installation of Windows NT, simply follow these steps:

1. Ensure that you have sufficient space on your hard drive for a second copy of Windows NT. Your second copy of Windows NT will only need to be the basic operating system—only a minimal amount of hard disk space will be required. Figure 100 to 150MB of hard disk space for this installation, depending on how much additional software and features you install.

2. Using the Windows NT installation boot diskettes, begin your installation. When prompted for a destination, simply specify a new directory. If you are far sighted enough, and are doing this before disaster has struck, you can install directly from the Windows NT distribution CD without using the boot diskettes. To do so, run the program WINNT32 /b to begin the installation process.

WARNING   Don't install to the same directory that your current working installation of Windows NT is installed into. That won't create a second copy of Windows NT.

---

3. The Windows NT setup program will configure the Boot Manager (creating new entries in the boot menu) so that you are able to choose which copy of Windows NT you want to boot.

Customizing the Boot Menu

Once you install a second copy of Windows NT, your boot menu will list both copies of Windows NT. This can be confusing since the descriptions will be almost identical.

There is a solution: the boot menu may be customized. The boot drive's root directory contains a file called BOOT.INI. This file includes the boot options for each copy of Windows NT that is installed. Note: Before you can edit BOOT.INI you need to remove the system, read-only, and hidden attributes using the command prompt command `c:\> attrib c:\boot.ini -r -s -h`. Don't forget to restore these attributes afterwards.

Included in this information is a text string that describes the installation:

```
[boot loader]
timeout=30
default=multi(0)disk(0)rdisk(0)partition(1)\WINNT40
[operating systems]
multi(0)disk(0)rdisk(0)partition(1)\WINNT40="Windows NT Server
4.00 DARK_STAR"
multi(0)disk(0)rdisk(0)partition(1)\WINNTBU="Windows NT Server
Version 4.00"
multi(0)disk(0)rdisk(0)partition(1)\WINNTBU="Windows NT Server
Version 4.00 [VGA mode]" /basevideo /sos
multi(0)disk(0)rdisk(0)partition(1)\WINNT40="Windows NT Server
4.00 DARK_STAR [VGA mode]" /basevideo /sos
```

Continued on next page

You may modify anything in the quoted strings, such as "Windows NT Server 4.0. DARK_STAR" in the above example. A suggestion is to call your backup installation of Windows NT just that—"Windows NT B/U." For example:

```
multi(0)disk(0)rdisk(0)partition(1)\WINNTBU="Windows NT Server
Registry B/U"
multi(0)disk(0)rdisk(0)partition(1)\WINNTBU="Windows NT Server
Registry B/U [VGA mode]" /basevideo /sos
```

Don't forget to use the Control Panel's System applet to change the default boot to the version of Windows NT that normally will be booted by default. After Windows NT is reinstalled, the latest installation is made the default operating system by the installation (setup) program.

To COPY or to XCOPY, That Is the Question

Users of FAT file systems can access the registry with a DOS boot disk, and users of both FAT or NTFS may gain access with a second copy of Windows NT as described above. Once a method to access the registry has been established it is a simple task to completely back up the registry.

Typically, I'll use a command window (a 'DOS box," or command prompt) because I use NTFS and have a second backup copy of Windows NT installed. I'll show how I back up the registry on my Windows NT Server.

Using the MD (make directory) or MKDIR command, I create a new directory called \RegBU on another drive (my system has four hard drives).

```
md d:\configbu
xcopy C:\winnt\system32\config\*.* D:\configbu\*.* /s
```

I then use the copy command (or xcopy) to copy the registry files in C:\winnt40\ system32\config directory to the RegBU directory. The directory winnt40 is where my main copy of Windows NT is installed.

This example would save a backup to a sub-directory on the D: drive. This is a good solution if the system (C:) drive becomes unreadable because the backup copy will still be accessible. Other alternatives include backing up to a removable (Zip) drive or a network drive on a different computer.

If things are going well, I also use PKZIP to back up the registry files to a set of diskettes. In my system, the files in my config directory are just over 10MB in size. Am I typical? No. I only have a few users in my user database, so my registry is smaller. PKZIP is able to compress the files down to only two diskettes, which is a reasonable number. Of course, if I used a Zip drive, I could put these files on a single cartridge, but that might be a waste of space.

Once you've copied your registry files to a safe location, simply remove the boot diskette (if used) and reboot the computer. This will give you a copy of the registry that is restorable later using an almost identical technique: boot to DOS and restore the files.

TIP

What the heck is a safe location? A safe location typically would be to another drive, a Zip drive, or perhaps even diskettes. Diskettes present a small problem in that the registry files are typically going to be a total of 10 to 20MB in size. Using a utility such as PKZIP will allow you to write these large files to a number of diskettes while at the same time compressing them, reducing the number of diskettes required to a minimum.

RDisk

RDisk is a utility that is part of Windows NT. It's used to create repair files for the system registry and to create an ERD (emergency repair diskette). Using RDisk is simple because it is run with a basic dialog interface, as shown below.

WARNING

RDisk only gives a partial backup of the system registry by default. This backup only includes the Administrator and Guest accounts from the user accounts database. Other account information contained in the SAM and Security hives, and possibly other registry information will be lost if the copy saved by RDisk is used to repair the system registry. This applies to the copy saved by RDisk to a diskette, or to the repair directory. Arrgggg! To prevent this, you would need to use RDisk with the /S or /S- options.

RDisk has been a part of Windows NT since version 3.5. This utility has two options that must be entered on the command line. Though RDisk has a simple user interface, neither of these options may be entered after RDisk has started.

The /S option causes RDisk to skip the initial user interface dialog box and immediately begin the creation of the repair files in the directory %SystemRoot%\ Repair. A prompt to create an ERD will be given after the repair files have been created.

The /S- option causes RDisk to skip the initial user interface dialog box and immediately begin the creation of the repair files in the directory %SystemRoot%\ Repair. No prompt to create an ERD will be given. Instead, RDisk will exit after the repair files have been created.

These options do two things: they cause RDisk to skip the user interface dialog box (see Figure 2.1) and they also tell RDisk to back up the SAM and SECURITY components of the registry. The default is not to back up either SAM or SECURITY, but to use the default SAM and SECURITY components that have only the default Administrator, Guest accounts, and passwords.

FIGURE 2.1:

RDisk's only user interface is a dialog box.

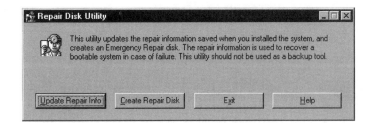

The Registry Won't Fit on the ERD Disk!

Do be aware that if there are a lot of users defined on your machine, the SAM and SECURITY files may be large and prohibit the creation of an ERD. See "RDisk Reports The Emergency Repair Disk Is Full," in the "Hints and Kinks from the Experts" section at the end of this chapter.

Also, Microsoft has a Knowledge Base article to describe steps to fix this problem. Search for article "Q130029, RDisk Reports The Emergency Repair Disk Is Full," and read this article, too.

What's on My ERD?

The Windows NT ERD contains a number of files in addition to the registry files. The files found on a typical ERD disk include:

AUTOEXEC.NT—Not part of the registry, this file is saved on the ERD. The AUTOEXEC.NT file is used to initialize the MS-DOS environment.

CONFIG.NT—Not part of the registry, this file is saved on the ERD. The CONFIG.NT file is used to initialize the MS-DOS environment.

DEFAULT._—This file contains the HKEY_USERS\.Default hive.

NTUSER.DA_—This file contains the new user profile. It is only present on Windows NT Version 4 and later.

SAM._—This file contains either the initial Administrator and Guest userid and passwords, or the entire SAM database; it depends on which option RDisk was run with. The registry hive HKEY_LOCAL_MACHINE\ SAM is contained in this file.

SECURITY—This file contains either the initial Administrator and Guest userid and passwords, or the entire SAM database; it depends on which option RDisk was run with. The registry hive HKEY_LOCAL_MACHINE\ Security is contained in this file.

SETUP.LOG—This file contains information about the initial setup of Windows NT. It is a critical file when restoring the registry using the Windows NT Setup program's repair facility.

software._—This file contains the registry hive HKEY_LOCAL_ MACHINE\Software information.

system._—This file contains the registry hive HKEY_LOCAL_ MACHINE\System information.

RegEdit—The Windows 95 Registry Editor

Using the Windows 95/98 Registry Editor, regedit.exe, and the procedures described below, you can make an additional copy of the registry and restore it by double-clicking a single icon. The Windows 95/98 Registry Editor, RegEdit, is included with Windows NT.

NOTE   If you are a system administrator and you have Windows 95/98 systems, the technique described below will work for these computers as well. Actually, they work better with Windows 95/98 than with Windows NT, but we'll keep that our carefully guarded secret.

If you follow the steps outlined shortly, you can create a copy of the system registry including everything except the security and SAM registry hives. When backing up a Windows NT Workstation on a network registry, RegEdit will usually use this technique to save everything needed.

There are other methods to back up the security database, though those methods are awkward and somewhat difficult to manage: it is easier to use the techniques described earlier in the chapter to do a complete registry backup.

Because the security and SAM hives are not backed up, this technique is not a complete backup technique. Rather, this is an interesting technique for backing up the other major parts of the registry—one that is very easy and quick to do.

To use RegEdit to back up the registry:

1. Run RegEdit. Either type the command **RegEdit** in a command window or click the Start button's Run selection. When the Run dialog box is displayed, type **RegEdit** on the Open: input area and click the OK button.

2. After RegEdit starts, note that "My computer" is highlighted. This ensures that the entire registry, and not just part of it, is backed up.

3. Select the Registry menu item Export Registry File.

4. RegEdit will display the File Save dialog box. Using the dialog box's toolbar, navigate to the desktop, type a name (for example, "Registry") in the Save File name box, and click Save.

5. Exit RegEdit.

This is easy and almost painless. Using this technique to back up the registry immediately after installation allows you to restore the system to a known state very easily and quickly. Simply double-click the file you created in step 5, above. When double-clicked, this file will be reloaded as the current registry.

NOTE   The saved registry file may be placed anywhere desired. In some cases, placing a registry restore capability on the user's desktop is tantamount to courting disaster. The user will click it just to see what will happen. One solution is to hide the file or save it to an offline storage location.

Realize that you will not be able to use this technique if you are unable to boot or run Windows NT. This is another good reason to have multiple backups of the registry in different formats.

NOTE When restoring the registry, several errors will be displayed. Some errors will state "System Process - Licensing Violation" and are to advise the user that the system has detected tampering with the product registration component of the registry. Click OK when these messages appear and also when a further error stating that it was not possible to write to the registry shows up. This final error is actually an artifact of the licensing violation errors and does not indicate a failure of the entire process.

To make the restored registry active, it is necessary to restart Windows NT. (Windows NT caches most of the registry while it is running.) There is no prompt to restart. However, some changes to the registry will not be reloaded until the system is restarted. Select Shut Down from the Start menu and select Restart the Computer in the Shutdown dialog box.

Restoring the Registry

To restore a registry, you must consider how the registry was saved. There are three ways to save a registry, each of which differs in just how much of the registry was saved and where the registry was saved:

- Backup programs typically copy the registry to a tape that the restore program will then restore to the original location.

- Copying the registry (as described above) creates identical copies of it, which may then be recopied back to the original registry locations.

- RDisk saves the registry into a special, compressed format that may only be restored by using the Windows NT setup program.

- RegEdit saves the registry in a text file with an extension of REG. Windows NT knows that this is a registry file because the REG file type is a registered extension and will reload the file automatically into the registry if the file is double-clicked in Explorer, or from the desktop. From a command prompt, enter the command `start filename.REG`, where filename is the name of the registry backup file.

Restoring from Tape

Restoring tape backup is a simple though time-consuming process. When the Windows NT backup and restore program is used, make sure that you select the option to restore the local registry. You will have to make the decision about restoring other files at this time based upon your circumstances. If you suspect that other system files may be corrupted, or if you are simply not sure of the state of the system, then I would recommend repairing Windows NT, or restoring the entire operating system and the registry at the same time. If you know that the registry is the only damaged component, a certain amount of time may be saved by simply restoring the registry and not other system files.

If you're using another backup program then simply follow the instructions provided with the program. The same general cautions about which files to restore (only the registry or the entire operating system) still apply. The main difference between most backup programs is the user interface.

NOTE When restoring from tape, be especially cautious that you do not restore the wrong version of the registry. Generally, you would want to make sure that you restore the most current working version of the registry.

Recovering a Copied Registry

A registry that has been backed up using copy or xcopy is restored in the opposite manner in which it was backed up. For example, if you have the NTFS file system then you would have to restart the system using your backup copy of Windows NT.

FAT and NTFS

When restoring a registry on a FAT-based file system running Windows NT, it will be necessary to boot either DOS or Windows 95/98. If you have dual boot installed (either DOS or Windows 95/98), it will be OK if you use the dual boot to get to the other operating system.

If you are restoring the registry on an NTFS system, then dual boot into the backup copy of Windows NT that you installed to back up the registry.

Important: Once running the alternate operating system, find your latest working copy of the registry *before* you copy it over the registry that you think is corrupted, and back up the current registry to another location. Take this precaution just in case the current registry is not the problem (it happens) and the backup copy is not as good as you think it is. Then you can follow these steps to restore your registry from a backup you have created:

1. Boot to another operating system: Windows NT, DOS or Windows 95/98 for FAT, and Windows NT for NTFS.

2. Save the current registry to a safe location just in case it is not the problem.

3. Copy your saved registry (from wherever it was stored) to the registry location.

4. Boot the original version of Windows NT and test to see if the restoration worked. If it didn't, keep reading, more golden tips are coming up soon.

RDisk Strikes Again—Using Setup to Recover

If there are no other backup copies of the original registry then it will be necessary to fall back on the ERD diskette, or the repair directory. This technique is fraught with perils, including the fact that the saved registry may not have all the necessary information. For example, if RDisk was run without the proper options, the SAM and Security hives will not be properly saved. Assuming that you have run RDisk frequently enough, then plunge in, the water's fine!

First, remember that the copies of the registry saved to the ERD and the repair directories are in a compressed format. Forget trying to restore them using some other method unless you're feeling brave (see sidebar).

Feeling Brave?

Actually, the registry files stored by RDisk appear to be compressed using the standard Windows NT compression program and API calls. The Windows NT Expand program expands these files very effectively. Try the command:

```
EXPAND inputfile outputfile
```

with copies of the registry files that RDisk saved. Make sure that you use copies of these files and that you save the output from Expand in a location where they won't overwrite any desired files.

Try using these expanded files with the techniques listed in "Recovering a Copied Registry," above.

Properly restoring the system registry from the repair directory, or from the ERD diskette, requires running the Windows NT Setup program. When it first starts, it examines the hard drive and looks for already installed copies of Windows NT and their repair directories. Once the examination is complete, Setup will give you four choices:

1. Help, which is invoked by pressing F1.

2. Setup Windows NT, invoked by pressing ENTER.

3. Repair a damaged Windows NT installation, by pressing R.

4. Quit, because this was all just a big mistake, by pressing F3.

Now, we know that we are in trouble at this point—the only choice is whether it might be possible to recover from the problems without doing a complete reinstallation of Windows NT.

Let's say that we are going to try to repair. First, we select the repair option, by pressing R. At this stage, the Setup program switches to repair mode and continues.

The next screen will display four choices. You may choose any combination or all of them:

Inspect registry files—This choice allows the repair program to check and repair the registry files. This is the option that most of us will be selecting if we are reading this book. The repair program will need either an ERD diskette or the files stored in the %SystemRoot%\Repair directory.

Inspect startup environment—The startup environment is the Boot Manager, which is called by the program contained in the boot sector. There are also other supporting files—including BOOT.INI, ntdetect.com, and others—which must be validated. The repair program will repair or replace these files as best as it can, but be prepared for some items to be restored to the state they were in when you installed Windows NT.

Verify Windows NT system files—Verifying the system files is a process where the repair program will go through the root directory and all the system directories (such as the Windows directory, and the system directories) and verify that each and every file is valid. This process is used when a hard disk error (especially on an NTFS volume) has made one or more system files invalid. Careful! You will loose all service packs installed to this repair process. Reinstall your service packs immediately after choosing this option.

Inspect Boot Sector—There are several reasons to inspect (and repair) the boot sector. For example, if you inadvertently install another operating system with boot sector virus infections, this could possibly damage the boot sector. The latter is especially the case with the FAT file systems.

All four of these selections will be selected by default. You may want to move the selector bar (use the arrow keys) to highlight and deselect any option that is not desired. The ENTER key is used to select or clear an option.

Once you have elected to continue, Setup will then do a device check. This is the same check that is done prior to an installation of Windows NT.

The next stage is to determine where the registry repair information will be coming from. Remember, you can use either the ERD or the copy stored in the repair directory. If you have multiple installations of Windows NT, be sure to choose the correct repair directory to repair from.

TIP

The ERD will tell Setup which copy of Windows NT you are attempting to repair. You *cannot* use the ERD from one installation of Windows NT to repair another installation of Windows NT. It just won't work.

If you don't have an ERD (or you don't want to use it) then Setup will search your drive for Windows NT. You may have multiple installations of Windows NT; this is common, considering how many times I've recommended installing at least two copies. If this is the case, Setup will list each installation of Windows NT that it finds.

Select the version of Windows NT you want to repair and press ENTER to repair the selected installation.

WARNING

Careful! Make sure you repair the right Windows NT installation if you have more than one copy of Windows NT installed. Nothing is worse than successfully repairing a copy of Windows NT that wasn't broken in the first place.

Next, Setup does a drive check. The message indicates that drives are being checked and the status indicator at the bottom of the screen shows the progress. Actually, Setup only checks the boot (C:) drive, but that's probably all that is needed right now.

The next prompt, which is displayed when you have elected to have the registry repaired, is to determine which hive or hives are to be repaired:

system—system configuration

software—software information

default—default user profile

ntuser.dat—new user profile

SECURITY—Security policy database

SAM—Security Account Manager database

You can choose any combination of hives to replace, but be careful: when replacing the SECURITY and SAM (both must be replaced together) you may lose user accounts if you have not fully backed up your registry using the RDisk /S option discussed earlier in this chapter.

Replacing some hives and not others might result in some problems when items in the registry have been updated since the registry was last saved. Typically, it is best to replace all files if possible to avoid any problems with different versions.

Once the registry has been updated, the Setup program will then prompt you to remove the diskette from its drive and reboot the computer. If all went well, the computer will reboot and run.

Loading a REG file

Any REG file created by RegEdit (discussed earlier) is usually loaded by simply double-clicking the REG file in the Explorer program. If the REG file is located on the desktop, then it may be double-clicked there, too.

Though there are few advantages to doing so, RegEdit will load a REG file. To load a registry file, select Registry ➤ Import Registry File from the RegEdit main menu. Actually, when you double-click on a REG file, Windows NT starts RegEdit to do the registry file load. The main advantage of loading a registry file from the RegEdit menu is that you'd be able to see the effect of the registry load in RegEdit.

A REG file, being a text file, may be *carefully* edited. Did I emphasize *carefully* enough? Realize you are making a registry change if you modify the REG file and then reload it.

> **NOTE**   It is not uncommon for applications to update the registry using a REG file during program installation time. This is one method used by software developers. Why? Simple: this allows the registry to be repaired, restoring the application's default values without having to reinstall the entire program.

Other Backup and Restore Programs

There are other registry backup and restoration programs. One excellent source for them is the Windows NT Resource Kit's RegBack and RegRest programs. Take a look at Chapter 4, "Registry Tools and Tips—Getting the Work Done," for a listing of the tools found in the Windows NT Resource Kit.

Hints and Kinks from the Experts

Here's another installment of good stuff from the Windows NT gurus. In your search for more information, frequent their sites on the Internet.

Why Don't My Changes to the Registry Take Effect?   Always reboot. Reboot after restoring any registry values. Many values are not reloaded by Windows NT except at boot time. There's nothing worse than wondering why your "fix" didn't work when it was simply not being loaded by Windows NT.

Users Never Have a Current ERD!   In most sites, users rarely have a current ERD when they need one. Do it for them with this procedure. Use the scheduler (AT command or a good one like OpalisRobot) on each workstation to schedule a RDisk.exe /S-. The batch file to schedule is:

```
%windir%\system32\rdisk.exe /s-
net use x: /delete
net use x: \\YourServer\RepairShare$ /persistent:no
if not exist x:\%computername% md x:\%computername%
Copy %windir%\repair\*.* X:\%computername%\*.*
net use x: /delete
exit
```

where %computername% is a sub-directoy of the hidden share on the server (one for each workstation). When you need an ERD for that workstation, just format a diskette on your server and copy the files from their wsX directory.

The scheduler must be run under the system context and allowed to interact with the desktop or under the context of an administrative user. If you use the system account, you can't schedule the copy because the system account has no network access. Use a ROBOT account with a non-blank, non-expiring password that is a member of the administrator group. Use full path names for all files.

Here is a sample schedule for Workstation "wsA":

```
AT \\wsA 01:00 /interactive every:M,T,W,Th,F,S,Su\YourServer\Repair-
Share$\Repair.bat
```

You can dress up the Repair.bat with logging, messaging, and so on.

(Courtesy of `http://www.jsiinc.com/reghack .htm`. Copyright © 1997 Jerold Schulman [JSI, Inc.] Used with permission.)

RDisk Reports The Emergency Repair Disk Is Full.   When you run RDisk.EXE or RDisk.EXE /S, the following files are updated in the %System-Root%\Repair directory:

> File Name Registry Hive Name
> AUTOEXEC.NT
> CONFIG.NT
> DEFAULT._ HKEY_USERS\.Default
> NTUSER.DA_ (NT V4.0 only)
> SAM._ Portions of HKEY_LOCAL_MACHINE\SAM
> SECURITY._ HKEY_LOCAL_MACHINE\Security
> SETUP.LOG
> software._ HKEY_LOCAL_MACHINE\Software
> system._ HKEY_LOCAL_MACHINE\System

If the total space for these files exceeds the size of the floppy, you receive the subject message.

You can reduce the size of the SETUP.LOG file by removing file from the [Files.WinNt] section that does not begin with %SystemRoot%\System32 or an equivalent. Make a backup first, such as SETUP.BAK. After the ERD is created, rename the \Repair\SETUP.BAK to \Repair\SETUP.LOG.

If you are running RDisk.EXE /S, the SAM contains 1K of data for each user account and 1K of data for each machine account. The SECURITY hive is even larger. You may have to forgo the /S option. You may even have to restore the original SAM and SECURITY from an older ERD. If you do, you must have at least one of the following to recover:

- Regback/Regrest from the Resource Kit

- ConfigSafe NT from `http://www.jsiinc.com/catalog.htm`

- A backup

- An alternate install of NT and to be safe, a copy of the %SystemRoot%\Repair directory

(Courtesy of Jerold Schulman)

I Can't Format a Disk/Create an Emergency Repair Diskette.   There are a number of possible problems. First, if you're using service pack 2, ensure you have the kernel fix applied. Also, some virus killers (such as Dr. Solomon's) lock up drives making a format impossible as NT thinks the drive is locked. This is why you can't create an emergency repair diskette. Stop the virus process using Control Panel services and click on the Virus Killer process and press Stop. Once the disk is formatted for the emergency repair diskette, go back to the Control Panel and start the Virus Killer process again.

(Courtesy of `http://www.ntfaq.com`. Copyright © 1998 John Savill [SavillTech Ltd]. Used with permission.)

When I Try and Create an Emergency Repair Diskette, I Get the Error Message, "One or more configuration files missing."   Run the RDisk /S a few times and this error will fix itself.

(Courtesy of John Savill)

What's the Difference between the Contents of the ERD and the Repair Directory?   The ERD and the repair directory contain the same files. One is as good as the other. However, you can have as many ERDs as you want while there can be only one repair directory. In fact, I'd recommend at least three or four ERDs for each Windows NT installation you have—more if you can find the diskettes.

Anatomy of the Registry— The Blood, Gore, and Guts

■ Of hives and bees—a registry overview

■ HKEY_LOCAL_MACHINE—the machine's configuration

■ HKEY_USERS—settings for users

■ HKEY_DYN_DATA—settings for PnP (Plug and Play)

■ NTUSER—the new user profile

■ Hints and kinks from the experts

In the previous chapter we talked about how a user might back up and restore the registry. In this chapter we will talk more about the details of what is actually in the registry. If you're only interested in recovering from a disaster and not interested in *what* the registry is, it might be possible to skip this chapter. However, if you're unsure about this, I'd recommend reading it anyway.

Now humor me for just a moment; I think I'm going to back up my registry. In fact, it is a good time for *you* to do a backup as well, since it is entirely possible that at any time you might have some kind of problem (or disaster) with the registry and really need that backup copy to restore it. Next, let some time pass by. Ah, that feels better—I've got a fresh backup copy of my registry just in case I do something stupid, and so do you—not that we ever do anything stupid, right?

The registry is subdivided into a number of clearly defined sections, called hives:

- HKEY_CLASSES_ROOT
- HKEY_CURRENT_USER
- HKEY_LOCAL_MACHINE
- HKEY_USERS
- HKEY_CURRENT_CONFIG
- HKEY_DYN_DATA

Some hives are less important than others. For example, if the Security Account Manager hive (SAM) is damaged, you can probably recover easily without serious permanent problems. You may possibly lose all of the user database, so no users would be able to log onto the server. However, as long as you can log on as Administrator, the worst case is that you would have to re-enter the other user information. The default SAM registry will contain at least the initial Administrator user ID and password, which you would have to know.

However, say you lose the system component of the registry without adequate backup. In that case it is unlikely that you'll be able to recover without reinstalling Windows NT, and that would be a painful experience at best.

Of Hives and Bees—A Registry Overview

The Windows NT registry (and the registry for Windows 95/98) is arranged into logical units called hives. Though I can't vouch for its truth, legend has it that some unnamed programmer at Microsoft seemed to see a logical relationship between the various keys in the registry and the structure of a bee hive. Now me, I just don't see this, so let's consider the two following alternative analogies:

- The registry is arranged just like the folders and files contained on your hard drive. Hives are analogous to directories, and keys are like files. In fact, this relationship is almost 100 percent parallel: Hives are usually shown separated by backslashes (just like directories on the drive), and keys typically (but not always) have values. Remember, a file may also be empty.

- The registry is arranged as a hierarchical database, nothing more, nothing less. If you are a database person, this view of the registry might make more sense to you. In truth, this arrangement is more like the registry's actual construction.

Specific data is assigned to a key. As I mentioned, some registry keys don't have a value set; this value is also acceptable.

WARNING   Be careful not to delete empty keys just because they are empty. Even though they don't have a value, their presence in the registry may be necessary for the health and well-being of Windows NT. Never, ever, delete a key unless you know that there will be no adverse side effects.

The Registry Hives

The registry is divided into five hives and every one is named with the prefix HKEY_. (Do we dare to guess that HKEY is short for hive key?) Each hive embodies a major section contained in the registry with a different functionality. These hives are discussed next.

Hives, Keys, and Values

In this book, I use a terminology similar to that used when referring to disk drives, directories, sub-directories, files, and the contents of files. Often Microsoft confuses the issue somewhat. I try to keep it clear:

Hive—A hive is similar to a directory on a drive. Located inside a hive may be keys (like files) or sub-hives (like sub-directories). A hive need not be the highest level; a hive may actually be a sub-hive inside another hive. An example of a hive in the registry is HKEY_LOCAL_MACHINE.

Sub-hive—A sub-hive is similar to a sub-directory on a drive. Located inside a sub-hive may be keys (like files) or other sub-hives (like sub-directories). A sub-hive may have one or more hives located above it and none or more sub-hives contained within it. Sometimes Microsoft refers to a sub-hive as a sub-key. An example of a sub-hive in the registry is HKEY_LOCAL_MACHINE\SAM.

Key—A key is similar to a file on a drive. A key may contain data, though a key may have no value set at all.

Value—A value is similar to a file's data. Each key will have one value (though the value may consist of many parts), or a key may have no value set at all. There is also something called the default value, which is used when appropriate.

HKEY_CLASSES_ROOT

The HKEY_CLASSES_ROOT branch contains information about both OLE and various file associations. The purpose of HKEY_CLASSES_ROOT is to provide for compatibility with the existing Windows 3.x registry.

The information contained in HKEY_CLASSES_ROOT is identical to information found in HKEY_LOCAL_MACHINE\SOFTWARE.

HKEY_CURRENT_USER

The HKEY_CURRENT_USER branch is used to manage specific information about the user who is currently logged on. This information includes:

- The user's desktop and the appearance and behavior of Windows NT 4 Server to the user.

- All connections to network devices, such as printers and shared disk resources.

- Desktop program items, application preferences, screen colors, and other personal preferences and security rights. They are stored for later retrieval by the system when the user logs on.

All other environment settings are retained for future use.

By accessing the roaming user profile, Windows NT is able to make any workstation that the user logs onto appear the same to the user. Domain users need not worry about having to set up or customize each possible workstation that they will be using.

Information contained in HKEY_CURRENT_USER is updated as users make changes to their environments.

HKEY_LOCAL_MACHINE

The HKEY_LOCAL_MACHINE branch contains information about the computer that is running Windows NT. This information includes applications, drivers, and hardware. There are five separate keys contained within the HKEY_LOCAL_MACHINE:

HARDWARE—HARDWARE is the key used to save information about the computer's hardware. It is always re-created when the system is booted, this allows new hardware to be easily added. Changes to this key are not meaningful. Contained within the HARDWARE key are the following four sub-keys:

DESCRIPTION—DESCRIPTION contains information about the system, including the CPU, FPU, and the system bus. Under the system bus is information about I/O, storage, and other devices.

DEVICEMAP—DEVICEMAP contains information about devices (keyboards, printer ports, pointers, and so on.)

OWNERMAP—OWNERMAP contains miscellaneous information about some of the PCI-based devices, such as SCSI, NIC, or video adapters.

RESOURCEMAP—RESOURCEMAP contains information about the HAL (Hardware Abstraction Layer). Remember, as we approach the year 2000, HAL is not a talking computer on a spaceship, HAL is the hardware. Also contained are I/O devices, drivers, SCSI adapters, system resources, and video resources.

SAM—The Security Account Manager (SAM), stores information about users and domains in the SAM key. This information is not accessible using any of the resource editors. Rather, this information is better managed using the administrator's User Manager program.

SECURITY—SECURITY contains information about local security and user rights. A copy of the SAM key is found in the SECURITY key. As with SAM, the SECURITY key is not accessible using the resource editors, and the information is best modified using the administrator's tools.

SOFTWARE— SOFTWARE contains information about installed system and user software, including descriptions. There should be sub-keys for each installed product where the product will store information—including preferences, configurations, MRU (most recently used files) lists, and other application modifiable items.

SYSTEM—SYSTEM contains information about the system start-up, device drivers, services, and the Windows NT 4 Server configuration.

HKEY_USERS

The HKEY_USERS key contains information about each active user who has a user profile. A minimum of two keys are in the HKEY_USERS key: .DEFAULT and the ID for the currently logged-on user. The purpose of the .DEFAULT key is to provide information for users who log on without a profile.

Personal profiles are contained in the %SystemRoot%\Profiles folder, unless roaming profiles are used, in which case a copy will be stored there, but the original will reside on a server.

HKEY_CURRENT_CONFIG

The HKEY_CURRENT_CONFIG key is new to Windows NT 4. It contains information about the system's current configuration. This information is typically derived from HKEY_LOCAL_MACHINE\SYSTEM\ and HKEY_LOCAL_MACHINE\SOFTWARE, though HKEY_CURRENT_CONFIG does not contain all the information that is contained in the source keys.

HKEY_DYN_DATA

The HKEY_DYN_DATA key is also new to Windows NT 4. It contains information about the system's PnP (Plug and Play) status. However, since Windows NT 4 does not support PnP, this key is empty. Probably, when it is released, Windows NT 5 will fully implement this key. Attempts to open this key will fail because it is not supported yet.

Registry Key Value Types

Values have different types:

REG_BINARY—REG_BINARY represents binary values. They may be edited or entered as hexadecimal or binary numbers. Figure 3.1 shows the RegEdt32 registry editor's Binary Editor dialog box. Regedit has a similar edit window, though it is not as flexible in how data is entered.

FIGURE 3.1:

The Binary Editor window for RegEdt32

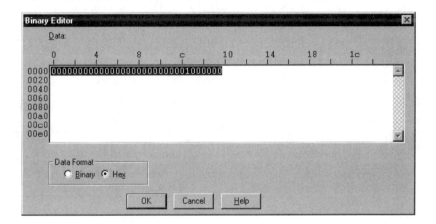

REG_SZ—REG_SZ is used for registry keys that contain strings. Editing is easy; just type in the new string. Case is preserved, but realize that the string is initially selected, so be careful not to inadvertently delete it. Strings are of fixed length and are defined when the key is created. Figure 3.2 shows a string being edited in the String Editor window. A string key may be made longer; it will be reallocated if this happens.

REG_EXPAND_SZ—REG_EXPAND_SZ is used if the key is to contain a string that may be expanded. Some keys may need to contain values that reference environment variables, much like a batch file. For example, if a string contains the field %SystemRoot%\System32, and it is necessary for the %SystemRoot% part of the string to be expanded to the value that is assigned to it in the environment, this string must be a REG_EXPAND_SZ string. The result of the expansion would then be passed to the requestor. %SystemRoot% is a standard environment variable containing the location, drive, and directory where Windows NT has been installed. The same dialog as REG_SZ is used to enter a REG_EXPAND_SZ key as shown in Figure 3.2.

FIGURE 3.2:

The String Editor window for RegEdt32

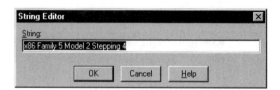

REG_DWORD—REG_DWORD is used to store a 32-bit value in the key, entered as decimal, hexadecimal, or binary. The Editor window allows entering only valid numeric data to help save us from sloppy typing, as Figure 3.3 shows.

FIGURE 3.3:

The DWORD Editor window for RegEdt32

REG_MULTI_SZ—REG_MULTI_SZ is used to store multiple strings in a single registry key. Normally, a string resource in the registry may contain only one line. However, the multi-string type allows a string resource in the registry to hold mutiple strings as needed. Figure 3.4 shows a multi-string being edited. Only one line is present in this example. As well, the REG_MULTI_SZ type is not supported by the Windows 95/98 registry editor, RegEdit. If a REG_MULTI_SZ item is edited with RegEdit, it is possible to corrupt the data that is contained in it.

REG_FULL_RESOURCE_DESCRIPTOR—REG_FULL_RESOURCE_ DESCRIPTOR is used to manage information for hardware resources. No one should edit the items that appear in the Resource Editor fields. Figure 3.5 shows RegEdt32 displaying a disk resource object. However, these objects are not normally changed manually with the resource editors.

FIGURE 3.4:

The Multi-String Editor window for RegEdt32

FIGURE 3.5:

The Resources window for RegEdt32 (editing a disk resource)

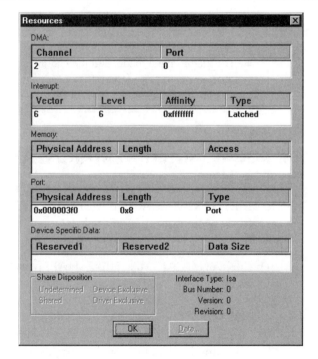

REG_NONE—REG_NONE is an identifier used when there is no data stored in the key. It doesn't take a rocket scientist to figure out that there is no editor for the none type.

REG_UNKNOWN—REG_UNKNOWN is used when the key's data type cannot be determined.

HKEY_LOCAL_MACHINE—The Machine's Configuration

The HKEY_LOCAL_MACHINE hive contains information about the current hardware configuration of the local computer. The information stored in this hive is updated using a variety of processes, including the Control Panel, hardware and software installation programs, administrative tools, and sometimes automatically by Windows NT.

It is important not to make unintended changes to the HKEY_LOCAL_MACHINE hive. A change here could quite possibly render the entire system unstable.

NOTE

All the settings in the HKEY_LOCAL_MACHINE hive are recomputed at boot time. If a change has been made, and the change is causing problems, first try rebooting the system. The Windows NT Boot Manager should rebuild the HKEY_LOCAL_MACHINE hive at the reboot time, discarding any changes made.

HKEY_LOCAL_MACHINE\HARDWARE—The Installed Hardware Hive

The HKEY_LOCAL_MACHINE\HARDWARE hive contains information about the hardware configuration of the local machine. Everything hardware related (and I do mean everything) will be found in this hive.

The HKEY_LOCAL_MACHINE\HARDWARE hive is subdivided into four sub-hives:

DESCRIPTION—DESCRIPTION contains descriptive information about each device. This descriptive information includes both a verbal description and information, such as basic configurations, and so on.

DEVICEMAP—DEVICEMAP contains information about devices, including locations in the registry where the device's full configuration is saved.

OWNERMAP—OWNERMAP contains information about removable PCI bus type devices. These devices are devices plugged into the system's

PCI bus, but generally not those permanently installed on the system's motherboard. However, not all PCI type devices will be listed in OWNERMAP.

RESOURCEMAP—RESOURCEMAP contains translation information about each major component that is installed in the system. Most consist of a set of entries called .Raw and .Translated.

DESCRIPTION

Within the HKEY_LOCAL_MACHINE\HARDWARE\DESCRIPTION hive is a wealth of information about the installed hardware. The only sub-hive, SYSTEM, describes the CPU and I/O fully. The following hives are contained in the SYSTEM sub-hive:

CentralProcessor—The CentralProcessor hive contains information about the CPU. This includes speed, which is an identifier that contains the CPU's model, family, and Stepping. Also included in this hive is vendor information; for example, a "real" Intel CPU has the VendorIdentifier string "GenuineIntel."

FloatingPointProcessor—The FloatingPointProcessor hive describes the system's FPU (Floating Point Unit) in a set of entries similar to that of the CPU. The fact that the typical CPU has an integral FPU is not considered here; the FPU will be listed separately, regardless.

MultiFunctionAdapter—The MultiFunctionAdapter hive describes the system's bus (PCI), any PnP BIOS installed (regardless of the fact that Windows NT 4 doesn't support PnP), and other devices, including the controllers for disk drives, keyboards, parallel and serial ports, and the mouse. For mice that are connected to a serial port, the mouse will be found under the serial port, while mice that are connected to a PS/2 mouseport will be shown connected to a pointer controller as a separate device.

Typically, the DESCRIPTION hive can be used to determine what hardware is installed (and being used) and how the installed hardware is connected. However, some devices, such as storage devices (hard drives, SCSI, CD-ROM, video, and network interface cards), are not listed in HKEY_LOCAL_MACHINE\HARDWARE\DESCRIPTION. Instead, they are listed in HKEY_LOCAL_MACHINE\HARDWARE\DEVICEMAP. Why? Because these devices are not detected at boot-up stage; instead, they are detected when they are installed.

DEVICEMAP

The HKEY_LOCAL_MACHINE\HARDWARE\DEVICEMAP hive contains information about devices, arranged in a similar fashion to the HKEY_LOCAL_ MACHINE\HARDWARE\DESCRIPTION hive discussed earlier in this chapter. In the DEVICEMAP hive are found the following hives:

KeyboardClass—KeyboardClass points to the hive that manages information about the keyboard itself.

KeyboardPort—KeyboardPort points to the hive that manages information about the keyboard interface unit, often called the 8042 after the original chip that served as the keyboard controller in the original PC.

PARALLEL PORTS—PARALLEL PORTS points to the hive that manages information about the parallel printer ports.

PointerClass—PointerClass points to the hive that manages information about the system mouse.

PointerPort—PointerPort points to the hive that manages information about the port that the system mouse is connected to.

Scsi—Scsi is a complex hive with information about each SCSI port found on the computer. A note about what is considered a SCSI port is in order. Actually, Windows NT pretends that IDE devices, and many CD-ROM devices that are connected to special interface cards, are SCSI devices. This is a management issue. Windows NT is not converting these devices to be SCSI, nor is Windows NT using SCSI drivers, rather Windows NT is simply classing all these devices under a common heading.

SERIALCOMM—SERIALCOMM points to the hive that manages information about the available serial ports. If the system mouse is connected to a serial port, and not to a PS/2 mouse port, that port will not be listed in the SERIALCOMM hive.

VIDEO—VIDEO points to the hive that manages the video devices. There are typically two devices defined in VIDEO: One is the currently used adapter, and the second is a backup consisting of the previously installed, usually the generic VGA, adapter's settings to use as a backup in the event of a problem with the video system.

OWNERMAP

The HKEY_LOCAL_MACHINE\HARDWARE\OWNERMAP hive is a simple hive with descriptions for devices connected to an external PCI bus. These devices (often SCSI, video, and network interface cards) are listed with a key that Windows NT uses and the internal device driver name.

The HKEY_LOCAL_MACHINE\HARDWARE\OWNERMAP hive is new to Windows NT 4.

RESOURCEMAP

The RESOURCEMAP sub-hive is used by all the various hardware device drivers to map resources that the driver will use. Each RESOURCEMAP entry will contain information about usage of:

- I/O ports
- I/O memory addresses
- interrupts
- direct memory access (DMA) channels and so on

The organization of the RESOURCEMAP hive is that there are entries for a class of device (such as VIDEO), under these entries are found sub-hives for a number of different video devices.

HKEY_LOCAL_MACHINE\SAM—The Security Access Manager

Contained in HKEY_LOCAL_MACHINE\SAM is information used by the Windows NT security system. User information (permissions, passwords, and the like) is contained within this key.

This information is typically set using the User Manager or User Manager for Domains.

NOTE   The SAM hives (both in HKEY_LOCAL_MACHINE\SAM\SAM and HKEY_LOCAL_MACHINE\SECURITY\SAM) should only be modified using the User Manager administrative programs. Attempts to modify information that is in the SAM hives typically results in disaster. For example, users will be unable to log on, wrong permissions will be assigned, and so on.

The two SAM hives (HKEY_LOCAL_MACHINE\SAM\SAM and HKEY_LOCAL_MACHINE\SECURITY\SAM) are mirrored. Changes made to one are automatically reflected in the other.

NOTE   Can't see the SAM or Security hives? Use REGEDT32 to select the hive you cannot see and then select Security ➤ Permissions from the main menu. Next, change the Type of Access from Special Access to Full Control.

WARNING   Following the advice in the above note is dangerous. Once a user has full access to the SAM and Security hives, the user may make changes and modifications that could cause all sorts of problems. Don't do this unless you have a full backup of your registry, including the SAM and Security hives, as described in Chapter Two, "README.1st—Preventing Disaster!"

HKEY_LOCAL_MACHINE\Security—The Windows NT Security Hive

Contained in the hive HKEY_LOCAL_MACHINE\Security is information relevant to the security of the local machine. This information includes:

- user rights
- password policy
- membership of local groups

This information is typically set using the Administrative User Manager or User Manager for Domains programs.

NOTE   The Security hives should only be modified using the User Manager or User Manager for Domains administrative programs. Attempts to modify information in the Security hive typically result in disaster. For example, users are unable to log on, wrong permissions are assigned, and so on.

HKEY_LOCAL_MACHINE\Software—The Installed Software Information Hive

The HKEY_LOCAL_MACHINE\Software registry hive is the storage location for all software installed on the computer. The information contained in HKEY_LOCAL_MACHINE\Software is available to all users and consists of a number of standard sub-hives as well as a few sub-hives that may be unique to each computer.

One computer on my network, a Windows NT Server, has the following sub-hives in HKEY_LOCAL_MACHINE\Software. These sub-hives correspond to items that I have installed on my computer:

3Com—3Com contains information specific to 3Com software that is installed. In the case of this computer, the installed devices are 3Com network interface cards.

Adobe—Adobe contains information about the copy of Adobe's Acrobat program that was recently installed.

Dragon Systems—Dragon Systems contains information about a voice recognition program called Naturally Speaking.

Federal Express—Federal Express contains information about the FedEx online access and support I have on my computer. All of my FedEx airbills are produced by computer, making shipments much easier.

INTEL—Intel contains information about the Intel 3D Scalability Toolkit that I installed at some point. I don't remember when or why, but it's there.

Intuit—Intuit contains information specfic to the financial software that is their specialty. I've found their products to be good performers. We all hope that Intuit will realize that they must support Windows NT with their products in the future.

Qualcomm—Qualcomm contains information specific to the Eudora e-mail program. The nice thing about Eudora is that there is a free version for private use.

The following are system sub-hives probably installed on your computer; however, some of these sub-hives, such as ODBC and Clients, may not be present on some minimal installations:

Classes—The Classes sub-hive contains two types of items. First are file-type association items. For example, a typical association entry might have the name DIB, with a string that associates this name with the application PaintShopPro, a graphics editing program.

Second are COM (Common Object Model) associations. For example, the name .DOC is associated with the WinWord application in Microsoft Word for Windows or with WordPad, the default viewer for DOC document files. Both WordPad and WinWord may be embedded in other applications. For instance, Outlook, Microsoft's upscale e-mail system, uses Word formatted documents and embeds either Word for Windows or WordPad to display and edit these documents.

Clients—The Clients sub-hive contains client-server relationships. For example, Microsoft Outlook is a multipurpose program with e-mail, a calendar, contact lists, news, and other features. Each of these parts of Outlook has a complex series of calling protocols that are defined in the Clients sub-hive.

Description—The Description sub-hive contains names and version numbers for software installed on the local computer. Though any vendor may use this sub-hive, the author can only see one entry, which is entered during installation of Windows NT. Microsoft RPC (Remote Procedure Call) has several entries in this sub-hive.

Microsoft—The Microsoft sub-hive stores a number of items that pertain to Microsoft products or parts of Windows NT. There can be as few as 20 or as many as 100 entries in the Microsoft sub-hive.

ODBC—The ODBC sub-hive stores items that pertain to Open DataBase Connectivity, which allows applications to retrieve data from a number of different data sources. Many users install ODBC, either realizing that it is being installed, or as a side effect of installing another product.

Program Groups—Under Windows NT 4, this sub-hive contains one value, ConvertedToLinks, which is used to indicate whether the program groups were converted. A value of one (0x1) shows that the conversion is complete. Even a Windows NT 4 system installed on a new computer that didn't require conversion will have this value.

Secure—If you say so. The Secure sub-hive is the location in which any application may store "secure" configuration information. Only an Administrator may modify this sub-hive, so mere mortal users can't change secure configuration information. Not many, if any, applications use the Secure sub-hive.

Windows 3.1 Migration Status—The sub-hive Windows 3.1 Migration Status is used to indicate if the computer was upgraded from Windows 3.*x* to Windows NT 4. Though at one time there were many upgrades, more users today are likely to be doing clean installations—virtually all existing Windows 3.*x* systems have already been upgraded. Two sub-hives exist: IniFiles and REG.DAT. These values show whether the INI and Reg.dat files have been migrated successfully to Windows NT 4 formats.

HKEY_LOCAL_MACHINE\System— The System Information Hive

The HKEY_LOCAL_MACHINE\System sub-hive is used to hold start-up information used by Windows NT when booting. This sub-hive contains all the data that is stored and not re-computed at boot time.

NOTE   A full copy of the HKEY_LOCAL_MACHINE\System information is kept in the file SYSTEM.ALT, found in the %SystemRoot%\System32\config directory.

The HKEY_LOCAL_MACHINE\System hive (aka, the System hive) is organized into control sets (such as Clone, ControlSet001, ControlSet002, and Current-ControlSet) containing parameters for devices and services.

The main control sets are:

Clone—The Clone control set is the volatile copy of the ControlSet (usually ControlSet001) that was used to boot the system. Created by the system Kernel during initialization, this hive is not accessible from the Registry Editor. This sub-hive is used by the Service Controller system (SCREG.EXE).

ControlSet001—The ControlSet001 set is the Current and the Default control set used to boot Windows NT normally. Mapped to CurrentControlSet at boot time, and copied to the volatile sub-hive Clone (see preceding control set), ControlSet001 is the most critical component in the registry in the normal boot-up process.

ControlSet002—ControlSet002 is a backup control set from the Last-KnownGood boot that is used to boot from when the default control set (ControlSet001) fails or is unusable for some reason.

ControlSet003—ControlSet003 is a backup control set from the Last-KnownGood boot that may be used to boot from when the default control set (ControlSet001) fails or is unusable for some reason.

ControlSet00n (where n is greater than three)—ControlSet00n are the backup control sets used for special purposes, not much documentation exists on higher numbered control sets.

CurrentControlSet—The CurrentControlSet is the control set that Windows NT has booted from. The CurrentControlSet is usually mapped to ControlSet001.

There are three other items in the HKEY_LOCAL_MACHINE\System hive:

DISK—The DISK sub-hive contains items for each mapped CD-ROM drive. For example, I map my CD-ROM drives to drive letters after S, so I have three entries in this sub-hive mapping each CD-ROM drive to a different drive letter. This sub-hive is updated by the Administrator's tool, Disk Administrator.

Select—This sub-hive contains four keys. It also has information on which control set was booted and which sub-hive is the LastKnownGood set. Also, if there is a "failed" control set, the failed control set's identity will be found in the Select sub-hive.

Setup—The Setup sub-hive contains information used by setup to configure Windows NT. This information includes locations of drives and directories; the setup command line; and a flag telling if setup is currently in progress.

The HKEY_LOCAL_MACHINE\System hive is critical to both the boot process and to the operation of the system. Microsoft has created a number of tools and processes that help protect the HKEY_LOCAL_MACHINE\System hive information. These include the LastKnownGood boot process, which allows mapping in a known (or so we hope) copy of the control set allowing the system to boot if the original control set is too damaged to be booted.

When modifying the control sets, be aware of the process of booting and creating the control sets. Generally, modifying a backup control set won't affect the system.

When Is the Current Control Set the LastKnown-Good Control Set?

At some point in the boot process the current control set (contained in the sub-hive Clone) will be copied into the LastKnownGood control set. In early beta releases of Windows NT 4, this was done as soon as the CTRL+ALT+DEL logon dialog box appeared, that is, before a user had logged on. This was a problem if the initial user was unable to log on.

In the released version of Windows NT 4, the process of replacing the LastKnownGood control set is done after the initial logon is performed. This allows the system to catch any problems related to the logon process.

WARNING   Do not, I repeat, *do not*, boot using the LastKnownGood control set unless it is necessary! Any changes made to the system during the previous session will be lost, gone, forever and forever!

HKEY_USERS—Settings for Users

Current user configurations are saved in HKEY_USERS. This hive contains two entries.

NOTE   Actually, HKEY_USERS may contain more users. See the section, "NTUSER—The New User Profile," later in this chapter for information on how more users might be added, and why.

In HKEY_USERS there are typically two keys. The first key, .DEFAULT, is the default user profile. This profile is used for any users who log on without having their own profile created. For users who have their own profile, their profile is loaded and stored as the second key found in HKEY_USERS.

The second key, the user profile for the user who is currently logged on, appears as something like this:

S-1-5-21-45749729-16073390-2133884337-500

This second key is the key for a specific user's profile. The profile would be either the user's own profile or copied from the .DEFAULT profile if the user has not established his or her own profile.

This long, magical registry key needs some explanation. The number, as a whole, is called a SID (Security Identifier). There is a lot of information in a SID. For example, the ending three- or four-digit number is used to identify both the user, and for some users, the types of user. Table 3.1 lists a number of general user types that might be assigned. The most commonly seen value is 500, which is assigned to the system administrator account.

TABLE 3.1:   Common SID Values Used by Windows NT

UserGroup	SID
DOMAINNAME\ADMINISTRATOR	S-1-5-21-xxxxxxxxx-xxxxxxxxxx-xxxxxxxxxx-500
DOMAINNAME\GUEST	S-1-5-21-xxxxxxxxx-xxxxxxxxxx-xxxxxxxxxx-501
DOMAINNAME\DOMAIN ADMINS	S-1-5-21-xxxxxxxxx-xxxxxxxxxx-xxxxxxxxxx-512
DOMAINNAME\DOMAIN USERS	S-1-5-21-xxxxxxxxx-xxxxxxxxxx-xxxxxxxxxx-513
DOMAINNAME\DOMAIN GUESTS	S-1-5-21-xxxxxxxxx-xxxxxxxxxx-xxxxxxxxxx-514

General users might be assigned SIDs ending in four-digit numbers starting at 1000. My domain has a user called Pixel, whose SID ends in 1003, and another user, Long, whose SID ends in 1006. Get the picture?

There are also a number of built-in and special groups of SIDs, as shown in Tables 3.2 and 3.3.

TABLE 3.2:   The Windows NT Built-In Local Groups

Built-In Local Groups	SID
BUILTIN\ADMINISTRATORS	S-1-2-32-xxxxxxxxx-xxxxxxxxxx-xxxxxxxxxx-544
BUILTIN\USERS	S-1-2-32-xxxxxxxxx-xxxxxxxxxx-xxxxxxxxxx-545
BUILTIN\GUESTS	S-1-2-32-xxxxxxxxx-xxxxxxxxxx-xxxxxxxxxx-546
BUILTIN\POWER USERS	S-1-2-32-xxxxxxxxx-xxxxxxxxxx-xxxxxxxxxx-547
BUILTIN\ACCOUNT OPERATORS	S-1-2-32-xxxxxxxxx-xxxxxxxxxx-xxxxxxxxxx-548
BUILTIN\SERVER OPERATORS	S-1-2-32-xxxxxxxxx-xxxxxxxxxx-xxxxxxxxxx-549
BUILTIN\PRINT OPERATORS	S-1-2-32-xxxxxxxxx-xxxxxxxxxx-xxxxxxxxxx-550
BUILTIN\BACKUP OPERATORS	S-1-2-32-xxxxxxxxx-xxxxxxxxxx-xxxxxxxxxx-551
BUILTIN\REPLICATOR	S-1-2-32-xxxxxxxxx-xxxxxxxxxx-xxxxxxxxxx-552

TABLE 3.3:   The Windows NT Special Groups

Special Groups	SID
\CREATOR OWNER	S-1-1-0x-xxxxxxxxx-xxxxxxxxxx-xxxxxxxxxx-xxx
\EVERYONE	S-1-1-0x-xxxxxxxxx-xxxxxxxxxx-xxxxxxxxxx-xxx
NT AUTHORITY\NETWORK	S-1-1-2x-xxxxxxxxx-xxxxxxxxxx-xxxxxxxxxx-xxx
NT AUTHORITY\INTERACTIVE	S-1-1-4x-xxxxxxxxx-xxxxxxxxxx-xxxxxxxxxx-xxx
NT AUTHORITY\SYSTEM	S-1-1-18-xxxxxxxxx-xxxxxxxxxx-xxxxxxxxxx-xxx

Naturally, there are many more SID codes and definitions. The above lists simply show a few of the more commonly used SIDs.

NOTE   Remember to differentiate between the HKEY_USERS hive and the HKEY_CURRENT_ USER hive. HKEY_CURRENT_USER contains a pointer that references the current user in HKEY_USERS.

The content of a user's profile, as it is found in the HKEY_USERS hive, is interesting. For example, the following keys are present in a typical user's profile (Usually, there is nothing to guarantee that they will all be present, or that others might be added.):

AppEvents—AppEvents contains information about events in a hive called EventLabels. This information includes a text label for the event, such as the event close, which has the label "Close program". These labels are used for a number of purposes, but one that most of us see is in the Control Panel's Sounds applet. A second section in AppEvents is Schemes, which lists labels for each application that uses specific sounds for its own events.

Console—Console contains the default command prompt configuration. This configuration may be customized for each command prompt individually, or it is possible in this hive to change the global default, which would be used for all new command prompts that are created. For an example of command prompt customization, open a command window and select Properties from the system menu. There are more settings that may be configured in the registry than are found in the Properties dialog box.

Control Panel—Control Panel contains information saved by many of the Control Panel's applets. Typically, these are default, or standard, values that are saved here, not user settings, which are stored elsewhere.

Environment—Environment contains the user environment variables for a user. Generally, the System Properties applet, in the Environment tab, is used to set user and system environment values.

Keyboard Layout—Keyboard Layout contains the keyboard configuration. Most users, at least those in the U.S., will have few or no substitutions. However, users who are using special keyboards, or non-U.S. English, will have some substitutions for special characters found in their languages.

Network—Network contains mappings for each network drive connected to the computer. Information about the connections includes the host (server), remote path, and user name used for the connection. The Network hive is not typically found in the .DEFAULT hive because users with no user profile are not automatically connected to a remote drive.

Printers—Printers contains mappings for each remote (network) printer connected to the computer. Information about the printer connection includes the host (server) and the DLL file used to manage the connection.

The Printers hive is not typically found in the .DEFAULT hive because users with no user profile are not automatically connected to a remote printer.

Software—Software contains information about software installed, including components of Windows NT, such as Schedule, Notepad, and so on. Also included in Software is Windows NT itself, with configuration information specific to the currently logged-on user.

UNICODE Program Groups—UNICODE Program Groups contains information about program groups that use UNICODE. More commonly found on computers configured for languages other than English, UNICODE is the scheme for displaying characters from other alphabets on computers.

HKEY_CURRENT_CONFIG—The Current Configuration Settings

The registry hive HKEY_CURRENT_CONFIG is created from two registry keys, HKEY_LOCAL_MACHINE\SYSTEM and HKEY_LOCAL_MACHINE\SOFTWARE. As this key is created dynamically, there is little value in modifying any of the objects found in the HKEY_CURRENT_CONFIG hive.

The HKEY_CURRENT_CONFIG hive is composed of two major sub-hives:

Software—Software contains current configurations for some software components. A typical configuration might have keys under Software for Microsoft Internet Explorer, for example.

System—Contains information about hardware. The most common device found in this key is the video display adapter (found in virtually all configurations) and sometimes information about the default video modes as well. The video mode settings contained here are typical for any video system: resolution, panning, refresh rates (Didn't you wonder where refresh rates were saved?), and BitsPerPel (color depth).

Generally, you would modify the source settings in HKEY_LOCAL_MACHINE\SYSTEM\ControlSet001\Hardware Profiles\Current\System\CurrentControlSet\Services\<device>\Device0, where <device> is the device being modified. For example, my Matrox Millennium is listed under mga_mil. There is another device called mga, also, which is identical in configuration.

> **TIP**
>
> For more information about the source for HKEY_CURRENT_CONFIG's source, take a look at HKEY_LOCAL_MACHINE, described earlier in this chapter.

HKEY_DYN_DATA—Settings for PnP (Plug and Play)

In Windows 95/98, the HKEY_DYN_DATA hive contains information about Plug and Play devices. Although Windows NT 4 does not support Plug and Play completely, there are vestiges of the PnP support in the operating system. One of these is the HKEY_DYN_DATA hive in the registry. Currently, with Windows NT 4, this hive is empty. Such is life! In Windows NT 5, we can expect full support for PnP.

With Windows 95/98, the HKEY_DYN_DATA hive contains two sub hives— one for PnP devices, the other used for the Windows 95/98 Performance Monitor. Didn't realize there was one, did you?

> **TIP**
>
> Wonder where Windows NT performance monitor information is contained? Since Windows 95/98 uses HKEY_DYN_DATA, and Windows NT doesn't, the performance data must be somewhere. To find the answer to this question, take a look at Chapter 10, "The Registry Meets the Performance Monitor."

NTUSER—The New User Profile

With Windows NT 4 networks, it is possible to make a modification to the NTUSER.DAT file, which contains the new user profile, and have this change affect all new users created after the change is made.

It is possible to modify HKEY_CURRENT_USER in NTUSER to set settings such as internationalization, colors, schemes, and other items.

Windows NT's installation process will create a default user profile. Whenever a new user logs onto a workstation or domain, this default user profile will then be copied to the user's profile. After that, the user may modify this default profile to his or her own requirements and needs.

As an example, Windows NT's default language is typically U.S. English. (There are other language editions of Windows NT; however, for this example we'll assume you are using the U.S. English version of Windows NT.) Whenever a new user logs on, the user will have U.S. English as his or her language, even if the system administrator has selected a different, non-English locale.

To modify the default new user's profile, you must perform the following steps.

WARNING   Caution: This technique is an advanced use of the Registry Editor and you must exercise care not to inadvertently modify the wrong registry or the wrong keys. Back up the registry *before* doing the following.

The default user profile is saved in the disk directory at %SystemRoot%\ Profiles\Default User\ with the name NTUSER.DAT. There is an entire configuration for new users in this directory—check out the Start Menu, Desktop, and other directories, too. You will find that interesting modifications may be made enabling new users to become proficient quickly without spending too much time customizing their computers.

First, to make this new user profile accessible to remote user, users other than those who log on locally, you must copy the Default User directory to the share named Netlogon. This share is typically located in the directory at %SystemRoot%\ System32\Repl\Import.

If there are BDCs (Backup Domain Controllers), you would actually edit the file in the Export directory (same initial path) because this directory is locally replicated to the Import directory and to the other BDC Import directories, although it might be located elsewhere. The Netlogon share can be located quickly by typing the following command:

```
net share
```

at a command prompt. The computer's shares will be displayed.

One way to copy these files is to create a new custom profile and copy the new custom profile using the Control Panel's System-User Profiles applet.

Follow these steps to modify the default new user profile in your new default user directory (Remember to create a new Default User directory, saving the current Default User directory as a backup.):

1. Start REGEDT32 using either a command prompt or the Start menu's Run command. Don't use Regedit for this process.

2. Click on the title bar of the HKEY_USERS on Local Machine window to make the window active.

3. Choose Registry ➤ Load Hive from the REGEDT32 menu.

4. Open the hive found in %SystemRoot%\Profiles\Default User. (If your system is configured with different directory names, choose the correct name.) This hive has the file name of NTUSER.DAT.

5. REGEDT32 will prompt for a new Key Name. Use the name NTUSER.

6. Change whatever keys in NTUSER that need to be modified. There is a slew of changeable items in the new profile, including AppEvents, Console, Control Panel, Environment, Keyboard Layout, Software, and UNICODE Program Groups. When adding new keys, do be careful to ensure that all users have at least read access to the new keys. No read access means that the key won't be accessible to the user.

TIP　　To set the permissions for a key, select the key, and then select Security ➤ Permissions from the REGEDT32 menu. Ensure that the group Everyone has at least read access. Resist the urge to give everyone more than read access to this key, too. Too much power can be a dangerous thing!

---

7. After making all modifications to NTUSER, choose Registry ➤ Unload Hive from the REGEDT32 menu.

8. Exit REGEDT32.

Once this profile is saved in the Netlogon share location, each time a new user logs on, the user will get this new profile.

Hints and Kinks from the Experts

Another installment of good stuff from the Windows NT gurus. In your search for more information, frequent their sites on the Internet. (See Appendix C, "Where Can I Get More Help?")

The Windows NT 4 Workstation Resource Kit

First, from Microsoft, is the Microsoft Windows NT Workstation Resource Kit 4.0. This resource kit is different from the Windows NT 4 Server Resource Kit. If you have both Server and Workstation systems installed, it might be a good idea to get both resource kits.

Chapter 23, "Overview of the Windows NT Registry," is a valuable resource for finding information about the registry and how it is used. I'd recommend reading Chapter 23 maybe two or three times!

How Can I Tell What Changes Are Made to the Registry? Using the regedit.exe program it is possible to export portions of the registry. This feature can be used as follows:

1. Start the Registry Editor (RegEdit.exe).

2. Select the key you want to monitor.

3. Select Registry ➢ Export registry file.

4. Enter a filename (if you want to export the whole registry, select Export Range All) and click OK.

5. Perform the change (install some software or change a system parameter).

6. Rerun steps 1 to 4 using a different filename.

7. Run the two files through a comparison utility, for example windiff.exe.

8. If you are using windiff, select File ➢ Compare Files, and you will be prompted to select the two files to compare.

9. Once compared, a summary will be displayed stating whether or not there are any differences. To view the changes, double-click on the message.

10. Press F8 to view the next change, or select View ➢ Next Change.

You have now found what changed.

(Courtesy of John Savill)

CHAPTER
FOUR

4

Registry Tools and Tips—
Getting the Work Done

- RegEdit

- RegEdt32

- RDisk

- The Windows NT Server Resource Kit

- The Microsoft System Policy Editor

- Hints and kinks from the experts

There are a number of excellent tools for users of Windows NT. First, coming directly from Microsoft as part of Windows NT are RegEdit and RegEdt32, the two registry editors. Two, did I say *two* registry editors? Why do we need two of them, anyway? Actually, each registry editor has its advantages and disadvantages. RegEdit is the registry editor created for Windows 95. This editor allows a few functions that RegEdt32 doesn't, such as importing and exporting registry files, and excellent search capability.

RegEdt32 is the "native" Windows NT registry editor. An MDI (multiple document interface) application, RegEdt32 displays each of the main hives in the registry in its own window. RegEdt32 has powerful administrative tools that RegEdit doesn't support, including read-only mode and security configuration, which allows you to restrict access to some registry hives, for example.

Both of these registry editors are valuable. I use either one depending on what I am doing, and my mood. I find RegEdit easier to use, while RegEdt32's got much more power. Not included with Windows NT directly, the Windows NT Resource Kit offers a number of excellent registry tools, too. These tools are:

CompReg—Run at a command prompt, CompReg will compare two local or remote registry keys, either Windows NT or Windows 95/98, and report the differences.

DelSrv—DelSrv is a service removal utility.

REG—Run at a command prompt, REG allows flexible manipulation of the registry. REG replaces a number of the other Resource Kit components, as noted in this chapter.

RegBack—Run at a command prompt, RegBack is a registry backup tool used to back up hives to devices other than tape. Remember, the Windows NT backup program supports tape devices only.

RegChg—Run at a command prompt, RegChg will allow changing a registry entry.

RegDel—Run at a command prompt, RegDel will allow deleting keys from the local registry or from a remote registry.

RegDir—Run at a command prompt, RegDir will display a directory type listing of a local or remote registry.

RegDmp—Run at a command prompt, RegDmp will dump a local or remote registry, with copious comments.

RegEntry—RegEntry is a powerful help file that lists many of the Windows NT registry hives, keys, and values. Tons of valuable advice is found in this help file, easily navigated because of the online search capabilities.

RegFind—Run at a command prompt, RegFind will search and/or replace data values in a local or remote registry.

RegIni—Run at a command prompt, RegIni will modify the SYSTEM and SOFTWARE hives.

RegKey—RegKey is a Windows-based utility to change logon and FAT file system options. This utility would fit well in the Windows NT Control Panel.

RegRead—Run at a command prompt, RegRead will search the HKEY_LOCAL_MACHINE registry hive in a local or remote registry.

RegRest—Run at a command prompt, RegRest is the complement to RegBack. RegRest restores backups made with RegBack.

RegSec—Run at a command prompt, RegSec lists the major hives (sections) in the local registry.

RestKey—Restores a key saved by RegSave, aka SaveKey.

RegChg—Run at a command prompt, RegChg will allow changing a remote registry entry.

SaveKey—Originally known as RegSave, SaveKey saves a key to a file that may later be reloaded as needed.

SecAdd—Run at a command prompt, SecAdd removes the Everyone group from a specified Registry key in the HKEY_LOCAL_MACHINE hive. SecAdd may also add read privileges to a user on a specified registry key.

The majority of the Windows NT Resource Kit's utilities are command prompt driven. However, being experienced users, we are not afraid of a command prompt, are we?

TIP

Found a program you don't know about? When in doubt, enter a command with either no options, or a /? option, and the command should display some form of help. Not all display significant help, and some do not provide any help at all. However, the Windows NT Resource Kit utilities won't cause damage if this help convention is used.

RegEdit

RegEdit is the Windows 95/98 registry editor. Microsoft was smart enough to make RegEdit work well with both Windows 95/98 and Windows NT, allowing Windows NT users the ability to choose between registry editors.

One of the nicest things about RegEdit is its simplicity. A quick user interface, easy to understand options, and a clean, uncluttered look make RegEdit a favorite for many users.

Registry Changes Are Permanent!

All changes made with RegEdit are immediate and for all intents—permanent! Though you can go back and manually undo a change made with RegEdit, generally, everything that you change with RegEdit affects the current registry. Unlike RegEdt32, RegEdit does not have a read-only mode. There is no safety net, nothing to catch your bloopers, and generally, you'll have to clean up your own mess.

In other words, you are editing the real, working, live, honest-to-goodness registry—not a copy. There is no save command in RegEdit; you type in a change, and it is saved right then and there.

So, make sure you have a backup of the registry files before diddling with registry.

Using RegEdit

Using RegEdit is as simple as starting it. From a command prompt, typing **RegEdit** will start the program. You can also select Start ➤ Run, type in **RegEdit**, and click the OK button to start RegEdit.

Once started, RegEdit will display the current registry (see Figure 4.1). By default, RegEdit opens the local registry. However, it is possible to open a registry on a remote computer by selecting Registry ➤ Connect Network Registry and entering the name of the computer whose registry is to be opened.

RegEdit has a straightforward menu. The Registry selection allows saving and loading text-based REG (registry) files, connecting to and disconnecting from a network registry, and printing the current branch or the entire registry.

RegEdit opens the current, local registry automatically.

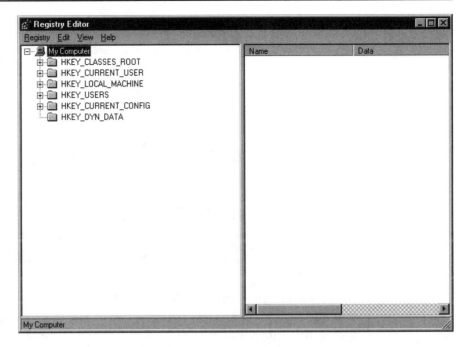

NOTE The typical Windows NT registry will be several thousand to hundreds of thousands of lines long. The registry on the author's server is over 130,000 lines. At 66 lines per page, that would be just about 2,000 pages. About, you say? Yes, many registry lines would require more than one line to print, so it would actually be much more than 2,000 pages.

The Edit menu selection allows the user to create a new key, or data value. Data types in RegEdit are restricted to String, Binary, and DWORD types. If there is a need to create a registry data type unique to Windows NT, it will be necessary to use RegEdt32 to create these data types.

The Edit menu also allows the user to delete an object, rename a hive or key, or copy a key name to a new name. Search facilities consist of finding the desired item.

Importing and Exporting Registry Hives and Keys

Exporting a registry hive (or the entire registry, if necessary) is a powerful feature of RegEdit. Once a registry is open, selecting a hive (or My Computer to export the entire registry) allows exporting the registry hive; see Figure 4.2.

FIGURE 4.2:

Exporting the current hive of a selected branch (hive) is easy!

A hive is exported into a text-based file. This file has no comments; some of the Resource Kit registry tools do comment exported sections of the registry. However, the file may be opened with most any text editor (such as Notepad), searched, and even modified. Any changes made to the exported text file may be incorporated into the registry by simply reimporting this file.

Importing a file that RegEdit had previously exported (see the next sidebar) is as simple as selecting Registry ➤ Import Registry File and entering the name of the registry file to import.

What Is an Exported Registry File?

A registry file exported by RegEdit will start with a line containing REGEDIT4. The next line following REGEDIT4 will be the first hive exported in a hierarchical format:

```
REGEDIT4
[HKEY_LOCAL_MACHINE]

[HKEY_LOCAL_MACHINE\HARDWARE]

[HKEY_LOCAL_MACHINE\HARDWARE\DESCRIPTION]
```

Generally, a full export of a registry will start with an export of the HKEY_LOCAL_MACHINE hive, as the above example shows.

The contents of an exported registry are arranged in the file as a hive (fully qualified, enclosed in brackets), followed by each key, with the key's data value after an equal sign:

```
[HKEY_LOCAL_MACHINE\HARDWARE\DESCRIPTION\System\FloatingPoint-
Processor\0]
"Component
Information"=hex:00,00,00,00,00,00,00,00,00,00,00,00,01,00,00,00
"Identifier"="x86 Family 5 Model 4 Stepping 3"
"Configuration
Data"=hex(9):ff,ff,ff,ff,ff,ff,ff,ff,00,00,00,00,00,00,00,00
```

The above example shows the three keys that the FloatingPointProcessor hive contains.

Why export the registry? First, none of the search capabilities in any of the registry editors are optimal. (Well, that's my opinion!) Loading an exported registry file into an editor allows you to quickly search for strings using the editor's search capability.

Another benefit is that it is easy to export the registry before installing an application or system extension. After an installation, it is also a good idea to export the registry. Then, using one of the system comparison tools (such as FC), you can compare the two versions of the registry and see what the installation has changed. Bingo—a quick way to see what's happening to the registry on installations.

Connecting to and Disconnecting from Remote Registries

When RegEdit starts, the local registry is opened. Once started, it is then possible to open the registry on a remote computer. Actually, it is possible to connect to many remote registries at one time (see Figure 4.3). Hopefully, this will make remote registry maintenance somewhat easier. Some functionality doesn't span multiple registries (such as searching), but generally, everything that may be performed on a local registry may be also performed on a remote registry.

TIP　　　　Once finished with a remote registry, it is a very good idea to disconnect from it. This may help prevent unexpected modifications to the wrong registry.

With a remote registry connected, you may not close, or disconnect, the local registry. This leaves it up to the user to make sure that if changes are made, they are made in the correct registry.

FIGURE 4.3:

A remote registry, and the local one, open at the same time in RegEdit.

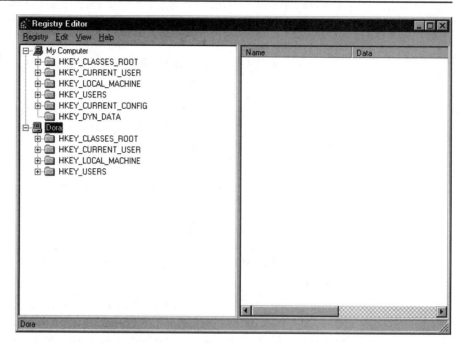

Printing the Registry

Printing a registry hive or sub-hive is possible in RegEdit. As mentioned previously, printing an entire registry is not a swell idea—you'd have to make a major investment in paper and printer supplies. Typically, a registry would require thousands of pages to print.

Printing sections of a registry hive can be very useful where a paper record is needed, or where one might need something to take to a meeting. The limits of printed registries are simply that searching them might be difficult.

Printing is more easily done if you select the hive or sub-hive to print, then select Registry ➤ Print from RegEdit's main menu. The Print dialog box, shown in Figure 4.4, will allow you to edit the branch to be printed (with the current hive as the default).

NOTE   The results of printing a registry report are almost identical to exporting the sub-hive, with the exception that on a printed report the initial line in an exported registry file (REGEDIT4) will not be present.

FIGURE 4.4:

RegEdit's Print dialog printing the sub-hive
HKEY_LOCAL_MACHINE\
HARDWARE\DESCRIPITON\
System\CentralProcessor.

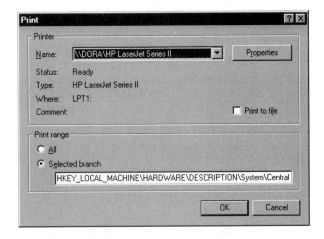

TIP

Is it readable, or usable? Generally not. The RegEdit print facility is basic and simply wraps lines at 80 characters. Any line more than 80 characters long will fold and be difficult to read. A better solution is to export the sub-hive and load the export file into a word processor, format it so that it is readable, and print it from the word processor.

Creating, Deleting, and Renaming Entries

RegEdit allows the user to quickly create, delete, and rename an entry.

Entries may consist of sub-hives or data values.

Creating a New Sub-Hive   A new sub-hive may be created quickly by following these steps:

1. Select the hive or sub-hive where the new sub-hive is to be created.

2. Select Edit ➤ New ➤ Key. Notice that Microsoft seems to have misused the term "key" in this instance when they wrote RegEdit.

3. RegEdit will create the new sub-hive, giving it a default name of "New Key #n" where *n* is a number beginning with 1. You will have the opportunity to edit the new sub-hive's name, which you should do at this time. Give the sub-hive a meaningful name, or the name that is expected for this sub-hive.

Once the new sub-hive has been created, it may then be populated with additional sub-hives or key and data values.

NOTE

A hive or sub-hive may contain both key and data values and other sub-hives at the same time.

Creating a New Key and Data Value Pair A new key and its corresponding data value may be created quickly by following these steps:

1. Select the hive or sub-hive where the new key and data value is to be created.

2. Select Edit ➢ New and then either String Value, Binary Value, or DWORD Value, depending on the type of data that this key will have. Again, notice that Microsoft seems to have misused the term "key" in this menu when they wrote RegEdit. You should select the data type for your key.

3. RegEdit will create the new key, giving it a default name of "New Value #n" where *n* is a number beginning with 1. You will have the opportunity to edit the new key's name, which you should do at this time. Give the key a meaningful name, or the name that is expected for it. Press the Enter key to save the new name.

4. To enter data into the new key, double-click the key. The correct edit box will be displayed, allowing the data to be edited.

Once the new key has been created, its data may be entered as necessary.

NOTE

A key need not have a data value entered. A key is valid without any data, though no data defaults vary depending on the type of data the key contains: String values have a zero-length string as default. Binary values have a zero-length binary value (different from having a value of zero). DWORD values have a value of zero.

Figure 4.5 shows RegEdit with a new sub-hive containing a sub-hive, a string value, a binary value, and a DWORD value, exactly as created by RegEdit. Note that I've named the initial sub-hive "Test Hive."

Each of the three new keys and values are defaults: All could be edited at any time. Selecting the key and clicking Edit ➢ Rename changes the key name.

You may double-click or right-click, also known as *context-clicking,* on the item to change the key's data value.

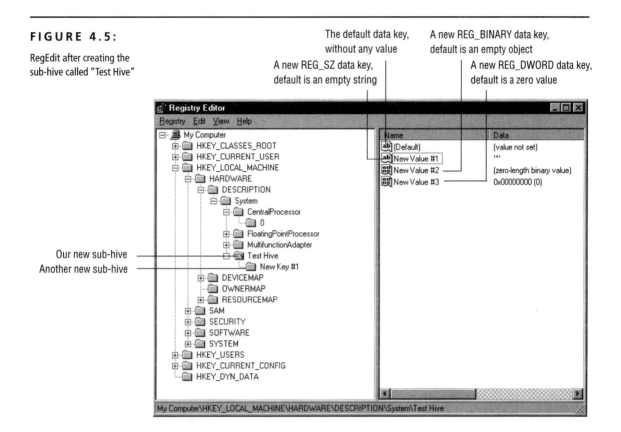

FIGURE 4.5:

RegEdit after creating the sub-hive called "Test Hive"

The default data key, without any value

A new REG_SZ data key, default is an empty string

A new REG_BINARY data key, default is an empty object

A new REG_DWORD data key, default is a zero value

Our new sub-hive
Another new sub-hive

Copying Key Names

Is this as simple as it seems? No, not really.

Copy Key Names, found in RegEdit's Edit menu, will copy the hive or sub-hive's name to the Clipboard. The information is copied in text format and may then be pasted into other applications or word processors as needed. For example, the new hive created for Figure 4.5, when copied, places the following text into the Clipboard:

HKEY_LOCAL_MACHINE\HARDWARE\DESCRIPTION\System\Test Hive\New Key #1

This means it is not necessary to manually type in long registry keys.

Searching: Find and Find Next

Searching a registry is one of the most important tasks that can be done. Before you make a modification, do debugging, or start browsing, it is usually necessary to search for something.

Now, as we've mentioned previously, RegEdit's search capabilities are a bit limited. However, RegEdit does have the best search of the two registry editors; RegEdt32 is more limited in its searching capabilities.

> **NOTE**
>
> RegEdit searches downward only. If what you are searching for is located above the current selection, you'll never find it. When in doubt, start at My Computer, and you can be assured that the search will include the entire registry.

Searching allows you to look at keys (hives and sub-hives), values (keys), and data (data values). You may choose to search any or all of these (see Figure 4.6), and the search may also be limited to whole strings only, which applies to searching text strings exclusively.

FIGURE 4.6:

RegEdit's search engine goes down only.

> **NOTE**
>
> RegEdit's search is not case specific, so strings to be searched for may be entered in lowercase if desired. This is nice, since the case of many registry entries is rather mixed.

Once the search finds the item searched for, it will stop on the word(s) found. If RegEdit's search is unable to find the string entered, RegEdit will display an error dialog box.

Tips for RegEdit Users

RegEdit offers the ability to export the registry, or parts of the registry, to a text file. This file may be used for any of the following:

- A snapshot of the condition of the registry at the time the export was made.

- A limited backup of the registry that might have value in restoring the registry in the event there is a failure.

- A file that when compared with another export file can quickly show differences between the two versions of the registry.

- A file that may be edited using any text editor (Notepad, for example), and the results of the editing may be incorporated into a registry using RegEdit's import facilities.

RegEdit allows adding simple hives, sub-hives, and keys (with limited data types) to any registry. Though RegEdit won't add the more complex data types that Windows NT supports (such as data types REG_MULTI_SZ, REG_FULL_RESOURCE_DESCRIPTOR, and so on) much work with the registry is done using the simple character and numeric data types.

RegEdt32

RegEdt32 is designed for the Windows NT registry directly. (RegEdit was actually designed for the Windows 95/98 registry.) Unlike RegEdit, RegEdt32 works as an MDI program, opening each of the main hives in the registry in a different window. This application model offers both a good side and a bad side. Each hive is kept separate, which means you don't inadvertently move from one hive to another, especially when doing searches; but at the same time, when searching, this can be difficult because things are not always where one expects them.

RegEdt32 is actually more powerful than RegEdit. Additional functionality includes management of security (noticeably missing on Windows 95/98 machines), more control of how data is displayed, more options, and the ability to add more data types to a registry.

Using RegEdt32

Using RegEdt32 is not difficult. It may be started from a command prompt, or from the Windows NT Start menu's Run command. Like any other command or program, a shortcut may be added to the Start menu for RegEdt32 as well, although I don't recommend doing so. RegEdt32 is a dangerous tool that should not be too easy for the uninitiated user to have access to.

When started, RegEdt32 opens the local registry. It is possible to open the registry on a remote computer as well; however, when editing a remote registry not all hives will be available.

Opening and Closing

RegEdt32 allows you to open and close both the local and remote registries. To open a local registry, select Registry ➢ Open Local. This will open the local registry without further ado. To close the currently selected registry, which may be either the local registry or a remote registry, click on any window in the registry to be closed, then select Registry ➢ Close.

NOTE   RegEdt32 allows closing all registries so that nothing is open. If this happens, you can either restart RegEdt32, or select Registry ➢ Open Local to open the local registry.

Remote Registries

Selecting Registry ➢ Select Computer will open remote registries. The Select Computer dialog box that appears in Figure 4.7 shows all computers accessible on the network. Select or double-click the computer whose registry is to be opened and click OK.

The remote computer's registry hives that may be opened are displayed, and a warning dialog will advise you if not all hives could be opened.

NOTE   Not all remote computers will allow you to edit, or open, their registry remotely. Windows 95/98 machines must specifically authorize remote registry editing (Windows NT systems do this automatically).

RegEdt32 is ready to open
the registry on the remote
computer DORA.

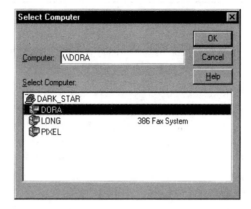

WARNING   As with a local registry, any changes made to a remote registry take effect immediately. There is no saving, no tossing the changes away, no just closing RegEdt32
and losing the changes. Once entered, the change takes effect, with possible dis-
astrous results for remote users who may not even realize that their registry was
modified.

Loading and Unloading

RegEdt32 allows a sub-hive to be loaded into the current registry. This sub-hive
may be modified and later unloaded. Why, one might ask?

There are several reasons for loading and unloading hives into RegEdt32. A
classic example was given in Chapter 3, "Anatomy of the Registry—The Blood,
Gore, and Guts." This example, configuring a modified new user profile, is contained in the file NTUSER.DAT.

In NTUSER.DAT is the HKEY_CURRENT_USER hive. Within this hive are settings, such as internationalization, colors, schemes, and other items.

Windows NT's installation process will create a default user profile—nothing
spectacular, a very plain configuration. Whenever a new user logs onto a workstation (or domain), this default user profile will be copied to the user's profile.
After that, the user may modify this default profile to his or her own requirements and needs. Of course, we might want to establish some organizational
defaults, such as a company scheme.

WARNING   The techniques shown next are advanced use of the registry editor, and you must exercise tons of care not to inadvertently modify the wrong registry, or wrong keys. Back up the registry *before* doing the following.

The default user profile is saved in the following disk directory:

%SystemRoot%\Profiles\Default User\

The name of the user profile is NTUSER.DAT. There is an entire configuration for new users in the directory %\SystemRoot %\Profiles\Default User—check out the Start Menu, Desktop, and other directories, too. You will find interesting modifications may be made enabling new users to become proficient quickly without spending too much time customizing their computers.

First, to make this new user profile accessible to remote users (users other than those who log on locally), you must copy the Default User directory to the share named Netlogon. This share is typically located in the directory at

C:\WINNT40\system32\Repl\Export

Placing files in Export will cause replication to copy it locally to Import, along with any BDCs (Backup Domain Controllers). Note that the share might be located elsewhere. The Netlogon share can be located quickly by typing the following command prompt command:

`net share`

The computer's shares will be displayed by the `Net Share` command.

One process to copy these files is to create a new custom profile, and copy the new custom profile using the Control Panel's System applet's User Profiles tab.

Do the following to modify the default new user profile (Remember to create a new Default User directory, saving the current Default User directory as a backup.):

1.   Start REGEDT32 using either a command prompt or by selecting Start ➢ Run. Don't use RegEdit for this process.

2.   Click on the title bar of the HKEY_USERS on Local Machine window to make the window active.

3. Choose Registry ➤ Load Hive from the REGEDT32 menu.

4. Open the hive found in %SystemRoot%\Profiles\Default User. (If your system is configured with different directory names, choose the correct name.) This hive has the filename of NTUSER.DAT.

5. REGEDT32 will prompt for a new Key Name. Use the name NTUSER.

6. Change whatever keys in NTUSER that need to be modified. There is a slew of changeable items in the new profile, including AppEvents, Console, Control Panel, Environment, Keyboard Layout, Software, and UNICODE Program Groups. When adding new keys, do be careful to ensure that all users have at least read access to the new keys. No read access means that the key won't be accessible to the person named "user."

TIP

To set the permissions for a key, select the key, and then select Security ➤ Permissions from the REGEDT32 menu. Ensure that the Everyone group has at least read access. Resist the urge to give everyone more than read access to this key. Too much power can be a dangerous thing!

7. After making all modifications to NTUSER, choose Registry ➤ Unload Hive from the REGEDT32 menu.

8. Exit REGEDT32.

Once this profile is saved in the Netlogon share location, each time a new user logs onto the network, the user will get this new profile.

Save Sub Key

Save Sub Key allows saving of a sub-hive and the sub-hive's contents. The data that is saved is written in text format, which may be edited. Information on the hive and keys is found in the saved file. Extensive data about the registry hive, including the date the registry file was last written to, is also saved in this file. Relatively easy to read, the file's size will be many, many times larger than the registry, as the small example in Figure 4.8 shows.

Just a suggestion: Don't print these files without first determining just how long they are. A simple hive was almost seven hundred lines of output.

FIGURE 4.8:

An example of the Save Sub Key saved file

```
                            HARDWARE\DESCRIPTION\System
          :                 System
          : Time:           4/29/98 - 8:58 AM

                            Component Information
                            REG_BINARY

      00 00 00 00 00 00 00 00 - 00 00 00 00 00 00 00 00
      ......

                            Configuration Data
                            REG_FULL_RESOURCE_DESCRIPTOR
                               Interface Type:    Invalid
                               Bus Number:        -1
                               Version:           0
                               Revision:          0
                               Partial Descriptor 0
                                  Resource:       Device Specific
                                  Disposition:    Undetermined
                                  Reserved1:      0x00000000
                                  Reserved2:      0x00000000
                                  Data:
      80 00 f7 03 00 00 3f 00 - 1f 00 01 00              ......?.....

                            Identifier
                            REG_SZ
                            AT/AT COMPATIBLE
```

Save Key

Save Key allows you to save a hive and the hive's contents. RegEdt32 writes the data saved in a binary format, no hacking or editing is allowed here. This file may be later reread using the Restore option in the Registry menu. The file is saved to the filename and extension you specify, unlike RegEdit, which automatically uses an extension of REG.

NOTE   Actually, to save a hive, you must have sufficient privilege to read the entire key. If you do not have this privilege, you will get the error message, "Insufficient privilege to save the key." Use the Permissions option in the Security menu to alter permissions if this becomes a problem.

Information saved by Save Key contains unqualified hive and key information. For example, if you save the HKEY_LOCAL_MACHINE\HARDWARE\ DESCRIPTION\System key, the only name saved to the file will be System.

The HKEY_LOCAL_MACHINE\HARDWARE\DESCRIPTION\ component of the hive name will *not* be saved. Again, think about how file and directory names are sometimes either fully qualified, or not.

Restoring

Restoring is what those guys on TLC (The Learning Channel) do to old furniture, right? Well, maybe so, but it's also possible to restore a hive in the registry using RegEdt32. The process is straightforward, although like everything else, you must have something to restore from.

Using Save Key (in the Registry menu), you can save a registry hive to a file. Since the file extension is user determined, it will be a really good idea to keep file names as descriptive as possible.

NOTE   When a hive is restored, the data overwrites the existing hive. It becomes permanent, as everything that RegEdt32 does is immediately written to the registry.

WARNING   More important—when a hive is restored, it is written on top of the currently selected hive. Make sure that the hive you are restoring belongs at the current selection. Again, make sure you name your file well so that you know exactly which hive a given file represents. Imagine coming back to a saved file, perhaps weeks later, and trying to restore it without knowing which hive it was saved from.

A suggestion: If there is a strong desire to play with the save and restore functionality of RegEdt32, install a practice copy of Windows NT. Don't do this on a working version—at least not a copy of Windows NT that you, or anyone else, cares about.

WARNING   Even *much* more important: Restoring a hive may override the read-only mode option—it will write to the registry no matter what! Care to guess how I found out?

When a hive is restored, the selected hive itself, which will be replaced, will not be renamed, even though the contents of the hive will be replaced.

Printing the Registry

If you select Registry ➤ Printer Setup from the Registry menu, this will take you to a standard printer configuration dialog box. Printing sub-hives of the registry with RegEdt32 results in a much nicer printout than is printed with RegEdit. The printout consists of virtually the same data that the Save Sub Tree in the Registry menu saves. An example of what a printout might look like is shown under "Save Sub Key", earlier in this chapter.

TIP   Be careful not to select too much to print. RegEdt32's printout capabilities can generate massive reports.

Adding Hives and Keys

Adding hives, keys, and data values is easy enough with RegEdt32. First, make sure the registry is not in read-only mode (see "Setting Options," later in this chapter). Next, select the hive where the new sub-hive or key is to be located. The RegEdt32 Edit menu then provides the tools to add the new item.

Adding Hives   A new sub-hive may be created by selecting Edit ➤ Add Key. The Add Key dialog box (see Figure 4.9) will allow specifying the name, and optionally, a class. Again, we are faced with the confusion between hives and keys with the registry editor.

NOTE   In one help paragraph, a Microsoft author switched between "key" and "hive" several times in the three sentences. Even Microsoft's writers were confused by the terminology, and rightly so.

FIGURE 4.9:

RegEdt32 allows adding
sub-hives with the Add Key
dialog box.

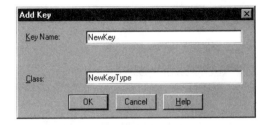

A sub-hive may be assigned a class. The class may be any of the following:

- REG_BINARY

- REG_SZ

- REG_EXPAND_SZ

- REG_DWORD

- REG_MULTI_SZ

- A user-supplied string describing the sub-hive's type

However, since sub-hives are not normally assigned a value, the class attribute is rarely used, and most often the class attribute is simply left blank.

Adding Keys and Values A new key and data type may be added by selecting Edit ➤ Add Value. The Add Value dialog box (see Figure 4.10) requires that the Value Name be entered, and a Data Type be selected.

FIGURE 4.10:

Adding a key is done using
the Add Value dialog box.

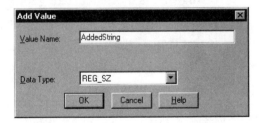

Unlike sub-hives, a key must have a data type. Valid selections for the data type are:

- REG_BINARY

- REG_SZ

- REG_EXPAND_SZ

- REG_DWORD

- REG_MULTI_SZ

The specialized types, such as REG_FULL_RESOURCE_DESCRIPTOR, may not be selected using the RegEdt32 Add Value dialog box, shown in Figure 4.9. (I'll leave it up to you to figure out how to create a key with a non-standard data type, with this hint: it can be done.)

Once the new key is created, one of the data value editors (see Figure 4.11) appropriate for the data type selected will be displayed.

FIGURE 4.11:

The RegEdt32 String Editor, just after I entered a new text string

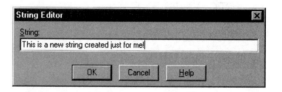

Once a key had been created, its data may be edited with a different editor. However, the contents may not make much sense when displayed using the wrong format. Select a key, then in the Edit menu, select one of the following choices:

Binary—Edits the item in binary format.

String—Edits the item in string format.

DWORD—Edits the item in the DWORD format. It will truncate objects longer than 4 bytes.

Multi String—Edits the item using the multi-line string editor.

WARNING   Remember that editing an object that is more than 4 bytes long into the DWORD editor will truncate the object to 4 bytes, permanently, irrevocably, without recourse, when you click OK.

NOTE
It is not possible to change a key's data type without creating a new key. Start by renaming the key to be changed to a temporary name. Next, create a new key with the original name, using the new data type. Finally, using the Clipboard, edit the original key, copy the key's data to the Clipboard, then edit the new key, and paste the data into the new key.

Deleting the Unwanted Getting rid of the unwanted is easy. Select the object, either a sub-hive or a key, to be deleted and then either select Edit ➤ Delete or just press the Delete key. RegEdt32 will prompt to confirm that the object is to be deleted if the Confirm on Delete option is selected. See "Confirm on Delete," later in this chapter.

WARNING
Once deleted, 'tis gone forever! Be careful not to delete anything that will be wanted later.

Searching for a Hive Value

The RegEdt32 search is somewhat different from that found in RegEdit. Unlike RegEdit, RegEdt32 is able to search either up or down and match case. Figure 4.12 shows the Find dialog box.

FIGURE 4.12:

The RegEdt32 Find dialog is better at searching criteria, but what is searched for is more limited.

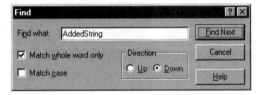

However, there is one big *gotcha*: RegEdt32 is able to search only on hive and sub-hive names. RegEdt32 is not able to find keys, or data, which is a major limitation if you ask me. (OK, they did ask me, but I didn't say anything at the time.)

If the search fails (which it usually does for me, since I'm always searching for data or for keys, not hives), a small dialog box will tell you that the item was not found. Don't forget to search in both directions if you are in the middle of the registry.

Security

Security is paramount in a Windows NT installation. The registry, just like the NTFS file system, may be protected from unauthorized access. This can be a critical issue because Windows NT supports remote registry editing.

NOTE   It is possible to make changes in a registry from another computer without the recipient of these changes even knowing that a change has been made.

RegEdit does not support any security modifications. If a hive is not accessible to RegEdit, the user is unable to view the hive or change it, depending on the level of access being granted. However, the RegEdt32 Security menu allows you to change the security attributes for a hive and any sub-hives, if desired.

Permissions   You may set permissions by selecting Security ➤ Permissions. When Permissions is selected, the Registry Key Permissions dialog box is displayed (see Figure 4.13). The currently selected key (sub-hive) is displayed along with the current permissions granted. Default permissions are typically, but not always, ones that everyone can read; the Administrator accounts and the system both have full control.

FIGURE 4.13:

RegEdt32 setting the permissions on the Central-Processor hive

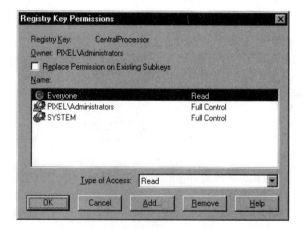

The Registry Key Permissions dialog box will list the hive name, referred to as Registry Key in the dialog box, and the owner. The checkbox, Replace Permission on Existing Subkeys, allows changing both the selected hive and any sub-hives contained in the selected hive.

In the list box are the current permissions, organized by Name. Select one name (Each must be modified separately.) and then the type of access may be set. Selections in Type of Access include the following:

Read—Allows the selected user to read, but not modify the object.

Full Control—Allows the selected user to read, write, and do all other operations to the object.

Special Access—Allows the selected user to change the following attributes (see Figure 4.14):

Full Control—Allows the selected user access to all of the operations listed here.

Query Value—Allows the selected user to have read access.

Set Value—Allows the selected user to have write access.

Create Subkey—Allows the selected user to create a sub-hive.

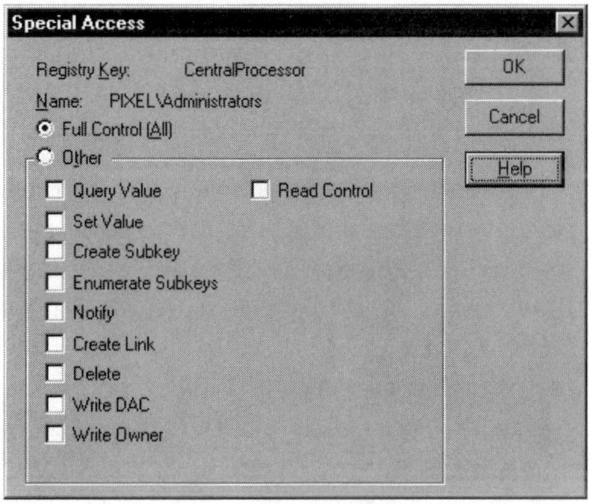

FIGURE 4.14:

RegEdt32 allows the owner to set security for every hive in the registry.

Enumerate Subkeys—Allows the selected user to obtain a list of sub-hives contained within the object.

Notify—Tells Windows NT to notify the owner when the object is modified.

Create Link—Allows the selected user to create a link to the object from another object.

Delete—Allows the selected user to delete the object.

Write DAC—Allows the selected user to modify Discretionary Access Control information.

Write Owner—Allows the selected user to modify the owner record information.

Read Control—Combines standard read, query value, enumerate subkeys, and notify permissions.

WARNING   Of course, the standard warnings apply: *Do not grant more permission than is necessary to do the job.* Understand what permissions are being granted (see the previous list) and consider granting permissions temporarily, removing anything granted as soon as it is not necessary.

Auditing   Auditing, when mentioned with the word "government" we generally get weak in the knees and start sweating profusely. However, auditing registry interaction can be somewhat less troublesome and very beneficial to the user.

Auditing, like permissions, is based on users. When Auditing is selected in the Security menu, the Registry Key Auditing dialog box (see Figure 4.15) is displayed. For an object that has not had any auditing set, the dialog box will be blank. The first thing to do is to check the Audit Permissions on Existing Subkeys option. Next, click the Add button to add new users to the Name list (see Figure 4.16). In the Add Users and Groups dialog box, both groups, and individual users, may be selected. To select specific users, first click the Show Users button. Select one name in the Names list and click the Add button to add that name to the list of names to be audited. Once all names to be audited have been added, click the OK button to close Add Users and Groups.

FIGURE 4.15:

Set the auditing permissions, either by individual user or by groups.

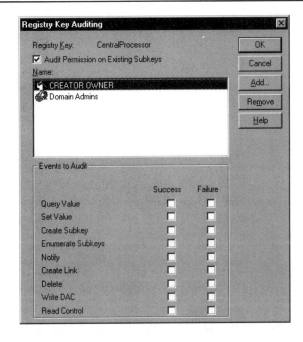

FIGURE 4.16:

Add users or groups to be audited in this dialog box.

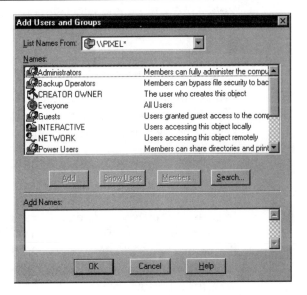

Next, in the Registry Key Auditing dialog box, select one of the names in the Name list, and set specific permissions in the Events to Audit list. Events that may be audited include:

Query Value—Is audited whenever the user or group in the Name list reads the object.

Set Value—Is audited whenever the user or group in the Name list writes to the object.

Create Subkey—Is audited whenever the user or group in the Name list creates a sub-hive.

Enumerate Subkeys—Is audited whenever the user or group in the Name list enumerates a list of sub-hives contained within the object.

Notify—Is audited whenever the user or group in the Name list does anything that generates a notification to the owner.

Create Link—Is audited whenever the user or group in the Name list creates a link to the object from another object.

Delete—Is audited whenever the user or group in the Name list deletes the object.

Write DAC—Is audited whenever the user or group in the Name list modifies the Discretionary Access Control information

Write Owner—Is audited whenever the user or group in the Name list modifies the owner record information.

Read Control—Is audited whenever the user or group in the Name list does anything that includes a standard read, query value, enumerate subkeys, or notify permissions.

Success and/or failure may be audited. Either or both may be selected if desired:

Success—Whenever a successful operation of this type is done, auditing information is saved. This mode is useful when creating a log of information about changes to the registry. The Success auditing can help one go back and determine what changes were made to the registry in an attempt to fix the problem.

Failure—Whenever an unsuccessful operation of this type is done, auditing information is saved. Whenever security is an issue (anytime there is more than one user), failure auditing can help point to attempts to compromise system security.

TIP

Select audit success for critical objects that shouldn't be changed often. Select audit failure for any object that is security related.

Owner   I own things, you own things. To keep the records straight, there are things like titles for cars, deeds for property, and other documents that trace ownership of anything that is non-trivial. With computers, especially Windows NT, ownership is an important thing. I "own" my computer, and probably, I don't want you messing with it.

When using NTFS, ownership may be set for files with Windows NT. As well, objects in the registry may have ownership, too. Ownership implies ultimate control: The owner may restrict access, audit, do whatever he or she wants.

The Owner selection in the Security menu of RegEdt32 allows one to take "ownership" of a registry object. The Owner dialog box is shown in Figure 4.17.

FIGURE 4.17;

The Owner dialog lists the current owner and allows setting ownership to the current user.

The owner of any object may allow or disallow another user from taking ownership; however, once another user has ownership, the original owner's rights are terminated.

NOTE

Both the current owner and the system administrator may assign ownership of the object to a user or to the system administrator.

Setting Options

RegEdt32 has a number of options that you may set. For example, the font may have the following options set: auto refresh, read-only mode, confirmations on delete, or save options on exit.

Font   Fonts, used to display all registry information, may be changed as necessary. Most often this is either a personal preference or it is necessary due to multiple language support. For example, you may be running RegEdt32 on one computer and remotely editing a registry on another computer, where the registry has strings that are in a different language or character set.

A standard Font dialog box (see Figure 4.18) will be displayed, allowing selection of the font, style (regular, italic, bold, or bold italic), and font size. As well, it is possible to select the Script (language) support, as well. Choices for Script include Western, Hebrew, Central European, and others.

FIGURE 4.18:

Setting fonts can be a personal preference, or they may support a different language or character set.

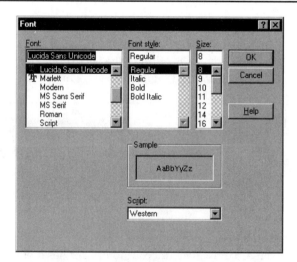

Auto Refresh   Auto Refresh is used to update all the RegEdt32 registry windows for the local registry. The choices are the following:

- Auto Refresh (in the Options menu) is checked; Refresh All and Refresh Active on the View menu will be disabled.

- Auto Refresh (in the Options menu) is not checked; Refresh All and Refresh Active on the View menu will be enabled.

Auto Refresh is active whenever it is checked in the Options menu.

NOTE   Auto Refresh cannot be used with a remote registry. Even if Auto Refresh is checked, remote registries will not be updated, nor will the Refresh All and Refresh Active selections be enabled in the View menu. When editing remote registries, always turn off Auto Refresh.

Read-Only   Read-only is used to make the current registry uneditable. This functionality serves as a safety net making it possible to browse the registry without being able to make any changes to it.

When read-only is active, it will be checked.

WARNING   Unless specifically editing a registry, it is best to keep read-only checked at all times. Making an inadvertent change to the registry can be the beginning of the end of the Windows NT installation!

Confirm on Delete   Whenever Confirm on Delete is active, RegEdt32 will notify the user with a Warning dialog box (see Figure 4.19) to confirm the deletion. The amount of time lost using Confirm on Delete is minimal compared to inadvertently deleting an object that is necessary to the well-being of Windows NT.

FIGURE 4.19:

Confirm on Delete warns you each time you delete an object.

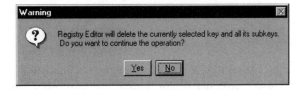

Confirm on Delete is active whenever there is a check next to it in the Options menu. Confirm on Delete is not available when RegEdt32 is in read-only mode.

Save on Exit   Options, such as those previously listed, may be either temporary (for the current session) or permanent. The Save on Exit selection on the Options menu allows RegEdt32 to save options whenever exiting.

WARNING   Only the settings of options are saved on exit. All changes to the registry are saved as they are made. There is no separate saving of the registry.

Tips for RegEdt32 Users

Several tips come to mind when using RegEdt32.

First, when saving a hive using Save Key (under Registry in the menu), make absolutely sure that the filename saved to is descriptive enough to enable restoring the hive at a later time. RegEdt32 does no checking of whether a hive being restored is the same hive as the one being replaced.

Second, as with RegEdit, be aware that printing can create reports of incredible size. Do not print the entire registry, especially if you are over the age of 22 or so: Life is just too short.

Finally, the RegEdt32 Save Subtree As functionality allows saving a detailed text report, identical to the printed report, to a disk file. This report could then be loaded into a text editor or word processor, allowing editing and later printing.

RDisk

RDisk is the Windows NT utility used to back up the system registry. RDisk is capable of backing up to a location on the hard drive (the repair directory) and to a diskette. The diskette version of this information is called the ERD (emergency repair diskette) and contains a complete copy of the registry that may be used to recover the system registry in the event of damage to the working copy of the registry.

Generally, copies of the registry contained in the repair directory, or on the ERD, are only usable with the Windows NT Setup program's repair facility. This may seem to limit their usefulness. However, when disaster strikes, anything is better than nothing. Actually, spending half an hour running the Setup repair is a small price to pay to recover from a damaged registry.

There can be only one repair directory on a Windows NT system, always at %SystemRoot%\Repair. However, there may be many ERDs in existence at one time.

TIP   Actually, you can copy the files in the repair directory to another save location, as well, then copy them back to the repair directory if necessary. Make sure that *all* files are copied or backed up, and restored as a set—don't attempt to back up only some of the files in the repair directory.

RDisk Options

RDisk runs with only one option, /S. The /S option comes in two flavors: RDisk /S and RDisk /S-. Using either /S option will cause RDisk to run in a non-interactive mode, without displaying the initial RDisk dialog user interface (see Figure 4.20).

FIGURE 4.20:

RDisk has a simple user interface, consisting of one dialog box.

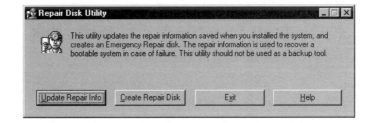

The RDisk options are:

No options selected—Open the RDisk user interface dialog box (Figure 4.19), allowing users to determine whether to update the repair information found in the %SystemRoot%\Repair directory, and whether to create a new ERD. When RDisk is used with no options, neither the SAM nor the SECURITY hives are saved.

/S—No initial RDisk user interface dialog box is displayed. This option tells RDisk to create a full backup of the entire registry, including the SAM and SECURITY hives. A prompt will then be made (see Figure 4.21) to ask if the user wishes to create a new ERD, and if so, RDisk will prompt for a diskette to be inserted.

/S—No initial RDisk user interface dialog box is displayed. This option tells RDisk to create a full backup of the entire registry, including the SAM and SECURITY hives. No opportunity to create an ERD is made.

FIGURE 4.21:

Setup allows you to create an ERD that preserves the registry as it is when Windows NT is first installed.

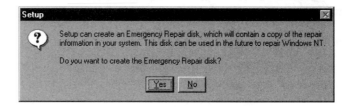

WARNING Microsoft recommends not using either /S or /S- on systems where there are a large number of users and groups defined in the SAM and SECURITY hives. Doing so might create a save set that is too large to fit on a single ERD diskette.

Creating an Emergency Repair Disk

To create an ERD, follow these steps:

1. Start RDisk without any options, or use the /S option. The /S- option will not allow creating an ERD.

2. If RDisk was started with no options, select Create Repair Disk from the Repair Disk Utility dialog box.

3. At the prompt to insert a diskette (see Figure 4.22), insert a diskette containing nothing of value. The diskette will be formatted by the RDisk utility.

FIGURE 4.22:

RDisk will format and write registry backup files to the ERD diskette.

---

4. Once RDisk is done, it will return to the original RDisk dialog box. You may then create another ERD, update the repair information on the hard disk, or exit.

> **NOTE** Remember to remove the floppy diskette from the drive once RDisk finishes writing the repair information to it. Attempting to boot this diskette won't cause a problem; however, it will have to be removed before the system can be rebooted.

Saving to the Repair Directory

RDisk can save to the repair directory. To update the %SystemRoot%\Repair directory, follow these steps:

1. Start RDisk without any options, or use the /S, or /S- options. If RDisk was started with either the /S or /S- options, the repair information will automatically be updated, and RDisk will exit automatically.

2. When RDisk is started with no options, select Update Repair Info from the Repair Disk Utility dialog box.

3. When RDisk is started with no options, a prompt is displayed to confirm that previously saved repair information will be overwritten (see Figure 4.23). Click the Yes button to continue.

FIGURE 4.23:

RDisk prompts before over-writing repair information when started with no options.

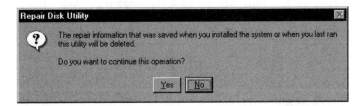

4. Once RDisk is done, it will return to the original RDisk dialog box. You may create an ERD or exit.

> **NOTE** If you create an ERD, either before or after updating repair information, remember to remove the floppy diskette from the drive once RDisk finishes writing the repair information to it—that way if the system is rebooted, it won't boot the ERD.

The Windows NT Server Resource Kit

The Windows NT Resource kit contains a number of very useful registry tools. Many of these tools run from a command prompt, although one has a Windows type interface.

If nothing else, the Windows NT Resource Kit is an excellent source of both information and a whole bunch of really neat utilities and tools for the Windows NT user. There are two resource kits available—one oriented toward the Windows NT Workstation user, and another larger kit aimed toward the Windows NT Server user. Larger organizations with both servers and workstations will want to consider having both kits, although the Windows NT Server Resource Kit has all the utilities (and more) from the Windows NT Workstation Resource Kit, and the text of the Windows NT Workstation Resource Kit on the enclosed CD.

> **NOTE**
>
> While I've got you in a spending mood, consider a subscription to Microsoft's TechNet program, which costs under $500. TechNet consists of monthly updates to a large CD-ROM collection containing a vast amount of technical information oriented toward system administrators. I don't know what I'd do without my TechNet subscription.

Many of the utilities in the Windows NT Resource Kit are either poorly documented or not documented at all. This is particularly true of the ones for manipulating the registry. This chapter contains the only available documentation that I know of for many of these commands.

COMPREG.EXE

CompReg is a Windows NT or Windows 95/98 32-bit character-based command-line program. It will display the differences between two local or remote registries. This program will run equally well under Windows NT and Windows 95/98. Currently, CompReg is at version 1.01. CompReg's command line is:

```
COMPREG <1> <2> [-v] [-r] [-e] [-d] [-q] [-n] [-h] [-?]
```

In this command line, <1> <2> represents the local or remote hives to compare. The default hive is HKEY_CURRENT_USER. An example is \\PIXEL\HKEY_LOCAL_MACHINE\Software. The root hives may be abbreviated as the following:

HKEY_LOCAL_MACHINE—lm

HKEY_CURRENT_USER—cu

HKEY_CLASSES_ROOT—cr

HKEY_USERS—us

The second argument, <2>, may be simply a computer name. In this case, the same hive is compared in both registries (see Table 4.1).

TABLE 4.1 CompReg Options

Option	Description
-v	Use the verbose mode, which will display both differences and matches in the two registries.
-r	Recurse into any "dead" hives (that is, hives that exist in only one hive).
-e	Set the error level to the last error code, rather than setting the error level.
-d	Display only keys, and not data values.
-q	Quiet mode, display only differences.
-n	Do not use color output.
-h	Display help screen.
-?	Display usage screen.

An example of executing CompReg is listed next. The lines shown as responses would vary for each execution of CompReg. Think of CompReg as working in a similar manner as the FC (file compare) command.

```
COMPREG "\lm\system\currentcontrolset\control\session manager" \\pixel
1 \DOS Devices!Mouse REG_SZ,[\Device\PointerClass0]

1 \Environment!DirCmd REG_SZ,[/o:gn /x]

1 \Environment!MSINPUT REG_SZ,[C:\Program Files\Microsoft Hardware]

1 \Environment!NTRESKIT REG_SZ,[C:\NTRESKIT]

1 \Environment!PROCESSOR_IDENTIFIER REG_SZ,[x86 Family 5 Model 4 Step-
ping 3, GenuineIntel]
```

```
2 \Environment!PROCESSOR_IDENTIFIER REG_SZ,[x86 Family 5 Model 2 Step-
ping 4, GenuineIntel]

1 \Environment!PROCESSOR_REVISION REG_SZ,[0403]
2 \Environment!PROCESSOR_REVISION REG_SZ,[0204]

1 \Environment!Path REG_EXPAND_SZ,[%SystemRoot%\system32;%System-
Root%;%SystemDrive%\rbin;%SystemDrive%\bin;C:\NTRESKIT;C:\NTRESKIT\Perl
;C:\PROGRA~1\MICROS~1\Office]
2 \Environment!Path REG_EXPAND_SZ,[%SystemRoot%\system32;%SystemRoot%]

1 \Environment!prompt REG_SZ,[$v$t$h$h$h $p$_]

1 \Executive!PriorityQuantumMatrix
REG_BINARY,[e0517ae800000000a26fbc01]
2 \Executive!PriorityQuantumMatrix
REG_BINARY,[40c8285800000000596dbd01]

1 \KnownDLLs!MSRATING REG_SZ,[MSRATING.DLL]

1 \KnownDLLs!NETAPI32 REG_SZ,[NETAPI32.DLL]

1 \KnownDLLs!SHDOCVW REG_SZ,[SHDOCVW.DLL]

1 \KnownDLLs!SHLWAPI REG_SZ,[SHLWAPI.DLL]

1 \KnownDLLs!URL REG_SZ,[URL.DLL]

1 \KnownDLLs!URLMON REG_SZ,[URLMON.DLL]

1 \KnownDLLs!WININET REG_SZ,[WININET.DLL]

1 \Memory Management!LargeSystemCache REG_DWORD,[1]
2 \Memory Management!LargeSystemCache REG_DWORD,[0]
1 \Memory Management!PagingFiles REG_MULTI_SZ,[C:\pagefile.sys 64
114|D:\pagefil e.sys 32 64|E:\pagefile.sys 64 128|]
2 \Memory Management!PagingFiles REG_MULTI_SZ,[C:\pagefile.sys 75|]

1 !LicensedProcessors REG_DWORD,[4]
2 !LicensedProcessors REG_DWORD,[2]
```

```
1 !RegisteredProcessors REG_DWORD,[4]
2 !RegisteredProcessors REG_DWORD,[2]

End of search : 20 differences found.

Windows NT Version 4.0  14:56:51 C:\NTRESKIT
```

CompReg is most useful when there are a number of computers with identical configurations. This happens often in corporate environments and in educational institutions, computer labs and such.

DELSRV.EXE

This command-line utility unregisters a service with the service control manager. While not specifically a registry tool, DelSrv does its job by modifying the registry. DelSrv also does its job by making changes in the control sets. Changes are made to ControlSet001 and CurrentControlSet. These changes are to delete the specified service from the Services hive.

WARNING   Sure, you can delete it, but what happens if you want it back? Deleting a service in error can be the beginning of the end! A repair of Windows NT using Setup might recover the system, but the only reasonable thing to do is restore from a backup. As DelSrv is totally undocumented, I did a backup (actually two backups), exported the registry using RegEdit, ran DelSrv, exported the registry a second time, and compared the results. Oh, and I restored my registry by re-importing the registry I exported before running DelSrv.

When DelSrv completes unregistering the service, the program displays the confirmation message, "The command completed successfully." If DelSrv fails (for a service that doesn't exist, for example), it will display the message, "Error touching service," indicating that the service was not found. There are no other messages produced by this rather simple program.

REG.EXE

Reg.exe is a tool combining the functionality of a number of the other command-line driven Windows NT 4 Resource Kit registry tools. This tool is included with release 2 of the Resource Kit, so you may not have Reg.exe in your resource kit. It improves the interaction between the command line and the registry, and is somewhat easier (and a whole lot more consistent) to use than the handful of other utilities.

Reg.exe has the following functionalities:

- Add
- Backup
- Copy
- Delete
- Load
- Query
- Restore
- Save
- Unload
- Update

In this section we'll cover each functionality, showing parameters and results as an example of how to use of Reg.exe.

ADD

The add function, invoked with the command `reg add <options>`, is used to add an object (sub-hive or data key) to the registry. Options required include the registry object to be added with the object's value, an optional machine name (additions may be made to remote registries), and an optional data type, as described next.

The command line for add is:

```
REG ADD RegistyPath=value [data type][\\Machine]
```

As with other registry tools, the registry path to be queried may be a ROOTKEY or a hive (with or without a data key). The ROOTKEY may consist of one of the following (HKLM is assumed if none is entered.):

HKLM—HKEY_LOCAL_MACHINE

HKCU—HKEY_CURRENT_USER

HKCR—HKEY_CLASSES_ROOT

HKU—HKEY_USERS

HKCC—HKEY_CURRENT_CONFIG

The hive will be further qualified to determine the object to be added.

The data type parameter will be one of the following; the default, if the data type is not specified, is to use REG_SZ:

- REG_SZ

- REG_DWORD

- REG_EXPAND_SZ

- REG_MULTI_SZ]

An example of executing the add command follows:

```
Windows NT Version 4.0    8:56:09 C:\
REG ADD HKLM\Software\MyCo\MyApp\Version=1.00
The operation completed successfully.


Windows NT Version 4.0    9:00:48 C:\
REG query HKLM\Software\MyCo\MyApp\Version
REG_SZ            Version 1.00

Windows NT Version 4.0    9:00:59 C:\
```

BACKUP

The backup function, invoked with the command `reg backup <options>`, is used to save the registry object specified to the file specified. Options required include the registry path to be saved, the output filename, and an optional machine name (saves may be made on remote registries).

The command line for backup is the following:

```
REG BACKUP RegistyPath OutputFileName [\\Machine]
```

As with other registry tools, the registry path to be queried may be a ROOTKEY or a hive, with or without a data key. The ROOTKEY may consist of one of the following; HKLM is assumed if none is entered:

HKLM—HKEY_LOCAL_MACHINE

HKCU—HKEY_CURRENT_USER

HKCR—HKEY_CLASSES_ROOT

HKU—HKEY_USERS

HKCC—HKEY_CURRENT_CONFIG

Only HKLM (HKEY_LOCAL_MACHINE) and HKU (HKEY_USERS) may be specified when copying objects to a remote registry.

NOTE Notice that reg save and reg backup are identical in functionality.

An example of executing the save command is shown next. In this example, I've saved a small sub-hive to the file C:\temp\MyCo.reg:

```
Windows NT Version 4.0    9:34:19 C:\
REG backup  HKLM\Software\MyCo\MyNewApp c:\temp\MyCo
The operation completed successfully.


Windows NT Version 4.0    9:34:21 C:\
dir c:\temp\myco.*
 Volume in drive C is (c) - Boot drive
 Volume Serial Number is CC56-5631

 Directory of c:\temp

07/17/98  09:34a                    8,192                    MyCo
            1 File(s)              8,192 bytes
                          183,407,104 bytes free

Windows NT Version 4.0    9:34:27 C:\
```

COPY

The copy function, invoked with the command `reg copy <options>`, is used to copy the registry object specified to a new name. Options required include the registry path to be copied (the source) and a destination name.

The command line for copy is the following:

```
REG COPY OldPath [\\Machine] Newpath [\\Machine]
```

As with other registry tools, the registry path to be copied (both the old path and the new path) may be a ROOTKEY or a hive. The path may be specified with or without a data key. The ROOTKEY may consist of one of the following; HKLM is assumed if none is entered:

HKLM—HKEY_LOCAL_MACHINE

HKCU—HKEY_CURRENT_USER

HKCR—HKEY_CLASSES_ROOT

HKU—HKEY_USERS

HKCC—HKEY_CURRENT_CONFIG

Only HKLM (HKEY_LOCAL_MACHINE) and HKU (HKEY_USERS) may be specified when copying objects to a remote registry.

NOTE   Consider the case where a registry object is copied from one registry to another registry, on a different machine. This command is more powerful than is apparent at first glance.

The hive may be further qualified to determine the contents of a specific sub-hive or data key. If no data key is specified, all the data keys in the sub-hive will be copied. An example of executing the copy command follows:

```
Windows NT Version 4.0   9:10:52 C:\
REG query HKLM\Software\MyCo\MyApp\

Listing of [Software\MyCo\MyApp\]

REG_SZ          Version 1.00
```

```
Windows NT Version 4.0   9:15:18 C:\
REG copy HKLM\Software\MyCo\MyApp\ HKLM\Software\MyCo\MyNewApp
The operation completed successfully.


Windows NT Version 4.0   9:15:43 C:\
REG query HKLM\Software\MyCo\MyNewApp

Listing of [Software\MyCo\MyNewApp]

REG_SZ          Version 1.00

Windows NT Version 4.0   9:15:51 C:\
```

DELETE

The delete function, invoked with the command `reg delete <options>`, is used to delete the specified registry object. Options required include the registry path to be deleted; an optional machine name (Queries may be made on remote registries.); and an optional parameter, /F, that forces the deletion without recourse.

The command line for delete is the following:

```
REG DELETE RegistyPath [\\Machine] [/F]
```

As with other registry tools, the registry path to be queried may be a ROOTKEY or a hive (with or without a data key). The ROOTKEY may consist of one of the following (HKLM is assumed if none is entered.):

HKLM—HKEY_LOCAL_MACHINE

HKCU—HKEY_CURRENT_USER

HKCR—HKEY_CLASSES_ROOT

HKU—HKEY_USERS

HKCC—HKEY_CURRENT_CONFIG

Only HKLM (HKEY_LOCAL_MACHINE) and HKU (HKEY_USERS) may be specified when deleting objects from a remote registry.

The hive deletion may be forced by using the /F option. This option will force the deletion without any prompt or confirmation. Microsoft recommends that the /F option be used only with extreme care. I agree.

An example of executing the delete command is shown next. Notice that I had to respond with a y to the prompt to delete the specified object:

```
Windows NT Version 4.0   9:05:30 C:\
REG query HKLM\Software\MyCo\MyApp\Version
REG_SZ          Version 2.00

Windows NT Version 4.0   9:09:30 C:\
REG delete HKLM\Software\MyCo\MyApp\Version
Permanently delete registry value Version (Y/N)? y
The operation completed successfully.


Windows NT Version 4.0   9:09:40 C:\
REG query HKLM\Software\MyCo\MyApp\Version
The system was unable to find the specified registry key.

Windows NT Version 4.0   9:09:43 C:\
```

LOAD

The load function, invoked with the command `reg load <options>`, is used to load the registry object from the file specified. The object must have been saved using the reg save or reg backup commands. Options required include the name of the file to load from, the registry path to be restored, and an optional machine name. (Restorations may be made to remote registries.)

The command line for restore is the following:

```
REG LOAD FileName keyname [\\Machine]
```

As with other registry tools, the registry path to be queried may be a ROOTKEY or a hive, with or without a data key. The ROOTKEY may consist of one of the following; HKLM is assumed if none is entered:

HKLM—HKEY_LOCAL_MACHINE

HKCU—HKEY_CURRENT_USER

Only HKLM (HKEY_LOCAL_MACHINE) and HKU (HKEY_USERS) may be specified in this command.

Objects in the sub-hive will be loaded, overwriting existing objects if there are any. An example of executing the load command follows:

```
Windows NT Version 4.0    9:47:58 C:\
 REG load c:\temp\myco  HKLM\TEMP\
The operation completed successfully.


Windows NT Version 4.0    9:48:01 C:\
reg query HKLM\TEMP /s

Listing of [TEMP\]

REG_SZ            Version 1.00

Windows NT Version 4.0    9:48:35 C:\
```

QUERY

The query function, invoked with the command `reg query <options>`, is used to search the registry for a specific data key and display its contents. Options required include the registry path to be queried; an optional machine name (Queries may be made on remote registries.); and an optional parameter, /S, that forces a query of all sub-hives.

The command line for query is as follows:

```
REG QUERY RegistyPath [\\Machine] [/S]
```

As with other registry tools, the registry path to be queried may be a ROOTKEY or a hive, with or without a data key. The ROOTKEY may consist of one of the following; HKLM is assumed if none is entered:

HKLM—HKEY_LOCAL_MACHINE

HKCU—HKEY_CURRENT_USER

HKCR—HKEY_CLASSES_ROOT

HKU—HKEY_USERS

HKCC—HKEY_CURRENT_CONFIG

The hive may be further qualified to determine the contents of a specific sub-hive or data key. If no data key is specified, all data keys in the sub-hive will be retrieved. An example of executing the query command follows:

```
Windows NT Version 4.0    8:54:08 C:\
REG QUERY HKLM\Software\Microsoft\ResKit\Setup\InstallDir
REG_SZ          InstallDir      C:\NTRESKIT

Windows NT Version 4.0    8:54:11 C:\
```

RESTORE

The restore function, invoked with the command `reg restore <options>`, is used to restore the registry object from the file specified. The object must have been saved using the reg save or reg backup commands. Options required include the name of the file to restore from, the registry path to be restored, and an optional machine name. (Restorations may be made to remote registries.)

The command line for restore is the following:

```
REG QUERY FileName RegistyPath [\\Machine]
```

As with other registry tools, the registry path to be queried may be a ROOTKEY or a hive, with or without a data key. The ROOTKEY may consist of one of the following; HKLM is assumed if none is entered:

HKLM—HKEY_LOCAL_MACHINE

HKCU—HKEY_CURRENT_USER

HKCR—HKEY_CLASSES_ROOT

HKU—HKEY_USERS

HKCC—HKEY_CURRENT_CONFIG

Only HKLM (HKEY_LOCAL_MACHINE) and HKU (HKEY_USERS) may be specified when copying objects to a remote registry.

Objects in the sub-hive will be restored and overwritten by the information contained in the specified file. An example of executing the restore command is the following:

```
Windows NT Version 4.0    9:39:17 C:\
 REG backup  HKLM\Software\MyCo\MyNewApp c:\temp\MyCo
```

```
The operation completed successfully.

Windows NT Version 4.0    9:40:20 C:\
 REG restore c:\temp\myco  HKLM\Software\MyCo\MyNewApp
Are you sure you want to replace Software\MyCo\MyNewApp (Y/N) y
The operation completed successfully.



Windows NT Version 4.0    9:40:44 C:\
```

SAVE

The save function, invoked with the command `reg save <options>`, is used to save the registry object specified to the file specified. Options required include the registry path to be saved, the output file name, and an optional machine name. (Saves may be made on remote registries.)

The command line for save is the following:

```
REG SAVE RegistyPath OutputFileName [\\Machine]
```

As with other registry tools, the registry path to be queried may be a ROOTKEY or a hive (with or without a data key). The ROOTKEY may consist of one of the following (HKLM is assumed if none is entered):

HKLM—HKEY_LOCAL_MACHINE

HKCU—HKEY_CURRENT_USER

HKCR—HKEY_CLASSES_ROOT

HKU—HKEY_USERS

HKCC—HKEY_CURRENT_CONFIG

Only HKLM (HKEY_LOCAL_MACHINE) and HKU (HKEY_USERS) may be specified when copying objects to a remote registry.

An example of executing the save command is shown next. In this example, I've saved a small sub-hive to the file C:\temp\MyCo.reg:

```
Windows NT Version 4.0    9:16:27 C:\
REG save  HKLM\Software\MyCo\MyNewApp c:\temp\MyCo.reg
The operation completed successfully.
```

```
Windows NT Version 4.0   9:18:35 C:\
dir c:\temp\myco.reg
 Volume in drive C is (c) - Boot drive
 Volume Serial Number is CC56-5631

 Directory of c:\temp

07/17/98  09:18a                  8,192                MyCo.reg
            1 File(s)          8,192 bytes
                         183,407,104 bytes free

Windows NT Version 4.0   9:19:08 C:\
```

UNLOAD

The unload function, invoked with the command `reg unload <options>`, is used to unload (delete) the registry object specified. The object must be a single level sub-hive, such as HKLM\TEMP, in order to use unload. Options required include the name of the sub-hive to unload and an optional machine name. (Objects may be unloaded from remote registries.)

The command line for restore is the following:

```
REG UNLOAD keyname [\\Machine]
```

As with other registry tools, the registry path to be queried may be a ROOTKEY or a hive, with or without a data key. The ROOTKEY may consist of one of the following; HKLM is assumed if none is entered:

HKLM—HKEY_LOCAL_MACHINE

HKCU—HKEY_CURRENT_USER

Only HKLM (HKEY_LOCAL_MACHINE) and HKU (HKEY_USERS) may be specified in this command.

Objects in the sub-hive will be unloaded and will not be saved. There is no recovery in the event of a user error with this command. An example of executing the unload command is the following:

```
Windows NT Version 4.0   9:47:58 C:\
REG unload HKLM\TEMP\
The operation completed successfully.
```

```
Windows NT Version 4.0    9:48:01 C:\
reg query HKLM\TEMP /s

The system was unable to find the specified registry key.

Windows NT Version 4.0    9:48:35 C:\
```

UPDATE

The update function, invoked with the command `reg update <options>`, is used to update an existing object (sub-hive or data key) to the registry. Options required include the registry object to be added (with the object's value) and an optional machine name. (Updates may be made to remote registries.)

The command line for udpate is the following:

```
REG UPDATE RegistyPath=value [\\Machine]
```

As with other registry tools, the registry path to be queried may be a ROOTKEY or a hive, with or without a data key. The ROOTKEY may consist of one of the following; HKLM is assumed if none is entered:

HKLM—HKEY_LOCAL_MACHINE

HKCU—HKEY_CURRENT_USER

HKCR—HKEY_CLASSES_ROOT

HKU—HKEY_USERS

HKCC—HKEY_CURRENT_CONFIG

The hive will be further qualified to determine the object to be added.

Here is an example of executing the **update** command (First I show the original value, then I update the object, then I show the new value.):

```
Windows NT Version 4.0    9:00:48 C:\
REG query HKLM\Software\MyCo\MyApp\Version
REG_SZ        Version 1.00

Windows NT Version 4.0    9:01:33 C:\
REG update HKLM\Software\MyCo\MyApp\Version=2.00
The operation completed successfully.
```

```
Windows NT Version 4.0   9:03:47 C:\
REG query HKLM\Software\MyCo\MyApp\Version
REG_SZ          Version 2.00

Windows NT Version 4.0   9:03:53 C:\
```

REGBACK.EXE

RegBack allows you to back up pieces of the registry, known as hives, while the system is running and has them open.

The required privilege, SetBackupPrivilege (SetBackupPrivilege is called the "Back up files and directories privilege" in the User Manager.) is required to use RegBack. Typically, Administrators and Backup Operators have this privilege by default; however, other users may be assigned it as necessary.

The RegBack program will not succeed if the hives being backed up do not fit on the target device, such as a diskette. A suggestion is to use RegBack with the destination being a hard drive, and then move the resultant backup to diskettes using either the Windows NT Backup command, or perhaps using PKZIP or one of the other available file compression utility programs to copy the backup file to diskette.

RegBack will not copy any files in system32\config that are not opened by the registry—use copy, xcopy, or another file copy program to back up these files.

Use the following command to back up the entire registry:

```
regback <directory argument>
```

RegBack typically expects the name of an existing, and preferably empty, directory (or drive) as the destination. Each registry file will be backed up to a filename that is the same as the original filename for the registry file.

Use the following command to back up a specific hive:

```
regback <filename> <hivetype> <hivename>
```

This version will back up either the machine, or users' hive, or any root hive.

If the specified output filename exists, RegBack will preserve the existing file, and simply end with an error. If running the registry backup with a batch file, test for the existence of the output file and either rename it, or delete it as necessary.

The resulting backup file(s) may be restored using the RegRest program, as shown in the next section.

RegBack, when run from a batch file, will signal the following error values (which you may test for):

0—successful backup of the registry files

1—for a hive that required a manual backup

2—all other errors

Generally, Microsoft recommends that if you have a tape device installed, you should use NTBackup instead of RegBack.

Here is an example run of executing RegBack:

```
Windows NT Version 4.0  13:27:45 C:\NTRESKIT
REM-Create a destination location, before running RegBack
Windows NT Version 4.0  13:29:21 C:\NTRESKIT
md \temp\regback

Windows NT Version 4.0  13:35:41 C:\NTRESKIT
regback c:\temp\regback
saving SECURITY to c:\temp\regback\SECURITY
saving SOFTWARE to c:\temp\regback\software
saving SYSTEM to c:\temp\regback\system
saving .DEFAULT to c:\temp\regback\default
saving SAM to c:\temp\regback\SAM

***Hive = \REGISTRY\USER\S-1-5-21-45749729-16073390-2133884337-500
Stored in file \Device\Harddisk0\Partition1\WINNT40\Profiles\Adminis-
trator\NTUSER.DAT
Must be backed up manually
regback <filename you choose> users S-1-5-21-45749729-16073390-
2133884337-500


Windows NT Version 4.0  13:36:05 C:\NTRESKIT
```

In the above example, the hive indicated (the currently logged on user) could not automatically be backed up. Therefore, RegBack told me that I had to back up this hive manually. I did this by issuing the following command:

```
regback c:\temp\regback\Admin users S-1-5-21-45749729-16073390-
2133884337-500
```

```
saving S-1-5-21-45749729-16073390-2133884337-500 to
c:\temp\regback\Admin

Windows NT Version 4.0  13:41:12 C:\NTRESKIT
```

I simply cut and pasted RegBack's message line indicating the command to use, and edited in the destination directory and filename to use. RegBack did all the work for me.

REGREST.EXE

RegRest is a program used to restore registry files backed up using RegBack (discussed in the previous section). RegRest uses the RegReplaceKey API to perform its magic. It saves the original hive in a SAV file, and then moves (not copies) the backup registry file to the %SystemRoot%\System32\config directory. Since RegRest uses move, and not copy, the backup files *must* reside on the same volume as %SystemRoot%.

WARNING   Because of the way that RegRest works (moving and renaming registry files), it is imperative that the system be rebooted for the restored registry files to take effect.

Usage of RegRest is similar to RegBack, with the addition of a specified location for the original registry files that RegRest will save as a precaution against disaster. The command syntax for a basic restoration of the registry is the following:

```
regrest <new files> <save files>
```

In this syntax, <new files> is the location of the backup created with RegBack. The <save files> location is where the current registry files will be backed up. Both <new files> and <save files> should be on the same volume (drive) as %SystemRoot% for RegRest to work correctly.

RegRest will warn of any hives needing to be restored manually. Use this syntax to manually restore these hives:

```
regrest <newfilename> <savefilename> <hivetype> <hivename>
```

In this syntax, <newfilename> is the name used to back up the specified hive with RegBack, and <savefilename> is the location and name of the file to be used to back up the existing hive. Additionally, <hivetype> is either "machine" or "users"; <hivename> is the name of an immediate subtree of HKEY_LOCAL_MACHINE or HKEY_LOCAL_USERS.

Here is a RegRest session:

```
Windows NT Version 4.0  14:04:10 C:\NTRESKIT
regrest c:\temp\regback c:\temp\regback\regrest

replacing SECURITY with c:\temp\regback\SECURITY
replacing SOFTWARE with c:\temp\regback\software
replacing SYSTEM with c:\temp\regback\system
replacing .DEFAULT with c:\temp\regback\default
replacing SAM with c:\temp\regback\SAM

***Hive = \REGISTRY\USER\S-1-5-21-45749729-16073390-2133884337-500
Stored in file \Device\Harddisk0\Partition1\WINNT40\Profiles\Adminis-
trator\NTUSER.DAT
Must be replaced manually
regrest <newpath> <savepath> users S-1-5-21-45749729-16073390-
2133884337-500

You must reboot for changes to take effect.

Windows NT Version 4.0  14:04:50 C:\NTRESKIT
```

Finally, replacing the current user, using the second form of RegRest (again, a simple cut and paste saves much error-prone typing.):

```
regrest c:\temp\regback\admin c:\temp\regback\regsave\admin users S-1-
5-21-45749729-16073390-2133884337-500
replacing S-1-5-21-45749729-16073390-2133884337-500 with c:\temp\reg-
back\admin
newfile='c:\temp\regback\admin'
savefile='c:\temp\regback\regsave\admin'

Windows NT Version 4.0  14:07:10 C:\NTRESKIT
```

If RegRest fails, it will indicate a failure code and return an error value to the caller. For example, this would happen if RegRest was run from a batch file.

REGCHG.EXE

RegChg, sometimes casually called RegChange, is used to change a registry key from a command-line prompt. This small program uses RegSetValue to change the value of the registry key.

RegChg takes the following four parameters:

Path—Is the hive (fully qualified, except that HKEY_LOCAL_MACHINE may not be specified).

EntryName—Is the name of the key to be changed.

Type—Is the data type, the following data types may be used:

- REG_FULL_RESOURCE_DESCRIPTOR
- REG_RESOURCE_LIST
- REG_MULTI_SZ
- REG_LINK
- REG_DWORD_BIG_ENDIAN
- REG_DWORD_LITTLE_ENDIAN
- REG_DWORD
- REG_BINARY
- REG_NONE
- REG_EXPAND_SZ
- REG_SZ

Value—Is the new value to be assigned to the key.

RegChg returns the following messages when it completes:

Invalid EntryName—Is displayed whenever the entry name (key) specified is not valid.

Error n—Is displayed when any other errors are detected, where n is a numeric value. Error 6 is displayed when the path is invalid.

The command completed successfully—Is displayed whenever RegChg completes successfully.

Here is a sample run of RegChg:

```
RegChg HARDWARE\DESCRIPTION\System\NewKey NewValue REG_SZ "My New
Value"
```

This example changes the value stored in the key NewValue, which is stored in the hive HKEY_LOCAL_MACHINE\HARDWARE\DESCRIPTION\System\ NewKey to a string with the type of REG_SZ, which contains "My New Value".

> **WARNING** RegChg will only change objects located in the HKEY_LOCAL_MACHINE hive. Attempts to change other hives will fail, usually with an error message, "Error 6." Painfully descriptive error message, right?

> **NOTE** The RegChg utility is no longer supplied. It is now part of reg.exe in the latest update of the Windows NT Resource Kit.

REGDEL.EXE

RegDel is a command-line program that may be used to delete a sub-hive under the HKEY_LOCAL_MACHINE hive. RegDel will not delete a key value, however. RegDel will work with both the local registry and with remote registries.

Here is an example of the usage for RegDel:

```
regdel "RegistryPathToDelete"
regdel -r \\ServerName "RegistryPathToDelete"
regdel -l \ServerName "RegistryPathToDelete"
```

The -l option is undocumented and unsupported. I would recommend not using it.

> **WARNING** Unlike RegChg, RegDel does not print any success or error messages, set error codes, or prompt for confirmation before deleting the sub-hive specified. Be most careful that a needed sub-hive of the registry is not deleted in error, because that could spell the absolute end of the world as far as Windows NT is concerned.

Here is a sample run of RegDel:

```
RegDel HARDWARE\DESCRIPTION\System\NewKey
```

In the above example, the sub-hive NewKey (created to test RegChg, discussed earlier in this chapter) is deleted from the registry. The sub-hive HKEY_LOCAL_MACHINE\HARDWARE\DESCRIPTION\System\NewKey is deleted without confirmation or warning.

WARNING   RegDel does not prompt for confirmations before deleting a sub-hive. It takes but a slip on the keyboard, hitting Enter instead of \, to blow away important parts of the registry without any recourse other than to restore the registry, or reinstall Windows NT. For this reason, I recommend using RegDel only in batch files and not at a command prompt.

NOTE   The RegDel utility is no longer supplied. It is now part of reg.exe in the latest update of the Windows NT Resource Kit.

REGDIR.EXE

RegDir is a command-line program that lists objects in a local or remote registry. Like the file system DIR command, RegDir is able to *recurse* (list sub-hives).

Here is an example of the usage for RegDir:

```
REGDIR [-h hivefile_hiveroot | -w Win95_Directory | -m \\machinename]
[-i n] [-o outputWidth] [-r] registryPath
```

In this usage, the options are defined as follows:

-h—Is the local root hive to display.

-w—Uses the Windows 95/98 registry specified, not a Windows NT registry.

-m—Opens a remote Windows NT registry on the specified computer.

-i n—Indents sub objects by n (default is four) spaces.

-o—Sets the output width to the specified value. The default is 80 if the output is to the screen, and 240 when output is redirected to a file.

-r—Tells RegDir to recurse (view) into sub-hives, listing all sub-hives and keys.

The registryPath specifies the base sub-hive to start the listing from. There are several predefined prefixes defined in RegDir:

\Registry—Resolves to the base registry (allowing access to HKEY_USERS, and HKEY_LOCAL_MACHINE).

\Registry\Users—Resolves to HKEY_USERS.

\Registry\Machine—Resolves to HKEY_LOCAL_MACHINE.

\HKEY_LOCAL_MACHINE—Resolves to HKEY_LOCAL_MACHINE.

USER:—Resolves to HKEY_CURRENT_USER.

Here is a sample run of RegDir:

```
Windows NT Version 4.0  16:42:20 C:\NTRESKIT
regdir \registry\machine\hardware\description\system
\registry\machine\hardware\description\system
    Component Information = REG_BINARY 0x00000010 \...
    Identifier = AT/AT COMPATIBLE
    Configuration Data = REG_FULL_RESOURCE_DESCRIPTOR 0x00000078 \...
    SystemBiosDate = 08/28/97
    SystemBiosVersion = REG_MULTI_SZ "Award Modular BIOS v4.51PG"  \...
    VideoBiosDate = 13/12/95
    VideoBiosVersion = REG_MULTI_SZ "VGA/VBE BIOS, Version V1.9 "  \...
    CentralProcessor
    FloatingPointProcessor
    MultifunctionAdapter


 Windows NT Version 4.0  16:42:24 C:\NTRESKIT
```

In this example, the objects in the HKEY_LOCAL_MACHINE\HARDWARE\ DESCRIPTION\System sub-hive are listed. The objects that have no "= value" following the name are themselves sub-hives. For example, CentralProcessor is a sub-hive of the System sub-hive.

NOTE
The RegDir utility is no longer supplied, it is now part of reg.exe in the latest update of the Windows NT Resource Kit.

REGDMP.EXE

RegDmp is a utility used to dump, in a formatted fashion, part or all of the registry. RegDmp offers the ability to detect any REG_SZ strings not having the (typically required) trailing null character to signify the end of the string. Not writing a trailing null character (a hex 0x00) is a common programming error.

Here is an example of the usage of RegDmp:

```
REGDMP [-h hivefile_hiveroot | -w Win95_Directory | -m \\machinename]
[-i n] [-o outputWidth] [-s] [-o outputWidth] registryPath
```

In this example, the options are defined as follows:

-h—Is the local root hive to display.

-w—Uses the Windows 95/98 registry specified, not a Windows NT registry.

-m—Opens a remote Windows NT registry on the specified computer.

-i n—Indents sub objects by n (default is four) spaces.

-o—Sets the output width to the specified value. The default is 80 if output is to the screen, and 240 when output is redirected to a file.

-s—Tells RegDmp to write only summary output, which truncates output lines to a readable length.

The registryPath specifies the base sub-hive to start the listing from. There are several predefined prefixes defined in RegDir:

\Registry—Resolves to the base registry (allowing access to HKEY_USERS, and HKEY_LOCAL_MACHINE).

\Registry\Users—Resolves to HKEY_USERS.

\Registry\Machine—Resolves to HKEY_LOCAL_MACHINE.

\HKEY_LOCAL_MACHINE—Resolves to HKEY_LOCAL_MACHINE.

USER:—Resolves to HKEY_CURRENT_USER.

NOTE
When RegDmp detects a REG_SZ or REG_EXPAND_SZ type string missing a trailing null character, the string will be prefixed with the message "(*** MISSING TRAILING NULL CHARACTER ***)." When a Unicode string does not have the correct multiple of characters, the message "(*** Length not multiple of WCHAR ***)" will be prefixed.

Here is a sample run of RegDmp:

```
Windows NT Version 4.0  18:46:16 C:\NTRESKIT
regdmp  HKEY_LOCAL_MACHINE\hardware\description\system\CentralProcessor
HKEY_LOCAL_MACHINE\hardware\description\system\CentralProcessor
    0
        Component Information = REG_BINARY 0x00000010 0x00000000
0x00000000 \
                                0x00000000 0x00000001
        Identifier = x86 Family 5 Model 4 Stepping 3
        Configuration Data = REG_FULL_RESOURCE_DESCRIPTOR 0x00000010 \
                            0xffffffff 0xffffffff 0x00000000
0x00000000
        VendorIdentifier = GenuineIntel
        ~MHz = REG_DWORD 0x000000e9


Windows NT Version 4.0  18:46:24 C:\NTRESKIT
```

This example shows a dump of the CentralProcessor sub-hive of the registry. This hive has information about the installed CPU.

RegDmp's output file follows these rules:

1. Use a semicolon as the first non-blank character in a line, to denote a comment line.

2. Continuation lines are marked with a backslash (\) character as the last non-blank character in the line. All characters, from the backslash to the first non-blank character in the next line, will be ignored including the backslash, but excluding the first non-blank character.

3. Use indentation to indicate the tree structure of registry keys. RegDmp indents four spaces by default.

4. With key names, leading and trailing space characters are ignored and not included in the key name, unless the key name is surrounded by quotes ("). Embedded spaces are part of a key name, except for at the equal (=) and at sign (@) characters, which are special (see item 7).

5. Each key name may be followed by an ACL (Access Control List), a series of blank separated decimal numbers enclosed in brackets (for example, [17 18]). ACL numbers and their meanings are listed in Table 4.2.

TABLE 4.2: ACL Values and Descriptions

ACL Values	Description
1	Administrators Full Access
2	Administrators Read Access
3	Administrators Read and Write Access
4	Administrators Read, Write, and Delete Access
5	Creator Full Access
6	Creator Read and Write Access
7	World Full Access
8	World Read Access
9	World Read and Write Access
10	World Read, Write, and Delete Access
11	Power Users Full Access
12	Power Users Read and Write Access
13	Power Users Read, Write, and Delete Access
14	System Operators Full Access
15	System Operators Read and Write Access
16	System Operators Read, Write, and Delete Access
17	System Full Access

Continued on next page

TABLE 4.2 CONTINUED: ACL Values and Descriptions

ACL Values	Description
18	System Read and Write Access
19	System Read Access
20	Administrators Read, Write, and Execute Access
21	Interactive User Full Access
22	Interactive User Read and Write Access
23	Interactive User Read, Write, and Delete Access

6. When there is a left bracket ([) and an equal sign (=) on the same line, the line is a registry value. When the string is [DELETE], RegIni will delete this key (or sub-hive).

7. Default keys: A key without a name, or a key having a name of @ (at sign), signifies an empty (or default) value. For ease of use, the value name may either be omitted or specified as an @ for a default key.

NOTE   Because of the syntax required, any object name that has leading or trailing spaces, quotes, an equal sign (=), or an at sign (@) in the name must be enclosed in quotes (").

8. Valid data value types and formats to follow are listed in Table 4.3.

TABLE 4.3: Data Type and Description

Data Type	Description of Data
REG_SZ	Text string quoted if there are leading quotes or spaces
REG_EXPAND_SZ	Text string quoted if there are leading quotes or spaces
REG_MULTI_SZ	Multiple, quoted text strings, each separated by a blank, for example, "string1," "string2," and so on

Continued on next page

TABLE 4.3 CONTINUED: Data Type and Description

Data Type	Description of Data
REG_DATE	The date, in the format of mm/dd/yyyy HH:MM DayOfWeek
REG_DWORD	A 4-byte number, in decimal, or hexadecimal (prefixed with 0x)
REG_BINARY	Count of the number of bytes in the object, then one or more DWORD values of data
REG_NONE	Count of the number of bytes in the object, then one or more DWORD values of data
REG_RESOURCE_LIST	Count of the number of bytes in the object, then one or more DWORD values of data
REG_RESOURCE_REQUIREMENTS	Count of the number of bytes in the object, then one or more DWORD values of data
REG_RESOURCE_REQUIREMENTS_LIST	Count of the number of bytes in the object, then one or more DWORD values of data
REG_FULL_RESOURCE_DESCRIPTOR	Count of the number of bytes in the object, then one or more DWORD values of data
REG_MULTISZ_FILE	The name of a file containing the text (formatted in the same way as REG_MULTI_SZ) to be used for the object's value
REG_BINARYFILE	The name of a file containing the value to be used for the object's value (formatted in the same manner as a REG_BINARY type object)

9. When REG_SZ and REG_EXPAND_SZ have either leading or trailing spaces, or quotes, in the text, the text must be surrounded by quotes ("). A string may contain embedded quotes, as neither RegDmp, nor RegIni will scan the interior of a string for quotes.

10. REG_BINARY data values consist of an initial number specifying the length of the object (excluding the length specification), and zero or more DWORD values specifying the object's data. Numbers may be in either decimal, or in hexadecimal (if prefixed with a 0x). Excess data values will be ignored.

REGFIND.EXE

No, RegFind won't "find" your registry. Actually, if the registry is lost, you're probably in deep trouble anyway—utilities won't help in this case. RegFind is a quick utility used to find and optionally replace objects in the registry.

WARNING   Like many of the Windows NT Resource Kit utilities, RegFind can be a powerful tool, very useful in destroying the registry with only a few keystrokes. Be careful when using RegFind, especially when using the replace option.

Here is a sample run of RegFind:

```
REGFIND [-h hivefile_hiveroot | -w Win95_Directory | -m \\machinename]
[-i n] [-o outputWidth] [-p RegistryKeyPath] [-z | -t DataType] [-b | -
B] [-y] [-n] [searchString [-r ReplacementString]]
```

In this example of RegFind, the options are defined as follows:

-h—Is the local root hive to display.

-w—Uses the Windows 95/98 registry specified, not a Windows NT registry.

-m—Opens a remote Windows NT registry on the specified computer.

-i n—Indents sub objects by n (default is four) spaces.

-o—Sets the output width to the specified value. The default is 80 if the output is to the screen, and 240 when the output is redirected to a file.

-s—Tells RegDmp to write only summary output, which truncates the output lines to a readable length.

The registryPath specifies the base sub-hive to start the listing from. There are several predefined prefixes defined in RegDir:

\Registry—Resolves to the base registry (allowing access to HKEY_USERS, and HKEY_LOCAL_MACHINE).

\Registry\Users—Resolves to HKEY_USERS.

\Registry\Machine—Resolves to HKEY_LOCAL_MACHINE.

\HKEY_LOCAL_MACHINE—Resolves to HKEY_LOCAL_MACHINE.

USER:—Resolves to HKEY_CURRENT_USER.

-t—Specifies the data types that RegFind is to search for:

- REG_SZ
- REG_MULTI_SZ
- REG_EXPAND_SZ
- REG_DWORD
- REG_BINARY
- REG_NONE

The default search, if not specified, is all string types.

-b—Is valid when searching for strings. It tells RegFind that all searches should also search inside REG_BINARY data objects. This is done because it is common to store strings in REG_BINARY data type objects. If specifying this option with the replace option, the replacement string must be exactly the same length as the original binary string.

-B—Works like –b (explained previously), but searches for ANSI character set versions in the REG_BINARY values.

-y—Specifies that RegFind will search for strings without regard for case.

-n—Tells RegFind to search both hives and key names in addition to data values. Do not specify –n with the –t (data type) option.

-z—Specifies that RegFind will test each REG_SZ and REG_EXPAND_SZ string for a trailing null value. Additional tests will be made to ensure that Unicode strings are of the proper byte pairing. (There are an even number of bytes in each Unicode string.) When -r is specified, the given replacement string is ignored, and RegFind will instead search for missing trailing nulls and unbalance Unicode strings and fix all invalid occurrences found.

searchString—Specifies the string to be searched for. Quote all strings that contain embedded blanks or tabs. Not specifying a searchString will force RegFind to search for all objects of the desired type.

-r replacementString—Specifies the optional string to replace the search string whenever a match is found.

NOTE   Both the searchString and replacementString must be of the type specified to the -t switch.

For REG_SZ and all other string types—The search and replacement strings must be quoted strings if there are embedded white characters.

For REG_DWORD—The search and replacement strings must be a single number (for example, 0x1000 or 4096).

For REG_BINARY—The search and replacement strings must be a number specifying the number of bytes in the string, optionally followed by the actual bytes, with a separate number for each DWORD (4 bytes). For example, a 6-byte REG_BINARY string would be "0x06 0x12345678 0x1234".

If only a length is specified, RegFind will search for all REG_BINARY values having the specified length. Do not specify the length only with the –r replacement string option.

If RegFind is replacing strings, RegFind will display the value after performing the replacement. To see the strings prior to changing, use RegFind without the –r option.

NOTE   When RegFind detects a REG_SZ or REG_EXPAND_SZ type string missing a trailing null character, the string will be prefixed with the message "(*** MISSING TRAILING NULL CHARACTER ***)." When a Unicode string does not have the correct multiple of characters, the message, "(*** Length not multiple of WCHAR ***)," will be prefixed.

RegIni.EXE

RegIni is a powerful tool to use to populate a registry with entries contained in a file. Input files for RegIni may be created by hand, using the format described here, or they may be output files from RegDmp (which was described previously).

Here is a sample run of RegIni:

```
RegIni [-h hivefile_hiveroot | -w Win95_Directory | -m \\machinename]
[-i n] [-o outputWidth] [-b] textFiles...
```

In this example usage of RegIni, the options are defined as follows:

-h—Is the local root hive to display.

-w—Uses the Windows 95/98 registry specified, not a Windows NT registry.

-m—Opens a remote Windows NT registry on the specified computer.

-i n—Indents sub objects by n (default is four) spaces.

-o—Sets the output width to the specified value. The default is 80 if the output is to the screen, and 240 when the output is redirected to a file.

-b—Specifies that RegIni should be backward compatible with older versions of RegIni. Early versions of the RegIni program did not support continued lines or quoted strings. Early versions of RegIni did not support comment lines either.

TextFiles—Names the input file used by RegIni. This file may be in either ANSI or Unicode format. For an understanding of the format of a RegIni input file, see the description of RegDmp's output file, described earlier in this chapter.

REGKEY.EXE

RegKey is a cool little program (see Figure 4.24) that allows customizing a few of Windows NT's logon and initialization settings. This utility is one of the few Windows NT Resource Kit registry tools that is equipped with a Windows interface. This program is such a gem, I'd have written it myself—if it had not already been written by Eric. (He didn't give his last name.)

FIGURE 4.24:

RegKey's user interface dialog allows setting both logon and FAT file system parameters.

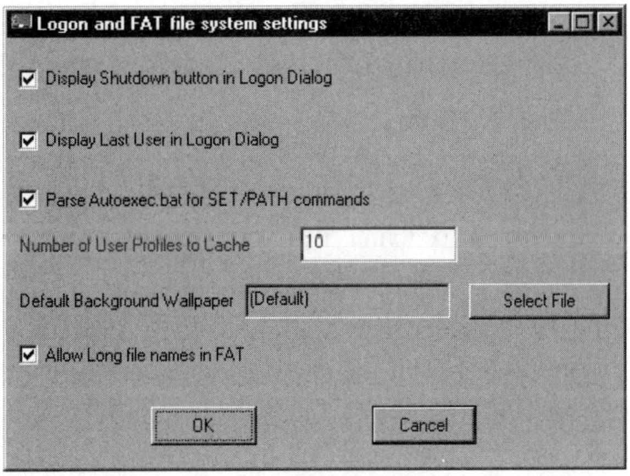

Using RegKey is simple. There is no command-line processing, no passed arguments—everything is presented in one simple dialog box. Most of the settings RegKey can modify are specific to logging on. One option allows configuration for support of long filenames on FAT volumes.

NOTE   When making changes using RegKey, any changes you make require that the computer be restarted for the changes to take effect.

RegKey allows setting the options discussed next.

The Shutdown Button in Logon Dialog

Windows NT Workstation and Windows NT Server both have a button labeled "Shutdown" in the logon dialog box. This button is enabled on Windows NT Workstation and disabled on Windows NT Server. Now, on the surface this makes sense: Who wants any joker that can get near a Windows NT Server to shut down the system without logging on? However, I begged to differ, and Microsoft realized that there was logic in allowing users to change the default behavior of the Shutdown button. (OK, OK, I admit it, Microsoft did not change anything for me, they just told me where the change had to be made.)

With RegKey it is easy to change the default behavior; simply check (or uncheck) the Display Shutdown button in Logon Dialog option as desired.

NOTE   I have the Shutdown button enabled on my servers. However, since no one is allowed to touch the servers but me, it is OK. Let's face it, if someone wants to shut down the server, there is always the power switch, which is *much* nastier.

The Display of Last User Logged On in Logon Dialog

When Windows NT displays the Logon dialog box, it is possible to set whether the last user who logged on will be displayed in the Logon dialog box. This can be handy for computers that are frequently used by the same person. This allows the user to type in only the password (No, that can't be defaulted.) rather than typing in the username and password.

For computers frequently used by a number of different people, it probably would be best if the last logged on user's name isn't displayed. This way there is no temptation to try to log on to another user's userid.

Enable or disable the display of the last user logged on by checking or unchecking Display Last User in Logon Dialog as desired.

Parse Autoexec.bat for Set and Path Commands

One problem for users who are either dual-booting or have upgraded from Windows 95/98 or DOS is that their autoexec.bat file contains many lines setting environment variables, and a path command as well.

As well, some ill behaved applications don't realize that they are installing on Windows NT and they modify the autoexec.bat file. They will add or modify the set and path variables with wild abandon, not realizing that these changes would normally not be noticed by Windows NT.

Fortunately, Microsoft recognized the existence of this problem. Windows NT can scan existing autoexec.bat files and use the set and path statements; path actually sets an environment variable. On my dual boot system, this feature has made switching between the two systems a piece of cake.

Enable or disable the parsing of the autoexec.bat for set and path lines by checking or unchecking `Parse Autoexec.bat for SET/PATH` commands as desired.

Autoexec Who, Config Who?

Which autoexec, and why is there a config.sys in Windows NT? We all know that Windows NT doesn't boot the same way as DOS or Windows 95/98. Windows NT doesn't typically parse or execute either the autoexec.bat or config.sys files, except as noted previously.

But, there is an autoexec and a config that Windows NT does fully process. (OK, as well as it can—there are limits.) These two files are called autoexec.nt and config.nt. Each is used whenever a basic command session is started, not when Windows NT is booted.

It is possible in a command session to specify a different config and autoexec to be used. This option is set in the Properties dialog for the command prompt. Right-click on the command prompt's shortcut and select Properties. Then select the Program tab in the Properties dialog box. Click on the Windows NT button to display the Windows NT PIF settings.

The parsing of set and path commands in the autoexec.bat file is done during boot-up; the use of autoexec.nt and config.nt is done during a command session.

Number of Cached User Profiles

Windows NT is able to cache zero to 50 previous successful logons locally. This is typically done on systems where a domain controller is used to validate logons and security. Sometimes, the PDC (Primary Domain Controller) is not available, even then it is still possible to provisionally log on the user, using locally stored logon credentials.

The number of cached logons defaults to 10; however, it may be set to any number between zero and 50. Setting this value to zero disables logon caching. This is quite useful in very high security environments where it is unacceptable to cache any sensitive logon information. Setting to higher numbers is useful on pooled computers where many users might logon frequently.

When the domain controller is unavailable and the user can be logged on using the cache, this message appears:

> "A domain controller for your domain could not be contacted. You have been logged on using cached account information. Changes to your profile since you last logged on may not be available."

If caching has been disabled, or if a user's logon information is not in the cache, this message is displayed:

> "The system cannot log you on now because the domain <name of domain> is not available."

Enable, disable, and configure logon caching by setting Number of User Profiles to Cache to a value between zero (disable caching) and 50 (the maximum number of cached users).

Default Background Wallpaper

What is displayed on the screen of a Windows NT system, before a user logs on, can be customized. RegKey allows setting the logo that is displayed. Typically, this is done under the Logon dialog box, although the dialog box may be moved. Other parameters may be modified, too. However, these changes must be made manually to the registry.

NOTE   We'll cover these types of modifications later in the book in Chapter 16, "Introduction to HKEY_CURRENT_USER and HKEY_USERS."

The specifications for the file used for the logo are simple; it must be a bitmap (16 or 256 colors) saved in the %SystemRoot% directory. It may be something as simple as a company logo or perhaps your favorite scanned photo

Enable the use of non-default wallpaper by clicking the Select File button to display the Select Bitmap dialog box. Select a BMP file, preferably from the default, %SystemRoot% directory. Then click the Open button to return to RegKey.

NOTE   Make sure that whatever bitmap is selected, it is not located on a network share. This share may not be present when the computer is logged off.

Allow LFNs on FAT Volumes

Some operating systems and tools are not compatible with LFNs (Long File Names). These are becoming less problematic because Windows 95/98 supports LFNs. Windows NT, by default, will create LFNs on FAT volumes. LFNs on non-FAT volumes are not a problem because these other operating systems and utilities cannot access information on an NTFS volume.

WARNING   Be very careful about whether you change the support for LFNs on FAT volumes. Major problems can arise if this support is turned off, such as installed applications failing to run properly and even instability of the operating system.

REGREAD.EXE

As yet another look at the registry program, RegRead reads the HKEY_LOCAL_ MACHINE hive on a remote, or local, computer. The program is simple, with only a few options.

Here is a sample run of RegRead:

```
RegRead \\ServerName <RegistryPath> <KeyName>
```

In this example, \\ServerName is the name of a server. To view a local registry, enter the name of the local server.

RegistryPath is the optional name of the HKEY_LOCAL_MACHINE registry sub-hive. If not specified, HKEY_LOCAL_MACHINE will be used, which is supplied by default by RegRead.

KeyName is the name of a specific registry key, if not specified, all keys in the hive will be displayed.

Odd Error Messages?

The author of RegRead coded two error messages that are not strictly polite. I doubt that RegRead will actually print these messages, but maybe someone else will see them. The messages are:

- Error: unable to open key. You are a nerd.

- Error: unable to open key. You are a losing Weenie.

NOTE   The Regread.exe utility is no longer supplied. It is now part of reg.exe in the latest update of the Windows NT Resource Kit.

REGSEC.EXE

RegSec lists the major hives in the registry. Although I've checked as much as I could, I can find no other use for this program. RegSec takes no options or command-line parameters.

An example of executing RegSec is:

```
Windows NT Version 4.0  13:20:40 C:\WINNT40\system32
RegSec
HKEY_LOCAL_MACHINE
HKEY_USERS
HKEY_CURRENT_USER
HKEY_CLASSES_ROOT

Windows NT Version 4.0  13:20:47 C:\WINNT40\system32
```

NOTE   The Regsec.exe utility is no longer supplied. It is now part of reg.exe in the latest update of the Windows NT Resource Kit.

SAVEKEY.EXE

Originally called RegSave, SaveKey is a utility that saves a sub-hive from the registry hive HKEY_LOCAL_MACHINE to a file. The format of the file is the same as the RegEdt32 Save Key in the Registry menu.

The usage of SaveKey is as follows:

```
SaveKey hive filename
```

In this syntax, the following are defined as:

> **hive**—Is the name of a sub-hive contained within the HKEY_LOCAL_MACHINE hive. Do not specify HKEY_LOCAL_MACHINE when giving the sub-hive name.
>
> **filename**—Specifies the name of the output file to write to.

An example of executing SaveKey is:

```
Windows NT Version 4.0  13:28:09 C:\WINNT40\system32
savekey HARDWARE\DESCRIPTION\SYSTEM c:\temp\savekey.key

Windows NT Version 4.0  13:28:31 C:\WINNT40\system32
```

Of course the standard filename cautions apply; make sure you name the output file with a name that tells you what the file contains—the output file is in binary format, making it difficult (if not impossible) to determine the hive contained at a later date.

NOTE   The SaveKey utility is no longer supplied. It is now part of reg.exe in the latest update of the Windows NT Resource Kit.

RESTKEY.EXE

Originally called RegSave, RestKey is a utility that reloads a sub-hive from a file to the registry hive HKEY_LOCAL_MACHINE. The format of the file is the same as the RegEdt32 Save Key function, or SaveKey saves (discussed previously).

The usage of RestKey is as follows:

```
RestKey hive filename
```

In this syntax, the following are defined as:

hive—Is the name of a sub-hive to be restored, contained within the HKEY_LOCAL_MACHINE hive. Do not specify HKEY_LOCAL_MACHINE when giving the sub-hive name.

filename—Specifies the name of the input file to restore from.

An example of executing RestKey is:

```
Windows NT Version 4.0  13:28:09 C:\WINNT40\system32
savekey HARDWARE\DESCRIPTION\SYSTEM c:\temp\savekey.key

Windows NT Version 4.0  13:28:31 C:\WINNT40\system32
```

Of course, the standard filename and content cautions apply; make sure you are restoring from the right file and that the file's contents are intended for the hive being restored.

> **NOTE**
> The RestKey utility is no longer supplied. It is now part of reg.exe in the latest update of the Windows NT Resource Kit.

RREGCHG.EXE

RRegChg is used to change a registry key on a remote computer from a command-line prompt. This small program uses RegSetValue to change the value of the registry key.

RRegChg takes five parameters:

```
RegChange //server Path EntryName Type Value
```

These parameters are defined as:

//Server—Is the name of the server to be changed.

Path—Is the hive fully qualified, except that HKEY_LOCAL_MACHINE may not be specified.

EntryName—Is the name of the key to be changed.

Type—Is the data type from the list below:

- REG_FULL_RESOURCE_DESCRIPTOR

- REG_RESOURCE_LIST

- REG_MULTI_SZ

- REG_LINK

- REG_DWORD_BIG_ENDIAN

- REG_DWORD_LITTLE_ENDIAN

- REG_DWORD

- REG_BINARY

- REG_NONE

- REG_EXPAND_SZ

- REG_SZ

Value—Is the new value to be assigned to the key.

RRegChg returns the following messages when it completes:

Invalid EntryName—Is displayed whenever the entry name (key) specified is not valid.

Error n—Where n is a numeric value, is displayed when any other errors are detected. (Error 6 is displayed when the path is invalid.)

The command completed successfully—Is displayed whenever RRegChg completes successfully.

An example of RRegChg follows:

```
RegChg \\DORA HARDWARE\DESCRIPTION\System\NewKey NewValue REG_SZ "My
New Value"
```

This example changes the value stored in the key NewValue, contained in the hive HKEY_LOCAL_MACHINE\HARDWARE\DESCRIPTION\System\NewKey, to a string with the type of REG_SZ, containing "My New Value."

NOTE   The RRegChg utility is no longer supplied. It is now part of reg.exe in the latest update of the Windows NT Resource Kit.

WARNING   RRegChg will only change objects located in the HKEY_LOCAL_MACHINE hive. Attempts to change other hives will fail, usually with an error message "Error 6." (Painfully descriptive error message, right?)

SECADD.EXE

This program is used to remove the Everyone group from a specified registry key in the HKEY_LOCAL_MACHINE hive or to add read privileges to a user on a specified registry key.

Here is an example of executing SecAdd:

```
RegSecAdd -l KeyName to remove the Everyone group locally.
RegSecAdd -r \\ServerName KeyName to remove the Everyone group
remotely.
RegSecAdd -l -a KeyName UserName to add read permissions to a key
locally.
RegSecAdd -r -a \\ServerName KeyName UserName to add read permissions
to a key remotely.
```

In this example, the options are defined as follows:

-l—Performs operations on a local registry.

-r—Performs operations on the specified computer whose name is specified in the \\ServerName parameter.

\\ServerName—Is the name of the remote server to be accessed and modified.

-a—Adds read permissions to the key KeyName, for user UserName for example, `RegSec -l -a software\microsoft DORA\SpecialUser`.

The Microsoft System Policy Editor

The System Policy Editor is a tool allowing users to set policy. Many of the changes made by the System Policy Editor are to the registry, so although the System Policy Editor is not thought of as a registry tool, we'll document it here anyway.

First, modifying the registry using the System Policy Editor is a wise move—it will validate your changes, preventing you from doing something that may have seemed logical to you, but actually was not.

The System Policy Editor allows opening of either a policy file (with the extension of POL) or a computer. It uses a simple user interface, as shown in Figure 4.25. When you click on an object, the object's Properties dialog box will be displayed. In Figure 4.25, Local Computer and Local User are both objects that may be opened.

FIGURE 4.25:

The System Policy Editor displays the Properties dialog when an icon is clicked. Then you can open the tree to see specific settings.

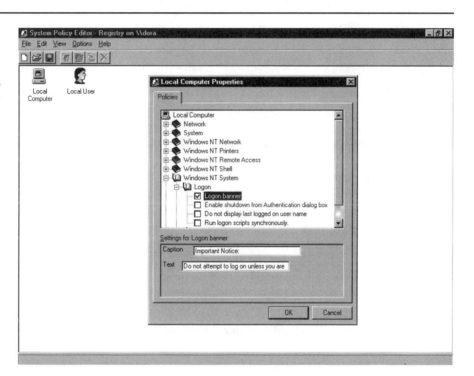

With the System Policy Editor, the Local Computer entry may display eight items, all applicable for a Windows NT system. For a Local User, the Properties dialog may have six items. In both cases the items displayed are unique; there is no overlap.

WYSIWYG? from System Policy Editor?

What is displayed in the Properties dialog boxes is dependent on which template(s) are loaded. With Windows NT, there are three templates supplied by default:

COMMON.ADM–Is common to both Windows NT and Windows 95/98.

WINNT.ADM–Contains specific settings for Windows NT.

WINDOWS.ADM–Contains specific settings for Windows 95/98.

There are two sections in all ADM files, CLASS MACHINE and CLASS USER, which define how settings are applied.

ADM files are text files, which may be modified to suit the user's needs. A competent user should be able to write an ADM file, or modify an existing one without too much trouble. However, those pesky "make sure you have good backup" warnings also apply if you customize your ADM files.

As the previous sidebar says, the System Policy Editor is usable for Windows 95/98 clients, enabling some remote administration of these machines. However, the System Policy Editor has not been well tested on these two platforms.

Typically, for all users (Windows NT and Windows 95/98), you may modify the following categories:

Control Panel—Allows restricting the display of the Control Panel.

Desktop—Allows/disallows the user to change wallpaper and/or color schemes.

Shell—Allows you to:

- Remove the Run command from the Start menu.
- Remove folders from Settings on the Start menu.
- Remove the Taskbar from Settings on the Start menu.
- Remove the Find command from the Start menu.
- Hide drives in My Computer.

- Hide Network Neighborhood.

- Hide the Entire Network in Network Neighborhood.

- Hide all items on the Desktop.

- Disable the Shut Down command.

- Not save settings at exit.

System—Allows you to:

- Disable Registry editing tools.

- Run only allows Windows applications.

For Windows NT users you may modify the following categories:

Windows NT Shell—Consists of three sections (Custom User Interface, Custom Folders, and Restrictions), which allow setting the following:

Custom User Interface—Sets Custom Shell.

Custom Folders—Sets Custom Programs folder.

Custom Folders—Hides Start menu subfolders.

Custom Folders—Sets Custom Startup folder.

Custom Folders—Sets Custom Network Neighborhood.

Custom Folders—Sets Custom Start menu.

Restrictions—Uses only approved shell extensions.

Restrictions—Removes File menu from Explorer.

Restrictions—Removes common program groups from Start menu.

Restrictions—Disables context menus for the taskbar.

Restrictions—Disables Explorer's default context menu.

Restrictions—Removes the Map Network Drive and Disconnect Network Drive options.

Restrictions—Disables Link File Tracking.

Windows NT System—Consists of four choices:

- Parse Autoexec.bat

- Run logon scripts synchronously
- Disable Task Manager
- Show welcome tips at logon

For Windows 95, you may modify the following categories:

Windows 95 Control Panel—Consists of four sections (Network, Printers, Passwords, and System) which allow setting the following:

Network—Restricts Network Control Panel.

Printers—Restricts printer settings.

Passwords—Restricts Passwords Control Panel.

System—Restricts System Control Panel.

Windows 95 Shell—Consists of one section, Custom folders, which allows the following settings:

- Custom Programs folder
- Custom desktop icons
- Hide Start menu subfolders
- Custom Startup folder
- Custom Network Neighborhood
- Custom Start menu

Windows 95 System–Consists of one section, Restrictions, which allows you to:

- Disable the MS-DOS prompt.
- Disable the single-mode MS-DOS apps.

Windows 95 Network—Consists of one section, Sharing, which allows you to:

- Disable file sharing.
- Disable print sharing.

For any type of machine (Windows NT or Windows 95/98), you may modify the following:

Network—Consists of one choice:

System policies update—Remotes update.

System—Consists of two sections, SNMP and Run, which allow you to set:

SNMP—Communities

SNMP—Permitted managers

SNMP—Traps for Public community

Run—Items that are executed at startup

For Windows NT-only machines, you may modify:

Windows NT Network—Consists of one section, Sharing, which allows you to:

- Create hidden drive shares (workstation).
- Create hidden drive shares (server).

Windows NT Printers—Consists of three choices:

- Disable browse thread on this computer
- Scheduler priority
- Beep for error enabled

Windows NT Remote Access—Consists of four choices:

- Max number of unsuccessful authentication retries
- Max time limit for authentication
- Wait interval for callback
- Auto Disconnect

Windows NT Shell—Consists of one section, Custom shared folders, which contains four choices:

- Custom shared Programs folder

- Custom shared desktop icons
- Custom shared Start menu
- Custom shared Startup folder

Windows NT System—Consists of two sections, Logon and File System:

Logon—Allows Logon banner.

Logon–Enables shutdown from Authentication dialog box.

Logon—Does not display last logged on username.

Logon—Runs logon scripts synchronously.

File system—Does not create 8.3 file name for long filenames.

File system—Allows extended characters in 8.3 filenames.

File system—Does not update last access time.

Windows NT User Profiles—Consists of four sections:

- Delete cached copies of roaming profiles
- Automatically detect slow network connections
- Slow network connection timeout
- Timeout for dialog boxes

For Windows 95 machines, you may modify the following:

Access control—Consists of one section:

- User-level access control

Logon—Consists of three sections:

- Custom logon banner
- Require validation by network for Windows access
- Allow logon without name or password

Passwords—Consists of four sections:

- Hide share passwords with asterisks
- Disable password caching

- Require alphanumeric Windows password

- Min Windows password length

Microsoft Client Service for NetWare networks—Consists of four sections:

- Preferred server

- Support long filenames

- Search mode

- Disable automatic NetWare login

Microsoft Client for Windows networks—Consists of three sections:

- Log on to Windows NT

- Workgroup

- Alternate workgroup

File and printer sharing—Consists of two sections:

- Disable file sharing

- Disable printer sharing

Dial-up networking—Consists of one section:

- Disable dial-in

Windows 95 System—Consists of three sections (SNMP, Network paths, and Profiles):

SNMP—Enables Internet MIB (RFC1156).

Network paths—Enables Network path for Windows setup.

Network paths—Enables Network path for Windows tour.

Profiles—Enables user profiles.

For each item, choices may range from a simple disable or enable of the property to setting of text, additional options, and so on. For instance, Figure 4.26 shows the Local Computer Properties dialog box, where I've selected Local computer, Network, System policies update, and Remote update. Displayed in the Settings for Remote update at the bottom of the dialog box are some additional settings that I can change for this item.

FIGURE 4.26:

Setting Remote update properties displays additional choices.

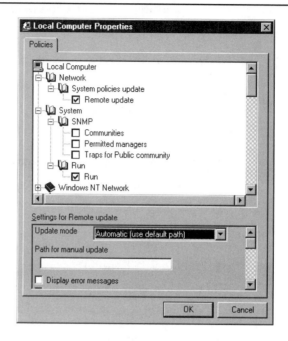

Hints and Kinks from the Experts

In this chapter's Hints and Kinks, we cover a few hints on using the two registry editors.

How Do You Restrict Access to the Registry Editor?   Using the registry editor regedt32.exe, follow these steps:

1. Highlight HKEY_USERS and Load Hive from the Registry menu.

2. Browse to their profile directory and select NTUSER.DAT.

3. When prompted for Key Name, input their UserID.

4. Navigate to \Software\Microsoft\Windows\CurrentVersion\Policies.

5. If no System sub-key exists in Policies, add it. Then select Add Value of DisableRegistryTools under the System key using type REG_DWORD and set it to 1.

6. Unload Hive from the Registry menu.

(Courtesy of John Savill)

Should You Use REGEDIT.EXE or REGEDT32.EXE?   You can use either for NT. RegEdit does have a few limitations, the largest limitation is that it does not support the full RegEdt32 data types, such as REG_MULTI_SZ. So, if you edit this type of data with RegEdit, RegEdit will change its type.

RegEdit is based on the Windows95 version and has features that RegEdt32 lacks, such as search. In general, RegEdit is nicer to work with. RegEdit also shows your current position in the registry at the bottom of the window.

(Courtesy of John Savill)

How Do You Restrict Access to a Remote Registry?   Access to a remote registry is controlled by the ACL on the key winreg.

To set access, follow these steps:

1. Start the registry editor (regedt32.exe).

2. Move to HKEY_LOCAL_MACHINE\SYSTEM\CurrentControlSet\Control\SecurePipeServers.

3. Check for a key called winreg. If it does not exist, create it (select Edit ➤ Add Key).

4. Select the winreg key by clicking on it.

5. Select Security ➤ Permissions.

6. Click the Add button and give the user read access.

7. Once added, click on the user and select Special Access.

8. Double-click on the user and you can select which actions the user can perform.

9. Click OK when finished.

It is possible to set up certain keys to be accessible even if the user does not have access by editing the value HKEY_LOCAL_MACHINE\SYSTEM\CurrentControlSet\Control\SecurePipeServers\winreg\All. (Use regedt32.) You can add paths to this list.

(Courtesy of John Savill)

For more information, see the Knowledge Base article, "Q153183," at `http://www.microsoft.com/kb/articles/q153/1/83.htm`.

PART II

Advanced Registry Stuff

Associations, Linkages, and OLE—How Confusing Can This Get?

- Introduction to OLE

- Client-Server OLE applications

- How linkages are made between applications

- Hints and kinks from the experts

How's this for good government?

If the U.S. government has no knowledge of aliens, then why does Title 14, Section 1211 of the Code of Federal Regulations, implemented on July 16, 1969, make it illegal for U.S. citizens to have any contact with extraterrestrials or their vehicles?

First, let's start out with a few ground rules:

- There is no way to learn all about OLE in one chapter.

- Even OLE experts are not really experts.

- There are a number of good books on OLE; but, unless you are programming, avoid them.

- If you don't understand everything about OLE after reading this chapter, don't feel bad.

- The author takes no responsibility for what happens when you wake up at 2 A.M. and shout, "Now I understand!"

Most programmers don't do the groundwork required for OLE. Instead, they use development systems, such as Microsoft's Developer Studio, to do most of the difficult parts. Today, a programmer can create an OLE application almost as quickly as any other type of application.

Most applications manage their initial OLE setup by themselves. Some applications rely on their installation programs to do the OLE setup. And some applications do both—use the installation program to set up OLE, and if the configuration becomes damaged, the program also has the ability to repair the damage to the extent that it can reconfigure the OLE components.

There are a few things that some of us are asking. First, what is OLE? Second, what does OLE have to do with the registry? And why do we have to worry about it? Do we mention DDE? And where, oh where, does the Clipboard fit into this mess?

OK, stay tuned for answers to all of these questions.

Introduction to OLE

OLE (Object Linking and Embedding) is a technology that allows applications to share data and functionality easily. I like that. Sounds good. It's quick and easy to understand, it's basically accurate.

Kraig Brockschmidt is probably the best known expert on OLE. Here's how he describes its evolution:

> *Windows API (Application Programming Interfaces) evolved into Windows Objects, which eventually became what we know as OLE.*

Kraig admits it's not that simple, but basically OLE developed by evolution not by revolution.

Way back in the good old days, Windows was much simpler and easier to understand. In its first incarnation, Windows allowed virtually no inter-process communications. There was the Clipboard (which we still know and love) where one program could post data, and another program could then (hopefully) read that data. But that interaction required user interaction. The user was required to select the data to be placed in the Clipboard; take steps to put the selected data in the Clipboard; then in the recipient application, take steps to retrieve the data stored in the Clipboard.

Problems arose. First, the basic Clipboard supported only a very limited range of data types. Programs could exchange data in various basic formats (text and binary, for the most part), but these formats were sorely lacking the flexibility to express any object that was composed of compound data.

Compound Data?

Compound data is data that contains information in multiple formats. The easiest type of compound data to envision is a word processing document that includes some images. At this point, the program can't just toss that document and its images on the Clipboard. After all, how does the program identify the format of that data? If it says binary, no other application will be able to understand or use the data. If it says text, what happens when an application tries to use the data and encounters the images? Does it delete the images? Sure, that would work, but if the user wanted the complete document, including the images, he or she would be most unhappy about the results.

As well, Microsoft realized quickly that applications needed a direct, application-to-application communication method that didn't rely on the Clipboard. Quickly or slowly, depending on your point of view, the concept of DDE (Dynamic Data Exchange) was born. Actually "conceived" would be a better description because DDE wasn't viable in its original format. As it grew, DDE did allow applications to communicate data. However, there were still problems. With DDE, there was no way for applications to find out about their partners. Most DDE applications were written specifically as pairs. For applications from two independent sources, DDE was unlikely to be useful because the developers would have to cooperate in order to use it.

OLE became the next stage in the development of inter-application communications and data sharing. OLE allowed applications to interact with each other without knowing, in advance, about the other application. Magic, really.

The Clipboard

The Clipboard is the original and most basic method to transfer data between applications. The Clipboard supports both inter-application transfers (between two applications) and intra-application transfers (between the same application).

There is only one object in the Clipboard at any one time. There are some complex rules on how things are done with the Clipboard, such as the following:

- An application cannot assume that an object placed in the Clipboard will remain there after the application releases the Clipboard. Therefore, the Clipboard cannot be used as a temporary storage location.

- The format of the object in the Clipboard must be in one of the standard formats (listed in the next paragraph), or the application placing the data on the Clipboard must be prepared to render or display the Clipboard's contents.

- Some objects may be placed in the Clipboard that are in a format that is not native to Windows. These objects require the application that places the object to be available to display or render the object if necessary.

Windows NT is able to support the following types of data in the Clipboard, without creating custom formats:

CF_BITMAP—A bitmap (image)

CF_DIBV—A DIB (Device Independent Bitmap)

CF_DIBV5—A version 5 bitmap (only available on Windows NT 5)

CF_DIF—A DIF (Data Interchange Format) object

CF_DSPBITMAP—A private format bitmap

CF_DSPENHMETAFILE—An enhanced metafile display format object

CF_DSPMETAFILEPICT—A metafile-picture display format object

CF_DSPTEXT—A text display format object, with private format

CF_ENHMETAFILE—An enhanced metafile object

CF_GDIOBJFIRST through **CF_GDIOBJLAST**—A range of integer values for application-defined GDI (Graphical Device Interface) objects

CF_HDROPV—A handle of type HDROP, identifying a list of files

CF_LOCALE—Locale information

CF_METAFILEPICT—A metafile picture object

CF_OEMTEXT—A text format in the OEM (original equipment manufacturer) character set

CF_OWNERDISPLAY—An object of owner display format

CF_PALETTE—A color palette object

CF_PENDATA—An object containing data for the pen extensions to the Microsoft Windows for Pen Computing

CF_PRIVATEFIRST through **CF_PRIVATELAST**—A range of integer values for private Clipboard formats

CF_RIFF—A sound object too complex for the CF_WAVE format

CF_SYLK—An object in Microsoft Symbolic Link (SYLK) format

CF_TEXT—A plain text format object

CF_WAVE—An audio object, using PCM (Pulse Code Modulation)

CF_TIFF—A tagged-image file format

CF_UNICODETEXT—A text object using the 2-byte Unicode character set

As this list shows, Windows supports a lot of different formats, without any programmer intervention. However, there are lots of situations where these formats are not adequate. In those cases, the application serving (placing) the data on the Clipboard may register a new format with Windows. To enable viewing of the Clipboard data, it will be necessary to also have code that will display the Clipboard data.

DDE

DDE, or Dynamic Data Exchange, has been part of Windows since the early days. An Excel spreadsheet (the client) for managing stock market information is an example of DDE. A second software application that actually retrieves the stock prices (quotes) is the server. As well, there is an application that goes to the Internet and gets current stock market quotes (the server). The two programs need to interact dynamically (after all, prices change), so using the Clipboard is not optimal: You want your spreadsheet updated dynamically and efficiently, without any user interaction.

Through a process of broadcasting, Excel (the client) establishes a communications link with the server. Excel broadcasts its requests and the server responds that it is able to fulfill this request. A DDE linkage is established, allowing Excel to request information from the server as necessary.

As an example, the user may be interested in a particular list of stocks. Excel would then tell the server to check these stocks and provide the current quote for them. As well, Excel might have a timer loop that repeats this process every five minutes, providing the user with up-to-date stock quote information.

As another example, the user may request a one-time quote on a stock of interest. Maybe the user is interested in just how well Microsoft (MSFT) is doing on the stock exchange. Perhaps the user's spreadsheet has a section where he or she types in the stock name. The user enters the name and the quote comes back.

Either the client or the server can perform automatic updating. Client initiated updates might be on a time-based basis, or when the user makes a change if the data retrieved was relatively static. Servers might initiate an update whenever the server recognizes that the information the user is requesting has become out of date.

OK, no one said DDE was easy. If they did, they didn't tell the truth. DDE is complex and very difficult to understand or use. Programmers exposed to DDE shuddered and desperately searched for better alternatives. Some programmers kludged together broadcast messages to pass simple data, but for many, DDE was still the best (only) method to exchange data between two applications.

Why Is It Difficult to Exchange Data?

Most of the problems are directly related to memory protection; memory objects belonging to one application cannot be accessed by other applications.

When an object is placed in the Clipboard, the memory that the object occupies is given to Windows. From that point onward, Windows owns the object, and the application that placed the object in the Clipboard loses control of the object. This means that whenever an object is placed in the Clipboard, the application will usually make a copy of the object and place the copy in the Clipboard, keeping the original object for the application's use.

The DDE process uses the Clipboard to transfer large blocks of data, too. Typically, the server application would place the data on the Clipboard and then use DDE to tell the client application about the data. Also, small data objects might be passed directly from the server application to the client application as part of the DDE conversation.

What Is OLE?

OLE means Object Linking and Embedding. That says it all. With DDE, and with the Clipboard, applications only passed data and did not pass any functionality. With OLE, we expand on what the server application is able to do for the client.

OLE allows a server to not only pass data back and forth, but also to pass programming functionality between the server and the client. The server is able to do something that the client wishes done. However, the client program's developer does not have to develop all this functionality if it exists already.

As an example, say we have the nifty e-mail system called Outlook. Outlook has a simple, built-in e-mail editor. However, some users want (demand, actually) more functionality in their e-mail editors. They want formatting, macros, even included images, and other nifty stuff. Word for Windows actually would do everything that the user wants.

Wouldn't it be nice if the Outlook development team could borrow part of Word for Windows? Now, it would make little sense for the Outlook development team to sneak into the Word group's office, and steal the code for Word for Windows. After all, they'd then have to maintain it, and Word's one big puppy— major maintenance blues there.

What's the next best thing? First, let's let the Word developers continue to maintain Word. Second, let's get Word to work for us. We know that the developers on the Word team included OLE server technology into Word; Word has client OLE technology too, in case you wondered. However, we find that the Outlook team can't really expect the Word team to put special stuff into Word for them, so what can they do?

Things are not so bad here; because Word is an OLE-compliant application, all Outlook has to do is to ask Word, "What can you do for me?" This is done by first checking with the server at the most basic OLE level (a level that all OLE applications must support). This level allows the client to ask the server what functionalities are supported.

Realize that when we talk about functionalities being supported, we are not talking about "Do you support italic text?" Rather, what we are asking are questions, such as, "Do you support embedding?" or, "Do you support automation?" The server is then able to tell the client exactly what it is able to do. In the case of Outlook using Word to edit e-mail, Outlook asks if the application can be embedded, and Word responds in the affirmative.

> **NOTE** You might ask, Peter, why are you are adding yet another term, *OLE automation*? This process allows the client application to take control of the server, and it lets the server see the client as a user. The client is able to actually click buttons and otherwise interact with the server application.

Now read on.

Embedding

With embedding, an object (which could be either a data object, or server functionality) is embedded into the client application or the client application's data. When we embed Word into Outlook, we create a window, and using OLE, we tell Word to use this window to interact with the user. As well, we tell Word how it should appear to the user; for example, Outlook customizes Word's toolbars.

This embedding works regardless of whether Word is running or not. If Word is running, anything that Word is currently doing is unaffected by having Word embedded into Outlook's e-mail editing system. In fact, the OLE server treats these as separate instances of the program, which are kept separate. There are advantages, however, if the server is already running, it is not necessary to load a second copy of the server. Instead, the executable code is shared between the two instances.

When objects are embedded, there is a private copy of the object that the client owns. The server may update the client's object, though the server won't change any other instances of the data.

Each time an object is embedded, there will be a new copy of the object. For complex objects, graphics and so on, this can consume substantial system resources.

Object Linking

Object linking is a mysterious technology where one application creates an object that is subsequently used by another application. An object that is linked remains the property of the creating application, and there is only one copy of the object.

The creating application is called the server. The application that is linked to the object is called the client. When the server updates the object, the client gets a message and the object display in the client is updated as necessary. Some objects are not visible, so there is no display update necessary.

The closest thing to showing how linking works is to look at Windows itself. There are a number of icons on your Desktop. Most are called shortcuts, which are denoted by that funny up-pointing arrow image in the lower-left corner. Think of these shortcuts as links. Open the properties for a shortcut and go to the Shortcut tab. In the Target edit box, you will see the name of the file that is associated with this shortcut (link). If you have a dozen shortcuts to the same file, each shortcut will open the same copy of the program. There won't be a dozen copies of the program.

OLE Controls AKA ActiveX

In our previous examples, the server application was a typical Windows program. These applications could be considered a native Windows application. For example, Word for Windows is a server application. Word has a user interface and it runs on its own, without needing any client to embed the Word object.

Sometimes the server application doesn't have a native, stand-alone mode. That is, these applications don't have a user interface—no window, no direct way for the user to interact with the program. These applications are called ActiveX controls; they used to be called OLE Controls. ActiveX controls are commonly used with programs, such as Internet Explorer and other Web browsers; however many programs can use ActiveX controls.

NOTE   An ActiveX control may only be embedded and may never be run by itself.

A typical user may have a large number of ActiveX controls installed, and the user may never know it. It is not uncommon for a user to download ActiveX controls from the Internet without ever realizing that this has happened.

VBX, What's a VBX?

VBX, or Visual BASIC, controls were the first generation of ActiveX controls. When VBX controls were first developed, they served in dialog boxes as custom controls; things, such as progress bars and so on, were all conceived as VBX controls first.

Generally, a VBX control doesn't handle data, while an ActiveX control might. As well, VBX controls were created with Visual BASIC only. Programmers who developed in C/C++, for example, had difficulty creating their own VBX controls. However, Microsoft eventually did develop a system to create VBX controls using development platforms other than Visual BASIC.

Eventually, Microsoft realized that the concept of VBX (embeddable controls) was a good one, and that these controls were here to stay. In came the OCX (OLE Control) technology; it was development-platform independent, usage-platform independent, and more flexible.

Evolution and the name game reared their heads again. Microsoft moved to ActiveX controls more as a change in name than in function. It is not uncommon to see ActiveX controls referred to as OCX controls, and vice versa.

Some ActiveX controls display data. Some don't do anything other than provide some form of user interface. These controls were found on one computer:

- BtnMenu Object
- CarPointProximityCtrl
- ChatShowClt Object

- DirectAnimation Java Classes

- HHCtrl Object

- Internet Explorer Classes for Java

- IPTDImageControl.SImage

- Label Object

- Microsoft MSChat Control Object

- Microsoft Search Settings Control

- Microsoft XML Parser for Java

- PopupMenu Object

- Win32 Classes

All of these controls were installed in the %SystemRoot%\Occache directory. If you are not using Internet Explorer or are not active on the Internet, you probably won't have many of these controls.

Liar, Liar, Pants on Fire!

Remember when I said previously that OLE Controls don't have a user interface? Well actually, I lied a little. Some OLE Controls can be run using rundll32 as the server application. Rundll32 doesn't have a user interface either, and any control that works with rundll32 must be written specifically for this type of usage. For example, the OLE Control Active Movie control can be run with the command:

```
%SystemRoot%\System32\rundll32.exe amovie.ocx,RunDll
```

This will open the Active Movie OLE Control (RunDll provides a main window for the control.), and Active Movie will then display an Open File dialog box. You might select an Active Movie file (Try clock.avi in the Windows NT %SystemRoot% directory.) and run it using amovie.ocx. This is possible because Active Movie was written to work with RunDll, and as such, it works. Try this trick with most any other OLE Control, and you will get the message, "Missing entry point RunDll," which indicates that the entry point passed in the command was not found.

Oh, yes, you can also pass parameters to your OLE Control with the command:

```
RunDll:%SystemRoot%\System32\rundll32.exe amovie.ocx,RunDll
%SystemRoot%\clock.avi
```

Continued on next page

This command would load Active Movie, load clock.avi, and allow the user to interact with the control. Try it. Better yet, try this:

```
%SystemRoot%\System32\rundll32.exe amovie.ocx,RunDll /play /close
%SystemRoot%\clock.avi
```

Don't mistakenly insert spaces between the executable file (amovie.ocx in the previous example), the comma, and the entry point (RunDll in the previous example). This will break RunDll without telling you why it failed.

Get the hint? We passed a parameter to the Active Movie control to play the clock.avi file, then to close it when it is done. Active Movie loaded the file specified, played the file, and closed it —all without user intervention.

Oh, don't blame me if the clock.avi file is a bit annoying.

Actually, RunDll will run more than OLE Controls—RunDll will (or at least attempt to) execute any executable file, including DLL (Dynamic Link Library) and EXE (EXEcutable). This is true as long as the file's entry point is known and the file to be executed follows the RunDll protocol. For more information, see Microsoft Knowledge Base article "Q164787," which can be viewed at http://support.microsoft.com/support/kb/articles/q164/7/87.asp. It was originally written for Windows 95/98 and contains information helpful to Windows NT users also.

Client-Server OLE Applications

Client-server OLE applications make up a substantial number of programs on most Windows computers. Even though the user may be unaware of what client-server OLE applications are installed, there are many.

One of the best designed and best integrated set of applications is Microsoft Office, currently released as Office 97. It combines word processing (Word for Windows), spreadsheets (Excel), a database system (Access), a presentation program (PowerPoint), and a host of utilities (such as Microsoft Draw 98 Drawing, Chart, and so on). Each of the main applications in Microsoft Office works as both client and server applications. Some applications—such as the Word Art and Chart utilities—are not designed to run as clients. For example, take Word for Windows (a program that at least I know how to use).

Word, as a client is . . . Word. Open Word and edit a document. Write a short letter to someone, it doesn't matter who. Create something, about a page long, three or four paragraphs. You have Word's functionality in all these paragraphs; everything you did was done using Word and nothing else.

Now things start to get really exciting. Insert an object. For grins, insert a drawing into a Word document. Click on Insert ➤ Object. Word displays the Object dialog box that will list all the OLE server objects that can be embedded (see Figure 5.1). Actually, OLE uses an API call to display the dialog box.

FIGURE 5.1:

Inserting a Microsoft Draw 98 Drawing is as easy as selecting it from the Object dialog box.

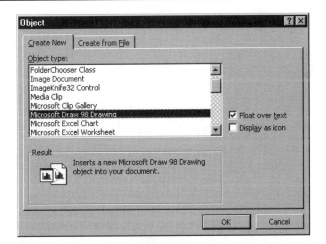

Some servers work by totally embedding themselves into Word. For example, Microsoft Draw 98 Drawing will replace Word's menu with the Microsoft Draw 98 Drawing menu and display the Microsoft Draw 98 Drawing tool bars, and so on—all without any user intervention (whammo, check Figure 5.2).

It is quite incredible that Microsoft Draw 98 Drawing works without Microsoft Word having prior knowledge of it. Actually, Word gives control to Microsoft Draw 98 Drawing whenever a Microsoft Draw 98 Drawing object is selected. Microsoft Draw 98 Drawing then displays its own menu items along with Word's Window menu so that the user can switch between Word documents if necessary—just like I'm doing while I write this chapter.

When a Microsoft Draw 98 Drawing object is not selected, Word takes control of the user interface, and the Word menu structure is restored (see Figure 5.3).

FIGURE 5.2:

Microsoft Draw 98 gives the user a new menu, new toolbars—it just takes over.

Microsoft Draw98 menu

Microsoft Draw98 toolbars

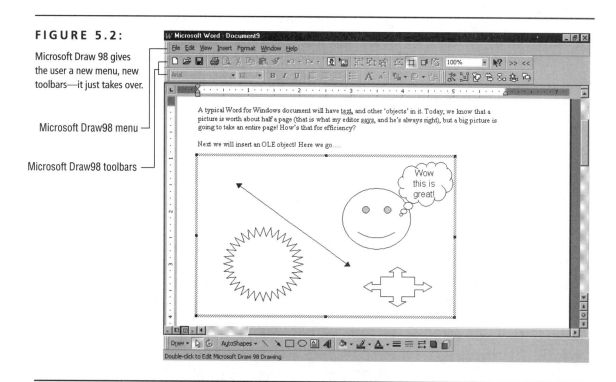

FIGURE 5.3:

Microsoft Word restores its own menu and toolbars when Microsoft Draw 98 is not active.

Microsoft Word menu

Microsoft Word toolbars

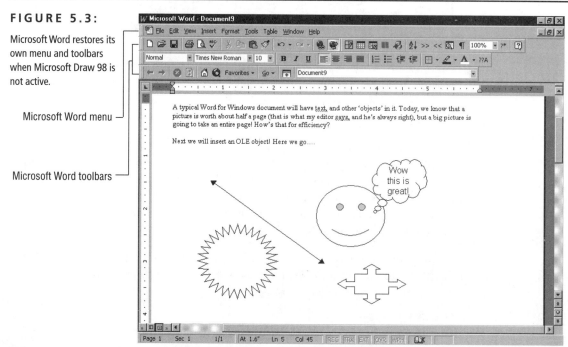

Context switching between Word and Microsoft Draw 98 Drawing is done by the user whenever the user selects something in the document. If the user selects something from Microsoft Draw 98 Drawing, Microsoft Draw 98 Drawing is put in control; otherwise, Word takes control.

There's a lot of magic going on behind the scenes here. When a complex document that contains OLE objects is saved, the OLE objects are saved by their servers when and where instructed to do so by Word.

Oops, topic drift. I'm trying to make everyone an OLE expert. Let's see if we can wrap this up in a nutshell, then connect everything with the registry.

So, in a nutshell:

- Client applications may have OLE objects embedded into their documents, and/or have OLE server functionality embedded into their basic functionality.

- This embedding is done at runtime, so the developer knows nothing about what embedding will be done when the program is being written.

- When a client application wants to embed an OLE object, the client application will call OLE to display the Insert Object dialog box to the user. The user then selects the object that is to be embedded.

- Whenever the object is selected, OLE allows the client's user interface (menus and toolbars, for example) to be turned over to the server application.

- Server applications may edit the object in place, or may create a special editing window, which may have menu/toolbar support, as appropriate. Usually, complex objects are edited in their own windows just to keep things simpler for the user.

- OLE uses the registry to learn about server applications that may be embedded.

- OLE server and client applications are identified to Windows NT by CLSIDs; call 'em UUIDs, or GUIDs if you want, 'tis the same thing. A CLSID is a long string of numbers that may be considered unique.

- The server application is able to use OLE to tell the client what capabilities the server has. This allows the client to behave in a predictable manner.

NOTE   It is possible to embed a purely functional OLE object into a document. This is done from time to time with database programming with OLE Controls (ActiveX), and OLE applications that don't have instance-specific data, such as the Microsoft Comic Chat control.

OK, I've prattled on about OLE long enough (Is that a wild cheer I hear?), so let's get to the registry component of OLE.

OLE and the Registry

Wow, now we're back to the registry. That was a lot of stuff to cover, just to get a handle of the basics of OLE.

OLE works extensively with the registry. When an application registers itself with OLE as a potential server application, this registration process consists of adding a number of entries into the registry. For OLE applications, such as ActiveX controls, these entries are relatively simple and easy to follow.

More complex OLE applications, take Microsoft Word for Windows as an example, have hundreds of entries in the registry and are typically difficult to understand.

Let's take a look at a simple OLE control—the ActiveX control called the Comic Chat control. Comic Chat is an application available from Microsoft to allow users to use the Internet chat facility. There are hundreds of chat servers—try chat.msn.com, chat.microsoft.com, or any other IRC chat server. Chat can be fun.

Yes, Comic Chat can be embedded into a Word document. This usage, though not typical, is legitimate. Check out Figure 5.4 to see Word and Comic Chat working together.

NOTE   Some versions of ActiveX controls, such as Comic Chat, don't work well when embedded into Word. They do not properly size themselves and tend to resize their display in unexpected ways. This is not acceptable behavior, I might add.

Microsoft Comic Chat is a large application that doesn't allow a lot of interaction with other documents or other applications. But why would you, a user, want other interaction? Easy! One, classic example is to embed Comic Chat into a Web page, which is a document whose application is the web browser. Another example is to embed Comic Chat into an e-mail message. Ding! Did the light go off? E-mail everyone on your team and include in the message the details of a virtual meeting both on an IRC chat server and on the client.

FIGURE 5.4:

Embedding Microsoft Comic Chat adds a new dimension to your Word documents.

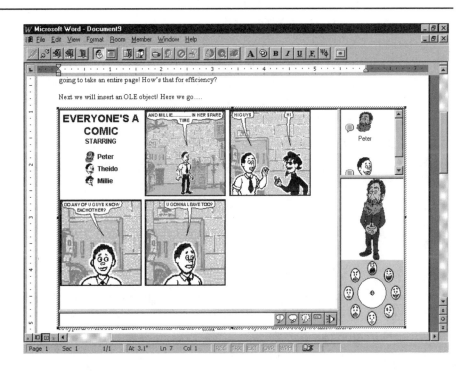

So, we have a Microsoft Comic Chat OLE server application implemented as an ActiveX control. Let's take a look at the registry entries for Comic Chat.

First, are the entries in HKEY_LOCAL_MACHINE\SOFTWARE\Classes\ CLSID. These entries define much of the OLE interface:

```
{241AF500-8FB6-11CF-ADC5-00AA00BADF6F}]
@="Comic Chat Room"
```

NOTE   The previous lines above are arranged as the hive and sub-hives, followed by any data keys that these hives might contain. A data key in the form of @=value denotes the default value entry found in every registry hive.

The first sub-hive contains the CLSID for the Comic Chat server. This CLSID happens to be 241AF500-8FB6-11CF-ADC5-00AA00BADF6F, although other versions of Comic Chat might have a different CLSID. The default data variable contains a string describing the program. Notice that this string is also found in the second section of the registry, [HKEY_LOCAL_MACHINE\SOFTWARE\Classes\Comic-Chat.Room.1], described next.

```
{241AF500-8FB6-11CF-ADC5-00AA00BADF6F}\AuxUserType]
@=" "
```

The AuxUserType hive is used for short, people-readable names for the application. These short names are then incorporated into menus, both regular and pop-up. Microsoft recommends that the names in AuxUserType be limited to not more than 15 characters.

This example shows one name for the application—the string Room:

```
{241AF500-8FB6-11CF-ADC5-00AA00BADF6F}\AuxUserType\2]
@="Room"
```

This example shows another name for the application—the string chat:

```
{241AF500-8FB6-11CF-ADC5-00AA00BADF6F}\AuxUserType\3]
@="chat"
```

Take this entry:

```
{241AF500-8FB6-11CF-ADC5-00AA00BADF6F}\DefaultExtension]
@=".ccr,Microsoft Chat Room (*.ccr)"
```

In this entry, the DefaultExtension hive is used to hold the extension that will be suggested for the default when a File Save As or File Open is done.

Take this next entry:

```
{241AF500-8FB6-11CF-ADC5-00AA00BADF6F}\DefaultIcon]
@="C:\\PROGRA~1\\MICROS~2\\CChat.exe,1"
```

In this entry, the DefaultIcon hive holds information about the icon that will be used. This icon is an icon index in the executable file listed. Though the executable file need not be the OLE control, it is strongly advised that they be the same.

The following entry, which works with the Microsoft OLE DocObject technology, may contain information about the capabilities of the OLE object:

```
{241AF500-8FB6-11CF-ADC5-00AA00BADF6F}\DocObject]
@="0"
```

In the next entry, the InprocHandler32 sub-hive tells the system what in-process handler will be used.

```
{241AF500-8FB6-11CF-ADC5-00AA00BADF6F}\InprocHandler32]
@="ole32.dll"
```

Many applications use OLE32.DLL as their in-process handler, although this is not a requirement.

Another commonly used in-process handler is MAPI32.DLL, which is used by many mail-enabled objects:

```
{241AF500-8FB6-11CF-ADC5-00AA00BADF6F}\Insertable]
@=" "
```

Intended for future use (Windows 95/98 and/or Windows NT 5), the following entry indicates to the system that the application should be listed in the insert list of the Insert New dialog box:

```
{241AF500-8FB6-11CF-ADC5-00AA00BADF6F}\LocalServer32]
@="C:\\PROGRA~1\\MICROS~2\\CChat.exe"
```

The next entry contains the application's fully qualified path and executable file name. This string is not a REG_EXPAND_SZ, so substitution variables should not be used:

```
{241AF500-8FB6-11CF-ADC5-00AA00BADF6F}\MiscStatus]
@="32"
```

Table 5.1 lists the flag values allowed in MiscStatus.

TABLE 5.1: Flag Values That Are Allowed in the MiscStatus Object

Flag (Value) in Decimal	Flag (Value) in Hex	Description
1	0x0001	Object is recomposed when resized.
2	0x0002	Object is only available as an icon.
4	0x0004	Object is used in insert mode, not replace mode.
8	0x0008	Object is static.
16	0x0010	Object can't link inside.
32	0x0020	Object can be linked by OLE 1.

Continued on next page

TABLE 5.1 CONTINUED: Flag Values That Are Allowed in the MiscStatus Object

Flag (Value) in Decimal	Flag (Value) in Hex	Description
64	0x0040	Object is a link object.
128	0x0080	Object is inside out.
256	0x0100	Activate the object when it is visible.
512	0x0200	Object's rendering is device independent.

NOTE

In MiscStatus, values may be combined, using a binary, or bitwise; the easiest way to do a bitwise is to simply add the values. For example, an application with the flags Object Can be linked by OLE 1 (32) and Activate the object when it is visible (256) would store a value of (256 + 32) = 288 in MiscStatus.

In this entry, the Printable hive denotes an OLE object that will support the IPrint method:

```
{241AF500-8FB6-11CF-ADC5-00AA00BADF6F}\Printable]
@=" "
```

For an insertable object, there must be an associated ProgID value. This value consists of a short name, a type, and a numeric value:

```
{241AF500-8FB6-11CF-ADC5-00AA00BADF6F}\ProgID]
@="ComicChat.Room.1"
```

A registry section will be created with this name (see next entry), where more registry values will be stored for this object:

```
{241AF500-8FB6-11CF-ADC5-00AA00BADF6F}\Verb]
@=" "
```

Verbs indicate types of action that the object may take. Always numbered consecutively in the registry, there are three components to verb entries, as shown here:

```
{241AF500-8FB6-11CF-ADC5-00AA00BADF6F}\Verb\0]
@="&Edit,0,2"
```

This sample verb, Edit, shows three things. First, the text used in the menu, &Edit. The & indicates that the letter following it will be underscored and used as a hotkey value.

Second, the first number, 0, is the menu flags value. Valid values (Although not all may be used with OLE menus, such as MF_OWNERDRAW.) are shown in Table 5.2.

TABLE 5.2: Flag Types Allowed

Flag Name	Value	Description
MF_STRING	0x000	The menu item is a string.
MF_ENABLE	0x000	The menu item is enabled.
MF_UNCHECKED	0x000	The menu item is unchecked.
MF_INSERT	0x000	The menu item is an inserted item.
MF_BITMAP	0x004	The menu item is a bitmap.
MF_CHECKED	0x008	The menu item is checked.
MF_DISABLED	0x002	The menu item is disabled.
MF_GRAYED	0x001	The menu item is dimmed.
MF_OWNERDRAW	0x100	The menu item is an owner-draw item.

Third, the second number, 2, is the verb flag. There are only two possible values for this entry as shown in Table 5.3.

TABLE 5.3: Verb Flag Names

Verb Flag Name	Value	Description
OLEVERBATTRIB_NEVERDIRTIES	1	Indicates that the verb does not modify the object, so the object will not require storing in persistent storage.
OLEVERBATTRIB_ONCONTAINERMENU	2	Indicates that the verb should appear on a pop-up menu.

There is a second section of the registry for the Comic Chat OLE object. This section, in HKEY_LOCAL_MACHINE\SOFTWARE\Classes, is named Comic-Chat.Room.1. This name was defined in the preceding ProgID entry.

In the ComicChat.Room.1 hive, there are two data keys:

```
[HKEY_LOCAL_MACHINE\SOFTWARE\Classes\ComicChat.Room.1]
@="Comic Chat Room"
"EditFlags"=hex:00,00,01,00
```

The first data key is the default value that contains the name (text) that will be used in the insert list of the Insert Object dialog box. The second value contains the edit flags, expressed as hex values:

```
[HKEY_LOCAL_MACHINE\SOFTWARE\Classes\ComicChat.Room.1\CLSID]
@="{241AF500-8FB6-11CF-ADC5-00AA00BADF6F}"
```

The CLSID contains the object's CLSID.

The next entry, which works with the Microsoft OLE DocObject technology, may contain information about the capabilities of the OLE object:

```
[HKEY_LOCAL_MACHINE\SOFTWARE\Classes\ComicChat.Room.1\DocObject]
@="0"
```

Intended for future use (Windows 95/98 and/or Windows NT 5), this entry indicates to the system that the application should be listed in the insert list of the Insert New dialog box:

```
[HKEY_LOCAL_MACHINE\SOFTWARE\Classes\ComicChat.Room.1\Insertable]
@=" "
```

The protocol sub-hive is used for compatibility with OLE 1 container (client) applications:

```
[HKEY_LOCAL_MACHINE\SOFTWARE\Classes\ComicChat.Room.1\protocol]
@=" "
```

There is one sub-hive in protocol, called StdFileEditing. Within StdFileEditing there are a number of items, as shown here:

```
[HKEY_LOCAL_MACHINE\SOFTWARE\Classes\ComicChat.Room.1\protocol\Std-
FileEditing]
@=" "
```

The default entry in StdFileEditing is an empty string:

```
[HKEY_LOCAL_MACHINE\SOFTWARE\Classes\ComicChat.Room.1\protocol\Std-
FileEditing\server]
@="C:\\PROGRA~1\\MICROS~2\\CChat.exe"
```

The first sub-hive in StdFileEditing is the server sub-hive. Inside the server is the default string that contains the fully qualified name of the server executable file. As this string is REG_SZ, do not use any substitutable variables, such as %SystemRoot%, in this string:

```
[HKEY_LOCAL_MACHINE\SOFTWARE\Classes\ComicChat.Room.1\protocol\Std-
FileEditing\verb]
@=""
```

The next sub-hive in StdFileEditing is verb. Inside verb will be found one or more numbered sub-hives; numbers begin with 0 and should be consecutive. Each verb that the OLE application uses in a menu will be included, as shown here:

```
[HKEY_LOCAL_MACHINE\SOFTWARE\Classes\ComicChat.Room.1\protocol\Std-
FileEditing\verb\0]
@="&Edit"
```

This verb is the Edit menu selection. The text used in the menu is &Edit. The & indicates that the letter following it will be underscored and used as a hotkey value.

How Linkages Are Made between Applications

OK, now we'll take a look at a few of the mechanisms that Windows NT uses to manage OLE applications, CLSIDs, and the user interface.

First, let's confuse applications and documents. Considering them to be identical for now will ease some of the issues here. OLE is one complex puppy, so anything we can do to understand it is OK. Later in this chapter, I'll spend some time pointing out what the issues are between a document and an application.

OK, so the user's application wants to use OLE. There are a couple of ways this can happen:

- The application can be written from the get-go to use OLE controls. Not many applications are written that way, but some are.

- The application can be written to allow the user to embed OLE objects into it. Most OLE applications are written this way.

Everyone Uses OLE

Everyone uses OLE, we just don't realize it. The Windows NT and Windows 95/98 operating systems use OLE to perform a number of useful tasks. OLE is a built-in, not an added-on-later, part of Windows NT.

Explorer, the Windows NT user interface, relies on OLE for many of its abilities. For example, take a look at your Desktop. Do you understand what is going on there? Probably not. Do you care? Maybe, and a bit of understanding can help later when you decide to customize your Desktop. Much of the functionality that you see on your Desktop is created by one program, Explorer. Explorer is the program that paints your Desktop background; puts up those icons (such as the pesky and difficult to remove Recycle Bin, My Briefcase, and My Computer, for example); and manages aspects of the user interface, such as property sheets and context menus. This is all done with the very valuable assistance of OLE.

Let's give OLE a big hand—it does a lot for us.

Neither of these two scenarios is mutually exclusive. For example, an application could have both methods built into it.

In either case, the server (the OLE object that the client will be using) must be registered. When registered, the server's basic properties will be listed in the registry, in the [HKEY_LOCAL_MACHINE\SOFTWARE\Classes] and [HKEY_LOCAL_MACHINE\SOFTWARE\Classes\CLSID] sections. This information in the registry provides the client with the minimum (got that, minimum) amount of information needed to interact with the OLE server.

However, the client application needs to know more about the server. Questions about what the server does, what is expected, whether in-place editing is supported, and what information or data is communicated between the server and the application all must be determined.

An ActiveX control, for example, probably won't have any data that is stored in the client's document. Most ActiveX controls are used to display information for the user. However, what information is displayed varies greatly.

Some ActiveX controls display information whose contents may vary only in detail. A classic example of this type of ActiveX control is a real-time clock control—the control retrieves the time from the system and displays the time in a specified format. Another controls data changes in content, but not type. For example, the Comic Chat control always displays IRC chat sessions, though the sessions might vary widely. However, a Microsoft Draw 98 Drawing server's data and type both would change from invocation to invocation. Who knows what the user might try to display in the Microsoft Draw 98 Drawing control? The display could be anything from a company logo to a cheery holiday greeting.

Regardless, each server must communicate with the client application. The client always initiates communications between a server and a client; otherwise, how'd the server know a client needed it? This communication is done using a technique called *querying the interface*. The server will respond with information about exactly what the server can do.

Embedded Documents

Embedded documents will have references to each OLE object that they have. Unlike when OLE controls are used with an application (remember, we blurred this distinction in the previous section), OLE objects in a document can and do vary greatly. Each document is unique—one document may contain no OLE objects, while the next may contain many different objects.

Transportability is a critical issue. Say I create a chapter for my publisher and embed an OLE object into the document. Then I e-mail that document to my editor. When the editor opens the document and wants to have access to the object, the OLE server application will have to be installed on the computer. It is not necessary that the OLE server be installed in the same directory, or in any specific directory. OLE uses the registry to take care of locating the server and activating it as necessary. I might have the OLE server installed in a directory on my Q: drive, while my editor might have the same server located on the C: drive, and the executable filename may well be different in each installation, too. Regardless, as long as the ProgID value is identical, Windows NT will be able to locate the server and launch it.

Critical items in the registry are those entries shown in the previous sections of this chapter. If you find it necessary to move an OLE server's files from one location to another, it may be possible to edit the registry and change the file locations that are stored in entries, such as:

```
[HKEY_LOCAL_MACHINE\SOFTWARE\Classes\CLSID\{241AF500-8FB6-11CF-ADC5-
00AA00BADF6F}\DefaultIcon]
@=
```

```
[HKEY_LOCAL_MACHINE\SOFTWARE\Classes\CLSID\{241AF500-8FB6-11CF-ADC5-
00AA00BADF6F}\LocalServer32]
@=

[HKEY_LOCAL_MACHINE\SOFTWARE\Classes\ComicChat.Room.1\protocol\Std-
FileEditing\server]
@=
```

NOTE   Before making any change such as this, be sure your backups are up-to-date.

WARNING   Don't even consider moving system OLE servers and objects. Anything supplied with Windows NT that is OLE related should be left where it is. This is because it is possible that there are references to these objects in places other than the registry.

Fixing an OLE Disaster

Common OLE problems arise when a user inadvertently deletes the OLE server files, often in an ill advised attempt to clean up hard disk space, while the OLE registry entries remain in the registry. Several tricks can be tried to recover from this. First, attempt to reinstall a new copy of the OLE server in the original location. This will probably work in most cases. However, if you cannot reinstall, maybe you don't know where the source files are located, consider restoring the files from a backup.

As a last resort, try to remove the registry entries for the OLE server. This probably will result in your registry and system becoming unstable, but if it is unusable anyway, what do you have to lose? Check the sections listed here for entries about the OLE server:

- [HKEY_LOCAL_MACHINE\SOFTWARE\Classes\CLSID\
- [HKEY_LOCAL_MACHINE\SOFTWARE\Classes\

Doing this will require some detective work. You will have to search the registry using either RegEdit, or by exporting the registry to a text file and using a text editor's search. While searching, note all locations where the OLE server is mentioned. There will be at least two, the two mentioned in the previous list; although some OLE components may have more entries.

Disaster typically raises its ugly head when there are multiple dependencies between a number of OLE objects. The fix here may be to restore if possible.

Another disaster point is when a new application installs an OLE object that conflicts with an existing one. Typically, the two OLE objects would have different CLSIDs. However, it is possible that the CLSIDs are identical, although in theory, this should not happen. When a second copy of an OLE object is installed, the object's ProgID will be adjusted, though the user will frequently see two OLE objects in the Insert Object dialog box with the same name. Often, only one of the objects will work correctly.

Hints and Kinks from the Experts

OK, there is a shortage of hints from the experts on OLE. I thought about making up some hints, but decided not to. I've included one hint from John Savill.

A Service Or Driver Failed To Start and the Event Viewer Has Taken a Vacation. If you receive a message that a service or driver has failed to start, you are instructed to check the Event Viewer for details.

If Event Viewer has gone on vacation (all your All Users folders are gone) and/or no Network icon displays in the Control Panel, you may have a missing or corrupted Ole32.dll in the %SystemRoot%\System32 folder. Install a copy from the CD-ROM or from your latest Service Pack or Hotfix, then reboot your system.

(Courtesy of John Savill)

CHAPTER

SIX

6

Why, Oh Why, Are There SYSTEM.INI and WIN.INI Files?

- SYSTEM.INI

- WIN.INI

- Hints and kinks from the experts

OK, so we have a registry, and that registry was supposed to replace the SYSTEM.INI and WIN.INI files that the first 16-bit versions of Windows were plagued with.

If you have been a Windows user for more than a few years, you're probably well aware of the issues evolving around the WIN.INI and SYSTEM.INI files. These files contained almost all of the information used to configure Windows; there were other configuration files, such as PROTOCOL.INI, used to store network information. When the time to design Windows NT and Windows 95/98 arrived, those wonderful software guys at Microsoft decided that there were some problems with using INI files. Several problems became apparent. Users would edit these files, often without regard for the consequences of making changes. Sometimes these changes were totally inadvertent. Some editors (typically those used to doing word processing) would add, remove, or even change some characters without explicitly telling the user. An example is the use of quotes around strings, where the word processor would stick in stylized quotes.

Another problem that became more apparent as time went on was that the SYSTEM.INI and the WIN.INI files were growing at an alarming rate. As users added software, fonts, and system components, these files grew. The result was that the primitive search routines employed in these early versions of Windows could not efficiently search for entries in the file.

A third problem was that applications were able to modify system entries in the WIN.INI and SYSTEM.INI file with impunity. A rogue application could butcher these files and no one would be the wiser until the damage caused a failure of the operating system—no protection or security was available.

These problems prompted Microsoft to move to a more efficient method of storing information that both Windows and user applications could access easily and efficiently. The registry—a binary, tree-oriented database—is quick and easy to work with. Changes to existing products as they were migrated to 32-bit environments, such as Windows NT and Windows 95/98, presented a few problems for programmers to resolve. However, moving to the registry-based model also presented a few problems for those applications that were already in existence. These applications were often called *legacy applications*. They already existed either on the user's computer(s) or as products that were being sold, but would not be updated for some time.

NOTE   Today, there are still many 16-bit applications being sold on the Windows platform. This is three years after the introduction of Windows 95, a 32-bit platform that supports 32-bit applications very well. We can even assume that in the foreseeable future, there will always be at least one 16-bit application being sold or used somewhere. Old habits, and old software, die hard.

These problems include:

- Existing 16-bit applications must be supported in executable form. That is, an application that expects WIN.INI and SYSTEM.INI files to exist must be able to use them.

- Some 16-bit applications do not have access to registry manipulation APIs. These applications must be supported using the pre-existing WIN.INI and SYSTEM.INI files also.

To handle these problems, Microsoft wisely decided to retain support for both WIN.INI and SYSTEM.INI. Windows would no longer use these files, but they would be available to any applications that chose to access or utilize them.

In this chapter, we'll take a look at the SYSTEM.INI and WIN.INI files that Windows NT provides. The default files are not too large, although the WIN.INI file might become larger when users install more 16-bit applications. The SYSTEM.INI file might also grow as the user adds items that are not designed to work with Windows NT.

There is one other INI file that Windows NT supports: The Windows 16-bit File Manager uses WINFILE.INI. Virtually all Windows NT installations will have an empty WINFILE.INI file. Unless you are running a 16-bit version of File Manager, the version supplied with Windows NT is 32-bit, no entries will be added to WINFILE.INI. Generally, the only time that WINFILE.INI will be used is when a user is dual-booting between Windows NT and Windows 3.1x or WFG (Windows for Workgroups). Dual-booting to one of these old versions of Windows is becoming exceedingly rare.

Windows NT and versions of Windows prior to Windows 95/98 could be installed into the same directory and coexist happily. (Windows 95/98 does not support installing both in the same directory, so don't try it.) We'll refer to the case where both Windows 3.1x and Windows NT are installed in the same directory as a dual Windows environment installation.

NOTE　Windows NT and Windows 3.1*x* must be installed in the same directory for the dual environment configuration to work. It is not possible to have them in different directories.

With this configuration, the user is able to boot into Windows or Windows NT as desired. This is slightly different from doing an upgrade, when Windows NT replaces the existing version of Windows.

When there is a dual Windows environment installation, Windows NT will manage the coordination (updating of the WIN.INI and SYSTEM.INI files) of the two different environments. When Windows NT is started, it will read the WIN.INI and SYSTEM.INI files and incorporate any changed information into the registry, if these changes are appropriate for Windows NT. This way, any changes made by a Windows 3.1*x* application will be reflected in the registry, if appropriate.

When Windows NT shuts down, it will update the WIN.INI and SYSTEM.INI to reflect any changes that are appropriate for the Windows 3.1*x* environment.

Since both environments are not running at the same time, the user is assured that anything changed in one environment will change in the other environment.

NOTE　Note that if there is no dual environment installation (That is, Windows 3.1*x* is not installed in the same directory as Windows NT.), the WIN.INI and SYSTEM.INI will not contain any environment information at all. Instead, these files will contain only user application–related information.

When Windows applications write the WIN.INI or SYSTEM.INI files, and those applications use the Windows NT registry updating APIs, the information that would have been stored in the INI file will be stored in the registry. This is subject to the exclusions discussed next.

NOTE　In addition to the WIN.INI and SYSTEM.INI files, any file listed in the HKEY_LOCAL_MACHINE\SOFTWARE\Microsoft\Windows NT\CurrentVersion\ IniFileMapping section (that is, the INI file or the registry) will also be updated using the Windows NT registry updating APIs. INI files in the IniFileMapping section will be updated based on the rules explained next.

Windows NT will search the IniFileMapping section for the application's section. If the section is found, it is used. If no application section is found, Windows NT will search for an INI file to use.

NOTE   Any application that directly opens an INI file, perhaps using the 16-bit INI file-processing APIs will bypass the registry file entirely.

SYSTEM.INI

Located in the SYSTEM.INI file are a few entries that the Windows NT Setup program supplies by default. Here is a typical SYSTEM.INI file:

```
; for 16-bit app support
[386Enh]
woafont=dosapp.fon
EGA80WOA.FON=EGA80WOA.FON
EGA40WOA.FON=EGA40WOA.FON
CGA80WOA.FON=CGA80WOA.FON
CGA40WOA.FON=CGA40WOA.FON

[drivers]
wave=mmdrv.dll
timer=timer.drv

[mci]
```

This file contains three sections ([386Enh], [drivers], and [mci]) and only a few entries in these sections. Entries are primarily for fonts (in the [386Enh] section), and two drivers used with Windows NT:

mmdrv.dll—A driver that is used for multimedia (sound) support.

timer.drv—A driver that is used to provide timer support.

As well, your SYSTEM.INI file may contain other entries and other sections if you are using 16-bit incompatible applications. These applications would use the WIN.INI file to write application-specific information, typically, in sections created for the application.

Most of the Windows NT system entries were moved from the SYSTEM.INI file to the registry hive HKEY_LOCAL_MACHINE\Software\Microsoft\Windows NT\ CurrentVersion\WOW. This hive contains many entries that would be found in a Windows 3.1*x* installation.

NOTE   Windows NT cannot use any 16-bit screen savers because they do not perform correctly when used in the Windows NT environment. Any entry, such as scrnsave .exe found in the [BOOT] section of the SYSTEM.INI file, will not be migrated to Windows NT.

WIN.INI

Few entries are located in the WIN.INI file, except for computers that have been used for some time and have had additional software or components installed.

The default WIN.INI file contains only four sections; none of them has any entries:

```
; for 16-bit app support
[fonts]
[extensions]
[mci extensions]
[files]
```

A computer with a few more miles on it might look something like this:

```
; for 16-bit app support
[fonts]
[extensions]
[mci extensions]
[files]
[Mail]
MAPI=1
MAPIX=1
OLEMessaging=1
CMC=1
CMCDLLNAME=mapi.dll
CMCDLLNAME32=MAPI32.DLL
```

```
Exchange=C:\Program Files\Windows NT\Windows Messaging\exchng32.exe
MAPIXVER=1.0.0.1
[SciCalc]
layout=0
[MSReport]
ProgramDir=C:\msreport\msreport.exe
[WinZip]
win32_version=6.1-6.2
Name=Peter D. Hipson
SN=9999999
[fedex]
stringsaved=FALSE
[FedEx Ship]
NetworkEnabled=0
LocalPath=C:\fedex20\
NetworkPath=C:\fedex20\
[WinMem]
DispFlags=508
X=768
Y=688
Width=256
Height=64
[MAPI 1.0 Time Zone]
Bias=12c
StandardName=Eastern Standard Time
StandardBias=0
StandardStart=00000A0005000200000000000000000000
DaylightName=Eastern Daylight Time
DaylightBias=ffffffc4
DaylightStart=00000400010002000000000000000000
ActiveTimeBias=f0
```

This computer has a number of additional applications installed. These applications are a mixture of system components and added-on programs from a variety of sources:

Mail—The entries in the [Mail] section are used to describe the mail interface that is installed on this computer.

SciCalc—The Windows Calculator adds this entry to the WIN.INI file indicating what mode (standard or scientific) the Calculator is in.

MSReport—Microsoft Report is a bug reporting tool used by Microsoft beta testers.

WinZip—WinZip is a front-end to the very popular DOS-based PKZIP program. WinZip adds both a Windows interface and the ability to handle long filenames to PKZIP.

FedEx—FedEx is a shipper whose computerized shipping manager makes creating shipments and airbills and tracking shipments much easier.

FedEx Ship—FedEx Ship is the actual shipping program used to create air-bills.

WinMem—This is a Windows memory application.

MAPI 1.0 Time Zone—This contains the settings for the MAPI (Mail Application Programming Interface) time zone information. This information is used to time/date stamp e-mail messages.

Now, you may have noticed that some of these programs are not 16-bit applications. The first application, Mail, is most certainly part of the 32-bit e-mail system. Why does it have entries in the WIN.INI file? This allows 16-bit applications to know something about the already installed e-mail interface.

Is SciCalc a 32-bit program? Yes, of course it is. So why does SciCalc store information in WIN.INI if it is not going to interact with other 16-bit applications? Got me! Somewhere a program has not done a good job of converting the Calculator program from a 16-bit application that couldn't use the registry to a 32-bit program that could. Remember—32-bit applications can use INI files, including WIN.INI; although it is strongly recommended that they do not. These same issues apply to WinZip, the FedEx applications, and WinMem.

Why do MAPI 1.0 Time Zone settings exist? I'd guess that, like the Mail entries, these entries are used to help 16-bit applications, although I would not place any money on that.

WIN.INI system-based settings are stored in the registry in a number of sub-hives. Table 6.1 shows some of these settings and their locations. This is mostly of interest to users who are using dual environments, such as Windows 3.1x and Windows NT, in the same directory.

TABLE 6.1: Sections Found in WIN.INI

Section in WIN.INI	Windows NT Registry Path	Description
[colors]	HKEY_CURRENT_USER\Control Panel\Colors	Colors used in the display of Windows
[compatibility]	HKEY_LOCAL_MACHINE\SOFTWARE\Microsoft\Windows NT\CurrentVersion\Compatibility	Compatibility issues for existing legacy software
[desktop]	HKEY_CURRENT_USER\Control Panel\Desktop	The Desktop properties set by the user using either the Desktop Properties dialog box or the Control Panel
[embedding]	HKEY_LOCAL_MACHINE\SOFTWARE\Microsoft\Windows NT\CurrentVersion\Embedding	OLE servers as created by applications and systems during installation time
[extensions]	HKEY_CURRENT_USER\SOFTWARE\Microsoft\Windows NT\CurrentVersion\Extensions	File associations used by Explorer
[fonts] and [fontSubstitutes]	HKEY_LOCAL_MACHINE\SOFTWARE\Microsoft\Windows NT\CurrentVersion \Fonts HKEY_LOCAL_MACHINE\SOFTWARE\Microsoft\Windows NT\CurrentVersion\FontSubstitutes	Fonts used by Windows
[intl]	HKEY_CURRENT_USER\Control Panel\International	Regional settings set by the Control Panel's Regional Settings applet
[mci extensions]	HKEY_LOCAL_MACHINE\SOFTWARE\Microsoft\Windows NT\CurrentVersion\MCI Extensions	The Media Control Interface settings and extensions

Continued on next page

TABLE 6.1 CONTINUED: Sections Found in WIN.INI

Section in WIN.INI	Windows NT Registry Path	Description
[network]	HKEY_CURRENT_USER\SOFTWARE\Microsoft\Windows NT\CurrentVersion\ Network\Persistent Connections (for drives); HKEY_LOCAL_MACHINE\SYSTEM\Control\Print (for printers)	Network drive and printer settings
[ports]	HKEY_LOCAL_MACHINE\SOFTWARE\Microsoft\Windows NT\CurrentVersion\Ports	Describes ports (comm and printer) with settings
[printerPorts] and [devices]	HKEY_LOCAL_MACHINE\SOFTWARE\Microsoft\Windows NT\CurrentVersion\PrinterPorts and \Devices	Describes printer ports and devices used for output
[sounds]	HKEY_CURRENT_USER\Control Panel\Sounds	Describes the sounds that occur when an event happens
[TrueType]	HKEY_CURRENT_USER\Software\Microsoft\Windows NT\CurrentVersion\TrueType	Describes the TrueType font options
[Windows Help]	HKEY_CURRENT_USER\Software\Microsoft\Windows Help	Describes the WinHelp settings
[Windows]	HKEY_LOCAL_MACHINE\SOFTWARE\Microsoft\Windows NT\CurrentVersion\Winlogon	Describes the various Windows settings used by the user

Some items are never migrated in a dual environment system. These items (listed next) are usually not moved to the registry either due to their complexity or for other reasons:

- [Ports], [Devices], and [PrinterPorts] are migrated during the migration process as part of installation; these settings are not used by Windows NT for any purpose.

- Persistent shares and users as used by Windows for Workgroups, not Windows 3.1x, however.

- Default domain and user ID from Windows for Workgroups or the LANMAN.INI.

- Individual user profiles that are maintained by WINLOGIN.

- Changes that users make in their copies of the Main, Startup, Games, and Accessories Program Manager groups.

- MS-DOS drive letters are managed using the Windows NT Disk Administrator. (Drive letters usually vary between Windows 3.1x and Windows NT due to how drives are detected, and the possible presence of non-Windows 3.1x compatible drive formatting, such as NTFS drives.)

- Auto Arrange, Minimize on Run, and Save Settings on Exit options for Program Manager, these settings are not type compatible. (Program Manager uses strings, while Windows NT uses DWORD values for these settings.)

- DOS command window font details.

Hints and Kinks from the Experts

Here are some SYSTEM.INI and WIN.INI hints from our experts.

Is Your Network Plagued with Browser Elections? A *browser election* is a normal network occurrence. An election provides a means to guarantee that there is never more than one master browser present in a domain/workgroup. A master browser is elected in the following priority:

- NT Server installed as PDC

- NT Server

- NT Workstation

- Other server

A PDC (Primary Domain Controller) is automatically the Domain Master Browser, even if "IsDomainMaster=Yes" is set in the registry on another NT Server in the domain.

If you are running workgroup servers (which contain no domain controller), and you want to force a specific server to be the preferred master browser, set the following registry entry on that server to Yes:

```
HKEY_LOCAL_MACHINE\SYSTEM\CurrentControlSet\Services\Browser\Parameters\
IsDomainMaster
```

To prevent an NT Workstation or Server (non-PDC) from acting as a browser, set the following entry to No:

```
HKEY_LOCAL_MACHINE\SYSTEM\CurrentControlSet\Services\Browser\Parameters\
MaintainServerList
```

To prevent a WFWG system from acting as a browser, create and/or set the following statement in the [Network] section of SYSTEM.INI of the WFWG client:

```
MaintainServerList=No.
```

Other valid entries are Yes and Auto.

Windows 95 machines can only participate in a browser election if they are configured for file and/or print sharing. This is accomplished in the Control Panel Networks applet. To set or check the browser settings, scroll to File and Printer Sharing for Microsoft Networks. Highlight this entry and click the Properties button. Select Browse Master and choose from Disabled, Enabled, or Automatic.

(Courtesy of Jerold Schulman)

Where Does Windows NT Store the SYSTEM.INI Info for 16-bit Programs?   The WOW key at HKEY_LOCAL_MACHINE\Software\Microsoft\ Windows NT\CurrentVersion\WOW stores configuration data for the Win16 on Win32 subsystem, aka Windows on Windows.

The WOW key contains sub-keys that have the same names as headings in the SYSTEM.INI file. The value entries in these sub-keys are the same as the values in the 16-bit Windows 3.x SYSTEM.INI file.

(Courtesy of Jerold Schulman)

Does Unattended Setup Sometimes Ignore Win31Upgrade=no in Your Unattended Answer File?   If you do not want to upgrade an existing Windows 3.x installation during Unattended Setup, you should have a Win31Upgrade=no statement in your Unattended Windows NT Setup Answer file.

You must also hide the old Windows installation from Windows NT Setup. If you don't hide it, Setup will only honor your Win31Upgrade=no if it has insufficient room on the Windows drive, or if it suspects that Windows 95 is installed. If it finds Shell32.dll, User32.dll, Kernel32.dll, and Gdi32.dll in the system directory; it will think Windows 95 is installed.

If Setup finds WIN.COM, WIN.INI, or SYSTEM.INI in the Windows directory and autoexec.bat in the root; it will think Windows 3.x is installed.

Since Setup only searches for Windows in the PATH as defined in C:\autoexec.bat, the best way to hide the Windows 3.x installation is to edit autoexec.bat and remove all references to Windows from the path.

(Courtesy of Jerold Schulman)

CHAPTER
SEVEN

7

Getting Rid of the Unwanted

- Removing things

- Possible problems, quick fixes

- RegClean

- RegMaid

- CleanReg

- Hints and kinks from the experts

Sometimes we don't have what we want in the registry. Other times, we have too much of what we *don't want* in the registry. This chapter covers the second case.

We install software, try it, don't like it, and remove it. Things come and things go, sometimes intentionally, sometimes by accident. But whatever the cause or reason, any computer that has been running Windows NT for more than a few months will probably have a few entries in the registry that do nothing more than clutter it up. Additionally, there will perhaps be a few unlucky users who will have some entries that are doing something that they really don't want to happen.

The classic problem is that we are not always good at removing things we install. Many software programs come with uninstall programs, but many others don't. Sometimes we lose track of an application—usually because, in a moment of weakness, we delete the application's directory without properly uninstalling the application. Desperation for even a few more MB of hard disk space will make us do strange things.

Have you ever installed an application on a secondary drive only to later have that secondary drive fail? Maybe you have a good backup, maybe not. Perhaps you just want to do a general housecleaning. For whatever the reason, this chapter will deal with the very difficult task of trying to remove unwanted things from the registry without having to reinstall Windows NT.

WARNING   Have I already said this? *Back up your registry before doing anything described in this chapter*. Manually removing items from a registry is perhaps the *easiest way to trash everything.* Back up, back up, and back up again.

This chapter will cover the problems associated with removing items from the registry. This chapter also covers three utilities that help clean up the registry: RegClean, RegMaid, and CleanReg.

Removing Things

Successfully removing anything from the registry can be most difficult. A classic example of what happens when you remove one item, maybe a sub-hive or a data key, is that Windows NT does something unexpected. Maybe Windows NT won't boot anymore. Maybe it boots, but a component or application won't run. Whatever.

The next step is to decide if it is better to try to restore things to their original state (by reinstalling the component or application), or to try to remove the offending item(s). If a backup exists for both the registry and the files for the item in question, restoring to get the system back to a working state will probably be a good starting point. A stable system that is not experiencing difficulties is much easier to work on than a system that fails for unexplained reasons.

Once the system is restored, try an established method for removing the component, such as the Add/Remove Programs applet in the Control Panel or the application's uninstall program.

If there is no backup of the registry or component, then a different attack must be undertaken. There are three possible avenues of attack:

- Try reinstalling the component. Often, the installation program will restore any registry entries that are necessary for the component to run. Typically, any customization done since the last installation will be lost, but that's life.

- Try finding an uninstall program. First check the Add/Remove Programs applet in the Control Panel. If the component is listed, run uninstall from there. If the component is not listed, check the component's directories. List all the executable files: files with the EXE or BAT extensions. If there is one that is named uninstall, or remove, this may be the program that you need. Also, don't forget to check the component's documentation regarding uninstallation procedures.

- If there is no uninstall program, and the application must be removed, you may have to do it manually. If this is the case, read on.

NOTE   Some components, especially those that are system components, make so many changes to the registry that it is impossible to remove them manually. This is particularly true for components that have replaced an already existing component, such as upgrading to a new version. Though you can remove the entries for the component in question, you cannot restore the entries that have been changed by the component to their original state—especially if you don't know their original state. Changes to the registry are usually not well logged, so there is typically little to tell you what has changed over time.

Possible Problems, Quick Fixes

This section discusses some possible problems and solutions that I've found.

The Application or System Was Deleted

The application or system was deleted, perhaps in error. In this case, you would try the following potential fixes:

- Try restoring the application's files.

- If that fails, try reinstalling the application.

- If that fails, try removing the application with the application's uninstall program, then try reinstalling the application.

Another Application Has Overwritten the Application's Files

In this case, a new application installation has overwritten another application's files. OK, this was an error, but you inadvertently installed application X in application Y's directory. It's rare, but sometimes the two applications have the same default installation directory. More often, we simply make a mistake and choose the wrong directory. Most application setup programs won't warn us that the path we have chosen already exists—major bummer.

Some hints for recovering an application include:

- First, use the new application's uninstall program to uninstall the new application. If the new application has been used, and there are user documents or data files, back these up. However, for now, just get rid of that new application.

- Next, try restoring the application's files. If that fails, try reinstalling the application.

- If that fails, try removing the application with the application's uninstall program and then try reinstalling the application.

There Is an Error Reading the Application's Files

Suppose there is an error reading the application's files, or the application crashes (faults) when executed. In this case, the application's files are probably damaged. What happened? There are several possibilities and some of them are very ugly. Maybe one or more files were overwritten by a user error. In this case, things don't look too bleak. Generally, you can recover from this situation by restoring the application's files.

Maybe another application or the operating system overwrote one or more files. This is rare, but it could happen. Check file dates to try to determine when the file overwrites occurred and see if there is a way to determine the culprit. Restore the correct files. Consider setting permissions to read/execute for everyone except an administrative userid that you use only to manage these files. Using file system permissions allows you to get immediate notification when a file overwrite occurs.

There Is an Error Reading the Drive

Well, actually this is the beginning of the end of the world.

First, run chkdsk and determine what Windows NT is able to do to fix the problem. Realize that when Windows NT fixes a file on an NTFS drive, it doesn't fix the file; it only makes the file readable. Windows NT is not able to recover the file's contents—if it could, everything would be all right. Windows NT gives a message that file so-and-so has been repaired, but it is somewhat misleading in that respect. However, you must do this repair to be able to replace the file with the right one.

When chkdsk runs, it will tell you if there are any damaged files. Windows NT is able to recover from minor problems and errors on the drive. Don't worry about these types of errors. It is not unusual to have a drive reported as having minor errors—such is life in the fast lane, or the fast drive lane in this case.

After running chkdsk, you must make a decision. A backup, at this point, can't hurt, but don't back up over any existing backups. Use a fresh tape (or whatever your backup program backs up to) and put this backup to the side. Here are the actions I'd take, in order of preference:

1. Replace the drive and restore (to the new drive) from the most recent, known good backup. Since drives usually fail in stages, a little bit at a time, it is

possible that your backups are not going to help as much as you'd like. This is a value call—if you are confident that a recent backup is OK, try it. If you are not confident of your more recent backups, you may need to try something else. As errors develop over time, they often contaminate all backups long before they are discovered.

2. Reformat the failing drive and restore from a known good backup.

3. Restore the entire drive from a known good backup without reformatting. This is sometimes necessary if for some reason the drive can't be formatted.

4. Try to restore specific files known to be defective, either from backups or from the application distribution media.

RegClean

Microsoft created a program that automates cleaning the registry. This program is available from several sources, I recommend that you retrieve it directly from Microsoft's Internet site at `http://support.microsoft.com/download/support/mslfiles/regclean.exe`.

There are several versions of RegClean, this URL gives the most recent version, RegClean 4.1a. This version was released in early 1998. It is fully compatible with Windows NT 4, although there may be a need to update to a later version of the OLE driver OLEAUT32.DLL. This update is included with the distribution of RegClean. Documentation on how to install the driver is also included in the RegClean readme.txt file.

Using RegClean is simple, just follow these steps:

1. Download the RegClean.EXE file from Microsoft's Internet site, as previously shown, or use the FTP site at `ftp://ftp.microsoft.com/Softlib/MSLFILES`.

2. Execute the RegClean.EXE file to start the self-extractor program. Alternatively, you may use either WinZip or PKUNZIP on the RegCleanEXE distribution file to extract the program and other files.

3. Files contained in the RegClean.EXE distribution file include:

   OADIST.EXE—This is the update for OLEAUT32.DLL, if needed.

   README.TXT—This is a text file with instructions on how to use RegClean and information about OADIST.EXE.

REGCLEAN.EXE—This is the real RegClean.EXE program, which is an executable Windows NT application.

4. Execute the RegClean.EXE program that is extracted.

NOTE   RegClean.EXE writes a program called RegClean.EXE. Confused? Well, you should be. The file RegClean.EXE that you download (about 800KB in size) is a self-extracting Zip file. One of the files contained in RegClean.EXE will be RegClean.EXE— the real program. In order for both files to coexist, the self-extracting RegClean.EXE file must write its output to a different directory or drive. RegClean.EXE cannot extract to its own directory.

Do I Need to Update OLEAUT32?

If you receive the message(s):

```
REGCLEAN.EXE is linked to missing export OLEAUT32.DLL:421
```

and

```
A device attached to the system is not correctly functioning
```

it is probable that you will need an updated OLEAUT32.DLL file.

OLEAUT32 is installed with Internet Explorer 3.x or later, so most of the users who are affected by this problem have earlier versions of Windows NT, such as Windows NT 3.51.

Installing OLEAUT32 is a simple process—just execute the OLEDIST.EXE file that is extracted from the RegEdit.EXE file (see step 2 in the "RegClean" section).

Running RegClean

Executing RegClean is simple; it doesn't care what directory it is run from. However, RegClean will save undo information to the directory that it has been executed from.

Start RegClean either by choosing Start ➤ Run, using a command-prompt window, or by running Explorer. Once started, RegClean will display a window similar to the one shown in Figure 7.1. In this window, the lower status bar and the descriptive text just above it will indicate the progress of RegClean's initial pass through the registry.

FIGURE 7.1:

RegClean has just two buttons: Fix Errors and Exit. The Fix Errors button is initially labeled "Start," even though RegClean starts automatically.

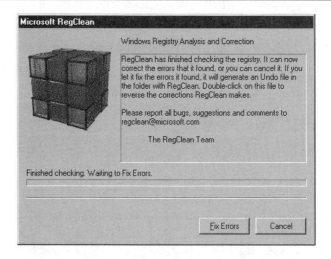

Once RegClean finishes the scan of the registry, it will advise the user either that it has not found any registry errors (This usually happens if you run RegClean frequently.) or that RegClean can correct the errors found. Clicking the Fix Errors button will tell RegClean to clean the registry. Clicking on Cancel will cause RegClean to exit without doing anything else.

If RegClean doesn't find any errors, the message shown in Figure 7.2 is shown. This message tells you that there were no errors detected in the registry.

FIGURE 7.2:

If RegClean finds no errors, this message is shown.

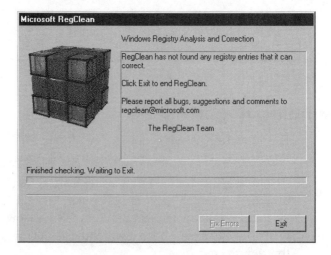

As RegClean cleans the registry, it will write a registry file to the drive that Reg-Clean was run from. This registry file may be used to restore the registry to the same condition that it was in before running RegClean.

The registry save file created by RegClean is named in the following manner:

UNDO computer yyyymmdd hhmmss.REG

In the file, "computer" will be the name of the computer whose registry was cleaned; you may keep a single copy of RegClean and then link to and execute it from many other computers. The "yyyymmdd" is the year, month, and day that Reg-Clean was executed; and "hhmmss" is the time of day that RegClean was executed.

Undoing RegClean

After RegClean runs, it is important to make sure that all applications and systems are still functioning correctly. If you find that something has broken (This is unlikely, but could happen.), it is imperative that you restore the registry to its original state immediately. To do this, simply use Explorer and double-click the REG backup file created by RegClean. See Figure 7.3 for an example of this.

FIGURE 7.3:

RegClean creates the Registration Entries files whose filenames all start with "Undo."

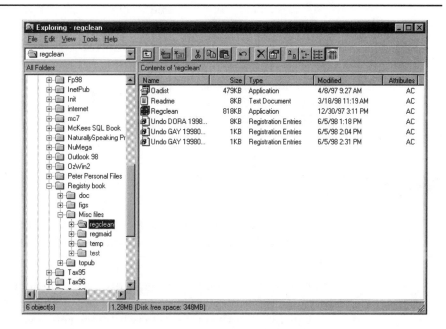

Be careful that you select the correct REG backup file if there is more than one. Remember, you can tell Explorer to list files in date/time order, making the selection process much simpler.

Sometimes, users find that they are unable to undo the changes. Windows NT will give an error when the registry backup file created by RegClean is double-clicked. The user (That's you.) will get one or more errors that indicate a problem has occurred. These errors are caused by a problem with the registry, not with the REG file.

To fix this problem, follow these steps:

1. Open Explorer and select View ➤ Options.

2. Select the File Types tab in the Options dialog box.

3. In the Registered File Type List box, select Registration Entries.

4. Click the Edit button in the Options dialog box.

5. In the Edit File Type dialog box, select Merge in the Actions list box. Then click the Edit button in the Edit File Type dialog box.

6. Enter the name `regedit.exe "%1"` in the Editing action for type: Registration Entries dialog box. The name is entered in the Application used to perform action dialog box control. Include the double quotes around the %1 entry.

7. Click OK in all open dialog boxes.

After doing this, you should be able to restore registry entries from a REG registry backup file. It is rare that the Registration Entries configuration becomes corrupted. However, Microsoft mentions that this may be a problem with RegClean.

RegMaid

Like RegClean, RegMaid is a utility that helps Windows NT users clean up their registries. RegMaid is much more interactive than RegClean; RegMaid actually has a user interface.

The program is available from several sources. I recommend that you retrieve it directly from Microsoft's Internet site at `ftp://ftp.microsoft.com/Softlib/MSLFILES`. Like RegClean, there may be other versions of RegMaid, and I'd recommend that you use Microsoft's version found at their previously given address.

The current version of RegMaid, 1.1, was stated as being released in 1995. This version is fully compatible with Windows NT 4 and was actually last revised in late 1997. The changes in the revision were slight.

NOTE RegMaid, unlike RegClean, comes with source code. That's right, you can customize RegMaid to do specific cleanups as desired. To rebuild RegMaid, you will need a copy of Microsoft Visual C++. However, to ensure that the correct directory structure for Visual C++ is maintained, be sure to use either the RegMaid self-extractor or the /d PKUNZIP option.

Using RegMaid is simple, just follow these steps:

1. Download the RegMaid.EXE file from Microsoft's Internet site at `ftp://ftp.microsoft.com/Softlib/MSLFILES`.

2. Execute the RegMaid.EXE file to start the self-extractor program. Alternatively, you may use either WinZip or PKUNZIP on the RegMaid.EXE distribution file to extract the program and other files. If you are using PKUNZIP, use the /d option to force the creation of sub-directories.

NOTE If you use PKUNZIP to extract the RegMaid programs without using the /d option, you will receive a message that there are two copies of RegMaid.hlp. Select Overwrite to retrieve the correct help file.

3. Files contained in the RegMaid.EXE distribution file include an executable copy of RegMaid.EXE, help files, and the program's source files. There are just under one hundred files contained in the RegMaid distribution package.

4. Execute the RegMaid.EXE program that is extracted. When RegMaid is extracted properly, you will be provided with a directory called RegMaid/Release. RegMaid and the necessary support files will be found in the Release directory. They may be copied to any location the user desires.

RegMaid's primary user interface is the toolbar; like almost all Windows applications, RegMaid has a full function menu, too. The toolbar buttons allow the user to quickly navigate through the registry objects that RegMaid has found suspect. The user may easily and quickly delete any of these objects that he or she desires.

Careful. Unlike RegClean, RegMaid doesn't create a recovery file. Once RegMaid removes a registry entry, it will be difficult to restore it. Before running RegMaid, it would be very wise to fully back up the registry. This will also facilitate recovery from any blunders that RegMaid might make.

RegMaid contains four views:

- CLSID view
- ProgId view
- TypeLib view
- Interface view

These views are discussed next. They are intended to be used in order, starting with the first view. There is a Refresh button on RegMaid's toolbar, and it is recommended that the user refresh after deleting objects, before moving to a new view, and after moving to a new view.

CLSID View

The first view that RegMaid displays is the CLSID view. This view lists objects, their names, and CLSIDs. The CLSID View looks for CLSIDs (OLE components) that either don't have a handler or server, or the handler or server specified is missing, probably because the file or directory was deleted.

Valid handlers are:

- InProcHandler
- InProcHandler32
- InProcServer
- InProcServer32
- LocalServer
- LocalServer32

Notice that each handler or server comes in two flavors, either 16-bit or 32-bit. Generally, Windows NT components will be 32-bit. However, some systems and components do use these entries, including some versions of Microsoft Word BASIC.

Take a look at Figure 7.4.

FIGURE 7.4:

RegMaid's report for the CLSID view shows three objects that have problems with their handlers.

```
                                                                    RegMaid
HKEY_CLASSES_ROOT: CLSID entries
-------------------------------------------------------------------------------
---X--          RRA Object - Slave
                {B556A5A1-BAF6-11ce-A0A7-00AA006EC279}        DS\Repl.RRASLAVE
                InprocHandler    =
                InprocHandler32  =
                InprocServer     =
                InprocServer32   =           C:\Program Files\Windows CE Services\srra.dll
                LocalServer      =
                LocalServer32    =

---X--              CPrm Object
                {B2A2EA33-737D-11ce-BC3F-00AA006116DB}        DS\Repl.CPrm
                InprocHandler    =
                InprocHandler32  =
                InprocServer     =
                InprocServer32   =           C:\Program Files\Windows CE Services\prm.dll
                LocalServer      =
                LocalServer32    =

---X--              Stm Object
                {a417bc01-7be1-11ce-ad82-00aa006ec559}        DS\Repl.Stm
                InprocHandler    =
                InprocHandler32  =
                InprocServer     =
                InprocServer32   =           C:\Program Files\Windows CE Services\stm.dll
                LocalServer      =
                LocalServer32    =
```

Three items are listed in Figure 7.4:

- BRA Object–Slave

- CPrm Object

- Stm Object

Each of these three items was installed to support a Windows CE computer, which is a typical PDA (Personal Digital Assistant) that is no longer used with this computer. Where'd the files go? No, I didn't delete the directory, and the installation still works. I'd wonder why these three DLL files were not found, except that I installed this product to beta test Windows CE, and it is not uncommon for beta products to enter extraneous registry entries and missing files. I'm not using Windows CE on my Windows NT computer anymore. I connect the

Windows CE machine to my Notebook because the notebook is considerably easier to connect a serial device to.

I have two courses of action. I can tell RegMaid to clean up these entries automatically. To do this, I must select an entry (see Figure 7.5), then click the Delete button in the toolbar; or select Clean Up ➢ Delete Entries.

FIGURE 7.5:

RegMaid's CLSID view showing my three objects that should be fixed

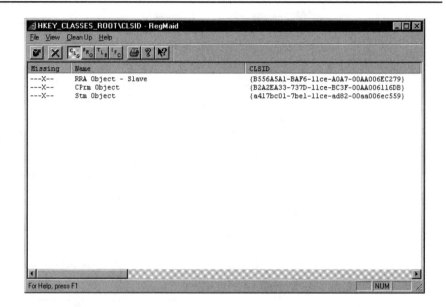

A second, and perhaps better, way is to simply uninstall the Windows CE support. Start the Add/Remove Programs applet in the Control Panel and select the program, application, component, or whatever it is that you want to remove. In my case, I'd select Windows CE Services 2.1 (Remove Only) and remove the product. Doing this would be an option only because I am not using this product anymore. If the product were still in use, this would not be an option.

Regardless of what I did, after fixing the problem, I'd next click on the Refresh button in RegMaid and make sure that no new entries showed up in the CLSID view. If nothing new showed up, I'd go on to the next view: ProgId. If any new entries did appear, I'd follow this process a second time.

Once you are happy with the items in CLSID view, move on to ProgId view.

ProgId View

The ProgId view contains items that are associated with the registry's ProgID entries. Entries in ProgId view (see Figure 7.6) list a name, a CLSID, and a ProgID name. As with the CLSID view, it is imperative to determine exactly what each entry listed is for, and why there is an error. Unlike CLSID problems, the ProgID entries are not simply a matter of a missing file—in this case, we are dealing with registry entries that are corrupt, or more likely, missing.

FIGURE 7.6:

RegMaid's ProgId view shows those entries with invalid ProgID entries.

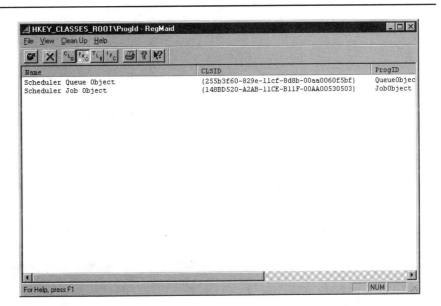

Generally, it is safe to remove these entries. As with any other registry change, back up the registry first.

NOTE   Right from the start, most Windows NT systems have several entries that show invalid ProgID entries. For Scheduler Queue Object and Scheduler Job Object, these entries are found in all Windows NT systems. No documentation exists with regard to their use or necessity, other than that they are used to process JOB or QUE file types. No actions are specified for either use.

TypeLib View

RegMaid will search all entries in the HKEY_CLASSES_ROOT\Typelib section of the registry to determine if there is an associated TLB (TypeLib) file. If the file cannot be found based on the entry, RegMaid will report that entry.

Here, I have to disagree with RegMaid's documentation. My recommendation is to do the following:

- For any TypeLib entry with an entry in one (or more) of the file columns, search for the file on the hard drive. If the file is found, but at a different location from where the registry entry says it should be, you may consider updating the registry manually to show the correct path name. I've found that about half of the entries flagged bad in the TypeLib view are marked this way because the path to the file was incorrect.

- For any TypeLib entry that lists two or more versions (see Figure 7.7), it is possible that one version has improper entries, while the other version may be OK. Typically, when a new version of a product is installed, the older version may not be completely removed from the registry. In this situation, I'd recommend leaving these entries in the registry without change, or deleting the version that has incomplete values. RegClean actually does a proper job of cleaning up this type of registry chaff.

FIGURE 7.7:

This TypeLib entry lists two versions. The first version, 1.1, doesn't have complete information, while the second, 1.21, does.

WARNING   Generally, my recommendation is to err on the cautious side. If in doubt, don't use RegMaid to delete the entry. RegClean does a much better job of cleaning and repairing the TypeLib entries than RegMaid does.

Interface View

The Interface view searches the HKEY_CLASSES_ROOT\Interface hive entries. Each entry that has a TypeLib sub-hive is checked to determine that there is a match between the TypeLib entry's CLSID and a valid OLE object found in the HKEY_CLASSES_ROOT\Typelib sub-hive. If no entry is found in HKEY_CLASSES_ROOT\Typelib, RegMaid will flag the line.

RegMaid claims that entries that don't match may be safely deleted. However, I recommend that you not allow RegMaid to fix this error—RegMaid will delete the entire sub-hive in HKEY_CLASSES_ROOT\Interface instead of deleting the suspect TypeLib entry. As well, RegClean does not flag this discrepancy as an error.

WARNING   If you wish to invoke RegMaid's delete on an Interface view item, back up the registry or sub-hive in question before continuing. Blind deleting like this will probably lead to disaster, sooner or later.

Recommendations for RegMaid

There are several recommendations to follow before using RegMaid:

1. Make a full backup of the registry before starting RegMaid.

2. Be careful about what is removed with RegMaid. RegMaid does not have any methodology to recover from errors, either its own or yours.

3. The CLSID view entries may be safe to delete, but do review each of them first.

4. The ProgId view entries are probably safe to delete, although you should review each of them first, as well.

5. The TypeLib and Interface view entries probably should not be deleted unless you are absolutely sure that these entries are not being used.

The best course of action with RegMaid is to keep RegEdit open at the same time. For each entry that RegMaid finds suspect, find the entry in the registry. See if you can determine what RegMaid is unhappy about. Can you fix the problem? For example, is the path missing or invalid? If either of these is the case, fix it. Is the problem caused by multiple versions of software within the ProgId or the

TypeLib entries that have one valid version and another invalid version? If so, consider manually deleting the invalid version, while retaining the valid one. RegMaid will attempt to delete all versions when one version is found invalid.

Run RegClean before running RegMaid. RegClean will clean many problem entries that RegMaid will find. RegClean will create a REG file that allows restoring these entries if desired, so there is an additional recovery path that RegMaid doesn't offer.

Consider rewriting RegMaid to write a recovery file for each item deleted. Since Microsoft supplies the source code file for RegMaid, a recovery file would not be difficult to create if you are a C/C++ programmer.

WARNING   Use RegMaid with caution!

CleanReg

Matt Pietrek, a columnist for *Microsoft System Journal* and a developer at NuMega Labs, created a program called CleanReg for an article he wrote for *MSJ*. This very clever utility may be obtained from several sources. First, if you have access to a subscription to MSDN (Microsoft Systems Developer Network), the source for CleanReg is available on the MSDN CD-ROM. Second, if you have a subscription to *MSJ* and still have the September 1996 issue, the source is located on page 77. Finally, the source code is available at `http://www.microsoft.com/msj/code1993 to1997/MSJSEP96.ZIP`.

In addition, checking out Microsoft's entire MSJ Web site at `http://www .microsoft.com./msj/` will reveal lots of good information, especially for programmers. For example, all source code from back issues is available by clicking on the Back Issues link and scrolling to the desired issue.

CleanReg works a bit differently from RegClean and RegMaid. CleanReg looks at registry entries and attempts to find filenames. Whenever CleanReg finds what it thinks is a filename, it searches for the file.

Pietrek had to overcome several difficulties when he wrote CleanReg. For one thing, he had to determine what constitutes a valid filename. With long filenames, Pietrek correctly states that the following is actually a valid file name (Try it, I did.): "foo -p .exe".

So You Say CleanReg Won't Compile Right?

There is a problem with CleanReg and some later versions of Microsoft Visual C++. Microsoft Visual C++ will indicate an error in clnregui.cpp with the WinMain function. The error indicates that WinMain has been either redefined or overloaded. The error is in the types assigned to the parameters of the WinMain function. Changing the WinMain parameter list to what I have shown here will clear this problem. Simply add all characters and lines shown in bold in the listing fragment to your version of clnregui.cpp:

```
    TEXT("CD-ROM) for all documentation questions.");


    // int PASCAL WinMain( HANDLE hInstance, HANDLE hPrevInstance,
    //                     PSTR lpszCmdLine, int nCmdShow )
    // Function parameters cleaned 6/8/98 by Peter D. Hipson
    int PASCAL WinMain(
        HINSTANCE hInstance,
        HINSTANCE hPrevInstance,
        LPSTR lpszCmdLine,
        int nCmdShow )


    {
        InitCommonControls();      // Gotta do this for treeview con-
    trols
```

Fix the WinMain function before correcting any errors, such as an error calling the Dialog-Box() function a bit later in the WinMain function, because these other errors are caused by the incorrect WinMain parameters.

The author has successfully compiled CleanReg with Microsoft Visual Studio 6.0 after fixing the WinMain line.

But, in the registry, what's to differentiate the filename "foo -p .exe" from the executable foo taking the parameter, "-p .exe"? Is there a standard in the registry? No, not really. Is there a standard anywhere else? Yes, somewhat. For a command passed to the operating system, it is expected that the executable filename will be enclosed in quotes (") if it is not a short (8.3) name. That is, if we have the file "foo -p .exe", and we want to execute this file, we must enter the command exactly as:

```
    "foo -p .exe"
```

There will be an error if we enter the name like this, without quotes:

foo -p .exe

In this case, the operating system will assume that the name of the executable file is "foo", and will then attempt to pass the parameter(s) -p .exe to that file.

NOTE   Sometimes Windows NT is able to correctly determine the filename even if it is a long name. In these cases, Windows NT usually is able to determine the filename if the name doesn't contain any spaces or other special characters.

Entries in the registry don't have set, fixed rules. Programmers of applications have been known to code exactly what they expect and not to bother considering any other application or system convention. Now, some programmers have adopted a convention that Microsoft uses for many registry entries. It involves filenames and parameters—don't quote the filename, but instead, quote the parameters, if there are any, such as in this example:

    foo "-p .exe"

This works well, but unless you know this rule is being followed, it is difficult to determine whether the programmer is following this rule, or simply being lazy about including quotes in the following string:

    foo -p .exe

This leads us right back to the original problem: What constitutes a valid filename in a registry entry and what does not? In the end, you, the user, will have to determine whether a filename is valid when running CleanReg. Some simple tricks of the trade will be helpful. When given a path, take the name up to the first non-alpha character, append *.* to that name, and try to find the file with the DIR command in a command window. (An alpha character is either a letter, a number, or one of the allowed special characters.)

For example, when searching for

    C:\temp\foo –p .exe

take the first part, up to the first invalid character (the space)

    C:\temp\foo

append *.* to this name

    C:\temp\foo*.*

and do a DIR command

`DIR C:\temp\foo*.*`

The DIR command will list all files beginning with foo, allowing you to determine if the file in question is foo, foo.exe, foo –p.exe, or whatever. Then you may make an educated guess with CleanReg as to whether to remove the file's entry in the registry or not, depending on the search.

CleanReg allows the user to remove either a single data key or a hive. When removing a hive, CleanReg will delete all sub-hives contained in the subject hive. This should raise a note of caution with you—be careful not to delete too much when using CleanReg.

Figure 7.8 shows CleanReg running on a system that has been installed for some time. Notice that there are probably almost two hundred various entries that CleanReg has found that are suspect. A manual check showed that about 80 percent of these entries really were bad.

FIGURE 7.8:

CleanReg listing a whole bunch of bad entries in the registry

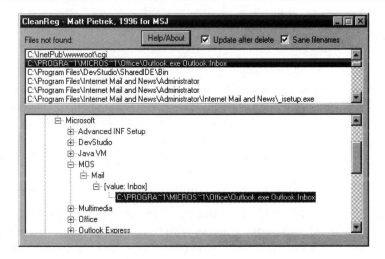

CleanReg has two checkboxes in the user interface:

> **Sane filenames**—A "filename" means that there's a ":\" near the beginning of the string that CleanReg is checking. If Sane filenames is checked, CleanReg assumes that characters like "/" and "-" aren't part of the filename, although they're technically legal.

Update after delete—This option tells CleanReg to update the display after the user deletes anything. Checking this option could slow things down a bit when the user's registry is large, so the use of this option is up to the user, based on experience.

Some entries to suspect and delete are those that point to the temp directory. These files are usually artifacts of checking out a file and having the file appear in a program's MRU (most recently used) list. Or, perhaps a program was temporarily installed into the temp directory to be checked out. My temp directory is C:\temp. My rule is that anything in the temp directory may be deleted at any time. Nothing to be saved should ever be placed in the temp directory.

Many applications store their MRU in the registry in a sub-hive called Recent File List. Any entries in these sub-hives can normally be removed manually with few bad effects. However, using the application to clear the MRU list may be the best alternative if possible; some applications don't have a mechanism to clear the MRU list.

Some applications save work or other files in the temp directory, too. Generally, these applications are robust enough that they will not fail should these files be deleted. Any critical work file will typically be kept open by the application just so the user is unable to delete the file.

> **NOTE** CleanReg doesn't see hidden files or directories. Be careful that you don't mistake a file that is hidden, one that has the hidden attribute, with a file that is truly missing. In a command-prompt window, you can determine a file's attributes with the ATTRIB command. In Windows, use Explorer's options to turn on the display of files with the hidden attribute.

When Matt wrote CleanReg, he wisely decided not to check for files on floppy drives or other drives with removable media, such as CD-ROM drives. CleanReg does check for files on currently accessible network drives. However, be careful of the case where a CD-ROM is accessed over a network.

To use or make changes to Pietrek's program, download the original source from Microsoft and compile it, or see if you can find an executable version of CleanReg on the Internet.

Hints and Kinks from the Experts

Here is a registry cleanup hint from our experts.

How Can I Clean Up/Remove Invalid Entries from the Registry?

Microsoft has released a utility called RegClean that will go through your machine's registry and delete any unused/unnecessary keys. The current version is 4.1a and can be downloaded from `http://support.microsoft.com/download/support/mslfiles/RegClean.exe`.

Once downloaded, just click on the executable, and it will check your registry. After the check is complete, you will be given an option to fix errors. You may do so by clicking the Fix Errors button. To exit, you can click the Exit button.

RegClean creates an uninstall file in the directory where RegClean is located. RegClean will use the name "Undo <machine name> <yyyymmdd> <hhmmss> .reg"; for example, "Undo workstation 19980320 104323.reg". To undo the changes, just double-click this file.

See `http://support.microsoft.com/support/kb/articles/q147/7/69.asp` for more information.

(Courtesy of John Savill)

CHAPTER
EIGHT

8

Recovering from Disaster or Avoiding Icebergs

- To repair or to replace

- Stabilizing the system

- Analysis

- Using RegClean, RegMaid, and CleanReg to fix things up

- Possible problems, quick fixes

- Manually removing registry entries

- Hints and kinks from the experts

Disaster usually strikes when least expected. There it is, usually late at night, just when things are sailing smoothly along, and whammo! A server fails, maybe with an infamous "blue screen of death"—when a system error occurs in Windows NT that is so severe that it cannot continue, it displays a blue screen with white characters in text mode telling about the error.

Disaster can also strike when Windows NT boots. Maybe the system starts fine, then mysteriously crashes in any of a thousand ways after a few minutes, a few hours, or even a few days. Or maybe, just maybe, out of the blue something happens and the system becomes unstable.

Sometimes we have to figure out what happened. Maybe a hardware problem precipitated the failure. Or perhaps a failing hard drive with a bad sector in an infrequently used section of a system file caused the problem. Maybe, and this one is nasty, there's a bad spot in the registry. When disaster strikes, a methodical approach to recovery is the only reasonable path to follow. You can try the shotgun technique: Replace things randomly until something fixes the problem. Or you can use a more logical technique: Analyze the problem and apply fixes in a systematic method. I vote for the latter; I've tried shotgun type repairs, and they are so difficult to do that in the long run, only the most inexperienced user will try to fix a problem using such a random technique.

WARNING   Have I already said this? *Back up your registry* before doing anything described in this chapter. Manually removing items from a registry is perhaps the *easiest way to trash everything!* Back up, back up, and back up again.

If I haven't mentioned it, read Chapter 7, "Getting Rid of the Unwanted," as well. Sometimes the unwanted is the root cause of all of our problems.

What Fails Most Often?

The things that cause serious problems with Windows NT registries and installations are:

- Software that has been removed without using the software's uninstallation program. Removing software without using the uninstallation program leaves entries in the registry pointing to files that are no longer there.

Continued on next page

- Software that has not been properly installed, perhaps because there was insufficient disk space for the software's files. In this case, the installation program probably updated the registry before the file copy process had completed; it then failed to undo the registry update after the file copy process failed.

- Software where the files have been damaged, often by installing either the wrong software or wrong software version into a directory where another software program or version has already been installed. Some problems arise when software versions become mixed, or when one or more files cannot be properly updated by the installation process.

To Repair or to Replace?

The Windows NT installation program allows you to repair a broken installation of Windows NT. This is nice. This is good. This can be dangerous, too.

Generally, the repair options in the Windows NT installation program simply allow you to replace the Windows NT system files with fresh copies from the distribution media. These system files are the same files that were installed when the system was originally installed. Now how can that be bad? Well, if you have installed a Service Pack, such as Service Pack 4, you may find that when you refresh the Windows NT installation, part of your Service Pack goes away. But some things, like registry entries, won't go anywhere. This can result in some rather strange problems, to say the least. Sometimes it becomes a catch-22 situation. You can't refresh the Windows NT installation because a Service Pack is installed; but you can't remove the Service Pack (most service packs have an uninstall process) because the system won't run; and if you force a refresh of the system files, the system won't run to allow you to install the Service Pack. Oops, you're stuck, again.

NOTE   *Catch-22* is the title of a popular book by Joseph Heller. This term describes a situation where two actions are mutually dependent and cannot be done separately. However, they can't be done at the same time, either. This is the situation where you can't reinstall the Windows NT system files and the Service Pack at the same time, although to run Windows NT, you might need the Service Pack.

What do you do? Try refreshing the Windows NT installation using the repair options in the Windows NT installation program. Immediately following that, install the same or a higher-level Service Pack than was installed originally on the system. That should refresh the Windows NT installation and the Service Pack installation. Of course, if you refresh the Windows NT installation and the system won't run afterwards, you do have a problem; it may be time to reinstall Windows NT from scratch.

> **NOTE** At least one supplier of Windows NT backup and restore software noted the following scenario and problem. Let's say you have a system where the system drive has failed. You replace the drive and install a minimum copy of Windows NT to run the restore program to recover the original disk's contents from backup. The original system included a Service Pack. You will probably find that you can't complete the restore. The problem is that the minimum copy of Windows NT must have the same Service Pack installed as the original copy of Windows NT; otherwise, you are restoring mismatched files into the system directories.

Stabilizing the System

Once a disaster has occurred, the first step is to stabilize the system. It is important that you prevent further problems or damage. Once the system is stabilized, it will be much easier to fix the problem(s) and get everything performing at its best.

Stabilization can be done as a step-by-step analysis. Consider the first step, discussed next. Can you do what this step calls for? If so, after doing so, does the system work right? If not, read step 1 and see if any of the hints and suggestions might apply to your system. I can't list every possible problem or fix, but I'll try to cover the most common ones here in this chapter.

When this chapter doesn't help, consider Microsoft's Internet News Server at `msnews.microsoft.com`. This news server is accessible using one of the Microsoft news programs, such as Outlook Express or Microsoft News; or by using an Internet news program, such as Agent from Forte or any of the other Internet news programs available to users.

A few of the newsgroups to check on `msnews.microsoft.com` include:

- `microsoft.public.windowsnt.misc`

- `microsoft.public.windowsnt.apps`
- `microsoft.public.windowsnt.setup`

Posting a query in one of these newsgroups will certainly create some response. Whether the respondents are able to assist you is something that you won't know until you try. I've posted a number of questions over the years; I've gotten help about half the time, and usually when I did not receive a useful reply, I did get the feeling that people on the newsgroup had at least tried to assist with a solution.

WARNING   Be careful not to lose your LastKnownGood configuration. When Windows NT boots successfully, it will overwrite the LastKnownGood configuration with the current configuration. This could be cause for great gnashing of teeth later on. Try very hard to back up the registry and the operating system (discussed next) if at all possible.

Step 1—Anyone Got a Spare Operating System?

Can you boot the system into a different operating system or a different copy of Windows NT? If not, go to Step 2.

By booting into a different operating system or a different copy of Windows NT, you will be able to possibly preserve (back up) the existing registry and hard drives, and even to do tests on the system's hardware.

Once you've gotten booted and running, back up immediately.

WARNING   When backing up, do not back up to existing backup tapes. Use new tapes so that you do not overwrite any existing backups. There is a very high probability that you will be making a backup of information that is not good, while any existing backup (especially older backups) may have valid copies that you may have to restore later. If necessary, go out and buy a new set of backup tapes.

Once the computer is booted into another copy of the operating system, do the following:

1. Back up the registry files. Use the techniques described in Chapter 2, "README.1ST—Preventing Disaster." Basically, copy the directory from the copy of Windows NT that failed. This copy of the registry will be found

in the Windows NT installation directory, system32\config, of the failed copy of Windows NT. For example, this directory may be named c:\windows\system32\config. Any process used to back up this directory and its files will be useful. Copy the directory to removable media, such as a Zip drive or a network drive. Even diskettes can be used, although the size of many registry files will necessitate the use of many diskettes.

2. Back up the entire system. Use the booted operating system's backup program to create a copy of the system exactly as it was when it failed. Don't delete anything, don't rename anything, don't change anything. Get a backup—just in case you are wrong about the problem and need to restore everything to the state that it was in when it failed. More than one time, I've hacked about on a failing system only to realize after I've done considerable damage and that the problem was somewhere else. When this happens, it is really nice to be able to restore the drive to undo your own self-induced damage.

3. Back up any drives used to hold components and applications. This generally will mean doing a complete backup of all of the system's hard drives.

4. Run diagnostic software on the computer. Check the drives (fully, including a surface scan if possible), memory, and CPU before going any further. Sometimes a system will boot another operating system even when there is a hardware failure—perhaps the other operating system doesn't have any critical components in the area of memory that is bad. (Windows NT pushes the hardware very hard, while Windows 95/98 is less demanding on the system and memory.) If you suspect bad memory, many computers will allow you to set, in the BIOS, the maximum amount of memory to be used. However, if the bad memory is in the first few MB, it is unlikely that there will be enough memory to boot Windows NT. In this case, swapping the bad RAM with good units can help diagnose the problem.

Diagnostic software? Where do I get diagnostic software? There are several good commercial test programs, such as Q&A Plus, that may be used to test computer hardware. These programs allow the user to determine if the system is performing correctly. Be careful with any diagnostic software, especially when checking storage media. Some diagnostic program functions may be destructive to data on drives. Be sure to follow all program instructions carefully and heed all warnings.

Step 2—Can You Boot the System in Normal Mode?

If you can boot the system in its normal mode, go to Step 3. Otherwise, read on.

Debugging Mode

First, try booting in the debugging mode. This is the mode shown in the Windows NT boot menu, which is where you select the version of Windows NT to boot; see Figure 8.1.

FIGURE 8.1:

The boot menu allows you to boot in VGA mode. This mode is the 640x480 standard VGA mode, which is useful if the video drivers are a problem.

```
OS Loader V4.00

Please select the operating system to start:

     Windows NT Workstation Version 4.00
     Windows NT Workstation Version 4.00 [VGA mode]
     Microsoft Windows 98

Use ↑ and ↓ to move the highlight to your choice.
Press Enter to choose

Seconds until highlighted choice will be started automatically: 30
```

The debugging mode will eliminate graphics driver issues because it will boot in 640x480 standard VGA mode. This mode also uses the standard VGA video drivers, eliminating the possibility that the video driver is at fault.

NOTE   It is important to note that the Windows NT debugging mode is not the same as the safe boot mode in Windows 95/98. Windows 95/98 offers more flexibility in its safe mode than Windows NT does. However, don't underestimate Windows NT's debugging mode.

Using LastKnownGood

The LastKnownGood menu is accessible during the boot process when you press the spacebar *as soon as you see the prompt* shown in Figure 8.2. Pressing the spacebar will display the screen shown in Figure 8.3.

FIGURE 8.2:

Pressing the spacebar at this prompt invokes the Hardware Profile/Configuration Recovery menu.

```
OS Loader V4.00
.

Press spacebar NOW to invoke Hardware Profile/Last Known Good menu
```

FIGURE 8.3:

The Hardware Profile/Configuration Recovery Menu allows you to use the LastKnownGood configuration to boot Windows NT.

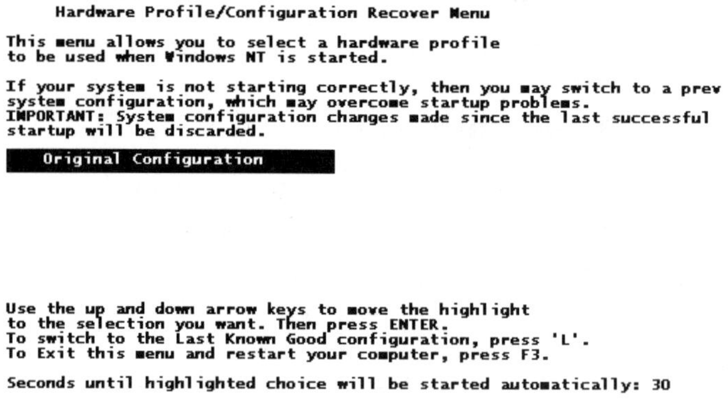

```
        Hardware Profile/Configuration Recover Menu

This menu allows you to select a hardware profile
to be used when Windows NT is started.

If your system is not starting correctly, then you may switch to a prev
system configuration, which may overcome startup problems.
IMPORTANT: System configuration changes made since the last successful
startup will be discarded.

    Original Configuration




Use the up and down arrow keys to move the highlight
to the selection you want. Then press ENTER.
To switch to the Last Known Good configuration, press 'L'.
To Exit this menu and restart your computer, press F3.

Seconds until highlighted choice will be started automatically: 30
```

Take a close look at Figure 8.3 and notice the line that states:

"To switch to the Last Known Good configuration, press 'L'."

This line tells you that if you press the L key, Windows NT will use the LastKnownGood configuration to boot. This action is not immediate; instead, the screen changes as shown in Figure 8.4.

FIGURE 8.4:

The Hardware Profile/Configuration Recovery menu changes when the L key is pressed.

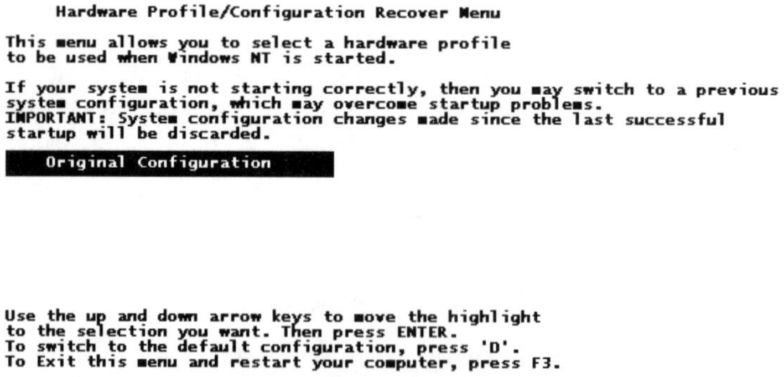

```
        Hardware Profile/Configuration Recover Menu

This menu allows you to select a hardware profile
to be used when Windows NT is started.

If your system is not starting correctly, then you may switch to a previous
system configuration, which may overcome startup problems.
IMPORTANT: System configuration changes made since the last successful
startup will be discarded.

    Original Configuration




Use the up and down arrow keys to move the highlight
to the selection you want. Then press ENTER.
To switch to the default configuration, press 'D'.
To Exit this menu and restart your computer, press F3.
```

After selecting the LastKnownGood configuration, it is still necessary to press Enter to continue the boot process. Once a key has been pressed in this screen, the boot process for Windows NT is placed on hold indefinitely until Enter is pressed.

WARNING Remember, once the LastKnownGood configuration is booted, it becomes the current configuration (the CurrentControlSet) and the current configuration that would have been booted will be discarded. Anything installed after the previous boot will be lost.

Control Sets, Control Sets, and More Control Sets

After booting using the LastKnownGood configuration option to perform the boot, your registry will "grow" a new ControlSet. This ControlSet will be numbered one higher than the currently known highest ControlSet. For example, if your system has ControlSet001 and ControlSet002, a new ControlSet called ControlSet003 will also be created. In this situation, one ControlSet is the one that failed, one is the current ControlSet, and one is the LastKnownGood configuration. After booting my system, the LastKnownGood configuration had the following ControlSets:

ControlSet001—Was marked as the ControlSet that failed. This was the ControlSet that would have been booted if the LastKnownGood configuration had not been chosen.

ControlSet002—Was marked as the LastKnownGood ControlSet. This is the ControlSet that will be booted if the LastKnownGood configuration is selected at the next boot.

ControlSet003—Was marked as the current ControlSet—the ControlSet being used to boot the system. Prior to booting, this ControlSet was marked as LastKnown-Good. This ControlSet is also mapped to the CurrentControlSet.

If you manage to boot the LastKnownGood configuration, consider yourself lucky; the system should be stable, although it probably will be missing whatever software and hardware was installed during the last session. However, this should be only a minor problem. In this case, consider what was installed during the last session. Think very carefully as to whether it makes sense to reinstall the same item a second time. Consider setting up a test machine, or another installation of Windows NT, to install the system that caused the problems and see if this other installation also fails.

If you are successful in using the LastKnownGood configuration to boot, it usually will be safe to delete the application's files and directories because the registry should not have any entries for this application. However, having a backup is vital at this stage.

NOTE   Instead of deleting files and directories, do this: Use either Explorer or the MOVE command at a command prompt to rename the directory. I usually prefix the original directory with DELETE_, which is very visual. Then, I don't do anything for a week or so. If the system displays no odd behavior, I back up the directory and delete it from the drive. Did you notice what I said? I *back up the directory* before deleting it. Again, a backup is very good insurance.

Step 3—Does the System Run without Crashing?

Say the system boots in normal mode; or by following Step 2, you have the system booted using the LastKnownGood configuration. Now, does the system run without crashing? If yes, go to Step 4. Otherwise, read on.

First, since the system boots, it is probably almost right. But "almost" covers a really wide territory. Does the system boot, but then crash almost immediately? Or, does the crash come sometime later? Can you cause it to crash by running an application or performing a specific task? Does the crash seem to happen at random times, or does there seem to be some rhyme and reason to the crash? We're in detective mode now.

The System Boots but Then Crashes Almost Immediately   This situation is virtually as bad as a system that won't boot. The crash is probably caused by something that is starting up when the system starts. Try this: Start the system, but don't log on. Just sit and watch for at least twice as long as it normally takes to crash. Does it crash? If it does, this is probably due to some system component. You are probably stuck with little or no hope except to reinstall Windows NT, or to restore from a backup.

If the system doesn't crash immediately, the crash is probably due to something that is being loaded for the user. Log on as another user. Does it crash? If it does, the problem is probably something that is common to all users. Check out the common Startup directory, all users\Start Menu\Programs\Startup, and clean it out. Try the user again. If it fails again, you are probably stuck with either a restore or a reinstallation.

If the system doesn't crash in this situation, you may be saved yet. Check the failing user's Programs\Startup directory in the Start menu. Check all the Programs\Startup directories for that matter, cleaning out each one; put anything contained in the Startup directories into temporary directories. Once you have cleaned out the Startup directories, log on again as the user who causes the system to fail. If the system doesn't fail (You're almost home free now.), check the entries that were in the Startup directory. Consider manually starting each one, then wait for a reasonable period of time to see if the system fails or not. This will almost certainly help localize the problem to a single entry in the Startup directory.

How do you get to the Startup directory if the system keeps failing? Again, you can rely on your old friend, the dual boot. (You did create a dual-boot system as I described in Chapter 2, "README.1ST—Preventing Disaster", right?) Boot the backup operating system and use it to allow you to clear out the Startup directories. Just make absolutely sure you are deleting the *correct* Startup directories.

Some additional locations that items may run from include:

HKEY_LOCAL_MACHINE\Software\Microsoft\Windows\Current-Version\Run

HKEY_LOCAL_MACHINE\Software\Microsoft\Windows\Current-Version\RunOnce

HKEY_LOCAL_MACHINE\Software\Microsoft\Windows\Current-Version\RunServices

HKEY_LOCAL_MACHINE\Software\Microsoft\Windows\Current-Version\RunServicesOnce

HKEY_LOCAL_MACHINE\Software\Microsoft\Windows NT\Current-Version\Winlogon\Userinit

HKEY_CURRENT_USER\Software\Microsoft\Windows\Current-Version\Run

HKEY_CURRENT_USER\Software\Microsoft\Windows\Current-Version\RunOnce

HKEY_CURRENT_USER\Software\Microsoft\Windows\Current-Version\RunServices

HKEY_CURRENT_USER\Software\Microsoft\Windows\Current-Version\RunServicesOnce

HKEY_CURRENT_USER\Software\Microsoft\Windows NT\Current-Version\Windows, run and Load keys

The Crash Comes Sometime Later.   How much later? Minutes, hours, or days? A crash that comes many hours or days later is probably not related to the registry. A crash that happens a few minutes later is almost identical to the above situation where the crash is virtually immediate. But a crash that happens some minutes or even an hour later could easily be a registry entry gone awry. How does this happen? When Windows NT starts, it will start up many services and devices. Some services are slow to start and other services start, but then spend some time initializing.

Try this: In the all users\Start Menu\Programs\Startup directory, put in a link to taskmgr.exe. This will launch the Windows NT Task Manager application. Look at what Task Manager is saying. Sort the entries in the Processes tab by CPU usage. Do you see an application that is jumping up in CPU utilization just before the system crashes? Consider that this may be the problem.

OK, let's say you have a suspect. Task Manager shows a big chunk of CPU utilized by a particular application. Let's call this application badapp.exe. (Great name, isn't it?) What do you do? First, it would be nice to simply tell Windows NT not to load or execute badapp.exe. However, it may be virtually impossible to do that since this application may be launched by a registry entry. Remember, there are six places in the registry that function much like the various Programs\Startup directories.

What is the next best thing? If you have nothing to lose, consider temporarily renaming the file. Boot into your backup operating system and use it to rename the file, giving it a new temporary filename. I would add the prefix BAD_ to the original filename, making it easy to find later. Just make absolutely sure you are renaming the *correct* file.

After renaming the file, restart the original Windows NT installation. You should expect to see at least one message informing you that the file you renamed can't be found, and you can *probably* ignore this. Probably, but not always. If the file is a necessary part of the operating system, Windows NT probably won't start. Arrgggg! Such is life; in this case, an operating system restoration or repair can be the only solution.

Can You Cause the System to Crash?   Sometimes the system will remain totally stable until we do a specific thing.

In this case, there are two possible courses of action. If the application worked at one time and just recently started to fail, something has happened either to the application's files or to the application's registry entries. In either case, a good course of action is to simply try reinstalling the application.

If possible, try removing the application before doing the reinstallation; be sure to back up any user data files first, though. Sometimes installation programs don't always write over some files if they already exist.

If the application never worked on your system, again, there is but one alternative: Uninstall the application, post haste. Sadly, some applications are poorly written and don't have an uninstall program. With due caution (make backups), rename the application's directory to something you'll notice, so that in a week or so, if the system remains stable, you can delete the directory.

Once the application's directory has been renamed, restart the system and see if there is any instability. If things are stable after a day or two, use a registry cleanup tool such as RegClean, CleanReg, or RegMaid to extract any registry entries for this application. My choice would be to use CleanReg (see Chapter 7, "Getting Rid of the Unwanted") because CleanReg will check more than just the OLE entries.

The Crash Happens after a Specific Time.   If the system always seems to crash after a specific time, check to make sure that there are no time-based applications or commands that run. (The Windows NT AT command is a suspect here.) What other things happen at the time? Is the time absolute or relative to boot? If absolute, suspect that something is being started at the specific time or shortly before. If relative, look for something that is being started with the system boot-up, but maybe taking a very long time to initialize because it fails. Note that some systems are timing interdependent, which means that Process A must start after Process B. Again, beware of any catch-22 situations where two processes are mutually dependent.

Step 4—Do the System Components and Sub-Systems Run OK?

If you find that your system will run indefinitely without failing, you may have good reason to suspect that an installed application is the problem. You randomly run applications and eventually something fails.

At this point you say *voilà*, I've found the problem. Alas, it is not that simple. You may find the problem's trigger, but the odds are high that the problem itself is somewhere else.

Narrow down inter-dependencies between applications by running only one at a time. Start Windows NT, then start and use one application. This works well for most applications, but when you have two applications designed to work together, this may not be a viable way to troubleshoot the problem.

Review your list of recently installed applications. Anything installed just before the system became unstable should be suspect.

If the application has never worked on your system, again there is but one alternative: Uninstall the application if possible.

NOTE   A possible test is to create a second, clean installation of Windows NT and install the suspect application under the second copy of Windows NT. That will be a good indicator as to whether the application will be able to run under Windows NT without problems. Using a clean installation of Windows NT will help minimize unwanted interaction between two applications.

If your application doesn't have an uninstall program, it is often more difficult to uninstall the program. If so, make a backup and rename the application's directory. Rename the directory to something you'll notice, so that in a week or so, if the system remains stable, you can delete the directory.

Once the application's directory has been renamed, restart the system and see if there is any instability. If things are stable after a day or two, use a registry cleanup tool such as RegClean, CleanReg, or RegMaid to extract any registry entries for this application. My choice would be to use CleanReg (see Chapter 7, "Getting Rid of the Unwanted") because CleanReg will check more than just the OLE entries.

Step 5—Do Installed Applications Run OK?

If installed applications run OK, go to Step 6. (Remember to check the Event Viewer.) Otherwise, read on.

What is happening? Probably, something has corrupted the registry or there is a hardware problem. First, back up the system fully. Then, run sufficient diagnostics to rule out any hardware problems. Finally, try restoring the registry. Start with the most recent backup—not the one you made before running diagnostics, but the most recent regularly scheduled backup. If the most recent backup doesn't solve the problem, continue working back through older backups to see if one of them will restore system stability.

Be aware that by going back through older backups, you only want to restore system files and the registry—for example, you do not want to restore user files.

Step 6—Is the System Generally Stable?

If the system is generally stable, go to Step 7. Otherwise, read on.

If a system is unstable, and the instability cannot be traced to a specific application or component, this usually points to a hardware problem. In this situation, analysis of the failures is important. These steps may help in diagnosing and fixing the problem:

- Run all possible hardware checks and diagnostics.

- Swap out whatever hardware parts may be replaced easily.

- Install and run a second copy of Windows NT with all the software and components that the failing system uses.

- Reinstall (repair) the failing installation of Windows NT.

- Reinstall the applications and optional components.

Step 7—Then What Is the Problem?

What is the problem, then, if the system will start, run, and shut down OK; and doesn't crash or otherwise fail? There can be serious problems even when a system doesn't crash.

Take the situation when the computer's hardware is simply overwhelmed by the demands that the operating system and applications place on it. Running some applications—for example, server components such as SMS, SQL Server, and Exchange Server—will quickly bring a substandard system to its knees.

Use the Windows NT Performance Monitor to analyze system performance problems. This program is able to monitor all Windows NT performance indicators and indicators for a number of add-on components, such as Exchange Server, SQL Server, and others.

Analysis

The first step is analysis. First, ask yourself what changed. Analysis of the problem means that we must determine why the computer worked yesterday but doesn't work today. For example, did we:

- Remove any software or system components?
- Clean up the drive, deleting files that we thought were unneeded?
- Install any new applications?
- Upgrade any applications?
- Upgrade the operating system (Install any Service Packs?)
- Change system hardware?
- Experience a power failure or fluctuation?

To keep this chapter from becoming a general system failure analysis tool, I'll limit the effects of these items to what might happen to the registry.

Using RegClean, RegMaid, and CleanReg to Fix Things Up

The next step is to decide if it is better to try to restore things to their original states either by reinstalling the component or application, or by removing the offending item.

If there is a backup of the registry and the item in question, restoring to get the system back to a working state will probably be a good starting point. A stable system that is not experiencing difficulties is much easier to work on than a system that fails for unexplained reasons.

Once the system is restored, try the established method for removing the component, such as the Add/Remove Programs applet in the Control Panel or the application's uninstall program.

If there is no backup of the registry or component, a different attack must be taken. There are three possible avenues of attack:

- Try reinstalling the component. Typically, the installation program will restore any registry entries that are necessary for the component to run. Often, any customization done since the last installation will be lost, but that's life.

- Try finding an uninstall program. First, check the Add/Remove Programs applet in the Control Panel. If the component is listed, run uninstall from there. If the component is not listed, then check the component's directories. List all the executable (EXE) files. If there is one that is named uninstall or remove, this may be the program that you need. Don't forget to check the component's documentation regarding uninstallation procedures, too.

- If there is no uninstall program, and the application must be removed, and you are going to have to do this manually; read on.

NOTE Some components, especially those that are system components, make so many changes to the registry that it is impossible to remove them manually. This is especially true for components that have replaced an already existing component as in the case of upgrading to a new version. Though you can remove the entries for the component in question, you cannot restore the entries that the component has changed to their original state; this is especially true if you don't know their original state. Changes to the registry are usually not well logged, so there is typically little to tell you what has changed from time to time.

Possible Problems, Quick Fixes

Some possible problems that cause the system to fail include those listed next. There are other problems too, so don't consider this list to be exhaustive.

The Application or a System Component Was Deleted

Say the application or a system component was deleted, perhaps in error. In this case, you would do the following:

- Try restoring the application's files. Running the application's installation program may be the best way to restore files, though many applications allow a single file to be restored from the distribution media. Be aware that some applications store the files on the distribution media in compressed format, so that the only way to restore a single file may be to reinstall the entire application.

- If that fails, try reinstalling the application. Reinstalling the application may be necessary when the application's files are not accessible on the distribution media. Be aware that some installation programs will delete user configurations and other items that either you or other users have modified since the original installation.

- If that fails, try removing the application with the application's uninstall program, then reinstall the application. Some applications try to be smart and only reinstall those files and components that have not already been installed. In this case, we may be trying to replace a file that we suspect has been corrupted, or trying to restore registry entries, and the setup program doesn't realize that. It's just trying to save us some time! (Some time-saver, huh?) In this case, it will probably be necessary to remove the original application (Use its uninstall program, if there is one.) before reinstalling it.

Another Application Has Overwritten the Application's Files

In this case, a new application has been installed, and this new installation has overwritten a previously installed application's files. OK, this was probably an error, but you inadvertently installed the new application in the existing application's directory. This sometimes happens when the two applications have the same default installation directory. More often, we simply make a mistake and choose the wrong directory. Most application setup programs won't warn that the path already exists. Major bummer. Here are some things to do when you suspect that an application's files have been overwritten:

- First, use the new application's uninstall program to uninstall the new application. If the new application has been used, and there are user document or data files, back up these files. However, get rid of that new application; you can reinstall it later. If there is no automated uninstall for the new application that you are removing, and you must remove it manually, make certain to clean up as many of the new application's registry entries as possible. If you don't, and you reinstall the new application into a new directory, the setup program may not properly update the registry because it thinks the application has already been installed.

- Next, restore the application's files, perhaps from a known good backup. If that fails, try reinstalling the application from the original distribution media.

- If that fails, try removing the original application with the application uninstall program and then reinstall the original application.

There Is an Error Reading the Application's Files

If there is an error reading the application's files, or the application crashes (faults) when executed, the application's files are probably damaged. What happened? There are several possibilities and some of them are very ugly, by the way.

Maybe one or more files were overwritten by user error. In this case, things don't look too bleak. Generally, a restore of the application's files will recover from this situation. Use a known good backup or reinstall from the distribution media.

Maybe another application or the operating system overwrote one or more files. This is rare, but it could happen. Check file dates to try to determine when the file overwrites occurred and see if there is a way to determine the culprit. Restore the correct files and consider setting permissions to read/execute for everyone but an administrative userid that you won't use except to manage these files. Using file system permissions allows you to get immediate notification when a file overwrite occurs.

WARNING   Permissions are the Windows NT way to protect applications and system files from unauthorized changes. Always set permissions so that most users, other than those who must have higher level permissions, have read/execute permissions only. Allowing all users to have write permissions for system and application executable files is not a very good move, no matter how trusted the users are. Eventually, someone will unintentionally overwrite something, delete a file, or do some other damage.

There Is an Error Reading the Drive

Well, actually this is the beginning of the end of the world.

First, run chkdsk and determine what Windows NT is able to do to fix the problem. Realize that when Windows NT fixes a file on an NTFS drive, it doesn't fix the file; it only makes the file readable. Windows NT is not able to recover the file's contents—if it could, everything would be all right. Windows NT gives a message that says file so-and-so has been repaired, which is somewhat misleading in this respect. However, you must do this repair to be able to replace the file with the right one.

When chkdsk runs, it will tell you if there are any damaged files. Windows NT is able to recover from minor problems and errors on the drive. Don't worry about these types of errors; it is not unusual to have a drive reported as having minor errors.

After running chkdsk you must make a decision. A backup at this point can't hurt, but don't back up over any existing backups. Use a fresh tape, or whatever your backup program backs up to, and put this backup to the side. Here are the actions I'd take, in order of preference:

1. Replace the drive and restore to the new drive from the most recent known good backup. Since drives usually fail in stages, a little bit at a time, it is possible that your backups are not going to help as much as you'd like. This is a judgment call—if you are confident that a recent backup is OK, try it. If you are not confident of your more recent backups—often errors develop over time and contaminate all backups long before they are discovered—don't use the backup.

2. Reformat the failing drive and restore from a known good backup.

3. Restore the entire drive from a known good backup without reformatting. This is sometimes necessary if, for some reason, the drive can't be formatted.

4. Try to restore specific files known to be defective, either from backups or from the application distribution media.

If there is an error reading the application's files, or the application crashes (faults) when executed, the application's files are probably damaged. What happened? There are a few possibilities. Maybe one or more files were overwritten by user error. In this case, things don't look too bleak. Generally, a restore of the application's files will recover from this situation.

Maybe another application or the operating system overwrote one or more files. This is rare, but it could happen. Check file dates to try to determine when the file overwrites occurred, and see if there is a way to determine the culprit. Restore the correct files and consider setting permissions to read/execute for everyone but an administrative userid that you won't use except to manage these files. Using file system permissions allows you to get immediate notification when a file is overwritten.

Manually Removing Registry Entries

Sometimes when repairing a problem, it is necessary to remove entries manually. In Chapter 7, "Getting Rid of the Unwanted," we described three programs that will automate the process of registry entry removal. In this chapter, we cover manual removal techniques.

Manual removal techniques are even more dangerous than using a program to clean out entries. Removing things by hand is tedious, and you won't be able to fully check registry integrity this way. Backups are in order before even thinking of starting to manually remove an entry from the registry.

Finding Entries

The first thing that must be done is to find all the entries relative to the problem. This means you have to do a search.

First, searching the registry with the registry editors is possible but not optimal. RegEdit has the best search capabilities. Launch RegEdit and select My Computer. Next, select Registry ➢ Export Registry File. This will write the entire registry, excluding items such as the security hives, to a text file.

Next, use a text editor to find your problem application. Sounds too easy, doesn't it? However, finding the application may present a few problems. What do you search for? Try searching for the executable name or directory name. Or, try searching for the known name of the application you are looking for. If none of these work, search for things such as the application's document file extension, if it has one.

In HKEY_LOCAL_MACHINE\SOFTWARE there may be entries for applications. Many applications install sub-hives here, but others do not. If looking for a potentially optional component of Windows NT, check the HKEY_LOCAL_MACHINE\SOFTWARE\Microsoft\Windows\CurrentVersion and HKEY_LOCAL_MACHINE\SOFTWARE\Microsoft\Windows NT\CurrentVersion sub-hives. Virtually everything that is part of the Windows NT operating system and from Microsoft should have entries in these two sub-hives.

Still having problems finding your application? Try reading through the registry line by line. Start in the CLSID section, HKEY_LOCAL_MACHINE\SOFTWARE\Classes\CLSID, and in HKEY_CLASSES_ROOT. Both of these are good sections to start with.

Visually scan the registry, starting with HKEY_CLASSES_ROOT, then HKEY_LOCAL_MACHINE, to see if any entries match anything that you can associate with the errant application. Look at the program's name, its publisher—anything that might be a link. At this point, you are in detective mode.

> **NOTE**   Ever wonder how hackers break into systems? Oftentimes, it's by doing things just like this. They read anything about the system they can find. In short, they do just what you'll be doing.

Once you find something that matches what you are looking for, see if there is a CLSID (class ID) for it. Searching for a CLSID will be helpful in finding other entries in the registry for that application or component.

Most of the time, the application will have entries grouped together under a sub-hive. Some applications will have other entries that tend to float, but these are rather unusual.

Removing Entries

Warning: First, realize that if you are trying to remove entries from the registry, you should have exhausted all other alternatives; removing these entries is your last resort short of reinstalling Windows NT. Got that? The odds are very good that if you start hacking away at the registry, you'll destroy it.

But, if you have nothing to lose, and you want to learn about the registry, this can be a way to do so. Back up the registry. I'd recommend having a parallel installation of either Windows NT or Windows 95/98 that you can boot to when you have totally destroyed your installed registry; this will allow you to restore the registry with a minimum of grief.

If you don't have a parallel installation of Windows NT or Windows 95/98, now would be as good a time as any to install one.

To remove items, use RegEdit or RegEdt32. The delete capabilities of both of these programs are adequate. Select the entry (data key, hive, or sub-hive) to be deleted and remove it. Don't forget that the registry editor is editing the actual working registry; once you delete something, there is no easy way to restore it.

With the registry editors, you may want to consider saving any major sub-hives to disk files before deleting them. By saving these sub-hives to the disk, you will be able to restore them should you find that you've deleted the wrong thing. It is possible to delete items from the registry that will make it impossible to start or run Windows NT. Having a complete backup of the registry that is restorable without using the affected copy of Windows NT is a very good idea.

Hints and Kinks from the Experts

Here are some hints from our experts.

When You Run a Repair, Setup Refuses to Recognize or Repair Your Installation.   While hacking the registry one day, I destroyed my installation so thoroughly that NT would not boot and setup would not repair it. The NTFS file system was still intact, but the registry was so damaged that setup did not recognize it as a valid installation. While I could have restored, I would have lost four hours of work.

To fix this problem, boot to an alternate installation of NT and expand each hive on your ERD, or original %SystemRoot%\Repair folder, to the original %SystemRoot%\System32\Config folder as shown here:

```
expand c:\winnt\Repair\Software._ C:\WINNT\system32\config\Software
expand c:\winnt\Repair\Software._ C:\WINNT\system32\config\Software.sav
expand c:\winnt\Repair\Default._ C:\WINNT\system32\config\default
```

```
expand c:\winnt\Repair\Default._ C:\WINNT\system32\config\default.sav
expand c:\winnt\Repair\SAM._ C:\WINNT\system32\config\sam
expand c:\winnt\Repair\SAM._ C:\WINNT\system32\config\SAM.sav
expand c:\winnt\Repair\Security._ C:\WINNT\system32\config\security
expand c:\winnt\Repair\Security._ C:\WINNT\system32\config\security.sav
expand c:\winnt\Repair\System._ C:\WINNT\system32\config\system
expand c:\winnt\Repair\System._ C:\WINNT\system32\config\SYSTEM.ALT
expand c:\winnt\Repair\System._ c:\WINNT\system32\config\system.sav
```

Here is an example of the response:

```
expand c:\winnt\Repair\Software._ C:\WINNT\system32\config\Software
Microsoft (R) File Expansion Utility Version 2.50
Copyright (C) Microsoft Corp 1990-1994. All rights reserved.
Expanding c:\winnt\repair\software._ to C:\WINNT\system32\config\
Software.
c:\winnt\repair\software._: 1242580 bytes expanded to 6377472 bytes,
413% increase.
```

If the files required to boot your alternate installation are damaged or missing, you will need a boot floppy.

After expanding these files, I was able to boot; and in my case, I was fully recovered. You may need to repair boot records using your ERD.

(Courtesy of Jerold Schulman)

Build an NTFS or FAT boot floppy. The Microsoft Knowledge Base article "Q119467," describes the process of building a boot floppy for an NTFS partition. This is useful if you accidentally replace the boot disk hardware driver or lose your Boot Manager, and no ERD is available.

The procedure in the article did not work in my environment, but the following process did allow me to successfully boot. Try the method in "Q119467," first.

If the "Q119467," method fails, try this:

1. Since some of these files are hidden/system/read-only, go to Explorer Options ➤ View and check the box labelled "show all files" and uncheck the box labelled "hide files."

2. Use DISKCOPY to copy the first Setup Disk.

3. Delete all files on this new boot floppy.

4. If DOS is installed, copy NTDETECT.COM and BOOTSECT.DOS to the floppy from your root.

5. Copy NTLDR from your root to the floppy, renaming it SETUPLDR.BIN.

6. COPY NTBOOTDD.SYS from your root to the floppy. This is a copy of your SCSI driver. If you don't have a SCSI NT disk, you don't need this. If you have a SCSI NT disk, and the SCSI BIOS is enabled, you don't need this; but it is a good idea to protect against SCSI BIOS failure, which will prevent booting.

7. Create a BOOT.INI as follows or just copy your C:\BOOT.INI (Spacing is very important.):

```
[boot loader]
timeout=10
default= scsi(0)disk(0)rdisk(0)partition(1)\WINNT
[operating systems]
scsi(0)disk(0)rdisk(0)partition(1)\WINNT="Windows NT Server
Version 4.0"
```

In this listing, WINNT is my NT directory; no drive letter is allowed. "Windows NT Server Version 4.0" could be any character string, such as "Glad I had this BOOT FLOPPY!"

It is a good idea to have a second instance of NT installed on a different partition, preferably on a different disk. This will ensure that you can always boot if the second instance of Windows NT is referenced in this BOOT.INI. You will also be able to boot to this alternate instance to repair your primary instance.

(Courtesy of Jerold Schulman)

Programming and the Registry—A Developer's Paradise?

■ Windows NT registry API functions

■ To MFC or not to MFC? that is the question

■ Hints and kinks from the experts

Disclaimer #1: I'm a C/C++ programmer, so this chapter will deal with C/C++ programming. However, to be fair, I've included some Visual Basic for Applications registry programming in Chapter 13, "Microsoft Office." All of the programming techniques discussed in that chapter can be used with virtually any version of Visual Basic.

Disclaimer #2: I'm a Microsoft Visual C++ programmer. However, any development platform that uses MFC (Microsoft Foundation Classes) will be compatible with this chapter's content. As well, those registry manipulation techniques that are part of the Windows NT API (Application Program Interface) are exposed in all development platforms as standard Windows NT API calls. So, if you are not using Visual C++, don't despair: Your system will be sufficiently similar. You should experience only minor problems in using everything discussed in this chapter with other languages and compilers on your system.

Disclaimer #3: I could write an entire book on programming for the Windows registry. Remember, programming is an art, not a science; and there are many, many different ways to write your applications. Use MFC, don't use MFC, use C++ and classes, don't use C++ and classes, use a dialog interface, use a window interface, use a command-prompt interface, and so on. I didn't spend a lot of time on the interface in this chapter; instead, I worked more on the actual calls and functions that you, a programmer, would be using.

NOTE   Much of what this chapter covers is directly applicable to both Windows NT and Windows 95/98. In Windows 95/98, many registry entries are in different locations, although the concepts are basically identical for the programmer. The operating system does a good job of masking or hiding these differences.

Remember the registry's history. You see, the history of the registry is important in trying to understand how the various registry functions work and the parameters that are passed to these functions. Originally, what is now the registry was, once upon a time, a set of INI files (specifically WIN.INI and SYSTEM.INI). As well, each application had its own INI file. An application could store information in the WIN.INI and SYSTEM.INI files, but that practice didn't gain much acceptance for a number of reasons, including performance and file bloat.

Much of the code that updated INI files was updated and reworked so that applications could be easily modified to work with the registry. In some cases, the applications didn't need to be modified at all; in other cases, there were minor modifications. However, all in all, you will see a lot of excess baggage in some registry functions. In some cases you will see that, even today, the same functions will still work with INI files if need be.

NOTE   The INI files of old were divided into sections called *profiles*. A profile section was typically dedicated to an application or module.

Windows NT Registry API Functions

The registry is manipulated by means of a number of registry functions. These functions are prefixed with the word "Reg". The final part of the name describes the function's actual purpose in life. Table 9.1 lists these functions, along with a short description of their functionality.

T A B L E 9 . 1 : Windows NT and Windows 95/98 Registry Functions with Descriptions

Function	Description
RegCloseKey	Closes the connection between the application and a specific registry object. The function RegOpenKey opens this connection.
RegConnectRegistry	Allows an application to modify a remote registry. It will establish a connection with the registry on a specified remote computer.
RegCreateKey	Creates a new registry sub-hive. This simple function allows no options; see RegCreateKeyEx for a more powerful version of this API.
RegCreateKeyEx	Creates a new registry sub-hive. This function allows setting security, options, and classes.
RegDeleteKey	Deletes an existing sub-hive that has been opened with RegOpenKey.
RegDeleteValue	Deletes an existing data key that has been opened with RegOpenKey.
RegEnumKey	Enumerates all the sub-hives starting with the specified hive or sub-hive. One object will be returned for each call to RegEnumKey, until the function returns the value ERROR_NO_MORE_ITEMS. This function exists for compatibility with earlier versions of Windows; programmers for Windows NT should use RegEnumKeyEx.

Continued on next page

TABLE 9.1 CONTINUED: Windows NT and Windows 95/98 Registry Functions with Descriptions

Function	Description
RegEnumKeyEx	Enumerates all the sub-hives, starting with the specified hive or sub-hive. One object will be returned for each call to RegEnumKeyEx until the function returns the value ERROR_NO_MORE_ITEMS. This function will retrieve the class name, the time of last modification, and the object's name.
RegEnumValue	Enumerates all the data keys in the specified hive or sub-hive. One object will be returned for each call to RegEnumValue until the function returns the value ERROR_NO_MORE_ITEMS. This function will retrieve the name, the value, and the type for the object.
RegFlushKey	Causes any changes made to a registry entry to be written to the actual registry. This implies only simple buffering because, generally, changes to the registry are immediate.
RegGetKeySecurity	Retrieves the security attributes for a given registry object; the security may be set (changed) if the user has sufficient privileges.
RegLoadKey	Creates a new sub-hive under either HKEY_USERS or HKEY_LOCAL_MACHINE; the information to create the new sub-hive is contained in a file, the name of which is passed to the function.
RegNotifyChangeKeyValue	Tells the system to inform the caller if the specified object is changed or if the object's attributes are changed. If the object is deleted, no notification is sent. The notification is processed using an event handler in the calling application.
RegOpenKey	Used to open a registry object, this function is called before many other registry functions. The handle returned by RegOpenKey is then passed to other registry functions that require a registry handle. Microsoft recommends that RegOpenKeyEx be called by Windows NT and Windows 95/98 applications.
RegOpenKeyEx	Used to open a registry object, this function is called before many other registry functions. The handle returned by RegOpenKey is then passed to other registry functions that require a registry handle. RegOpenKeyEx handles security and other options that RegOpenKey does not handle.
RegQueryInfoKey	Returns information about the specified object.
RegQueryMultipleValues	Returns information about the data keys in a specified sub-hive.

Continued on next page

TABLE 9.1 CONTINUED: Windows NT and Windows 95/98 Registry Functions with Descriptions

Function	Description
RegQueryValue	Returns the value of the default (unnamed) data key associated with each hive and sub-hive. Microsoft recommends that RegQueryValueEx be called by Windows NT and Windows 95/98 applications.
RegQueryValueEx	Returns the value of the default (unnamed) data key associated with each hive and sub-hive. RegQueryValueEx handles security and other options that RegQueryValue does not handle.
RegReplaceKey	The registry is stored as a series of files, one file for each of the main hives. Upon restarting, the RegReplaceKey function tells the operating system to use a different file for this hive. This function is typically used for backing up and restoring the registry and for disaster recovery.
RegRestoreKey	Restores the hive's or sub-hive's contents from a file. The RegRestore-Key function will restore multiple objects, as many as are contained in the registry file provided.
RegSaveKey	Saves the hive's or sub-hive's contents to a file. The RegSaveKey function will save multiple objects, as many as are specified to the registry file provided.
RegSetKeySecurity	Sets the specified object's security attributes. The user must have sufficient privileges to use this function.
RegSetValue	Sets the value of the default (unnamed) data key associated with each hive and sub-hive. Microsoft recommends that RegSetValueEx be called by Windows NT and Windows 95/98 applications.
RegSetValueEx	Sets the value of the default (unnamed) data key associated with each hive and sub-hive. RegSetValueEx handles security and other options that RegSetValue does not set.
RegUnLoadKey	Removes from the registry the specified object(s).

There are a number of different functions that were designed to work with the older INI files. These functions are considered obsolete by Microsoft, although they still allow support for legacy applications. These functions should not be incorporated into new code, although they may be encountered in legacy code. Use the functions described in Table 9.1 for new work. The functions that are considered obsolete are listed in Table 9.2.

TABLE 9.2: Obsolete Windows NT (and Windows 95/98) Registry Functions, with Descriptions

Function	Description
GetPrivateProfileInt	Returns an integer data key value from the specified location.
GetPrivateProfileSection	Returns an entire sub-hive's contents.
GetPrivateProfileSectionNames	Returns the names in a sub-hive.
GetPrivateProfileString	Returns a string data key value from the specified location.
GetPrivateProfileStruct	Fetches a private structure from the specified location, comparing the checksum retrieved with the checksum that was written when the object was saved.
GetProfileInt	Returns an integer data key value from the specified location.
GetProfileSection	Returns an entire sub-hive's contents.
GetProfileString	Returns an integer data key value from the specified location.
WritePrivateProfileSection	Saves or writes to the specified location an entire sub-hive's contents.
WritePrivateProfileString	Writes to the specified location a data key string value.
WritePrivateProfileStruct	Writes to the specified location, saving a checksum that is written with the object.
WriteProfileSection	Writes an entire sub-hive's contents.
WriteProfileString	Writes to the specified location a data key string value.

In many cases, these functions will map directly into the registry, in the entry under HKEY_LOCAL_MACHINE\SOFTWARE\Microsoft\Windows NT\CurrentVersion\IniFileMapping. This mapping allows many legacy applications that used the WIN.INI, SYSTEM.INI, or CONTROL.INI files to continue to function correctly. This functionality is supported under Windows NT only and does not apply to Windows 95/98 or any other version of Windows. However, for new code, do not use these functions: Use the newer functions described earlier in this chapter in Table 9.1.

Writing an application that uses the registry API calls is simple and straightforward. For example, an application that queried the registry for a certain object's value might be as simple as:

1. Open the object.

2. Query the object's contents.

3. Close the object.

Let's try that. In Windows NT, we have some advantages in that we can write console applications that interact with the registry. OK, Windows 95/98 has many of these advantages, too. Although console applications are not always the most user-friendly, they are very quick and easy to write; and since this is not a programming book, we'll develop our example program as a console application.

To develop any application using Visual C++, we use the new project wizard. Why not, after all, this wizard saves us a lot of work. Follow these steps:

1. In Visual C++ select File ➤ New.

2. Select the Projects tab in the New dialog box.

3. Select Win32 Console Application in the Project Type list.

4. Provide a name for the project (Reg1) and a location, then click OK.

5. Open the newly created Reg1.cpp file and drop in the code shown in Listing 9.1. It is best if you download the code from `http:\\www.sybex.com` (Click on Catalog, type the name of the book or the ISBN [1983], and press Enter.) and cut and paste to save time and to avoid typing errors. However, if you do not have Internet access, you may type in this code directly.

6. Build the project.

7. Correct your typing errors.

8. Rebuild the project and try out Reg1.

If you are not using Visual C++, these steps may need to be slightly modified for your development system. Regardless, the basics are the same: Create a new, empty console application and, in the main source file, add the code from Listing 9.1.

Listing 9.1:   *Reg1.cpp: A Program to Access the Registry*

```cpp
// Reg1.cpp : Defines the entry point for the console application.
//

#include "stdafx.h"
#include "windows.h"
#include "winreg.h"
#include <winerror.h>
#include "stdio.h"
```

```
int main(int argc, char* argv[])
{
#define MAX_VALUE_NAME 4096          // How big things can get
CHAR    ClassName[MAX_PATH] = "";  // Buffer for class name.
CHAR    KeyName[MAX_PATH];          // Name for the data key
char    *szHive = "HARDWARE\\DESCRIPTION\\System";
char    szBufferReturn[MAX_VALUE_NAME];
char    szData[MAX_VALUE_NAME];           // Data value returned
DWORD   dwcClassLen = MAX_PATH;    // Length of class string.
DWORD   dwcMaxClass;               // Longest class string.
DWORD   dwcMaxSubKey;              // Longest sub key size.
DWORD   dwcMaxValueData;           // Longest Value data.
DWORD   dwcMaxValueName;           // Longest Value name.
DWORD   dwcSecDesc;                // Security descriptor.
DWORD   dwcSubKeys;                // Number of sub keys.
DWORD   dwcValues;                 // Number of values for this key.
DWORD   dwType = 0;                // Type of data such as REG_SZ;
DWORD   i = 0;
DWORD   nBufferReturnSize = sizeof(szBufferReturn);
DWORD   nDataSize = MAX_PATH;      // Data value buffer size
DWORD   dwcValueName = MAX_VALUE_NAME;
DWORD retCode;
FILETIME ftLastWriteTime;                 // Last write time.
HKEY    hKey = NULL; // Handle for the registry key
HKEY    hKeyResult;
long    nReturnCode = 0;
PHKEY   phkResult = &hKeyResult; // Result code hole!

    printf("Reg1: version 1.02\n");
    hKey = HKEY_LOCAL_MACHINE;
    hKeyResult = HKEY_LOCAL_MACHINE;

    // First open the key specified in szHive:
    if ((nReturnCode = RegOpenKeyEx(hKey,
        szHive,
        0,
        KEY_ENUMERATE_SUB_KEYS|KEY_EXECUTE|KEY_QUERY_VALUE,
        &hKeyResult
        )) == ERROR_SUCCESS)
    {// Get Class name, Value count. Display for the user.
        retCode = RegQueryInfoKey (hKeyResult,     // Key handle.
```

```
                ClassName,         // Buffer for class name.
                &dwcClassLen,      // Length of class string.
                NULL,              // Reserved.
                &dwcSubKeys,       // Number of sub keys.
                &dwcMaxSubKey,     // Longest sub key size.
                &dwcMaxClass,      // Longest class string.
                &dwcValues,        // Number of values for this key.
                &dwcMaxValueName,  // Longest Value name.
                &dwcMaxValueData,  // Longest Value data.
                &dwcSecDesc,       // Security descriptor.
                &ftLastWriteTime); // Last write time.

        printf("\n\nLooking at HKEY_LOCAL_MACHINE\\%s\n\n", szHive);

        printf (
            "ClassName, '%s' \n"
            "dwcClassLen, '%ld'\n"
            "dwcSubKeys, '%ld'\n"
            "dwcMaxSubKey, '%ld'\n"
            "dwcMaxClass, '%ld'\n"
            "dwcValues, '%ld'\n"
            "dwcMaxValueName, '%ld'\n"
            "dwcMaxValueData, '%ld'\n"
            "dwcSecDesc, '%ld'\n",
            ClassName,         // Buffer for class name.
            dwcClassLen,       // Length of class string.
            dwcSubKeys,        // Number of sub keys.
            dwcMaxSubKey,      // Longest sub key size.
            dwcMaxClass,       // Longest class string.
            dwcValues,         // Number of values for this key.
            dwcMaxValueName,   // Longest Value name.
            dwcMaxValueData,   // Longest Value data.
            dwcSecDesc);       // Security descriptor.

        printf("\n\n");

        for (i = 0, retCode = ERROR_SUCCESS; retCode == ERROR_SUCCESS;
            i++)
        {
            retCode = RegEnumKey (hKeyResult, i,
                KeyName, MAX_PATH);
```

```
        if (retCode == (DWORD)ERROR_SUCCESS)
            printf("Sub-hive name = '%s'\n", KeyName);
}

retCode = ERROR_SUCCESS;

printf("\n\n");

// Next get the value stored in Identifier:
for (i = 0; i < 100 && nReturnCode == ERROR_SUCCESS; i++)
{
    nBufferReturnSize = sizeof(szBufferReturn);
    szBufferReturn[0] = '\0';
    nDataSize = sizeof(szData);
    szData[0] = '\0';

    if ((nReturnCode = RegEnumValue(
        hKeyResult, i,
        szBufferReturn, &nBufferReturnSize,
        NULL,
        &dwType,
        (LPBYTE)szData, &nDataSize
        )) == ERROR_SUCCESS)
    {
        printf("Identifier is '%s'\n\n", szBufferReturn);
        nBufferReturnSize = sizeof(szBufferReturn);

        if (dwType == REG_SZ)
        {
            printf("Identifier contains '%s' REG_SZ \n\n",
            szData);
        }
        else
        {
            printf("Identifier contains a non-string'\n\n");
        }
    }
    else
    {// We're done, check for errors now:
```

```
                    if (nReturnCode != ERROR_NO_MORE_ITEMS)
                    {// No need to tell we are at end of list...
                        nBufferReturnSize = sizeof(szBufferReturn);

                        FormatMessage(FORMAT_MESSAGE_FROM_SYSTEM, NULL,
                            nReturnCode, 0, szBufferReturn,
                            nBufferReturnSize, NULL);

                        printf("RegEnumValue() %ld failed '%s'!\n\n",
                            nReturnCode, szBufferReturn);

                        printf("RegEnumValue() failed!\n\n");
                    }
                }
            }
            // When done, always close the key!
            RegCloseKey(hKey);
    }
    else
    {
        nBufferReturnSize = sizeof(szBufferReturn);

        FormatMessage(FORMAT_MESSAGE_FROM_SYSTEM, NULL, nReturnCode,
            0, szBufferReturn, nBufferReturnSize, NULL);

        printf("RegOpenKey() %ld failed '%s'!\n\n",
            nReturnCode, szBufferReturn);
    }

    return 0;
}
```

NOTE   If so desired, users may also download the entire project from the Web site; all of the files in the project are zipped into a single file called reg1.zip.

NOTE   This is when I usually regale the reader with my first Windows program. It took me about six months to get the basics of my first Windows interface displayed on the screen, and there was no functional code in that interface. Today, with Visual C++ and the wizards, I can do that six months of work in about ten minutes. Progress, ah progress, and to think there are those who'd choose to stifle this innovation.

A program that uses a few of the registry APIs can be written in only a few lines. Listing 9.1 shows the main source file for just such a program.

The program in Listing 9.1 also requires simple stdafx.cpp and stdafx.h files. Listing 9.2 shows the stdafx.cpp file and Listing 9.3 shows the stdafx.h header (include) file for Reg1.cpp.

Listing 9.2:   *stdafx.cpp: The Support Pre-compiled Header File for Reg1*

```
// stdafx.cpp : source file that includes just the standard includes
//    Reg1.pch will be the pre-compiled header
//    stdafx.obj will contain the pre-compiled type information

#include "stdafx.h"

// TODO: reference any additional headers you need in STDAFX.H
// and not in this file
```

Listing 9.3:   *stdafx.h: The Support Pre-compiled Header File for Reg1*

```
// stdafx.h : include file for standard system include files,
//  or project specific include files that are used frequently, but
//      are changed infrequently
//

#if
!defined(AFX_STDAFX_H__BD7FBDE9_14B4_11D2_88CB_0060970BB14F__INCLUDED_)
#define AFX_STDAFX_H__BD7FBDE9_14B4_11D2_88CB_0060970BB14F__INCLUDED_

#if _MSC_VER > 1000
#pragma once
#endif // _MSC_VER > 1000
```

```
// TODO: reference additional headers your program requires here

//{{AFX_INSERT_LOCATION}}
// Microsoft Visual C++ will insert additional declarations immediately
before the previous line.

#endif //
!defined(AFX_STDAFX_H__BD7FBDE9_14B4_11D2_88CB_0060970BB14F__INCLUDED_)
```

To create your own Reg1 program, simply plug these files into a project. Since this program doesn't have a Windows user interface, the output is done using simple printf statements.

NOTE   The Reg1 program, though nominally a C++ program, is basically a standard C program. Although it would be very easy to include additional C++ (and even MFC) code, I chose to keep this program as simple as possible.

Now, let's take a closer look at the Reg1 program. The first step after basic program initialization is to open a registry sub-hive:

```
if ((nReturnCode = RegOpenKeyEx(hKey,
       szHive,
       0,
       KEY_ENUMERATE_SUB_KEYS|KEY_EXECUTE|KEY_QUERY_VALUE,
       &hKeyResult
       )) == ERROR_SUCCESS)
{// Get Class name, Value count. Display for the user.
```

In this code, I call RegOpenKeyEx() and save the return code; the error handler will use the return code to display an error message, if appropriate. If RegOpenKeyEx returns ERROR_SUCCESS, the registry sub-hive was opened successfully. In hKey, the base hive is given to RegOpenKeyEx. We initialize this to HKEY_LOCAL_MACHINE. We initialize the desired hive to be opened in szHive. The desired hive to open is hard coded as "HARDWARE\\DESCRIPTION\\System". Finally, hKeyResult will contain the handle to the hive that has been opened if the function is successful.

Once opened, the next step is to get some information about our hive:

```
retCode = RegQueryInfoKey (hKeyResult,             // Key handle.
             ClassName,          // Buffer for class name.
```

```
             &dwcClassLen,       // Length of class string.
             NULL,               // Reserved.
             &dwcSubKeys,        // Number of sub keys.
             &dwcMaxSubKey,      // Longest sub key size.
             &dwcMaxClass,       // Longest class string.
             &dwcValues,         // Number of values for this key.
             &dwcMaxValueName,   // Longest Value name.
             &dwcMaxValueData,   // Longest Value data.
             &dwcSecDesc,        // Security descriptor.
             &ftLastWriteTime);  // Last write time.
```

The call to RegQueryInfoKey returns the following information about the hive, as shown in Table 9.3.

TABLE 9.3: Information Returned by RegQueryInfoKey()

Variable in Reg1 (The user may specify a different name.)	Description
ClassName	Class name (This field may be blank under Windows 95/98.)
dwcClassLen	Length of class string buffer and the returned length of the class string
dwcSubKeys	Number of sub-hives in this hive
dwcMaxSubKey	Longest object name
dwcMaxClass	Longest class string
dwcValues	Number of data keys in this sub-hive
dwcMaxValueName	Longest value name
dwcMaxValueData	Longest value data
dwcSecDesc	Security descriptor
ftLastWriteTime	Last write time for Windows NT

Once we have some information about the sub-hive, we display this information for the user and carry on.

The next step in our simple program is to display all the sub-hives that are contained within our target hive. This process is done in a simple loop where we enumerate all the sub-hives and print the results of this enumeration. We monitor the results of the RegEnumKey function call until an error is returned. Most loops would check the return value to determine what the error was, in order to build in error recovery; in our simple program, this is unnecessary.

```
        for (i = 0, retCode = ERROR_SUCCESS; retCode == ERROR_SUCCESS;
i++)
        {
            retCode = RegEnumKey (hKeyResult, i,
                KeyName, MAX_PATH);

            if (retCode == (DWORD)ERROR_SUCCESS)
                printf("Sub-hive name = '%s'\n", KeyName);
        }
```

The next step is to get each data key's name and value. Due to the simple nature of this program, I only display keys that have a data type of REG_SZ and skip other keys. However, adding a more complex case statement would allow displaying all the different data types.

As in code where we enumerate the sub-hives, the printing of data key values is done using a loop and a test to ensure that the enumeration function, RegEnum-Value, returns successfully.

This loop is done in two steps. The first is to get the data key's name; the second is to get the actual data value contained in the data key. Separate printf statements display this data for the user, as appropriate:

```
        for (i = 0; i < 100 && nReturnCode == ERROR_SUCCESS; i++)
        {
            nBufferReturnSize = sizeof(szBufferReturn);
            szBufferReturn[0] = '\0';
            nDataSize = sizeof(szData);
            szData[0] = '\0';

            if ((nReturnCode = RegEnumValue(
                hKeyResult, i,
                szBufferReturn, &nBufferReturnSize,
                NULL,
                &dwType,
                (LPBYTE)szData, &nDataSize
                )) == ERROR_SUCCESS)
            {
                printf("Identifier is '%s'\n\n", szBufferReturn);
                nBufferReturnSize = sizeof(szBufferReturn);
```

```
                    if (dwType == REG_SZ)
                    {
                        printf("Identifier contains '%s' REG_SZ \n\n",
                        szData);
                    }
                    else
                    {
                        printf("Identifier contains a non-string'\n\n");
                    }
                }
                else
                {// We're done, check for errors now:
                    if (nReturnCode != ERROR_NO_MORE_ITEMS)
                    {// No need to tell we are at end of list...
                        nBufferReturnSize = sizeof(szBufferReturn);

                        FormatMessage(FORMAT_MESSAGE_FROM_SYSTEM, NULL,
                            nReturnCode, 0, szBufferReturn,
                            nBufferReturnSize, NULL);

                        printf("RegEnumValue() %ld failed '%s'!\n\n",
                            nReturnCode, szBufferReturn);

                        printf("RegEnumValue() failed!\n\n");
                    }
                }
            }
            // When done, always close the key!
            RegCloseKey(hKey);
        }
```

This is error handling at its simplest. We save the return code from a registry function call. If the return is not ERROR_SUCCESS, something went wrong. In this case, we can use FormatMessage to create a more user-friendly error message, which we can print on the screen for the user:

```
else
{// Could not open the registry object!
    nBufferReturnSize = sizeof(szBufferReturn);
```

```
FormatMessage(FORMAT_MESSAGE_FROM_SYSTEM, NULL, nReturnCode,
    0, szBufferReturn, nBufferReturnSize, NULL);

printf("RegOpenKey() %ld failed '%s'!\n\n",
    nReturnCode, szBufferReturn);
}
```

For a Windows program, the message probably would have been best placed in a message box.

Does FormatMessage Always Return the Best Message?

It probably does, but not always; the problem is exactly as it seems. Regardless, whatever FormatMessage does return is better than just displaying an error code value to the user.

Take this example of an error message:

```
"Error number 259 occurred".
```

Descriptive? No.

Useful? No.

User-friendly? No.

The better result comes from FormatMessage, formatted in a string:

```
"The Error 'No more data is available.' occurred in the call to
RegEnumValue"
```

This message, though not perfect, is much better and provides useful information to the user of the program. Programmers who display meaningless numbers in their error messages without explanatory text should be banned from ever using a computer again.

One caution, however: The error strings returned by FormatMessage may contain a trailing newline. It may be necessary to pare these from your error messages.

The results of an execution of Reg1 are shown in Figure 9.1. Even when run under Windows 95/98, Reg1 will provide useful output (although different from Windows NT). This shows the compatibility between the Windows NT registry and the registry found in Windows 95/98.

FIGURE 9.1:

Reg1, a simple command-prompt application, gives us lots of interesting information about a registry sub-hive.

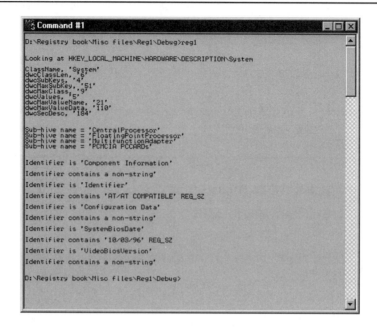

NOTE   Check this book's Web site at http:\\www.sybex.com (Click on Catalog, enter the book title or ISBN [1983], and press Enter.) for complete source code for the Reg1 program.

To MFC or Not to MFC? That Is the Question

C++, MFC (Microsoft Foundation Classes), and the concept of object-oriented programming (aka OOP) have all hit the big time. Some programmers actually believe that it is not possible to use old C calls in a C++ program. Actually, it is fully possible to use the Windows API calls in any program, whether the program is C, C++, MFC, or whatever. However, Microsoft did bundle a few of the registry functions into MFC to make programming a bit easier. For example, the CWinApp class contains a number of both documented and undocumented registry manipulation functions.

First, the good news: Some registry functions are available in CWinApp. Now, the bad news: There are not many registry functions available in CWinApp. Basically, the functions listed in Table 9.4 are available to programmers directly. But don't despair—you can just call the plain old Windows API registry functions as well.

TABLE 9.4: Registry Functions That Are Part of CWinApp.

Function, with Parameters Passed	Documentation	Description
void SetRegistryKey(LPCTSTR lpszRegistryKey)	Yes	This overloaded function fills in m_pszRegistryKey variable using the passed string. This string would typically contain the company name. m_psz-RegistryKey is used to create the necessary hive(s) under HKEY_CURRENT_USER\software\m_pszRegistryKey\m_pszProfileName. m_pszProfile-Name is set to m_pszAppName by SetRegistryKey.
void SetRegistryKey(UINT nIDRegistryKey)	Yes	This overloaded function fills in m_pszRegistryKey variable from a string contained in the application's string resources. This string would typically contain the company name. m_psz-RegistryKey is used to create the necessary hive(s) under HKEY_CURRENT_USER\software\m_pszRegistryKey\m_pszProfileName. m_pszProfile-Name is set to m_pszAppName by SetRegistryKey.
HKEY GetSectionKey(LPCTSTR lpszSection)	No	Returns hKey for HKEY_CURRENT_USER\Software\RegistryKey\AppName\lpsz-Section, creating it if it doesn't exist, where RegistryKey is the company name as stored in m_pszRegistryKey and App-Name is the application name as stored in m_pszAppName. The caller must close the hKey returned.

Continued on next page

T A B L E 9 . 4 C O N T I N U E D : Registry Functions That Are Part of CWinApp.

Function, with Parameters Passed	Documentation	Description
HKEY GetAppRegistryKey()	No	Returns hKey for HKEY_ CURRENT_USER\Software\ RegistryKey\AppName, creating it if it doesn't exist, where RegistryKey is the company name as stored in m_psz- RegistryKey, and AppName is the application name as stored in m_pszAppName. The caller must close the hKey returned.
UINT GetProfileInt(LPCTSTR lpszSection, LPCTSTR lpszEntry, int nDefault)	Yes	Calls GetSectionKey() to open lpszSection, then calls Reg- QueryValueEx() to get the value for the key specified in lpsz- Entry. Returns nDefault if the entry is not found. Works on an INI file if a call to Set- RegistryKey() has not previously been made.
BOOL WriteProfileInt(LPCTSTR lpszSection, LPCTSTR lpszEntry, int nValue)	Yes	Calls GetSectionKey() to open lpszSection, then calls RegSet- ValueEx() to set the value for the key specified in lpszEntry. Returns FALSE if the entry cannot be set. Works on an INI file if a call to SetRegistryKey() has not previously been made.
CString GetProfileString(LPCTSTR lpszSection, LPCTSTR lpszEntry, LPCTSTR lpszDefault = NULL)	Yes	Calls GetSectionKey() to open lpszSection, then calls Reg- QueryValueEx() to get the value for the key specified in lpsz- Entry. Returns lpszDefault if the entry is not found. Works on an INI file if a call to Set- RegistryKey() has not previously been made.

Continued on next page

TABLE 9.4 CONTINUED: Registry Functions That Are Part of CWinApp.

Function, with Parameters Passed	Documentation	Description
BOOL WriteProfileString(LPCTSTR lpszSection, LPCTSTR lpszEntry, LPCTSTR lpszValue)	Yes	Calls GetSectionKey() to open lpszSection, then calls RegSetValueEx() to set the value for the key specified in lpszEntry. Returns FALSE if the entry cannot be set. Works on an INI file if a call to SetRegistryKey() has not previously been made.
BOOL GetProfileBinary(LPCTSTR lpszSection, LPCTSTR lpszEntry, LPBYTE* ppData, UINT* pBytes)	Yes	Calls GetSectionKey() to open lpszSection, then calls RegQueryValueEx() to get the value for the key specified in lpszEntry. The size of the buffer to return the data in is specified by pBytes. The parameter pBytes will be set to the size of the returned data. Works on an INI file if a call to SetRegistryKey() has not previously been made.
BOOL WriteProfileBinary(LPCTSTR lpszSection, LPCTSTR lpszEntry, LPBYTE pData, UINT nBytes)	Yes	Calls GetSectionKey() to open lpszSection, then calls RegSetValueEx() to set the value for the key specified in lpszEntry. The buffer containing the data to save is pData, and the data's size is specified by nBytes. Works on an INI file if a call to SetRegistryKey() has not previously been made.
LONG DelRegTree(HKEY hParentKey, const CString& strKeyName)	No	Deletes the specified sub-hive from the specified parent. Since a registry sub-hive may not be deleted unless it is empty in Windows NT, a helper function is used to recursively delete further sub-hives and keys.

NOTE

A bright programmer could write a wrapper around the Windows API registry functions if desired. However, there's a reason that Microsoft didn't already do that: Actually, you'd gain no additional functionality or usability. On the other hand, it might be possible to improve the registry access, especially searching for and retrieving specific keys, with a C++ registry class. I'll leave it up to you to design your own registry class.

The process for using the CWinApp registry functions is simple:

1. Call CWinApp::SetRegistryKey() to tell MFC that your application is going to work with the registry rather than a separate INI file.

2. Call the functions to retrieve or set values in the registry.

There is no closing code needed unless a call has been made to one of the following CWinApp functions:

- `HKEY GetSectionKey(LPCTSTR lpszSection)`

- `HKEY GetAppRegistryKey()`

If one of these functions is used, be sure that your application does a proper close of the registry key returned. Of course, check to ensure that the function didn't fail.

Hints and Kinks from the Experts

Our experts are not programmers, but here we go.

How Do I Migrate My Older Application to Support the Registry?

There are two problems here: program conversion and user migration. First, the application must be modified to use the registry. Replace all calls that access the application's INI file with calls that access the registry. Establish the application's registry hive, using the following convention:

HKEY_CURRENT_USER\Software*company**application*

In this convention, *company* is your company name, or a name or word closely associated with your company; and *application* is the name of this particular application. If your company produces many applications, and they share some items in common, it may be useful to create both a sub-hive for each specific application and a separate sub-hive (called Common) for items that are shared between two or more applications or components.

The second issue is migration of user data from the INI file to the registry. This can be done at either of two points—either during installation/upgrade time or the first time the application is executed. In either case, the process is identical.

A helper program or function must be created. This helper will read the INI file using INI file I/O routines. Then the helper will write registry entries based on the INI file's contents.

Hint: Once the INI file has been transferred to the registry, consider marking it read-only. This will prevent additional manual modifications by the user. As well, add a comment at the top of the INI file describing the move to the registry and advising the user that the INI file is no longer used.

Say something like: "The information in this INI file has been moved to the registry. Items in this file will be ignored *by application name version n* and later." Of course, fill in *application name* and *version n* with your application's name and version.

(Courtesy of Peter D. Hipson)

CHAPTER

TEN

10

The Performance Monitor Meets the Registry

- PerfMon1—a program to access HKEY_PERFORMANCE_DATA

- The program

- Adding performance data to the registry

- Hints and kinks from the experts

There is a part of the registry that we've not discussed yet. That is the registry hive HKEY_PERFORMANCE_DATA, the registry's performance hive. This registry hive contains the necessary information to allow an application to successfully interact with and display performance data. It is also hidden from the registry editors—it is contained in a place in the registry that is only accessible programmatically. Otherwise, it's not visible or editable.

Although it is somewhat more difficult to access than other registry hives, this difficulty can be overcome using the tools provided in the Windows header file, winperf.h, distributed with Visual C++. In addition, in this chapter we'll show you a simple program we've created for browsing HKEY_PERFORMANCE_DATA. The program is called PerfMon1. Keep in mind that the program as presented in this chapter is only an example and doesn't actually do any useful retrieval of data—adding that functionality is left up to you.

> **NOTE** Are the performance data and HKEY_PERFORMANCE_DATA really part of the registry? Well, that's a good question. They're hardly ever mentioned, and show up in only eleven TechNet articles. Basically, it seems obvious that they weren't part of Microsoft's original conception of the registry. HKEY_PERFORMANCE_DATA is an example of Microsoft *extending* the registry functionality and interface to provide special services.

PerfMon1—A Program to Access HKEY_PERFORMANCE_DATA

To keep our example as simple as possible, I've forgone any semblance of a user interface. This program is a simple console application, displaying its voluminous data using printf() statements.

> **NOTE** When you're using PerfMon1, I suggest you use I/O redirection and capture the data into a file. The file may be subsequently edited or browsed easily. PerfMon1 might typically print over 50,000 lines of output; watching all of this scroll past on the screen won't be any fun.

The performance data is entirely contained within the HKEY_PERFORMANCE_ DATA hive with the exception of the object and counter names and help information, which is contained in the sub-hive HKEY_LOCAL_MACHINE\SOFTWARE\ Microsoft\Windows NT\CurrentVersion\Perflib\009.

Appendix D, "Performance Counters and Descriptions," lists all the available counters and objects contained in the registry. Let's take a look at a part of Perf-Mon1's output and compare the output to the items listed in Appendix D.

An Example Portion of PerfMon1 Output

First, let's look at PerfMon1's output:

```
PerfMon1 - Check out HKEY_PERFORMANCE_DATA!
Index: 2
        Counter: 10
        Counter: 12
        Counter: 14
        Counter: 16
        Counter: 18
        Counter: 20
        Counter: 146
        Counter: 150
        Counter: 240
        Counter: 242
        Counter: 244
        Counter: 246
        Counter: 406
        Counter: 674
        Counter: 44
        Counter: 686
        Counter: 688
        Counter: 690
        Counter: 660
        Counter: 662
        Counter: 1342
        Counter: 1344
        Counter: 1346
        Counter: 1348
        Counter: 1350
        Counter: 1350
```

```
Index: 238

    Instance '0'
            Counter: 6
            Counter: 142
            Counter: 144
            Counter: 148
            Counter: 696
            Counter: 698
            Counter: 1334
            Counter: 1336
            Counter: 1338
            Counter: 1340
```

Descriptions of PerfMon1's Performance Counters

Comparing the preceding portion of PerfMon1's output to what we can find described in Appendix D, we see the following (I've made the comments more relevant here, to explain what these numbers mean.):

Index: 2—Index 2 is System object. The System object will contain a number of counters. Check this out: Start the Windows NT Performance Monitor, and select Edit ➤ Add To Chart. The Add to Chart dialog box (see Figure 10.1) shows the System object selected and also displays some of the counters found in System. The Counter Definition area contains the description for the highlighted counter.

Counter: 10—Counter 10 is File Read Operations/sec, not shown in the list; it is further down on the list of System counters. The next six counters (12 through 150) are also not visible. The Windows NT Performance Monitor will sort items in the Counter list, though the counters are not sorted in any particular order in the registry.

Counter: 12—Counter 12 is the counter for File Write Operations/sec.

Counter: 14—Counter 14 is the counter for File Control Operations/sec.

Counter: 16—Counter: 16 is the counter for File Read Bytes/sec.

Counter: 18—Counter 18 is the counter for File Write Bytes/sec.

Counter: 20—Counter: 20 is the counter for File Control Bytes/sec.

Counter: 146—Counter: 146 is the counter for Context Switches/sec.

FIGURE 10.1:

The Performance Monitor's Add to Chart dialog box shows the System object and some counters.

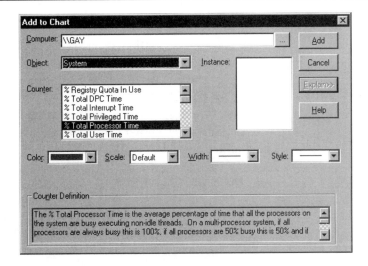

Counter: 150—Counter: 150 is the counter for System Calls/sec.

Counter: 240—Counter 240 is % Total Processor Time, as shown in Figure 10.1. A good question to ask is why does the eighth counter in the System object become the currently selected counter? When the folks at Microsoft designed the Performance Monitor, they decided to include an index to tell applications which counter to display first; there is also a corresponding index for objects. In the case of the System object, the index for the counter to select is 8 (numbered from 0). Thus, if you count down in the list of counters (10, 14, 16, 18, 20, 146, 150, and so on), we see that the counter number 8 is % Total Processor Time.

With our PerfMon1 listing, we can see that System object has a total of 26 counters. The ones we haven't described are for other related counters.

Referring back to the next object in the PerfMon1 report, the next index in the Performance Monitor system is number 238, or, in more friendly terms, Processor. This object is a bit different from System, but why? Well, you may remember from our forays into HKEY_LOCAL_MACHINE\Hardware\Description\System\ CentralProcessor that our system in this example has only one CPU. If this were a multi-CPU system, we would have an Instance '0', an Instance '1', and so forth, with one instance for each CPU that was installed. This tells us that the Processor object is capable of monitoring each CPU in a multiprocessor environment separately. Actually, this is the only way that the Processor performance data may be monitored; there is no aggregate data for this object.

Index: 238—As mentioned earlier, Index 238 is the Processor object. Like the System object, the Processor object also contains a number of counters. Again, try starting the Windows NT Performance Monitor. Next select Edit ➤ Add To Chart. The Add to Chart dialog box (see Figure 10.2) shows the Processor object selected and also displays some of the counters found in Processor. The Counter Definition area contains the description for the highlighted counter.

Instance '0'

Counter: 6—Counter: 6 is the counter for % Processor Time.

Counter: 142—Counter: 142 is the counter for % User Time.

Counter: 144—Counter: 144 is the counter for % Privileged Time.

Counter: 148—Counter: 148 is the counter for Interrupts/sec.

Counter: 696—Counter: 696 is the counter for % DPC Time.

Counter: 698—Counter: 698 is the counter for % Interrupt Time.

FIGURE 10.2:

The Performance Monitor's Add to Chart dialog box shows the Processor object and some counters.

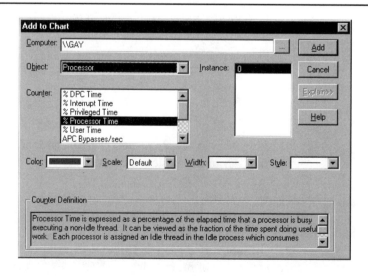

Counter: **1334**—Counter: 1334 is the counter for DPCs Queued/sec.

Counter: **1336**—Counter: 1336 is the counter for DPC Rate.

Counter: **1338**—Counter: 1338 is the counter for DPC Bypasses/sec.

Counter: **1340**—Counter: 1340 is the counter for APC Bypasses/sec.

Again, as with System, Processor counters are displayed in sorted order, with the counter for % Processor Time being the first, or initially selected, counter.

The Program

Since PerfMon1 is the main topic of this chapter, let's take a look at it.

Listing 10.1 contains the main program, PerfMon1.CPP, a very simple program that is used to access performance counters and objects stored in the registry. To create PerfMon1, see the instructions for creating a project in Chapter 9, "Programming and the Registry—a Developer's Paradise?"

Listing 10.1:   *PerfMon1.CPP*

```
// PerfMon1.cpp : Defines the entry point for the console
application.
//

#include "stdafx.h"

#include <windows.h> // Standard windows header
#include <winperf.h> // Performance monitor definitions
#include <stdio.h>   // printf() and other I/O stuff
#include <malloc.h>  // memory allocation definitions.

#define BUFFERSIZE 8192 // initial buffer size,
#define INCREMENT 1024  // If too small, increment by this
size

int main(int argc, char* argv[])
```

```
{
// These objects are shown in winperf.h:
PPERF_DATA_BLOCK          PerfDataBlock = NULL;
PPERF_OBJECT_TYPE         PerfObjectType;
PPERF_INSTANCE_DEFINITION PerfInstanceDefinition;
PPERF_COUNTER_DEFINITION  PerfCounterDefinition;
PPERF_COUNTER_DEFINITION  PerfCurrentCounter;
PPERF_COUNTER_BLOCK       PerfCounterBlock;

// Program variables:
DWORD    BufferSize = BUFFERSIZE; // Size of our buffer.
DWORD    nShort;        // If TRUE, display minimal data
DWORD    i;             // Index
DWORD    j;             // Index
DWORD    k;             // Index

    printf("PerfMon1 - Check out HKEY_PERFORMANCE_DATA!\n");

    // Check options, /S for short output display!

    nShort = FALSE;

    if (argc > 1)
    {
        if (argv[1][0] == '/' && (argv[1][1] == 'S' ||
            argv[1][1] == 's'))
        {
            nShort = TRUE;
        }
    }

    // Allocate an initial buffer, which we'll resize later.
    PerfDataBlock = (PPERF_DATA_BLOCK) malloc(BufferSize);

    while (RegQueryValueEx(HKEY_PERFORMANCE_DATA,
        "Global", NULL, NULL, (LPBYTE) PerfDataBlock,
        &BufferSize) == ERROR_MORE_DATA)
    {// The buffer is too small, so expand it! .
        BufferSize += INCREMENT;
        PerfDataBlock = (PPERF_DATA_BLOCK) realloc(PerfData-
Block,
            BufferSize);
    }
```

```
    // Buffer is sized OK now, let's get the first object!
    PerfObjectType = (PPERF_OBJECT_TYPE)((PBYTE)PerfDataBlock
+
        PerfDataBlock->HeaderLength);

    // loop through objects in HKEY_PERFORMANCE_DATA
    for (i = 0; i < PerfDataBlock->NumObjectTypes; i++)
    {
        if (nShort)
        {
            printf("Index: %ld\n", PerfObjectType->
                ObjectNameTitleIndex);
        }
        else
        {
            printf("\n");
            printf("Index to name in Title Database %ld\n",
                PerfObjectType->ObjectNameTitleIndex);
            printf("Length of this object definition %d\n",
                PerfObjectType->TotalByteLength);
            printf("Length of object definition %ld\n",
                PerfObjectType->DefinitionLength);
            printf("Length of this header structure %ld\n",
                PerfObjectType->HeaderLength);
            printf("use by analysis program to point to "
                "retrieved title string %ld\n",
                PerfObjectType->ObjectNameTitle);
            printf("Index to Help in Title Database %ld\n",
                PerfObjectType->ObjectHelpTitleIndex);
            printf("Used by analysis program to point to "
                "retrieved title string %ld\n",
                PerfObjectType->ObjectHelpTitle);
            printf("Object level of detail %ld \n",
                PerfObjectType->DetailLevel);
            printf("Number of counters in each counter "
                "block %ld \n",
                PerfObjectType->NumCounters);
            printf("Default counter to display %ld \n",
                PerfObjectType->DefaultCounter);
            printf("Number of object instances %ld\n",
                PerfObjectType->NumInstances);
            printf("Instance name Code page, or 0 if "
                "UNICODE %ld\n",
```

```
                      PerfObjectType->CodePage);
            printf("Sample Time in 'Object' units %ld\n",
                PerfObjectType->PerfTime);
            printf("Frequency of 'Object' units %ld\n\n",
                PerfObjectType->PerfFreq);
        }

        // next get the counter block, containing counter
        // information!
        PerfCounterDefinition = (PPERF_COUNTER_DEFINITION)
            ((PBYTE)PerfObjectType +
            PerfObjectType->HeaderLength);

        if (PerfObjectType->NumInstances > 0)
        {// first instance:
            PerfInstanceDefinition =
                (PPERF_INSTANCE_DEFINITION)
                ((PBYTE)PerfObjectType +
                PerfObjectType->DefinitionLength);

            // Next instance loop:
            for(k = 0; k < (DWORD)PerfObjectType->NumIn-
stances; k++)
                {
                if (nShort)
                {
                    printf("\n\tInstance '%S'\n",
                        (char *)((PBYTE)PerfInstanceDefini-
tion +
                        PerfInstanceDefinition->NameOffset));
                }
                else
                {
                    printf("\n\tUnicode name of this instance"
                        " '%S'\n",
                        (char *)((PBYTE)PerfInstanceDefinition
+
                        PerfInstanceDefinition->NameOffset));
                    printf("\tLength including the subsequent"
                        " name %ld\n",
                        PerfInstanceDefinition->ByteLength);
                    printf("\tTitle Index to name of 'parent'"
                        " object %ld\n",
```

```
                            PerfInstanceDefinition->
                            ParentObjectTitleIndex);
                    printf("\tIndex to instance of parent "
                        "object %ld\n",
                        PerfInstanceDefinition->
                        ParentObjectInstance);
                    printf("\tA unique ID used instead of"
                        " matching the name to identify this"
                        " instance, -1 = none %ld\n",
                        PerfInstanceDefinition->UniqueID);
                    printf("\tLength in bytes of name;"
                        " 0 = none %ld\n\n",
                        PerfInstanceDefinition->NameLength);
                }

                PerfCurrentCounter = PerfCounterDefinition;

                // Get first counter in this instance
                PerfCounterBlock =
                    (PPERF_COUNTER_BLOCK)((PBYTE)
                    PerfInstanceDefinition +
                    PerfInstanceDefinition->ByteLength);

                // Then retrieve all counters in this instance
with
                // a loop:
                for(j = 0; j < PerfObjectType->NumCounters;
j++)
                {
                    if (nShort)
                    {
                        printf("\t\tCounter: %ld\n",
                            PerfCurrentCounter->
                            CounterNameTitleIndex);
                    }
                    else
                    {
                        printf("\t\tLength in bytes of"
                            " this structure %ld \n",
                            PerfCurrentCounter->ByteLength);
                        printf("\t\tIndex of Counter name"
                            " into Title Database %ld\n",
                            PerfCurrentCounter->
```

```
                                     CounterNameTitleIndex);
                                printf("\t\tretrieved title string
'%s'\n",

tle);
                                    PerfCurrentCounter->CounterNameTi-

                                printf("\t\tIndex of Counter Help
into"
                                    " Title Database %ld\n",
                                    PerfCurrentCounter->
                                    CounterHelpTitleIndex);
                                printf("\t\tretrieved title string
'%s'\n",

tle);
                                    PerfCurrentCounter->CounterHelpTi-

                                printf("\t\tPower of 10 by which to"
                                    " scale %ld\n",
                                    PerfCurrentCounter->DefaultScale);
                                printf("\t\tCounter level of detail"
                                    " (for controlling display"
                                    " complexity %ld\n",
                                    PerfCurrentCounter->DetailLevel);
                                printf("\t\tType of counter %ld\n",
                                    PerfCurrentCounter->CounterType);
                                printf("\t\tSize of counter in bytes
%ld\n",
                                    PerfCurrentCounter->CounterSize);
                                printf("\t\tOffset to the first byte
of"
                                    " this counter %ld\n",
                                    PerfCurrentCounter->CounterOff-

set);

                                printf("\n\n");
                        }

                        // Get next counter.
                        PerfCurrentCounter =
                            (PPERF_COUNTER_DEFINITION)
                            ((PBYTE)PerfCurrentCounter +
                            PerfCurrentCounter->ByteLength);
                } // for loop

                // next instance, coming up next!
```

```
                    PerfInstanceDefinition =
                        (PPERF_INSTANCE_DEFINITION)
                        ((PBYTE)PerfCounterBlock +
                        PerfCounterBlock->ByteLength);
                } // for loop

        } // if (PerfObjectType->NumInstances > 0)
        else
        {// Get the first counter.
            PerfCounterBlock = (PPERF_COUNTER_BLOCK)
                ((PBYTE)PerfObjectType +
                PerfObjectType->DefinitionLength);

            // Get counters in a loop:
            for(j = 0; j < PerfObjectType->NumCounters; j++)
            {
                if (nShort)
                {
                    printf("\tCounter: %ld\n",
                        PerfCounterDefinition->
                        CounterNameTitleIndex);
                }
                else
                {
                    printf("\tLength in bytes of this"
                        " structure %ld \n",
                        PerfCounterDefinition->ByteLength);
                    printf("\tIndex of Counter name"
                        " into Title Database %ld\n",
                        PerfCounterDefinition->
                        CounterNameTitleIndex);
                    printf("\tretrieved title string '%s'\n",
                        PerfCounterDefinition->CounterNameTi-
tle);
                    printf("\tIndex of Counter Help into"
                        " Title Database %ld\n",
                        PerfCounterDefinition->
                        CounterHelpTitleIndex);
                    printf("\tretrieved title string '%s'\n",
                        PerfCounterDefinition->CounterHelpTi-
tle);
                    printf("\tPower of 10 by which to scale
%ld\n",
```

```
                                PerfCounterDefinition->DefaultScale);
                        printf("\tCounter level of detail"
                            " (for controlling display complexity"
                            " %ld\n",
                            PerfCounterDefinition->DetailLevel);
                        printf("\tType of counter %ld\n",
                            PerfCounterDefinition->CounterType);
                        printf("\tSize of counter in bytes %ld\n",
                            PerfCounterDefinition->CounterSize);
                        printf("\tOffset to the first byte of"
                            " this counter %ld\n",
                            PerfCounterDefinition->CounterOffset);
                        printf("\n\n");
                    }

                    // Data is (LPVOID)((PBYTE)PerfCounterBlock +
                    // PerfCounterDefinition->CounterOffset);

                    PerfCounterDefinition =
                        (PPERF_COUNTER_DEFINITION)
                        ((PBYTE)PerfCounterDefinition +
                        PerfCounterDefinition->ByteLength);
                } // for loop

            } // else if (PerfObjectType->NumInstances > 0)

            // Get the next object to monitor
            PerfObjectType = (PPERF_OBJECT_TYPE)((PBYTE)PerfOb-
jectType +
                PerfObjectType->TotalByteLength);

        } // Done! Go home and be sweet about it.

    return(0);
}
```

Our performance information access program is simple and does not do much more than describe the counters that are found in the registry. Of course, most performance monitoring programs will want the actual performance data values too.

If we take a look at the PERF_COUNTER_DEFINITION structure, we will see that the last three items defined in this structure are CounterType, CounterSize, and CounterOffset. These three items represent the specific information needed to access a particular performance counter. Of course, to use the counter in a meaningful way, you'd also have to (at least) scale and format the counter properly, and then display it.

The following code segment shows the definition of the PERF_COUNTER_DEFINITION object:

```
typedef struct _PERF_COUNTER_DEFINITION {
    DWORD           ByteLength;
        // Length in bytes of this structure
    DWORD           CounterNameTitleIndex;
        // Index of Counter name into Title Database
    LPWSTR          CounterNameTitle;
        // Initially NULL, for use by analysis
        // program to point to retrieved title string
    DWORD           CounterHelpTitleIndex;
        // Index of Counter Help into Title Database
    LPWSTR          CounterHelpTitle;
        // Initially NULL, for use by analysis program
        // to point to retrieved title string
    LONG            DefaultScale;
        // Power of 10 by which to scale chart line
        // if vertical axis is 100
        // 0 ==> 1, 1 ==> 10, -1 ==>1/10, etc.
    DWORD           DetailLevel;
        // Counter level of detail (for controlling
        // display complexity)
    DWORD           CounterType;
        // Type of counter
    DWORD           CounterSize;
        // Size of counter in bytes
    DWORD           CounterOffset;
        // Offset from the start of the PERF_COUNTER_BLOCK
        // to the first byte of this counter
} PERF_COUNTER_DEFINITION, *PPERF_COUNTER_DEFINITION;
```

Notice the last item in the PERF_COUNTER_DEFINITION: CounterOffset. This variable is defined as the offset from the start of the PERF_COUNTER_BLOCK for this counter. This finds the counter in question. The CounterSize variable (just above CounterOffset) tells us how many bytes the counter in question occupies. Many counters are 4 bytes (a DWORD) in length.

Another important item for the counter is CounterType, a DWORD that describes the counter's type, as shown in Table 10.1. A mapping of the bits in CounterType follows.

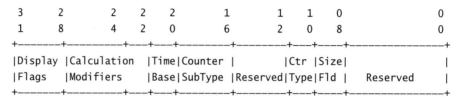

```
3       2         2   2   2       1       1   1   0               0
1       8         4   2   0       6       2   0   8               0
+--------+----------+---+---+--------+--------+---+----+----------------+
|Display |Calculation|Time|Counter |        |Ctr |Size|                |
|Flags   |Modifiers  |Base|SubType |Reserved|Type|Fld |    Reserved    |
+--------+----------+---+---+--------+--------+---+----+----------------+
```

The CounterType field is bitmapped and contains a lot of valuable information about the counter, as described in Table 10.1.

TABLE 10.1:   The Bits in CounterType

First Bit	Final Bit	Description
0	7	Reserved
8	9	Size field indicating the size, ranging from 0 size to variable length binary
10	11	Type of the counter: number, counter, text or 0
12	15	Reserved
16	19	The counter's type: hex, decimal, or decimal scaled (for counters); value, rate, fraction, and so on (for numbers); and other values (for text or 0 counter types)
20	21	The time base for the counter: either timer ticks, timer 100 nanoseconds, or an object-based timer
22	23	Calculation modifier, used for delta counters
24	27	Calculation modifier, used with inverse, or multi-counters
28	31	Display format flag describing how to display this counter's data

The best information on these values is contained in winperf.h, one of the better documented header files for Windows NT.

To access a counter, see Listing 10.1 earlier in this chapter, where PerfCounter-Block is used. Initially, it is set to the first counter:

```
PerfCounterBlock = (PPERF_COUNTER_BLOCK)((PBYTE)PerfInstanceDefinition
+
                    PerfInstanceDefinition->ByteLength);
```

We can access the data using the following line of code:

```
Data = (LPVOID)((PBYTE)PerfCounterBlock + PerfCounterDefinition->Coun-
terOffset);
```

When using the code described here, be certain to properly de-reference the pointers.

Adding Performance Data to the Registry

The first part of this chapter delves into accessing pre-existing performance data in the registry. It is also possible to add performance data to the registry for your own systems and applications. To do this, you must design your application or system to keep counters and modify the application or system to write these counters into the registry. Use the techniques described in the Microsoft Resource Kit Version 3.5, Chapter 13, "Adding Application Performance Counters." This reference is available on the TechNet CD from Microsoft.

The process of adding performance data to the registry involves creating a DLL for collecting performance information. This DLL must have (at least) the Collect entry point functionality. The entry point names may be determined at product design phase. When installed, your installation program *must* specify the entry point names. Below is a list of possible entry points used to support performance monitoring.

Library—The name of the DLL file that your application must have to collect performance data.

Collect—The routine that I used to report performance data upon request; this function is required.

Open—The function that is used to initialize the performance monitoring; this function is not required if the application is able to update performance counters without requests.

Close—The function that terminates the collection of performance data; as with Open, the Close function is not strictly required.

A program called LODCTR is used to update the registry and add performance counters for an application. To use LODCTR, it is necessary to write an INI file. This process is well documented in the Microsoft Resource Kit Version 3.5, Chapter 13.

Here is an example of performance counters added to the registry of one Windows NT Server installation for the IIS Gopher Service:

```
[HKEY_LOCAL_MACHINE\SYSTEM\ControlSet001\Services\GOPHERSVC\Performance]
"Library"="gdctrs.DLL"
"Open"="OpenGdPerformanceData"
"Close"="CloseGdPerformanceData"
"Collect"="CollectGdPerformanceData"
"Last Counter"=dword:000007b8
"Last Help"=dword:000007b9
"First Counter"=dword:00000792
"First Help"=dword:00000793
```

In this example, the library to monitor performance data is called dgctrs.dll. There are function entry points defined for Open, Close, and Collect. Your application may add these entries at program installation time, or the first time the program is executed.

The final four entries—Last Counter, Last Help, First Counter, and First Help—are created automatically by LODCTR when counters are loaded; your application should not need to modify these four entries.

An example of a LODCTR INI file follows:

```
[info]
applicationname=MyApp
symbolfile=symfile.h

[languages]
009=English

[text]
```

```
OBJECT_1_009_NAME=MyApp
OBJECT_1_009_HELP=Monitor performance statistics for MyApp

DEVICE_COUNTER_1_009_NAME=Transactions
DEVICE_COUNTER_1_009_HELP=Number of transactions processed/second

DEVICE_COUNTER_2_009_NAME=LostCustomers
DEVICE_COUNTER_2_009_HELP=Number customers lost due to slow transac-
tions
```

This example is simple. There are two counters with descriptive text and only one language. A real application might have many counters, depending on the application's complexity.

In summary, to create performance monitoring, follow these steps:

1. Create the necessary registry entries as described earlier in this section for Library, Open, Close, and Collect.

2. Move or otherwise place a copy of the file specified in the Library entry to the %SystemRoot%\System32 directory.

3. Use the LODCTR program to integrate the INI file's counter entries into the registry.

Hints and Kinks from the Experts

Although not exactly programming oriented, the following hints are performance related.

Finding That Memory Leak Using Windows NT 4.   Much has been written about using Performance Monitor to detect and isolate memory leaks. Two Microsoft Knowledge Base articles on the subject are "Q130926" and "Q150934." While these standard protocols work, the hit-and-miss method of finding the leaking process can be very time-consuming. Here is an alternate method:

1. Start PMON.EXE from the Resource Kit.

2. Monitor paged and non-paged pool usage; these are the last two items in the second row. If these are increasing over time, you have a memory leak.

3. Monitor the commit counters in the second row. Increasing numbers over several hours indicate a probable leak.

4. Monitor the Commit Charge column. The process with the leak will have an increasing value.

5. To make it easier to monitor, copy the output to the Clipboard and paste it into Notepad. You can save the output as a file and compare it with later outputs.

Do this about once an hour over the duration of your testing.

(Courtesy of Jerold Schulman)

Allowing Ordinary Users to Monitor Server Performance.   How do you allow ordinary users to monitor server performance? Start by granting read access to the following server files:

- %windir%\system32\PERFCxxx.DAT

- %windir%\system32\PERFHxxx.DAT

The basic language ID for the system is xxx, 009 for U.S. English. Subtract 400 from HKEY_USERS\<SID of local server user>\Control Panel\International\ Locale to determine the basic language ID.

If the files are missing or corrupt, expand them from the CD-ROM. Using REGEDT32, give the user at least read access to the following:

- HKEY_LOCAL_MACHINE\Software\Microsft\Windows NT\ CurrentVersion\Perflib and all of its sub-keys

- HKEY_LOCAL_MACHINE\System\CurrentControlSet\Control\ SecurePipeServers\winreg

When adding objects to monitor, the user can select the \\Server.

(Courtesy of Jerold Schulman)

PART III

Windows System Registry Entries

CHAPTER

ELEVEN

11

The Windows NT User Interface—Changing How It Looks

- The Desktop

- Other user interface settings

- Console and command-prompt settings

- Hints and kinks from the experts

Have you ever noticed? Anybody going slower than you is an idiot, and anyone going faster than you is a moron.

George Carlin

The Windows NT user interface is probably the most modified part of Windows NT. Virtually all users change some part of the user interface at some time in their usage of Windows NT.

Many user interface registry modifications are easy to do and they are relatively safe. Messing up a registry entry for the user interface will usually not break the operating system. Typically, it will just make things either less friendly or not so pretty. However, there are some changes that can cause serious damage to the system, making it necessary to restore the registry from a backup.

Many parts of the user interface may be changed with the Display applet in the Control Panel. The registry controls everything—the Desktop, how things look, fonts, dialog box styles, colors, and DOS command-prompt windows.

There are some shortcuts. For example, you can use the Policy Editor under Start ➣ Programs ➣ Administrative Tools (Common); the RegKey utility in the Resource Kit (see Chapter 4, "Registry Tools and Tips—Getting the Work Done"); and a few other tools to implement many of the settings. But the really interesting settings that are often wanted, but seldom used, must be set using either very special tools, or by direct, manual manipulation of the registry.

In this chapter, we'll cover each of the user interface items and describe each item, its location in the registry, and any tool available to manipulate it.

When you need to create a new key for setting values, make sure that you choose the correct data type for the key. Many keys are REG_SZ, but hold a numeric value. Be careful not to create these keys with the wrong data type, such as REG_DWORD, because Windows NT won't recognize the value.

Here Are a Couple of Things to Consider

Many of the settings for the user interface won't take effect until you log on the next time.

Typically, many settings are the REG_SZ type. To show values stored in these settings, the value is enclosed in double quotes (") so that you will clearly see the value. When entering these values, don't enter the quotes.

WARNING   Do I have to say it? Back up your registry before making changes in it. Admittedly, changing the HKEY_USERS hive is less dangerous than changing HKEY_LOCAL_ MACHINE, for example, but there are hazards in making any changes to the registry.

The Desktop

The Desktop is the single most modified part of the Windows NT user interface. Users quickly put on a bitmap for their wallpaper, set a background pattern, customize the size and configuration of windows, and change colors—all with wild abandon.

One of the first things we do is load the Microsoft Windows NT themes application, which is available from Microsoft as part of the Windows NT Resource Kit. Themes allows loading of any Windows 95/98-compatible theme; this saves time when configuring one's Desktop.

Users can create themes themselves or get them from a variety of sources. Many users rely on the themes that come with the Windows NT Resource Kit, Windows 95/98, or from a number of sites on the Internet.

NOTE   I won't get into the issues of copyrights and themes. There are a number of themes that surely impinge upon the rights of others, for example, *Star Trek*, *Star Wars*, *Three Stooges*, *The Simpsons*, and a host of other themes floating around on the Internet. Some are licensed, and most are the creation of the fans who have made these themes available to the public, usually for free. If you use a particular theme, whether you pay for it or not is a value decision that you will have to make. Myself, I'd prefer that everyone respected the intellectual property rights of others.

Though many modifications mentioned in this chapter may be done using various Properties dialog boxes, some cannot be done except by modifying the registry. Of course, I recommend using the easiest method to change things when possible—that would be the Properties dialog box, in most cases.

The registry hive HKEY_USERS\.DEFAULT\Control Panel\Desktop contains the settings used by Windows NT when no user is logged on. Notice that this sub-hive includes many settings that probably won't mean much to the system. In the "no user logged on" mode, Windows NT *normally* doesn't display icons or much of anything else. Notice I said "normally"; there are ways to force Windows NT to do just this. For example, you can allow services to interact with the Desktop and start the service before a user logs on.

The registry hive HKEY_USERS\<SID>\Control Panel\Desktop is the hive used to hold the current user's Desktop settings. Note that the <SID> (Security IDentifier) is a placeholder for a user's SID. Usually, finding your SID is easy; just take a peek at the HKEY_USERS hive. There will be two sub-hives: .DEFAULT (for use when no user is logged on) and a sub-hive identified by a SID value— this is your SID.

Backgrounds and Wallpapers

At some point, every user has probably wondered about the difference between a background and wallpaper. Both are bitmaps; the background bitmap is typically small, consisting of one or two colors. Wallpaper is usually an image that covers some, or all, of the exposed Desktop.

The background is under everything else. When drawing, the first thing that Windows NT does with the Desktop is to draw the background bitmap in the background color selected. The Windows NT default is pea-green—not my favorite color. If no background bitmap is selected, Windows NT by default draws the background as a solid color.

NOTE   We'll talk about changing that pea-green background color later, don't worry. Having a solid color background can improve system performance when compared to having a bitmap for the background.

Once the background is drawn, Windows NT draws the wallpaper. Wallpaper is drawn in one of three modes:

Centered—One copy of the wallpaper is drawn in the center of the screen.

Tiled—The first copy of the wallpaper is drawn in the upper-left corner of the screen; additional copies are drawn below and to the left to fill the entire screen with the wallpaper bitmap. Some bitmaps are designed to fit together well, hiding this seam; while other bitmaps present a jagged, clumsy look when tiled.

Stretched—This refers to the Windows NT Plus! functionality. Plus! is built into Windows NT and is not an option as it was with Windows 95. In this case, Windows NT automatically stretches the wallpaper bitmap to fit the screen dimensions. This is the most commonly used mode, and it is also the most inefficient one.

NOTE   If you primarily use one resolution, you can improve performance by doing the following: When using a bitmap as wallpaper in stretched mode, consider using a graphics editor to stretch the bitmap to the screen's resolution. Then, select the Centered option to display the wallpaper. Windows NT's Desktop update may be substantially improved by doing this.

After drawing the wallpaper, Windows NT draws objects, such as Desktop icons and other windows.

Icons and their labels are handled in a special manner. The icon image is drawn over the wallpaper. Next, the area under the icon's label is filled with the background color, but not the background pattern; the label's background is a solid color. Next the text for the icon is drawn, so what you see under the text of an icon is not the wallpaper, but the background color or bitmap.

As well, there are two sets of background/wallpaper settings. Windows NT maintains one set for each user, although you can only access the settings for your userid when logged on. Another collection of settings is used to customize what is displayed before any user logs on. In theory, anyone can change the settings for Windows NT to display before any user logs on. This is done by modifying the HKEY_USERS\.default sub-hive settings.

The registry entries affecting background and wallpaper display are discussed next.

Wallpaper

Wallpaper is a string that must contain the filename of the file to be used for the wallpaper. The name, data type, and typical or default value are as follows:

Wallpaper

Type: REG_SZ

Typical value: (Default)

The file should be a standard (noncompressed) Windows NT bitmap, and the resolution should be compatible with the current display mode. If the resolution is different from the display mode, it is not the end of the world, but the quality of the display will be compromised.

If you are specifying a file that is not in the %SystemRoot% path, be sure to include a fully qualified path name. Generally, the Display Properties dialog box in Windows NT will include path-name information regardless of where the file is located.

This parameter is compatible with both specific users and the .DEFAULT user sub-hives. It allows you to configure the Desktop display before any user has logged on. When configuring the Desktop display before a user has logged on, consider placing your company logo there!

WallpaperStyle

WallpaperStyle tells Windows NT to stretch or compress a wallpaper bitmap that is different from the Desktop in size or resolution to fit the Desktop fully. The name, data type, and a typical or default value are as follows:

> WallpaperStyle
>
> Type: REG_SZ
>
> Typical value: 0

If carried to extremes, this mode can result in a Desktop that is visually unappealing. Generally, if the wallpaper image is close to the size of the Desktop, the appearance will be acceptable. Certain bitmaps stretch better than others, so if in doubt, try it.

The WallpaperStyle parameter is compatible with both specific users and the .DEFAULT user sub-hives. It allows you to configure the Desktop display before any user has logged on. For the .DEFAULT user configuration, consider stretching either wallpaper that is a different size from the default logon screen or wallpaper that is designed to be stretched.

TileWallpaper

The wallpaper may be tiled or centered using TileWallpaper. The name, data type, and a typical or default value are as follows:

> TileWallpaper

Type: REG_SZ

Typical value: 0

It is possible to have a single copy of the wallpaper that is not centered; see the sections "WallpaperOriginX" and "WallpaperOriginY," discussed next. To center the wallpaper, set this parameter to 0; to tile the wallpaper, set this parameter to 1.

This parameter is compatible with both specific users and the .DEFAULT user sub-hives. It allows you to configure the Desktop display before any user has logged on. For the .DEFAULT user configuration, consider tiling a wallpaper that is either a small bitmap or that is designed to be tiled.

WallpaperOriginX

WallpaperOriginX allows the user to set the origin for both tiled and untiled wallpaper displays as shown here. This registry object is as follows:

WallpaperOriginX

Type: REG_SZ

Typical value: 0

It's useful if, for example, you want to set your wallpaper to be in one of the corners of the Desktop. This parameter works with both centered and tiled wallpapers.

This parameter is compatible with both specific users and the .DEFAULT user sub-hives. It allows you to configure the Desktop display before any user has logged on. For the .DEFAULT user configuration, consider re-centering the wallpaper to provide an aesthetically pleasing Desktop. I find that having a small company logo in the lower-right corner of the screen can be pleasing!

WallpaperOriginY

The WallpaperOriginY allows the user to set the origin for both tiled and untiled wallpaper displays. The name, data type, and a typical or default value are as follows:

WallpaperOriginY

Type: REG_SZ

Typical value: 0

It's useful if, for example, you want to set your wallpaper to be in one of the corners of the Desktop. This parameter works with both centered and tiled wallpapers.

This parameter is compatible with both specific users and the .DEFAULT user sub-hives. It allows you to configure the Desktop display before any user has logged on. For the .DEFAULT user configuration, consider re-centering the wallpaper to provide an aesthetically pleasing Desktop. I find that having a small company logo in the lower-right corner of the screen can be pleasing!

Pattern

Pattern contains the pattern that is drawn using the background Desktop color. It is stored as a string containing eight numbers. The name, data type, and a typical or default value are as follows:

>Pattern
>
>Type: REG_SZ
>
>Typical value: (None)

Each number is converted to a line in a bitmap. Each 1 in the binary number will represent the Desktop color.

This parameter is compatible with both specific users and the .DEFAULT user sub-hives. This allows you to configure the Desktop display before any user has logged on. For the .DEFAULT user configuration, consider using a pattern when stretched or tiled wallpaper is not being used.

Task Switching

Task switching is usually done with the keystroke combination Alt-Tab, although some of us use the Taskbar. The Task Switch dialog box can be configured by the user if he or she so desires.

Settings for this dialog box are simple to implement. Since there is no task switching before a user logs on, these settings are only meaningful to users who are logged on. Though the settings can be set for the .DEFAULT user, they will have no useful effect.

CoolSwitch

CoolSwitch is used to control whether or not a task change window is displayed. An example of this registry item is as follows:

> CoolSwitch
>
> Type: REG_SZ
>
> Typical value: 1

Originally, versions earlier than Windows NT 4 used two styles of task switching. In *direct switching*, the system cycled through the running applications as the task switch key stroke combination was pressed. Usually, only the application's title bar was made active until the user released the task switch key. The second method of task switching, *CoolSwitch*, was used to display a dialog box, similar to that used in Windows NT 4, to allow the user to select the application to switch to. Windows NT 4 only supports the second method. Therefore, the CoolSwitch enabling registry key is not used in Windows NT 4. Setting this entry to any value other than 1 seems to have no effect. It is not recommended that this key be changed, so that compatibility with future upgrades of Windows NT will be retained.

CoolSwitchColumns

The number of columns in the CoolSwitch dialog box is set using CoolSwitch-Columns, as shown here. An example of this registry item follows:

> CoolSwitchColumns
>
> Type: REG_SZ
>
> Typical value: 7

The CoolSwitch dialog box displays icons for each running application that has a window that can be displayed. The CoolSwitch dialog box displays icons in rows and columns. Applications and components that do not have a main window will not be displayed because they cannot be switched to using the task switch keys.

The number of columns, the number of icons across, displayed in the CoolSwitch dialog box is set by this registry key. The default value, 7, is a reasonable choice for most resolutions. However, users may find that with low-resolution displays, fewer columns may be more appropriate. Users with high-resolution displays, running a large number of applications concurrently, might want more columns displayed.

NOTE Are more applications running than will fit in the CoolSwitch dialog box? No problem, CoolSwitch will scroll the icons automatically as the user presses the task switch keystroke combination. However, setting both CoolSwitchColumns and CoolSwitchRows to 1 won't create a single icon CoolSwitch dialog.

CoolSwitchRows

The number of rows in the CoolSwitch dialog box is set using CoolSwitchRows. The name, data type, and a typical or default value follow:

CoolSwitchRows

Type: REG_SZ

Typical value: 2

The CoolSwitch dialog box displays icons for each running application that has a window that can be displayed. The CoolSwitch dialogue box displays icons in rows and columns. Applications and components that do not have a main window will not be displayed because they cannot be switched to by using the task switch keys.

The number of rows, the number of icons up and down, displayed in the CoolSwitch dialog box is set by this registry key. The default value, 2, is a reasonable choice for most users.

Moving Windows

One of the nice things about Windows is its ability to drag things. Windows may be moved using a drag operation, and objects may be dragged and dropped. We can also move windows either by using the keyboard or by simply clicking on the title bar and dragging the window itself.

Icons and objects may both be dragged. This includes selections in documents for those applications that support drag-and-drop. Clicking on the object selects it, and moving the mouse begins a drag-and-drop operation.

There are three registry entries for dragging that are specific to Windows NT: DragFullWindows, DragHeight, and DragWidth. DragFullWindows specifies whether a window's content will be displayed (full content drag) while moving it, or whether only the window's outline will be displayed. The other two entries specify the size the box must be in a drag operation before Windows NT will consider the object as actually being dragged.

Why change the size of the drag box? Some users who have difficulty controlling the amount that they move the mouse may find it preferable to set a larger drag area.

DragFullWindows

Earlier versions of Windows only supported a mode called outline dragging. DragFullWindows allows dragging both a window and the window's contents. The name, data type, and a typical or default value for this registry item are shown here:

DragFullWindows

Type: REG_SZ

Typical value: 1

This was necessary primarily due to the incredible lack of performance of early CPUs and video systems. Newer hardware, improvements in video driver technology, and other changes have brought full-window dragging to Windows NT.

To drag the entire window with contents, set this parameter to 1; to drag only a window outline, set this parameter to 0.

There is not much dragging done before a user logs on, so these entries probably won't matter much to the .DEFAULT configuration.

DragHeight

DragHeight determines the height of the rectangle used to detect the start of a drag operation. The name, data type, and a typical or default value for this registry item are shown here:

DragHeight

Type: REG_SZ

Typical value: 2

The object is clicked and the mouse pointer is moved more than DragHeight and/or DragWidth, and Windows NT will assume that a drag operation is being performed.

DragWidth

DragWidth determines the width of the rectangle used to detect the start of a drag operation. The name, data type, and a typical or default value for this registry item are shown here:

DragWidth

Type: REG_SZ

Typical value: 2

The object is clicked and the mouse pointer is moved more than the DragWidth (and/or DragHeight), and Windows NT will assume that a drag operation is being performed.

The Cursor

The cursor can be configured somewhat. The only parameter that can be set for the cursor (sometimes called the *text caret*) is the blink rate. Some video systems, such as portables and video projection systems, don't react well to fast blink rates. Setting the CursorBlinkRate (discussed next) to a higher value may make the cursor easier to see.

CursorBlinkRate

CursorBlinkRate specifies in milliseconds the blink rate of the cursor. The name, data type, and a typical or default value for this registry item are shown here:

CursorBlinkRate

Type: REG_SZ

Typical value: 530

A smaller value will make the cursor blink faster, while larger values make it blink slower.

NOTE   Where'd that odd value of 530 milliseconds come from? Why not just use 500 milliseconds, which is half a second? Got me. I know this is a holdover from the earliest versions of Windows, though.

Menus and the Windows 95 User Interface

The Windows 95/98 user interface allows users more flexibility when selecting menu items. Menu selections follow the cursor better in Windows NT 4 and display cascading menus as the cursor is positioned over them. Try your Start menu for a good example of menu cascading.

The MenuShowDelay entry in the registry controls cascading menu delays. This entry is discussed next.

MenuShowDelay

MenuShowDelay controls how long Windows NT will delay before showing a cascading menu. The name, data type, and a typical or default value for this registry item are shown here:

> MenuShowDelay
>
> Type: REG_SZ
>
> Typical Value: 400

If the user pauses on a menu item that has a cascading menu under it, after the period of time specified in milliseconds, the cascading menu will be displayed automatically.

Slower processors may work better with a smaller value. However, generally, the default of 400 milliseconds works well in all Windows NT installations.

Keyboard Settings

InitialKeyboardIndicators is used to set or clear keyboard toggle keys, such as Num Lock and caps lock. The name, data type, and a typical or default value for this registry item are shown here:

> InitialKeyboardIndicators

Type: REG_SZ

Typical value: 0

The Num Lock key can be problematic because many users wish to have it turned on at the time they log on. There are two ways to ensure that this happens. One way is to turn on the Num Lock key then press Ctrl-Alt-Delete and select the Logoff button. Alternately, in the registry, change the user's setting in either HKEY_USERS\<SID>\Control Panel\Keyboard or HKEY_CURRENT_USER\Control Panel\Keyboard. Change the data key InitialKeyboardIndicators from whatever value it already has to 2. This will force the Num Lock key to be on.

NOTE   Other values in the Keyboard data key also may be used to control the other toggle keys, such as Caps Lock and Scroll Lock.

The Mouse and the Microsoft Intellimouse

There are a number of settings for the mouse and the new Microsoft Intellimouse. The Intellimouse has a design with a new feature—a wheel that is used to scroll windows. As Microsoft's Intellimouse support improves, more and more applications will work with the scroll wheel. The scroll wheel has a switch that functions as a separate button. This button may be assigned its own functionality.

WheelScrollLines

Only meaningful for the Intellimouse, this data key specifies the number of lines to scroll whenever the mouse wheel is moved. The name, data type, and a typical or default value are shown here:

WheelScrollLines

Type: REG_SZ

Typical value: 3

The wheel has discrete degrees of movement that provide tactile feedback to the user. The default value is to scroll both up and down three lines.

I took some time to experiment with using the wheel, or Intellimouse, for scrolling. Before long, it became second nature. It can be very fast and easy to use.

NOTE   Be sure to get Microsoft's latest driver for the Intellimouse. Alhough there is some native support for wheel mice in Windows NT, the latest drivers offer much improved performance.

DoubleClickHeight and DoubleClickWidth

These two settings control how much the mouse may move before Windows NT won't consider two clicks in quick succession to be a double-click. Their names, data types, and typical or default values are shown here:

DoubleClickHeight

DoubleClickWidth

Type: REG_SZ

Typical value: 4

For most users, the default values are fine. However, users with notebook computers that don't have good pointer resolution and users with handicaps may wish to make the double-click tolerance higher, especially when the users are working with a high-resolution screen.

Other User Interface Settings

There are a few other user interface settings that you can use with Windows NT. Some of these just don't fit well in the previous section, so we'll give them their own home.

Change Your Favorites with User Shell Folders\Favorites

Displaying Internet Explorer's Favorites list in the Start menu allows you to quickly jump to an Internet Explorer favorite item. To do so, follow these steps:

1. At a command prompt, create a new directory (using the command MD) named WWW in the following location: "%USERPROFILE%\Start Menu\WWW". Be sure to include the quotes in this command because this is a long filename.

2. Copy all your favorites, typically in %UserProfile%\Favorites, to your new directory at "%USERPROFILE%\Start Menu\WWW".

3. In the registry, go to HKEY_CURRENT_USER\Software\Microsoft\ Windows\CurrentVersion\ Explorer\User Shell Folders.

4. Edit the data key Favorites and change its value to "%USERPROFILE%\ Start Menu\WWW". This will force Internet Explorer to use your new Favorites directory instead of your original favorites.

Customize the Properties Pop-up Menu

To customize the generic Properties pop-up menu to add an Open With menu selection, do the following:

1. In HKEY_CLASSES_ROOT* create a new sub-hive, called openas.

2. In HKEY_CLASSES_ROOT*\openas, created in step 1 create a sub-hive called "command".

3. In HKEY_CLASSES_ROOT*\openas\command change the data key, which is named (default) in RegEdit or <no name> in RegEdt32 to have the value "%SystemRoot%\System32\rundll32.exe %SystemRoot%\System32\ shell32.dll,OpenAs_RunDLL %1"

Custom Icons on the Desktop

It is possible to use the Display Properties dialog box in the Control Panel to change the icon for the following objects: My Computer, Network Neighborhood, Recycle Bin (full), and Recycle Bin (empty). Fine and dandy. But what about the other system icons?

The icon that is most often changed is that yellow folder icon that is used when Windows NT displays a directory on the Desktop. With all those bright colors and complex icons, the yellow folder icon is just a bit plain. That one's easy to fix; you can change the icon in the Properties dialog for the specific folder.

Other icons can be more problematic. For example, changing some of the icons on the Desktop can be most intimidating. Table 11.1 lists some of the Windows NT Desktop objects that have icons that are difficult to change.

TABLE 11.1: CLSIDs for Some Desktop Objects

Name	CLSID
Inbox	00020D75-0000-0000-C000-000000000046
Internet Explorer 1.0	0002DF01-0000-0000-C000-000000000046
Internet Explorer 2.x/3.x/4/x	FBF23B42-E3F0-101B-8488-00AA003E56F8
Microsoft Outlook	00020D75-0000-0000-C000-000000000046
My Computer	20D04FE0-3AEA-1069-A2D8-08002B30309D
Network Neighborhood	208D2C60-3AEA-1069-A2D7-08002B30309D
Recycle Bin	645FF040-5081-101B-9F08-00AA002F954E
The Internet	3DC7A020-0ACD-11CF-A9BB-00AA004AE837
The Microsoft Network (MSN)	00028B00-0000-0000-C000-000000000046

NOTE   The Recycle Bin has three default icons: one for empty, one for full, and one that Windows NT displays. You must change the icon that is named (default) in RegEdit or <no name> in RegEdt32, when either or both of the empty or full icons are changed. See the sidebar, "The Recyce Bin's Icons," later in this chapter for more information on changing the Recycle Bin's icons.

To change the Desktop icon for one of the above mentioned objects, go to HKEY_CLASSES_ROOT\CLSID in the registry and scroll down until you find the CLSID (from Table 11.1) for the item that you wish to change. Open the hive and open the sub-hive named DefaultIcon under that hive.

In the DefaultIcon sub-hive there will be a default entry, REG_SZ, containing the path to the icon to display. Simply change that path to another icon path.

Figure 11.1 shows the registry entry for the Recycle Bin. This entry is the most complex of the Desktop icons, in that the Recycle Bin will automatically switch between an icon representing the full or empty state as necessary. Windows NT always displays the icon that is in the (default) entry and doesn't know about any other entries in the DefaultIcon sub-hive. Getting ideas here? You can hide a few icon definitions in the DefaultIcon sub-hive for later manual retrieval if you want.

FIGURE 11.1:

The Recycle Bin has two icons, plus the (default) entry for icons. You can change both the empty and full icons if you want. All the other objects only have the (default) entry.

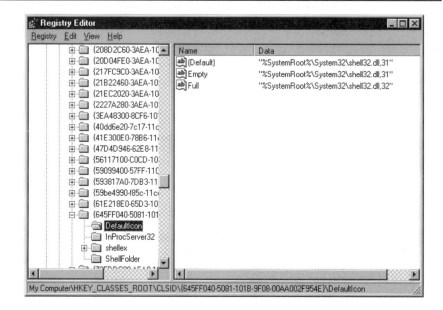

The Recycle Bin's Icons

The Recycle Bin has two icons: one for empty and one for full. You may change either or both. If you check the Recycle Bin's sub-hive, you will see how they are arranged (see Figure 11.1). Either the empty icon or the full icon will match the icon specified in the (default) entry. You must maintain this relationship. For example, if the empty icon entry matches the (default) entry, change both at the same time to the same value. The Recycle Bin automatically changes the default icon depending on its state by copying either the full or empty icon description to the (default) entry.

Windows NT displays only the icon in the data key, named (default) in RegEdit, or <no name> in RegEdt32 entry because Windows NT knows nothing about the Recycle Bin, the empty or full icons, or the state of the Recycle Bin.

If the Recycle Bin's icons get out of sync, drop a file into the Recycle Bin, then empty it. This should force the Recycle Bin to re-synchronize the displayed icon.

Want More Icons?

There are two main sources of icons in Windows NT. The first, `shell32.dll`, has several of the icons used by Windows NT for many components. Most of the program's executable files contain icons, too.

Another file that contains only icons is `moricons.dll`. This file is found in the `%SystemRoot%\System32` directory. This file contains hundreds of icons of all different types. If you find that none of the icons in `shell32.dll` are to your liking, check out the `moricons.dll` file.

Enhancing the Start Menu

You may add a number of new entries to the Start menu, such as a quick shortcut to specific Control Panel applets. This process is not really a registry modification; but you do use CLSIDs , so we'll pretend that it is.

A folder named with *<any name>*.*<{CLSID}>*, as shown in the following format example, is handled differently by Windows NT. Windows NT will use Explorer to display the part of the name before the period. (Remember, Explorer is used to display the Start menu, too.) The part after the period, the CLSID number, will be used to fill in the directory structure.

For example, a directory named Control Panel.{21ec2020-3aea-1069-a2dd-08002b30309d} will display the word Control Panel in Explorer and in the Start menu. The following Windows NT components will support this behavior:

- Control Panel.{21EC2020-3AEA-1069-A2DD-08002B30309D}

- Printers.{2227A280-3AEA-1069-A2DE-08002B30309D}

- Dial-Up Networking.{992CFFA0-F557-101A-88EC-00DD010CCC48}

- Recycle Bin {645FF040-5081-101B-9F08-00AA002F954E}.

NOTE   When creating one of these special folders, don't forget to enclose the CLSID in curly braces. It won't work otherwise. The name, the portion before the period, may be any name that you desire.

Sounds That Microsoft Never Gave Us

It is possible to add new sounds to Windows NT. For example, every time you start RegEdit, you could have Ringin.wav play that nice bell sound that can't be ignored.

NOTE This process requires setting the (default) variable and works best if done with RegEdit. RegEdt32 will work, however. Instead of performing step 5 in the following instructions, use the Sounds applet in the Control Panel to set the value. RegEdt32 will not automatically create a (default) variable. RegEdt32 calls the (default) variable <No Name>. However, the Sounds applet will allow you to fill in the (default) variable.

To add new sounds, follow these steps:

1. Start RegEdit (or RegEdt32) and open the sub-hive HKEY_CURRENT_USER\AppEvents\Schemes\Apps.

2. Create a new sub-hive named RegEdit; use the name of the program that you are adding sounds for.

3. In your new RegEdit hive, create a sub-hive called Open.

4. In your new Open hive, create a sub-hive called .Current. Don't forget the leading period.

5. In your .Current sub-hive, set the (default) variable to Ringin.wav. Remember that when using RegEdt32, the (default) variable will display as <No Name>, if it exists.

Once the registry entries in steps 2, 3, and 4 have been completed; you may also use the Sounds applet in the Control Panel to set the sound played. This will make setting the sounds easier because the Sounds applet permits browsing and previewing sounds.

Make DLL Files Show Their Own Icons

DLL files, when displayed in Explorer, are all displayed as a generic DLL icon. This generic icon conveys no information about the DLL file, other than the fact that the file is a DLL.

Many DLL files have one or more icons. The technique described in this section will force Explorer to display the DLL's first icon, if there is one, or the generic Windows file icon if there is no icon in the DLL file.

Change the value contained in HKEY_CLASSES_ROOT\dllfile\DefaultIcon to the string "%1". The original value, "%SystemRoot%\System32\shell32.dll,-154", is the generic icon for DLL files and won't be used anymore.

Easter Egg Hunt?

As many of us know, Microsoft programmers put little credits screens and other goodies into each Microsoft product. These screens are popularly called Easter Eggs because they are meant to be found by users, perhaps by accident. Windows NT 4 and Windows 95/98 each have at least one of these.

Windows NT contains several Easter Eggs. They are placed in the OpenGL 3D Text screen saver.

To display the Easter Egg, follow these steps:

1. Open the Display Properties dialog box either by context-clicking (right-clicking) on the Desktop or by using the Control Panel.

2. In the Screen Saver tab, select the 3D Text (OpenGL) screen saver.

3. Click on the Settings button.

4. In the Display group's Text box, enter the word **Volcano**.

5. Change any other settings you wish and click OK.

6. Click the Preview button.

You will see a list of all the volcanoes for the U.S. west coast.

Or, try this:

1. Open the Display Properties dialog box either by context-clicking (right-clicking) on the Desktop or by using the Control Panel.

2. In the Screen Saver tab, select the 3D Text (OpenGL) screen saver.

3. Click on the Settings button.

4. In the Display group's Text box, enter the words **Not Evil**. That's two words, folks!

5. Change any other settings you wish and click OK.

6. Click the Preview button.

You will see a list of all the Windows NT developers.

Console and Command-Prompt Settings

All Windows NT installations will have a sub-hive under HKEY_CURRENT_ USER called Console. Under Console in some installations there will be a second sub-hive called Command Prompt. This section describes customizing these two areas of the user interface. The values discussed in this section affect console and command-prompt windows that do not have a custom configuration created.

> **NOTE**   The Command Prompt sub-hive will not be created until the user changes the screen colors or font of the command-prompt window and saves the changed settings.

All changes to the Console sub-hive will change the default values for all command-prompt windows created after the change takes effect. Once a window has been opened, use the Properties dialog box to change the window's attributes.

The user may create additional sub-hives under the HKEY_CURRENT_ USER\Console hive. Name each sub-hive created with the same name as a console window's title. When Windows NT creates a console window with the same name as a sub-hive found in HKEY_CURRENT_USER\Console, Windows NT will use the setting in this sub-hive to configure the window's default view.

Foreground and Background Colors

A command prompt's foreground and background colors may be changed by the user. I prefer a light gray background with black characters; or sometimes I use dark blue characters. There are three areas that affect colors: the color table entries, the command-prompt window colors, and the pop-up window colors.

By modifying the color table entries, ColorTable00 through ColorTable15, a custom color pallet can be created. Windows NT allows modification of the color pallet in the Properties dialog box, although some users may be able to use the registry for this.

Setting the foreground and background indexes into the color table entries changes the window colors. Indexes are stored for both foreground and background as a single DWORD entry.

ColorTable00 through ColorTable15

The color table is used to allow users to select colors for fonts and backgrounds. The names, data types, and typical or default values are as follows:

ColorTable00 through ColorTable15

Type: REG_DWORD

Typical value: (RGB value, varies)

The default colors for a command window are white on a black background. You can display the command window's Properties dialog box from the window's system menu. Or you can open a command window, choose properties, and right-click on the window's title bar.

The Properties dialog box contains four tabs. Choose the final tab, labeled "Colors". In this tab, the user is allowed to choose a color for both the window's and the pop-up window's background and foreground from the standard 16-color palette. See Figure 11.2.

FIGURE 11.2:

The Colors tab allows setting colors and color palettes.

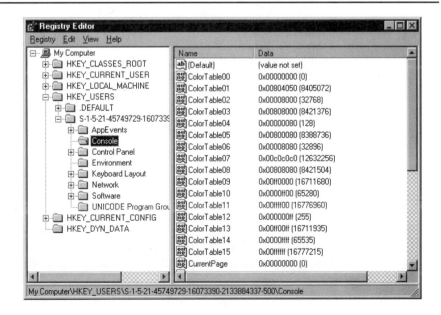

The standard palette allows selecting the rather common and mundane colors. It also allows the user to customize colors using a set of edit controls. Some users will want the custom colors to be available. An alternative to setting these colors manually, one by one, is to change them in HKEY_CURRENT_USER\Console.

Each color index is expressed as a DWORD, consisting of red, green, and blue values; such as 00RRGGBB. Each color value may range from 0 to 255.

PopupColors

A pop-up window can be used to inform the user of some action or problem. It may have its colors set independently from the colors of the command window itself. The name, data type, and a typical or default value follow:

PopupColors

Type: REG_DWORD

Typical value: 0xF5

The DWORD value is split into two 4-bit nibbles; 1 byte is used and the other 3 are ignored. This allows both the foreground and background color indexes to be specified. These colors are indexes to the ColorTablenn entries. The first 4 bits, 5 in the preceding typical value, are the foreground color index. The second 4 bits, the F in the preceding typical value, are the background color index.

ScreenColors

Command windows may have both foreground and background colors set using ScreenColors. The name, data type, and typical or default value follow:

ScreenColors

Type: REG_DWORD

Typical value: 0x07

The DWORD value is split into two 4-bit nibbles; 1 byte is used and the other three are ignored. This allows both the foreground and background color indexes to be specified. These colors are indexes to the ColorTablenn entries. The first 4 bits, 7 in the preceding typical value, specify the foreground color index. The second 4 bits, the 0 in the preceding typical value, specify the background color index.

Memory Used by Command-Prompt Windows

A couple of settings control the memory used by a command-prompt window. This memory is only for the display and does not affect memory available for applications, for example.

CurrentPage

CurrentPage specifies the current page to use. This is a system variable that should not be reset by the user. The name, data type, and typical or default value follow:

> CurrentPage
>
> Type: REG_DWORD
>
> Typical value: 0x3

ScreenBufferSize

This entry specifies the size of the screen buffer. The buffer size is specified as a height and width value. The name, data type, and typical or default value follow:

> ScreenBufferSize
>
> Type: REG_DWORD
>
> Typical value: 0x190050

The DWORD value is split into two halves, allowing both the width and height of the screen buffer to be specified in characters. The low order word specifies the width, while the high order word specifies the height. For example, 0x00190050 specifies a screen buffer that is 0x19 (25) lines high and 80 characters wide.

Cursors

The cursor attributes may be set to allow the cursor size to be customized. The standard cursor for a Windows NT command-prompt window is a modified underline cursor with the option of setting this cursor to a block cursor of varying size. I say modified underline cursor because it is actually a very short block cursor that looks like an underline.

CursorSize

CursorSize specifies the amount of the character cell that will be filled with the cursor. The name, data type, and typical or default value follow:

CursorSize

Type: REG_DWORD

Typical value: 0x19 (That's 25 in decimal.)

The Properties dialog allows setting the cursor to three sizes: Small, Medium, and Large (see Figure 11.3). Actually, this value may be a number between 0, no cursor will be displayed, and 99, a full block cursor will be displayed.

FIGURE 11.3:

The Options tab allows setting many different options, such as three different cursor sizes.

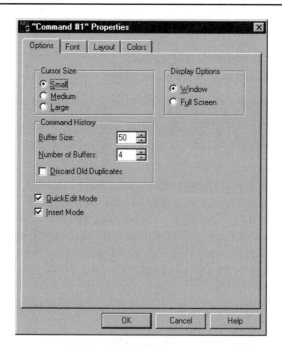

Keep in mind that the cursor consists of discrete lines and it is based on the command-prompt window's font size. As the font size gets larger, the user has more control over the size of the cursor.

NOTE   Windows NT does not have any provision for a non-blinking cursor. Such is life—it just blinks on and on and on.

Fonts

Font attributes may be set, in a limited fashion, from the Font tab of the command-prompt Properties dialog box (see Figure 11.4). More full control is available to users in the registry. Setting font values requires an understanding of fonts, especially when using complex ones, such as TrueType.

FIGURE 11.4:

The Font tab allows setting some font specifications. More flexibility may be gained by directly manipulating the registry.

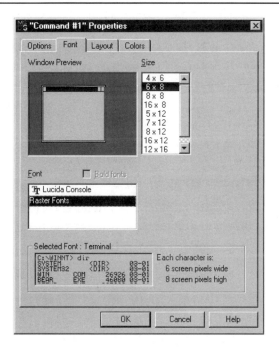

For simple changes, such as font size and so on, use the Properties dialog box. To select fonts that are not available normally, or sizes that the dialog box doesn't allow to be set, direct manipulation of the registry is the way to go.

FaceName

FaceName specifies the font used to display characters in a command-prompt window and is by default a raster font. The name, data type, and typical or default value follow, the value is blank by default:

> FaceName
>
> Type: REG_SZ
>
> Typical value:

A *raster font* is created in a cell, say 8 dots wide by 12 dots high, producing a monospaced font. Raster fonts are faster for Windows NT to process, but usually don't have much size flexibility. They are also generally lower in quality due to size constraints. Complex fonts, such as the TrueType fonts, are infinitely variable in size and are typically a higher quality when displayed in larger sizes. However, a complex font, such as a TrueType font, requires more system resources (CPU capacity) to display because the font must be created when it is used.

Most command windows use the default font, which is an undefined raster font. The font size may vary depending on screen resolution, although a default size in most installations is 8x12, providing a reasonable, readable display.

FontFamily

FontFamily specifies the font family for the window's display font. There are a number of different families, such as TrueType and raster. The name, data type, and typical or default value follow:

> FontFamily
>
> Type: REG_DWORD
>
> Typical value: 0

This entry is a DWORD, with values ranging from:

0—Don't care which is used

10—Roman family

20—Swiss family

30—Modern family

40—Script family

50—Decorative family

As the most flexible font family specification is 0 or "don't care," most users do not change this value.

WARNING   Before setting font family values, be sure to understand what a family value is and how it is specified. Setting an invalid family value may cause the display to be different from what was expected.

FontSize

FontSize specifies the value for the font displayed. The name, data type, and typical or default value follow:

FontSize

Type: REG_DWORD

Typical value: 0

The DWORD value is split into two halves, allowing both the width and height of the characters to be specified. The low order word specifies the width, while the high order word specifies the height. For example, 0x0008000C specifies a character that is 8x12 in size.

FontWeight

The FontWeight value specifies whether a font is bold or light. The name, data type, and typical or default value follow:

FontWeight

Type: REG_DWORD

Typical value: 0

A default value of zero specifies a default character that is not bold. Values range from 0 to 1000, with typical values shown in Table 11.2.

TABLE 11.2: FontWeight Values

Description	Value
Don't care how bold	0
Thin	100
Extralight	200
Light	300
Normal	400
Medium	500
Semibold	600
Bold	700
Extrabold	800
Heavy	900

NOTE   The Don't care (0) value will be equated with the normal level (400) of bolding.

A generic bold/non-bold may be set from the Command Prompt's Properties Font tab when displaying a TrueType font. Raster fonts may not be made bold.

What the Window Looks Like

The appearance of the command-prompt window may be changed in a number of ways (see Figure 11.5). Direct manipulation is possible: For example, the window location can be set using a simple drag-and-drop procedure.

Other window attributes can be set using the registry or the Properties dialog box for the command-prompt window.

FIGURE 11.5:

The Layout tab allows setting the size, position, and buffer size of the screen.

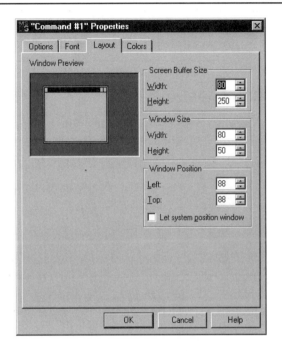

FullScreen

FullScreen specifies whether the console session is either full screen or windowed. The name, data type, and typical or default value follow:

FullScreen

Type: REG_DWORD

Typical value: 0

Most users window their command sessions for ease of use. The two values allowed for this entry are as follows:

1—Full screen mode

0—Windowed mode

NOTE This option is usable only on Windows NT running on Intel x86 machines. RISC systems allow only windowed mode.

WindowSize

WindowSize specifies the size of the command-prompt window. It is specified as a height and width value. The name, data type, and typical or default value follow:

> WindowSize
>
> Type: REG_DWORD
>
> Typical value: 0x190050

The DWORD value is split into two halves, allowing both the width and height of the screen buffer to be specified in characters. The low order word specifies the width, while the high order word specifies the height. For example, 0x00190050 specifies a screen buffer that is 0x19 (25) lines high and 80 characters wide.

WindowPosition

WindowPosition specifies the Window's location on the Desktop relative to the upper left corner. The name, data type, and typical or default value for this registry item are as follows:

> WindowPosition
>
> Type: REG_DWORD
>
> Typical value: 0x000000000

This position is specified as a number of pixels in the x and y axes.

The DWORD value is split into two halves, allowing both the x and y axes of the window to be specified in pixels. The low order word (A DWORD consists of two words.) specifies the width, while the high order word specifies the height. For example, 0x00000000 specifies that the command prompt will be located in the upper left part of the Desktop at screen coordinates 0,0.

NOTE   When WindowPosition is set using the Properties dialog, Windows NT keeps the user from entering a value that might cause the window to be placed entirely off the Desktop. However, when setting these values manually, there is no safeguard to prevent placing the window off the screen. This presents some interesting possibilities.

The Command History Buffer

The command history buffer is activated with the up and down arrow keys. It may be configured both in the command prompt's Properties dialog box and in the registry. The buffer size, the number of buffers, whether duplicates are stored, and so on may all be set.

Why do we set the number of commands stored in a buffer and the number of buffers, as well? I haven't found a satisfactory answer to this question. I am not aware of advantages of having multiple smaller buffers versus having a few large buffers. Microsoft has not clarified this.

The command history management is actually performed by a program called DosKey, which is loaded by Windows NT every time a command-prompt session is started. DosKey allows the definition of keys, the creation of macros, and so on.

For more information on DosKey, enter the command **DosKey /?** at any command prompt. The help screen will assist you in using DosKey.

HistoryBufferSize

Windows NT maintains a command buffer that allows users to recall previously entered commands for re-execution. The name, data type, and typical or default value are shown here:

> HistoryBufferSize
>
> Type: REG_DWORD
>
> Typical value: 0x32 (That's 50 in decimal.)

This command buffer is activated using the up and down arrow keys. The history buffer size is specified in number of commands stored.

A number of buffers can be set in the Command Prompt Properties dialog regardless of whether duplicate commands are saved or not.

HistoryNoDup

HistoryNoDup specifies whether duplicate entries that allow users to recall previously entered commands for re-execution will be retained in the command buffer. The name, data type, and typical or default value are shown here:

HistoryNoDup

Type: REG_DWORD

Typical value: 0x0

This command buffer is activated using the up and down arrow keys. The history buffer size is specified in number of commands stored.

This key controls whether duplicate commands are saved or not. Values allowed in this entry are as follows:

1—Discard duplicates

0—Keep duplicates

NumberOfHistoryBuffers

NumberOfHistoryBuffers specifies the size of the Windows NT command buffer. The name, data type, and typical or default value are shown here:

NumberOfHistoryBuffers

Type: REG_DWORD

Typical value: 0x4

The command buffer is activated using the up and down arrow keys.

This entry allows you to specify how many buffers are to be used; see the previous section, "HistoryBufferSize." The default value, 4, is usually adequate for most users.

Miscellaneous Settings

A couple of settings that don't seem to fit into other categories are covered here. Settings for the default value of insert mode and the setting for the QuickEdit feature are both helpful to users.

InsertMode

A command-prompt window allows a default insert/overwrite mode; the default may be changed by pressing the Insert key on the keyboard. The name, data type, and typical or default value are shown here:

> InsertMode
>
> Type: REG_DWORD
>
> Typical value: 1

Most users set insert on (This is my preference.), although some users find overwrite mode is more convenient for them.

QuickEdit

QuickEdit is a mode that allows the user to quickly mark, copy to the Clipboard, and paste information from the Clipboard with the mouse. The name, data type, and typical or default value are shown here:

> QuickEdit
>
> Type: REG_DWORD
>
> Typical value: 0

Values allowed in this mode are QuickEdit disabled, which allows normal editing and is signified with a value of 0; and QuickEdit enabled, which is signified with a value of 1.

CompletionChar

CompletionChar is located in HKEY_USERS/Software/Microsoft/Command Processor. This registry data key tells Windows NT to complete a partially typed filename when the user presses a specified key. The name, data type, and typical or default value are shown here:

CompletionChar

Type: REG_DWORD

Typical value: 0

Many users set this key's value to 9, the numeric value for the tab key. Other keys could be used, but be careful not to select a key that is already used with Windows NT.

After setting this value and logging on again, open a command window. Next, in the root directory, type the command **DIR w**.

Next, press the Tab key or whatever key you assigned to the command completion key. Notice how Windows NT now cycles through each directory or file that begins with the letter w.

NOTE   The sub-hive Command Processor may not be present for users who have upgraded from earlier versions of Windows NT. If this sub-hive is missing, create it and the `CompletionChar` data key. Be sure to preserve both case and spaces in these names and to assign the key's data type as REG_DWORD, in order to ensure that they work correctly.

Hints and Kinks from the Experts

Here are some hints from our experts.

Do Your Users Close the Logon Script Window?   If your users close the logon script window, you may hide it to prevent users from doing this. First, navigate to HKEY_USERS\<each user>\Console. Next, select Edit or Add Value, as appropriate, and add/edit the two following REG_DWORD values:

- WindowSize, with the Radix at Hex, set it to 050005

- WindowPosition, with the Radix at Hex, set it to 04FF06FF

This makes the window very small and positions it off screen so users can't see it and, hence, can't close it.

If this window is invoked when running a command prompt, just maximize it, right-click the title bar, and size/position it using the Layout tab in the Properties dialog box. When you click OK, check Modify shortcut.

(Courtesy of Jerold Schulman)

How Can I Get Windows NT to Use My Keyboard Layout During Logon?   To get Windows NT to use a specified keyboard layout during logon, perform the following steps:

1. Edit HKEY_USERS\.DEFAULT\Keyboard Layout\Preload.

2. Double-click on 1 and change the number to your local layout, which is at HKEY_CURRENT_USER\Keyboard Layout\Preload\1. (You may also change HKEY_USERS\.DEFAULT\Control Panel\International\Locale to this value, but this is not mandatory.)

3. Log off and then log on.

(Courtesy of Jerold Schulman)

CHAPTER

TWELVE

12

Networking and Registry System Entries

- System entries

- Networking

- Disk, directory, and related entries

- Other hardware support entries

- Non-User-Interface software configuration entries

- Hints and kinks from the experts

The Windows NT internal registry entries probably occupy about half of the registry for a typical user. Only after adding many applications does this proportion change much.

Many networking and system registry modifications are easy to do, although unlike changes to the user interface, they can be dangerous. Making a change that is improper can break the operating system, which may prevent you from booting your system. There are many changes that will cause serious damage to the system when done improperly, necessitating restoration of the registry from a backup.

Most networking changes should be done using the Control Panel's Network applet. The main reason for this is that after the changes are made, the Network applet will check the registry to ensure that all networking registry entries are valid. This is not an exhaustive, problem-finding check, rather; the Network applet just updates some entries if updating is necessary. In other words, don't rely on this updating to detect errors. This updating is done during the binding phase.

Do I Always Have to Reboot?

Many times when we use the Network applet to make a change to the registry, we get a message that Windows NT must be restarted to allow the changes to take effect.

Although there are times when Windows NT will work fine without being rebooted, I recommend that you always reboot when the Network applet tells you to do so. If you have systems or software that slow down the rebooting process, such as Microsoft Exchange Server, consider disabling these systems or software while making changes to the networking registry components.

NOTE   Many of the settings for networking won't take effect until you restart the system. Simply logging on again isn't sufficient.

WARNING   Do I have to say it again and again? Back up your registry before making changes in it! Changing the system and networking sections of the registry are extremely dangerous. These sections are some of the most sensitive and difficult ones to modify.

System Entries

System entries are found in many of the registry hives. Most system entries are located in HKEY_LOCAL_MACHINE, HKEY_CURRENT_USER (HKEY_ USERS), and HKEY_CURRENT_CONFIG. We can basically ignore HKEY_CURRENT_ CONFIG, since it contains only a reference to the CurrentControlSet sub-hive contained in HKEY_LOCAL_MACHINE. That is, modifying an object in HKEY_ CURRENT_CONFIG\System would simply modify the corresponding object in HKEY_LOCAL_MACHINE\System. Ditto for HKEY_USERS, since this information is available in HKEY_CURRENT_USER as well.

So at this point, if you examine HKEY_LOCAL_MACHINE you'll see most of the configurations that Windows NT uses for the system. The entries can be divided into a number of major areas, such as networking, disk, and other hardware support, and non-user-interface software configurations.

Networking

Networking is a major component of Windows NT. Virtually every Windows NT user is networked, with many users connected to complex networks.

Often, changes to the network configuration are done using the Control Panel's Network applet. In fact, I'd recommend that you use the Network applet whenever possible, because it is much more difficult to make serious, damaging errors using the Network applet.

Many of the network configuration settings are contained in the sub-hive HKEY_ CURRENT_USER\Software\Microsoft\WindowsNT\CurrentVersion\ Network\. Additionally, other hives in HKEY_LOCAL_MACHINE and elsewhere control the networking environment.

Windows NT handles network issues differently from other Windows NT components, such as video. For example, the network card's configuration is done at a different time from any other interface adapter. Also, the network card configuration is done somewhat differently. These differences are due to the deep-rooted nature of networking with Windows NT.

Once network settings have been initialized, only the most trivial changes may be made to them without necessitating a reboot. Windows NT will advise you, often too frequently, that you must reboot before your changed settings will take effect. Generally, the cautions are accurate—they won't take effect. Sometimes, it is necessary to defer rebooting until a later time, particularly when the computer is a vital network server.

NOTE   Sometimes, you must make two or three different sets of changes at a given time, and NT may tell you after each one that it requires a reboot. Now, if you had infinite time (Anybody got a few hours to spare?), you could go ahead and reboot every time NT suggests it. Often, however, you can skip the reboot until you have made the last change. Then when you reboot you can have all the changes take effect at the same time.

Persistent Connections

Persistent connections are connections to network resources—typically, file-based resources—that are restored each time the user logs on. There are also non-persistent connections that are lost when the user logs off. Persistence is determined when the connection is made.

Here is a connection made from a command prompt, using the NET USE command:

```
NET USE [devicename | *] [\\computername\sharename[\volume] [password |
*]]
        [/USER:[domainname\]username]
        [[/DELETE] | [/PERSISTENT:{YES | NO}]]
```

The NET USE command allows the user to specify persistence, although the default is for the connection to be persistent. When using Explorer to map a network drive, the dialog box used has a checkbox labeled "Reconnect at Logon." When checked, this option creates a persistent connection. Regardless of the method used to create the connection, maintenance of persistence is the same: Either the connection is restored when the user logs on the next time, generally the default, or the connection is lost when the user logs off.

Other than a data key named "Order," which specifies the order for the shared directory connections (If you edit it, the order in the dropdown changes.), the only key in the sub-hive HKEY_CURRENT_USER\Software\Microsoft\Windows NT\ CurrentVersion\Network\Persistent Connections that seems to do anything significant is the data key SaveConnections. This data key specifies the default value used with Explorer when mapping a network drive. The value in the Map Network Drive dialog's Reconnect at Logon checkbox is stored in this data key. If this key is missing, Explorer will assume that the value is Yes.

Just Because Microsoft Says It, Doesn't Mean It's Always So

Concerning persistent connections, the Microsoft Resource Kit for Windows NT states the following about HKEY_CURRENT_USER\Network:

"This key is no longer used. In previous versions of Windows NT, it stored persistent connections. Persistent connections are now stored in HKEY_CURRENT_USER\Software\Microsoft\Windows NT\CurrentVersion\Network\Persistent Connections."

However, with some computers, I've noticed that Windows NT still stores the persistent connection information in HKEY_CURRENT_USER\Network, and not in the sub-hive it identifies in the Resource Kit. This is an example of how you should always check the system itself rather than simply trusting the documentation.

RestoreConnection

Ghosted connections are persistent connections that exist when the actual connection to the server has not been re-established after the user logs on. For example, say user John has persistent connections to 10 network drives. Each time John logs on, Windows NT could restore each network connection, establishing connections with each server. However, what happens when this is done? First, restoring a number of connections is slow. Second, if one or more servers is unavailable at logon time, John will get some sort of message telling him that a connection could not be made. Both situations are problematic because John is always in a hurry. He knows that some of the servers are not available, but he doesn't care because he won't be using those connections until he knows the server is accessible.

Ghosted connections are used when a user doesn't need or want an actual connection until the connection is actually going to be used. Once the user uses the connection, Windows NT will make the necessary connection. In some instances, this technique can cause problems; for example, there will be a delay the first time that an inactive, ghosted connection is used. To avoid such problems, it is possible to disable ghosting with the following registry key:

RestoreConnection

Type: REG_DWORD

Typical value: 0

Values used in this data key are as follows:

0–Ghost the connection, restoring each connection only when the connection is needed.

1–Connection is restored when the user logs on.

This data key is found in HKEY_LOCAL_MACHINE\SYSTEM\Current-ControlSet\Control\NetworkProvider. This data key doesn't exist by default and must be created in order to be used.

OptionalNames

Care to make your server appear as if it had a split personality? This one is easier done than said. In the registry hive HKEY_Local_Machine\System\CurrentControl-Set\Services\LanmanServer\Parameters you may add the following data key:

OptionalNames

Type: REG_SZ or REG_MULTI_SZ

Typical value: "SPLIT"

The system must be rebooted for this change to take effect, but that is a small price to make your network appear to be larger than it really is.

Why do this? Several reasons. Say you add a new server. Eventually, this new server will replace an old, preexisting server. You know that many users have persistent connections to the old server. You create your new server with the name you choose, which will necessarily be different from the old server since it is still in use on the network. You set up the new server, test it, and all is well.

At some quiet time, like when no clients are logged on, you migrate all resources from the old server to the new server. Then you turn off the existing server. Finally, just add the OptionalNames data key using the name of the existing server. Tell users that you are migrating to the new server and that they should use the new server's name, not the old name, whenever they make new connections.

Users will eventually migrate to the new server's name, or you can migrate them manually without disrupting the system.

Improving Network Performance

There are several networking settings that may be used to improve performance. Increasing buffering usually improves performance if sufficient memory is available. The following registry keys, found in HKEY_LOCAL_MACHINE\ System\ CurrentControlSet\Services\LanmanWorkstation\Parameter, can help improve network performance. Some of these data keys may not exist on your system. If they don't exist, it will be necessary to create them.

First, modify or add a MaxCmds value of type REG_DWORD:

MaxCmds

Type: REG_DWORD

Typical value: 15

This registry data key may contain a value between 0 and 255. Since the default value is only 15, our recommendation is to increase it by steps of five, monitoring performance with each change.

Both MaxThreads and MaxCollectionCount also affect network performance:

MaxThreads

Type: REG_DWORD

Typical value: 15

This registry data key should contain the same value as MaxCmds, shown in the previous example.

MaxCollectionCount

Type: REG_DWORD

Typical value: 16

Specify the buffer used for the "character-mode named pipe" writes. You may choose a value up to 65535.

Disk, Directory, and Related Entries

There are probably a thousand different registry entries that affect disk drives. Unfortunately, many are specific to a given hardware configuration. The odds that any two computers would have the same hardware configuration are somewhat remote, unless you bought them all on the same day from the same vendor and had since made all changes yourself. Also, the number of different permutations of hardware makes it difficult to localize common entries that would be significant to the majority of us. However, even with these staggering obstacles, I've plowed ahead and found as many generic disk registry entries as I could. Let's hope that these will answer most of your questions.

Moving Windows NT to a New Directory

In Knowledge Base article "Q154129," Microsoft outlines how to change the name of the directory that Windows NT is installed in. This is not an everyday action. However, for users who have upgraded earlier versions of Windows NT that were installed in a directory with the version number as part of the directory name, this process may make the installation look cleaner. For example, let's say you upgraded an installation of Windows NT 3.51 that was installed in the directory WNT351. You'd like to rename this directory WNT400 to reflect the current version number. Another example involves installing the new version of the operating system into a temporary directory, such as NewWNT, so that you have both versions of Windows NT installed at the same time.

There are two distinct possibilities here. First, if you have installed Windows NT on an NTFS partition, it will be necessary to follow one process. If Windows NT is installed on a FAT partition, another somewhat simpler process may be followed.

To make this change, use whichever method matches the formatting of the Windows NT installation system partition.

FAT System Partitions: First Steps

Users who have installed Windows NT on a FAT partition have a somewhat simpler task. FAT doesn't support security and is compatible with DOS and Windows 95/98, so a boot diskette made on a DOS or compatible machine can be used to access the files on the hard drive.

Microsoft Says "No" to Be Safe

Microsoft doesn't recommend or support renaming the Windows NT system directory. (Can we blame them?) This means that if something goes wrong, you could be up the creek without a paddle. For this reason, before doing this, do a full backup to ensure that you are able to restore the original configuration just in case something goes wrong.

My own precaution is to carefully check applications that have been installed to ensure that none are expecting Windows NT to be installed in a fixed location.

One test to perform first is dumping the registry and searching for the directory, such as C:\WNT351, in the registry. RegEdit and RegEdt32 could also do this search, but a dump edited with a good text editor may work better.

NOTE

I recommend that you have sufficient disk space to hold two copies of the operating system temporarily. This allows you to retain your original installation until you are able to ensure that the change in directory names is working correctly. If you retain two copies, be sure to rename the original so that the system won't see it.

Users of NTFS have to install a second copy of Windows NT to change the installation directory. Luckily, users of FAT partitions don't have to do this. For FAT based systems, perform the following steps:

1. Open a command-prompt window. Type the command **attrib -r-s c:\boot.ini**.

2. Create a bootable DOS diskette. Copy the XCOPY, EDIT, and MOVE command files. Make sure they are compatible with the version of DOS that the diskette was created with.

3. Boot your computer from the bootable DOS disk. Test to ensure that the XCOPY, EDIT, and MOVE commands function correctly. If they are not correctly functioning, correct this problem before continuing.

4. After ensuring that the necessary commands work, make a directory, using the MD command, with the new name that you wish to run Windows NT from—for example, type **MD WNT400**.

5. Use the XCOPY command to copy all the files and sub-directories from the original Windows NT system directory to your new Windows NT system directory.

NOTE

Use the XCOPY command option /E to ensure that even empty sub-directories are copied. There may be empty sub-directories that are necessary for the system to work correctly.

6. Using the EDIT command, change the BOOT.INI file. Edit and change the following lines:

```
multi(0)disk(0)rdisk(0)partition(2)\WNT351="Windows NT Server Version
3.51"
multi(0)disk(0)rdisk(0)partition(2)\WNT351="Windows NT Server Version
3.51" /basevideo /sos
```

Both lines contain a directory reference, in our example, it is WNT351. Change both to read:

```
multi(0)disk(0)rdisk(0)partition(2)\WNT400="Windows NT Server Version
4.00"
multi(0)disk(0)rdisk(0)partition(2)\WNT400="Windows NT Server Version
4.00" /basevideo /sos
```

7. In both cases, the comment in quotes may be changed as well. This comment is used to allow the user to select the operating system and options to be started at boot time.

NOTE

It is not necessary, but may be desirable, to change the attributes in the BOOT.INI file. If you do reset the attributes to System and Read Only, do so after everything is working correctly.

8. Remove your DOS boot diskette and attempt to reboot the system. If Windows NT reboots and runs correctly, continue.

9. Follow the steps outlined later in this chapter under "Completing the Move."

10. Reboot the system. If Windows NT reboots and runs correctly, rename the original Windows NT directory, WNT351 in our example, to a different name (say, WNT351_OLD). Do not delete this directory yet—wait until you have tested the change.

11. Now set the attributes back on BOOT.INI, use the command `attrib c:\boot.ini +r +s`.

12. After a suitable test period with no problems, typically several weeks, back up and then delete the original installation directory that you renamed in step 10.

NTFS System Partitions: First Steps

Users who have installed Windows NT on an NTFS partition have a somewhat more difficult task. NTFS is not accessible from DOS or Windows 95/98, at least not easily accessible in a read/write mode. Because of this limitation, it will be necessary to install a second operating system that is compatible with NTFS—Windows NT.

NOTE   I recommend that you have sufficient disk space to hold two copies of the original operating system temporarily as well as a third, basic installation of the operating system. This allows you to retain your original installation until you are able to ensure that the change in directory names is working correctly. If you retain two copies, be sure to rename the original so that the system won't see it.

To change the system directory name when NTFS is installed, follow these steps:

1. Install a new, temporary copy of Windows NT (If you don't already have one installed, that is.) into a new directory. It is not necessary to install this copy of Windows NT on the boot drive. However, doing so will make things slightly easier.

2. Open a command-prompt window. Type the command `attrib -r-s c:\boot.ini`.

3. Restart the computer, booting your new temporary copy of Windows NT.

4. Log on to Windows NT and open a command window.

5. Make a directory, using the MD command, with the new name that you wish to run Windows NT from; for example, type **MD WNT400**.

6. Use the XCOPY command to copy all the files and sub-directories from the original Windows NT system directory to your new Windows NT system directory.

NOTE

Use the XCOPY command option /E to ensure that even empty sub-directories are copied. There may be empty sub-directories that are necessary for the system to work correctly.

7. Using the edit command, change the BOOT.INI file. Edit and change the following lines, where WNT351 is the original directory that Windows NT was installed in:

```
multi(0)disk(0)rdisk(0)partition(2)\WNT351="Windows NT Server Version
3.51"
multi(0)disk(0)rdisk(0)partition(2)\WNT351="Windows NT Server Version
3.51" /basevideo /sos
```

Both lines contain a directory reference, in our example, it is WNT351. Change both to read:

```
multi(0)disk(0)rdisk(0)partition(2)\WNT400="Windows NT Server Version
4.00"
multi(0)disk(0)rdisk(0)partition(2)\WNT400="Windows NT Server Version
4.00" /basevideo /sos
```

In both cases, the comment in quotes may be changed as well. This comment is used to allow the user to select the operating system and options to be started at boot time.

NOTE

It is not necessary, but may be desirable, to change the attributes on the boot.ini file. If you do not immediately reset the attributes to System and Read Only, do so after everything is working correctly.

8. Attempt to reboot the system, selecting your original installation of Windows NT. If the system reboots OK, continue.

9. Follow the steps outlined under the next section, "Completing the Move."

10. Again, attempt to reboot the system, selecting your original installation of Windows NT. If the original version of Windows NT reboots and runs correctly, rename the original Windows NT directory, WNT351 in our example, to a different name (say, WNT351_OLD). *Do not delete this directory yet—test the system thoroughly first!*

11. Now set the attributes back on BOOT.INI, using the command **attrib c:\boot.ini +r +s**.

12. After a suitable test period with no problems, typically several weeks, back up and then delete the original installation directory that you renamed in step 10.

Completing the Move

Regardless of whether you have an NTFS or FAT partition, the steps described here must also be taken in addition to the ones presented in the separate NTFS and FAT discussions. The file setup.log is used by both RDisk and by Windows NT's Setup and Service Pack setup programs. This file must be modified. Additionally, the registry itself will have many hard-coded references to the Windows NT system directory. These references must be changed as well.

Perform the following steps on your FAT or NTFS system to complete the renaming process:

1. Back up the file setup.log to setup.bak using the COPY command.

2. Open the file setup.log in the %SystemRoot%\Repair directory with a text editor, such as the command prompt's EDIT command or Notepad.

3. Globally change all references to the original installation directory with the new name that you have chosen.

A short section of a typical setup.log file is shown below. As an example, I've used underlines here to highlight the lines that would have to be changed:

```
[Paths]
TargetDirectory = "\WNT351"
TargetDevice = "\Device\Harddisk0\partition1"
SystemPartitionDirectory = "\"
SystemPartition = "\Device\Harddisk0\partition1"
[Signature]
Version = "WinNt4.0"
[Files.SystemPartition]
ntldr = "ntldr","2a36b"
NTDETECT.COM = "NTDETECT.COM","b69e"
[Files.WinNt]
\WNT351\Help\31users.hlp = "31users.hlp","12bfc"
\WNT351\Help\acc_dis.cnt = "acc_dis.cnt","cc99"
\WNT351\Help\acc_dis.hlp = "acc_dis.hlp","b82c"
\WNT351\inf\accessor.inf = "accessor.inf","13070"
\WNT351\system32\acledit.dll = "acledit.dll","2be50"
```

NOTE

Be careful not to change anything other than the installation directory name in this file, or the Windows NT setup repair process will not be able to repair the system at a later time.

It will be necessary to scan the system registry to ensure that there are no hard-coded references to the installation directory. I found that there were almost two thousand hard-coded references to the Windows NT installation directory in a well-used Windows NT Server installation. Each of these references would have to be changed. Follow these steps to determine all hard-coded references to the installation directory for Windows NT:

1. Using RegEdit, export the entire registry to a file called orig.reg. To do so, select My Computer in the registry tree display.

2. Use a text editor's search and replace commands to change all occurrences of the original Windows NT installation directory name to the new directory name.

3. Reintegrate your edited registry into the original registry; either double-click on the exported registry in the Explorer or issue the command **START orig.reg** at a command prompt.

NOTE

This process is somewhat complex and difficult. There is a good chance that when you've finished, the system will not work correctly. Always make sure you have a good backup for restoring in case the change fails.

Upgrade Blues

Windows NT is sold in two flavors: upgrade and full installation. You can usually get an upgrade for an existing product at a considerable discount over the cost of an entire new product license. Generally, the product is identical in both versions, but in the upgrade version, the Setup program will confirm that you actually have the original product.

The test to see if there is an original product to upgrade is relatively simple, but not flawless. The upgrade version of Windows NT will check the hard drive for a version of Windows that may be upgraded. If none is found, you will be prompted to insert a disk for the original product to prove you have a product that may be upgraded.

One problem comes about when you install the Windows NT upgrade on a system and you later need to reinstall a new copy of Windows NT in the same directory. It is possible that the Windows NT Upgrade Setup program won't work correctly, because it may think that you don't have a product that is included in the upgrade offer when it only finds Windows NT version 4 on the drive.

NOTE   If you are installing a second copy of Windows NT, the upgrade program will work. It only fails when reinstalling over the original installation.

There is a quick workaround for this problem:

1. Edit the registry sub-key HKEY_LOCAL_MACHINE\Software\Microsoft\ Windows NT\CurrentVersion. Change the data key CurrentVersion to 3.5.

2. Edit the registry sub-key HKEY_LOCAL_MACHINE\System\Setup. Check the data key SystemSetupInProgress. If necessary, reset it to 0.

3. Edit the registry sub-key HKEY_LOCAL_MACHINE\System\Setup. Check the data key UpgradeInProgress. If necessary, reset it to 0. If this key does not exist, don't worry about it; it is not necessary to add it.

4. If a Service Pack has been installed, it would be a very wise move to remove it before reinstalling Windows NT. Otherwise, problems with the TCP/IP drivers may result in system instability. After reinstalling Windows NT, reinstall the last Service Pack. Remember, Service Packs are cumulative, so only the highest numbered Service Pack need be installed. Install any hotfixes that have been applied to the original system.

5. If RAS (Remote Access Service) is installed on this computer, it is imperative that the Service Packs be uninstalled. (RAS has been substantially changed with each Service Pack.) However, some users are unable to remove the Service Packs without breaking other critical parts of Windows NT. In that case, restore the file %Systemroot%\System32\drivers\tcpip.sys from the original Windows NT distribution CD-ROM or from the Service Pack uninstall directory %SystemRoot%\\$NtServicePackUninstall$.

NOTE   To recover a file from the Windows NT distribution CD-ROM, you must use the **EXPAND** command from a command prompt. Typing **EXPAND /?** will give you more information on using EXPAND.

Where Was Windows NT Installed From?

Many of us change the drive letters assigned to the CD-ROM drives after the Windows NT installation is completed. It is a simple process and helps provide order in the system, especially if you are like me and add and remove drives frequently.

In my system, all CD-ROM drives are assigned drive letters ranging from S: to Z:. There are four servers with between one and three CD-ROM drives each. Shares are made with the same drive letters used on each networked computer. This way, a reference to S: on a computer on the network will always access the same CD-ROM drive and usually the same CD-ROM, too.

Reassigning the CD-ROM drive letters makes the system more manageable, but there is one problem. Every time you want to make a setup change to Windows NT and the Windows NT's Setup or Configuration programs need to access the original Windows NT CD-ROM, the prompt will be for the CD drive letter that Windows NT was installed from. This drive letter will be different from the new, reassigned CD-ROM drive letter.

The location of the original installation source CD-ROM is stored in the registry sub-hive HKEY_LOCAL_MACHINE\SOFTWARE\Microsoft\Windows NT\CurrentVersion in the data key Sourcepath. Also check the registry sub-hive HKEY_LOCAL_MACHINE\SOFTWARE\Microsoft\Windows\CurrentVersion\Setup, data key SourcePath, and data key Installation Sources. Data key installation sources is a binary key, so edit this one with caution. Change both instances of SourcePath to "X:\I386", where X: is the CD-ROM drive letter.

I'm Full, Burp

Windows NT will give a warning when free space on the drive falls to less than 10%. This percentage works well with smaller 1 or 2GB hard drives, but when the drive is large (9GB or more), the amount of free space can be almost a full gigabyte when the warning is given.

To fix this problem, it is possible to alter the Percentage Free parameter, changing it from 10% to a more reasonable value for your system. Edit the hive HKEY_LOCAL_MACHINE\System\CurrentControlSet\Services\LanmanServer\Parameters. Add a new REG_DWORD data key named DiskSpaceThreshold. Edit this data key and set its value to the percentage of free space at which you want the warning to be given. For example, set the value to 5 to give a warning when there is less than 5% free space remaining.

NOTE DiskSpaceThreshold will affect all drives. Consider the effect when your system has a mix of small and large drives.

Why Is Windows NT Asking for a Disk in the Drive?

From time to time, we get into a situation with Windows NT in which there is no disk or CD-ROM in the disk drive. This might happen when we start an application or a service or at some other time. After checking whether the drive specified is missing from the path statement, check something less obvious. Check the subhive HKEY_LOCAL_MACHINE\SYSTEM\SETUP. If it contains a data key named WinntPath, delete this key and restart Windows NT.

NOTE How does a CD-ROM or diskette drive get into the path? Most often this happens either due to a user error or an application installation that has gone awry. Some applications allow execution from the CD-ROM drive, but don't realize that the application, or a disc, isn't always going to be available in the drive. If the message from Windows NT that no disc is in the drive is satisfied by inserting any disc, the message is not significant and you should try one of the fixes just discussed.

Remove Context Menu Items, Map Network Drive, and Disconnect Network Drive

It is easy to remove both the Map Network Drive and Disconnect Network Drive selections in the Explorer context menu (and the Tools menu) for drives. A simple change to the registry tells Explorer not to display either of these entries. Here's how:

In the registry hive HKEY_CURRENT_USER\Software\Microsoft\Windows\ CurrentVersion\Policies\Explorer, change (or add, if the data key doesn't exist) the following data key:

NoNetConnectDisconnect

Type: REG_DWORD

Typical value: 1

This registry key supports two values. When the value is 1, then the Map Network Drive and Disconnect Network Drive menu selections are available. When the value is 0, the Map Network Drive and Disconnect Network Drive menu selections are not available. This setting may also be made using the Policy Editor, as described in Chapter 4, "Registry Tools and Tips—Getting the Work Done."

More Than Two IDE Controllers in Windows NT

Most computers now come with two built-in IDE controllers. The hardware will usually map one controller to the PCI bus, and one to the IDE bus. (The PCI bus IDE controller may exhibit better performance.) Both IDE controllers may be accessed by Windows NT if desired, and Windows NT doesn't require modifications to access up to two IDE controllers.

Several configurations are possible with the two IDE controllers. One configuration is to have four hard drives. Today, IDE drives are available in sizes that rival SCSI drives. A very reasonable configuration with as much as 36GB of hard disk space can be created using all four IDE drives.

NOTE IDE and ESDI drives are basically the same to Windows NT, so actually it's possible to add additional ESDI controllers with the techniques discussed in this section. Of course, ESDI drives and ESDI controllers are scarcer than hen's teeth, but that's not the issue here.

Another popular configuration is one or two hard drives on the PCI IDE controller (This allows maximum performance with the hard drives.) and one or two CD-ROM drives on the other second IDE controller. Due to inherent low performance of CD-ROM drives, CD-ROM drives are best connected to the slower of the two IDE controllers.

Windows NT supports up to two standard IDE controllers. However, it is possible to add a third or fourth IDE controller to many systems. I'm not going to comment on the availability of hardware to do this type of configuration, other than to say that many IDE controller cards are available, some of which offer substantial performance.

NOTE One hard drive and one CD-ROM drive? Resist the urge to connect these two devices to a single IDE controller. Some systems will limit the hard drive's performance to the slowest device on the IDE controller—and this slowest device will always be the CD-ROM drive. So, unless you want your hard drive to perform like a CD-ROM drive, keep these two devices on different controllers.

NOTE Only perform this procedure if your computer is an Intel *x*86 system or if you are only using two IDE controllers. The changes described below only work with *x*86 systems; Windows NT supports two IDE systems without any modifications.

Each IDE controller is numbered. The primary IDE controller is numbered 0 and the secondary IDE controller is numbered 1. An added third IDE controller would be numbered 2, a fourth would be numbered 3, and so forth. Keep this concept in mind as we go about adding a third or fourth (or fifth. . .) IDE controller:

1. In RegEdit or RegEdt32, open the registry sub-hive HKEY_LOCAL_MACHINE\SYSTEM\CurrentControlSet\Services\Atdisk and add a new sub-hive named "PARAMETERS."

2. Open this newly created PARAMETERS hive and create a sub-hive named with the number for the controller to be added. For example, create a sub-hive named "2" if you are adding a third new IDE controller, or "3" for a fourth new IDE controller.

3. Open the sub-hive that you named in step 2 and create the following three data keys:

BaseAddress	Type: REG_DWORD	Typical value: Use the IDE controller's Data Register's physical address. Configure the controller so that this address does not conflict with any existing IDE controllers or other installed devices.
DriveControl	Type: REG_DWORD	Typical value: Use the IDE controller's Drive Control Register's physical address. Configure the controller so that this address does not conflict with any existing IDE controllers or any other installed devices. Typically, this address is at BaseAddress + 0xE.

Interrupt	Type: REG_DWORD	Typical value: Use the IDE controller's IRQ (Interrupt Request) address. Configure the controller so that this address does not conflict with any existing IDE controllers or any other installed devices.

Saving Share Information

Windows NT shares are often used by many people and they may be lost when a clean installation of Windows NT must be made. We clean install for a number of reasons. Perhaps we clean install when we find our system unstable for reasons that cannot be traced to a specific point in time or when backups cannot be depended upon. As well, sometimes the system hardware configuration is changed (for example, a new server is installed), which necessitates a clean installation.

> **NOTE** Before following these steps, realize that any existing shares may be overwritten by the process described.

For servers with a large number of shares, re-entering each share manually can be a time-consuming process. The following registry trick is easier:

1. Start RegEdit.

2. Open the sub-hive HKEY_LOCAL_MACHINE\SYSTEM\CurrentControlSet\ Services\LanmanServer\Shares.

3. Select Registry ➤ Export Registry File.

4. Enter a filename for saving the Shares sub-hive. Preferably, save this file to a floppy disk or another non-volatile location. The Selected Branch button should be selected, and the branch to be saved should read HKEY_LOCAL_ MACHINE\SYSTEM\CurrentControlSet\Services\LanmanServer\Shares.

5. After reinstalling Windows NT, insert the diskette with the file saved in step 4, and type the command **START *filename*.REG** at the command prompt. Use the filename you saved in step 4.

6. Check to ensure that the shares have been properly incorporated into the registry.

NOTE   Macintosh shared volumes will not be saved using these techniques.

NOTE   When using this technique at upgrade time, check to ensure that the new version of Windows NT saves share information in the same location as the previous version; otherwise the changes won't have the desired effect.

Other Hardware Support Entries

There are thousands of other hardware support entries. I've gathered a few for this chapter and grouped them by major components—serial ports, printer ports, and so on.

Serial Ports

HKEY_LOCAL_MACHINE\System\CurrentControlSet\Services\Serial contains a number of parameters that help control the system's utilization of the basic serial ports. Many Windows NT computers use one of these serial ports for a mouse or other pointing device, and one serial port is typically connected to a modem or other communications device. An Intel *x*86 system may have between zero and four serial ports, though most systems are configured with two of them.

Ports on virtually all Windows NT systems utilize the 16550 UART (Universal Asynchronous Receiver/Transmitter) chip to manage the serial communications at the hardware level. The 16550 UART has a buffer for both transmission and reception, allowing up to 16 bytes of data to be buffered. This lessens the load on the main CPU when serial communications are being performed. Many of the serial port's settings are configurable with the Control Panel's Ports applet.

Settings made with the Control Panel's Ports applet are stored in the registry sub-hive at HKEY_LOCAL_MACHINE\System\CurrentControlSet\Services\Serial\Parameters. This hive contains a number of basic settings for each port and settings used for defaults for each port that is configured.

There are additional settings that a user may configure outside the Control Panel's Ports applet. To set these settings, it will be necessary to make several additions to the registry. Under the sub-hive HKEY_LOCAL_MACHINE\System\CurrentControlSet\Services\Serial\Parameters, it will be necessary to create one or more sub-hives. Name each sub-hive with a number as shown here:

Serial0	Serial port 1, com1:
Serial1	Serial port 2, com2:
Serial2	Serial port 3, com3:
Serial3	Serial port 4, com4:

NOTE   I don't recommend setting parameters for the serial port dedicated to the pointing device if there is a serial mouse or other serial-connected pointing device connected to the computer—your pointing device may not work correctly if you do this.

Once you have created your sub-hives, go to the sub-hive for the port to be modified. In our example, we'll modify COM1—that is, HKEY_LOCAL_MACHINE\System\CurrentControlSet\Services\Serial\Parameters\Serial0. Add the following data keys to the sub-hive. The first data key, DosDevices, is the name that DOS will use for the device:

DosDevices

Type: REG_SZ

Typical value: a string

The string contained in this data key is used to name the port for access from a command prompt. Typical names would be (as for our example) COM1, or perhaps, SERIAL1. There is no need to specify a colon in this name. This data key is required. If it is not included, Windows NT will generate an error.

PortAddress is the hardware I/O address for the device:

PortAddress

Type: REG_DWORD

Typical value: 0x3F8

This DWORD value, almost always expressed in hexadecimal, is the port address. There are standard addresses for communications ports; although users with special hardware, perhaps a multi-port add-on card, may be using special addresses. This data key is required. If it is not included, Windows NT will generate an error.

DisablePort indicates whether Windows NT should treat this device as disabled, and not allow access to the device once initialized. Its name, type, and default value follow:

> DisablePort
>
> Type: REG_DWORD
>
> Typical value: 0

A value of 0, the default, allows full access to the port. When set to 1, the device is deleted and cannot be accessed after the port has been initialized.

ForceFifoEnable tells Windows NT to use or not use the hardware FIFO buffers. Its name, type, and typical default value follow:

> ForceFifoEnable
>
> Type: REG_DWORD
>
> Typical value: 1

If the UART supports a buffer, Windows NT will normally enable the buffer. However, some hardware and some UART chips are not known for their reliability when the buffer is used. This data key allows you to disable the buffer. A value of 1 enables support for the buffer; 0 disables the buffer support. This data key is not required and should be used only if it is needed.

Printer (Parallel) Ports

HKEY_LOCAL_MACHINE\System\CurrentControlSet\Services\Parallel contains a number of parameters that help control the system's utilization of the basic parallel or printer ports. Many Windows NT computers use one of these parallel ports connected to a standard printer. An Intel *x*86 system may have between zero and two parallel ports, although most systems are configured with only a single parallel port.

Ports on virtually all Windows NT systems utilize a standard printer driver chip as the hardware interface. This chip is configurable in the BIOS, and may allow either one-way (to the printer) or two-way (both to the printer and from the printer to the computer) communications. Additionally, printer port configurations allow for high-speed communications. High-speed communications are important when you are printing complex images (bitmapped, for example) and a large amount of data must be transferred between the computer and the printer. Some printers also have a scanning mode. These printers require both high-speed printer ports and ports that support bidirectional data transfers. Many of the parallel port's settings are configurable with the Control Panel's Ports applet.

Settings made with the Control Panel's Ports applet are stored in the registry sub-hive at HKEY_LOCAL_MACHINE\System\CurrentControlSet\Services\Parallel\Parameters. This hive contains a number of basic settings for each port and settings used for defaults for each port that is configured.

There are additional settings that a user may configure outside the Control Panel's Ports applet. It will be necessary to make several additions to the registry for these settings. Under the sub-hive HKEY_LOCAL_MACHINE\System\CurrentControlSet\Services\Parallel\Parameters, it will be necessary to create one or more sub-hives. Name each sub-hive with a name and a number, as shown here:

Parallel0   Parallel port 1, LPT1:

Parallel1   Parallel port 2, LPT2:

Once you have created your sub-hives, go to the sub-hive for the port to be modified. In our example, we'll modify LPT1—that is, HKEY_LOCAL_MACHINE\System\CurrentControlSet\Services\Parallel\Parameters\Parallel0. Add the following data keys to the sub-hive. DosDevices contains the name that a DOS application would use to refer to the port:

DosDevices

Type: REG_SZ

Typical value: a string

The string contained in this data key is used to name the port for access from a command prompt. Typical names would be LPT1, or perhaps PRT1. There is no need to specify a colon in this name. This data key is required. If it is not included, Windows NT will generate an error.

PortAddress is the I/O address for the parallel port:

PortAddress

Type: REG_DWORD

Typical value: 0x278

This DWORD value, almost always expressed in hexadecimal, is the port address. There are standard addresses for parallel (printer) ports, although users with special hardware (perhaps a multi-port add-on card) may be using special addresses. This data key is required. If it is not included, Windows NT will generate an error.

DisablePort, when set, tells Windows NT to not allow access after initializing the port:

DisablePort

Type: REG_DWORD

Typical value: 0

A value of 0, the default, allows full access to the port. When set to 1, the device is deleted and cannot be accessed after the port has been initialized.

Interrupt specifies the hardware IRQ (Interrupt Request) value:

Interrupt

Type: REG_DWORD

Typical value: 0x5

For parallel (printer) ports, an IRQ of 5 is used. Many printer ports do not support IRQs. Check and set this value in the system BIOS.

Non-User-Interface Software Configuration Entries

Some settings affect the user interface and the system equally. Where do we place these entries? Winlogon is a section in the registry that holds settings used for the users log, and so on.

Password Expires in *n* Days

The password expiration message is given to the user a certain number of days before the password expires. In Windows NT 4, this message may be configured at the client by following these steps:

1. Start RegEdit or RegEdt32.

2. Open HKEY_LOCAL_MACHINE\Software\Microsoft\Windows NT\ CurrentVersion\Winlogon.

3. Add this data key, or modify it if it already exists:

   PasswordExpiryWarning

   Type: REG_DWORD

   Typical value: 14

This entry holds the number of days that the "password expires" warning will be displayed.

Domain Refresh Interval

The domain list is refreshed whenever the workstation is unlocked, providing that the workstation has been locked for more than 120 seconds. (A user can lock their workstation by pressing Ctrl+Alt+Del.) On many networks, refreshing the domain list can result in a significant delay before the user regains control of their system.

This problem may be somewhat alleviated by increasing the minimum "locked time" setting (in essence, gambling that the domain list won't have changed during that time), which you do by modifying the following data key:

   DcacheMinInterval

   Type: REG_DWORD

   Typical value: 120

This value contains the number of seconds that the system must have been locked before the registry will force the system to refresh the domain list. Values may range from a minimum of 120 seconds, the default, to a maximum of 86,400 seconds.

Hints and Kinks from the Experts

Here are some hints and kinks from our experts on Windows NT networking and system entries.

Where Does a DHCP Client Store Lease Information?   DHCP (Dynamic Host Configuration Protocol) clients store information locally so that they can attempt to lease the same IP address and still function if the DHCP server is down. A Windows NT client stores DHCP information in the registry at HKEY_LOCAL_MACHINE\SYSTEM\CurrentControlSet\Services\<Network Adapter>\Parameters\Tcpip.

A Windows 95 client stores DHCP information in the registry at HKEY_LOCAL_MACHINE\SYSTEM\CurrentControlSet\Services\VxD\DHCP\DHCPInfo00.

Windows for Workgroups with TCP/IP-32 stores the DHCP-related information in the DHCP.bin file in the <WINDOWS_SYSTEM_ROOT> subdirectory. This file is in binary format.

LAN Manager 3 and LAN Manager for MS-DOS 2.2c clients both store the local DHCP-related information in the DHCP.prm file in the <NETWORK_ROOT> directory. This file is in a binary format.

(Courtesy of Jerold Schulman)

Does Your 100MB Ethernet TCP/IP Network Perform Poorly?   If your 100MB Ethernet TCP/IP network performs poorly, it could be due to ACK collisions. You can contact your NIC manufacturer to see if there is a way to increase the interframe gap.

The Intel EtherExpress 100B adapters have the following registry parameter: HKEY_LOCAL_MACHINE\SYSTEM\CurrentControlSet\Services\e100bx\Parameters. The x represents the number of your interface card.

Add the following Value to enable an adaptive algorithm:

Value name: Adaptive_ifs

Type: REG_DWORD

Value setting: 1

Setting the value to 0 will disable it. A value of 2 to 200 sets a predefined inter-frame gap if you want to measure collisions at 20, 40, 60, and so on; be sure to pick one with a low collision rate and good performance.

If you have a different NIC, edit HKEY_LOCAL_MACHINE\SYSTEM\CurrentControlSet\Services\Tcpip\Parameters instead, adding the following:

Value name: TcpWindowSize

Type: REG_DWORD

Value setting: 2920 (decimal)

TIP This tip is for 100MB Ethernet TCP/IP networks only. Using this parameter on a 10MB network, WAN, FDDI, Token Ring, or anything else will impact performance.

(Courtesy of Jerold Schulman)

Learn Common Registry Entries for Networking Programs. The HKEY_CURRENT_USER\Software\Microsoft\Windows NT\CurrentVersion\Network\Program name contains configuration data that is common for programs that view and maintain the network. Program names are sub-keys, such as Browser Monitor, Event Viewer, Server Manager, User Manager, and so on. Table 12.1 shows some of the common entries in the registry for networking programs. All the entries are type REG_SZ.

TABLE 12.1: Common Registry Entries for Networking Programs

Value	Default	Description
SaveSettings	1	1=Options are saved and the user's choices are restored when the user starts the program again. 0=Options are not saved. This entry needs to be 1 for most other entries to work.
Confirmation	1	Is confirmation for deletion or changes required? 1=Yes; 0=No.
FontFaceName	none	Sets the font that is used if different from default.

Continued on next page

TABLE 12.1 CONTINUED: Common Registry Entries for Networking Programs

Value	Default	Description
FontHeight	0	0=Use the default point size for the font.
FontItalic	0	0=Not italic; 1=Italic.
FontWeight	0	0=Use the default font weight. 400=Standard weight. 700=Bold. 900=Heavy.
SortOrder	depends on program	For Event Viewer: 0=Oldest first; 1 (default)=Newest first. For User Manager: 0=Sort by full name; 1 (default)=sort by username.
Window PosX PosY SizX SizY	*xyxy*0	Sets the four pixel coordinates that define the size and position of the window. When followed by 0, it means the window was not minimized when closed. When followed by 1, it means it *was* minimized.

Reduce Network Delay.   When TCP/IP network activity is light, delays may be encountered with the default request buffer size, 4356 (decimal). The range of this parameter is 512 to 65536 bytes. Testing has shown that in most standard Ethernet environments, 14596 (decimal) is a better choice if the memory is available. To reduce network delay, perform the following steps:

1. Edit HKEY_LOCAL_MACHINE\System\CurrentControlSet\Services\ LanmanServer\Parameters.

2. Add the following:

   Value name: SizReqBuf

   Type: REG_DWORD

3. Restart the computer.

(Courtesy of Peter D. Hipson)

PART IV

More Common Registry Entries

CHAPTER
THIRTEEN

13

Microsoft Office

- Microsoft Office shared components

- Changes made by Microsoft Office Setup

- The REG and SRG files

- Microsoft Office system configuration information

- Microsoft Office user configuration information

- Using the Registry from Microsoft Office applications

- Hints and kinks from the experts

Why would anyone expect him to come out smarter? He went to prison for three years, not Princeton.

—Boxing promoter Dan Duva on Mike Tyson hooking up again with promoter Don King

This chapter is a bit different from some of the others. Although we could just list every registry entry for Microsoft Office, the chapter would quickly become boring, and it would be the largest chapter in the entire book. Instead, I'm going to focus on particular Office-related topics that affect the registry:

- Microsoft Office Shared Components and how they are interlinked to form a cohesive product

- Changes made by the Microsoft Office Setup program

- The REG and SRG files that come with Microsoft Office

- How to modify Microsoft Office configuration information

- How to customize and copy user information between users

- Programming the registry using Microsoft Office's VBA (Visual BASIC for Applications)

NOTE   The information in this chapter refers to Microsoft Office 97 Professional Edition, the release that is current as this book was being written. Later versions of Office are due out in the next year or so, 1999 or perhaps 2000, and hopefully much of this chapter's information will be usable with these future releases.

This chapter tells you how to repair your Office 97 registry entries. If Office 97 is not running correctly, the problem may be more involved than just a damaged or missing registry entry. For example, it is entirely possible that *files* are either corrupted or missing, also. For this reason, don't look at this chapter as being a save-all. Rather, try fixing the registry, but if that doesn't have the desired effect, try reinstalling the malfunctioning Office components.

I'd never suggest that you try to restore the Office products by first restoring a backup of the files and then adding registry entries. Though this might work, you could expect that there would be other subtle things that would have to be done, such as adding critical shared DLL files to the Windows NT SYSTEM32 directory.

Most of Microsoft Office's registry modifications are performed by one of two processes. The first process is the Setup program. This program will add, subtract, and otherwise modify a number of registry entries, all of which are critical to the running of Microsoft Office.

The second process is a group of registry modification files, with the extensions of REG and SRG. These files are contained in directories on the Microsoft Office distribution CD-ROM.

Repairs to Microsoft Office are relatively easy. On the one hand, some components reinstall well. Reinstalling Microsoft Word, on the other hand, may overwrite your normal.dot file. We suggest, therefore, that you save or otherwise back up user-modified Microsoft Office files, such as the document templates (normal.dot is one of these), before reinstalling Microsoft Office.

NOTE   Notice that there are also components listed in this registry section that are *not* part of the basic Microsoft Office package, such as a listing for Microsoft Publisher.

Microsoft Office Shared Components

Microsoft Office consists of a number of components. We all know about the big ones—Word, Excel, Access, and PowerPoint. But a number of small helper applications that we don't always see or know about are also included with Microsoft Office. For instance, there is Microsoft Chart, a charting program that can be used with Word; Excel; and Access.

These are the Microsoft Office shared components:

Equation Editor	Used to create visually appealing equations
WordArt	Allows simple drawing that may be embedded into documents
Graph	A basic graphing tool
Organization Chart	Allows drawing and maintenance of basic organizational charts
Media Player	An embeddable media player; most useful in embedding video clips into PowerPoint presentations

ClipArt Gallery A collection of clip art from Microsoft Power-Point that may be used to improve the visual appeal of documents

With the possible exception of the ClipArt Gallery, which consists mostly of images, the shared components are usually ActiveX embeddable components. The embedding is performed using CLSIDs that are inserted into the registry by the Microsoft Office installation process. The significant Microsoft Office CLSIDs are shown in Table 13.1.

TABLE 13.1: Microsoft Office CLSIDs That May Be Installed with Office

CLSID	Usage
{00020344-0000-0000-C000-000000000046}	The MAPI (mail program interface) remote logon handler
{00020420-0000-0000-C000-000000000046}	Internally used by proxy stub
{00020810-0000-0000-C000-000000000046}	Microsoft Excel
{00020810-0000-0000-PIAF-S-13Bo84-000046}	Microsoft Excel
{00020820-0000-0000-C000-000000000046}	MSBiff (binary file converter)
{00020900-0000-0000-C000-000000000046}	Search for Microsoft Word 6.*x*
{00020D05-0000-0000-C000-000000000046}	Mail File Attachment
{00020D09-0000-0000-C000-000000000046}	Mail Message Attachment
{00020D30-0000-0000-C000-000000000046}	International Program Manager handler
{00020D31-0000-0000-C000-000000000046}	International Program Manager Note handler
{00020D32-0000-0000-C000-000000000046}	International Program Manager Document handler
{00020D33-0000-0000-C000-000000000046}	International Program Manager Resend handler
{00020D34-0000-0000-C000-000000000046}	International Program Manager Any Report handler
{00020D35-0000-0000-C000-000000000046}	International Program Manager Post handler

Continued on next page

TABLE 13.1 CONTINUED: Microsoft Office CLSIDs That May Be Installed with Office

CLSID	Usage
{00020D75-0000-0000-C000-000000000046}	Inbox (Exchange/Outlook)
{00021302-0000-0000-C000-000000000046}	RTF support for Microsoft Works for Windows 3.*x*
{00030000-0000-0000-C000-000000000046}	Microsoft Biff (binary file exchange)
{00030003-0000-0000-C000-000000000046}	RTF support for Microsoft Word for Windows 2.*x*
{00031001-0000-0000-C000-000000000046}	RTF support for Word for Macintosh
{00031002-0000-0000-C000-000000000046}	RTF support for Word for Macintosh
{00031009-0000-0000-C000-000000000046}	RTF support for Word for WordPerfect for DOS
{0003100A-0000-0000-C000-000000000046}	RTF support for Word for WordPerfect 6.*x*
{0003100B-0000-0000-C000-000000000046}	RTF support for Word for Lotus 123
{00031016-0000-0000-C000-000000000046}	RTF support for Word for Lotus 123
{00031017-0000-0000-C000-000000000046}	RTF support for Word for Lotus 123
{00031018-0000-0000-C000-000000000046}	RTF support for Word for WordPerfect for DOS
{0006FE01-0000-0000-C000-000000000046}	Exchange (Outlook) WordMail Mail Message handler
{0006FE02-0000-0000-C000-000000000046}	Exchange (Outlook)
{0006FE04-0000-0000-C000-000000000046}	Exchange (Outlook)
{0006FE05-0000-0000-C000-000000000046}	Exchange (Outlook)
{000c0114-0000-0000-c000-000000000046}	Support for IMsoTbFrame Proxy/Stub Factory
{11943940-36DE-11CF-953E-00C0A84029E9}	Unknown
{2542F180-3532-1069-A2CD-00AA0034B50B}	Display engine for the Font Property Page
{28cddbc2-0ae2-11ce-a29a-00aa004a1a72}	RTF support for Microsoft Works for Windows 4.0
{3FA7DEB3-6438-101B-ACC1-00AA00423326}	MAPI 1.0 Session (v1.0)

Continued on next page

TABLE 13.1 CONTINUED: Microsoft Office CLSIDs That May Be Installed with Office

CLSID	Usage
{3FA7DEB4-6438-101B-ACC1-00AA00423326}	MAPI 1.0 Session (v1.0)
{3FA7DEB5-6438-101B-ACC1-00AA00423326}	MAPI 1.0 Session (v1.0)
{4d2f086c-6ea3-101b-a18a-00aa00446e07}	MAPIPSFactory
{6316D324-2238-101B-9E66-00AA003BA905}	Exchange Extensions Conflict Note
{7BF80981-BF32-101A-8BBB-00AA00300CAB}	Picture class
{B54DCF20-5F9C-101B-AF4E-00AA003F0F07}	Unknown
{BB2B65B0-241E-101B-9E67-00AA003BA905}	Exchange Extensions Conflict Note
{BEF6E003-A874-101A-8BBA-00AA00300CAB}	Font
{C20D7340-5525-101B-8F15-00AA003E4672}	Microsoft Access (Jet) support.
{DDF5A600-B9C0-101A-AF1A-00AA0034B50B}	Support for the Color Property Page
{FB8F0823-0164-101B-84ED-08002B2EC713}	Support for the Font Property Page
{FB8F0824-0164-101B-84ED-08002B2EC713}	Support for the Picture Property Page
{FC7AF71D-FC74-101A-84ED-08002B2EC713}	Support for the Picture Property Page

NOTE   Note that not all of the CLSIDs shown in Table 13.1 will always be installed. Most of us install only part of Microsoft Office, and therefore only some of the CLSIDs will be present in the registry. A missing CLSID doesn't signify an error or problem in itself.

Changes Made by Microsoft Office Setup

The Microsoft Office Setup program first adds and sometimes removes a number of registry entries. Actually, a full installation process could modify over a thousand registry entries. (Now you see why I don't just list them all!) Each entry that is modified, deleted, or added by the Setup program is done that way because the entry is based on information specific to the current installation. For example, an entry that has the installation directory, which the user may change at setup time, must be modified by Setup. This cannot be done using a REG file, such as those described later in this chapter, because the REG file technique cannot take into account user preferences.

The main controlling file for the Microsoft Office Setup program is called OFF97PRO.STF. It is located in the root directory of the Microsoft Office CD-ROM drive. This file is fully editable with any text editor, but don't try altering it—it contains a script that drives the Setup program. The STF file contains entries that control which files are copied and where; which registry entries to delete, add, and modify; and everything else that must be done to install Microsoft Office.

The OFF97PRO.STF file includes:

- 19 registry searches
- 53 retrievals of path names
- 1418 additions to the registry
- 2 checks of the registry
- 28 checks for registry equality
- 9 registrations of type libraries
- 29 self-registrations
- 21 retrievals of the Windows path
- 73 creations of strings of REG_SZ type
- 6 creations of REG_DWORD type objects
- 35 registry entry removals
- 9 registry tree deletions
- 3 copies of registry key values
- 6 items that are specifically not removed if encountered
- 1 copy of INI file values to the registry

These are just the registry manipulation instructions; there are over 5500 lines that perform other tasks.

The REG and SRG Files

Microsoft Office uses a number of registry updating files. These files update registry entries that do not change from one installation to another. There are two types of files, REG and SRG. The difference between these two file types is that a REG file may be used to directly update the registry using RegEdit, while a SRG file is not compatible with RegEdit.

Table 13.2 lists the four REG files that are included with Microsoft Office, along with their size in bytes. These REG files are spread between a number of directories, as appropriate for each product.

TABLE 13.2: Microsoft Office SRG Registry Update Files

Registry Update File	Size
X:\OFFICE\WMS\COMMON\MAPIRPC.REG	11,886
X:\OFFICE\WMS\COMMON\MDISP32.REG	3,061
X:\OFFICE\WORDMAIL\WORDMAIL.REG	2,286
X:\VALUPACK\PPT4VIEW\OLE2.REG	27,026

Table 13.3 shows the 28 SRG files that are included with Microsoft Office. Like the REG files, these SRG files are spread between a number of directories, as appropriate for each product.

TABLE 13.3: Microsoft Office SRG Registry Update Files

Registry Update File	Size
X:\AAMSSTP\BS96SE.SRG	1,787
X:\OFFICE\EXCEL8.SRG	37,509
X:\OFFICE\FATNS.SRG	6,001
X:\OFFICE\GRAPH8.SRG	5,297
X:\OFFICE\HLINK.SRG	457

Continued on next page

TABLE 13.3 CONTINUED: Microsoft Office SRG Registry Update Files

Registry Update File	Size
X:\OFFICE\MISC.SRG	5,438
X:\OFFICE\MISC2.SRG	504
X:\OFFICE\MSACCESS.SRG	28,561
X:\OFFICE\MSOFFICE.SRG	1,194
X:\OFFICE\OUTLOOK.SRG	39,779
X:\OFFICE\PP8.SRG	33,197
X:\OFFICE\PPT2HTML.SRG	2,359
X:\OFFICE\SCHDPLS.SRG	2,641
X:\OFFICE\WINWORD8.SRG	26,907
X:\OFFICE\WIZARD.SRG	15,794
X:\OS\MSAPPS\ARTGALRY\ARTGALRY.SRG	6,421
X:\OS\MSAPPS\DATAMAP\MSMAP.SRG	3,085
X:\OS\MSAPPS\EQUATION\EQNEDT32.SRG	4,402
X:\OS\MSAPPS\ORGCHART\ORGCHART.SRG	4,599
X:\OS\MSAPPS\PHOTOED\PHOTOED.SRG	9,902
X:\OS\SYSTEM\EFDOCX.SRG	17,232
X:\OS\SYSTEM\T2EMBED.SRG	856
X:\TEMPLATE\ACALLLNG.SRG	3,039
X:\TEMPLATE\ACALLSHT.SRG	2,691
X:\TEMPLATE\ACMINLNG.SRG	5,605
X:\TEMPLATE\ACMINSHT.SRG	5,273
X:\TEMPLATE\ACTYPLNG.SRG	6,863
X:\TEMPLATE\ACTYPSHT.SRG	5,603

NOTE The SRG files may be edited with a standard text editor. Their format is simple, and could easily be adapted to update the registry if necessary.

Microsoft Office System Configuration Information

Microsoft Office stores information about common configuration settings in the registry hive at HKEY_LOCAL_MACHINE\SOFTWARE\Microsoft\Office\. This hive contains a sub-hive called 8.0 (for the current version number of Microsoft Office, Office 97). The next version of Office will probably be stored in a sub-hive named 9.0.

Under the sub-hive 8.0 are further sub-hives for each installed Office component. Don't be surprised if there are sub-hives for Microsoft Office components that are not installed. Some components set items for other components regardless of whether these components are installed or not.

For example, on my computer, I have the following major sub-hives:

Access—Microsoft Access, a full-featured Desktop database system

Common—Items common to more than one Microsoft Office component

Excel—Microsoft Excel, a spreadsheet program

New User Settings—Settings used for new users who do not have any user-specific settings

Outlook—Microsoft's advanced e-mail client

PowerPoint—Microsoft's presentation program

Publisher—A publishing and layout program not specifically part of Microsoft Office, but available separately

Word—Microsoft's well-known word processor, used to write this book

Wrapper—Used to support the use of the New dialog box by Microsoft Office applications

Each of these hives contain more hives and information. For example, I don't actually have Access installed, but Microsoft Office Setup included the Access sub-hive, regardless. The Access sub-hive has entries for the following items:

- Access
- Access\Clipboard Formats
- Access\FullProduct
- Access\Jet
- Access\Menu Add-Ins
- Access\Options
- Access\Report Formats
- Access\Speller
- Access\Wizards

We'll describe each of these sub-hives in detail in the next section.

Access—Microsoft Access

The Microsoft Access database program is Microsoft's main entry into desktop database systems. Though Microsoft also offers a product called FoxPro (and more appropriately, Visual FoxPro), FoxPro is not part of the Office suit.

In the Access sub-hive are a number of sub-hives, including the ones discussed here.

Access\Clipboard Formats

The entries in the Clipboard Formats sub-hive describe special formats that Microsoft Access is able to process. This list includes the formats in the form of data keys, and descriptive information on the handler for the format. A typical entry might be:

```
HTML (*.html)

Type: REG_SZ

Typical value: soa800.dll,30,html,HTML,HTML(*.html),1
```

This entry indicates that Access will use soa800.dll to read this type of data. The entry also provides information to Access about what is needed to invoke the code in the DLL file. A typical installation might define five or more Clipboard formats.

Access\FullProduct

The FullProduct sub-hive doesn't have any entries defined in my installation.

Access\Jet

Microsoft Jet is the engine that Microsoft Access uses to access the actual database files. Microsoft has exposed the Jet engine to other application software, allowing developers to create programs. These programs are able to create, read, and write Microsoft Access-compatible databases.

Microsoft Jet is a complex, high-performance database engine. There are several additional interfaces in the Jet engine, allowing programming interoperability between Access-compatible software and other database systems, including:

- SQL Database
- Microsoft Access
- Microsoft Active Server Pages (ASP)
- Microsoft IIS (Internet Information Server)
- Rich Text Format (RTF)
- Word for Windows Merge

Access\Menu Add-Ins

Access may be expanded or enhanced by using menu add-in programs. Some menu add-ins supported by Microsoft Access include:

- Add-In Manager
- Database Splitter
- Linked Table Manager
- Switchboard Manager

Each of these add-ins are defined in registry entries in the Access\Menu Add-Ins sub-hive.

Access\Options

The state of certain Access Options is stored in the Options sub-hive. These options can vary greatly from installation to installation.

Access\Report Formats

The sub-hive Access\Report Formats stores the formats that Access is able to write reports in. Formats typically supported by most installations include:

- HTML
- Microsoft Excel
- MS-DOS Text
- Rich Text Format (RTF)

Access\Speller

Like the other members of the Microsoft Office family, Microsoft Access supports a spell-checking mode. Spell-checking is important if you or other users are as fumble fingered as I am. Without a spelling-checker, this book would be unreadable; and the editor, who had to work hard enough anyway, would have probably done nasty things to me.

Settings for spell-checking include:

- Custom Dictionary
- Ignore All Caps
- Ignore Mixed Digits
- Language ID (information about the current language being used)
- Suggest Always
- Suggest Main Dictionary Only

Access\Wizards

Access uses Wizards to perform a number of the more complex basic setup and processing tasks. Wizards allow inexperienced users to quickly become proficient and to get the maximum amount of use from Microsoft Access without spending a great deal of time learning the product.

The main categories of Wizards are:

- Control Wizards
- Data Files
- Form Wizards
- Preferences
- Property Wizards
- Query Wizards
- Replication Conflicts
- Report Wizards
- Table Wizards

Common—Items Common to More Than One Microsoft Office Component

Some parts of Microsoft Office are shared between many of the Microsoft Office applications. For example, that funny and entertaining Microsoft Office Assistant window (see Figure 13.1) allows a user to select Help quickly and easily. Other common information—such as Default Save, New, Templates, and so on—is stored in this section as well.

The following items are shared between multiple Microsoft Office applications:

Assistant—Manages the configuration and customization of the Microsoft Office Assistant. Me, I like that cute cat figure.

Default Save—Contains a prompt to tell users to be careful to save documents in formats that are compatible with other versions of Microsoft Office.

FileNew—Contains information about templates and new documents, such as the following:

LocalTemplates—Information on the location of templates

NFT—New File Template; used when creating new documents

NFT\General—General documents

NFT\General\Blank Database—Access databases

NFT\General\Blank Workbook—Excel documents

NFT\General\nft1—Binder documents

NFT\General\Normal—Word documents

FIGURE 13.1:

The Office Assistant is always there to provide help. A single click displays the Help balloon, as shown.

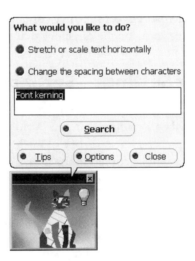

NOTE   What's Binder? It is surprising just how many experienced Microsoft Office users don't know what Binder is or how to use it. Microsoft Binder is a program that makes it possible to group all of your documents, spreadsheets, and presentations for a project into a single overall master document. A typical use for Microsoft Binder is to create a project proposal and presentation.

InstallRoot

InstallRoot contains the directory that Microsoft Office has been installed in.

InstallRootSR1

InstallRootSR1 contains the directory that Microsoft Office Service Release 1 has been installed in.

InstallType

When used, InstallType describes the installation type done by the user.

Excel—Microsoft Excel, a Spreadsheet Program

The Microsoft Excel sub-hive contains only one sub-hive: Excel\InstallRoot. This sub-hive contains the directory that Microsoft Excel has been installed in.

New User Settings—Settings for New Users

New User Settings is used to hold a template of settings used for new users. Remember, Windows NT and Windows 95/98 are multi-user operating systems. When a new user starts one of the Microsoft Office applications, the New User Settings will be copied to the user's own private profile. Once copied, these new settings will then be updated as the user configures the system to his or her desired settings.

Did a light go on here? If you're thinking it is easy to customize Microsoft Office for new users by changing entries in the New User Settings sub-hive, you're right. After modifying these settings, Microsoft Office will use whatever settings you apply.

NOTE   The usual caution applies here: Back up everything before making changes, and test out your new configuration fully before unleashing it on unsuspecting users. Nothing will foment a popular uprising faster than having the system work incorrectly.

The typical New User Settings sub-hive has entries for the following Microsoft Office products:

- Excel
- Outlook
- PowerPoint
- Query
- Word

How Do I Create a Custom New User Settings Configuration?

The easiest way to create a custom New User Settings configuration is to follow these steps:

1. Create a new, temporary userid.

2. Log on with that userid.

3. Start each Microsoft Office application and customize as needed.

4. Copy the relevant hives from HKEY_CURRENT_USER\Software\Microsoft\Office\8.0 to the New User Settings configuration.

It would be wise to do a final check of the new hives to ensure that nothing unwanted is moved in the copy process.

Outlook—The E-Mail Client

Outlook contains the settings for the Outlook e-mail client. Outlook is available as part of the Microsoft Office package; you may prefer obtaining Outlook 98, however, which is available directly from Microsoft.

I'll admit a preference for Outlook 98. It's a tool that I use every day for e-mail, calendar, and contact management tasks. Prior to Outlook 98, there was no viable export facility for contacts, so it was difficult to back up Outlook's contacts list. Outlook 98 offers substantial improvements over earlier versions of Outlook. I recommend that if you are considering Outlook, you get the latest version of it from Microsoft.

The Outlook sub-hive contains information on the following functionalities of Outlook. In this example, we are looking at the Outlook 98 registry entries:

AnimatedCursor—Outlook supports certain additional animated cursors, and this sub-hive contains information on the location of these cursors. There is no guarantee that there will be additional animated cursors installed, however.

Answer Wizard—The Answer Wizard is a supplementary help system that assists users in searching for additional help on problems they are having.

Categories—This entry includes categories of items in Outlook. For example, in my version I have Business, Holiday Cards, Competition, Favorites, Status, Gifts, Goals/Objectives, Hot Contacts, Ideas, International, Key Customer, Miscellaneous, Personal, Phone Calls, Suppliers, Strategies, Time & Expenses, VIP, Waiting, and Holiday.

Dataviz—This entry holds a flag indicating whether public folders are hidden or not.

NameSpaces—A NameSpace represents a data source, such as the MAPI message store.

OMI—This is the Outlook Internet e-mail system configuration.

Operations—This entry contains configurations of various operations that Outlook will perform, such as file import, file export, data link export, VCard import, Accounts import, Calendar import, and Eudora import.

OutlookToday—This entry contains configuration information for Outlook Today, if any exists.

Rules Wizard—This entry contains configuration information for the Outlook Rules Wizard, if any exists.

SchedPlusOption—This entry contains options and configuration information for the Outlook Schedule functionality.

SchedulingInformation—This entry contains options and configuration information for the Outlook Schedule functionality.

Scripting—This is the CLSID for the scripting manager.

SearchTypes—This is the table of CLSID entries for each search type.

Setup—This entry lists options chosen during setup.

UpgradePath—This is the path to be used for upgrade.

Outlook is one of the most complex components of Microsoft Office. It can be difficult to configure; but once it's set up, it provides flexibility and power, making it a valuable tool for any busy computer user.

PowerPoint—Microsoft's Presentation Program

Microsoft PowerPoint is a tool used to create presentations for display on a number of different media, including video screens, printed handouts, and slides. Microsoft PowerPoint is capable of such tricks as animation, sounds, and special effects, making it a good presentation and training tool. Many users are familiar with Microsoft PowerPoint, but most do not use this program to its fullest. Look at the supported features discussed in this section for some ideas of what can be done with this versatile program.

The following list contains items that are specific to PowerPoint:

Addins—Microsoft PowerPoint supports a number of add-in product functionalities. Some add-ins include auto-content and PowerPoint tools.

Answer Wizard—The Answer Wizard is a supplementary help system that assists users in searching for additional help on problems they are having.

AutoContent Wizard—Assists users in designing a presentation.

DLL Addins—These are add-in DLL files.

Document Routing—This is a flag to tell Microsoft PowerPoint whether or not to track status.

Export Modules—These are any modules used to export presentations to other formats, such as for an offline publishing or printing system.

InstallRoot—This is the root directory that Microsoft PowerPoint has been installed in.

OLE Play Options—This is any OLE multimedia support that is included. Typically, items in this sub-hive include sound and video support.

PPCentral—This consists of basic Microsoft PowerPoint options, many of which are configurable by the user.

Sound—This concerns sound formats, such as WAV, that are supported by Microsoft PowerPoint.

Sound Effects—These are the included sound effects that the user may use in a presentation. Microsoft PowerPoint includes the Typewriter, Whoosh, Laser, Camera, and Drive By effects.

Translators—These tools provide import and export support for other versions of Microsoft PowerPoint. The tools include export to Microsoft PowerPoint 7, and import to Microsoft PowerPoint 7 and Microsoft PowerPoint 4.

ValuPack—Specifies the location of the Microsoft Office ValuPack directory. Run VALUPK8.HLP to find out more about the ValuPack.

Viewer—This is the location for the Microsoft PowerPoint viewer, a stand-alone Microsoft PowerPoint display program.

Publisher—Microsoft's Layout Program

Microsoft Publisher is a mid-range page layout program that is well integrated with other Microsoft Office products. Using Microsoft Publisher is easy, and allows you to create professional documents that may be printed locally or sent to a printer/typesetter for duplication. The following list contains items specific to Microsoft Publisher:

ColorSchemes—Contains the definition of the Microsoft Publisher color schemes. Microsoft Publisher allows users to switch color schemes at any point by using a four-color palette.

Envelopes—Contains information on any envelopes defined.

HTML—Contains the filter to process HTML documents. Microsoft Publisher will publish in HTML if desired, allowing the creation of Web pages from other existing documents with a minimum of effort.

HTMLCharacterEncodings—Character encoding for foreign languages is found here.

Mail Merge—Contains information on mail merge. Using the Microsoft Access Jet database engine, Microsoft Publisher is able to merge database information, creating custom documents as necessary.

Page Size—Defines custom page sizes, such as those required for business cards.

Printing—Contains information used by Microsoft Publisher to print user documents.

ProPrint—Contains information used by Microsoft Publisher to print using a high-end image processing system.

PubBackground—Contains the directory path to the Microsoft Publisher backgrounds that may be used with publications.

PubClipart—Contains the directory path to the Microsoft Publisher clip art that may be used with publications.

Recent File List—Holds the Microsoft Publisher MRU (Most Recently Used) file list.

Spelling—Contains spell-checking options.

Version—Version information is saved here.

WizType—Contains the Microsoft Publisher Wizards that are used to create basic publications with a minimum of effort.

Word—Microsoft's Word Processor

The Word sub-hive contains information about the directory that Microsoft Word was installed in. All of the remaining Word options are set in the user's configuration.

Wrapper—The New Dialog Box Support

The Wrapper sub-hive is used to implement file types that will be recognized by the File New dialog box. The list is a set of descriptions and extensions. The following list contains items specific to the Wrapper sub-hive.

FindFile\Filters—The entries here constitute the list of descriptions used in the New dialog box.

NewTypes—These entries constitute the list of file types used in the New dialog box.

Microsoft Office User Configuration Information

Much like the general setting described in the previous section, the settings discussed here control how Microsoft Office behaves. The main difference is that these settings control the behavior of Microsoft Office for a specific user—typically, you. Not all users will have these sub-hives, but most Microsoft Office users will have some, if not all, of them.

The best way to access these registry entries is through HKEY_CURRENT_USER\ Software\Microsoft\Office\8.0. Although they are also available in the HKEY_ USERS hive, using HKEY_CURRENT_USER instead will ensure that the correct set of entries (those for the currently logged on user) are always modified.

Some usage of these hives includes:

- Backing up the hive and saving it for another userid. This second userid could be the same user, but with a different userid. This allows the users to recover their entire configuration without changes.

- Modifying a specific user's entries. Maybe the organization name changes. We could rely on users to update their systems or simply go in and make the necessary changes for the users.

- Implementing a specific backup and restore for whatever reason the user wants.

NOTE Sometimes we just want to start over and redo our user settings from scratch. So, we uninstall Microsoft Office and do a new clean install. Bang! There are all our old settings back again—we can't seem to get rid of them. The reason for this is simple: Uninstalling doesn't remove these user configuration settings. Uninstalling only removes the system settings. It is actually not even necessary to uninstall to change the user configuration settings; simply delete the user's configuration.

Below are some of the common user configuration settings. These may be altered, following standard precautions about backing up, and will only affect the current user. Other users will not see any changes made to the HKEY_CURRENT_USER configuration.

Access

Microsoft Access user configurations are stored in sub-hives under the Access hive. The items found in this hive will vary greatly depending on the user's configuration and use of Access.

Binder

Any Binder user-specific settings are saved in this sub-hive.

Common

Items in the Common sub-hive are shared between more than one of the Microsoft Office applications. For example, the Microsoft Office Assistant is used by all the Microsoft Office products.

Commonly, any user-installed items, such as those from Visual Basic for Applications, will be stored in the Common sub-hive as well. See "Using the Registry from Microsoft Office Applications," later in this chapter.

Most Common sub-hives contain:

Assistant—Contains the settings for the Microsoft Office Assistant, including who the assistant is and other Microsoft Assistant configurations. To change these settings, left-context-click the Microsoft Office Assistant and select an item to change.

AutoCorrect—AutoCorrect is mostly used in Microsoft Word. It allows a word that is misspelled to be automatically corrected. Users of Excel, Power-Point, and Access will also find use for this functionality.

Cursors—Cursors displayed by Microsoft Office may be configured in this sub-hive. I've been unable to find any way other than registry manipulation to change Microsoft Office's cursor selections.

FileNew—Contains the configurations for the File New dialog box.

General—Contains the general settings for all Microsoft Office applications.

Internet—Contains the Internet settings for all Microsoft Office applications.

Open Find—Contains the settings for the Open dialog box.

Toolbars—Contains the Toolbar configuration and settings.

UserInfo—Contains information about the current user.

Draw

Microsoft Draw is a helper application that is used to allow editing and drawing within Microsoft Office documents. Primarily an OLE server application, Microsoft Draw is not designed or intended to be used as a stand-alone application.

Excel

The user's entire Excel configuration is contained in the Excel sub-hive. Items in this sub-hive include:

Init Commands—Contains the commands used to initialize Excel.

Init Menus—Contains information used to initialize Excel's menu.

Line Print—Contains Lotus macro line printing settings.

Microsoft Excel—Contains Basic configuration settings.

Recent File List—Contains the list of the most recently used files.

Spell Checker—Contains the options for configuration of the spelling checker.

WK? Settings—Contains the settings for the Lotus open and save feature.

Graph

Microsoft Graph is a helper application that is used to allow editing and inclusion of simple graphs and tables within Microsoft Office documents. Primarily an OLE server application, Microsoft Graph is not designed or intended to be used as a stand-alone application.

Outlook

Outlook's configuration settings are contained in this sub-hive. Settings for the following areas are included:

Appointment—Contains the appointment book configuration information.

AutoNameCheck—Contains the setting that indicates whether to automatically check names in the Send-to and CC lines of messages.

Categories—Contains the message categories.

Contact—Contains the contact (names) list management configuration and options.

Dataviz—Contains the interface with external data sources such as the PAB (Personal Address Book) and other data sources.

Item Toolbars—Contains the Toolbar configurations.

Journal—Contains the Outlook Journal, used to track items.

Journal Entry—Contains the Outlook Journal configuration.

Message—Contains the message box configuration.

Note—Contains the note configuration.

Office Explorer—Contains the configuration of the Office Explorer.

Office Finder—Contains the Office Finder configuration and settings.

OMI Account Manager— Contains the Outlook Internet e-mail system configuration.

Options—Contains various miscellaneous settings.

Printing—Contains the printing options and configuration.

Report—Contains the reporting options and configuration.

Scripting—Contains the scripting driver's CLSID.

Security—Contains the security settings.

Setup—Contains the setup options and settings.

Task—Contains the task options and settings.

Today—Contains the Outlook Today settings.

WAB—Contains the settings for the Windows Address Book.

Wizards—Contains the Wizard settings.

PowerPoint

Microsoft PowerPoint user settings are saved in this sub-hive.

Publisher

Microsoft Publisher user settings are saved in this sub-hive. They include the following:

Preferences—Contains the user preferences and settings.

Tracking Data—Contains the tracking items.

UserInfo—Contains the information specific to the current user, including the following:

- OtherOrganization

- Personal

- PrimaryBusiness

- SecondaryBusiness

Query

Contains information for the Microsoft Query program, if installed and used. Microsoft Query is useful for peeking at various data sources, such as database files created by any ODBC-compliant application.

Word

The user configuration of Microsoft Word is saved in this sub-hive. Items saved here include:

Custom Labels—Holds information that is used when printing on labels. Users may create their own custom label to match their label stock.

Data—Information contained includes the Word MRU (Most Recently Used) file list. This list is hidden in another object and is not editable.

Default Save—Contains the default save format.

Help—Contains the Help file information.

List Gallery Presets—Contains binary information about presets for the list gallery.

Options—Holds various Microsoft Word options and settings.

Stationery—Contains information used primarily when Microsoft Word is the e-mail editor.

Text Converters—Contains the filters used to convert documents saved as text files into Word:

Import\MSPAB—Filter for importing from Microsoft Personal Address Book

Import\OUTLOOK—Filter for importing from Microsoft Outlook

Import\SPLUS—Filter for importing from Microsoft Schedule Plus

Wizards—Contains configurations for the various Word Wizards

WordMail—Contains WordMail settings that are used when Word is used as the e-mail editor.

Using the Registry from Microsoft Office Applications

Okay, in our final section of this chapter, let's figure out how to manipulate the registry from a Microsoft Office application. That's right, if you wanted to, you could write an entire registry editor using Microsoft Word.

Most Microsoft Office users won't have a great need to save items in the registry. But, if you find that you need to save information that must be persistent between sessions, saving this information in the registry can be an excellent method.

The example we'll use here is Sybex's system that authors use to manage their books. This system allows the author to automatically name his or her files; insert pertinent information, such as the book's title and ISBN; and allow defaults for a vast number of different options that authors and editors like to use.

This system works by having the author enter some information at the beginning of a new project. This information is entered using a simple dialog box that was created with Microsoft Office's Visual Basic for Applications. The information is then written into the registry, in the user's section, under the hive HKEY_CURRENT_USER\Software\Microsoft\Office\8.0\Common\Sybex. You would use a different name than Sybex, of course.

Figure 13.2 shows the registry hive Sybex and the data keys that have been saved in it. These keys can be modified from various places in Word, where Sybex has added functionality.

FIGURE 13.2:

The Sybex sub-hive has a lot of information about this book.

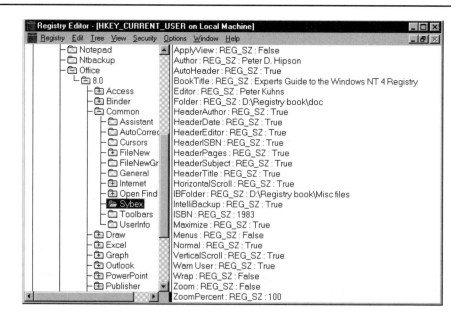

The Sybex options, stored in the Sybex sub-hive, are generally modified using the Sybex Options dialog box. This dialog box (see Figure 13.3) is a multi-tab dialog box that is well designed to allow easy data entry. (A special thanks goes to the authors of this system—it is the best author support from a publisher that I've used to date!)

FIGURE 13.3:

The Sybex Author Template Options dialog box sets and resets options saved in the registry.

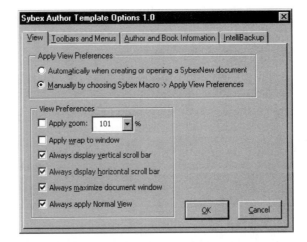

I'm going to show some of the code used to create this dialog box here. Your example does not need to be this complex. A simple single dialog box without tabs can be very effective in getting a user interface together.

First is the main function that displays the dialog box itself:

```
Sub DisplaySybexOptionsDialogBox()
    frmPreferences.Show
    frmPreferences.mlpTabs.Value = 0
End Sub
```

This code shows the dialog box frmPreferences, then exits. The frmPreferences dialog box takes care of actually initializing itself by reading the various registry entries and updating the dialog box appropriately.

Next, the function ApplyViewPreferences does the actual initialization by reading the appropriate registry hive and updating each of the controls located on the dialog box:

```
Sub ApplyViewPreferences()

'Allows user to manually apply view preferences stored in the Registry
```

```
Dim Sybex As String
Sybex = "HKEY_CURRENT_USER\Software\Microsoft\Office\8.0\Common\Sybex"
```

Which hive is the right hive? The hive location is stored in a simple string variable. This saves us a lot of typing and possible errors since spelling "Sybex" is so much easier than spelling that whole registry name:

```
'Quotes on "True" to avoid error if key does not exist
With ActiveWindow
```

Any line that begins with a leading single quote (') is a comment line. These comment lines will be ignored by the system and are only there for our own information. ActiveWindow tells the system to work with the active window. An example of conditional processing follows:

```
    If System.PrivateProfileString("", Sybex, "Zoom") = "True" Then
        .View.Zoom.Percentage = System.PrivateProfileString("", Sybex,
"ZoomPercent")
    End If
```

An If statement allows what is called *conditional processing*. When the subject of the If statement is True, the statement after the Then is executed. Conditional processing is the cornerstone of computer programming. Without conditional processing, programs as we know them could not exist.

In the previous example, if the following function:

```
System.PrivateProfileString("", Sybex, "Zoom")
```

returns a value of "True", we fill in the View.Zoom.Percentage with the value contained in the registry data key ZoomPercent. The function System.PrivateProfileString() returns the value that the data key contains if it exists. If the data key doesn't exist, the default, an empty string, is returned.

The following code is very similar. We check to see if the data key "Wrap" exists, and what its value is. If the value is "True", we set the variable View.WrapToWindow to True. Otherwise, we set the variable View.WrapToWindow to False.

```
    If System.PrivateProfileString("", Sybex, "Wrap") = "True" Then
        .View.WrapToWindow = True
    Else
        .View.WrapToWindow = False
    End If
```

This same process—of checking a registry data key for its value, setting a local variable to reflect the registry key's value, and checking the next registry data key in our list—is performed by checking each of the relevant registry data keys, as shown in the following:

```
If System.PrivateProfileString("", Sybex, "VerticalScroll") = "True"
Then
        .DisplayVerticalScrollBar = True
    Else
        .DisplayVerticalScrollBar = False
    End If

    If System.PrivateProfileString("", Sybex, "HorizontalScroll") =
"True" Then
        .DisplayHorizontalScrollBar = True
    Else
        .DisplayHorizontalScrollBar = False
    End If
```

Next, we check to see which of the user's toolbars are to be displayed. (The toolbars are specified by the user in the Toolbars and Menus tab [it's the second tab] of the dialog box.) Notice that in my registry example, I don't have the data key "Headings". This is because this option was never turned on, and the default, if missing, is off.

The same process is used for the Toolbars and Menus section of the dialog box:

```
'Headings toolbar
'this is problematic on some computers for some reason
'may need an On Error statement
On Error Resume Next
    If System.PrivateProfileString("", Sybex, "Headings") = "True" Then
        CommandBars("Heading Styles").Visible = True
    Else
        CommandBars("Heading Styles").Visible = False
    End If

'Text Styles toolbar
    If System.PrivateProfileString("", Sybex, "Text Styles") = "True"
Then
        CommandBars("Text Styles").Visible = True
    Else
```

```
            CommandBars("Text Styles").Visible = False
        End If

'List Styles toolbar

    If System.PrivateProfileString("", Sybex, "Lists") = "True" Then
        CommandBars("List Styles").Visible = True
    Else
        CommandBars("List Styles").Visible = False
    End If

'Sidebar Styles toolbar

    If System.PrivateProfileString("", Sybex, "Sidebar") = "True" Then
        CommandBars("Sidebars").Visible = True
    Else
        CommandBars("Sidebars").Visible = False
    End If

'Table Styles toolbar

    If System.PrivateProfileString("", Sybex, "Tables") = "True" Then
        CommandBars("Table Styles").Visible = True
    Else
        CommandBars("Table Styles").Visible = False
    End If

'Menu Preferences

'Style menu
        If System.PrivateProfileString("", Sybex, "Style") = "True"
Then
            If Is_Menu_Displayed("&Style") = False Then
                    CommandBars("The
Reservoir").Controls("&Style").Move _
                        Bar:=CommandBars("Menu Bar"), Before:=3
            End If
        Else
            If Is_Menu_Displayed("&Style") = True Then
                CommandBars("Menu Bar").Controls("&Style").Move
Bar:=CommandBars("The Reservoir")
```

```
                    End If
                End If

    'Sidebar menu

            If System.PrivateProfileString("", Sybex, "Sidebars") = "True"
    Then
                If Is_Menu_Displayed("Si&debar") = False Then
                    If Is_Menu_Displayed("&Style") Then
                        SidebarMenuPosition = 4
                    Else
                        SidebarMenuPosition = 3
                    End If
                    CommandBars("The
    Reservoir").Controls("Si&debar").Move _
                        Bar:=CommandBars("Menu Bar"), Before:=Sidebar-
    MenuPosition
                End If
            Else
                If Is_Menu_Displayed("Si&debar") = "True" Then
                    CommandBars("Menu Bar").Controls("Si&debar").Move
    Bar:=CommandBars("The Reservoir")
                End If
            End If

    'Element menu

            If System.PrivateProfileString("", Sybex, "Element") = "True"
    Then
                If Is_Menu_Displayed("E&lement") = False Then
                    If Is_Menu_Displayed("&Style") Then
                        If Is_Menu_Displayed("Si&debar") Then
                            ElementMenuPosition = 5
                        Else
                            ElementMenuPosition = 4
                        End If
                    Else
                        If Is_Menu_Displayed("Si&debar") Then
                            ElementMenuPosition = 4
                        Else
                            ElementMenuPosition = 3
```

```
                                End If
                        End If
                        'add the Element menu to the menu bar
                                CommandBars("The
Reservoir").Controls("E&lement").Move _
                                        Bar:=CommandBars("Menu Bar"), Before:=Element-
MenuPosition
                        End If
                Else
                        If Is_Menu_Displayed("E&lement") = "True" Then
                                CommandBars("Menu Bar").Controls("E&lement").Move
Bar:=CommandBars("The Reservoir")
                        End If
                End If


        'Sybex Macro menu check box


        If System.PrivateProfileString("", Sybex, "Sybex Macro") =
"True" Then
                If Is_Menu_Displayed("Sybe&x Macro") = False Then
                        CommandBars("The Reservoir").Controls("Sybe&x
Macro").Move _
                                Bar:=CommandBars("Menu Bar"), Before:=Command-
Bars("Menu bar").Controls.Count + 1
                End If
        Else
                If Is_Menu_Displayed("Sybe&x Macro") = True Then
                        CommandBars("Menu Bar").Controls("Sybe&x Macro").Move
Bar:=CommandBars("The Reservoir")
                End If
        End If

'Turn off the display of The Reservoir toolbar if it somehow made an
appearance
With CommandBars("The Reservoir")
    If .Visible = True Then .Visible = False
End With
```

After the user finishes with the dialog box and clicks the OK button, the registry is updated by the function All_OK(). If the user clicks the Cancel button instead of OK, everything is discarded without making any changes in the registry.

This function is virtually the opposite of the initialization code. Read the value of the dialog control and update the registry appropriately. First, a bit of house-keeping:

```
Sub All_OK()
Dim Sybex As String
Sybex = "HKEY_CURRENT_USER\Software\Microsoft\Office\8.0\Common\Sybex"

    frmPreferences.Hide
```

Start up the function and save the desired registry hive as a string to avoid having to retype mutiple times. Next, hide the dialog box from the user by using frm-Preferences.Hide.

Simply check each dialog item's state or value, as appropriate, and update the registry. For example, Apply View Preferences is controlled by a pair of radio buttons. Radio buttons are mutually exclusive—only one may be selected at a time. Since there are only two radio buttons for View Preferences, we need only check one of them because the other will be of the opposite value.

```
'View tab of Options dialog box
'Apply View Preferences group box: Automatically or Manually

If optAutomatically.Value = True Then
    System.PrivateProfileString("", Sybex, "ApplyView") = True
Else
    System.PrivateProfileString("", Sybex, "ApplyView") = False
End If
```

In the previous example, if the control optAutomatically.Value returns True, we set the registry data key ApplyView to True. Otherwise, we know that optManu-ally (the other control in View Preferences) will be True and we'd have to set ApplyView to False. (Refer to Figure 13.3 again.)

We continue in the same manner, checking the state or value of each of the dialog box controls, updating the registry as necessary. This process continues through each of the dialog box controls, updating the registry data keys to reflect the user's preferences.

TIP

Need a quick way to create a Visual Basic for Applications function? Simply create a macro and edit the macro's code. This will provide a quick way to start a function.

Confused about System.PrivateProfileString?

The first example in this section retrieved a value from the registry. This value was used to initialize the dialog box controls. In the second example, we set a registry data key value with the same function. How does it know the difference?

The magic is that the context of *how the call is made* tells Visual Basic for Applications *how to use it*. In the first instance, the call was within an If statement. In the second use, the call was part of an assignment statement. Visual Basic for Applications knows the difference.

Hints and Kinks from the Experts

Our experts don't have a lot of registry hints on Microsoft Office because overall, most serious problems with Microsoft Office require reinstallation of the product, usually due to problems with file corruption.

How to Disable That Leaky, Resource-Stealing FindFast.   If you remove the FindFast shortcut from the StartUp group, the index files are not removed from your partition. The Microsoft Office apps still continue to use these old index files whenever you use the Open dialogue box, which can cause delays in finding documents. The proper way to remove FindFast follows:

1.   Select Start ➤ Settings ➤ Control Panel ➤ Find Fast.

2.   Select an entry in Index for Documents In and Below and click Delete Index from the Index menu. Click OK until the index is deleted.

3.   Repeat step 2 until Index for Documents In and Below is empty.

4.   On the Index menu, click Close and Stop.

5.   Remove the FindFast shortcut from the StartUp group.

(Courtesy of Jerold Schulman)

CHAPTER
FOURTEEN

14

The Windows NT Service Pack 3

- Retrieving original registry files

- Registry entries added or modified during installation

- Font substitution entries

- Hints and kinks from the experts

The Windows NT Service Pack 3 fixes a number of the major problems that exist in Windows NT version 4. Not everything is perfect with Windows NT Service Pack 3, though, it still manages to break a few things! We'll not get into the good and the bad of Windows NT Service Pack 3; however, this chapter will cover the changes that Windows NT Service Pack 3 makes to the Windows NT registry.

In this chapter we'll try to understand the changes to the registry that the Windows NT Service Pack 3 installation program makes. We'll look at these changes on a component-by-component basis, just as they are handled by the Windows NT Service Pack 3 setup program.

NOTE
There are slight differences between Windows NT for the Intel platform and the other (RISC) platforms. These changes are primarily in the data stored in the registry and not in the registry structure itself.

Retrieving Original Registry Files

If the user requests it, the Windows NT Service Pack 3 installation process is able to save all the changes made during the installation process, allowing the user to uninstall the service pack if necessary. The files removed during installation and other information about the changes made are stored in the hidden directory %SystemRoot%\$NtServicePackUninstall$.

NOTE
The creation of an uninstallation directory does not address the problem of the user needing Windows NT Service Pack 3, but when installed, Windows NT Service Pack 3 breaks something that is also critical to the user's system.

TIP
Even though the uninstallation directory is hidden, you can still access this information by typing **CD %SystemRoot%\$NtServicePackUninstall$** at a command prompt.

Changes to the registry are documented in two locations. There will be a series of about 36 files named REG000??, where *??* is a sequential number. These files do not have an extension. Each of these files contains binary registry information. Additionally, the file uninst.inf also contains registry hive, sub-hive, and data key values. The information in uninst.inf is readable and editable with a standard text editor.

NOTE   For registry entries specific to NT Workstation and to IBM-6070 that are saved in a similar fashion, see the next sections.

Table 14.1 lists registry items that are saved in the event that the user wishes to uninstall Windows NT Service Pack 3. Most of the entries saved will be modified later by the Windows NT Service Pack 3 installation process.

TABLE 14.1: Registry Keys Saved by the Service Pack 3 Setup Program

Hive	Sub-Hive	Data Key (if specified)
HKEY_LOCAL_MACHINE	SYSTEM\CurrentControlSet\Control\Windows	CSDVersion
HKEY_LOCAL_MACHINE	SYSTEM\CurrentControlSet\Services\RPCLOCATOR	DependOnService
HKEY_LOCAL_MACHINE	SYSTEM\CurrentControlSet\Control\SecurePipeServers\winreg\AllowedPaths	Machine
HKEY_LOCAL_MACHINE	SOFTWARE\Microsoft\Cryptography\Defaults\ProviderTypes\Type001	
HKEY_LOCAL_MACHINE	SOFTWARE\Microsoft\Cryptography\Defaults\Provider\MicrosoftBaseCryptographicProviderv1.0	
HKEY_CLASSES_ROOT	DirectDraw	
HKEY_CLASSES_ROOT	DirectDraw\CLSID	
HKEY_CLASSES_ROOT	CLSID\{D7B70EE0-4340-11CF-B063-0020AFC2CD35}	
HKEY_CLASSES_ROOT	CLSID\{D7B70EE0-4340-11CF-B063-0020AFC2CD35}\InprocServer32	
HKEY_CLASSES_ROOT	CLSID\{D7B70EE0-4340-11CF-B063-0020AFC2CD35}\InprocServer32	ThreadingModel
HKEY_CLASSES_ROOT	DirectSound	

Continued on next page

TABLE 14.1 CONTINUED: Registry Keys Saved by the Service Pack 3 Setup Program

Hive	Sub-Hive	Data Key (if specified)
HKEY_CLASSES_ROOT	DirectSound\CLSID	
HKEY_CLASSES_ROOT	CLSID\{47D4D946-62E8-11cf-93BC-444553540000}	
HKEY_CLASSES_ROOT	CLSID\{47D4D946-62E8-11cf-93BC-444553540000}\InprocServer32	
HKEY_CLASSES_ROOT	CLSID\{47D4D946-62E8-11cf-93BC-444553540000}\InprocServer32	ThreadingModel
HKEY_CLASSES_ROOT	DirectDrawClipper	
HKEY_CLASSES_ROOT	DirectDrawClipper\CLSID	
HKEY_CLASSES_ROOT	CLSID\{593817A0-7DB3-11CF-A2DE-00AA00B93356}	
HKEY_CLASSES_ROOT	CLSID\{593817A0-7DB3-11CF-A2DE-00AA00B93356}\InprocServer32	
HKEY_CLASSES_ROOT	CLSID\{593817A0-7DB3-11CF-A2DE-00AA00B93356}\InprocServer32	ThreadingModel
HKEY_LOCAL_MACHINE	Software\Microsoft\DirectPlay\ServiceProviders\%SP_SERIAL%	
HKEY_LOCAL_MACHINE	Software\Microsoft\DirectPlay\ServiceProviders\%SP_SERIAL%	Guid
HKEY_LOCAL_MACHINE	Software\Microsoft\DirectPlay\ServiceProviders\%SP_SERIAL%	Path
HKEY_LOCAL_MACHINE	Software\Microsoft\DirectPlay\Service-Providers\%SP_SERIAL%	dwReserved1
HKEY_LOCAL_MACHINE	Software\Microsoft\DirectPlay\ServiceProviders\%SP_SERIAL%	dwReserved2
HKEY_LOCAL_MACHINE	Software\Microsoft\DirectPlay\ServiceProviders\%SP_SERIAL%\AddressTypes\{F2F0CE00-E0AF-11cf-9C4E-00A0C905425E}	
HKEY_LOCAL_MACHINE	Software\Microsoft\DirectPlay\ServiceProviders\%SP_MODEM%	
HKEY_LOCAL_MACHINE	Software\Microsoft\DirectPlay\Service-Providers\%SP_MODEM%	Guid

Continued on next page

TABLE 14.1 CONTINUED: Registry Keys Saved by the Service Pack 3 Setup Program

Hive	Sub-Hive	Data Key (if specified)
HKEY_LOCAL_MACHINE	Software\Microsoft\DirectPlay\ServiceProviders\ %SP_MODEM%	Path
HKEY_LOCAL_MACHINE	Software\Microsoft\DirectPlay\ServiceProviders\ %SP_MODEM%	dwReserved1
HKEY_LOCAL_MACHINE	Software\Microsoft\DirectPlay\ServiceProviders\ %SP_MODEM%	dwReserved2
HKEY_LOCAL_MACHINE	Software\Microsoft\DirectPlay\ServiceProviders\ %SP_MODEM%\AddressTypes\{78EC89A0-E0AF-11cf-9C4E-00A0C905425E}	
HKEY_LOCAL_MACHINE	Software\Microsoft\DirectPlay\ServiceProviders\ %SP_TCP%	
HKEY_LOCAL_MACHINE	Software\Microsoft\DirectPlay\ServiceProviders\ %SP_TCP%	Guid
HKEY_LOCAL_MACHINE	Software\Microsoft\DirectPlay\ServiceProviders\ %SP_TCP%	Path
HKEY_LOCAL_MACHINE	Software\Microsoft\DirectPlay\ServiceProviders\ %SP_TCP%	dwReserved1
HKEY_LOCAL_MACHINE	Software\Microsoft\DirectPlay\ServiceProviders\ %SP_TCP%	dwReserved2
HKEY_LOCAL_MACHINE	Software\Microsoft\DirectPlay\ServiceProviders\ %SP_TCP%\AddressTypes\{C4A54DA0-E0AF-11cf-9C4E-00A0C905425E}	
HKEY_LOCAL_MACHINE	Software\Microsoft\DirectPlay\ServiceProviders\ %SP_IPX%	
HKEY_LOCAL_MACHINE	Software\Microsoft\DirectPlay\ServiceProviders\ %SP_IPX%	Guid
HKEY_LOCAL_MACHINE	Software\Microsoft\DirectPlay\ServiceProviders\ %SP_IPX%	Path
HKEY_LOCAL_MACHINE	Software\Microsoft\DirectPlay\ServiceProviders\ %SP_IPX%	dwReserved1
HKEY_LOCAL_MACHINE	Software\Microsoft\DirectPlay\ServiceProviders\ %SP_IPX%	dwReserved2

Continued on next page

TABLE 14.1 CONTINUED: Registry Keys Saved by the Service Pack 3 Setup Program

Hive	Sub-Hive	Data Key (if specified)
HKEY_LOCAL_MACHINE	Software\Microsoft\Direct3D	
HKEY_LOCAL_MACHINE	Software\Microsoft\Direct3D\Drivers\RampEmulation	
HKEY_LOCAL_MACHINE	Software\Microsoft\Direct3D\Drivers\RampEmulation	Base
HKEY_LOCAL_MACHINE	Software\Microsoft\Direct3D\Drivers\RampEmulation	Description
HKEY_LOCAL_MACHINE	Software\Microsoft\Direct3D\Drivers\RampEmulation	GUID
HKEY_LOCAL_MACHINE	Software\Microsoft\Direct3D\Drivers\RGBEmulation	
HKEY_LOCAL_MACHINE	Software\Microsoft\Direct3D\Drivers\RGBEmulation	Base
HKEY_LOCAL_MACHINE	Software\Microsoft\Direct3D\Drivers\RGBEmulation	Description
HKEY_LOCAL_MACHINE	Software\Microsoft\Direct3D\Drivers\RGBEmulation	GUID
HKEY_LOCAL_MACHINE	Software\Microsoft\Direct3D\Drivers\Direct3DHAL	
HKEY_LOCAL_MACHINE	Software\Microsoft\Direct3D\Drivers\Direct3DHAL	Base
HKEY_LOCAL_MACHINE	Software\Microsoft\Direct3D\Drivers\Direct3DHAL	Description
HKEY_LOCAL_MACHINE	Software\Microsoft\Direct3D\Drivers\Direct3DHAL	GUID
HKEY_CLASSES_ROOT	CLSID\{25E609E0-B259-11CF-BFC7-444535540000}	
HKEY_CLASSES_ROOT	CLSID\{25E609E0-B259-11CF-BFC7-444535540000}\InProcServer32	
HKEY_CLASSES_ROOT	CLSID\{25E609E0-B259-11CF-BFC7-444535540000}\InProcServer32	ThreadingModel
HKEY_CLASSES_ROOTHKEY_CLASSES_ROOT	CLSID\{25E609E1-B259-11CF-BFC7-444535540000}	
HKEY_CLASSES_ROOT	CLSID\{25E609E1-B259-11CF-BFC7-444535540000}\InProcServer32	
HKEY_CLASSES_ROOT	CLSID\{25E609E1-B259-11CF-BFC7-444535540000}\InProcServer32	ThreadingModel
HKEY_LOCAL_MACHINE	SOFTWARE\Microsoft\DirectX	
HKEY_LOCAL_MACHINE	SOFTWARE\Microsoft\DirectX	InstalledVersion

Continued on next page

TABLE 14.1 CONTINUED: Registry Keys Saved by the Service Pack 3 Setup Program

Hive	Sub-Hive	Data Key (if specified)
HKEY_LOCAL_MACHINE	SOFTWARE\Microsoft\ActiveSetup\Installed-Components\{44BBA855-CC51-11CF-AAFA-00AA00B6015C}	
HKEY_LOCAL_MACHINE	SOFTWARE\Microsoft\ActiveSetup\Installed-Components\{44BBA855-CC51-11CF-AAFA-00AA00B6015C}	MicrosoftDirectX
HKEY_LOCAL_MACHINE	Software\Microsoft\WindowsNT\CurrentVersion\Font Substitutes	

Workstation-Only Registry Entries Saved

Table 14.2 lists the registry keys saved during installation, allowing the user to uninstall Windows NT Service Pack 3 and retain the old files. These items are specific to the Windows NT Workstation installation only and don't apply to Windows NT Server.

TABLE 14.2: NT Workstation Registry Keys Saved by the Service Pack 3 Setup Program

Hive	Sub-Hive	Data Key
HKEY_CURRENT_MACHINE	SYSTEM\CurrentControlSet\Control\Lsa	Notification Packages
HKEY_CURRENT_MACHINE	SYSTEM\CurrentControlSet\Control\Lsa\MSV1_0	Auth1

IBM 6070-Only Registry Entries Saved

The IBM model 6070 computer has a slight incompatibility with the standard Intel-based Windows NT. Therefore, there is a custom HAL (Hardware Abstraction Layer) for this computer, and there are some registry keys that are different for this specific computer.

Table 14.3 lists registry items that are saved to allow the user to uninstall Windows NT Service Pack 3. These items are only saved for the IBM 6070 systems and not for any other systems.

TABLE 14.3: IBM-6070–Only Registry Keys Saved by the Service Pack 3 Setup Program

Hive	Sub-Hive	Data Key
HKEY_CURRENT_MACHINE	SYSTEM\CurrentControlSet\Services\Atapi\ Parameters\Device0	DriverParameter
HKEY_CURRENT_MACHINE	SYSTEM\CurrentControlSet\Services\Atapi\ Parameters\Device1	DriverParameter

IIS-Only Registry Entries Saved

Microsoft's IIS (Internet Information Server) is used by many Windows NT users. A competent Web/FTP and Gopher server, IIS is finding great acceptance in the industry.

Table 14.4 lists registry items that are saved from the original registry in the event that the user wishes to uninstall Windows NT Service Pack 3. These items are only significant to IIS and not for any other systems.

TABLE 14.4: IIS-Only Registry Keys Saved by the Service Pack 3 Setup Program

Hive	Sub-Hive	Data Key
HKEY_CURRENT_MACHINE	SOFTWARE\Microsoft\Inetsrv\CurrentVersion	Description
HKEY_CURRENT_MACHINE	SOFTWARE\Microsoft\Inetsrv\CurrentVersion	ServiceName
HKEY_CURRENT_MACHINE	SOFTWARE\Microsoft\Inetsrv\CurrentVersion	Title
HKEY_CLASSES_ROOT	CLSID\{5a61f7a0-cde1-11cf-9113-00aa00425c62}	
HKEY_CLASSES_ROOT	Folder\shellex\PropertySheetHandlers\IISSEPage	
HKEY_CLASSES_ROOT	Folder\shellex\PropertySheetHandlers	
HKEY_CLASSES_ROOT	Folder\shellex\CopyHookHandlers\IISCopyHook	
HKEY_CLASSES_ROOT	*\shellex\CopyHookHandlers\IISCopyHook	
HKEY_CURRENT_MACHINE	SOFTWARE\Microsoft\Windows\CurrentVersion\ Shell Extensions\Approved	{5a61f7a0-cde1-11cf-9113-00aa00425c62}

Registry Entries Added or Modified during Installation

For all Windows NT systems, registry entries are added or changed during installation of Service Pack 3. Table 14.5 lists those items. Items specific to a certain system are described in later sections. The Type column is coded for setup and does not relate to the registry data types as described in Appendix B.

> **NOTE** Throughout this chapter, any data value that is enclosed in quotes would be entered without the quotes when placed in the registry.

TABLE 14.5: Registry Keys Added or Changed by the Service Pack 3 Setup Program

Hive	Sub-Hive	Data Key	Type	Value
HKEY_CURRENT_MACHINE	SYSTEM\CurrentControlSet\ Control\Windows	CSDVersion	0x10001	0x300
HKEY_CURRENT_MACHINE	SYSTEM\CurrentControlSet\ Services\RPCLOCATOR	DependOnService	0x10000	"LanmanWorksta-tion", "Rdr"
HKEY_CURRENT_MACHINE	SYSTEM\CurrentControlSet\ Control\SecurePipeServers\ winreg\AllowedPaths	Machine	0x10008	System\Current-ControlSet\ Services\ Replicator
HKEY_CURRENT_MACHINE	SOFTWARE\Microsoft\ Cryptography\Defaults\ Provider Types\Type 001	Name	0	Microsoft Base Cryptographic Provider v1.0
HKEY_CURRENT_MACHINE	SOFTWARE\Microsoft\ Cryptography\Defaults\ Provider\Microsoft Base Cryptographic Provider v1.0	Image Path	0	rsabase.dll
HKEY_CURRENT_MACHINE	SOFTWARE\Microsoft\Cryptogra-phy\Defaults\Provider\Microso ft Base Cryptographic Provider v1.0	Type	0x10001	1
HKEY_CLASSES_ROOT	DirectDraw			DirectDraw Object

Continued on next page

TABLE 14.5 CONTINUED: Registry Keys Added or Changed by the Service Pack 3 Setup Program

Hive	Sub-Hive	Data Key	Type	Value
HKEY_CLASSES_ROOT	DirectDraw\CLSID			{D7B70EE0-4340-11CF-B063-0020AFC2CD35}
HKEY_CLASSES_ROOT	CLSID\{D7B70EE0-4340-11CF-B063-0020AFC2CD35}			DirectDraw Object
HKEY_CLASSES_ROOT	CLSID\{D7B70EE0-4340-11CF-B063-0020AFC2CD35}\InprocServer32			ddraw.dll
HKEY_CLASSES_ROOT	CLSID\{D7B70EE0-4340-11CF-B063-0020AFC2CD35}\Inproc-Server32	ThreadingModel		Both
HKEY_CLASSES_ROOT	DirectDrawClipper			DirectDraw Clipper Object
HKEY_CLASSES_ROOT	DirectDrawClipper\CLSID			{593817A0-7DB3-11CF-A2DE-00AA00B93356}
HKEY_CLASSES_ROOT	CLSID\{593817A0-7DB3-11CF-A2DE-00AA00B93356}			DirectDraw Clipper Object
HKEY_CLASSES_ROOT	CLSID\{593817A0-7DB3-11CF-A2DE-00AA00B93356}\Inproc-Server32			ddraw.dll
HKEY_CLASSES_ROOT	CLSID\{593817A0-7DB3-11CF-A2DE-00AA00B93356}\Inproc-Server32	ThreadingModel		Both
HKEY_CLASSES_ROOT	DirectSound	DirectSound Object		
HKEY_CLASSES_ROOT	DirectSound\CLSID			{47D4D946-62E8-11cf-93BC-444553540000}
HKEY_CLASSES_ROOT	CLSID\{47D4D946-62E8-11cf-93BC-444553540000}			DirectSound Object
HKEY_CLASSES_ROOT	CLSID\{47D4D946-62E8-11cf-93BC-444553540000}\InprocServer32			dsound.dll

Continued on next page

TABLE 14.5 CONTINUED: Registry Keys Added or Changed by the Service Pack 3 Setup Program

Hive	Sub-Hive	Data Key	Type	Value
HKEY_CLASSES_ROOT	CLSID\{47D4D946-62E8-11cf-93BC-444553540000}\Inproc-Server32	ThreadingModel		Both
HKEY_CURRENT_MACHINE	Software\Microsoft\DirectPlay\Service Providers\%SP_SERIAL%			
HKEY_CURRENT_MACHINE	Software\Microsoft\DirectPlay\Service Providers\%SP_SERIAL%	Guid		{0F1D6860-88D9-11cf-9C4E-00A0C905425E}
HKEY_CURRENT_MACHINE	Software\Microsoft\DirectPlay\Service Providers\%SP_SERIAL%	Path		%11%\dpmodemx.dll
HKEY_CURRENT_MACHINE	Software\Microsoft\DirectPlay\Service Providers\%SP_SERIAL%	dwReserved1	1	00,00,00,00
HKEY_CURRENT_MACHINE	Software\Microsoft\DirectPlay\Service Providers\%SP_SERIAL%	dwReserved2	1	00,00,00,00
HKEY_CURRENT_MACHINE	Software\Microsoft\DirectPlay\Service Providers\%SP_SERIAL%\Address Types\{F2F0CE00-E0AF-11cf-9C4E-00A0C905425E}			
HKEY_CURRENT_MACHINE	Software\Microsoft\DirectPlay\Service Providers\%SP_MODEM%			
HKEY_CURRENT_MACHINE	Software\Microsoft\DirectPlay\Service Providers\%SP_MODEM%	Guid		{44EAA760-CB68-11cf-9C4E-00A0C905425E}
HKEY_CURRENT_MACHINE	Software\Microsoft\DirectPlay\Service Providers\%SP_MODEM%	Path		%11%\dpmodemx.dll
HKEY_CURRENT_MACHINE	Software\Microsoft\DirectPlay\Service Providers\%SP_MODEM%	dwReserved1	1	00,00,00,00

Continued on next page

TABLE 14.5 CONTINUED: Registry Keys Added or Changed by the Service Pack 3 Setup Program

Hive	Sub-Hive	Data Key	Type	Value
HKEY_CURRENT_MACHINE	Software\Microsoft\DirectPlay\Service Providers\%SP_MODEM%	dwReserved2	1	00,00,00,00
HKEY_CURRENT_MACHINE	Software\Microsoft\DirectPlay\Service Providers\%SP_MODEM%\Address Types\{78EC89A0-E0AF-11cf-9C4E-00A0C905425E}			
HKEY_CURRENT_MACHINE	Software\Microsoft\DirectPlay\Service Providers\%SP_TCP%			
HKEY_CURRENT_MACHINE	Software\Microsoft\DirectPlay\Service Providers\%SP_TCP%	Guid		{36E95EE0-8577-11cf-960C-0080C7534E82}
HKEY_CURRENT_MACHINE	Software\Microsoft\DirectPlay\Service Providers\%SP_TCP%	Path		%11%\"dpw-sockx.dll"
HKEY_CURRENT_MACHINE	Software\Microsoft\DirectPlay\Service Providers\%SP_TCP%	dwReserved1	1	F4,01,00,00
HKEY_CURRENT_MACHINE	Software\Microsoft\DirectPlay\Service Providers\%SP_TCP%	dwReserved2	1	00,00,00,00
HKEY_CURRENT_MACHINE	Software\Microsoft\DirectPlay\Service Providers\%SP_TCP%\Address Types\{C4A54DA0-E0AF-11cf-9C4E-00A0C905425E}			
HKEY_CURRENT_MACHINE	Software\Microsoft\DirectPlay\Service Providers\%SP_IPX%			
HKEY_CURRENT_MACHINE	Software\Microsoft\DirectPlay\Service Providers\%SP_IPX%	Guid		{685BC400-9D2C-11cf-A9CD-00AA006886E3}
HKEY_CURRENT_MACHINE	Software\Microsoft\DirectPlay\Service Providers\%SP_IPX%	Path		%11%\"dpw-sockx.dll"

Continued on next page

TABLE 14.5 CONTINUED: Registry Keys Added or Changed by the Service Pack 3 Setup Program

Hive	Sub-Hive	Data Key	Type	Value
HKEY_CURRENT_MACHINE	Software\Microsoft\ DirectPlay\Service Providers\%SP_IPX%	dwReserved1	1	32,00,00,00
HKEY_CURRENT_MACHINE	Software\Microsoft\ DirectPlay\Service Providers\%SP_IPX%	dwReserved2	1	00,00,00,00
HKEY_CURRENT_MACHINE	Software\Microsoft\Direct3D			
HKEY_CURRENT_MACHINE	Software\Microsoft\Direct3D\D rivers\Ramp Emulation			
HKEY_CURRENT_MACHINE	Software\Microsoft\Direct3D\D rivers\Ramp Emulation	Base		ramp
HKEY_CURRENT_MACHINE	Software\Microsoft\Direct3D\D rivers\Ramp Emulation	Description		Microsoft Direct3D Mono(Ramp) Software Emulation
HKEY_CURRENT_MACHINE	Software\Microsoft\Direct3D\D rivers\Ramp Emulation	GUID	1	20,6b,08,f2,9f,2 5,cf,11,a3,1a,00 ,aa,00,b9,33,56
HKEY_CURRENT_MACHINE	Software\Microsoft\Direct3D\D rivers\RGB Emulation			
HKEY_CURRENT_MACHINE	Software\Microsoft\Direct3D\D rivers\RGB Emulation	Base		rgb
HKEY_CURRENT_MACHINE	Software\Microsoft\Direct3D\D rivers\RGB Emulation	Description		Microsoft Direct3D RGB Software Emulation
HKEY_CURRENT_MACHINE	Software\Microsoft\Direct3D\D rivers\RGB Emulation	GUID	1	60,5c,66,a4,73,2 6,cf,11,a3,1a,00 ,aa,00,b9,33,56
HKEY_CURRENT_MACHINE	Software\Microsoft\Direct3D\D rivers\Direct3D HAL			
HKEY_CURRENT_MACHINE	Software\Microsoft\Direct3D\D rivers\Direct3D HAL	Base		hal

Continued on next page

TABLE 14.5 CONTINUED: Registry Keys Added or Changed by the Service Pack 3 Setup Program

Hive	Sub-Hive	Data Key	Type	Value
HKEY_CURRENT_MACHINE	Software\Microsoft\Direct3D\Drivers\Direct3D HAL	Description		Microsoft Direct3D Hardware acceleration through Direct3D HAL
HKEY_CURRENT_MACHINE	Software\Microsoft\Direct3D\Drivers\Direct3D HAL	GUID		1,e0,3d,e6,84,aa,46,cf,11,81,6f,00,00,c0,20,15,6e
HKEY_CLASSES_ROOT	CLSID\{25E609E0-B259-11CF-BFC7-444535540000}\			Microsoft DirectInput Object
HKEY_CLASSES_ROOT	CLSID\{25E609E0-B259-11CF-BFC7-444535540000}\ InProcServer32			%11%\dinput.dll
HKEY_CLASSES_ROOT	CLSID\{25E609E0-B259-11CF-BFC7-444535540000}\ InProcServer32	ThreadingModel		Both
HKEY_CLASSES_ROOT	CLSID\{25E609E1-B259-11CF-BFC7-444535540000}\			Microsoft DirectInput-Device Object
HKEY_CLASSES_ROOT	CLSID\{25E609E1-B259-11CF-BFC7-444535540000}\ InProcServer32			%11%\dinput.dll
HKEY_CLASSES_ROOT	CLSID\{25E609E1-B259-11CF-BFC7-444535540000}\ InProcServer32	ThreadingModel		Both
HKEY_CURRENT_MACHINE	SOFTWARE\Microsoft\DirectX			
HKEY_CURRENT_MACHINE	SOFTWARE\Microsoft\DirectX	Installed-Version	1	03,00,00,00
HKEY_CURRENT_MACHINE	SOFTWARE\Microsoft\Active Setup\Installed Components\{44BBA855-CC51-11CF-AAFA-00AA00B6015C}			

Continued on next page

TABLE 14.5 CONTINUED: Registry Keys Added or Changed by the Service Pack 3 Setup Program

Hive	Sub-Hive	Data Key	Type	Value
HKEY_CURRENT_MACHINE	SOFTWARE\Microsoft\Active Setup\Installed Components\ {44BBA855-CC51-11CF-AAFA-00AA00B6015C}	Microsoft DirectX	1	04,00,04,00,00, 00,44,00

Intel-Only Registry Entries Added or Modified

For Intel-based (x86) machines, only one registry entry is added. It is shown in Table 14.6.

TABLE 14.6: Intel x86 Registry Key Added or Changed by the Windows NT Service Pack 3 Setup Program

Hive	Sub-Hive	Data Key	Type	Data Value Used
HKEY_CURRENT_MACHINE	SOFTWARE\Microsoft\ Cryptography\Defaults\ Provider\Microsoft Base Cryptographic Provider v1.0	Signature	1	BD,9F,13,C5,92,12,2B, 72,4A,BA,B6,2A,F9,FC, 54,46,6F,A1,B4,BB,43, A8,FE,F8,A8,23,7D,D1, 85,84,22,6E,B4,58,00, 3E,0B,19,83,88,6A,8D, 64,02,DF,5F,65,7E,3B, 4D,D4,10,44,B9,46,34, F3,40,F4,BC,9F,4B,82, 1E,CC,A7,D0,2D,22,D7, B1,F0,2E,CD,0E,21,52, BC,3E,81,B1,1A,86,52, 4D,3F,FB,A2,9D,AE,C6, 3D,AA,13,4D,18,7C,D2, 28,CE,72,B1,26,3F,BA, F8,A6,4B,01,B9,A4,5C, 43,68,D3,46,81,00,7F, 6A,D7,D1,69,51,47,25, 14,40,00,00,00,00,00, 00,00,00

Alpha-Only Registry Entries Added or Modified

Table 14.7 describes the registry entry added for non-Intel–based machines, such as Digital Alpha.

TABLE 14.7: Alpha Registry Key Added or Changed by the Service Pack 3 Setup Program

Hive	Sub-Hive	Data Key	Type	Data Value Used
HKEY_CURRENT_MACHINE	SOFTWARE\Microsoft\ Cryptography\Defaults\ Provider\ Microsoft Base Cryptographic Provider 1.0	Signature	1	8A,06,01,6D,C2,B5,A2, 66,12,1B,9C,E4,58,B1, F8,7D,AD,17,C1,F9,3F, 87,E3,9C,DD,EB,CC,A8, 6B,62,D0,72,E7,F2,EC, D6,D6,36,AB,2D,28,EA, 74,07,0E,6C,6D,E1,F8, 17,97,13,8D,B1,8B,0B, 33,97,C5,46,66,96,B4, F7,03,C5,03,98,F7,91, AE,9D,00,1A,C6,86,30, 5C,C8,C7,05,47,ED,2D, C2,0B,61,4B,CE,E5,B7, D7,27,0C,9E,2F,C5,25, E3,81,13,9D,A2,67,B2, 26,FC,99,9D,CE,0E,AF, 30,F3,30,EC,A3,0A,FE, 16,B6,DA,16,90,9A,9A, 74,7A,00,00,00,00,00, 00,00,00

IBM 6070-Only Registry Entries Added or Modified

Table 14.8 lists registry items that are added or changed in the registry by Windows NT Service Pack 3. These items are only significant to IBM 6070 systems and not for any other systems.

TABLE 14.8: IBM 6070 Registry Keys Added or Changed by the Service Pack 3 Setup Program

Hive	Sub-Hive	Data Key	Type	Data Value Used
HKEY_CURRENT_MACHINE	SYSTEM\CurrentControlSet\ Services\Atapi\Parameters\ Device0	Driver-Parameter	0	BaseAddress = 0x1f0; Interrupt = 0x10
HKEY_CURRENT_MACHINE	SYSTEM\CurrentControlSet\ Services\Atapi\Parameters\ Device1	Driver-Parameter	0	BaseAddress = 0x170; Interrupt = 0x11

IIS-Only Registry Entries Added or Modified

Table 14.9 lists registry items that are added or changed in the registry by Windows NT Service Pack 3. These items are only significant to IIS and not to any other systems.

NOTE   For registry entries specific to IIS running on either NT Server or NT Workstation, see the sections following.

TABLE 14.9: IIS Registry Keys Added or Changed by the Service Pack 3 Setup Program

Hive	Sub-Hive	Data Key	Data Value Used
HKEY_CLASSES_ROOT	CLSID\{5a61f7a0-cde1-11cf-9113-00aa00425c62}		%IIS_SHELL_EXTENSION%
HKEY_CLASSES_ROOT	CLSID\{5a61f7a0-cde1-11cf-9113-00aa00425c62}\InProc-Server32		%65601%\w3scfg.dll
HKEY_CLASSES_ROOT	CLSID\{5a61f7a0-cde1-11cf-9113-00aa00425c62}\InProc-Server32	Threading-Model	Apartment
HKEY_CLASSES_ROOT	Folder\shellex\ PropertySheetHandlers		IISSEPage

Continued on next page

TABLE 14.9 CONTINUED: IIS Registry Keys Added or Changed by the Service Pack 3 Setup Program

Hive	Sub-hive	Data key	Data Value Used
HKEY_CLASSES_ROOT	Folder\shellex\PropertySheet-Handlers\IISSEPage		"{5a61f7a0-cde1-11cf-9113-00aa00425c62}"
HKEY_CLASSES_ROOT	Folder\shellex\CopyHook-Handlers\IISCopyHook		"{5a61f7a0-cde1-11cf-9113-00aa00425c62}"
HKEY_CLASSES_ROOT	*\shellex\CopyHookHandlers\IISCopyHook		"{5a61f7a0-cde1-11cf-9113-00aa00425c62}"
HKEY_CURRENT_MACHINE	SOFTWARE\Microsoft\Windows\CurrentVersion\Shell Extensions\Approved	{5a61f7a0-cde1-11cf-9113-00aa0 0425c62}	"%IIS_SHELL_EXTENSION%"

Server-Only IIS Registry Entries Added or Modified

Table 14.10 lists registry items that are added or changed in the registry by Windows NT Service Pack 3. These items are only significant to IIS when installed on a Windows NT Server and not for Workstation installations.

TABLE 14.10: Registry Keys Added or Changed for Server Versions of IIS

Hive	Sub-Hive	Data Key	Type	Data Value Used
HKEY_CURRENT_MACHINE	SOFTWARE\Microsoft\Inetsrv\CurrentVersion	Description	0	%SRV_IIS_30_NAME%
HKEY_CURRENT_MACHINE	SOFTWARE\Microsoft\Inetsrv\CurrentVersion	ServiceName	0	%SRV_IIS_30_NAME%
HKEY_CURRENT_MACHINE	SOFTWARE\Microsoft\Inetsrv\CurrentVersion	Title	0	%SRV_IIS_30_NAME%

Workstation-Only IIS Registry Entries Added or Modified

Table 14.11 lists registry items that are added or changed in the registry by Windows NT Service Pack 3. These items are only significant to IIS when installed on a Windows NT Workstation and not for Server installations.

TABLE 14.11: Registry Keys Added or Changed for Workstation Versions of IIS

Hive	Sub-Hive	Data Key	Type	Data Value Used
HKEY_CURRENT_MACHINE	SOFTWARE\Microsoft\ Inetsrv\CurrentVersion	Description	0	%WKS_IIS_30_NAME%
HKEY_CURRENT_MACHINE	SOFTWARE\Microsoft\ Inetsrv\CurrentVersion	ServiceName	0	%WKS_IIS_30_NAME%
HKEY_CURRENT_MACHINE	SOFTWARE\Microsoft\ Inetsrv\CurrentVersion	Title	0	%WKS_IIS_30_NAME%

Font Substitution Entries

There are a number of changes to the font substitution tables in Windows NT. These changes are based on country or region.

Users who are not using these languages will probably not need to worry about these settings, as they are relatively benign.

Eastern European

Table 14.12 lists registry items regarding Eastern European fonts that are added or changed by Windows NT Service Pack 3.

TABLE 14.12: Registry Keys Modified for Eastern Europe Fonts

Hive	Sub-Hive	Data Key	Data Value Used
HKEY_CURRENT_MACHINE	Software\Microsoft\ Windows NT\CurrentVersion\ FontSubstitutes	System,0	System,238
HKEY_CURRENT_MACHINE	Software\Microsoft\ Windows NT\CurrentVersion\ FontSubstitutes	Fixedsys,0	Fixedsys,238"
HKEY_CURRENT_MACHINE	Software\Microsoft\ Windows NT\CurrentVersion\ FontSubstitutes	Small Fonts,0	Small Fonts,238
HKEY_CURRENT_MACHINE	Software\Microsoft\ Windows NT\CurrentVersion\ FontSubstitutes	MS Serif,0	MS Serif,238
HKEY_CURRENT_MACHINE	Software\Microsoft\ Windows NT\CurrentVersion\ FontSubstitutes	MS Sans Serif,0	MS Sans Serif,238
HKEY_CURRENT_MACHINE	Software\Microsoft\ Windows NT\CurrentVersion\ FontSubstitutes	Courier,0	Courier New,238
HKEY_CURRENT_MACHINE	Software\Microsoft\ Windows NT\CurrentVersion\ FontSubstitutes	Arial CE,0	Arial,238
HKEY_CURRENT_MACHINE	Software\Microsoft\ Windows NT\CurrentVersion\ FontSubstitutes	Courier New CE,0	Courier New,238
HKEY_CURRENT_MACHINE	Software\Microsoft\ Windows NT\CurrentVersion\ FontSubstitutes	Times New Roman CE,0	Times New Roman,238
HKEY_CURRENT_MACHINE	Software\Microsoft\ Windows NT\CurrentVersion\ FontSubstitutes	Tms Rmn,0	MS Serif,238
HKEY_CURRENT_MACHINE	Software\Microsoft\ Windows NT\CurrentVersion\ FontSubstitutes	Helv,0	MS Sans Serif,238

Cyrillic

Table 14.13 lists registry items regarding Cyrillic fonts that are added or changed by Windows NT Service Pack 3.

TABLE 14.13: Registry Keys Modified for Cyrillic Fonts

Hive	Sub-Hive	Data Key	Data Value Used
HKEY_CURRENT_MACHINE	Software\Microsoft\ Windows NT\CurrentVersion\ FontSubstitutes	System,0	System,204
HKEY_CURRENT_MACHINE	Software\Microsoft\ Windows NT\CurrentVersion\ FontSubstitutes	Fixedsys,0	Fixedsys,204
HKEY_CURRENT_MACHINE	Software\Microsoft\ Windows NT\CurrentVersion\ FontSubstitutes	Small Fonts,0	Small Fonts,204
HKEY_CURRENT_MACHINE	Software\Microsoft\ Windows NT\CurrentVersion\ FontSubstitutes	MS Serif,0	MS Serif,204
HKEY_CURRENT_MACHINE	Software\Microsoft\ Windows NT\CurrentVersion\ FontSubstitutes	MS Sans Serif,0	MS Sans Serif,204
HKEY_CURRENT_MACHINE	Software\Microsoft\ Windows NT\CurrentVersion\ FontSubstitutes	Courier,0	Courier New,204
HKEY_CURRENT_MACHINE	Software\Microsoft\ Windows NT\CurrentVersion\ FontSubstitutes	Arial Cyr,0	Arial,204

Continued on next page

TABLE 14.13 CONTINUED: Registry Keys Modified for Cyrillic Fonts

Hive	Sub-Hive	Data Key	Data Value Used
HKEY_CURRENT_MACHINE	Software\Microsoft\ Windows NT\CurrentVersion\ FontSubstitutes	Courier New Cyr,0	Courier New,204
HKEY_CURRENT_MACHINE	Software\Microsoft\ Windows NT\CurrentVersion\ FontSubstitutes	Times New Roman Cyr,0	Times New Roman,204
HKEY_CURRENT_MACHINE	Software\Microsoft\ Windows NT\CurrentVersion\ FontSubstitutes	Tms Rmn,0	MS Serif,204
HKEY_CURRENT_MACHINE	Software\Microsoft\ Windows NT\CurrentVersion\ FontSubstitutes	Helv,0	MS Sans Serif,204

Greek

Table 14.14 lists registry items regarding Greek fonts that are added or changed by Windows NT Service Pack 3.

TABLE 14.14: Registry Keys Modified for Greek Fonts

Hive	Sub-Hive	Data Key	Data Value Used
HKEY_CURRENT_MACHINE	Software\Microsoft\ Windows NT\CurrentVersion\ FontSubstitutes	System,0	System,161
HKEY_CURRENT_MACHINE	Software\Microsoft\ Windows NT\CurrentVersion\ FontSubstitutes	Fixedsys,0	Fixedsys,161
HKEY_CURRENT_MACHINE	Software\Microsoft\ Windows NT\CurrentVersion\ FontSubstitutes	Small Fonts,0	Small Fonts,161

Continued on next page

TABLE 14.14 CONTINUED: Registry Keys Modified for Greek Fonts

Hive	Sub-Hive	Data Key	Data Value Used
HKEY_CURRENT_MACHINE	Software\Microsoft\ Windows NT\CurrentVersion\ FontSubstitutes	MS Serif,0	MS Serif,161
HKEY_CURRENT_MACHINE	Software\Microsoft\ Windows NT\CurrentVersion\ FontSubstitutes	MS Sans Serif,0	MS Sans Serif,161
HKEY_CURRENT_MACHINE	Software\Microsoft\ Windows NT\CurrentVersion\ FontSubstitutes	Courier,0	Courier New,161
HKEY_CURRENT_MACHINE	Software\Microsoft\ Windows NT\CurrentVersion\ FontSubstitutes	MS Sans Serif Greek,0	MS Sans Serif,161
HKEY_CURRENT_MACHINE	Software\Microsoft\ Windows NT\CurrentVersion\ FontSubstitutes	System Greek,0	System,161
HKEY_CURRENT_MACHINE	Software\Microsoft\ Windows NT\CurrentVersion\ FontSubstitutes	Fixedsys Greek,0	Fixedsys,161
HKEY_CURRENT_MACHINE	Software\Microsoft\ Windows NT\CurrentVersion\ FontSubstitutes	Small Fonts Greek,0	Small Fonts,161
HKEY_CURRENT_MACHINE	Software\Microsoft\ Windows NT\CurrentVersion\ FontSubstitutes	MS Serif Greek,0	MS Serif,161
HKEY_CURRENT_MACHINE	Software\Microsoft\ Windows NT\CurrentVersion\ FontSubstitutes	Arial Greek,0	Arial,161
HKEY_CURRENT_MACHINE	Software\Microsoft\ Windows NT\CurrentVersion\ FontSubstitutes	Courier New Greek,0	Courier New,161
HKEY_CURRENT_MACHINE	Software\Microsoft\ Windows NT\CurrentVersion\ FontSubstitutes	Times New Roman Greek,0	Times New Roman,161

Continued on next page

TABLE 14.14 CONTINUED: Registry Keys Modified for Greek Fonts

Hive	Sub-Hive	Data Key	Data Value Used
HKEY_CURRENT_MACHINE	Software\Microsoft\ Windows NT\CurrentVersion\ FontSubstitutes	Tms Rmn,0	MS Serif,161
HKEY_CURRENT_MACHINE	Software\Microsoft\ Windows NT\CurrentVersion\ FontSubstitutes	Helv,0	MS Sans Serif,161

Turkish

Table 14.15 lists registry items regarding Turkish fonts that are added or changed by Windows NT Service Pack 3.

TABLE 14.15: Registry Keys Modified for Turkish Fonts

Hive	Sub-Hive	Data Key	Data Value Used
HKEY_CURRENT_MACHINE	Software\Microsoft\ Windows NT\CurrentVersion\ FontSubstitutes	System,0	System,162
HKEY_CURRENT_MACHINE	Software\Microsoft\ Windows NT\CurrentVersion\ FontSubstitutes	Fixedsys,0	Fixedsys,162
HKEY_CURRENT_MACHINE	Software\Microsoft\ Windows NT\CurrentVersion\ FontSubstitutes	Small Fonts,0	Small Fonts,162
HKEY_CURRENT_MACHINE	Software\Microsoft\ Windows NT\CurrentVersion\ FontSubstitutes	MS Serif,0	MS Serif,162
HKEY_CURRENT_MACHINE	Software\Microsoft\ Windows NT\CurrentVersion\ FontSubstitutes	MS Sans Serif,0	MS Sans Serif,162

Continued on next page

TABLE 14.15 CONTINUED: Registry Keys Modified for Turkish Fonts

Hive	Sub-Hive	Data Key	Data Value Used
HKEY_CURRENT_MACHINE	Software\Microsoft\ Windows NT\CurrentVersion\ FontSubstitutes	Courier,0	Courier New,162
HKEY_CURRENT_MACHINE	Software\Microsoft\ Windows NT\CurrentVersion\ FontSubstitutes	Arial Tur,0	Arial,162
HKEY_CURRENT_MACHINE	Software\Microsoft\ Windows NT\CurrentVersion\ FontSubstitutes	Courier New Tur,0	Courier New,162
HKEY_CURRENT_MACHINE	Software\Microsoft\ Windows NT\CurrentVersion\ FontSubstitutes	Times New Roman Tur,0	Times New Roman,162
HKEY_CURRENT_MACHINE	Software\Microsoft\ Windows NT\CurrentVersion\ FontSubstitutes	Tms Rmn,0	MS Serif,162
HKEY_CURRENT_MACHINE	Software\Microsoft\ Windows NT\CurrentVersion\ FontSubstitutes	Helv,0	MS Sans Serif,162

Baltic

Table 14.16 lists registry items regarding Baltic fonts that are added or changed by Windows NT Service Pack 3.

TABLE 14.16: Registry Keys Modified for Baltic Fonts

Hive	Sub-Hive	Data Key	Data Value Used
HKEY_CURRENT_MACHINE	Software\Microsoft\ Windows NT\CurrentVersion\ FontSubstitutes	System,0	System,186
HKEY_CURRENT_MACHINE	Software\Microsoft\ Windows NT\CurrentVersion\ FontSubstitutes	Fixedsys,0	Fixedsys,186

Continued on next page

TABLE 14.16 CONTINUED: Registry Keys Modified for Baltic Fonts

Hive	Sub-Hive	Data Key	Data Value Used
HKEY_CURRENT_MACHINE	Software\Microsoft\ Windows NT\CurrentVersion\ FontSubstitutes	Small Fonts,0	Small Fonts,186
HKEY_CURRENT_MACHINE	Software\Microsoft\ Windows NT\CurrentVersion\ FontSubstitutes	MS Serif,0	MS Serif,186
HKEY_CURRENT_MACHINE	Software\Microsoft\ Windows NT\CurrentVersion\ FontSubstitutes	MS Sans Serif,0	MS Sans Serif,186
HKEY_CURRENT_MACHINE	Software\Microsoft\ Windows NT\CurrentVersion\ FontSubstitutes	Courier,0	Courier New,186
HKEY_CURRENT_MACHINE	Software\Microsoft\ Windows NT\CurrentVersion\ FontSubstitutes	Tms Rmn,0	MS Serif,186
HKEY_CURRENT_MACHINE	Software\Microsoft\ Windows NT\CurrentVersion\ FontSubstitutes	Helv,0	MS Sans Serif,186

Hints and Kinks from the Experts

Next, you'll find some hints and kinks from our experts on Service Packs.

How Do You Get Service Pack 3 for Windows NT?   You can get Service Pack 3.0 for Windows NT 4.0 from the Microsoft FTP site at ftp://ftp.microsoft .com/bussys/winnt/winnt-public/fixes/. An alternate Microsoft site is ftp://198.105.232.37/fixes/.

At either site, navigate to the country/product/ServicePack/Processor directory and choose the Service Pack .exe file, not the symbol file. The U.S.A. Service Pack for Intel processors would be at usa/nt40/ussp3/i386/. You must download and read the readme.txt at the Microsoft site.

WARNING   Service Pack 3 alters the ERD (Emergency Repair Disk) process. You must create an ERD by running RDisk /S after you successfully reboot from an SP3 installation. (Always keep multiple generations of the ERD and keep your last SP2 ERD until you are sure all is OK.) To use the ERD after SP3 is installed, you must update boot floppy 2 of the 3-diskette boot set. Copy the Service Pack to a temporary directory, switch to that directory, and type the service pack /x, for example: **nt4sp3_i /x**. Copy Setupdd.sys from the expanded Service Pack to boot floppy 2 of the 3-diskette set. It will replace the older version. If you ever recreate the boot floppies by running Winnt /ox or Winnt32 /ox from the CD-ROM, you must repeat this process.

Due to changes in the Registry Security Hive, the SAMSRV.DLL, SAMLIB.DLL, and WINLOGON.EXE have changed and previous versions of these files cannot access NT system security information. If you uninstall SP3, these files will remain. Do not replace them with older versions.

Be sure to check for Post-SP3 Hotfixes at `ftp://ftp.microsoft.com/bussys/ winnt/winnt-public/fixes/`. The following Microsoft Knowledge Base articles are relevant to Windows NT Service Pack 3:

- "Q146887" (You must read this!)
- "Q166730"
- "Q161372"
- "Q143474"
- "Q151082"
- "Q161990"
- "Q143475"
- "Q158423"
- "Q165333" (a KB article on new features)

NOTE   It is best to uninstall SP2 or SP3 prior to an update install. If you have RAS installed, you must uninstall the SP. If you cannot uninstall, expand <cd-rom>:\i386\ tcpip.sy%SystemRoot%\System32\drivers\tcpip.sys prior to doing the update install. This is also applicable to installing RAS after SP2/SP3.

(Courtesy of Jerold Schulman)

How Do You Implement Enhanced Password Functionality on NT 4 with SP2? Service Pack 2 for Windows NT 4 allows you to add the following enhancement to your password policies:

- Passwords must be a minimum of six characters in length.

- Password must include at least three of the following:
  - English uppercase letters
  - English lowercase letters
  - Numbers 0 through 9
  - Special characters (.,;:*&%!)

To implement these additional requirements, follow these steps:

1. Copy Passfilt.dll to your %windir%\System32 directory. (You may have to expand the Service Pack into a Temp directory to locate it.)

2. Edit HKEY_LOCAL_MACHINE\SYSTEM\CurrentControlSet\Control\Lsa.

3. Double-click on the Notification Packages value or add it as a REG_MULTI_SZ.

4. Insert the name of the DLL file, PASSFILT, beneath the FPNWCLNT if it is present. You must reboot for this change to take effect.

(Courtesy of Jerold Schulman)

How Do You Install a Service Pack with Hotfixes? KB article "Q166839," updated May 15, 1997, contains some useful information about installing Hotfixes with Service Pack 3, but it is incorrect and incomplete in the "How to" section.

Starting with Windows NT 4 Service Pack 3, Update.exe will update your NT 4 install to the service pack and will install any specified Hotfixes. The steps required to accomplish this are as follows:

1. Copy all service pack files to a directory, i.e. C:\SP3. You can expand a Service Pack by typing: **ServicePackFileName.exe /x**.

2. Create a sub-directory under SP3 called HOTFIX.

3. Copy Hotfix.inf and Hotfix.exe to this directory. I have a ZIP file that includes a sample combined Hotfix.inf.

   In the file Hotfix.inf, there is a comment line that shows which issues or problems the Hotfix will address. These issues or problems include the following:

   - Q143478 - oobfix_i
   - Q168748 - javafixi
   - Q154087 - lsa-fixi
   - Q170510 - w32kfixi
   - Q154174 - icmpfixi
   - Q146965 - admnsymi
   - Q154460 - chargeni

4. Copy the actual files that make up the Hotfixes into this directory. You may ignore the *.dbg files. You must expand the Hotfix .exe files in order by date, earliest first, so that you get the latest version of a duplicate file. Type **HotfixFileName.exe /x** to expand a Hotfix.

5. Open up the sample Hotfix.inf file and add the files in the appropriate sections from the expanded hotfix.inf.

6. Save your INF file and run update.exe. After the SP3 files are copied, you will be prompted to verify that you want to have Hotfixes installed. Choose Yes.

If you are prompted for the location of your Service Pack files, just point to the SP directory, i.e. SP3. If you uninstall the Service Pack, you will be prompted to remove the Hotfix.

(Courtesy of Jerold Schulman)

PART V

The Registry Reference

15

Introduction to
HKEY_CLASSES_ROOT

- GUIDs, UUIDs, and other funny numbers in Windows

- HKEY_CLASSES_ROOT

- Hints and kinks from the experts

Reality is that which, when you stop believing in it, doesn't go away.

—Philip K. Dick (1928-1982), U.S. science fiction writer

Much of the registry's contents deal with Windows NT, the system. These entries compromise about 90 percent of the registry just after Windows NT is installed, although as more and more applications are installed, this percentage will drop.

Is there anything to fear in the registry's system components? Absolutely! A wrong entry in some system entries will make the system unstable, unbootable, or just plain dead.

We'll cover the registry, hive by hive, pointing out some of the more important entries, some values, and some cautions to consider. This chapter and the three subsequent ones cover each of the major hives in the registry. This chapter covers HKEY_CLASSES_ROOT; Chapter 16 covers HKEY_CURRENT_USER and HKEY_USERS; Chapters 17, 18, and 19 cover HKEY_LOCAL_MACHINE; and Chapter 19 also covers HKEY_CURRENT_CONFIG.

The HKEY_CLASSES_ROOT branch contains information about both OLE and various file associations. The purpose of HKEY_CLASSES_ROOT is to provide compatibility with the existing Windows 3.x registry. The information contained in HKEY_CLASSES_ROOT is identical to information found in HKEY_LOCAL_MACHINE\SOFTWARE.

Before we talk too much about HKEY_CLASSES_ROOT, we'll delve into things like GUIDs, UUIDs, and funny registry numbers. Don't let this scare you—it is good (not absolutely necessary, just good) to understand what these numbers *really* are.

Knowing that you have backed up your registry *before* starting this chapter, let's dig in and see what's there.

GUIDs, UUIDs, and Other Funny Numbers in Windows

Windows NT, and Windows 95/98 for that matter, are just chock full of strange, long numbers. One type of number is the GUID (Globally Unique ID), aka UUID (Universally Unique ID). Regardless of which term is used, a GUID is *always* a unique number that is assigned to an application or component. Controls, applications, parts of Windows NT, software and components, tools, compilers—everything today has one or more GUIDs.

Used primarily with OLE (Object Linking and Embedding), GUIDs are used to link between a component and the operating system.

For example, Microsoft 97 has a GUID of {000209FF-0000-0000-C000-000000000046}. This is sufficiently unique enough that we can be sure that a request for this GUID will always match Microsoft Word, and not some other application. How can we say that? After all, although a GUID is long (It's a number with 16 bytes, or 128 bits.), what mechanisms are there to make sure that each programmer uses a unique GUID?

The process of obtaining a GUID is simple and, in most cases, doesn't even require that Microsoft be notified. Does that make you rather nervous? Fear not, Microsoft provides a tool to generate a GUID, and that tool takes some rather interesting steps to attempt to make each GUID unique.

First, a bit of history (just what you wanted). All Ethernet network interface cards (NICs) have a unique identifying number built into them. That's right, your NIC in your computer is different from the NIC of the computer in the office next door. This means that each computer with an NIC actually has a form of a serial number that is guaranteed to be unique.

The NIC's serial number is there to allow the hardware layer of the network to be able to distinguish between different computers on the network. An organization assigns part of this identifier to each manufacturer of NICs, and the manufacturer assigns the second part of the identifier to each NIC as it is assembled. Most NIC's have their id number written on a small sticker on the card, though in today's world, users and administrators have virtually no need for the NIC's ID.

The Microsoft GUID program takes the NIC's identifier number, which is unique; the current time and data information, hashed a bit; and a random number, and uses these to create the GUID. To have two identical GUIDs, it would be necessary to have two computers with the same NIC identifying numbers, at the same time (exactly, to the millisecond), and with the same random number.

In short, it is unlikely that two GUIDs would be the same. Even if a programmer were to take the same computer to get the command to run at *exactly* the same time, it is not reasonable that the random number would be the same on both runs. This is because the random number is not based on time or any other factor that a programmer might be able to influence. Hence, we can be reasonably sure that the GUID for each application will be unique.

There is actually one area where a GUID might not be unique: That is where a programmer intentionally copies the GUID for one program into another program. This could be unintentional, but more likely, the program would do this by design. I can't think of any valid reason why a programmer might create two applications with the same GUID, but I'm sure that someone will write and tell me why this could, or would, happen.

A GUID consists of five groups of digits in hexadecimal. Each group is separated by hyphens. These groups are arranged to display 4 bytes, 2 bytes, 2 bytes, 2 bytes, and 6 bytes—in that order—as the following GUID shows:

{000209FF-0000-0000-C000-000000000046}

It is common, although not specifically required, that a GUID will be enclosed in braces. However, whenever you encounter a number with the above arrangement of digits (8, 4, 4, 4, 12), you can generally assume that the number is a GUID.

A Rose by Any Other Name

A UUID and a GUID are just different names for the same thing. Ditto for CLSID (Class ID). CLSIDs, GUIDs, and UUIDs are all used to identify a specific class of objects. Treat a CLSID the same as you would treat a GUID or a UUID, and all will be well.

HKEY_CLASSES_ROOT

The HKEY_CLASSES_ROOT hive contains information about both OLE and various file associations.

WARNING   A little later in this chapter we'll start fiddling with the registry. You are an intelligent person; therefore, you know that you should back up your registry before you start. Please, do not change the registry without having a good backup that is easily restored.

HKEY_CLASSES_ROOT provides compatibility with the existing Windows 3.x registry; some applications and systems expect HKEY_CLASSES_ROOT to exist. The information contained in HKEY_CLASSES_ROOT is identical to information found in HKEY_LOCAL_MACHINE\SOFTWARE\Classes. Actually, these two hives are physically the same. A change made in one will automatically modify the other. Think of HKEY_CLASSES_ROOT as a house on the corner of an intersection. The house might have two addresses, one on each street. Remember: HKEY_CLASSES_ROOT is HKEY_LOCAL_MACHINE\SOFTWARE\Classes and HKEY_LOCAL_MACHINE\SOFTWARE\Classes is HKEY_CLASSES_ROOT.

Managing File Types and File Extensions

The HKEY_CLASSES_ROOT hive consists of a list of all file extensions (file types) known to your installation of Windows NT. Each time a new application is installed, the application should add or modify one or more extensions. This is done with the application's setup program, and this process should tell Windows NT that the application will handle (open, print, and so on) the file when users select it.

For example, the HKEY_CLASSES_ROOT hive for an Excel spreadsheet type file (any file that ends in XLS) is as follows:

```
HKEY_CLASSES_ROOT\.xls
HKEY_CLASSES_ROOT\.xls\Excel.Sheet.5
HKEY_CLASSES_ROOT\.xls\Excel.Sheet.5\ShellNew
HKEY_CLASSES_ROOT\.xls\Excel.Sheet.5\ShellNew\FileName = excel.xls

HKEY_CLASSES_ROOT\.xls\ExcelWorksheet
HKEY_CLASSES_ROOT\.xls\ExcelWorksheet\ShellNew
HKEY_CLASSES_ROOT\.xls\ExcelWorksheet\ShellNew\FileName = excel4.xls

HKEY_CLASSES_ROOT\.xls\ShellEx
HKEY_CLASSES_ROOT\.xls\ShellEx\{00021500-0000-0000-C000-000000000046}
HKEY_CLASSES_ROOT\.xls\ShellEx\{00021500-0000-0000-C000-
000000000046}\<NO NAME> = {83799FE0-1F5A-11d1-95C7-00609797EA4F}

HKEY_CLASSES_ROOT\.xls\ShellEx\{BB2E617C-0920-11d1-9A0B-00C04FC2D6C1}
HKEY_CLASSES_ROOT\.xls\ShellEx\{BB2E617C-0920-11d1-9A0B-
00C04FC2D6C1}\<NO NAME> = {9DBD2C50-62AD-11d0-B806-00C04FD706EC}
```

This is due to the complexity of the Microsoft Office product; after all, we pay a lot for those Office products.

Another example is for batch files with the extension of "BAT." The entry we find for batch files is as follows:

```
HKEY_CLASSES_ROOT\.bat
HKEY_CLASSES_ROOT\.bat\<No Name> = batfile
```

We see an identifier, which has no name, with a data value of batfile. Looking a bit further down the line (or down the registry's HKEY_CLASSES_ROOT hive, so to speak), we find an entry called batfile. Coincidence? Luck? Secret conspiracy? Here are the facts for batfile:

```
HKEY_CLASSES_ROOT\batfile
HKEY_CLASSES_ROOT\batfile\<NO NAME> = MS-DOS Batch File
HKEY_CLASSES_ROOT\batfile\EditFlags = 0x00000430

HKEY_CLASSES_ROOT\batfile\DefaultIcon
HKEY_CLASSES_ROOT\batfile\DefaultIcon\<NO NAME> = %SystemRoot%\Sys-
tem32\shell32.dll,-153

HKEY_CLASSES_ROOT\batfile\shell
HKEY_CLASSES_ROOT\batfile\shell\edit
HKEY_CLASSES_ROOT\batfile\shell\edit\<NO NAME> = &Edit

HKEY_CLASSES_ROOT\batfile\shell\edit\command
HKEY_CLASSES_ROOT\batfile\shell\edit\command\<NO NAME> =
%SystemRoot%\System32\NOTEPAD.EXE %1

HKEY_CLASSES_ROOT\batfile\shell\open
HKEY_CLASSES_ROOT\batfile\shell\open\EditFlags = 0x00000000
HKEY_CLASSES_ROOT\batfile\shell\open\command
HKEY_CLASSES_ROOT\batfile\shell\open\command\<NO NAME> = "%1" %*

HKEY_CLASSES_ROOT\batfile\shell\print
HKEY_CLASSES_ROOT\batfile\shell\print\command
HKEY_CLASSES_ROOT\batfile\shell\print\command\<NO NAME> = %System-
Root%\System32\NOTEPAD.EXE /p %1

HKEY_CLASSES_ROOT\batfile\shellex\batfile\shellex\PropertySheetHandlers
HKEY_CLASSES_ROOT\batfile\shellex\PropertySheetHandlers\PifProps
HKEY_CLASSES_ROOT\batfile\shellex\PropertySheetHandlers\PifProps\<NO
NAME> = {86F19A00-42A0-1069-A2E9-08002B30309D}
```

Now, the preceding set of entries tell us and Windows NT everything needed to handle a BAT file—the icon to display, how to edit it, how to open it, how to print it, and how to process (execute) it. Let's look at each section of this entry. Let's begin with the first section:

```
HKEY_CLASSES_ROOT\batfile
```

```
HKEY_CLASSES_ROOT\batfile\<NO NAME> = MS-DOS Batch File
HKEY_CLASSES_ROOT\batfile\EditFlags = 0x00000430
```

Initial handling for batch files includes (in an unnamed variable) the text string used both in Explorer for the file's properties dialog box, and in the Type field of Explorer's details list view. Modifying this string would change the behavior of Explorer, and Windows NT, for the properties that are displayed for a batch file.

The EditFlags variable is used to control how Windows NT processes the command.

EditFlags and Bitmapped Variables

EditFlags are bitmapped, with a few apparent bits.

EditFlags seem to affect the way that Windows NT and Windows NT's components, such as Internet Explorer, handle receiving certain files, as well as how files are processed:

EditFlag 0x02000000—For drives, directories, folders, and objects where action is taken without reservation

EditFlag 0x30040000—For batch files that are executed

EditFlag 0x30000000—For DOS applications, again usually executed ones

EditFlag 0x01000000—For DLL files that are not usually executed or opened directly

EditFlag 0xD8070000—For application files that may or may not be executed

One bitmapped bit that is documented is 0x00000100. When set, it tells the system to "Always ask before opening this type of file" whenever the file type is received using Internet Explorer.

The next section for batch files is as follows:

```
HKEY_CLASSES_ROOT\batfile\DefaultIcon
HKEY_CLASSES_ROOT\batfile\DefaultIcon\<NO NAME> = %SystemRoot%\System32\
shell32.dll,-153
```

The DefaultIcon entry specifies which icon Explorer displays in the Explorer program or on the Desktop, as appropriate. Notice that Explorer won't allow you to use the Explorer Properties dialog box to change the icon for a batch file. Here is where it is changed:

```
%SystemRoot%\System32\shell32.dll,-153
```

What does that magic line mean? First, the file named %SystemRoot%\System32\ shell32.dll is a DLL (Dynamic Link Library) file that has, in addition to other things, a whole bunch of icons. The second number is a bit of a mystery, right? First, it is negative; just how do you find a negative icon, anyway? Second, there doesn't seem to be any simple program or method to find which icon matches this magic number. The negative number isn't so difficult. Icons are stored as resources in executable files; EXE and DLL files are both executable, but other extensions are also executable and can have icons in them. Resources are numbered with signed numbers from zero to 65535 (a 2-byte value). These *resources* (icons, dialog boxes, and strings) have a number to identify them. Programmers, and programmer's tools, ignore the fact that these resources are stored with signed numbers, so our tools simply ignore the sign. A programmer sets the icon's identifier to 65383; and Windows, to make things easy for all of us, displays it as –153. So, the icon number, –153, is actually the icon number 65383.

Two DLL files with lots of icons in them are PIFMGR.DLL and shell32.dll. There are other files containing icons, too.

Let's look at the next section:

```
HKEY_CLASSES_ROOT\batfile\shell
HKEY_CLASSES_ROOT\batfile\shell\edit
HKEY_CLASSES_ROOT\batfile\shell\edit\<NO NAME> = &Edit

HKEY_CLASSES_ROOT\batfile\shell\edit\command
HKEY_CLASSES_ROOT\batfile\shell\edit\command\<NO NAME> =
%SystemRoot%\System32\NOTEPAD.EXE %1
```

The shell/edit section describes how the subject file is edited. The name of the context menu selection to edit is listed in a variable that has no name. (Right-click on the file in Explorer to see the context menu.) The default variable name for most programs is &Edit, which displays the word <u>E</u>dit. Whichever letter is preceded with an ampersand is the accelerator key's letter and will be underscored.

The section shell\edit\command contains a single, unnamed entry listing the editor to be used to edit the file. In the case of a batch file, the default editor is Notepad. If you have a favorite editor, you can plug it into this location to have it edit the file. Just remember that the editor must be able to open and save the file in the correct format. Fortunately for batch files, this is not difficult; they are plain text files with no special editing requirements. When the editor is called, the argument %1 will be substituted with the batch file's name, as shown here:

```
HKEY_CLASSES_ROOT\batfile\shell\open
HKEY_CLASSES_ROOT\batfile\shell\open\EditFlags = 0x00000000
HKEY_CLASSES_ROOT\batfile\shell\open\command
HKEY_CLASSES_ROOT\batfile\shell\open\command\<NO NAME> = "%1" %*
```

The shell\open section contains the code to execute the file. In the case of a batch file, the EditFlags value is 0x00000000. Notice the format of this command, especially the placement of the quotes: "%1" %*. This command string will have the initial (quoted) %1 substituted with the batch file's name and the second %* will be substituted with any parameters that the user passed to the command. If editing the data, be very careful not to place the quotes in the wrong place; don't quote the entire string, for example.

The next section in the batfile entries handles printing requests:

```
HKEY_CLASSES_ROOT\batfile\shell\print
HKEY_CLASSES_ROOT\batfile\shell\print\command
HKEY_CLASSES_ROOT\batfile\shell\print\command\<NO NAME> = %SystemRoot%\
System32\NOTEPAD.EXE /p %1
```

Printing, managed by the shell\print section, contains only one working entry under HKEY_CLASSES_ROOT\batfile\shell\print\command with a single, unnamed entry. This entry tells Explorer to print using Notepad, passing the filename and the /p option. The option /p is a relatively standard option telling the program to open the file, print it to the default printer, and then exit. Generally, the entire file will be printed, although it is possible that some applications may provide options for the print process. (Notepad is not silent or hidden; you will see it open, see the print dialog, and see Notepad close.)

After the printing entries, entries for property sheets for this object are next:

```
HKEY_CLASSES_ROOT\batfile\shellex
batfile\shellex\PropertySheetHandlers
HKEY_CLASSES_ROOT\batfile\shellex\PropertySheetHandlers\PifProps
HKEY_CLASSES_ROOT\batfile\shellex\PropertySheetHandlers\PifProps\<NO
NAME> = {86F19A00-42A0-1069-A2E9-08002B30309D}
```

The final part of the batfile registry entry contains entries for the PifProps. Mappings to programs for all CLSIDs are found in the CLSID part of HKEY_ CLASSES_ ROOT. Looking up our magic CLSID, {86F19A00-42A0-1069-A2E9-08002B30309D}, we find it is registered for shell32.dll, along with a few other settings. This tells us that the PIF (Program Interface File) manager is actually part of shell32.dll, and is used to display the property sheet for batch files:

```
HKEY_CLASSES_ROOT\CLSID\{86F19A00-42A0-1069-A2E9-08002B30309D}
HKEY_CLASSES_ROOT\CLSID\{86F19A00-42A0-1069-A2E9-08002B30309D}\<NO
NAME> = .PIF file property pages

HKEY_CLASSES_ROOT\CLSID\{86F19A00-42A0-1069-A2E9-08002B30309D}\
InProcServer32
HKEY_CLASSES_ROOT\CLSID\{86F19A00-42A0-1069-A2E9-08002B30309D}\
InProcServer32\<NO NAME> = shell132.dll
HKEY_CLASSES_ROOT\CLSID\{86F19A00-42A0-1069-A2E9-08002B30309D}\
InProcServer32\ThreadingModel = Apartment
```

Several items in the CLSID section are worth noting. First, InProcServer32 is the name for a section dealing with in-process servers. In this case, we are working with a 32-bit in-process server, but that's not important right now.

We get the name of the server, shell32.dll, from the variable with no name; and we get the threading model, Apartment, from the ThreadingModel entry. These are important and critical, since specifying the wrong ThreadingModel can cause data corruption. Other possible values for ThreadingModel are Single, Apartment, and Both; although it is unlikely that you will see Single specified.

One picture is worth a thousand words. Or so they say. Figure 15.1 shows the entries for a batch file (BAT) a bit more graphically.

As shown in Figure 15.1, batch files are a relatively more complex example of how a particular file type is processed. Some other types of files are simpler—for example, they may not support context menus—while some are much more complex. Each system will be different for optional components, although Windows NT components typically are similar regardless of the installation.

OK, what have we learned? First, for virtually any object that relates to a file (except My Computer, Network Neighborhood, Recycle Bin, and so on), we can set the text description, change the icon, set an editor to edit, set a printer to print, and control how the object is executed or opened, as appropriate. In fact, we can add almost any functionality to the context menu we might want to. For instance, we can set a second editor for batch files; we'll use the command prompt's editor.

This example uses RegEdt32. I'm going to start right from the beginning since this is our first registry hack, I mean "fix."

1.   Open RegEdt32. The current local registry will be displayed.

FIGURE 15.1:

The entries for BAT type files in HKEY_CLASSES_ROOT, showing their relationships

```
HKEY_CLASSES_ROOT\.bat
HKEY_CLASSES_ROOT\.bat\<No Name> = batfile

HKEY_CLASSES_ROOT\batfile
HKEY_CLASSES_ROOT\batfile\<NO NAME> = MS-DOS Batch File
HKEY_CLASSES_ROOT\batfile\EditFlags = 0x00000430

HKEY_CLASSES_ROOT\batfile\DefaultIcon
HKEY_CLASSES_ROOT\batfile\DefaultIcon\<NO NAME> = %SystemRoot%\System32\shell32.dll,-153

HKEY_CLASSES_ROOT\batfile\shell
HKEY_CLASSES_ROOT\batfile\shell\edit
HKEY_CLASSES_ROOT\batfile\shell\edit\<NO NAME> = &Edit

HKEY_CLASSES_ROOT\batfile\shell\edit\command
HKEY_CLASSES_ROOT\batfile\shell\edit\command\<NO NAME> = %SystemRoot%\System32\NOTEPAD.EXE %1

HKEY_CLASSES_ROOT\batfile\shell\open
HKEY_CLASSES_ROOT\batfile\shell\open\EditFlags = 0x00000000
HKEY_CLASSES_ROOT\batfile\shell\open\command
HKEY_CLASSES_ROOT\batfile\shell\open\command\<NO NAME> = "%1" %*

HKEY_CLASSES_ROOT\batfile\shell\print
HKEY_CLASSES_ROOT\batfile\shell\print\command
HKEY_CLASSES_ROOT\batfile\shell\print\command\<NO NAME> = %SystemRoot%\System32\NOTEPAD.EXE /p %1

HKEY_CLASSES_ROOT\batfile\shellex\batfile\shellex\PropertySheetHandlers
HKEY_CLASSES_ROOT\batfile\shellex\PropertySheetHandlers\PifProps
HKEY_CLASSES_ROOT\batfile\shellex\PropertySheetHandlers\PifProps\<NO NAME> = {86F19A00-42A0-1069-A2E9-08002B30309D}


HKEY_CLASSES_ROOT\CLSID\{86F19A00-42A0-1069-A2E9-08002B30309D}
HKEY_CLASSES_ROOT\CLSID\{86F19A00-42A0-1069-A2E9-08002B30309D}\<NO NAME> = .PIF file property pages

HKEY_CLASSES_ROOT\CLSID\{86F19A00-42A0-1069-A2E9-08002B30309D}\InProcServer32
HKEY_CLASSES_ROOT\CLSID\{86F19A00-42A0-1069-A2E9-08002B30309D}\InProcServer32\<NO NAME> = shell32.dll
HKEY_CLASSES_ROOT\CLSID\{86F19A00-42A0-1069-A2E9-08002B30309D}\InProcServer32\ThreadingModel = Apartment
```

2. Make HKEY_CLASSES_ROOT the top window either by selecting it in the Window menu or by clicking on it.

3. A batch file's extension is BAT, so find BAT in the list of extensions.

4. Open the BAT hive, where you will see that there is one unnamed entry with a data value of batfile. Figure 15.2 shows this entry.

5. Find the entry batfile in HKEY_CLASSES_ROOT and expand the shell sub-hive. The original shell sub-hive contains three entries: edit, open, and print.

6. Create a new sub-hive under shell and call this new sub-hive "NewEdit." (Sure, you can call this new sub-hive anything you want.)

7. In your NewEdit sub-hive, create an unnamed key with a data type of REG_SZ. In this key, put the text of the new command you are adding. In this example, we are adding the command-level editor (the editor displayed when you type edit at a command prompt), so I'm adding the string **&DOS Edit**. Take a gander at Figure 15.3 to see what we've done so far!

FIGURE 15.2:

Most extension entries have a single entry referring to a subsequent entry in HKEY_CLASSES_ROOT.

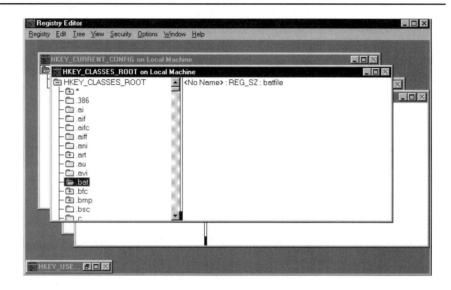

FIGURE 15.3:

RegEdt32 with NewEdit open, showing the unnamed key with the command's menu text

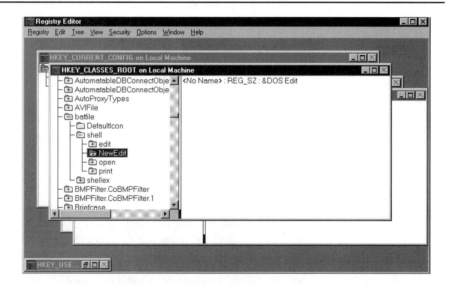

8. Under the NewEdit sub-hive, create a second sub-hive called **command**.

9. In the sub-hive command, create a new, unnamed key with a data type of REG_EXPAND_SZ. Make sure you use REG_EXPAND_SZ, and not REG_SZ, because this string will have an expansion variable embedded in it.

10. The string value for this new variable is the command itself. In our case, we are going to use the command editor, edit.com, which is located in %SystemRoot%\System32. Add this string as the following:

```
%SystemRoot%\System32\edit.com %1
```

The "%1" is a substitution variable, much like substitution variables in batch files, where Windows NT will substitute the name of the file to load into the editor. Figure 15.4 shows this change.

11. We are done with adding a new context menu selection. Close RegEdt32 and restart Windows NT.

FIGURE 15.4:

RegEdt32 with the new command added

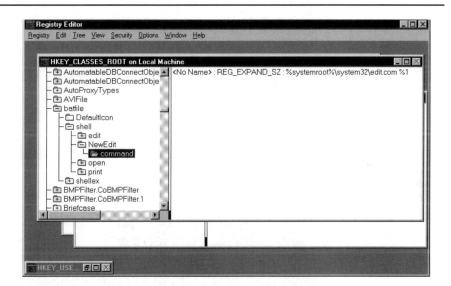

NOTE   Although not always necessary, I recommend that you restart Windows NT after each registry modification. Some parts of the registry are cached by Windows NT and changes won't become visible until after restarting Windows NT. Actually, much of HKEY_CLASSES_ROOT is cached, so a reboot is a really good idea here.

Figure 15.5 shows the new context menu in action. When the user clicks on the menu selection DOS Edit, the command prompt editor will open in its own window, and the selected file will be loaded, as shown in Figure 15.6.

FIGURE 15.5:

The new, modified context menu. Look—we now have a new editor to choose from.

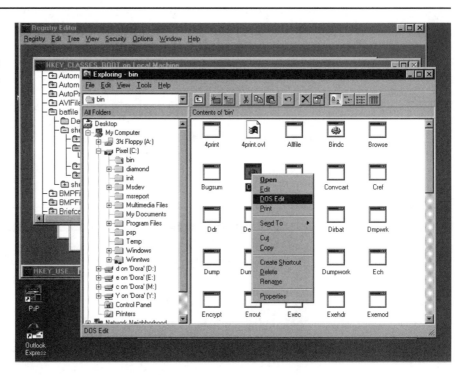

FIGURE 15.6:

Using a different editor may be just the trick for some users.

Editing with the command editor may be easier for some users, or maybe you have a favorite editor you would like to substitute.

All context menus in Explorer, which includes the desktop, may be modified using this technique. You can add selections for different file types, adding new actions to take, new editors, new print options, whatever.

Managing OLE and Embedding

The second function of HKEY_CLASSES_ROOT is to manage OLE and embedding. It is perhaps well beyond the scope of this book to really delve into the intricacies of OLE and embedding. But a quick introduction may be in order.

OLE (Object Linking and Embedding) is a basic functionality that Microsoft has been working on for the last 8 to 10 years. The origin of OLE, or at least the concepts surrounding OLE, are vague. Some of these techniques and functions can be traced back to the beginnings of Windows and something called DDE (Dynamic Data Exchange). DDE was one hell of a difficult thing to work with, and Microsoft quickly expanded it to make it more flexible.

OLE consists of a whole slew of features, but the main one we'll worry about today is the concept of embedding. *Embedding* is the process of using one application inside another application. Many of Microsoft's applications rely heavily on embedding. Outlook is one example; it's the Microsoft Desktop information management system that many of us use for e-mail. Outlook can use Microsoft Word as the preferred e-mail editor by embedding Word into Outlook's e-mail editor window. When this is done, Word's menus, tool bars, and other functions are all available to the user.

Figure 15.7 shows Word as the e-mail editor, running and editing a message to my editor. An invisible Word window exists with this chapter open. Using Word to edit an e-mail message doesn't affect Word's ability to be a word processor; although I do save my work before using Outlook.

There is nothing that would prevent you from writing an application that allowed Word to be embedded. For that matter, virtually all server applications can be embedded into a client application. There are established mechanisms to determine the server's capabilities, what is needed to embed, and so on; although it is well beyond the scope of this book to get into that topic. They say there are only about two programmers who really understand embedding and OLE, and they both work for Microsoft.

FIGURE 15.7:

Outlook's e-mail editor with Word embedded

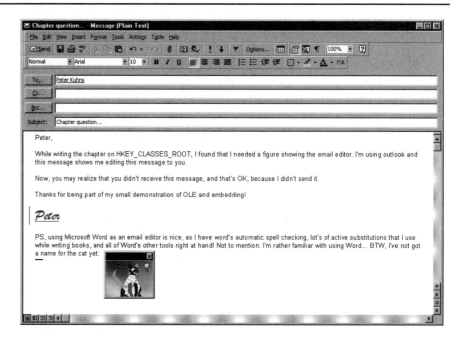

The Default Client—It's a Dirty Job but Someone Has to Do It

Windows NT offers what amounts to a default client application. It allows a server application that is incapable of running on its own a way to execute. This default client application is called RunDLL32.exe.

When RunDLL32 is executed, it is passed the name of the server, typically an ActiveX control (aka an OLE control); some actions, as in the case of the amovie.ocx /play and /close; and the name of the subject object, typically a file of some sort.

For example, the entry for the amovie.ocx, an ActiveX control used to display MPEG (video) files, is as follows:

```
%SystemRoot%\System32\RunDLL32.exe
%SystemRoot%\System32\amovie.ocx,RunDll /play /close %1
```

Continued on next page

In this example, RunDLL32 will load amovie.ocx (an ActiveX control), passing these four parameters:

RunDll—Tells amovie.ocx who the client is.

/play—Tells amovie.ocx to play the specified object, in this case the object is a file.

/close—Tells amovie.ocx to close after playing the specified object.

%1—Tells amovie.ocx which file contains the object to be played.

Delving into the Unknown

Regardless of how many viewer controls, applications, and whatever else is installed under Windows NT, there are going to be files that are handled. Windows NT refers to these files as *unknown*. When an unknown file is to be opened, Windows NT will display a dialog box called Open With. This dialog box, shown in Figure 15.8, allows the user to select an application to open files whose file type is currently not defined in Windows NT.

FIGURE 15.8:

Open With allows both opening a specific file of an unknown type, and setting a new default action for other files at the same time.

The Open With dialog will allow the user to select the application used to open the file. Also, if the Always use this program to open this file button is checked, Open With will create a new default handler for the file type.

Default handlers include most applications installed under Windows NT, which are those that are properly registered in the registry—that is, installed correctly. Also, several system components, including RunDLL32 (which allows running ActiveX controls), WinHlp32 (to open standard Windows help files), and Internet Explorer may be used as handlers.

Whenever a selection does not appear within the Open With dialog's list, clicking on the Other button allows the user to select any other executable program.

When the box labeled "Always use this program to open this file" is checked, new entries in HKEY_CLASSES_ROOT are created for this file type. These entries may then be edited or modified by the user, using the techniques previously shown, to change or enhance the behavior of the context menu.

Hints and Kinks from the Experts

In this chapter's Hints and Kinks, we cover a few hints for the HKEY_CLASSES_ROOT hive.

Define a Default Open When You Right-Click in Explorer.   When you right-click on a file with a known extension (in Explorer), you get a choice of how to open the file. If the extension is unknown, you get an Open With choice.

You can define a default Open choice for those unknown extensions and still have the Open With by amending the registry as follows:

1.   Open HKEY_Classes_root\unknown\shell in the registry editor.

2.   Double-click on Shell.

3.   Add Key open.

4.   With Open selected, add Key command.

5. With command selected, add a value with no name (leave it blank) and type **REG_EXPAND_SZ**.

6. Enter the full path to the executable, followed by a space and "%1". For example, Drive:\Directory\Program.exe "%1".

(Courtesy of Jerold Schulman)

Adding "Open with xyz" to Every Explorer Right-Click.   You can add a new option to every right-click by doing the following:

1. In the registry editor, edit the registry key HKEY_CLASSES_ROOT*.

2. Add a key called EditFlags with a type of REG_BINARY.

3. With the Hex button checked, enter a value for EditFlags of 02000000.

4. Open Explorer and select the File Types tab from the Options menu, displayed when selecting options in the View menu.

5. Highlight the * entry and click the Edit button.

6. Click the New button. In the Action box, type **open with xyz**. The xyz represents whatever program you want to run when the user selects the new menu selection.

7. In the Application box, browse to the program (xyz) you wish to use.

8. Click OK to close all dialog boxes.

Now, when you right-click in Explorer, you will always be able to "Open with xyz."

To restrict this functionality to unknown file types, perform the registry edit on HKEY_CLASSES_ROOT\Unknown, and modify the unknown selection (step 5) instead.

NOTE   This procedure will prevent you from using the Office 95 toolbar.

(Courtesy of Jerold Schulman)

CHAPTER

SIXTEEN

Introduction to HKEY_CURRENT_USER and HKEY_USERS

- HKEY_CURRENT_USER

- HKEY_USERS

- Hints and kinks from the experts

HKEY_CURRENT_USER and HKEY_USERS are hives dealing with users and user profiles. When first installed, Windows NT systems have two profiles configured: the default user, used by the system when no user is logged on; and a profile for the user who is currently logged on.

HKEY_CURRENT_USER is the profile for the currently logged on user. It is a link to the user's profile stored in HKEY_USERS. Changes made in HKEY_CURRENT_USER are also going to appear in HKEY_USERS and will be saved when the user logs off if the user doesn't have a mandatory profile.

HKEY_USERS contains the profile for the currently logged on user and the default profile, which is used when no user is logged on. All user profiles are stored as separate profile files and are loaded as needed. They are saved in the %SystemRoot%\Profiles\<userid> directory. The registry components of the user's profile are contained in the NTUSER.DAT files.

For example, consider our fictional user, Pixel:

1. The user Pixel logs onto the system.

2. Windows NT validates the userid and password with the Primary Domain Controller or the local machine's security manager if the user is not logging onto a domain.

3. The logon checks the user's profile status.

4. If the profile is local, or if the user is not logging on using a domain, the profile is loaded from the local machine.

5. If the user's profile is not local, the user is logging onto a domain or has a roaming or mandatory profile, the correct profile is loaded from the appropriate network share. The user's NTUSER.DAT file will be loaded into the registry's HKEY_USERS hive with a sub-hive name equal to the user's SID.

6. The user's profile is read from the server and updated as necessary to reflect the user's preferences. The user may log on at any computer in the domain and will be given the same profile regardless of which computer the user is using.

NOTE   Pixel, who's Pixel? Try Robert A. Heinlein's book, *The Cat Who Walked Through Walls* (ISBN 0-441-09499-6), to learn about the cat, Pixel.

In the process of loading the user's profile, the user's file NTUSER.DAT is loaded into HKEY_USERS. This hive contains the user's registry settings, everything that will later appear in the HKEY_CURRENT_USER hive. This becomes a hive with a name equal to the user's SID. The previously logged on user's profile is unloaded and saved to the location it was originally loaded from. This leaves HKEY_USERS with only two user profiles loaded at any given time.

> **WARNING**   Careful—backing up a server's registry doesn't back up each user's profile. It is necessary to completely back up the server's profiles directory, which contains information for each user who is defined on that machine and who has a profile stored there.

Users who don't have authority to modify their profile because they are using a mandatory profile may make changes; however, these changes will be lost when the user logs off.

> **WARNING**   What happens when the same userid, with a roaming profile, is used concurrently on two different computers? This situation is not well defined. It is not an error; however, only one of these multiple logged sessions will actually save the user's profile. The session that is the last to log off that will overwrite all other saves by other sessions.

The major user components in the registry are:

HKEY_CURRENT_USER—The HKEY_CURRENT_USER branch is used to manage specific information about the user who is currently logged on. Remember, changes made in HKEY_CLASSES_ROOT are automatically reflected in the user's information contained in HKEY_USERS.

HKEY_USERS—The HKEY_USERS key contains information about the system when no user is logged on, and also about the currently logged on user.

Again, a backup is vital. I've got to do one myself, so while I'm busy, why don't you do a registry backup, too.

HKEY_CURRENT_USERS

The HKEY_CURRENT_USER branch is used to manage specific information about the user who is currently logged on. This hive contains a complete profile of how Windows will look and behave for the user.

NOTE   If at any time it is desirable to modify Windows NT's look and feel (the profile) when no user is logged on, modify the entries in the HKEY_USERS\.DEFAULT sub-hive. There are parallel entries in this sub-hive for virtually every entry found in HKEY_CURRENT_USER. Realize that some changes won't be meaningful because they represent parts of the system that are inaccessible when a user is not logged on. Cute tricks include setting the wallpaper to be your company logo, setting a different screen saver, and so on.

Major sub-hives in HKEY_CURRENT_USER include the following:

AppEvents—This includes information about labels for events, such as Default Beep. Other information includes the sounds (such as the beeps, dings, and bongs) that Windows emits when things happen. The label entries are not normally edited, but can be changed if desired. The sounds are typically changed using the Control Panel's Sounds applet, although some sounds must be changed directly in the registry.

Console—The colors, font, and other command-window metrics are stored in this sub-hive. These settings apply to console windows only; other windows have their metrics stored elsewhere.

Control Panel—The Control Panel sub-hive is used to hold settings for some of the Control Panel's applets. Examples of settings saved here include Accessibility, Appearance, Mouse, and Keyboard.

Environment—The system environment strings are saved in the Environment sub-hive.

Keyboard Layout—The keyboard layout may be modified by users from this sub-hive, typically when a special-purpose keyboard is used.

Network—All drives where drive letters are mapped to are managed in the Network sub-hive. Explorer primarily manages drive mapping of network shares.

Printers—All printers, local and remote, are managed in the Printers sub-hive. Printer information is accessible in the system's Printer applet.

Software—Information about all installed software is stored in the Software sub-hive. Vendor typically arranges this information, although some applications may be in their own sub-hives.

Unicode Program Groups—This sub-hive contains information used by Program Manager. (Is anyone using Program Manager anymore?) The sub-keys found in Unicode Program Groups are in a binary format that is difficult to edit. (Have I ever seen entries in the Unicode Program Groups sub-hive? No, not yet.) Actually, users who upgraded from Windows NT 3.*x* may have entries in the Unicode Program Groups sub-hive. However, this sub-hive is not used by Windows NT version 4 or later.

Windows 3.1 Migrations Status—This sub-hive is contained only in systems that have been upgraded from Windows NT 3.*x*. This sub-hive contains the keys used to show the status of conversion of the Program Manager Group files (.GRP) and associated initialization (.INI) files that have been converted to Windows NT version 4 format. Deleting this key and not the Windows 3.1 Migration Status sub-hive causes Windows NT to attempt to convert the Program Manager files when Windows NT restarts. This reconversion may change the Start menu substantially.

Volatile Environment—Typically, this sub-hive contains only one entry, a key called LOGONSERVER that contains a string with the logon server (the server the user is currently logged on to). For example, my logon server is \\DORA.

AppEvents

AppEvents contains all the information that Windows NT uses to play sounds whenever an event happens. There are event labels for a number of events, as Table 16.1 shows. This table lists sounds found in virtually all Windows NT systems right from the first installation. Additionally, the AppEvents sub-hive contains definitions of what sounds to play when an event occurs. Finally, AppEvents also contains sound schemes for both default sounds and no sounds. Users may create new schemes, as desired, using the Control Panel's Sounds applet—more on that later.

TABLE 16.1: Windows NT Sounds That Are Found on Most Windows NT Systems

Sub-Hive	Default Text	Description
AppEvents\EventLabels\.Default	Default Beep	Default sound used when a sound is needed, but no specific sound has been defined
AppEvents\EventLabels\Activating-Document	Complete Navigation	Sound played when the navigation of an object is complete
AppEvents\EventLabels\AppGPFault	Program error	Sound played when a program returns an error
AppEvents\EventLabels\CCSelect	Select	Sound played when an object is selected
AppEvents\EventLabels\Close	Close program	Sound played when a program closes
AppEvents\EventLabels\Empty-RecycleBin	Empty Recycle Bin	Sound played when the recycle bin is emptied
AppEvents\EventLabels\MailBeep	New Mail Notification	Sound played when a new e-mail arrives
AppEvents\EventLabels\Maximize	Maximize	Sound played whenever a window is maximized
AppEvents\EventLabels\Menu-Command	Menu command	Sound played whenever a menu item is selected
AppEvents\EventLabels\MenuPopup	Menu pop-up	Sound played whenever a pop-up (context) menu item is selected
AppEvents\EventLabels\Minimize	Minimize	Sound played whenever a window is minimized
AppEvents\EventLabels\MoveMenuItem	Move Menu Item	Sound played whenever a menu item is moved
AppEvents\EventLabels\MSVC_HitBP	Breakpoint Hit	Sound played when a breakpoint in Microsoft Visual C++ has been reached (may not be present if Microsoft Visual C++ is not installed)
AppEvents\EventLabels\MSVC_OutputError	Error in Output	Sound played when an error in Microsoft Visual C++ has been detected (may not be present if Microsoft Visual C++ is not installed)

Continued on next page

TABLE 16.1 CONTINUED: Windows NT Sounds That Are Found on Most Windows NT Systems

Sub-Hive	Default Text	Description
AppEvents\EventLabels\MSVC_OutputWarning	Warning in Output	Sound played when a warning in Microsoft Visual C++ has been detected (may not be present if Microsoft Visual C++ is not installed)
AppEvents\EventLabels\Navigating	Start Navigation	Sound played when navigation begins
AppEvents\EventLabels\Open	Open program	Sound played when a program starts or opens
AppEvents\EventLabels\RestoreDown	Restore Down	Sound played when a window is restored from the maximized size to the normal size
AppEvents\EventLabels\RestoreUp	Restore Up	Sound played when a window is restored from the minimized size to the normal size
AppEvents\EventLabels\RingIn	Incoming Call	Sound played when an incoming telephony call is received
AppEvents\EventLabels\RingOut	Outgoing Call	Sound played when an outgoing telephony call is made
AppEvents\EventLabels\ShowBand	Show Toolbar Band	Sound played when the toolbar band is shown
AppEvents\EventLabels\SystemAsterisk	Asterisk	Sound played as the standard Windows NT asterisk sound
AppEvents\EventLabels\SystemExclamation	Exclamation	Sound played as the standard Windows NT exclamation sound
AppEvents\EventLabels\SystemExit	Exit Windows	Sound played when Windows is exited
AppEvents\EventLabels\SystemHand	Critical Stop	Sound played as the standard Windows critical stop sound
AppEvents\EventLabels\SystemQuestion	Question	Sound played as the standard Windows NT question sound
AppEvents\EventLabels\SystemStart	Start Windows	Sound played when Windows starts

Sounds based on events are set in the Control Panel's Sounds applet. This simple program is shown in Figure 16.1. Each event can have one sound assigned, and users are permitted to create and save event sound schemes.

FIGURE 16.1:

The Control Panel's Sounds applet sets sounds and sound schemes.

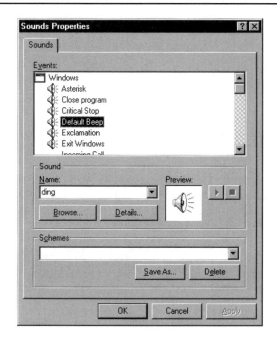

All sounds are rather meaningless unless the computer supports audio. Windows NT systems without sound compatibility will display these labels, and the user may set system sounds, but these sounds won't be played. After all, how can Windows play a sound without a sound system? (Experiments at the Dilbert facility using Elbonionans to make the appropriate sounds did not succeed well!)

Maybe, just maybe, there will be systems that don't have all of the above event labels. This is typically the case when a system administrator has substantially customized the installation and has deleted these objects. Although there may seem to be good reasons to delete event labels, it rarely is a good idea—more likely, it is a case of someone trying to generate work for themselves.

Once a system has more software applications, and perhaps hardware too, these products may add events. These events will require labels and (probably, although not necessarily) sounds.

Microsoft Office, for example, adds about 40 event labels; that's more than the default version of Windows. Microsoft's Developer Studio consists of a myriad of development tools, including Visual C/C++, Visual BASIC, Visual FoxPro, and others. It will also add many new events. Events and event labels can become overwhelming if lots of applications are installed.

We previously discussed labels for events. Next, we need a table of sounds to "play" when the event happens. These events are located in HKEY_CURRENT_USER\AppEvents\Schemes\Apps\.DEFAULT. This sub-hive contains entries to match each entry in the EventLabels sub-hive (listed in Table 16.1). Each sub-hive has at least two sub-hives: .Current and .DEFAULT. For example, HKEY_CURRENT_USER\AppEvents\Schemes\Apps\.Default\.DEFAULT contains the following:

> **.Current**—This sub-hive contains one unnamed key with the value of ding.wav, unless the user has changed the sound to be played. That is, when a default event (an event that doesn't have its own sound defined) occurs, Windows will play the ding.wav file.

> **.DEFAULT**—This sub-hive contains one unnamed key with the value of windows\Media\ding.wav. Windows NT will actually hard code the directory that Windows NT was installed in. If at some time the user selects the default sound in the Control Panel's Sounds applet, this is the one that will be chosen.

Additionally, if the user has defined one or more schemes, there will be an entry for each user-defined scheme. The name that will be used is a system generated hash of the user's scheme name. For example, I created a scheme called Peter's Scheme and Windows NT named the relevant sub-hives Peter'0.

Scheme names are contained in the HKEY_CURRENT_USER\AppEvents\Schemes\Names sub-hive. There will be one sub-hive for each scheme created by users, plus the two default ones: .Default and .None. The .Default sub-hive is the scheme used to restore the sounds to their default values. The .None sub-hive is a scheme used to turn off all sounds, which in some situations may be a really good move. There have been times when I wanted to use a really big hammer on someone's speakers. Oh, and by the way, each of these scheme sub-hives contains the username for the scheme.

Already we see the possibility to modify the default sounds so that there could be an organizational standard set of sounds. After all, a company with specialized sounds (for example, any company in the entertainment business) might really want their sounds to be the default sounds.

Selecting default sounds is done in the Schemes section of Control Panel's Sounds applet (see Figure 16.1). Select the Windows NT Default scheme to restore the defaults.

Selecting no sounds is done in the Schemes section of Control Panel's Sounds applet also (see Figure 16.1). Select No Sounds scheme to remove all sounds from events.

NOTE   Before selecting a scheme and making massive changes, it may be a good idea to save the current settings in a new scheme so that you can back out of an undesired change with only a little work. Schemes that are no longer needed may be deleted in the Control Panel's Sounds applet using the Delete button. Better safe than sorry.

Console

The HKEY_CURRENT_USER\Console sub-hive contains information used to configure the default sessions. Each entry sets parameters used for character-based applications; those with their own PIF files will use the PIF file settings rather than the settings in this sub-hive.

In Table 16.2, we are actually dealing with two-digit values (four of them in each ColorTable entry). A two-digit hex value can represent a value between 0 and 255 (that's 0 and 0xFF in hex). The table shows each key, a typical data value, and what the data value means.

T A B L E 16.2: Windows NT Console Settings Found on Most Windows NT Systems

Key	Typical Value	Description
ColorTable00	0x00000000	An RGB color value that is Black as night. RGB is additive, getting lighter as the values increase.
ColorTable01	0x00800000	Dark Red
ColorTable02	0x00008000	Dark Green
ColorTable03	0x00808000	Pea-Green color (or a Dark Yellow, you decide)

Continued on next page

TABLE 16.2 CONTINUED: Windows NT Console Settings Found on Most Windows NT Systems

Key	Typical Value	Description
ColorTable04	0x00000080	Defines Dark Blue.
ColorTable05	0x00800080	Defines Violet.
ColorTable06	0x00008080	Defines Dark Cyan.
ColorTable07	0x00c0c0c0	Defines Light Gray.
ColorTable08	0x00808080	Defines Darker Gray.
ColorTable09	0x00ff0000	Defines Bright Red.
ColorTable10	0x0000ff00	Defines Bright Green.
ColorTable11	0x00ffff00	Defines Yellow—or a really, really bright Pea Green.
ColorTable12	0x000000ff	Defines Bright Blue.
ColorTable13	0x00ff00ff	Defines Bright Violet.
ColorTable14	0x0000ffff	Defines Cyan.
ColorTable15	00x0ffffff	Defines White.
CurrentPage	0x00000000	Page zero is the current page.
CursorSize	0x00000019	The cursor is 25% of the character cell in size.
FaceName		Defines the name of the console font if defined. A default font is selected if none is defined.
FontFamily	0x00000000	Defines the console font family if defined. The default family for the selected font is used if none is defined; typical values include TrueType and Raster.
FontSize	0x00000000	Defines font size, the low word contains the character width; the high word contains the character height—for example, a font 8 x 16 would be 0x00080010.
FontWeight	0x00000000	Defines the weight (bolding) of the font, larger numbers are more bold.
FullScreen	0x00000000	Value of 0x00000001 is set if this window is full screen; value of 0x00000000 is set if the window is not full screen
HistoryBufferSize	0x00000032	Size of history buffer in commands, the hex value of 32 is 50 commands in decimal.

Continued on next page

TABLE 16.2 CONTINUED: Windows NT Console Settings Found on Most Windows NT Systems

Key	Typical Value	Description
InsertMode	0x00000000	Value of 0x00000001 is to use insert mode; 0x00000000 is to use overwrite mode.
NumberOfHistory-Buffers	0x00000004	Describes the number of history buffers used for this command session.
PopupColors	0x000000f5	Describes the color used for a pop-up window if displayed. The first 4 bits (f in the example) are the characters; the next 4 bits (5 in the example) are the foreground color. Indexes to the color values are defined in this table.
QuickEdit	0x00000000	Value set to 0x00000001 if quick-edit mode is enabled. Value set to 0x00000000 if quick-edit is not enabled. Quick edit allows quick cut and paste to the Clipboard.
ScreenBufferSize	0x00190050	Desribes the screen buffer size. In the example, 0x0019 = 25 in decimal and 0x0050 = 80 in decimal, therefore, the default screen buffer size is 25 x 80 in size. Other common sizes are 50 x 80 (0x00320050), or 43 x 80 (0x002b0050).
ScreenColors	0x00000007	Describes the index to colors for the screen. The next to last digit is index for characters, and last digit is the index for the background.
WindowSize	0x00190050	Describes the window size. In the example, 0x0019 = 25 in decimal and 0x0050 = 80 in decimal, therefore, the default screen buffer size is 25 x 80 in size. Other common sizes are 50 x 80 (0x00320050), or 43 x 80 (0x002b0050).

Colors are expressed in RGB as a 4-byte value. The first byte is ignored—actually, Windows uses it internally and it should always be set to zero. The second byte is red, the third byte is green, and the fourth and final byte is blue. For example, a color value of 0x00AA2020 is a dusky red, the same color as the windbreaker that I wear in the spring. I left the jacket in a restaurant the other day and called them to check to see if it was there. I described the color as an RGB color 170, 32, 32; and the person who owned the restaurant told me without any hesitation that it was there. Could the fact that I was the only one to leave a jacket there in weeks have anything to do with it?

TIP   Lazy and don't want to convert between hex and decimal using your fingers and toes—or just can't take off your shoes? The Windows NT Calculator program will convert between hex and decimal with ease. Just start Calculator and select View ➤ Scientific.

Hexadecimal and Colors

What the heck is hex? *Hexadecimal* numbers, usually just called "hex" for short, are expressed in base 16. We usually use base 10 to show a hex number, since there are only 10 numeric digits, 0 through 9. We also use the letters a through f for the missing six digits.

Computers are binary. They know only two number values: either 1 (on) or 0 (off). A single datum of computer data is called a *bit*, which represents either 0 or 1, and no other value in between.

In computers, numbers are stored in bytes, each comprised of eight bits. A byte's value may range from 0 to 255. Hex numbers are always prefixed with 0x and they may be either uppercase or lowercase, it doesn't matter. In hex, that value range is 0x00 to 0xFF.

Two bytes together (16 bits) form what is called a "WORD" (usually, but not always written in uppercase). A WORD, if unsigned, may represent a value from 0 to 65535. A signed WORD value represents a value of –32767 to 32767.

Four bytes together (32 bits) form what is called a "DWORD," short for double word. A double WORD, if unsigned, may represent a value from 0 to 4294967295. A signed double WORD represents a value from 2147483647 to –2147483647.

Often times programmers try to fit as much information as possible into a WORD or DWORD value. History has shown how this can backfire, but for some data, this technique works well. Color values are a case where three sets of values (one each for red, green, and blue) fit within the DWORD's 4 bytes.

Oh, and one more bit of confusion: Half a byte, 4 bits, is called a nibble. A nibble can hold a value between 0 and 15. Though nibbles are not used very often, there are several registry entries that do use 4-bit values.

Control Panel

The Control Panel sub-hive in the registry is where many of the Control Panel applets store settings and defaults. There are a number of sections that may vary depending on which Windows NT components are installed. Things that affect the number of sections include special mouse support, screen savers, and what optional things are installed. There may be some differences between a Windows NT Server and a Windows NT Workstation installation.

Information in this sub-key includes data stored in the WIN.INI and the SYSTEM.INI files on Windows 3.*x* and earlier.

The sections that show in many registries include:

Accessibility—Windows NT's features for users who require special support due to physical limitations; items such as a special keyboard, mouse, or sounds; and general support are covered in Accessibility.

Appearance—Windows NT's appearance and the Windows NT Schemes used for display configuration are covered in Appearance.

Cache—Unknown, don't you just hate it when there is a component that is both undocumented and apparently unused? I checked every Windows NT system I could, and the Cache sub-hive was empty on all systems—both Server and Workstation.

Colors—The colors for buttons, text—just about everything displayed to the user—are contained here.

Current—The currently loaded color scheme is contained here.

Custom Colors—Any user-defined color schemes are contained here.

Desktop—The Desktop configuration, colors, spacing metrics—everything about what the screen displays—is covered in this sub-hive.

International—Items dealing with the computer's location (country), including sorting orders, are contained here.

IOProcs—Media view file system control is found in IOProcs.

Keyboard—Configurations for the keyboard, such as initial state of the toggle keys for Caps Lock, Num Lock, and Scroll Lock; and delay and repeat rates are contained here.

MMCPL—Multimedia Control Panel settings are contained here.

Mouse—Mouse settings, such as speed, tracking, and other settings are contained here.

Patterns—Windows NT's patterns used to create backgrounds, such as Boxes, Critters, Diamonds, and so on are contained here.

Screen Saver.3DflyingObj—Configurations for this screen saver are contained here.

Screen Saver.3DPipes—Configurations for this screen saver are contained here.

Screen Saver.Bezier—Configurations for this screen saver are contained here.

Screen Saver.Marquee—Configurations for this screen saver are contained here.

Screen Saver.Mystify—Configurations for this screen saver are contained here.

Screen Saver.Stars—Configurations for this screen saver are contained here.

Sound—Information about sounds is contained here.

Sounds—One entry for something called SystemDefault is contained here.

In the remainder of this section, we'll take a look at some of these entries that seem interesting or can set data that cannot be set elsewhere. Most entries can be set using the Control Panel if the user desires.

Accessibility

The concept of allowing Windows NT to be accessible to users who have special needs is relatively new. Windows 95 was the first version of Windows to offer accessibility configurations. Windows NT 4, released after Windows 95, followed suit.

Accessibility is subdivided into eight sub-keys:

Keyboard Response—Items in Keyboard Response include the following:

AutoRepeatDelay—This key has a default value of 1000, one second. Increasing this value will increase the wait time before the keyboard auto-repeat kicks in.

AutoRepeatRate—This key has a default value of 500. Increasing this value will increase the repeat rate.

BounceTime—This key has a default value of zero. It is used to specify the amount of time a keystroke will be ignored after pressing and releasing a key. It helps eliminate false double keystrokes.

DelayBeforeAcceptance—This key has a default value of 1000. Increasing it will increase the amount of time that the key must be pressed before it registers as being pressed. Changing the default here is useful if a user has a tendency to hit keys by mistake.

Flags—This is a character field containing the default value of 82. It's used to enable or disable the previously discussed flags.

MouseKeys—Items in MouseKeys include the following:

MaximumSpeed—This key has a default value of 80. It is used to limit the maximum speed, in pixels per second, that the mouse cursor will move when a mouse movement key is held down.

TimeToMaximumSpeed—This key has a default value of 3000, three seconds, and is used to determine the amount of time required for the mouse pointer to reach full speed (specified in MaximumSpeed) when a mouse movement key is held down.

Flags—This is a character field containing the default value of 18. It is used to disable and enable the previously discussed flags.

SerialKeys—A special input device that is connected to a serial port, this device is used to emulate the keyboard and mouse on the computer. Typically, people who are unable to use standard keyboards take advantage of these devices. Each device is configured in its own manner, and registry entries will be specific to the device installed. For systems that do not have serial keyboard/mouse emulation devices configured, SerialKeys will have no entries. Otherwise, the following entries will be found:

ActivePort—This is the com port used with a default of COM1.

Baud—This is the serial speed, in baud, displayed as a hexadecimal number by default.

Port—This is the com port supported.

Flags—This is a value of 3 indicates the feature is supported.

ShowSounds—This sub-key is in the Sound tab of Accessibility Properties. ShowSounds has a single registry key and no other options as shown here:

On—A value of 0 is off, and a value of 1 is on.

SoundSentry—Inside the SoundSentry sub-hive, there are three or more keys, listed here:

FSTextEffect—This is full-screen text window (command- or character-based application) support. A value of 0 is off; non-zero is on.

TextEffect—This key is probably unused. The Accessibility Properties applet in Control Panel will reset TextEffect to 0 if it is non-zero.

WindowsEffect—A value of 0 indicates no Windows effects; 1 indicates flash active caption bar; 2 indicates flash active window; 3 indicates flash Desktop.

Flags—A value of 2 is off; a value of 3 indicates that SoundSentry is on.

StickyKeys—There is a single value in StickyKeys called Flags. Flags appears to be bitmapped, although the exact relationship between bits and settings is difficult to determine. However, the following known bits are:

0000 0000 0000 0001—The on/off bit, if 1, StickyKeys is off.

0000 0000 1000 0000—The Press modifier key twice to lock flag, if 0, the option is off.

0000 0000 0000 0100—The Use shortcut flag, if 0, use shortcut is off.

0000 0001 0000 0000—The Turn StickyKeys off if two keys are pressed at once flag, if 0, the option is off.

0000 0000 0101 0000—The Make sounds when modifier key is pressed flag, if both are 0, the option is off; if both are 1, the option is on.

TimeOut—There are two values in TimeOut that control when the accessibility options are turned off. They are based on non-use for a certain period of time.

Flags—A value of 2 is off and a value of 3 indicates that the option is enabled.

TimeToWait—The value, in milliseconds, that the computer has been idle before accessibility options are turned off. Five minutes is 300000.

ToggleKeys—There is a single value in ToggleKeys called Flags. A bitmapped value is used that has four known states, shown here:

26—Use ToggleKeys is off; Use ToggleKeys shortcut is off.

27—Use ToggleKeys is on; Use ToggleKeys shortcut is off.

30—Use ToggleKeys is off; Use ToggleKeys shortcut is on (not a meaningful choice).

31—Use ToggleKeys is on; Use ToggleKeys shortcut is on.

Appearance

What Windows NT looks like is contained in the Windows NT Schemes used for display configuration. Under Appearance, there is a single sub-hive called Schemes. In Schemes, there are keys, all REG_BINARY, containing definitions of the Windows NT standard color schemes, such as Lilac, Maple, Wheat, Windows Standard, and so on.

Each scheme in this sub-hive is loaded in the Control Panel's Display applet, which is also accessible from the Desktop's Properties menu. Looking in the Appearance tab, there is a drop-down list to select a scheme from.

It is quite possible to hack a scheme from the registry, although many of the parts of the scheme may be modified more easily in the Display Properties dialog box. Once modified, a new scheme may be saved for later reloading as needed.

Cache

This sub-hive seems to control how Windows NT's Control Panel displays its icons. Many Windows NT users do not have any entries in this sub-hive, while others do. An example of the Cache sub-hive is shown in Microsoft's Knowledge Base article "Q150541," which may be viewed at `http://support.microsoft.com/support/kb/articles/q150/5/41.asp`.

Colors

The colors for buttons, text, and just about everything displayed to the user are contained here. Sub-keys included in Colors and their default values are listed next. Keep in mind that more colors may be defined as more applications and components are installed on Windows NT.

Each key listed here has a string containing three numbers representing the red, green, and blue color levels. As the color value increases, the color becomes lighter, so that a value of 127 0 0 is a dark red, and a value of 255 0 0 is a bright red.

- `ActiveBorder= 92 192 192`
- `ActiveTitle=0 0 128`
- `AppWorkSpace=255 255 255`
- `Background=255 255 255`
- `ButtonFace=192 192 192`
- `ButtonHilight=255 255 255`
- `ButtonShadow=128 128 128`
- `ButtonText=0 0 0`
- `GrayText=128 128 128`
- `Hilight=0 0 128`
- `HilightText=255 255 255`
- `InactiveBorder=192 192 192`
- `InactiveTitle=192 192 192`
- `InactiveTitleText=0 0 0`
- `InfoText=0 0 0`
- `InfoWindow=255 255 255`
- `Menu=255 255 255`
- `MenuText=0 0 0`
- `Scrollbar=192 192 192`
- `TitleText=255 255 255`
- `Window=255 255 255`
- `WindowFrame=0 0 0`
- `WindowText=0 0 0`

Current

The sub-hive Current contains the currently loaded color scheme. One key, named Color Schemes, will contain the color scheme name. Also check HKEY_CURRENT_USER\ControlPanel\Appearance\Schemes for a list of schemes installed on the computer.

Custom Colors

The Windows NT common dialog called Colors allows you to define and save up to 16 custom color definitions. These custom colors are stored in the sub-hive called Custom Colors, in entries named ColorA through ColorP. Each entry consists of a six-digit string, in hexadecimal, nominally in RGB, for each custom color. The default value for each color is FFFFFF, or white.

Desktop

The configuration of the user's Desktop is contained in the sub-hive called Desktop. This hive contains between 25 to 50 different entries. Many of these items (see Table 16.3) may be adjusted in the various Properties dialog boxes, but some must be changed directly from the registry.

TABLE 16.3:   Windows NT Desktop Settings Found on Most Windows NT Systems

Entry	Typical Value	Description
AutoEndTasks	0	Sets the automatic task-ending mode that controls whether the system may automatically end a timed-out task without displaying a warning or prompt dialog box.
CoolSwitch	1	The fast task-switching mode, set to 0 to disable. CoolSwitch is not listed as being supported in Windows NT version 4 because the feature is always enabled.
CoolSwitchColumns	7	Sets the number of columns of icons present when the ALT+TAB dialog box is displayed.
CoolSwitchRows	3	Sets the number of rows of icons present when the ALT+TAB dialog box is displayed.
CursorBlinkRate	530	The time between blinks of the cursor, in milliseconds, the default value is 530 milliseconds.

Continued on next page

TABLE 16.3 CONTINUED: Windows NT Desktop Settings Found on Most Windows NT Systems

Entry	Typical Value	Description
DragFullWindows	0	The drag mode in Windows NT which supports either full window dragging or outline dragging; a value of 1 indicates that full windows dragging is enabled.
DragHeight	2	Sets the vertical size of the dragging box required before the mouse detects a drag operation.
DragWidth	2	Sets the horizontal size of the dragging box required before the mouse detects a drag operation.
FontSmoothing	2	Font smoothing makes certain fonts easier to read on high-resolution color adapters. It is set in the Display Properties' Plus! tab under Smooth edges of screen fonts.
GridGranularity	0	A grid that helps align objects on the Desktop may be enabled.
HungAppTimeout	5000	Sets the time, in milliseconds, before a hung application (one that does not respond) will cause Windows NT to display a dialog box to prompt the user to either wait or kill the application.
IconSpacing	75	Sets the icon spacing granularity for the Desktop.
IconTitleFaceName	MS Sans Serif	Sets the icon font name.
IconTitleSize	9	Sets the size of icon titles.
IconTitleStyle	0	Sets the icon title style.
IconTitleWrap	1	Sets the entry that controls whether icon titles will wrap or be displayed on only one line.
MenuShowDelay	400	The delay time set before showing a cascading menu; typical values are 0 to 400, although values can be higher.
Pattern	(None)	The pattern used under icon labels or exposed areas of the Desktop that the Desktop wallpaper doesn't cover, set in Display Properties ➤Background.
ScreenSaveActive	1	The screen saver displayed when the system has been inactive for a longer amount of time than is specified in ScreenSaveTimeOut, it is displayed when this value is set at 1.
ScreenSaverIsSecure	0	The screen saver will prompt for a password if this value is set at 1.

Continued on next page

T A B L E 1 6 . 3 C O N T I N U E D : Windows NT Desktop Settings Found on Most Windows NT Systems

Entry	Typical Value	Description
ScreenSaveTimeOut	1500	Sets the amount of time the computer is inactive, in seconds, before displaying the screen saver
SCRNSAVE.EXE	C:\WINNTWS\System32\sspipes.scr	The name of the current screen saver; in this example, the user has the OpenGL 3-D Pipes screen saver installed.
TileWallpaper	0	The wallpapering mode, if the value is set at 0, the wallpaper is centered using only a single copy. If the value is 1, the wallpaper is tiled starting in the upper-left corner.
WaitToKillApp Timeout	20000	Sets the amount of time that elapses, in milliseconds, before notifying users of any applications that are not responding properly when a logoff or shutdown command is received.
Wallpaper	C:\WINNTWS\SYBEX.bmp	Sets the name of the wallpaper file; a bitmap file.
WheelScrollLines	3	The number of lines that the Microsoft wheel mouse will scroll when the wheel is turned, the default value of 3 may be too much for some applications.

As the installation of Windows NT ages and more optional components are added, the number of entries in the Desktop sub-hive will increase. Many of the possible entries are self-explanatory. Generally, modifying a value won't cause a computer to crash, although the results may be unpleasant.

A sub-hive under Desktop, named WindowMetrics, contains one or two entries:

BorderWidth—Sets the width of a resizable window's border. A typical value is 1.

Shell Icon BPP—Sets the number of bit-planes for icons. A typical value is 16.

International

Items dealing with the computer's location (country), including sorting orders, are stored here. Most of these entries are set in the Control Panel using the Regional Settings Properties applet.

Generally, there is little need to manually set anything in International. The Regional Settings Properties dialog covers each entry fully and includes error checking.

IOProcs

Contained in IOProcs is a reference to a single file, MVFS32.DLL, which is not found on any system that I have checked. MVFS32.DLL is the Media View File System DLL used by some applications to view media files. There is a strong probability that this file system and IOProcs are not used by more recent applications. There are two Media View File System DLLs supplied with Windows NT 4: MVFS13N.DLL and MVFS14N.DLL. Like the Cache entry mentioned earlier in this chapter, this is almost a mystery entry. One Microsoft Knowledge Base entry does document a fix for a problem with Encarta 95 and Windows NT 3.5 that requires an entry in IOProcs for M12 = `mvfs1232.dll`. This is the only information available.

Keyboard

Configurations for the keyboard, such as the initial state of the toggle keys; Caps Lock, Num Lock, and Scroll Lock; and the delay and repeat rates are stored here.

A typical system will have these three entries:

InitialKeyboardIndicators—This is automatically set by Windows NT when users log off or when the system is shut down. It preserves the previous state of the Num Lock key. 0 turns off Num Lock when the user logs on, and 2 turns on Num Lock when the user logs on.

KeyboardDelay—This is the delay, when a key is held down, before the key auto-repeats. Values between 0 and 3 are accepted, with 0 being a delay of 250 milliseconds, and 3 being a delay of 1 second. These times are approximate.

KeyboardSpeed—This is the speed that a key auto-repeats. Choose a value between 0, which repeats at two characters per second, and 31, which repeats at 30 characters per second.

MMCPL

Some ODBC (Open Database Connectivity) and multimedia control panel settings are stored here. Many computers do not have any entries in the MMCPL. Some typical entries might include the following:

- NumApps=20

- H=230

- W=442

- X=88

- Y=84

It is possible to have multimedia control panel applets in other directories, with the exception of %SystemRoot%\System32, by specifying their names and paths in the MMCPL sub-hive.

Mouse

Mouse settings, such as speed and tracking, are set here. Typical settings include those shown in Table 16.4.

TABLE 16.4: Windows NT Desktop Settings Found on Most Windows NT Systems

Entry	Typical Value	Description
SwapMouseButtons	0	Right and left buttons swap if the value is 1.
DoubleClickSpeed	500	Sets the speed of pressing the mouse to activate a double-click.
DoubleClickHeight	4	Sets the amount of movement allowed (vertical) for a double-click to be valid.
DoubleClickWidth	4	Sets the amount of movement allowed (horizontal) for a double-click to be valid.

Continued on next page

TABLE 16.4 CONTINUED: Windows NT Desktop Settings Found on Most Windows NT Systems

Entry	Typical Value	Description
MouseThreshold1	6	Sets the motion factor that, when factored with MouseSpeed, controls the motion of the mouse.
MouseThreshold2	10	Sets the motion factor that, when factored with MouseSpeed, controls the motion of the mouse.
MouseSpeed	1	Sets the speed of the mouse pointer relative to the movement of the mouse.
SnapToDefaultButton	0	The mouse will snap to the default button in dialog boxes when this value is set to 1.
ActiveWindowTracking	0x00000000	The mouse will specify the active window when this value is set to 0x00000001.

Patterns

Windows NT's patterns used to create backgrounds, such as Boxes, Critters, and Diamonds, are set here. For Windows NT, patterns are expressed as an 8 x 8 box of color, either black for each 1 bit or the background color for each 0 bit. The first number represents the first, topmost, line in the pattern; the second number represents the second line in the pattern, and so forth.

Each line is a binary representation, for example, the Boxes pattern is:

Boxes=127, 65, 65, 65, 65, 65, 127, 0

These values are expressed as binary numbers, as shown in Table 16.5.

TABLE 16.5: Binary Values for Patterns

Decimal	Binary
127	0111 1111
65	0100 0001
65	0100 0001
65	0100 0001

Continued on next page

TABLE 16.5 CONTINUED: Binary Values for Patterns

Decimal	Binary
65	0100 0001
65	0100 0001
127	0111 1111
0	0000 0000

You can compare these binary numbers with the Boxes pattern. To do so, use the Edit Pattern button to view the pattern in the pattern editor. This fully shows the relationship between the bits and the pattern.

Be creative; you can cook up new patterns using the pattern editor. Just enter a new pattern name, click the Add button, and *voilà*, there is your new pattern. Just remember: It can be hard to be creative using an 8 x 8 cell.

Screen Saver.3DflyingObj

Configurations for the 3D Flying Objects (OpenGL) screen saver are saved in this hive. Actually, all necessary settings can be performed from the Screen Saver tab in the Display Properties dialog box. Select the 3D Flying Objects (OpenGL) screen saver and click the Settings button to configure these settings.

Screen Saver.3Dpipes

Configurations for the 3D Pipes (OpenGL) screen saver are saved in this hive. Actually, all necessary settings can be performed from the Screen Saver tab in the Display Properties dialog box. Select the 3D Pipes (OpenGL) screen saver and click the Settings button to configure these settings.

Screen Saver.Bezier

Configurations for the Bezier screen saver are saved in this hive. Actually, all necessary settings can be performed from the Screen Saver tab in the Display Properties dialog box. Select the Bezier screen saver and click the Settings button to configure these settings.

Screen Saver.Marquee

Configurations for the Marquee screen saver are saved in this hive. Actually, all necessary settings can be performed from the Screen Saver tab in the Display Properties dialog box. Select the Marquee screen saver and click the Settings button to configure these settings.

Screen Saver.Mystify

Configurations for the Mystify screen saver are saved in this hive. Actually, all necessary settings can be performed from the Screen Saver tab in the Display Properties dialog box. Select the Mystify screen saver and click the Settings button to configure these settings.

Screen Saver.Stars

Configurations for the Stars screen saver are saved in this hive. Actually, all necessary settings can be performed from the Screen Saver tab of the Display Properties dialog box. Select the Stars screen saver and click the Settings button to configure these settings.

Sound

Information about basic sounds is contained in the Sound sub-hive. Two entries that I've found, `Beep=yes` and `ExtendedSounds=yes`, both seem to be present on all systems.

`Beep=yes` is used to indicate whether Windows NT will make a warning beep when the user attempts to do something that is not allowed.

Sounds

The Sounds sub-hive contains one entry called `"SystemDefault"` that typically has a value of , (That is just a comma, nothing else.). Other entries in the Sounds sub-hive include the following:

- `Enable=1`
- `SystemAsterisk=chord.wav,Asterisk`
- `SystemDefault=ding.wav,Default Beep`

- `SystemExclamation=chord.wav,Exclamation`

- `SystemExit=chimes.wav,Windows Logoff`

- `SystemHand=chord.wav,Critical Stop`

- `SystemQuestion=chord.wav,Question`

- `SystemStart=tada.wav,Windows Logon`

It can be assumed that the Sounds hive contains information used by legacy systems. Each of these sounds is defined for use by Windows NT elsewhere in the registry.

Environment

The Control Panel's System Properties applet contains a tab called Environment. This tab is subdivided into two sections: System Variables and User Variables for <user>, where <user> is the currently logged on user (see Figure 16.2). Any environment variable defined in System Variables will be available to all users, while environment variables defined in User Variables for <user> will only be available to <user>.

FIGURE 16.2:

The Environment for each user is contained in HKEY_CURRENT_USER-\Environment.

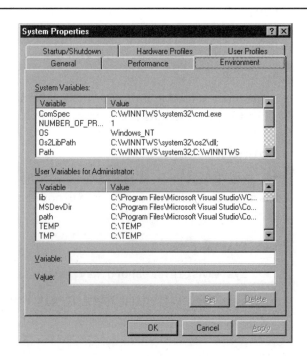

Notice in Figure 16.2 that the current user is Administrator. When the next user logs on, he or she will get a different environment.

There is little need to modify the HKEY_CURRENT_USER\Environment section directly. The Control Panel's System Properties dialog does a better job of modifying entries in Environment, and using System Properties is much safer than manually editing the registry.

WARNING   Avoid the urge to modify existing system properties system variables unless you understand the ramifications of making such a change. For instance, changing the entry NUMBER_OF_PROCESSORS from 1 to 2 won't give you an extra CPU.

Keyboard Layout

Keyboard Layout is used to allow users to change keyboard configurations, typically when users must work in two different languages. Since different languages may have different layouts (usually special symbols, such as currency and so on), Windows NT allows users to change the keyboard layout using the Control Panel's Keyboard and Regional Settings applets.

To configure multiple language support, the user must do the following:

1. Open Regional Settings Properties in the Control Panel.

2. Click and open the Input Locales tab.

3. If the languages and layouts desired are already installed in the Input Locales list, go to step 7.

4. Click the Add button.

5. In the Add Input Locale dialog, select the desired locale. Check or uncheck, depending on your preference, the Use default properties for the selected input locale. Click the OK button.

6. If you deselected Use default properties for this input locale, select the desired layout in the Input Locale Properties dialog box.

7. Check to ensure that the correct default is selected.

NOTE   You can have more than two input locales, although it may be unusual to have many different locales defined.

You can define a hotkey to switch locales. The default hotkey is Left Alt+Shift, although Ctrl+Shift may be chosen as an alternative hotkey. If no hotkey is desired, select None. If you select the No hotkey option, it probably would be a good idea to check the Enable indicator on Taskbar option, so that you can use the taskbar to switch input locales.

Now, back to our currently scheduled programming . . .

In HKEY_CURRENT_USER\Keyboard Layout, there are the following three sub-hives:

Preload—This sub-hive contains the keyboard layouts to be preloaded by Windows NT. Once preloaded, they may be selected using the Control Panel, hotkeys, or the Taskbar, as desired.

Substitutes—Any key substitutes will be defined in the Substitutes sub-hive. Key substitutes typically use the Dvorak keyboard layout. In Substitutes, a key named with the original locale is created with the value of the substituting layout. For instance, the Unites States English locale is 409. Also, 00000409 = 00000809 substitutes British English on the United States English locale.

Toggle—This sub-hive contains a single key whose data value will be 0 if no hotkey is defined, 1 if Left Alt+Shift is defined as the hotkey, and 2 if Ctrl+Shift is defined as the hotkey.

TIP
Tired of QWERTY? A different keyboard layout can be most useful if QWERTY is not your thing. Another type of keyboard layout is called Dvorak, which changes the location of the letters on the keyboard. Said to improve typing proficiency by a great deal, Dvorak has a slowly growing band of supporters. To select the Dvorak layout, select an Input Locale in Regional Settings, and click on Properties to modify the layout.

Generally, all modifications to HKEY_CURRENT_USER\Keyboard Layout should be done using either the Control Panel's Regional Settings' Input Locales or the Keyboard applet's Input Locales tab.

Network

HKEY_CURRENT_USER\Network contains configuration information for each network drive that the user has permanently mapped. Under Network you will find a sub-hive for each mapped drive letter.

For instance, if a user on Network Neighborhood selects a server, selects a share, right (context) clicks on the share, and selects Map Network Drive in the pop-up context menu; the Map Network Drive dialog box (Figure 16.3) will appear. This allows the user to select which drive letter is mapped to the network share. This sub-hive also contains the following:

- the path, which may not be modified

- a Connect As box, which allows you to access the drive as another user

- a checkbox called Reconnect at Logon, which is important because unchecking it will mean that the share is available only for the current session

FIGURE 16.3:

The Map Network Drive

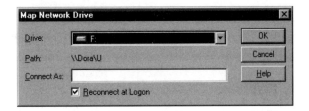

> **NOTE**   Any drives mapped without the Reconnect at Logon attribute will not be loaded into the HKEY_CURRENT_USER\Network sub-hive.

Network drives may be mapped as any unused drive letter, using either the current userid or another userid.

Once the user selects a drive (U: in our next example) and clicks the OK button, the registry's HKEY_CURRENT_USER\Network sub-hive will have F as the new sub-hive. The F sub-hive contains five key variables:

ConnectionType—The value of 0x1 is for drives; 0x2 is for printers.

ProviderName—The network provider, it is typically Microsoft Windows Network for Microsoft networking.

ProviderType—The Network provider's type is 0x20000 for Microsoft Windows networking.

RemotePath—The UNC (Universal Naming Conventions) path to the network share, \\Dora\U is the share named U on the server whose name is Dora.

> **UserName**—The name of the user for whom the share is established, it is either the current user's name or the name the user specifies in the Map Network Drive dialog box (Figure 16.3). The username syntax consists of domain\user, where *domain* is the user's domain and *user* is the userid.

Again, as with many other HKEY_CURRENT_USER entries, the entries in Network are easily manipulated without using the registry editor. If for some reason there are problems in deleting a connection, one fix would be to delete the sub-hive from the HKEY_CURRENT_USER\Registry sub-hive.

Shares can be established quickly from a command-line prompt by using the command-line syntax:

```
net use U: \\Dora\c
```

Here U: is the drive letter to be mapped and \\Dora\C is the share name. To get the full syntax of the net use command, type **net use /?** at a command-line prompt.

Printers

The HKEY_CURRENT_USER\Printers sub-hive contains information about printers—both local and remote.

Local Printers

Locally attached printers are typically served with two sub-hives in HKEY_CURRENT_USER\Printers. These sub-hives are as follows:

> **DevModes2**—The configurations for the printer, regardless of whether the printer is local or remotely attached, are stored in DevModes2. Each printer has a key entry, named for the printer, with a binary data value following it.

> **Settings**—This sub-hive contains binary objects for each attached printer.

Remote Printers

Locally attached printers are typically served with two sub-hives in HKEY_CURRENT_USER\Printers. These sub-hives are as follows:

> **Connection**—This sub-hive contains sub-hives for each remotely connected printer. Each sub-hive is named for the printer and contains two

objects: Provider, a variable that contains the name of the driving DLL file; and Server, a variable that contains the name of the server that the printer is attached to.

DevModes2—The configurations for the printer, regardless of whether the printer is local or remotely attached, are stored in DevModes2. Each printer has a key entry, named for the printer, with a binary data value following.

RemoteAccess

Remote Access, part of RAS (Remote Access Service), has an entry in HKEY_ CURRENT_USER\RemoteAccess. The RemoteAccess sub-hive contains connectoids for RAS. Connectoids? What the heck is a connectoid? A *connectoid* consists of all the information needed to implement a connection, typically to a remote computer.

The RemoteAccess sub-hive may include one key variable, called InternetProfile. Typically, the InternetProfile key contains a null (empty) string.

Software

Information about all installed software is stored in the Software sub-hive. This information is typically arranged by vendor, although some applications may be in their own sub-hives.

In a typical installation of Windows NT, with Microsoft Internet Explorer 4 installed, we see the Software hive has the following four sub-hives:

Microsoft—Information about many of the components that are part of Windows NT are found in the HKEY_CURRENT_USER\Software\ Microsoft hive. On a typical installation, we see about 30 entries. A better equipped installation could have twice the number of entries.

Below is a list of entries found in a typical system:

- Active Setup
- Advanced INF Setup
- Clock
- Command Processor

- Conferencing
- DataEnvironment Designer
- DevStudio
- Disk Administrator
- File Manager
- Full-Text-System
- IEAK
- Internet Explorer
- Java VM
- Microsoft Setup (ACME)
- Multimedia
- NetDDE
- Notepad
- Ntbackup
- Outlook Express
- Protected Storage System Provider
- RegEdt32
- Schedule+
- SystemCertificates
- User Location Service
- Visual Basic
- WAB
- WebPost
- Windows
- Windows Help
- Windows NT

- ODBC
- Policies
- VDO

On a more mature installation with more installed software, we see the Software hive expanded to cover more different product lines. Notice that products are arranged by the company who has produced the product or the product's functionality, such as ODBC, rather than by specific product. For example, if there were two Adobe products installed on the computer, the Adobe hive would have information about both products. Here is a list of entries found on a mature installation:

- Adobe
- Canon
- Dragon Systems
- Federal Express
- Forte
- Inetstp
- Microsoft
- Netscape
- ODBC
- Policies
- Qualcomm
- VDO
- Wang

Unicode Program Groups

This sub-hive contains information used by Program Manager. The question, of course, is who uses Program Manager anymore?

The sub-keys found in Unicode Program Groups are in a binary format that is difficult to edit. Have I ever seen entries in the Unicode Program Groups sub-hive? No, not yet. Wait a minute, I've never actually run Program Manager with Windows NT 4 yet, either.

After running Program Manager, creating a couple of personal groups and a few common groups, I now have entries in the Unicode Program Groups hive. As I mentioned before, these entries are in binary format and they are complex structures. As Microsoft recommends, editing these entries is best done using Program Manager.

> **NOTE**   Actually, users who upgraded from Windows NT 3.*x* may have entries in the Unicode Program Groups sub-hive; however this sub-hive is not used by Windows NT version 4 or later unless the user has configured or run Program Manager (ProgMan.EXE).

Windows 3.1 Migrations Status

This sub-hive is contained only in systems that have been upgraded from Windows NT 3.*x*. (There may be a few of these installations remaining.) The sub-hive contains keys that are used to show the status of conversion of the Program Manager Group files (.GRP) and associated initialization (.INI) files that have been converted to Windows NT version 4 format. Deleting this key, and not the Windows 3.1 Migration Status sub-hive, causes Windows NT to attempt to convert the Program Manager group files when Windows NT restarts. This reconversion may change the Start menu substantially, but should not cause serious damage.

Volatile Environment

Typically, this sub-hive contains only one entry, a key called LOGONSERVER. It contains a string with the logon server (the server the user is currently logged on to). For example, my logon server is \\DORA.

HKEY_USERS

The HKEY_USERS key contains information about each active user who has a user profile. There are a minimum of two keys in the HKEY_USERS key: .DEFAULT and the ID for the currently logged on user.

Hints and Kinks from the Experts

In this chapter's Hints and Kinks, we cover a few hints on using the two registry editors.

How Can I Audit Changes to the Registry?   Using the regedt32.exe utility, it is possible to set auditing on certain parts of the registry. I should caution you that any type of auditing is very sensitive lately, and you may want to add some sort of warning to let people know that their changes are being audited.

1. Start the registry editor (regedt32.exe).

2. Select the key you wish to audit, for example, KEY_LOCAL_MACHINE\ Software.

3. Select Security ➣ Auditing.

4. Check the Audit Permission on Existing Subkeys option if you want sub-keys to be audited also.

5. Click the Add button and select the users you want to be audited. Click Add, then click OK

6. Once there are names in the Names box, you can select which events are to be audited and whether success or failure is audited.

7. After filling in all the information, click OK.

You will need to make sure that Auditing for File and Object access is enabled. To do so, select User Manager ➣ Polices ➣ Audit.

To view the information, use the Event Viewer program and look at the Security information.

(Courtesy of John Savill)

Activate Screen Saver if No One Logs On. To activate a screen saver when no user is logged on, follow these steps:

1. Use RegEdit to edit the sub-hive HKEY_USERS \DEFAULT\Control Panel\Desktop.

2. Double-click ScreenSaveActive and set it to 1.

3. Double-click SCRNSAVE.EXE and enter the full path to the screen saver you want to use, such as scrnsave.scr or sstars.scr.

4. Double-click ScreenSaveTimeOut and enter the number of seconds of inactivity required before activation of the screen saver begins.

You will need to reboot for this to become effective.

WARNING   Never use anything other than the blank screen saver (scrnsave.scr) on a server because it will steal needed cycles.

(Courtesy of Jerold Schulman)

Define Initial Settings for New Users.   In other tips on these pages, you have seen registry hacks to the HKEY_CURRENT_USER hive. Any hack that you can make to KEY_CURRENT_USER can be made to the default user hive, as well.

To modify the default user hive, follow these steps:

1. Start RegEdt32.

2. Highlight the HKEY_USERS window.

3. Select Registry ➤ Load Hive.

4. Select the NTUSER.DAT file, usually from %windir%\Profiles\Default User directory.

5. Type **NTUSER** in the Key Name dialog box.

6. Now you can add or modify any key or value within this hive. When you finish, highlight NTUSER and select Security ➤ Permissions. Add Read permission to the Everyone group. Check the Replace Permission on Existing Subkeys box and click OK.

7. Select Registry ➤ Unload Hive and exit Regedt32.

8. Copy the profile to the Netlogon share on the PDC, which is usually at C:\%windir%\System32\Repl\Export\Scripts.

When a new user logs on, he or she will receive the default profile.

(Courtesy of Jerold Schulman)

Introduction to
HKEY_LOCAL_MACHINE

■ HKEY_LOCAL_MACHINE

■ Hints and kinks from the experts

The HKEY_LOCAL_MACHINE hive contains information about the system as it is currently running. Also contained within HKEY_LOCAL_MACHINE is information about users, groups, security, and installed software.

HKEY_LOCAL_MACHINE is subdivided into five sub-hives:

HARDWARE—Information about currently used hardware is contained in the HARDWARE sub-hive.

SAM—The Security Account Manager has information defining all uses who may use the computer. If the computer is a PDC/BDC, then the domain information is contained in the SAM sub-hive also.

SECURITY—The SECURITY sub-hive contains information about cached logons, policy, special accounts, and RXACT (registry transaction package).

SOFTWARE—Software information, a superset of the information contained in HKEY_CURRENT_USER, is located in the SOFTWARE sub-hive.

SYSTEM—The system definitions, control sets, information about removable media (CD-ROMs), and Windows NT setup are contained in the SYSTEM sub-hive.

So, you've backed up your registry before starting this chapter, right? Let's dig in and see what's there.

WARNING   If you touch *anything* in the HKEY_LOCAL_MACHINE hive, there's a good chance you'll trash your system registry. Really: HKEY_LOCAL_MACHINE is probably the most critical part of the registry, so *back up before you touch it*—before you even browse it!

HKEY_LOCAL_MACHINE

As I mentioned above, HKEY_LOCAL_MACHINE has five sections. Each section is separate, and can be dealt with separately. Even SAM, the Security Account

Manager, and SECURITY actually cover different aspects of security, so don't confuse 'em.

HARDWARE

The HARDWARE sub-hive describes the system's hardware. Most everything in the HARDWARE sub-hive is set during boot-up, by the NTDETECT.COM program or by the ARC (Advanced RISC Computer) database for users running Windows NT on RISC computers.

The sub-hive contains four sub-hives:

DESCRIPTION—The DESCRIPTION sub-hive contains information about the processor, math co-processor, and 'multi-function' adapters (devices such as the PCI bus, Plug-and-Play BIOS, and the ISA bus).

DEVICEMAP—In DEVICEMAP are sub-hives for most devices, such as the keyboard, mouse, serial ports, and video.

OWNERMAP—OWNERMAP includes a mapping of some PCI devices.

NOTE Windows NT has some problems dealing with the PCI bus, as PCI was designed to work integrally with Plug-and-Play, which Windows NT 4 does not support.

RESOURCEMAP—Items, such as HAL (Hardware Abstraction Layer), keyboard and pointer port(s), serial and parallel ports, SCSI devices (which include IDE drives too), and video information are found in RESOURCEMAP.

These sub-hives are covered fully later in this chapter. If you are having problems with your hardware (No, nothing here will help fix a broken keyboard!) interfacing with Windows NT, it is possible that something in the HARDWARE hive may help you fix the problem.

Before diddling with registry values in HKEY_LOCAL_MACHINE\ HARDWARE directly, first try the Control Panel. Many devices can be manipulated best using the Control Panel.

NOTE   Many times there will be sub-hives with numbers for names, starting at 0 (zero). Often there is only one of these sub-hives, though if there are multiple objects of the type described by a hive, there will be multiple sub-hives numbered 0 to n, where n is the number of objects –1. For example, a computer with four hard drives on a SCSI bus would have sub-hives named 0, 1, 2 and 3 in the HKEY_LOCAL_ MACHINE\HARDWARE\DESCRIPTION\System\MultifunctionAdapter\2\DiskCon-troller\0\DiskPeripheral.

Hardware Profiles, Or How Can I Make Windows NT More Hardware-Friendly?

Windows NT is capable of supporting multiple hardware configurations. This functionality is most useful for notebooks and other portable computers that use Windows NT.

NOTE   Don't confuse hardware profiles with user profiles. They are very different animals (Goodness. . . is he referring to users as animals?), covering completely different areas, hardware rather than users.

For instance, in the Control Panel's System Properties applet, selecting the Hardware Profiles tab allows a user to create multiple hardware profiles. To create a new configuration, select an existing configuration and click the Copy button. Enter a new name for the configuration (I used the name New Configuration in my example). Click OK after entering the new name. Select the new configuration you just created, and click the Properties button to display the dialog box as shown in Figure 17.1. Remember the dialog box's title will vary depending on what you named your new configuration.

For each configuration, it is possible to define the computer as portable, which is useful when there is docking support. When This Is a Portable Computer is checked, the docking state can be determined as one of the following:

- The docking state is unknown.
- The computer is docked.
- The computer is undocked.

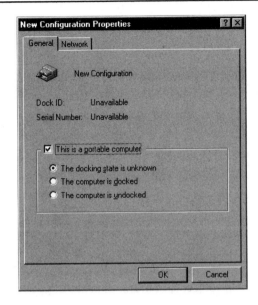

When creating a hardware profile, simply name it to reflect the configuration. For example, if creating a profile for the computer when it is docked in the docking station, name the profile Docked and make sure you select both This Is a Portable Computer and The Computer Is Docked. Then create a profile for the computer when not docked, name this profile UN-Docked and select This Is a Portable Computer and The Computer Is Undocked.

Sometimes it is necessary to create a profile that can be used when the portable computer is either docked or undocked. Two scenarios can be envisioned: one where the docking state is not important and another where the docking state is important. When the docking state is not important, it is possible to create a single profile with The Docking State Is Unknown checked.

DESCRIPTION

OK, first, the standard warning: Be very careful about making any changes in the DESCRIPTION sub-hive. Everything in the DESCRIPTION sub-hive is set during boot-up, by the NTDETECT.COM program or by the ARC database.

As this information is volatile (It is re-generated by the boot-up process.), it is neither practical nor meaningful to modify the data. You can use a program called

WinMSD to view information in these sub-hives. A shortcut to WinMSD, called Windows NT Diagnostics, can be found in Administrative Tools (Common).

There is a single sub-hive in DESCRIPTION called "System." The sub-hives inside System are listed as follows:

CentralProcessor   In the CentralProcessor sub-hive are sub-hives describing each processor found. For uniprocessor systems, a single sub-hive named "0," contains information about the processor. Multi-processor computers will have sub-hives named from "0" to "n," where n is the number of processors minus 1. The following list shows the configuration of an Intel Pentium system. Users with other processors or processors from other suppliers will see some different information, although the keys will be identical:

> **Component Information**—This key identifies information about the processor.

> **Configuration Data**—A REG_FULL_RESOURCE_DESCRIPTOR data object containing data about the processor

> **~MHz**—A DWORD value containing the CPU speed, this field may not be present or contain a value for some RISC processors.

> **VendorIdentifier**—The name of the company that manufactured the CPU as a text string; for example, an Intel Pentium will have "GenuineIntel" as the vendor identifier.

> **Identifier**—The CPU model and other CPU-specific identifying information, an Intel Pentium might have the string "X86 Family 5 Model 2 Stepping 4" as the identifier. This string can be used to selectively apply patches to correct known flaws in certain CPUs, for example.

FloatingPointProcessor   In the FloatingPointProcessor hive are sub-hives describing each floating point math co-processor found. For uniprocessor systems, a single sub-hive named "0" contains information about the co-processor. Multi-processor computers will have sub-hives named "0" to "n," where n is the number of processors minus 1. The following list shows an Intel Pentium system. Users with other processors or processors from other suppliers will see some different information, although the keys will be identical:

> **Component Information**—This key identifies information about the processor.

Configuration Data—A REG_FULL_RESOURCE_DESCRIPTOR data object containing data about the processor

Identifier—The CPU model and other CPU-specific identifying information, an Intel Pentium might have the string "X86 Family 5 Model 2 Stepping 4" as the identifier. This string can be used to selectively apply patches to correct known flaws in certain CPUs, for example.

MultifunctionAdapter   As with entries in CentralProcessor and Floating-PointProcessor, the entries in MultifunctionAdapter are created either by the hardware recognizer (NTDETECT.COM) for Intel-based systems or by the ARC database found on RISC computers.

> **NOTE**   Bus, who's got the bus schedule? Instead of MultifunctionAdapter used with ISA, MCA (Micro-Channel Architecture), and PCI bus machines; you may find EisaAdapter if your computer uses the EISA bus, and TcAdapter if your computer uses the TurboChannel bus architecture. Entries for both EisaAdapter and TcAdapter will be similar to those in MultifunctionAdapter; this varies based on what components are installed rather than on bus type.

Inside the MultifunctionAdapter hive are sub-hives describing the internal structure of the computer, bus structure, PnP (Plug-and-Play), BIOS (if PnP is installed), and devices installed on these buses.

It is not practical to describe all sub-hives that might be found for every different type of computer in the MultifunctionAdapter sub-hive. Instead, let's take a look at a typical system: an Intel motherboard, PCI bus, an IDE hard drive, and typical peripherals.

One or more entries will be found under MultifunctionAdapter. There will be one sub-hive for each bus controller (PnP is counted as a bus, and is included, though no devices are assigned to PnP). A typical PCI bus computer (virtually all PCI-based computers also have ISA bus support to allow using legacy interface cards) will have three entries:

0—The PCI bus, with keys for Component Information, Configuration Data, and Identifier

1—The PnP BIOS doesn't have a physical bus as such. PnP works with both the ISA bus, and the PCI bus in the computer. There are keys for Component Information, Configuration Data, and Identifier.

2—The ISA bus, with keys for Component Information, Configuration Data, and Identifier. The ISA bus hive will contain sub-hives for other devices such as disk controllers, keyboards, and printer and serial ports.

Rather than taking pages describing all possible entries for the Multifunction-Adapter hive, use RegEdt32 (in read-only mode, please!) and peruse this hive. Figure 17.2 shows most of the MultifunctionAdapter hive expanded, on a typical PCI bus computer.

FIGURE 17.2:

RegEdt32 shows the HKEY_LOCAL_MACHINE MultifunctionAdapter sub-hive's contents.

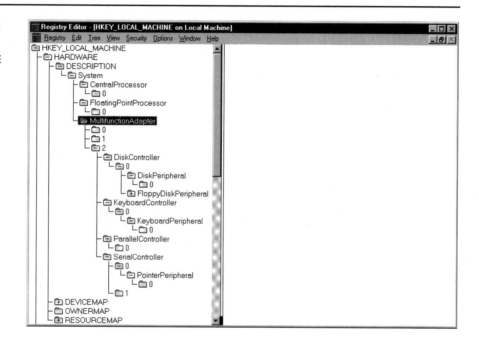

DEVICEMAP

In DEVICEMAP are sub-hives for devices such as the keyboard, mouse, serial ports, and video.

As with other parts of the HKEY_LOCAL_MACHINE\HARDWARE hive, DEVICEMAP is generated at boot-time, making modifications ill-advised. We can take a look at several parts of DEVICEMAP, however, which are either typical or have changed in Windows NT version 4.

Under DEVICEMAP is a sub-hive called "KeyboardClass." This sub-hive has an entry called \Device\KeyboardClass0, containing the data value \REGISTRY\ Machine\System\ControlSet001\Services\Kbdclass. This is a reference to HKEY_ LOCAL_MACHINE\SYSTEM\\ControlSet001\Services\Kbdclass, where the current keyboard configuration and settings are held.

In DEVICEMAP\SCSI is information pertaining to SCSI hard drives and to IDE (ATAPI) hard drives. Windows NT blurs the line between IDE drives and SCSI drives by listing both under the same registry entries.

The hives for a Windows NT system with one IDE drive is as follows:

```
Scsi
Scsi\Scsi Port 0
Scsi\Scsi Port 0\Scsi Bus 0\
Scsi\Scsi Port 0\Scsi Bus 0\Target Id 1
Scsi\Scsi Port 0\Scsi Bus 0\Target Id 1\Logical Unit Id 0
    Identifier = "Micropolis 2112A"
    Type = "DiskPeripheral"
```

These two keys identify a Micropolis 2112A 2GB IDE hard drive.

Another system is a small Windows NT Server working as a PDC (Primary Domain Controller) and as a file server (serves four hard drives and three CD-ROM drives). For a system with two IDE CD-ROM drives, a SCSI bus with four SCSI hard drives, and one SCSI CD-ROM drive, the sub-hives would look like this:

```
Scsi
Scsi\Scsi Port 0
    DMAEnabled = 00000000
    Interrupt = 0000000f
    IOAddress = 00000170
    Driver = "atapi"

Scsi\Scsi Port 0\Scsi Bus 0
Scsi\Scsi Port 0\Scsi Bus 0\Initiator Id 255
Scsi\Scsi Port 0\Scsi Bus 0\Target Id 0
Scsi\Scsi Port 0\Scsi Bus 0\Target Id 0\Logical Unit Id 0
    Identifier = "MATSHITACD-ROM CR-581-M 1.05"
    Type = "CdRomPeripheral"

Scsi\Scsi Port 0\Scsi Bus 0\Target Id 1
Scsi\Scsi Port 0\Scsi Bus 0\Target Id 1\Logical Unit Id 0
    Identifier = "MATSHITACD-ROM CR-581-M 1.05"
```

```
        Type = "CdRomPeripheral"

Scsi\Scsi Port 1
    DMAEnabled = 00000001
    Interrupt = 0000000a
    IOAddress = 00006300
    Driver = "aic78xx"

Scsi\Scsi Port 1\Scsi Bus 0
Scsi\Scsi Port 1\Scsi Bus 0\Initiator Id 7
Scsi\Scsi Port 1\Scsi Bus 0\Target Id 0
Scsi\Scsi Port 1\Scsi Bus 0\Target Id 0\Logical Unit Id 0
    Identifier = "QUANTUM FIREBALL_TM2110S300X"
    Type = "DiskPeripheral"

Scsi\Scsi Port 1\Scsi Bus 0\Target Id 2
Scsi\Scsi Port 1\Scsi Bus 0\Target Id 2\Logical Unit Id 0
    Identifier = "MICROP  2112-15MZ1001905HQ30"
    Type = "DiskPeripheral"

Scsi\Scsi Port 1\Scsi Bus 0\Target Id 4
Scsi\Scsi Port 1\Scsi Bus 0\Target Id 4\Logical Unit Id 0
    Identifier = "TOSHIBA CD-ROM XM-3301TA2342"
    Type = "CdRomPeripheral"

Scsi\Scsi Port 1\Scsi Bus 0\Target Id 5
Scsi\Scsi Port 1\Scsi Bus 0\Target Id 5\Logical Unit Id 0
    Identifier = "QUANTUM XP34301        1071"
    Type = "DiskPeripheral"

Scsi\Scsi Port 1\Scsi Bus 0\Target Id 6
Scsi\Scsi Port 1\Scsi Bus 0\Target Id 6\Logical Unit Id 0
    Identifier = "TOSHIBA MK537FB        6262"
    Type = "DiskPeripheral"
```

In this example, there are two IDE CD-ROM drives. Both are identical MATSHITA CR-581s; and one SCSI CD-ROM drive, a Toshiba XM-3301. There are four hard drives, all SCSI:

- Identifier = "QUANTUM FIREBALL_TM2110S300X"

- Identifier = "MICROP 2112-15MZ1001905HQ30"

- Identifier = "QUANTUM XP34301   1071"

- Identifier = "TOSHIBA MK537FB   6262"

How do we tell the differences between different drive types if they are all listed as SCSI? Well, actually, that's easy. Take a look at the different keys defined in the SCSI Port n entry, such as in this example:

```
Scsi\Scsi Port 0
    DMAEnabled = 00000000
    Interrupt = 0000000f
    IOAddress = 00000170
    Driver = "atapi"
```

In this example, the driver, atapi, tells us that the drive is an IDE drive. (ATAPI is short for AT Attachment Peripheral Interface and IDE is short for integrated drive electronics.)

Drives and Buses!

Under Windows NT, the ATAPI.SYS file is used to handle I/O for all PCI connected IDE devices. When the device is connected to an ISA bus controller, the I/O is managed by ATDISK.SYS, a different driver.

Sometimes, when upgrading from Windows NT 3.5x to Windows NT 4, the user will see the message that a driver didn't start. Checking the event log, the ATDISK driver will be shown as failing to start—in this case simply open the Control Panel's Devices applet, select ATDISK, and disable it.

OWNERMAP

No, not a map to your home or office! The OWNERMAP sub-hive provides a mapping of many PCI devices. OWNERMAP may be found on computers having other non-ISA buses than PCI.

Entries for each PCI bus adapter are contained in OWNERMAP, but not necessarily adapters connected to the internal PCI bus; these are managed differently. You will also find entries named for the PCI bus slot number, as PCI sees each slot. The data for each entry will be information for the device, such as the device's driver.

Are all PCI devices found in OWNERMAP? (The answer is no, and no, I can't explain the rules!) For example, on one Windows NT computer, the video adapter, a Matrox Millennium MGA, is not listed in OWNERMAP. Another computer, also running Windows NT, lists the video card. However, it is not fully supported by Windows NT.

An example of OWNERMAP follows:

```
HKEY_LOCAL_MACHINE\HARDWARE\OWNERMAP
    PCI_0_e = "\\Device\\Video0"
    PCI_0_6 = "\\Driver\\E190x"
```

> **NOTE**
>
> Windows NT has some problems dealing with the PCI bus, as PCI was designed to work integrally with Plug-and-Play, which Windows NT 4 does not support. Most problems become apparent when PCI systems are dual booted with Windows NT and Windows 95/98 as the two operating systems. Changes made with Windows 95/98 can cause problems with Windows NT as Windows NT will not detect these changes without a refresh (repair) re-installation of Windows NT or manipulation of the Control Panel.

RESOURCEMAP

RESOURCEMAP includes items such as HAL (Hardware Abstraction Layer), keyboard and pointer port(s), serial and parallel ports, SCSI devices (which include IDE drives too!), and video information. This sub-hive also includes data about I/O Channels, I/O ports and addresses, IRQ (Interrupt Request), and DMA (Direct Memory Access) channels. Everything in RESOURCEMAP is generated at boot time, so changes are transient at best.

RESOURCEMAP entries are based on hardware class, then device, as Figure 17.3 shows. In this figure, notice the VIDEO sub-hive has been opened showing three entries: ark, VgaSave, and VgaStart. Ark is the entry for the Diamond Stealth-64 PCI video card, which uses an ARK chipset; VgaSave and VgaStart are entries for standard VGA configurations that are used to restore or initialize the VGA video system.

FIGURE 17.3:

RegEdit showing the RESOURCEMAP hive with the VIDEO sub-hive expanded to show the three video drivers available

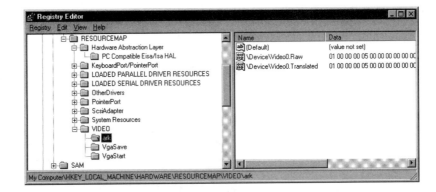

Each entry (sub-hive) in RESOURCEMAP consists of one or more sub-hives, containing two entries: .Raw and .Translated. These entries are used to hold information about the device resources in a special variable type called REG_RESOURCE_LIST. A two-stage editing process is used, where the object is opened and the Resource Lists edit box is displayed. In the Resource Lists edit box (shown in Figure 17.4), a resource may be selected, and the Display button clicked to display the Resources dialog box (see Figure 17.5). In Resources, you can see a myriad of information including DMA Channel, Interrupt (IRQ), Memory used (commonly with video cards and some network cards), Port used, and device-specific data.

FIGURE 17.4:

The Resource Lists box allows you to select a resource and click the Display button.

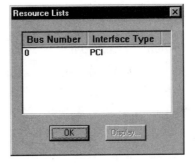

FIGURE 17.5:

The Resources dialog box displays information about resources.

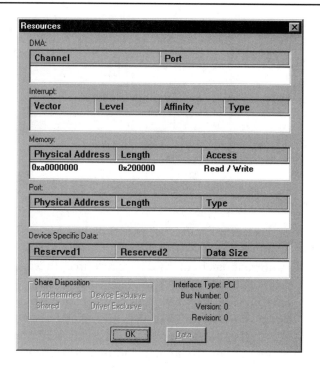

SAM

SAM, the Security Account Manager, is used to manage user accounts on the computer. When the computer is a PDC (Primary Domain Controller) or BDC (Backup Domain Controller), SAM contains information about all domain users.

Normally, SAM is protected against any viewing or tampering by users. That is good. After all, who wants the typical user going in and monkeying about with the user database? In a normal environment, changes to SAM are made with either the User Manager or User Manager for Domains found in the Administrative Tools section of the Start menu.

WARNING Again, standard warnings: any playing with the SAM may prevent one, more than one, or all, users from being able to log on. The ultimate result could be that the system may need to be restored from backup or re-installed. Be most cautious in making any changes in SAM—use the User Manager program to make changes.

SAM consists of a sub-hive, called (strangely enough) "SAM." Inside the SAM sub-hive are two sub-hives.

The first sub-hive, called "Domains," contains several objects. (We'll cover these in a minute, don't panic.) The second sub-hive, called "RXACT," contains, as far as I can determine, absolutely nothing. However, my experience with Microsoft has indicated that when one thinks that some component of the registry is empty, one is not looking at it correctly.

OK, back to the Domains sub-hive. Inside Domains are two sub-hives, called "Account" and "Builtin."

> **NOTE** Much of the data in the SAM hives is stored in a format that cannot be displayed or edited by the registry editor(s). Therefore, there is little possibility that you can edit these fields.

Domains\Account

The Account sub-hive contains virtually everything regarding the users and groups. Three sub-hives, Aliases, Groups, and Users hold information about aliases, groups, and users.

> **NOTE** For information on userids, see Chapter 3, "Anatomy of the Registry—the Blood, Gore, and Guts." The section entitled "HKEY_USERS, Settings for Users" contains a full reference on SIDs (Security IDentifiers), which are present throughout the SAM hive of the registry.

Domains\Account\Aliases   In Domains\Account the sub-hive, Aliases contains information on local groups defined in the registry by the system administrator. Local groups defined by the system are maintained in the Builtin sub-hive.

Under Aliases are sub-hives for each local group. (Our example in Figure 17.6 has one local account.) Aliases also contains a sub-hive called "Members" that lists the userids of each member of this group. Each user is identified by a DWORD hexadecimal number (see the next section). In our example, users 000003EC and 000003F3 are both members of the Local Programmers group.

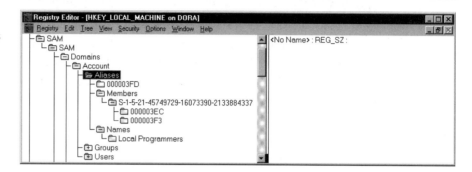

Domains\Account\Groups In Domains\Account the sub-hive Groups has a number of entries, all pertaining to user groups. For instance, on a PDC and BDC these three sub-hives will be found:

> **00000200**—This sub-hive, when expressed as decimal (512), indicates the sub-hive relates to the domain admins group.

> **00000201**—This sub-hive, when expressed as decimal (513), indicates the sub-hive relates to the domain users group.

> **00000202**—This sub-hive, when expressed as decimal (514), indicates the sub-hive relates to the domain guests group.

Quickly we realize that these first three entries are the default global or domain groups. If we have created any additional global groups, they will be found typically with identifiers, such as the following (Remember—this is an example.):

> **000003F9**—This sub-hive, when expressed as decimal (1017), indicates the sub-hive relates to the global group called Domain Workers. I created Domain Workers to cover a number of users who needed to access the entire domain to do certain work.

> **000003FA**—This sub-hive, when expressed as decimal (1018), indicates the sub-hive relates to the global group called Programmers. I created Programmers to cover users working in the R&D division, who needed to access the entire domain to do their work.

Table 17.1 shows common SID values: Pay particular attention to the ending digits. Notice that the final two groups, Domain Users and Domain Guests, are not present in the Account\Groups sub-hive in our example.

TABLE 17.1: Common SID Values for Domain (Global) Groups Used by Windows NT

Sub-Hive Name	Global (Domain) Group	SID
00000200	Domain Admins	S-1-5-21-xxxxxxxxx-xxxxxxxxxx-xxxxxxxxxx-500
00000201	Domain Guests	S-1-5-21-xxxxxxxxx-xxxxxxxxxx-xxxxxxxxxx-501
00000202	Domain Users	S-1-5-21-xxxxxxxxx-xxxxxxxxxx-xxxxxxxxxx-502

NOTE   Note that Windows NT will typically work in unit increments when creating groups and users, so the next group or user created would be 3FA (1018). Notice that the same numbering scheme is used for both groups and users, and these numbers start at 3E8, which is 1000 in decimal. Another interesting tidbit: Users and groups created by the system's administrator start with 1000 and are incremented sequentially.

Also in Groups is a sub-hive called "Names." Inside Names is the final piece of this puzzle. We find sub-hives matching those previously described, with the group names as their sub-hive name. All three of these default sub-hives contain a single, unnamed key containing data that neither registry editor is able to display or edit:

- Domain Admins
- Domain Guests
- Domain Users

Also within Names are the two groups added to this domain:

- Domain Workers
- Programmers

NOTE   Careful—Don't go jumpin' to no conclusions here. Do not assume that names listed in the Names sub-hive have a one-to-one correspondence with the entries above them. In our example, that relationship exists—but that is wholly coinciden-tal, because I managed to create groups in alphabetical order, the order that objects in the Names sub-hive are stored.

Taking a quick look at Figure 17.7, we see the relationships between the objects contained in the Groups sub-hive. Five sub-hives exist, one for each of the global groups we have (three default, supplied with Windows NT, and two added later by the system's administrator). We also see the Names sub-hive, which has five sub-hives, each with the name of a global or domain group. The first three are the three default global groups, and the last two are groups created by the system's administrator.

FIGURE 17.7:

The relationship between the five numbered sub-hives and the sub-hives in Names

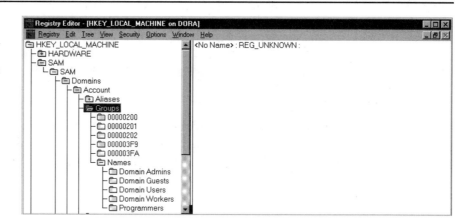

Domains\Account\Users   The final sub-hive within Domains\Account is Users. This sub-hive contains one entry for each user defined in the SAM. For PDC or BDC computers the number of users could be large. It is not uncommon for a large network to have hundreds, if not thousands, of users defined. Fortu-nately, this author has a small network so there are only a few users defined, making things a bit less cluttered.

Like groups, system-created users have numbers less than 3F8 (That's 1000.) and users created by the system administrator will have numbers equal to or greater than 3F8 (1000).

NOTE There will probably be gaps in the numbers. This is normal—once a userid has been deleted, Windows NT will not reuse the number. After all, there are lots of numbers to use, millions and millions of them to be exact.

Rather than list every userid and name on my system (You can see that I have 17 users defined: two defined by the system, and 15 defined by the system administrator.), let's just talk about a few of them. First, directly under Users (see Figure 17.8) are some numbered sub-hives. The first two sub-hives are predefined by the system:

000001F4—The system Administrator account has an SID ending in 500 (which is 0x1F4, funny how that worked out).

000001F5—The system Guest account has an SID ending in 501 (which is 0x1F5, just as funny how that worked out).

Check these two out in Table 17.1, noting the ending digits in the SIDs in the table, with the above hives. This is much too scary to be coincidence.

FIGURE 17.8:

Users and their attributes are contained within the Users and Users\Names sub-hives.

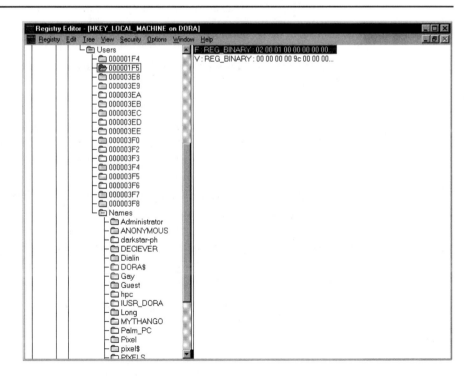

The next sub-hives (starting with 000003E8, which is 1000 in decimal and ending with 000003F8, or 1016) are created, one for each administrator-created userid. Each of these sub-hives contains two named keys, called "F" and "V." Feel free to guess as to the meanings of these names, and what the data contained within each contains. Some assumptions can be made; for instance, there must be an index between the sub-hives and their counterparts found in the Names sub-hive. Information, such as group membership, privileges, passwords, and all other data specified by the administrator must be contained in these variables, too.

In the Names sub-hive (again refer to Figure 17.8), we can see a number of user names found on my system. For example:

Administrator—The system-created system administrator account

ANONYMOUS—A userid used by IIS's FTP to allow users to FTP files anonymously

darkstar-ph—A userid used in-house to manage e-mail

DECIEVER—A userid used by a portable user

Dialin—Any user may dial in without a password using the userid Dialin.

DORA$—The computer name for the computer DORA (this server, actually)

The remaining entries (Gay, Guest, and so forth) and others not shown are similar. There is nothing unusual about them.

Any userid ending in a $ is a machine account, not a userid. There is always confusion about what constitutes a machine account and what constitutes a userid. To connect a computer to a server, the server must have both the computer's account and the user's account. Got that? Both must exist! Generally, when you create a new computer configuration, you create the computer name on that computer. The dialog box used to create the computer name has a section called "Create a Computer Account in the Domain," which when checked will create the computer account. Sometimes, however, it is necessary to create a Computer Account in a domain, and all documentation says to use the User Manager for Domains program without telling you about this neat trick. No one mentions the ending $, and computer accounts aren't visible in the User Manager for Domains.

Holy Mackerel, Batman, what's a user to do?

Computer Accounts for Everyday Administrators

There are, it seems, two ways to create a computer account.

First, in the User Manager for Domains, you can create a user account with a trailing $. This seems to create a valid computer account, although this is undocumented. Computer accounts created this way remain visible to the User Manager for Domains program.

A second method (A more approved method, I might add!) is to use the command prompt NET command, NET COMPUTER \\<*name*> /ADD, where <*name*> is the name of the computer to be added. Use NET COMPUTER \\<*name*> /DEL, where <*name*> is the name of the computer to be deleted.

Though Windows NT computers require a computer account on the server, actually Windows 95/98 computers do not seem to need one. Other computers, including Windows CE machines, have been known to require a computer account in addition to the user account. Try working without a computer account, and if the user is unable to log on, add a computer account to the user database and try again.

Well, we've covered global users and groups who are created by default by the system. Next, we'll cover local users and groups.

Domains\Builtin

Under SAM\Domains\Builtin, we find (as we did for SAM\Domains\Account) three sub-hives. These sub-hives perform a similar task to those in Domains\Account.

Domains\Builtin\Aliases   In Aliases, we find the group numbers for each of the local groups. For example, the local group 00000220, when viewed as a decimal number, is 544, which is the local administrators group. Figure 17.9 shows the Builtin sub-hive, fully expanded.

Each of these local groups is used to maintain and use the local machine. There are domain groups to perform remote maintenance. Table 17.2 shows the groups found in the default Builtin groups.

FIGURE 17.9:

Expanding Aliases shows we have eight built-in groups.

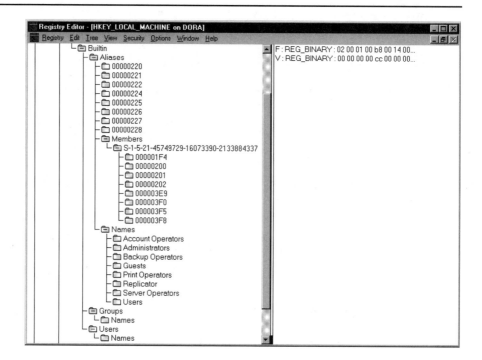

TABLE 17.2: The Windows NT Builtin Local Groups

Sub-Hive Name	Builtin Local Groups	SID
00000220	BUILTIN\ADMINISTRATORS	S-1-2-32-xxxxxxxxx-xxxxxxxxxx-xxxxxxxxxx-544
00000221	BUILTIN\USERS	S-1-2-32-xxxxxxxxx-xxxxxxxxxx-xxxxxxxxxx-545
00000222	BUILTIN\GUESTS	S-1-2-32-xxxxxxxxx-xxxxxxxxxx-xxxxxxxxxx-546
00000223	BUILTIN\POWER USERS	S-1-2-32-xxxxxxxxx-xxxxxxxxxx-xxxxxxxxxx-547
00000224	BUILTIN\ACCOUNT OPERATORS	S-1-2-32-xxxxxxxxx-xxxxxxxxxx-xxxxxxxxxx-548
00000225	BUILTIN\SERVER OPERATORS	S-1-2-32-xxxxxxxxx-xxxxxxxxxx-xxxxxxxxxx-549
00000226	BUILTIN\PRINT OPERATORS	S-1-2-32-xxxxxxxxx-xxxxxxxxxx-xxxxxxxxxx-550
00000227	BUILTIN\BACKUP OPERATORS	S-1-2-32-xxxxxxxxx-xxxxxxxxxx-xxxxxxxxxx-551
00000228	BUILTIN\REPLICATOR	S-1-2-32-xxxxxxxxx-xxxxxxxxxx-xxxxxxxxxx-552

NOTE Wonder what the xxxxx's in Table 17.1 and 17.2 are? They are a number generated at system installation time identifying the particular server or computer. The number, much like a GUID or UUID, is guaranteed to be unique.

Also present in Aliases is a sub-hive called Members. In this sub-hive are users and global groups who are members of local groups, identified by their SID suffix.

NOTE Remember: Global groups may be members of local groups, but local groups may not be members of global groups. Oh, and yes, local users may be members of global groups, too. Confused? Good, then I am not alone! Basically, the only member relationship not allowed is that local groups may not be members of global groups, and other than that anything goes.

Domains\Builtin\Groups   In Groups, we find a single sub-hive called Names. There appears to be no information stored in these sub-hives.

Domains\Builtin\Users   In Users, we find a single sub-hive called Names. There appears to be no information stored in these sub-hives.

RXACT

The hive HKEY_LOCAL_MACHINE\SAM\SAM\RXACT is undocumented. Contained within the RXACT sub-hive is a single, unnamed, REG_NONE type variable. Contained within this variable is a set of three DWORD values, one of which seems to change between installations, the other two of which don't seem to change. The values are in decimal 1, 1332588, and 1244820 on one machine. On another Windows NT installation, the values are in decimal 1, 1336468, and 1244820. The function of these values is unknown, although a guess might be that the password encryption algorithm uses them. Maybe and maybe not.

SECURITY

SECURITY? What is SECURITY? First, it is not something to depend on in your old age, that's assured!

In the HKEY_LOCAL_MACHINE\SECURITY hive, we find we have another hive that normally only the system has access to. Like SAM, discussed previously, we can change the access rights to the SECURITY sub-hive to allow us (the administrator) to browse, and (if you are daring, stupid, or both) modify items.

To change the access rights to SECURITY, select it in RegEdt32 and click the Security menu's Permissions selection. In the Registry Key Permissions dialog box, select your userid. In the Type of Access drop-down list, select Full Control, then click OK. It is imperative to be careful: Changing something improperly can lead to disaster.

Cache

Windows NT is able to cache zero to 50 previous successful logons locally. This is typically done on systems where a domain controller is used to validate logons and security. Sometimes (happens to all of us) the PDC (Primary Domain Controller) is not available, and then it is still possible to provisionally log on the user, using locally stored logon credentials.

NOTE   The number of cached logons defaults to 10; however it may be set to any number between zero and 50.

When the domain controller is unavailable and the user can be logged on using the cache, the following message appears:

> A domain controller for your domain could not be contacted. You have been logged on using cached account information. Changes to your profile since you last logged on may not be available.

If caching has been disabled or a user's logon information is not in the cache, this message displayed is:

> The system cannot log you on now because the domain *<name of domain>* is not available.

In the SECURITY\Cache hive are 11 cache entries (or more, or fewer, see "Number of Cached User Profiles" in Chapter 4, "Registry Tools and Tips—Getting the Work Done").

One entry is named NL$Control, and contains the cached entry of the currently logged on user.

NOTE   Actually, RegEdit can display REG_BINARY values better than RegEdt32. With RegEdit you are able to see both the hexadecimal values and an ANSI character representation, which is readable even with UNICODE characters.

The other entries in the Cache hive, 10 entries by default, are named "NL$1" through "NL$10." Each entry contains logon information for one of the previous ten people who logged on to the computer.

NOTE   The ten previous logged-on users are unique users. If a user logs on twice, there will be only one entry in the cache—each entry in the cache is for a unique user account.

Policy

Psst, hey buddy, you want to buy some insurance?

No, not that type of policy! SECURITY\Policy contains security settings for users, and groups, and other components.

There are a large number of sub-hives located under the Policy hive. These sub-hives include the following:

Accounts	PolPrDmN
DefQuota	PolPrDmS
Domains	PolPromot
PolAcDmN	PolRevision
PolAcDmS	PolSrvRo
PolAdtEv	PolState
PolAdtFl	QuAbsMax
PolAdtLg	QuAbsMin
PolMod	SecDesc
PolNxPxf	Secrets

Each sub-hive (excluding Accounts, Domains, and Secrets) is constructed in virtually the same manner: a single, unnamed data variable of type REG_NONE. This data variable will contain a binary value, the length of which depends on the entry's purpose.

The Accounts sub-hive will contain information on perhaps six or more different SIDs. Most of these SIDs are listed in Table 17.3, along with their descriptions.

TABLE 17.3: Some Users Listed in the Accounts Sub-Hive

Sub-Hive	Description
S-1-1-0	(everyone)
S-1-2-32-544	BUILTIN\ADMINISTRATORS
S-1-2-32-545	BUILTIN\USERS
S-1-2-32-546	BUILTIN\GUESTS
S-1-2-32-547	BUILTIN\POWER USERS
S-1-2-32-548	BUILTIN\ACCOUNT OPERATORS
S-1-2-32-549	BUILTIN\SERVER OPERATORS
S-1-2-32-550	BUILTIN\PRINT OPERATORS
S-1-2-32-551	BUILTIN\BACKUP OPERATORS
S-1-2-32-552	BUILTIN\REPLICATOR

The information contained for each sub-hive described in Table 17.3 is:

ActSysAc—A DWORD value, stored as binary (REG_BINARY) data, values range from 0x00000001 to 0x00000003.

Privilgs—Not found in all Policy\Accounts sub-hives, a variable length binary value

SecDesc—A variable-length binary value

Sid—A binary representation of the SID value for the sub-hive, the SID value is also used as the sub-hive name.

The Domain sub-hive will contain information on each domain, typically only one. The Domain hive will have a sub-hive for the domain that the computer belongs to, named with the domain server's SID.

Contained within this sub-hive are typically four sub-hives:

SecDesc—A binary value, probably variable length

Sid—A binary representation of the SID value for the sub-hive, the SID value is also used as the sub-hive name.

TrDmName—A binary value, containing both binary data, and the name of the domain

TrDmPxOf—A DWORD value

> **NOTE** A computer that is the domain server (PDC) will not have an entry in the Domain sub-hive.

The Secrets sub-hive will contain secret information. (Quiet, someone may be listening to this.) There are a number of sub-hives in Secrets. Big users of the Secrets sub-hive include Windows NT, and IIS (Internet Information Server).

Due to the nature of the data (No, not that it is secret, just that it is meaningless except to the application or system that is using it.), we won't cover it.

> **NOTE** Secret data is specific to the application that has stored the data there, and generally is not meaningful to users.

RXACT

RXACT seems to contain an uninitialized value of RXACT that is stored in SAM.

SAM

SECURITY\SAM is an identical copy of the SAM\SAM, which we covered previously.

SOFTWARE

The HKEY_LOCAL_MACHINE\SOFTWARE sub-hive contains a collection of sub-hives for various installed components and applications. Any application can create its own sub-hive (most do so when they install and store items such as file pointers, user initialization, etc.), although most often sub-hives are based on the organization producing the software, with further sub-hives for different applications. For example, Microsoft's entries might look like this (actually they are much more complex):

```
HKEY_LOCAL_MACHINE\SOFTWARE\Microsoft
HKEY_LOCAL_MACHINE\SOFTWARE\Microsoft\DrWatson
HKEY_LOCAL_MACHINE\SOFTWARE\Microsoft\Exchange
HKEY_LOCAL_MACHINE\SOFTWARE\Microsoft\IE4
HKEY_LOCAL_MACHINE\SOFTWARE\Microsoft\Internet Audio
```

Each of these entries will have one or more. (DrWatson has 12 keys with data values for different user settings and file names, set using DRWTSN32.EXE.)

Figure 17.10 shows the HKEY_LOCAL_MACHINE\SOFTWARE hive on a computer that has been running Windows NT for about 9 months, and has a number of software packages installed.

FIGURE 17.10:

The HKEY_LOCAL_MACHINE\SOFTWARE key can become large if many applications and system components are installed.

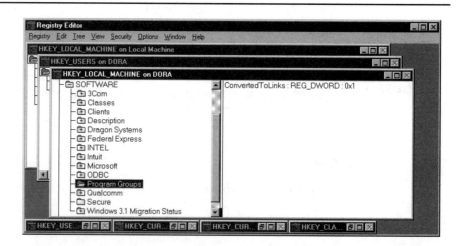

Now, you may think that I should say more about the HKEY_LOCAL_MACHINE\SOFTWARE hive here in this chapter; but no, I won't. There is just too much really good stuff in HKEY_LOCAL_MACHINE\SOFTWARE to not devote a complete chapter to it, so I've dedicated the next chapter (Chapter 18) to HKEY_LOCAL_MACHINE\SOFTWARE.

SYSTEM

HKEY_LOCAL_MACHINE\SYSTEM contains the system configurations. Sub-hives include:

Clone—When the system is booted, the boot-up ControlSet used is saved as HKEY_LOCAL_MACHINE\SYSTEM\Clone. When the boot is success-fully completed, the ControlSet pointed to by HKEY_LOCAL_MACHINE\SYSTEM\Select\LastKnownGood will be deleted, and the control set con-tained in Clone is moved to replace the deleted one. Clone is, therefore, empty immediately after booting, and cannot be accessed.

ControlSet001—Is a copy of the Current ControlSet.

ControlSet002—Is the LastKnownGood ControlSet used to boot from if there is a problem booting from the Current ControlSet.

CurrentControlSet—Is the ControlSet used to boot from.

DISK—Contains information about drive letters, volume sets, RAID (mir-rored, stripe, and stripe with parity), and CD-ROM and drive mapping.

Select—Contains information on which ControlSet is being used for what purpose.

Setup—Contains information about Windows NT's installation.

As with HKEY_LOCAL_MACHINE\SOFTWARE, HKEY_LOCAL_MACHINE\SYSTEM is a very important hive, and therefore we'll cover it fully in Chapter 19. No sense in overdoing it here.

Hints and Kinks from the Experts

In this chapter's Hints and Kinks, we cover a few hints on using the two registry editors.

How Do You Find Out Who Changed the @!#* Administrator's Password? To determine the UserName that changed the Administrator password, perform the following on the PDC:

1. Enable Success and Failure audits for File and Object Access using User Manager for Domains ➤ Policies ➤ Audit.

2. Using Regedt32, select the SAM key in HKEY_LOCAL_MACHINE and use Security ➤ Permissions to set Full Control for the Administrators local group. Check Change Permissions on Existing Subkeys.

3. Navigate to KEY_LOCAL_MACHINE\SAM\SAM\Domains\Account\ Users\000001F4. Select Security ➤ Audit Permissions and add the Administrators local group to the list. Select this group and enable Success and Failure auditing for Set Value events on this and all subkeys.

When a change is made to the Administrator account, the following event will indicate the UserName:

```
ID: 560
Source: Security
Type: Success Audit
Category: Object Access
```

(Courtesy of Jerold Schulman)

How Do You Identify Registry Hives in the Registry? Permanent keys, those not created at boot, are identified in the key at HKEY_LOCAL_MACHINE\ System\CurrentControlSet\Control\hivelist. The one exception is HKEY_CURRENT_USER, which is located at %SystemRoot%\Profiles\UserName.

The value entries identify the registry hives. All are type REG_SZ. Table 17.4 shows the permanent HKEY_LOCAL_MACHINE keys.

TABLE 17.4: Permanent HKEY_LOCAL_MACHINE Keys

Permanent Key	Typical Default Value	Comment
\REGISTRY\MACHINE\HARDWARE	None	The HKEY_LOCAL_ MACHINE\ Hardware key, recreated upon boot
\REGISTRY\MACHINE\SAM	\Device\Harddisk 0\Partition1 \WINNT\System32\Config\ SAM	HKEY_LOCAL_MACHINE\SAM
\REGISTRY\MACHINE\SECURITY	\Device\Harddisk 0\Partition1 \WINNT\System32\Config\ SECURITY	HKEY_LOCAL_MACHINE\Security
\REGISTRY\MACHINE\SOFTWARE	\Device\Harddisk 0\Partition1 \WINNT\System32\Config\ Software	HKEY_LOCAL_MACHINE\ Software
\REGISTRY\MACHINE\SYSTEM	\Device\Harddisk 0\Partition1 \WINNT\System32\Config\ System	HKEY_LOCAL_MACHINE\System
\REGISTRY\USER\.DEFAULT	\Device\Harddisk 0\Partition1 \WINNT\System32\Config\ Default	HKEY_USERS\.DEFAULT
\REGISTRY\USER\Security ID (SID)	\Device\Harddisk 0\Partition1 \WINNT\Profiles\Username\nt user.dat	The current user profile, if services are running under user accounts, their entries also located here

(Courtesy of Peter D. Hipson)

Introduction to HKEY_LOCAL_ MACHINE\SOFTWARE

- Classes

- Clients

- Description

- Microsoft

- ODBC

- Program groups

- Secure

- Windows 3.1 migration status

- Hints and kinks from the experts

The HKEY_LOCAL_MACHINE\SOFTWARE hive is used to contain information about software that has been installed on your system. Also contained within HKEY_LOCAL_MACHINE\SOFTWARE is some information about Windows NT, although the HKEY_LOCAL_MACHINE\SYSTEM hive also contains Windows NT information.

In a typical installation, HKEY_LOCAL_MACHINE\SOFTWARE is subdivided into a minimum of eight sub-hives:

- Classes

- Clients

- Description

- Microsoft

- ODBC

- Program Groups

- Secure

- Windows 3.1 Migration Status

For most installations there will be one or more additional sub-hives under HKEY_LOCAL_MACHINE\SOFTWARE. For example, systems might have sub-hives including:

- 3Com or the supplier of the computer's NIC (Network Interface Card)

- INTEL for software such as the Intel 3D Scalability Toolkit

- Intuit if you are using their accounting or tax software

- Qualcomm if using one of their e-mail or communications products

Of course, the number of sub-hives is limited only by the amount and types of software packages installed on the target computer. Go hog wild, install tons of stuff, and you'll have a big HKEY_LOCAL_MACHINE\SOFTWARE sub-hive.

WARNING   You *have* backed up your registry before starting this chapter, right?

In Case of Disaster

Be cautious! Blow a sub-hive or key, and you probably will have to re-install the product whose hive or key was damaged. If you're really unlucky, you may also have to re-install Windows NT if the application's install program doesn't properly repair the registry. If you find you have to re-install because you didn't have a good registry backup, follow these steps:

1. Reinstall the product without uninstalling the original installation. If this works, you may be able to recover your user settings, profiles, and such. If this doesn't work, try step 2.

2. Uninstall the product and then re-install. This probably will loose the user settings, profiles, and such; but that's life. If this doesn't work, try step 3.

3. Install a second copy of Windows NT, and install the product on the second copy of Windows NT into the product's original directory. If the product works on the second copy of Windows NT, try the first copy of Windows NT again. If it still doesn't work on the first copy but does work on the second copy, you'll have to restore everything from backups or re-install everything from scratch. Either way, you are in for a long, long night.

As I mentioned above, HKEY_LOCAL_MACHINE\SOFTWARE has at least eight sections. Each of the sections varies in size from small (Secure usually has nothing in it at all!) to huge (Microsoft has settings for every Microsoft application installed, and for some components of Windows NT also.)

NOTE A typical user's HKEY_LOCAL_MACHINE\SOFTWARE hive may contain only the Microsoft, Policies, and VDO sub-hives.

Classes

The HKEY_LOCAL_MACHINE\SOFTWARE\Classes sub-hive is a mapping of the HKEY_CLASSES_ROOT registry hive. This is done to ensure that both have the same set of mappings.

The description of HKEY_CLASSES_ROOT in Chapter 3, "Anatomy of the Registry—The Blood, Gore, and Guts," applies to all entries in HKEY_LOCAL_MACHINE\SOFTWARE.

Clients

The HKEY_LOCAL_MACHINE\SOFTWARE\Clients sub-hive contains information used by Windows NT for e-mail and related services. Users who have not installed any additional e-mail services will find Microsoft Exchange client defined as their Mail provider—Exchange is a default component of Windows NT.

Users who have installed Microsoft's Internet Explorer 4 or later will find that a typical installation of Internet Explorer 4 installs features, including the following:

> **Contacts**—The management of names, addresses (including e-mail addresses), phone numbers, etc. is done by Contacts. An integral component of Outlook Express and Outlook, Contacts provides a powerful tool for managing contacts and names.

> **Mail**—Internet Explorer 4 installs a product called Outlook Express, which is a scaled-down version of Microsoft's e-mail client, Outlook.

> **News**—The news client is a component in Outlook Express. Newsgroups are public (and private) forums on the Internet where users are able to speak their minds on various topics.

A full installation of Microsoft's Outlook would install even more components, including:

> **Calendar**—Outlook's calendar serves as an integrated time-management tool and a powerful scheduling tool.

> **Internet Call**—NetMeeting is a tool used to hold online, interactive meetings.

Typical sub-hives found in HKEY_LOCAL_MACHINE\SOFTWARE\Clients might include those shown in Figure 18.1. This figure shows a computer on which the full version of Outlook, Outlook Express, Forte Agent, and Eudora are all installed.

FIGURE 18.1:

Clients can include products from more than one software vendor—check out my five e-mail clients, all usable at the same time!

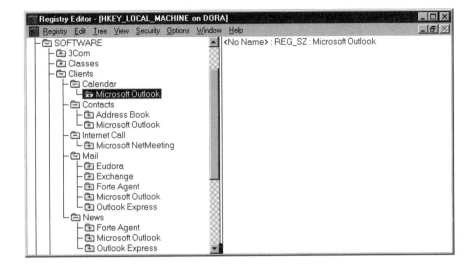

Why More Than One E-Mail Client?

OK, I can hear the questions now: Why the heck does this guy need so many e-mail clients? Yes, there is a good reason (At least I think so!):

1. I use Microsoft Outlook as my primary e-mail client. However. . .

2. I use Eudora to get messages from a mailing list that I belong to because most of the people on this list are not using Windows-compatible systems. The users don't receive Outlook-generated messages well. (Outlook creates two copies of the message, one in plain text and one in formatted text.) Also, as the mail list is archived, the Outlook-generated messages are too large for the archive.

3. I use Forte Agent to retrieve messages from news servers. I could use Microsoft's newsreader program, but I just like Agent. Because Agent can also send e-mail (in addition to news groups), it is listed as an e-mail program, too.

4. Exchange is (was) installed with Windows NT by default. Attempts to use Exchange will start Outlook, because Outlook's installation removes Exchange.

5. Outlook Express is installed with Internet Explorer 4. I have not used this program because I use Outlook.

Continued on next page

All of these e-mail addresses are an example of:

- How registry entries multiply (like rabbits!)
- How the entries get convoluted (like Exchange being deleted by Outlook, but entries for Exchange remaining in the registry, probably until hell freezes over)
- How products get installed without the user realizing that they have been installed (Outlook Express)

Now the question, since Exchange has been removed by the installation of Outlook, do I dare remove the Exchange entries from the Registry?

NO! Just I'll just leave them as they are.

Description

The hive HKEY_LOCAL_MACHINE\SOFTWARE\Description contains a sub-hive Microsoft, which contains a sub-hive Rpc, which in turn contains a sub-hive Uuid-TemporaryData. UuidTemporaryData contains two entries:

NetworkAddress—Contains the NIC's unique address (not a TCP/IP address). This address is used by the network to identify computers. Each NIC has a unique address. (This address could also be used by applications to identify a specific computer, something like a computer serial number.) This entry is updated automatically if the NIC address is changed. This value is typically called a 6-byte IEEE address.

NetworkAddressLocal—Contains a DWORD value, typically zero in value.

These entries are generally used by SQL Server and other utilities that will access the network directly. Some examples of direct network access applications include ISQL.EXE, SQLW.EXE, SQLEW.EXE, and PERFMON.EXE.

Microsoft

The Microsoft sub-hive in HKEY_LOCAL_MACHINE\SOFTWARE is the largest of the sub-hives in HKEY_LOCAL_MACHINE\SOFTWARE.

One typical installation of a Windows NT Server, with a number of applications from Microsoft installed, has the following sub-hives under HKEY_LOCAL_MACHINE\SOFTWARE\Microsoft:

Active Accessibility—Contains support for Microsoft Active Accessibility (MSAA). MSAA improves the access of command bars.

Active Setup—Currently used with Internet Explorer 4, Active Setup is the installation process for applications distributed by the Internet.

Advanced INF Setup—Contains support for setups based on INF files, used with Internet Explorer 4 and some Internet Explorer 4 components, such as Java.

AsyncMac—Also known as AsyMAC (media access control), contains an NDIS 3.0 MAC driver that is used with serial communications (RAS).

AudioCompressionManager—Contains support for the Microsoft Audio Compression Manager system.

Browser—Contains the configuration for the Computer Browser Service.

ClipArt Gallery—Contains information about ClipArt objects installed. Typically—but not always—installed with products such as Microsoft Office.

Code Store Database—Is used with objects, such as Java.

Conferencing—Supports Microsoft NetMeeting, a virtual conferencing/meeting system.

CRS—Contains the configuration for the Content Replication System.

Cryptography—Contains the management for the Microsoft CryptoAPI (Cryptographic Application Program Interface).

DHCPServer—Contains the support and configuration for DHCP (Dynamic Host Configuration Protocol), which, in a nutshell, allows dynamic (automatic) allocation of IP addresses in a TCP/IP network.

Direct3D—Contains Microsoft's high-performance 3D drawing API.

DirectPlay—Contains Microsoft's high-performance engine that provides a way for multi-player games to communicate using networks.

DirectX—Contains Microsoft's I/O system.

DownloadManager—Contains a system that allows files being transferred by Internet Explorer 4 to be downloaded in background mode, and can be suspended and resumed as desired.

DrWatson—Contains a system for providing information on application and system faults.

Exchange—Contains Microsoft's default e-mail client.

FrontPage—Contains Microsoft's application to develop and manage Internet Web pages.

IE4—Contains Microsoft's Internet Explorer 4.

INetMgr—The Internet Service Manager, used to manage Microsoft IIS (Internet Information Server).

Inetsrv—Contains Microsoft Internet Information Server.

INetStp—Contains configuration information for Microsoft IIS.

InfoViewer—Contains Microsoft Information Viewer, a data and information retrieval system, typically used with Microsoft TechNet and MSDN.

IntelliPoint—Contains support for the Microsoft Intellimouse, an enhanced pointing device.

InteractiveMusic—No, not karaoke. Microsoft Interactive Music is a system used to deliver music over the Internet.

Internet Account Manager—Is used to manage e-mail accounts.

Internet Audio—Audio may be sent to clients on the Internet using a number of different compression techniques, such as CCITT, Lernout & Hauspie, and Microsoft's encoding.

Internet Connection Wizard—The Internet Connection Wizard automates the steps used to connect a new user to the Internet.

Internet Explorer—Contains Microsoft Internet Explorer, currently version 4.01.

Internet Mail and News—Contains Internet Mail and News settings.

Internet Shopper—Contains Microsoft's client Internet commerce system.

Java VM—Contains the Java virtual machine configuration.

Jet—Contains the Microsoft Access database access engine, used by Microsoft Office and other applications.

KeyRing—Contains a small, usually metal, often lost, object used to hold keys. Or contains the Internet Information Server's Key Manager program.

Languages—Is used with Microsoft's Internet browser and server support, used to define file types (such as HTM, HTML, STM, STML, and ALX).

LanmanServer—Manages server support for SMB (Server Message Block) protocol, the core of Microsoft networking.

LanmanWorkstation—Manages client support for SMB (Server Message Block) protocol, the core of Microsoft networking.

Machine Debug Manager—Works to help define which processes should be debugged and which should be ignored.

Microsoft Chat Character Editor—Contains an add-on graphics editor for Microsoft Chat characters.

Microsoft Comic Chat—Contains Internet Chat, an interactive conferencing system with a graphic interface (using comic characters).

Microsoft Expedia—Contains Pocket Streets 98, Microsoft's road atlas program.

Microsoft FrontPage—Contains Microsoft's Internet Web page publishing utility.

Microsoft Image Composer—Contains Microsoft's graphic and image editing application.

Microsoft Reference—Contains a component of Microsoft office, providing a complete reference section.

MMCtlsForIE—Contains multi-media controls for Internet Explorer.

MOS—Contains configurations for Microsoft Office's Outlook and MsnAudio.

MS Setup (ACME)—The ACME setup is used for a number of Microsoft applications including—but not limited to—Internet Explorer 4, Publisher 98, TechNet, Office 97, and the Microsoft Windows NT Resource Kit.

Multimedia—Contains configurations for Active Movie, and DirectX components.

Ncpa—Contains the Network Control Panel applet's configuration information.

NdisWan—Contains the Network Device Interface Standard, used with a WAN (Wide Area Network), such as the Internet.

NetBIOS—Contains the Network Basic Input/Output System, used to control basic network communications, including the software interface and naming conventions.

NetBT—Contains the onfiguration for NetBIOS when implemented over TCP/IP.

NetDDE—Contains the configuration for Network Dynamic Data Exchange.

NwlnkIpx—Contains support for the Novell NetWare IPX protocol.

NwlnkNb—Contains the configuration for the NetWare network browser.

NwlnkSpx—Contains the configuration for the NetWare SPX protocol.

Office—Contains Microsoft Office, whichever version is installed, typically Office 97.

Ole—Contains basic configuration information for Object Linking and Embedding.

OS/2 Subsystem for NT—Contains basic support for OS/2 standards.

Outlook Express—Contains Microsoft's basic e-mail system, installed by default with Internet Explorer 4.

Pegasus—Contains winged horse of Greek mythology, or support for Windows CE 2.*x*.

Protected Storage System Provider—Contains an inaccessible sub-hive used to protect user security.

RAS—Contains configurations for the Remote Access Server, the dial-in component of Windows NT Server.

RasAuto—Contains configurations for the Remote Access Server AutoDial facility, used to automatically connect to a remote network.

RasMan—Contains the Remote Access Server manager program.

ReferenceTitles—Contains Microsoft Bookshelf (part of Microsoft Office) is included under ReferenceTitles.

RemoteAccess—Some settings for RAS (Remote Access Server) are included in this sub-hive.

ResKit—The Windows NT Resource Kit (either for server or workstation) basic setup settings.

Resource Kit—Contains the Windows NT Resource Kit components settings.

Rpc—Contains the configuration for Remote Procedure Calls is set in Rpc.

RPCLOCATOR—Is used with RPC (Remote Procedure Calls) to enable RPC applications to perform procedures on multiple remote computers.

Schedule+—Contains settings for Schedule+ or a substitute, such as Outlook or Exchange.

ScrptDbg—Contains Microsoft Office's script debugger settings.

Shared Tools—Lists and describes relationships with various Microsoft tools, which may be 'shared' using OLE.

SystemCertificates—Information about security certificates (used primarily with Internet Explorer) are stored in this sub-hive.

Tcpip—System configurations for TCP/IP are stored in this sub-hive. Computer-specific configuration information is stored elsewhere.

VBA—Microsoft Visual Basic for Applications, used with a number of Microsoft products, is configured here.

VisualStudio—Contains the configuration for Microsoft's Visual Studio, the development platform.

WAB—Not Windows Always Breaks... The WAB (Windows Address Book), used to manage addresses (different from Outlook's Contacts functionality), is configured in WAB.

Windows—A number of Windows configuration parameters are set here. See the second part of this section for more information on this sub-hive.

Windows Messaging Subsystem—Configurations for e-mail are contained here.

Windows NT—A number of Windows configuration parameters are set in this sub-hive. The second part of this section will document the NT sub-hive.

Wins—The Windows Internet Name Service, or WINS, is configured in this sub-hive.

Looking at the previous list, one should realize that there are many more possible sub-hives under Software. So many possibilities in fact that no single source could hope to document them all. Each installed application or component can and often does create a sub-hive in the HKEY_LOCAL_MACHINE\SOFTWARE hive.

Now, let's take a detailed peek into a few of the sub-hives found on virtually every Windows NT system.

NOTE   Some items below are specific to server installations, others are significant to workstation installations, and most are applicable to both servers and workstations. If known, I've indicated which ones are specific to which type of installation.

Even more interesting—and unexplainable—is the fact that there are both Windows *and* Windows NT sections in HKEY_LOCAL_MACHINE\SOFTWARE. Microsoft came up with Windows, then later developed Windows NT, and chose to group items whichever way they wanted. Were I to tell you that old stuff was in Windows and new stuff was in Windows NT, I'd be accused of making it all up (and rightly, I might add). There is little rhyme or reason to the organization and contents of these two sub-hives.

Windows

First and foremost, I know the question you are asking right now: Why is configuration for parts of Windows NT included in HKEY_LOCAL_MACHINE\SOFTWARE, and parts in other sections of the registry? Why isn't it all consolidated? Why spread it out? Why, oh why is this so hard to understand?

Well, I can't answer the last question, but I may be able to shed a bit of light on a few of the others. Many of the Windows NT components included in HKEY_LOCAL_MACHINE\SOFTWARE are components that are or were separate from

Windows NT. For example, Internet Explorer, Font support, even Explorer are separate from the base operating system. Yes, dear friends, you can run Windows NT version 4 without using Explorer—File Manager and Program Manager are still part of Windows NT. (No, I'm not going to comment on Windows NT 5's support for those antiquated user interface components!)

CurrentVersion

Under HKEY_LOCAL_MACHINE\SOFTWARE\Microsoft\Windows is a sub-hive called CurrentVersion. In CurrentVersion, there are a number of keys defining information about the current installation of Windows NT. Also found in CurrentVersion are a large number of sub-hives (which I've documented below, in separate sections) for various components of Windows NT.

The following are included in CurrentVersion:

CommonFilesDir—The directory where files used by more than one component are stored here. Typically, some DLL files and other support files are used by a number of other applications. Contained within the directory specified in the CommonFilesDir entry are a number of sub-directories containing either files or other sub-directories. Typically CommonFilesDir contains the value C:\Program Files\Common Files. Check your system for an idea of what is contained in the Common Files directory.

DevicePath—The location for all the INF files used to configure drivers for hardware devices are stored here. For example, the configuration file for modems made by Practical Peripherals is called MDMPP.INF (*mdm* for modems, *pp* for Practical Peripherals, and *inf* for the INF file type).

MediaPath—The absolute location for media files used by the system, for example, the sounds used by Windows for events and themes are stored here.

MediaPathUnexpanded—Contains the relative location (based on the installation-defined %SystemRoot% variable) for media files used by the system.

PF_AccessoriesName—The name for accessories, contains only the value "Accessories" by default.

ProgramFilesDir—Contains the absolute location for the Program Files directory. Uh-oh… Wondering how to rename the default location of Program Files? Guess what we have here! But check out the next entry also.

ProgramFilesPath—The path to the Program Files directory, the default is "C:" as specified in the variable %SystemDrive%. If you change the location of the Program Files directory, this is where. But check out the previous entry also, and make sure that each matches.

SM_AccessoriesName—The name for accessories, contains only the value "Accessories" by default.

Some 20 to 30 entries exist as sub-hives under CurrentVersion. The common ones are found in the next sections, by name.

CurrentVerson\App Paths

In a typical installation of Windows NT, one might find as many as 30 or 40 entries. A clean installation of Windows NT might have fewer than 10 entries, for example:

- `DIALER.EXE`
- `HYPERTRM.EXE`
- `PINBALL.EXE`
- `WORDPAD.EXE`

Even this "minimum" list could be smaller if Hyperterm or Pinball had not been installed on the computer.

Each sub-hive contains one required entry:

<No Name>—Is an unnamed key with a data value containing a string with the fully qualified path of the application, including the application's name and extension, typically .EXE.

Each sub-hive may contain one additional entry:

Path—Is a key with a data value containing a string with the fully qualified path of the application, typically used to locate supporting files, if necessary. Not all App Paths sub-hives have the Path key.

If an application component must be moved, check App Paths to see if the application is listed. If it is, when moving the component, make sure that the App Paths entries are updated to reflect the application's new location.

CurrentVersion\Controls Folder

In the Controls Folder sub-hive, there is a single binary key. Within this key is information used by the Control Panel to configure the display of Control Panel applets, including title information.

A number of Control Panel applets may also include sub-hives in the Controls Folder. For instance, when special handlers are used by the applets, typically done with OLE, a mapping of tabs in the Control Panel applet to OLE server is found in Controls Folder.

Next is an example of two Control Panel applets, Display and Mouse, and how their appearance and functionality is modified:

Display—Display may contain an entry to manage the Plus! tab in the Display Properties applet's main window. The Plus! tab allows the modification of features that have been installed in Windows 95 with the Plus Pack optional package.

Mouse—When a user installs Intellimouse support, a number of new tabs and controls are added to the Control Panel's Mouse applet. These tabs allow the configuration of the Intellimouse's wheel control, and allow other functionality to be exposed to the user.

There are probably other Control Panel applets that can and do use the Controls Folder sub-hive in addition to the two above examples.

CurrentVersion\DeleteFiles

When it is necessary to delete a system component from the desktop, the deletion is marked in the DeleteFiles\DesktopFiles sub-hive.

NOTE   Only system components (which, if deleted by the user, were probably deleted in error) are listed in DeleteFiles\DesktopFiles. User components are not listed here. Why? Because Windows NT will attempt to restore any deleted system desktop components if the user deletes them.

CurrentVersion\DeleteFiles\DesktopFiles—In a typical system, the only item that will be listed in this sub-hive might be the Inbox. This happens when Outlook is installed to replace Inbox as the e-mail system.

Some system customization tools will add additional items to the DeleteFiles\DesktopFiles sub-hive. They do this so that they can have their own application(s) replace the default components supplied by Microsoft. An example is to replace the Recycle Bin with a different application that may delete files in a different manner.

NOTE   My example of putting the Recycle Bin into the DeleteFiles\DesktopFiles sub-hive should not be attempted without making sure you have a good backup of everything. I can't promise that things will work well if you remove the Recycle Bin. Hee, hee. . . .

CurrentVersion\Explorer

Microsoft Explorer, which functions as the user interface for Windows NT, has a number of configuration options. Some options are set with various configuration dialog boxes, others must be set using one of the registry editors.

AlwaysUnloadDLL—Contains a single, unnamed string key, with a value of either 1 or 0.

AutoComplete—Contains a single string key, named UseAutoComplete. The default value is Yes.

BrowseNewProcess—Contains a single string key, named BrowseNewProcess. The default value is Yes.

CSSFilters—Contains a number of entries primarily for Internet Explorer. These entries are for OLE controls used for visual effects, such as blur, invert, glow, and shadow.

Desktop—Typically contains three entries, for Inbox, Recycle Bin, and The Internet. These are default items on the desktop.

FileTypesPropertySheetHook—Used by Internet Explorer, the entries in this sub-hive are used to display files, often containing MIME-encoded objects.

FindExtensions—Used by Internet Explorer, Outlook, and the Windows Address Book to manage their find functionality.

MyComputer—Used with the Start Menu (and elsewhere). Other entries found on some computers include dial-up networking and mobile devices:

NameSpace\Controls—Contains the Control Panel

NameSpace\Printers—Contains the Printers Panel

NewShortcutHandlers—Is used to manage items, such as property sheets.

RemoteComputer—Contains a sub-hive called NameSpace, which includes information on remote printers.

Shell Folders—Is used by the system to configure part of a user's profile. User profiles consist of two parts: the user's private items and a second common profile called All Users. The Shell Folders sub-hive contains four keys:

Common Desktop—Contains a pathname to the Windows NT Profiles directory. On many systems this will be C:\Windows\Profiles\All Users\Desktop.

Common Programs—Contains a pathname to the Windows NT Common Programs directory. On many systems this will be C:\Windows\Profiles\All Users\Start Menu\Programs.

Common Start Menu—Contains a pathname to the Windows NT Start Menu. On many systems this will be C:\Windows\Profiles\All Users\Start Menu.

Common Startup—Contains a pathname to the Windows NT Start Menu\Programs directory. On many systems this will be C:\Windows\Profiles\All Users\Start Menu\Programs\Startup.

ShellExecuteHooks—Is used by Internet Explorer to manage execution of shell extensions.

SmallIcons—On the Plus tab of the Display Properties dialog box, the Use large icons checkbox state. String values allowed are YES and NO.

Streams—Could be small rivers, seasonally may be dry. More likely, contains the status of the taskbar and tool bar and only one entry:

Desktop—Two entries, Default Taskbar and Default Toolbars, are the only entries found in this sub-hive.

Thumbnail View—Contains one key, called AutoExtract. The value will be either 0x1 or 0x0.

Tips—Contains money or value given to a person who serves you, or words of advice. OK, really: Tips are displayed on a dialog box when a user logs on, although most users turn off the tips as their second or third action after installing Windows NT. A total of 50 tips exist in Windows NT by default, but you could add more. And a tip for you: If you add more, Windows won't know about them.

User Shell Folders—Contains the folders used for users. Four keys exist in this sub-hive:

Common Desktop—Contains the path %SystemRoot%\Profiles\All Users\Desktop. This provides a path to the common desktop for users.

Common Programs—Contains the path %SystemRoot%\Profiles\All Users\Start Menu\Programs. This provides a path to the common Start Menu\Programs directory for users.

Common Start Menu—Contains the path %SystemRoot%\Profiles\All Users\Start Menu. This provides a path to the common Start Menu directory for users.

Common Startup—Contains the path %SystemRoot%\Profiles\All Users\Start Menu\Programs\Startup. This provides a path to the common Start Menu\Programs\Startup directory for users.

User Shell Folders\New—Usually empty, contains a location to put new common objects for users.

VolumeCaches—Is empty, except for the following sub-hives:

Active Setup Temp Folders—The description reads: "These files should no longer be needed. They were originally created by a setup program that is no longer running."

Downloaded Program Files—The description reads: "Downloaded Program Files are ActiveX controls and Java applets downloaded automatically from the Internet when you view certain pages. They are temporarily stored in the Downloaded Program Files folder on your hard disk."

Internet Cache Files—The description reads: "The Temporary Internet Files folder contains Web pages stored on your hard disk for quick viewing. Your personalized settings for Web pages will be left intact."

WindowsUpdate—Contains a single entry called UpdateURL, which contains a reference to the Windows Internet Connection Wizard.

CurrentVersion\Extensions

The Extensions sub-hive contains keys defining what program will be used to open a specific file type. Similar to the Classes sub-hives found elsewhere in the registry, Extensions is used only for added on, non-Microsoft applications. The Extensions sub-hive is used to show, for File Manager, the application that a user prefers to open a certain file with, for example RTF files might be opened with Word for Windows. This sub-hive does not appear to be used with Explorer, or Windows NT 4.

> **NOTE**
>
> Why have this in the registry if it is not used? Simple: Many legacy (older) applications will attempt to update the sub-hive even though it is not used. Also, since it is possible to use File Manager with Windows NT 4, there actually is a potential use for these entries.

CurrentVersion\Internet Settings

The Internet Settings sub-hive consists of settings used with the Internet, primarily with Internet Explorer. Two keys present in this hive include ActiveXCache, which points to a directory where Internet Explorer may cache ActiveX (OLE) controls; and CodeBaseSearchPath, which points to a Microsoft site where common code may be downloaded.

In addition to these two keys, there are a number of sub-hives contained in Internet Settings:

Accepted Documents—Some documents can be accepted as safe. These include Word, Excel, and PowerPoint documents. (No, there is no need to tell me about all those nasty Word viruses. I know.) Also considered safe are the GIF, bitmap, and JPEG image types.

ActiveX Cache—A second set of ActiveX control cache directories, two entries in this sub-hive allow two locations to store ActiveX controls that become installed on the user's system.

Cache—Contained in Cache are Internet Explorer's cache parameters: Cleanup factor, interval and time, a debug flag, freshness, and persistence.

These factors are set in Internet Explorer's Settings dialog box, on the General tab.

Cache\Paths—Internet Explorer stores Web pages and objects in a series of cache directories. The default is to have four cache directories, though the number of cache directories can be modified if necessary. For each cache directory, a sub-hive named path1, path2, … path$n$ (where n is the number of cache directories), is created. Each of the path sub-hives contains a path name and a size limit.

Cache\Special Paths—Several special directories are used by Internet Explorer. These are for cookies (small files stored on the computer by a Web site), and for the Internet Explorer history list.

Cookies—Contained in the Cookies sub-hive are keys to limit the size of the cookies directory, the cache prefix (cookie:), and the directory path. Cookies are often used to track a user's usage of a particular site, monitor favorite selections, and sometimes to gather information about the user. Virtually all cookie use is benign, intended to optimize the Web site's presentation to the user, or to cache user-specific information for re-use at a later time.

NOTE   Don't like cookies? Don't accept them, and clean out your cookies directory. Nothing evil will happen—a few Internet sites will deny access to clients who don't allow cookies, but this is rare.

History—Internet Explorer keeps a (limited) history of sites visited by the user. This list is kept in the directory named by the unnamed key in this sub-hive.

Last Update—This sub-hive contains information about the last version of Internet Explorer components to be installed. Information may consist of a product's date or a version number.

Cryptography\AUTH2UPD—Contains the version number of the currently installed cryptography component.

IEXPLOREV2—Contains the product date for Internet Explorer 2.

IEXPLOREV3—Contains the product date for Internet Explorer 3.

IEXPLOREV4—Contains the product date for Internet Explorer 4.

NOTE With the Internet Explorer Last Update information, it is not really possible to determine which, if any, versions are installed. It is safe to assume, however, that the latest version is probably the currently installed version. Of course, a user might have gone back to an earlier version—if so, it would not be possible to determine this from the Last Update sub-hive.

SO—So what? No, that's not it. SO is short for Security Options. You will find the Settings button on the Security tab of the Internet Options dialog box in Internet Explorer 4. Clicking on the Settings button will display the Security Settings dialog box. Here you will find security based options, including:

ACTIVE_CONTENT\ACTIVEX—Runs ActiveX controls and plug-ins.

ACTIVE_CONTENT\ENABLE—Downloads signed ActiveX objects.

ACTIVE_CONTENT\SAFETY—Initializes and scripts any ActiveX controls that have not been marked as safe.

ACTIVE_CONTENT\SCRIPTSAFE—Scripts any ActiveX controls that have been marked as safe.

ACTIVE_CONTENT\UNSIGNEDACTIVEX—Downloads unsigned ActiveX controls.

AUTH\LOGON—Sets how to handle logon credentials.

DOWNLOAD\FILEDOWNLOAD—Sets whether to download files or not.

DOWNLOAD\FONTDOWNLOAD—Sets whether to download and install fonts or not.

JAVAPER\JAVA—Sets Java permissions.

MISC\DRAGDROP—Sets whether to allow drag and drop or cut and paste of files.

MISC\FORMDATA—Sets submission of unencrypted form data.

MISC\INSTALLDT—Sets whether to allow installation of desktop items.

MISC\LAUNCHING—Sets whether to allow launching a file or application in an <IFRAME>.

MISC\SOFTDIST—Sets software channel permissions.

SCRIPTING\SCRIPT—Sets whether to allow active scripting.

SCRIPTING\SCRIPTJAVA—Whether to allow Java scripting.

SOIEAK—Security Options for IEAK (Internet Explorer Administration Kit), Internet Explorer may be installed from a product called the IEAK. With IEAK it is possible to customize the setup of Internet Explorer, presetting preferences and options to suit a particular set of circumstances. As with the SO options, previously listed, these settings will appear on the Security tab of the Internet Options dialog box in Internet Explorer 4. Clicking on the Settings button will display the Security Settings dialog box.

NOTE   These are not the only options or settings that may be configured with IEAK. IEAK allows customization of the installation for an ISP, for example, where the user's default home page will be the ISP's page.

ACTIVE_CONTENT\ACTIVEX—Runs ActiveX controls and plug-ins.

ACTIVE_CONTENT\ENABLE—Downloads signed ActiveX objects.

ACTIVE_CONTENT\SAFETY—Initializes and scripts any ActiveX controls that have not been marked as safe.

ACTIVE_CONTENT\SCRIPTSAFE—Scripts any ActiveX controls that have been marked as safe.

ACTIVE_CONTENT\UNSIGNEDACTIVEX—Downloads unsigned ActiveX controls.

AUTH\LOGON—Sets how to handle logon credentials.

DOWNLOAD\FILEDOWNLOAD—Sets whether or not to download files.

DOWNLOAD\FONTDOWNLOAD—Sets whether or not to download and install fonts.

JAVAPER\JAVA—Sets Java permissions.

MISC\DRAGDROP—Sets whether or not to allow drag and drop or cut and paste of files.

MISC\FORMDATA—Sets submission of unencrypted form data.

MISC\INSTALLDT—Sets whether or not to allow installation of desktop items.

MISC\LAUNCHING—Sets whether or not to allow launching a file or application in an <IFRAME>.

MISC\SOFTDIST—Sets software channel permissions.

SCRIPTING\SCRIPT—Sets whether or not to allow active scripting.

SCRIPTING\SCRIPTJAVA—Sets whether or not to allow Java scripting.

Subscription Folder—The subscription folder holds certain subscribed objects.

TemplatePolicies—These settings are used to initialize (and reset) the SO (Security Options) for Internet Explorer. The original factory default is Medium, which provides a reasonable medium between excessive safety and minimal safety.

High—Typically these settings will keep your system as safe as possible.

Low—These settings offer little safety to your system.

Medium—These settings offer a compromise between safety and ease of use.

Url History—Four entries in Url History manage the history list, including cache limit (number of entries in the history list), number of days to keep the cache (20 days is the default), and the directory where the history cache is kept.

UrlHistory—A single entry exists in this sub-hive; the number of days to keep the cache. The default is 20 days. It is possible that this entry is not used.

NOTE

Why Url History (with a space) and UrlHistory (no space)? The best guess is that some programmer somewhere in Microsoft forgot to type a space, and created (inadvertantly) a second registry entry in error.

User Agent—Contains a sub-hive used to manage MSN entries.

UA Tokens—Two entries for MSN (Microsoft Network) exist in this sub-hive, one for each version (2.0 and 2.5) of MSN.

ZoneMap—Four pre-defined zones are contained in Internet Explorer 4, which are groupings of Internet sites based on security issues. The user is able to set zone attributes (see SO, above) for each zone, and assign sites to a specific zone as desired. Contained in ZoneMap are entries defining which sites fit within a specific zone (local sites not in other zones, sites that bypass the proxy server, and all net (UNC) paths).

Domains—Typically contains an empty sub-hive.

ProtocolDefaults—Contains the various protocols allowed, such as file, ftp, and http.

Ranges—Contains a place where the buffalo roam, and also entries (if any) for zone ranges.

Zones—Contains definitions of the four default zones, plus the local computer (included but not a zone, as such).

0   The first zone is not a zone at all. Just your computer.

1   The local intranet zone is for sites within your own organization. Generally all the local intranet sites can be trusted.

2   The trusted sites zone is for intranet sites that you trust to have safe (for your computer, but not necessarily for you) content.

3   The everyone else zone is for sites that you have not placed in any other zone. This is the default zone.

4   The "I really don't trust this site" zone is where sites having content that is not tested, not known, or otherwise considered to be unsafe for your computer are. Maybe call this the *Twilight Zone*?

CurrentVersion\MCD

MCD is the OpenGL Mini-Client Driver. In this model, the driver is responsible for features that are accelerated using hardware, and software is used to handle all other features. MCD typically contains about six settings for MCD functionality. Most users only use OpenGL for screen savers. The Pipes screen saver is an example of an OpenGL program.

CurrentVersion\MMFiles

MMFiles (Multi-media) files are a common component to Windows NT. The advent of sound and high-performance video adapters in Windows NT computers has opened a new world of media to a platform that was not originally intended to be used this way. (Imagine: sounds and good video on a business system!)

Contained in MMFiles are graphics and media-related paths, such as the following:

> **GraphicsPath**—Typically contains C:\Multimedia Files\Graphics.
>
> **MyMediaPath**—Typically contains C:\Multimedia Files\My Media.
>
> **PalettePath**—Typically contains C:\Multimedia Files\Graphics\Color Palettes\Microsoft Image Composer.
>
> **<unnamed>**—Typically contains C:\Multimedia Files.

CurrentVersion\ModuleUsage

The ModuleUsage sub-hive contains a listing of modules, typically ActiveX controls and UUIDs (Uniform Unique IDs). In the sub-hives within ModuleUsage, there is information, such as owner (if known).

CurrentVersion\MS-DOS Emulation

When an MS-DOS application is opened and the application does not have its own PIF file, settings for the application's display are found in the MS-DOS sub-hive.

In MS-DOS is a single key named "DisplayParameters," which controls the display's attributes. Many different attributes are mapped to this single binary object, such as the following:

> **Font**—The sub-hive Font contains the name of the font that will be used for MS-DOS applications. The default is Lucida Console.

CurrentVersion\Nls

NLS (National Language Support) provides the support to manage and display characters using the UNICODE character sets. With UNICODE, it is possible to display characters from multiple languages at one time. It contains the following:

> **LocaleMapIDs**—Contains a table of lookup values for NLS languages.

CurrentVersion\Policies

CurrentVersion\Policies is used to manage RASC (Recreational Software Advisory Council) ratings. These settings are used with the Internet, Internet Explorer, and some games. The CurrentVersion\Policies hive contains a single sub-hive called "Ratings:"

Ratings—Contains two keys. FileName0 contains the name of the RSAC ratings definition file. This file is text and may be edited with NotePad. The second key, called "Key," contains a binary value.

.Default—The .Default sub-hive contains three ratings-oriented keys: Allow_Unknowns, Enabled, and PleaseMom. Each is a binary key.

.Default\http://www.rsac.org/ratingsv01.html—This sub-hive contains four DWORD values: l, n, s, and v.

CurrentVersion\RenameFiles

Sometimes it is necessary for an application, when it is being installed, to remove a file for some reason. (The reason would be specific to the application.) Rather than deleting these files, which the user might need at a later time should the application need to be removed, a common technique is to re-name the files. Then, if necessary, they may be renamed back to their original name.

A few of the applications that rename files are:

- Sa
- Win
- WinMail
- WinNews
- WordPadAttribSet

CurrentVersion\Run

Here is one of those areas in the registry that you want to find, but never seem to be able to. The CurrentVersion\Run hive contains the name of executables that will be run each time the system is started.

In one system that I have, the following are included in the CurrentVersion\Run hive:

BrowserWebCheck—Contains Internet Explorer's application, which uses pull technology to check currency of subscribed Web pages.

H/PC Connection Agent—Contains a program that checks for an HPC (Hand Held PC) to be connected. If the program detects the HPC, it will automatically initiate logon for the HPC.

POINTER—Contains an enhanced mouse system, part of the Microsoft Intellipoint program.

SystemTray—Contains the system tray.

TIPS—Contains the Mouse tips program.

Most Windows NT systems only have an entry for SystemTray in Current-Version\Run. The CurrentVersion\Run is much like the Start Menu\Programs\Startup directory—anything there will be run when a user logs on.

NOTE   By putting items in CurrentVersion\Run, then protecting the registry hive from modification, you can force users to open or run certain applications. They would be unable to change this behavior.

CurrentVersion\RunOnce

Once? When?

CurrentVersion\RunOnce allows a program to be executed the first time a user (any user) logs on, and does not allow the user to continue until they have exited the program(s).

Once the program has completed execution, Windows NT will delete it from the CurrentVersion\RunOnce hive.

A program to be run in CurrentVersion\RunOnce should be entered with a name as the key (The program's common name will work fine here.), and the string data for the program should be the program's fully qualified file name. For example:

```
JobRun = "C:\Jobs\JobRun.exe"
```

The key's data type should be REG_STRING.

The application will be run after the next user logs on. The computer will not need to be restarted.

CurrentVersion\RunOnceEx

Is used by system components and Internet Explorer to run setup and configuration components. Works much like CurrentVersion\RunOnce.

CurrentVersion\Setup

The Setup sub-hive contains information including the boot directory (typically C:\), the installation source directory (often the drive letter of your CD-ROM drive), and source path (often the same as the source directory).

Often after installing Windows NT, we find that we want to change the CD-ROM's drive letter. (I use drive letters after S for CD-ROM drives, for example.) If you don't tell Windows NT (in CurrentVersion\Setup) every time you attempt to change the installation of Windows NT (for instance, installing a new component or option), the Windows NT setup program will prompt you to insert the disk in the wrong drive, making the installation process more complicated. A simple change to the entries in this section will make the process much easier.

> **BaseWinOptions**—Contained in this sub-hive are a number of sub-components (about ten), all of which are controlled by INF files.

> **OptionalComponents**—OptionalComponents provides the status for each optional component that may be installed with Windows NT. In the OptionalComponents sub-hive is a list of optional components, and a set of corresponding sub-hives, one for each optional component.

CurrentVersion\SharedDlls

DLL (Dynamic Link Library) files may be shared between multiple applications. Windows NT maintains a list of all shared DLL files and a count of the number of applications using the shared DLL file.

When an application using a shared DLL file is removed (uninstalled), the count is decreased by one. If the count becomes zero, Windows NT will prompt you to remove the shared DLL file.

NOTE   Although this section implies that it is for DLL files only, actually any shared file may be managed using this feature.

CurrentVersion\Shell Extensions

Shell Extensions is a method used to extend and expand Windows NT's user interface and capabilities. Contained within the CurrentVersion\Shell Extensions hive is a sub-hive named Approved where all Shell Extensions are stored.

NOTE   For more information on Shell Extensions, check out Jeff Prosise's March 1995 MSJ article titled "Writing Windows 95 Shell Extensions."

CurrentVersion\ShellScrap

CurrentVersion\ShellScrap, on most systems, contains a single sub-hive, Priority-CacheFormats. In PriorityCacheFormats is a single data key, named "#3," which contains an empty string.

CurrentVersion\ShellServiceObjectDelayLoad

The ShellServiceObjectDelayLoad loads objects subject to a delay. The delay allows the operating system to finish initializing, establish connections, etc. Most systems with Internet Explorer 4 installed load WebCheck. WebCheck is responsible for subscription maintenance.

CurrentVersion\Telephony

Windows NT is designed to work with telecommunications. Modems and telephones are commonly used to establish remote connections (and voice calls, at times). Within the CurrentVersion\Telephony hive are a number of sub-hives:

Country List—Inside the Country List hive are about 240 sub-hives, one for each country defined. A typical country code is one to four digits, and matches the telephone company's country code. For example, the country code for Thailand is 66. (To make a long distance telephone call to Thailand, I'd dial 001-66 where the 001 is the overseas access code, and 66 is the country code.) Information in each country sub-hive includes:

CountryCode—Contains a DWORD value that should be equal to the country code. (Remember this value will be displayed in hexadecimal format.) It is possible that this code might have to be changed if a country's country code were to change, although this is unlikely.

Name—Contains a string with the country's name, Thailand in this example.

InternationalRule—Contains the rules used to dial numbers in this country. (See the next sidebar for more on rules.)

LongDistanceRule—Contains the rules used to dial long distance in this country. (See the next sidebar for more on rules.)

SameAreaRule—Containsthe rules used to dial local numbers in this country. (See the next sidebar for more on rules.)

TIP

Need a list of all the countries in the world? Here they are, along with the applicable telephone country codes. Export this sub-hive of the registry to a text file, and use an editor to clean up the list!

Rules, Rules, and More Rules

In the InternationalRule, LongDistanceRule, and SameAreaRule; you see a jumble of letters and numbers. Each has meaning. For example:

0-9   Indicates a number that is to be dialed as entered.

ABCD   Indicates touch-tone characters to be dialed, only usable on tone dial systems. (This sounds the special tones named A, B, C and D.)

E   Dial the country code.

F   Dial the area code or city code.

G   Dial the local number.

H   Dial the card number.

*   Dial a * tone.

Dial a # tone.

T   Indicates subsequent numbers dialed as tone dial.

P   Indicates subsequent numbers dialed as pulse dial.

Continued on next page

, Pause for a fixed period of time (typically 1 second).

! Flash the hook (1/2 second on-hook, 1/2 second off-hook).

W Wait for second dial tone (outside line dial tone).

@ Wait for silent answer (ringback followed by silence for five seconds).

$ Wait for calling-card prompt tone.

? Pause for user input.

Again, using Thailand as our example:

InternationalRule = 001EFG

(Dial 001, the country code, the city code, the local number.)

LongDistanceRule = 0FG

(Dial 0, the city code, the local number.)

SameAreaRule = G

(Dial the local number.)

That's all folks, an easy set of rules! With these rules it's easy to add new countries (they pop up all the time, right?) if necessary. What with the sometimes major changes to area codes, which are equivalent to city codes in other countries, it is sometimes necessary to modify the United States entry.

Set rules in the Change Calling Card dialog box by clicking the Rules button.

Locations—Each user may have zero, one, or more locations defined. (Actually, each user should have one location: the user's current, or home location.) Each location defined is stored in the Locations sub-hive, as Location0, Location1, etc. I've given an example, Location0:

Location0—Contains information entered in Dialing Properties dialog box.

Providers—Providers are the connection between Windows NT and the modem or other telecommunications device. The most common provider is the Unimodem driver, though there are also other drivers, including the TAPI interface.

CurrentVersion\Unimodem

The Unimodem driver is a universal modem driver (See, now Unimodem makes sense.) used to control virtually all industry-compatible AT-command modems, also known as Hayes-compatible. Most standard modems designed to be connected to POTS (Plain Old Telephone Service) lines—in other words, lines that are not digital—are controlled by the Unimodem Driver.

Also controlled by the Unimodem driver are direct connections between two computers connected via a serial cable. Though good speed performance cannot be achieved, serial cable connections are used when connecting some notebooks, and most PDA (Personal Digital Assistants) and HPC (Handheld Personal Computers). Note that some systems use an IR (infrared) link for these devices, too.

NOTE
Please note that Windows NT 4 and Windows CE version 1 are not compatible. It will be necessary to upgrade to Windows CE version 2.*x* or later to connect an HPC to your Windows NT system.

DeviceSpecific—A hive containing sub-hives for each connection. For example, a typical system will have a sub-hive under DeviceSpecific for each modem type installed, and one for direct serial cable connections if installed. Each entry contains information that the device, modem or connection, might send to the host computer.

CurrentVersion\Uninstall

In the Control Panel's Add/Remove Programs applet there is a list of applications that may be removed automatically. Using this feature, the user is assured that the removal will be smooth and will not cause problems with system stability.

WARNING
This assumes that the applications designer did a credible job of creating his remove system. If the application does not have a good uninstaller, you may still have problems. No one, other than the supplier of an application, can assure you that the uninstall will go smoothly. Before uninstalling anything, make absolutely sure you have a backup of the system, the application (all of it), and the registry. With good backups, it is possible, (although nothing is guaranteed), that you may be able to recover from an uninstall gone awry.

Located in the CurrentVersion\Uninstall hive will be a sub-hive for each component that may be automatically uninstalled. For example, in the Uninstall for IntelliPoint, you'll find the following:

> **IntelliPoint\DisplayName**—Contains a key the string Microsoft IntelliPoint.

> **IntelliPoint\UninstallString**—Contains a key containing the string `'C:\progra~1\MICROS~2\Mouse\UNINSTALL.EXE`.

When the user selects Microsoft IntelliPoint in the Add/Remove Programs applet, the program or object in the UninstallString will be executed, performing the uninstallation. Typically for a system component such as the IntelliPoint mouse driver to be uninstalled, it must re-install the original component.

TIP Ever manually uninstalled a program and then realized that the Add/Remove Programs list had an uninstall for the program? Easy fix: delete the applicable sub-hive from the CurrentVersion\Uninstall hive. Careful, don't remove the wrong one.

CurrentVersion\URL

Used with Internet Explorer, this hive provides a default prefix for a URL when the user does not enter one. For example, I'm in the habit of accessing my Web page by typing in the following:

```
www.mv.net/ipusers/darkstar
```

When in fact, I should type in the following:

```
http://www.mv.net/ipusers/darkstar
```

Internet Explorer, using information stored in CurrentVersion\URL, determines that the default prefix should actually be http://.

> **DefaultPrefix**—Contains the default prefix (usually http://) used when the user does not enter a prefix, and the initial characters of the URL do not tell Internet Explorer what prefix from the Prefixes list (below) to use. The default prefix could be changed if the user were using ftp or gopher, for example.

Prefixes—Contains a list of all valid prefixes, based on the initial part of the URL. For example, if the URL started with www, or www., the prefix would be http://. If the URL started with ftp, or ftp., then the prefix would be ftp://. Prefixes defined by default (You may add more if you wish.) are the following:

ftp—ftp://

ftp.—ftp://

gopher—gopher://

gopher.—gopher://

home—http://

home.—http://

mosaic—http://

mosaic.—http://

www—http://

www.—http://

Help

The Help sub-hive contains a list of help files and their locations. These are used when, inside an application, the user either presses F1 (for help), or selects the What's This button and clicks on a control or object in the application's user interface.

It is possible to remove entries from this section, if desired, when you know for sure that the help file is either no longer used or has been removed.

TIP　　If you find that pressing F1 or selecting What's This brings up a WinHelp error, indicating that WinHelp cannot find the help file, search for the file; and if you can find it, WinHelp will update this sub-hive to indicate this file's location.

ITStorage

Is used with the Microsoft HTML Help Control (an ActiveX control) to display help for HTML documents in Internet Explorer.

> **Finders**—For each type of HTML help files, an entry is created. Each entry has a name equal to the extension of the help file. For instance, the CHM HTML help files are listed as being serviced by a specific control, identified by a UUID.

Windows NT

Under HKEY_LOCAL_MACHINE\SOFTWARE\Microsoft is a sub-hive called Windows NT. Much like the Windows sub-hive (described previously) the Windows NT sub-hive sets a number of Windows NT operating parameters.

There is only one sub-hive in the Windows NT hive. This sub-hive, called "CurrentVersion," contains about 30 sub-hives and perhaps 15 data keys in a typical installation. Unlike the Windows sub-hive, the number of entries in Windows NT is relatively constant between different installations.

CurrentVersion

CurrentVersion contains a number of data keys. These data keys hold information about the installation:

> **CSDVersion**—Contains the level of the system. By level I mean which service packs have been installed (if any). Remember, service packs are cumulative—installing Service Pack 3 automatically installs both Service Pack 1 and Service Pack 2. Data in this key might be Service Pack 3.

> **CurrentBuild**—Contains an obsolete data key containing old version and build information. Do not use this key, use CurrentBuildNumber to determine the build of Windows NT that is running.

> **CurrentBuildNumber**—Contains a number indicating which build of Windows NT is running. For instance, the build number for Windows NT 4 is 1381. A higher number indicates a later operating system build. During the development process, build numbers are incremented each time the developers create a complete operating system, sometimes daily.

CurrentType—Contains information on whether the installation is uniprocessor, or multi-processor.

CurrentVersion—Contains the Windows NT version number, such as 4.0. Microsoft sometimes has sub-version numbers, such as 3.11 or 3.51. The next version of NT will be 5.0.

InstallDate—Contains information on the date that Windows NT was installed. This value is the number of seconds since January 1, 1970, and these dates remain valid until early 2038, not much of a Y2K problem there.

PathName—Contains information on the path that the Windows NT system is installed in.

Plus! VersionNumber—Plus!, installed as part of Internet Explorer 4, has a version number matching both Internet Explorer 4 and Windows NT 4.

ProductID—Contains the Windows NT product ID. If Windows NT is installed from something other than OEM media, the product ID will consist of a total of 20 digits: five lead digits, the first three digits of the user's CD key, the last seven digits of the user's CD key, and five trailing digits. The leading and trailing digit numbers will vary from installation to installation. For OEM media installations, the ProductID will be equal to the OEM CD key. In both cases the CD key is written on a small yellow sticker on the back of the CD jewel case.

RegisteredOrganization—Contains the name of your company or organization, as you entered it during setup. If your company or organization name changes, you may edit this key to change the name.

RegisteredOwner—Contains the name as you entered it during setup. If your name changes (maybe you inherited the computer from your predecessor?), you may edit this key to change the name.

Software Type—Contains the string SYSTEM.

SourcePath—Contains he path you used to install Windows NT from. If you re-assign CD-ROM drive letters (I do, to keep all CD-ROM drives at the end of the alphabet, using letters S through Z) you can edit this key to change where Windows NT is installed from. This path could be a network path, if the installation was made from a shared resource.

SystemRoot—Contains information used to create the %SystemRoot% environment variable, this is the base directory that Windows NT is installed in. Be cautious about changing this key and realize that Windows

NT, when booting, will update this registry entry anyway. There may be other locations where the Windows NT directory is coded without using %SystemRoot%. To change the directory without re-installing Windows NT, see the "Hints and Kinks from the Experts" section at the end of this chapter.

CurrentVersion\AeDebug

Windows NT will launch a debugger when there is an application or system failure. A debugger is a program that will either save information about the failure, or allow interactive debugging. Most users who are not developers will simply use DrWatson as their debugger. DrWatson is a simple program that saves vital information about what failed and why there was a failure to a debugging file.

For DrWatson users, the typical entries in AeDebug are as follows:

Auto—Is a string value containing 1 if automatic debugging is to be done, and 0 if no automatic debugging is done.

Debugger—Is the name of the default debugger. If you have another debugger installed other than DrWatson, your debugger will be listed here.

UserDebuggingHotKey—Allows a user to launch the debugger using a keystroke combination. Useful for developers, but the average user will find little use for this functionality.

DrWatson's Options

DrWatson, DRWTSN32.EXE, takes a number of command line options when launched:

- Use the –i option to (re)install DrWatson as the default debugger. This option would be used if a different debugger was installed at some point, and you now want to use DrWatson again.

- The –g option is ignored, but no error is generated. This option is used to maintain compatibility with 16-bit (Windows 95 and Windows 3.x versions of DrWatson).

- The –p <pid> option tells DrWatson to debug the Process ID specified.

- The –e <event> option tells DrWatson to debug the event specified.

- Use -? to display a simple help screen of options.

CurrentVersion\Compatibility

Within CurrentVersion\Compatibility are data keys for a number of legacy (older, pre-existing) applications that are not totally compatible with Windows NT. A flag value (a hexadecimal number, expressed as a string) tells Windows NT about the incompatibility, and allows Windows NT to modify the operating system's behavior to compensate for the application's incompatibility.

What does Compatibility do? During beta testing of the operating system, testers inform Microsoft of applications that do not perform correctly. Microsoft may contact the application's supplier, and work with them to make the program work correctly. For some applications, especially for applications where there is a large installed base of users, Microsoft will make patches to the operating system to allow that application to function correctly. Usually these patches consist of doing things that make the new version of the operating system look like the original version for that application. These patches are turned on and off with a set of binary switches—when the application is loaded, Compatibility is checked, and the necessary patches are turned on for that application.

NOTE	Realize that these patches will be only visible to the offending application and not to any others.

CurrentVersion\Drivers

Some drivers are installed using this section of the registry. In certain Windows NT installations two drivers—timer.drv, and mmdrv.dll are installed. Timer.drv is used to create certain timer functions on PC-compatible systems, and mmdrv.dll is the low-level wave, MIDI, and aux support driver.

CurrentVersion\drivers.desc

In CurrentVersion\drivers.desc are descriptions of certain drivers that may be installed under Windows NT. The descriptions are text, intended to be people readable.

CurrentVersion\Drivers32

Driver mapping for certain virtual devices, such as multi-media, is done in CurrentVersion\Drivers32. For instance, the data key midi = mmdrv.dll.

CurrentVersion\Embedding

Applications that may be embedded (such as PaintBrush, and Sound Recorder) are listed in data keys in CurrentVersion\Embedding.

CurrentVersion\File Manager

The CurrentVersion\File Manager has a sub-hive called AddOns.

> **AddOns**—Contains a sub-hive containing information on add-on software products for File Manager. WinZip is an add-on software product that fits into this category.

CurrentVersion\Font Drivers

In CurrentVersion\Font Drivers are any needed drivers used to display fonts. Usage of True Type fonts has minimized the usage of this sub-hive.

CurrentVersion\FontCache

The management of fonts is critical to system performance. Using a cache allows much better performance when displaying frequently used fonts. Windows creates bitmaps of the TrueType fonts, and then caches these bitmaps so that they do not have to be re-created.

In the CurrentVersion\FontCache sub-hive are three data keys:

> **MaxSize**—Maximum size of the font cache.
>
> **MinIncreSize**—The minimum increment size for the font cache.
>
> **MinInitSize**—The minimum initial size for the font cache.

TIP   Also in CurrentVersion\FontCache is a sub-hive. Do not modify these values except when absolutely necessary, for instance when dealing with non-English character sets, or when using Print Shop.

> **CurrentVersion\FontCache\LastFontSweep**—In this sub-hive is one variable:
>
> > **LastSweepTime**—A binary value indicating the last time the font cache was cleaned.

CurrentVersion\FontMapper

Font mapping is an internal component of Windows NT that compares the attributes for a font that is requested and is not available, and then matches these attributes with available physical fonts.

In CurrentVersion\FontMapper, attribute modifiers are supplied for the font mapper in Windows NT.

CurrentVersion\Fonts

In CurrentVersion\Fonts is a list of currently installed fonts. The list is comprised of keys in the form:

Font display name = fontfile

where Font display name is the display name, for example, "Arial (TrueType)"; and fontfile is the actual font file (arial.ttf, for Arial (TrueType)).

The information in Fonts is used by the Font applet in the Control Panel, and by applications (indirectly, through the operating system). It is possible to manually manipulate the font information; however, using the Fonts applet will make the process easier.

CurrentVersion\FontSubstitutes

Some fonts, commonly called for by applications, are not supplied with Windows NT 4. These fonts are older, bitmapped fonts that were commonly used with early versions of Windows and Windows NT, but are no longer supplied or directly supported. These fonts are simply mapped to newer TrueType fonts.

Fonts substitutions are:

Helv—MS Sans Serif

Helvetica—Arial

Microsoft Shell Dlg—MS Sans Serif

Times—Times New Roman

Tms Rmn—MS Serif

CurrentVersion\GRE_Initialize

The GRE (Graphic Rendering Engine) is used to display a few fonts that Windows NT supports. These fonts are bitmapped fonts (not TrueType). Fonts handled or remapped by GRE are:

FIXEDFON.FON—vgafix.fon

FONTS.FON—vgasys.fon

OENFONT.FON—vgaoem.fon

CurrentVersion\Image File Execution Options

Used for debugging objects such as services or DCOM, Image File Execution Options specifies what debugger to use for a specific service or DCOM object.

NOTE   Notice that the term *image file* refers to an executable image file, not a graphics file.

Your Image File Name Here without a path—In this sub-hive, which serves as an example, are data keys showing how to configure the debugger. More information on image file debugging is available from NuMega Lab's Web site at http://www.numega.com/newsletters/apr96.htm.

CurrentVersion\IniFileMapping

The sub-hive CurrentVersion\IniFileMapping is used to map ini files (as they were used with early versions of Windows) to registry hives. In all cases the entries in CurrentVersion\IniFileMapping point to other registry entries.

CurrentVersion\MCI

In CurrentVersion\MCI are the MCI (Media Control Interface) drivers. Most systems with an audio card will have four entries:

AVIVideo—Contains the AVI (video files) driver, mciavi.drv.

CDAudio—Contains the CD audio (music) player driver, mcicda.drv.

Sequencer—Contains the MIDI (sequencer) driver, mciseq.drv.

WaveAudio—Contains the wave file (audio files) driver, mciwave.drv.

CurrentVersion\MCI Extensions

The hive CurrentVersion\MCI Extensions holds multi-media file extensions, and the driver used to handle these objects. For example, the following entry:

```
mpeg = MPEGVideo
```

denotes that Windows NT should use the MPEGVideo driver to process mpeg files.

CurrentVersion\MCI32

In CurrentVersion\MCI32 are 32-bit MCI (Media Control Interface) drivers. Most systems with an audio card will have five entries:

AVIVideo—Contains the AVI (video files) driver, mciavi32.drv.

CDAudio—Contains the CD audio (music) player driver, mcicda.drv.

MPEGVideo—Contains the MPEG (video) driver, mciqtz32.dll.

Sequencer—Contains the MIDI (sequencer) driver, mciseq.drv.

WaveAudio—Contains the wave file (audio files) driver, mciwave.drv.

Note that in MCI32, some drivers are common with CurrentVersion\MCI.

CurrentVersion\Midimap

MIDI (Musical Instrument Digital Interface) is used to create music using sound (instrument musical note) definitions, combined with the music's score. The score (in a special format) tells the computer how to "play" each instrument. As might be expected, the computer does not make many mistakes, assuming the score has been properly entered into the MIDI file.

Better-quality sound systems use actual recordings of instruments playing specific notes to create a very high quality sound.

CurrentVersion\ModuleCompatibility

In CurrentVersion\ModuleCompatibility you will find entries much like in CurrentVersion\Compatibility. A flag value (a hexadecimal number, expressed as a string) tells Windows NT about the incompatibility, and allows Windows NT to modify the operating system's behavior to compensate for the application's incompatibility.

Each entry lists a module, and a compatibility flag. For example:

```
MYST = 0x8000
```

CurrentVersion\Network

In CurrentVersion\Network (only in HKEY_LOCAL_MACHINE) there are four sub-hives. There is some disagreement between what Microsoft documents should be in each sub-hive, and what experience shows is actually there.

Shared Parameters—Documented to hold the single data key named "Slow Mode," it is used to list which servers and domains will be accessed over a slow (typically dialup or modem), connection. Additional caching may be used on these connections, and some software compensates for slow connections.

SMAddOns—Contains a pointer to Server Manager extension .DLLs used to augment RAS.

UMAddOns—Contains a pointer to User Manager extension .DLLs used to augment RAS.

World Full Access Shared Parameters—Is documented to hold the data key ExpandLogonDomain, which contains a value (yes or no) that defines whether the Shared Directories list will be expanded by default in the Connect Network Drive dialog box. Experience shows that the data key named Slow Mode, used to list which servers and domains will be accessed over a slow connection (typically dialup or modem), is also present in this sub-hive, as is the data key RAS Mode.

CurrentVersion\NetworkCards

For each network card installed (remember, servers can have multiple cards) and for remote access (either RAS and/or DUN) there will be one entry in Current-Version\NetworkCards. Entries are named with numbers, beginning with 1. In each is a sub-hive called NetRules. An example, using a 3-Com 3C-590 PCI Ethernet card, is shown here:

1—Contains six keys, plus the sub-hive NetRules. The entries are:

```
Description : REG_SZ : 3Com Etherlink III Bus-Master Adapter
(3C590)
```

```
InstallDate : REG_DWORD : <a date, expressed as the number
of seconds since January 1, 1970>

Manufacturer : REG_SZ : 3Com

ProductName : REG_SZ : E159X

ServiceName : REG_SZ : E159x1

Title : REG_SZ : [1] 3Com Etherlink III PCI Buss-Master
Adapter (3C590)
```

The sub-hive 1\NetRules contains the following entries:

```
bindform : REG_SZ : "Ei59x1" yes yes container

class : REG_MULTI_SZ : Ei59xAdapter basic

InfName : REG_SZ : oemnad0.inf

InfOption : REG_SZ : 3C590

type : REG_SZ : ei59x ei59xAdapter
```

CurrentVersion\Perflib

Monitoring system performance is a critical part of managing a Windows NT Server. Performance Monitor allows graphing of between 500 and 800 different parameters. The number of parameters, which may be monitored, varies depending on system components, packages, and configurations.

CurrentVersion\Perflib\009—Is a sub-hive that contains the performance item names and descriptions. Each is listed in the Performance Monitor's Add to Chart dialog box. A REG_MULTI_SZ string contains the item name, and a second REG_MULTI_SZ string contains the item description.

Running Performance Monitor can be very instructional, especially for Windows NT Servers. With Performance Monitor it is possible to see which applications are "hogging" resources, making pigs of themselves, etc. Also, Performance Monitor is able to show usage for optional components such as Exchange Server, SQL Server, and IIS to name a few.

CurrentVersion\Ports

Ports (serial, printer, file, and network ports) are configured in the Current-Version\Ports sub-hive. For most ports, no entries are needed. For serial ports, the default settings (typically 9600, n, 8, 1 as set by the Control Panel's Ports applet) for some settings are stored here.

CurrentVersion\ProfileList

User profiles for each user who uses the computer are listed in the CurrentVersion\ProfileList sub-hive. A sub-hive is created for each user, named with the user's SID. Inside each of these sub-hives are five variables:

CentralProfile—Contains the location of the user's central profile, if the profile is not stored on the local machine. This location will be specified as a UNC path name.

Flags—Contains a DWORD value, typically 0x2.

ProfileImagePath—Contains the location of the users local profile. For users with a central profile, a local copy is kept in the eventuality that the central profile is unavailable.

Sid—Contains the user's SID, as a binary object.

State—Contains a DWORD value indicating the user's current state.

CurrentVersion\related.desc

Contains descriptions (if any) for items such as wave1 and wave2.

CurrentVersion\Time Zones

Windows NT is able to compensate for various time zones, and for DST (Daylight Saving Time) in those areas where DST is supported. Though technically there can only be 24 time zones (if we assumed even hours) actually there are several time zones where the time difference is only 30 minutes, and some time zones have different names depending on the country. Windows NT supports about 47 different time zones, spanning the entire world. These settings are used primarily by the Control Panel's Time and Date applet, or are passed to other applications as data.

Each time zone has information including the following:

Display—A string describing the time zone, such as `'Eastern Time (US & Canada)'`

Dlt—Contains a string describing the daylight time, such as `'Eastern Daylight Time'`

MapID—Contains a string containing coordinates for the world map displayed by the Control Panel's Date/Time Properties dialog box. Allows scrolling of the map, although unlike some versions of Windows 95, individual time zones are not highlighted.

TZI—Contains time zone information, a structure documented in KB article "Q115231."

CurrentVersion\Type 1 Installer

Adobe Illustrator Type1 fonts may be used with Windows NT by converting these fonts to TrueType fonts using the Control Panel's Fonts applet. Contained in the CurrentVersion\Type 1 Installer hive are three sub-hives:

Copyrights—Contains encoded copyright information for Type 1 fonts.

LastType1Sweep—Contains the time of the last Type 1 font sweep, if there was one.

Type 1 Fonts—Lists any Type 1 fonts installed.

CurrentVersion\Userinstallable.drivers

Any user-installed drivers are listed in the CurrentVersion\Userinstallable.drivers sub-hive. An example of a user-installed driver might be the Sound Blaster driver. This driver is not installed automatically by Windows NT.

The Sound Blaster driver, SNDBLST.DLL, is listed as the following:

```
Wave1 : REG_SZ : SNDBLST.DLL
```

CurrentVersion\Windows

In CurrentVersion\Windows (Remember we are still in the hive HKEY_LOCAL_ MACHINE\SOFTWARE\Microsoft\Windows NT.) are found five data keys.

Keys in this section are used to support both Windows NT as it currently runs (AppInit_DLLs), and for legacy application support (the other entries).

The keys in CurrentVersion\Windows are the following:

AppInit_DLLs—Tells Windows NT to attach the specified DLL (Dynamic Link Libraries) to all Windows applications. Loading any Windows application will, after the system has been restarted, load the specified DLLs. This feature is used for debugging and performance monitoring, for example.

Swapdisk—Is used to specify the location that Windows for MS-DOS in standard mode will swap non-Windows–based applications. Not terribly useful for Windows NT, and this entry is not specified in a default installation of Windows NT.

Spooler—Tells any applications that might check the win.ini file whether to use the spooler. A string (yes or no) tells the application whether the spooler will, or will not, be used.

DeviceNotSelectedTimeout—Tells the time, in seconds, that the system waits for an external device to be turned on. Specific printers may have their own values, set in the Printer Manager.

TransmissionRetryTimeout—Tells the System default time for the Print Manger to attempt to send characters to a printer. Specific printers may have their own values, set in the Printer Manager.

CurrentVersion\Winlogon

Ah, we've come to an important part of the registry. 'Bout time, you say?

WinLogon contains the configuration for the logon portion of Windows NT. Many logon defaults are stored in this sub-hive. Each important entry will be covered in detail. This first list shows those entries present on all Windows NT installations. A second list of optional components comes next.

AutoRestartShell—A value of 0x1 indicates that if the shell (usually Explorer) crashes, then Windows NT will automatically restart it. A value of 0x0 tells Windows NT to not restart the shell (the user will have to log off and log back on to restart the shell).

CachedLogonsCount—Contains the number of logons to be cached. If Windows NT is unable to find an authenticating PDC (Primary Domain

Controller), the information used in the cache will be used to authenticate the user's logon. The default value is 10 cached entries.

CachePrimaryDomain—Contains the name of the current domain. If no domain has been established, the value will be NEWDOMAIN.

DCache—Listed by some sources as not used by Windows NT 4, this entry does not contain any value in any system that I have examined.

DCacheUpdate—Listed by some sources as not used by Windows NT 4 this entry does have a value, which may be a date/time variable.

DebugServerCommand—The default value of this string is "no". Used with the internal Microsoft debug tool used to debug CSRSS.EXE, a Windows NT Executive subsystem used to perform graphics for text-mode applications.

DefaultDomainName—Contains the default domain name, usually the domain the user last logged onto. The default value is NEWDOMAIN.

DefaultUserName—Contains the name of the last user who logged on successfully. Displayed if DontDisplayLastUserName has a value of 0.

DontDisplayLastUserName—If this REG_STRING value is 0, the last user's name to successfully log on will automatically be displayed in the system logon dialog box. Setting this key to "1" will force users to enter both a user name, and a password to log on. If using automatic logon, make sure this key is set to "0".

LegalNoticeCaption—A dialog box may optionally be displayed prior to logging on a user. This key contains the dialog box's title. Typical usage of this dialog box is to advise users of organizational policy (such as a policy that a user may not install software without management approval). It is used with the key LegalNoticeText.

LegalNoticeText—A dialog box may optionally be displayed prior to logging on a user. This key contains the dialog box's text. Typical usage of this dialog box is to advise users of organizational policy (such as a policy that a user may not install software without management approval). Used with LegalNoticeTitle.

PowerdownAfterShutdown—For computers that support automatic power-down, Windows NT is able to perform power-down. Some computers (such as those with the ATX-style motherboards, or many notebooks) support automatic power-down. Set this string key to 1 to enable automatic power-down.

ReportBootOk—Is used to enable or disable automatic startup acceptance. This happens after the first successful logon. Use a value of 0 when using alternative settings in BootVerification or BootVerificationProgram.

Shell—The shell or user interface displayed by Windows NT once a user has successfully logged on is set with this key. The default value is Explorer .exe, though for users who insist, Program Manager, File Manager, or another shell program can be substituted. For users not using Explorer, entries in Shell might be: taskman, progman, wowexec. If the shell cannot be executed, then Windows NT will execute the programs found in the shell directory.

ShutdownWithoutLogon—The Windows NT logon dialog box has a button to shut down the system. For Windows NT Workstation users, this button is enabled, and for Windows NT Server users, this button is disabled. When ShutdownWithoutLogon is equal to 1, the button is enabled. Changing this button for a server can allow a non–logged on user to shut down the server—but then so will the power switch.

System—The default entry is lsass.exe, the Local Security Authority system. The lsass.exe program is the one that displays the logon dialog box (displayed when the user presses Ctrl+Alt+Del), and lsass.exe uses many of the entries in this sub-hive.

Userinit—This entry specifies the executable(s) that will be run when the user logs on. Typically, userinit.exe will start the shell program (see Shell, previously discussed), and nddeagnt.exe starts NetDDE (Network DDE).

VmApplet—Runs the Control Panel's System Properties applet.

There are a number of keys that don't exist by default in WinLogon. These keys may be added to modify the logon behavior of the system. The list below shows those WinLogon keys that I am aware of:

AllocateCDRoms—This data key is used to restrict access to the CDs in the CD-ROM drives to the currently logged on user only. Otherwise, if not restricted, CD-ROM contents and drives are accessible to all processes on the system.

AllocateFloppies—This data key is used to restrict access to the floppy disks in the floppy drives to the currently logged on user only. Otherwise, if not restricted, floppy contents and drives are accessible to all processes on the system.

AutoAdminLogon—When used with DefaultPassword and DefaultUser-Name, and when DontDisplayLastUserName is false (0), AutoAdmin-Logon logs on a user automatically without displaying the logon dialog box.

CacheLastUpdate—Is used internally by WinLogon and should not be modified.

CacheValid—Is used internally by WinLogon and should not be modified. The typical value is 1.

DcacheMinInterval—Contains a time, in seconds, which specifies the minimum time before the domain list cache is refreshed. Since refreshing the domain list cache may be a lengthy process, and as when a workstation is unlocked the cache is refreshed, it may be wise to change this value to a longer period of time. The range of this key is 120 to 86,400 seconds (that's one day).

DefaultPassword—Is used with AutoAdminLogon to provide password information for an automatic logon.

DeleteRoamingCache—To conserve disk space, locally cached profiles may be deleted when the user logs off using this key. Set DeleteRoaming-Cache to 1, and when the user logs off, their cached profile will be deleted. Computers used by a lot of users who have roaming profiles can create cached profiles that consume a substantial amount of disk space.

KeepRasConnections—Normally when a user logs off, all RAS sessions are canceled. By setting the key KeepRasConnections to 1, the system will keep these RAS sessions active through logons and logoffs. This is useful when there is a permanent connection to a WAN (such as the Internet) that must be maintained.

LogonPrompt—Placing a string (up to 255 characters) in this key allows displaying an additional message to users when they log on. This key is similar to the LegalNoticeText key in that it provides a method to advise all users who log on of something.

PasswordExpiryWarning—Provides a warning, in days, to users when their password is going to expire. The default is 14 days, though a shorter period—typically five days—is often used.

ProfileDlgTimeOut—Contains the amount of time, in seconds, that a user must respond to the choice of using a local or a roaming (remote) profile. The default time out period is 30 seconds.

RASForce—Is used to force checking of the Logon Using Dialup Networking checkbox in the logon dialog box. If RASForce is set to 1, then it is checked; if 0, then it is unchecked. This is meaningful only if RAS is installed, and the computer is a member of a domain.

RunLogonScriptSync—Windows NT is able to run both the logon script (if there is one) and the initialization of the Program Manager shell at the same time. If RunLogonScriptSync is set to 1, the logon script will finish before Windows NT will start to run Program Manager.

SlowLinkDetectEnabled—Determines if slow link detection is enabled. Used with roaming (remote) profiles, to help minimize the amount of time a user might have to wait before a local profile is used.

SlowLinkTimeOut—Sets the time (in milliseconds) that the system will wait for a slow connection when loading a user's profile.

Taskman—When the name of an alternative task manager is specified, Windows NT will use the specified program. The default task manager is taskmgr.exe.

Welcome—Allows specifying text that will be displayed in the title of the logon and lock/unlocked screens. Include a leading space in this text to separate your text from the default title, which is retained.

WARNING   Be careful of both DefaultPassword and AutoAdminLogon because their use can create security problems if misused. Do not auto-logon a user with special privileges, and resist the urge to auto-logon the system administrator for servers. The password stored in DefaultPassword is not encrypted, and AutoAdminLogon doesn't know or care who is sitting in front of the machine when it starts up and logs on the user.

Many of these settings may be modified with the System Policy Editor.

CurrentVersion\WOW

WOW, or Win-16 on Win-32, is a system where legacy 16-bit Windows applications may be run on newer 32-bit Windows NT systems. WOW emulates Windows 3.1 in standard (not enhanced) mode.

In CurrentVersion\WOW are eight sub-hives, as described next.

boot—In boot are drivers (communications, display, mouse, keyboard, etc.) used to emulate the Windows 3.1 mode.

boot.description—This sub-hive contains a description of the computer system (hardware) such as display, keyboard, and mouse. Also included is the language support requirement, English (American), for instance.

Compatibility—The concept of compatibility and applying minor patches to the operating system to allow legacy applications that are not directly compatible with the newer version, is an old concept. In this case compatibility is maintained between the 3.1 emulation and earlier versions of Windows.

keyboard—The keyboard driver DLL file, the keyboard type, and sub-type are located in this sub-hive.

NonWindowsApp—Could contain two entries, ScreenLines and SwapDisk. Generally this section is not used in WOW, unless these lines existed in the previous installation of Windows 3.x.

SetupPrograms—Contains a list of commonly known installation and setup programs.

standard—Contains entries from the standard mode settings of SYSTEM.INI. If Windows NT was installed as an upgrade for Windows 3.x, and SYSTEM .INI had modifications affecting standard mode (the mode that WOW runs in), these entries will be moved to this sub-hive.

WowFax—Contains only the sub-hive SupportedFaxDrivers.

WowFax\SupportedFaxDrivers—Contains the name of the supported fax drivers. The only entries, by default, are for WinFax, E-FAX, MAXFAXP, Quick Link II Fax, Quick Link Gold, and Procomm Plus.

ODBC

ODBC (Open DataBase Connectivity) is a system for Windows (both Windows NT and Windows 95/98) used by applications to share data stored in databases.

With ODBC, an application is able to open a database written by another application and read (and sometimes update) data in the database using a set of common API (Application Program Interface) calls.

ODBC, having been around for a while, originally worked using a setup file called ODBCINST.INI. Today that file's contents have been moved to the registry as a sub-hive under ODBC, called (guess!) ODBCINST.INI.

In the ODBCINST.INI sub-hive will be information about each installed driver. Drivers commonly installed include Access, Oracle, SQL Server, FoxPro, Dbase, and text files.

NOTE   To learn more about ODBC, I would recommend one of my programming books for database programmers, such as *Database Developer's Guide with Visual C++ 4* (Que, ISBN 0-672-30913-0). Though this book is out of print, copies are still available from some sources, and libraries.

Program Groups

In Program Groups are Program Manager's program groups. This sub-hive will be empty if this is a clean installation of Windows NT (not upgraded from Windows NT 3.*x*, for example.) However, if a user runs Program Manager and creates any groups, then these groups will appear in the Program Groups hive.

Also in Program Groups is a single key:

ConvertedToLinks—This key indicates that program groups were converted to Explorer links. If this key is equal to 0x0, or does not exist, Windows NT will attempt to convert program groups to links.

Secure

No documentation on the HKEY_LOCAL_MACHINE\Software\Secure sub-hive exists. No entries seem to exist in this hive.

Windows 3.1 Migration Status

The HKEY_LOCAL_MACHINE\SOFTWARE\Windows 3.1 Migration Status sub-hive is used to tell Windows NT that the system has (already) migrated the existing Windows 3.*x* INI and REG.DAT files to Windows NT 4. For users who are dual-booting Windows 3.*x* and Windows NT 4, deleting this key will allow a subsequent re-migration at any time should software installed under Windows 3.*x* be moved to Windows NT 4.

When the Windows 3.1 Migration Status hive is deleted, Windows NT will, on the next boot, prompt the user to migrate. Afterwards, Windows NT will re-create the key and sub-keys as needed.

Hints and Kinks from the Experts

In this chapter's Hints and Kinks, we cover a few hints on using the two registry editors.

How Do You Change the Default WinNT Install Path?   If you want to change where NT expects to find the NT CD, edit HKEY_LOCAL_MACHINE\ SOFTWARE\Microsoft\Windows NT\CurrentVersion\Sourcepath and HKEY_ LOCAL_MACHINE\SOFTWARE\Microsoft\Windows\CurrentVersion\Setup\ Sourcepath.

If your CD drive is D: and you are working with an Intel-based machine, the value should be D:\I386 and D:\ respectively.

(Courtesy of Jerold Schulman)

Why Does WinNT Run an Unknown Job at Login? If you can't find it in the startup groups, do the following:

1. Check HKEY_CURRENT_USER\Software\Microsoft\Windows NT\ CurrentVersion\Windows.

2. Load and/or run data keys.

3. Remove the offending program.

Here are other places where a program can be loaded at startup in NT:

- In the Startup folder for the current user and all users.

- In the registry, in the following places:

  - HKEY_LOCAL_MACHINE\Software\Microsoft\Windows\ CurrentVersion\Run

- HKEY_LOCAL_MACHINE\Software\Microsoft\Windows\CurrentVersion\RunOnce

- HKEY_LOCAL_MACHINE\Software\Microsoft\Windows\CurrentVersion\RunServices

- HKEY_LOCAL_MACHINE\Software\Microsoft\Windows\CurrentVersion\RunServicesOnce

- HKEY_CURRENT_USER\Software\Microsoft\Windows\CurrentVersion\RunOnce

- HKEY_CURRENT_USER\Software\Microsoft\Windows\CurrentVersion\RunServices

- HKEY_CURRENT_USER\Software\Microsoft\Windows\CurrentVersion\RunServicesOnce

(Courtesy of Peter D. Hipson)

How Do You Uninstall Apps Without Add/Remove Or an Uninstall Program?   If you want to uninstall an application that has no uninstall program and is not listed in the Add/Remove applet of Control Panel (or the uninstall doesn't work), just delete the directory files. Drill down HKEY_LOCAL_MACHINE\SOFTWARE\ and HKEY_CURRENT_USER\SOFTWARE. Locate the application's entries and delete them.

Use Explorer to remove the entries from the Start Menu in either %windir%\Profiles\All Users\Start Menu\Programs\ and/or %windir%\Profiles\YourId\Start Menu\Programs\.

If there is an entry in the Add/Remove list, edit HKEY_LOCAL_MACHINE\SOFTWARE\Microsoft\Windows\CurrentVersion\Uninstall. Locate the entry and delete it.

If the app has a service, edit HKEY_LOCAL_MACHINE\System\CurrentControlSet\Services. Scroll down until you locate the service, then delete it.

If this app starts automatically and there is no entry in the StartUp folder(s), use Regedt32 to edit HKEY_CURRENT_USER\Software\Microsoft\Windows NT\CurrentVersion\Windows. Load and run data keys. Next, remove the offending value and reboot.

(Courtesy of Jerold Schulman)

CHAPTER

NINETEEN

19

Introduction to HKEY_LOCAL_MACHINE\SYSTEM and HKEY_CURRENT_CONFIG

- Clone

- HKEY_CURRENT_CONFIG

- HKEY_CURRENT_CONFIG\Software

- HKEY_CURRENT_CONFIG\System

- Hints and kinks from the experts

The HKEY_LOCAL_MACHINE\SYSTEM hive contains information about the system and system configuration. HKEY_LOCAL_MACHINE\SYSTEM is subdivided into seven sub-hives in a typical installation:

Clone—This is the control set used to boot the computer. Because Clone doesn't really exist, at no time should you have any content in the Clone sub-hive, and the sub-hive should appear as inaccessible (grayed out) to you in RegEdt32.

ControlSet001—This is the primary ControlSet, which is used by default to boot Windows NT.

ControlSet002—The backup ControlSet, ControlSet002 is used to boot in the event that ControlSet001 has failed.

CurrentControlSet—This is the ControlSet that Windows NT has booted from. It is typically a mapping of ControlSet001 or ControlSet002.

DISK—These are the parameters that are managed by the Disk Administrator program. Included are CD-ROM mappings and other binary information.

Select—This is a small sub-hive that contains information about which ControlSet has been used to boot the computer.

Setup—This is a small sub-hive with information about the initial setup (installation) of Windows NT.

Some systems will have slightly different names for the two numbered ControlSets. Some computers won't have a ControlSet002. For example, your computer might only have the following:

- ControlSet001

- ControlSet003

It is also possible, but unlikely, that there may be more than two numbered ControlSets.

Each ControlSet consists of two sub-hives: Control and Services.

What Are Mapped Registry Sub-Hives?

Some registry sub-hives (ControlSets in particular) are often mapped to multiple names. The process is simple. Consider the mythical Fizbin Company, the proud maker of Fizzits. (You do use Fizzits, don't you?) Fizbin found that with a high-tech product such as Fizzits, it was necessary to have a high-tech company. They also wanted to make it seem as if they were more international than they really were.

However, Fizbin has a number of stodgy stockholders, most of whom have never seen or used a Fizzit, and have only a vague idea of what a Fizzit is or does. These stockholders were dead set against renaming the company for any reason.

A compromise was reached. The company would remain named the Fizbin Company. However, when doing business, they would use the name International Fizbin. Regardless of which name was used, it was the same company. A letter written to the president of International Fizbin would still be directed to the president of Fizbin Company—they had one company, it just had two names. So, when the president of Fizbin Company hired a new marketing manager, she was also automatically the marketing manager of International Fizbin, too.

Clone

Clone is the Clone sub-hive that is actually the ControlSet used to boot the computer. Clone's contents are then renamed to become other registry entries. The contents are not mapped because this process deletes them from Clone. At no time should you have any content in the Clone sub-hive, and the sub-hive should appear as inaccessible (grayed out) to you in RegEdt32. (RegEdit will display Clone, showing it as an empty sub-hive). Clone is created during kernel initialization and is used by the Service Controller (SCREG.EXE).

NOTE   Attempting to open Clone will always generate this error in RegEdit: "Cannot open Clone: Error while opening key." RegEdt32 will not display an error, but will not open Clone either.

CurrentControlSet

The CurrentControlSet is the ControlSet used to boot the computer. It is copied from ControlSet001, or one of the other numbered ControlSets if ControlSet001 failed to boot, and is the main ControlSet as a mapping of ControlSet001. Except for the contents of keys that may be different, ControlSet002 (or ControlSet003, if that is what your computer has) is identical to CurrentControlSet.

CurrentControlSet consists of four sub-hives:

Control—This sub-hive consists of information used to control how Windows NT operates. This information controls everything from boot-up, to networking parameters, to Windows, to WOW (Windows on Windows).

Enum—Information about hardware, hardware state, legacy devices, and so on is contained in this sub-hive.

Hardware Profiles—Windows NT may be configured to have one or more hardware profiles. The use of hardware profiles is most helpful when running Windows NT on portable computers, particularly those with docking stations.

Services—Services, such as support for hardware, are managed in this sub-hive. Services may be changed using the Control Panel's Services applet.

Control

The Control sub-hive has a number of data keys used for booting and system initialization. Control also contains about 30 sub-hives.

Control's data keys are:

CurrentUser—This entry is the name of the currently logged on user. Actually, this entry always has the default value USERNAME because Windows NT does not update it.

RegistrySizeLimit—If the registry size limit has been changed from the default value of 8MB, RegistrySizeLimit will contain the maximum registry size in bytes. Though users are only able to set the registry size limit in MB, Windows NT will store the value as a DWORD containing the maximum registry size in bytes.

SystemStartOptions—This entry contains options for start-up that are passed from firmware or the start-up contained in BOOT.INI. Options could include debugging information (such as a debugging port and the debugging port parameters) and perhaps information on the system root directory to be used.

WaitToKillService—This entry contains a time period in milliseconds to wait before killing a service when Windows NT is shutting down. If this value is too small, Windows NT may kill a service before it has finished writing its data; if too large, a hung service will delay Windows NT shutdown. It is best to leave the WaitToKillService value at its default value of 20000 unless you know you are having a problem.

BootVerificationProgram

One entry, ImagePath, is a data key with a string variable that is used in Boot-VerificationProgram. This key will contain the filename of the boot verification program. Enter an empty string, or delete this key if no boot verification program is used.

It is also necessary to set ReportBootOk to 1 in HKEY_LOCAL_MACHINE\ Software\Windows NT\CurrentVersion\WinLogon. If ReportBootOk is 0, automatic (default) start-up acceptance is disabled. This happens after the first logon that is successful. ReportBootOK is defined in Chapter 18, "Introduction to HKEY_LOCAL_MACHINE\SOFTWARE."

Class

The Class sub-hive contains a number of GUIDs (Globally Unique IDs), one each for the following:

- Display adapters
- Keyboard
- Sound, video, and game controllers
- Modem
- Mouse
- Network adapters
- Ports (COM & LPT)

- Printer
- SCSI controllers
- Other devices
- Tape drives

Each of these sub-hives contains a number of possible data keys:

(Default)—This is the default name as a string; for example, "Mouse." When using RegEdt32, the name (Default) is shown as <No Name>, in either case this is the same entry.

Class—This is the device's class as a single word with no embedded spaces. It is a string that is similar to the default entry.

Icon—This is an index to the object's icon.

Installer32—This is a string pointing to the program or system to install this type of device. Many devices are installed with the Control Panel.

Default Service—This is a string defining the default service, usually the same as the Class entry.

NoDisplayClass—This is a flag, 1 or 0, indicating whether or not to display the class.

LegacyInfOption—This is a string with information about legacy support. It is usually a string name for the device, similar to the Class entry.

Entries do not have all possible keys. The data keys (Default) and Class are universal to all sub-hives, while Icon and Installer32 are found in most (but not all) sub-hives.

ComputerName

ComputerName contains two sub-hives and no data keys:

> **ActiveComputerName**—This sub-hive includes a single data key, ComputerName, with a string containing the computer name.
>
> **ComputerName**—This sub-hive contains a single data key, Computer-Name, with a string containing the computer name.

Yes, both sub-hives contain exactly the same thing.

CrashControl

CrashControl brings to mind all kinds of marvelous things. However, Crash-Control is actually a basic function for Windows NT that is used when Windows NT fails at the system level. CrashControl options are generally set using the System applet in the Control Panel, which is shown in Figure 19.1.

FIGURE 19.1:

The System Properties
Startup/Shutdown tab

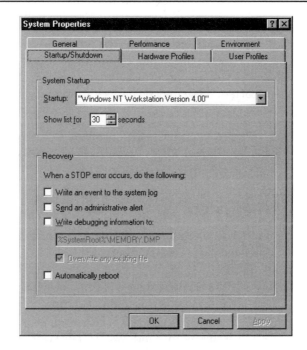

CrashControl options are set in the Recovery section at the bottom of the dialog box.

There are six data keys in CrashControl:

AutoReboot—The Automatically Reboot control state is set to zero if there is no automatic reboot after a STOP error.

CrashDumpEnabled—This is the Write Debugging Information To control state. It is set to zero if no dump is to be written after a STOP error.

DumpFile—This is the text control just under the Write Debugging Information To control. It is set to the name of the debugging file. This file will be as large as (or slightly larger than) the physical memory installed in the computer. Make sure the device to receive this file is large enough to hold the file.

LogEvent—This is the Write an Event to the System Log control state. It is set to zero if no event log entry is to be written after a STOP error.

Overwrite—This is the Overwrite Any Existing File control state. It is set to zero if there is no automatic reboot after a STOP error. If set, Windows NT will create a new debugging file with a new name.

SendAlert—This is the Send an Administrative Alert control state. It is set to zero if no administrative alert is to be sent after a STOP error.

Each of these may be best set from the System Properties applet in the Control Panel.

All data keys in CrashControl are REG_DWORD except for DumpFile, which is REG_EXPAND_SZ. Some references indicate that these data keys are REG_SZ; this information is incorrect.

FileSystem

Entries in FileSystem vary based on which file system(s) is installed. There are three data keys in FileSystem:

Win31FileSystem—When this key is set to 1, LFNs (Long File Names) will be disabled. This maintains compatibility with older operating systems, such as Windows 3.1. However, using this option may create compatibility issues with Windows NT 4 or Windows 95/98 and should be set only if absolutely necessary. Also, do not set this option except immediately after installing Windows NT. If you do, it may cause existing, installed applications to fail.

Win95TruncatedExtensions—The following behavior will take place depending on the setting of this option: Say you have two files, smith.htm and jones.html. If Win95TruncatedExtensions is equal to 1, the command DEL *.htm will delete both files. The command DEL *.html will delete only jones.html. When Win95TruncatedExtensions is equal to 0, the command DEL *.htm will delete only smith.htm. The command DEL *.html will delete only jones.html.

NtfsDisable8dot3NameCreation—If set to 1, Windows NT will not automatically generate standard 8.3 compatible filenames. Without 8.3 filenames, any legacy DOS or Windows 3.*x* applications lacking LFN support will fail. They will not be able to open or otherwise use any file that has an LFN unless the file is renamed to a valid 8.3 filename.

NOTE   Note that some applications, including Microsoft Office 97, will not even install if NtfsDisable8dot3NameCreation is set.

WARNING   As mentioned, be careful about changing these options. Once installed, some systems do not expect that the state of the FileSystem data keys will change, or that support for LFNs will change, either. This is especially true when changing from allowing LFNs to not allowing them.

GraphicsDrivers

By default, the GraphicsDrivers sub-hive contains one sub-hive called DCI (Display Control Interface). This standard sub-hive contains a data key named Timeout, which has a default value of 7.

NOTE   Microsoft has dropped DCI support for Windows NT 4.

As well, there is one optional entry in GraphicsDrivers: DisableUSWC. With certain higher-performance video cards, Uncached Speculative Write Combining (USWC) memory is uncached. As well, certain computers have a memory conflict with USWC that may cause the user interface to fail to respond after certain drag-and-drop operations. The DisableUSWC data key does not have a value; its presence in the registry is sufficient to turn off USWC. This type of error is rare.

GroupOrderList

Each service in HKEY_LOCAL_MACHINE\System\CurrentControlSet\Services is listed in GroupOrderList along with a binary value indicating the order in which the group is to be loaded at system start-up time. Systems typically have the following groups:

- Base
- Extended base
- Filter
- Keyboard Class
- Keyboard Port
- Ndis
- Parallel arbitrator
- Pointer Class
- Pointer Port
- Primary Disk
- SCSI CDROM Class
- SCSI Class
- SCSI miniport
- SpoolerGroup
- System Bus Extender
- Video
- Video Init
- Video Save

Hivelist

Hivelist contains the following data keys listing registry hives and their source files. \REGISTRY\MACHINE\HARDWARE does not have a source file because this hive is created dynamically at boot time.

- \REGISTRY\MACHINE\HARDWARE =

- \REGISTRY\MACHINE\SECURITY = \Device\Harddisk0\Partition1\WINNTWS\System32\Config\SECURITY

- \REGISTRY\MACHINE\SOFTWARE = \Device\Harddisk0\Partition1\WINNTWS\System32\Config\SOFTWARE

- \REGISTRY\MACHINE\SYSTEM = \Device\Harddisk0\Partition1\WINNTWS\System32\Config\SYSTEM

- \REGISTRY\MACHINE\SAM = \Device\Harddisk0\Partition1\WINNTWS\System32\Config\SAM

- \REGISTRY\USER\.DEFAULT = \Device\Harddisk0\Partition1\WINNTWS\System32\Config\DEFAULT

- \REGISTRY\USER\S-1-5-21-45749729-16073390-2133884337-500 = \Device\Harddisk0\Partition1\WINNTWS\Profiles\Administrator.000\ntuser.dat

Here is some further information about the preceding names:

\REGISTRY—Is the name for the registry itself.

\MACHINE—Is HKEY_LOCAL_MACHINE.

\USER—Is HKEY_USERS.

As well, HKEY_DYN_DATA has no source file, nor does it have any contents. HKEY_CURRENT_CONFIG is dynamically created at boot time. HKEY_CLASSES_ROOT is created from other registry entries at boot time. HKEY_CURRENT_USER is created when a user logs on.

IDConfigDB

The IDConfigDB hive is the identification for the current configuration. This hive contains four data keys:

CurrentConfig—Indicates which ControlSet is being used.

IsPortable—A value of 1 indicates that this is a portable computer.

PropertyProviders—This data key specifies the name of the DLL file used to display property sheets. The default is profext.dll.

UserWaitInterval—This data key specifies the period of time a user waits. In the Hardware Profile/Configuration Recovery menu, the default choice will be taken if the user waits the time specified in UserWaitInterval. The value is specified in seconds, the default value is 30 seconds.

IDConfigDB also contains the hardware profiles in the Hardware Profiles sub-hive.

The Windows NT installation process will create one configuration for the user. This default configuration is called "Original Configuration." Any additional configurations that users create will also appear in the Hardware Profiles sub-hive.

See the Hardware Profiles tab in the System applet for the Control Panel to get more information about setting up multiple hardware profiles.

Keyboard Layout

There are two sub-hives in Keyboard Layout, each dealing with supporting MS-DOS applications to use languages other than US English:

DosKeybCodes—Contains a list of keyboard layouts and a two-letter (MS-DOS compatible) country code.

DosKeybIDs—Contains a list of keyboard layouts and keyboard ID values.

NOTE   See the Knowledge Base article "Q117850", titled "MS-DOS 6.22 COUNTRY.TXT File," for more information about support for MS-DOS applications.

Keyboard Layouts

Keyboard Layouts contains sub-hives for each possible keyboard layout that Windows NT supports for Windows applications. (The information for DOS application keyboard layout is under the "KeyboardLayout" section of this chapter.) Each layout sub-hive contains two entries:

Layout File—The name of the DLL file that manages the keyboard using that character set, for example, the Icelandic keyboard layout DLL file is named kbdic.dll.

Layout Text—A string identifying the keyboard layout, for example, for Iceland, the string is "Icelandic."

It is possible, though difficult, to create custom keyboard layouts.

Support is available to Windows NT users who wish to use the Dvorak keyboard layouts. Use the Regional Settings applet in the Control Panel to select either the Dvorak right- or left-hand layout. No special hardware is required, though the markings on the standard keyboard will be incorrect. This is because the Dvorak keyboard has a different keyboard layout where letters are arranged based on how often they are used.

LSA

LSA, the Local Security Authority, is used to locally validate security for user rights, secret objects, and trusted domain objects. LSA uses the msv1_0 DLL file to do the actual validation of security. Within the LSA hive is a sub-hive called msv1_0. This sub-hive contains items for msv1_0.

WARNING   Microsoft strongly recommends that you do not touch anything in the LSA sub-hive. An incorrect entry or change could render the system in a state where no users are able to log on, and a complete restoration of the system would be necessary.

MediaProperties

MediaProperties is a hive used primarily to describe MIDI properties. Media-Properties contains sub-hives to describe any MIDI schemes (custom configurations in the Control Panel Multimedia Properties applet) that a user has created.

MediaResources

MediaResources is a hive used to describe the resources available for multimedia (specifically for MIDI) on the computer.

Two sub-hives exist in this section:

MIDI—Contains sub-hives for each physical and virtual device that is installed. The device sub-hives contain definitions for instruments that the user has defined.

NonGeneralMIDIDriverList—Resource definitions (including instrumentation) for users with non-general type MIDI hardware are defined here.

NetworkProvider

The NetworkProvider hive supplies a home for the settings that are made in the Network applet of the Control Panel. These settings are in the Network Access Order tab, which is only visible if your computer is connected to two or more networks. The settings are controlled by a list box that allows the user to move up or down a specific network provider.

If using RAS (Remote Access Service), there is an option to disable automatic (ghosted) restoration of network connections at logon. Most users prefer to have connections restored automatically at logon. If RAS is not installed, enable ghosted connections by putting in the RestoreConnection data key in the NetworkProvider hive. This REG_DWORD data key may contain either a 0x1 or a 0x0 value. If the value is 0x0, Windows NT will ghost connections.

Active   The Active sub-hive, though documented as a possible sub-hive, has not been observed in any Windows NT 4 installations.

Order   Order indicates the specific order of network providers as shown in the Network Access Order tab of the Control Panel's Network applet. This list is a comma-separated set of names. The default for a standard Microsoft Networking network is the single name LanmanWorkstation. This is applicable regardless of whether the computer is a server or a workstation. There is one data key in Order: ProviderOrder. It is a REG_SZ string containing a comma-separated list of providers. The default value is LanmanWorkstation

ShortName   The ShortName sub-hive, though documented as a possible sub-hive, has not been observed in any Windows NT 4 installations.

NLS

The NLS (National Language Support) functionality of Windows NT is defined in the NLS hive. There are three possible sub-hives in NLS. However, the OEM-Locale sub-hive is not present in all installations of Windows NT; it is used when an OEM has customized Windows NT for a specific locale.

CodePage   CodePage contains a series of data keys. Each key is named to match a code page ID with a REG_SZ value equal to the filename for that code page. For code pages with no supporting file, the data key's value will be an empty string.

CodePage also includes the following additional data keys:

ACP—The active (or default) code page used by Windows NT

MACCP—The Macintosh active code page

OEMCP—The OEM (Original Equipment Manufacturer) code page to translate ANSI characters

OEMHAL—The OEM display of extended characters at a command prompt

Language　The Language sub-hive contains entries used to identify files that support different languages. Each data key is named with the ID for a language with a REG_SZ data value equal to the name of the file to support that language. If the language is not supported (the support files have not been installed), the data key's value will be an empty string.

OEMLocale　Not normally present on systems, the OEMLocale sub-hive is added by OEMs to support systems in their specific locale. Entries in OEMLocale are similar to the CodePage sub-hive.

OEMLocale contains a series of data keys. Each key is named to match a code page ID with a REG_SZ value equal to the filename for that code page. For code pages with no supporting file, the data key's value will be an empty string.

NOTE　The OEMLocale sub-hive is only checked if a specific locale ID is not found in the default locale file (LOCALE.NLS).

Print

The Print hive contains all the information accessed by Windows NT when a printer is being used. In addition to the sub-hives documented next, there are also a few data keys in the Print hive:

BeepEnabled—Enables or disables a beep when a printer error is detected. Set to 0x1 to turn on beeps.

MajorVersion—The version number's high digit(s); for a product with the version of 4.3, the major version would be 4.

MinorVersion—The version number's low digit(s); for a product with the version of 4.3, the minor version would be 3.

NoRemotePrinterDrivers—Contains the name of print drivers that cannot be used with remote connections. This data key typically has "Windows NT Fax Driver" as a value.

PortThreadPriority—The Windows NT kernel priority for the printer driver. A value of 0 indicates normal priority; –1 indicates lower than normal priority; and 1 indicates a higher than normal priority.

PriorityClass—Used to set the priority class for the print spooler, a value of 0 (or no value) indicates a default priority class. The default priority class is 7 for workstations and 9 for servers. Coding any other value will be translated to the priority class for servers, 9.

SchedulerThreadPriority—Sets the priority for the scheduler. Setting SchedulerThreadPriority to 1 sets the priority to be above normal; 0 sets the priority to normal; and –1 (0xFFFFFFFF) sets the priority to be below normal.

The Print hive contains five sub-hives, which are discussed next.

Environments   The Environments hive contains sub-hives for each possible platform. Each platform hive contains two sub-hives: Drivers and Print Processors. The platform sub-hives are:

Windows 4.0—This sub-hive is used for Windows 95 drivers.

Windows NT Alpha_AXP—This sub-hive provides support for Digital Alpha systems.

Windows NT PowerPC—This sub-hive provides support for PowerPC systems.

Windows NT R4000—This sub-hive provides support for the MIPS R4000 systems.

Windows NT x86—This sub-hive provides support for Intel-based systems.

Each platform sub-hive contains:

Drivers—Contains the driver information for each print driver that is installed. Each installed printer will be installed in a separate sub-hive that is named for the printer. Printer Driver configuration sub-hives are contained in a sub-hive named Version-0, for Windows NT 3.1; Version-1, for Windows NT 3.5; and Version-2, for Windows NT 4. Each printer driver sub-hive contains the following data keys:

Configuration file—The DLL file that holds the printer configuration

Data file—The PPD or DLL file containing printer data

Datatype—The data type, such as RAW; most printers leave this field blank.

Dependent files—Any files that the printer driver is dependent on

Driver—The name of the printer driver DLL file

Help File—The name of the printer driver help file

Monitor—The print processor will direct its output to a Print Monitor if one is defined

Version—The printer driver version number. It is a value of 0 for Windows NT 3.1, 1 for Windows NT 3.5, and 2 for Windows NT 4.

Print Processors—There are one or more print processors with Windows NT. The default processor is WinPrint (winprint.dll).

Forms   By default, forms that are used when printing documents are defined in the Forms sub-hive. However, a user may also specify a custom form. In most installations of Windows NT, the following forms are defined:

- A2 420.0 x 594.0 mm
- B3 364.0 x 515.0 mm
- Foolscap 13.50 x 17.00in
- #10 Env. 9.50 x 4.12 in
- DL Env. 220.0 x 110.0 mm
- Fanfold 9.50 x 11.00 in
- Fanfold 12.00 x 8.50 in
- Fanfold 14.50 x 11.00 in

- Letter+ 9.00 x 13.30 in
- A4+ 223.5 x 355.6 mm

Custom forms may be created using the Printers applet in the Control Panel. To do this, follow these steps:

1. Select File ➤ Server Properties. The Forms tab includes a button to create a new form.
2. Click Create a New Form.
3. Change the name in Form Description.
4. Change the sizes and margins to match your form.
5. Save the form.

NOTE   The Metric/English Units control is for display—all forms may be displayed in either metric or English units, subject to the user's preferences.

Monitors   No, not that big thing on your desk. A monitor for printing is a program that receives messages from a networked printer and displays information to the user. The printer may be either locally connected to a computer, or connected directly to the network with a network card that is installed inside the printer. When a printer is connected to the network, the management of the printer is a bit more difficult. In this case, a Printer Monitor program is used to receive messages from the printer and to process these messages for the user.

Each type of networked printer varies and there are different monitors designed to work with each printer. Monitors exist for Hewlett Packard, Lexmark, Digital, and other network printers.

There are also monitors for locally connected printers. These monitors are more generic in nature—they work with any printer connected to the printer port. Default monitors include PJL (Printer Job Language) and Local Port.

Printers   Each printer installed is given a sub-hive under the Printer hive. The printer's hive name is the same as the printer's description; by default this is also the system name for the printer.

A printer's sub-hive is comprised of one sub-hive and the following data keys:

Attributes—The printer attributes, for example, those set in the Scheduling tab of the printer's property page

ChangeID—This data key is a funny number that is not documented anywhere. Every time you change something on the printer, ChangeID changes, too. It is used to track changes.

Datatype—The type of data that is passed to the printer, such as RAW

Default DevMode—The printer's default DevMode structure

Default Priority—The default priority

Description—A printer description provided by the user

DnsTimeout—The amount of time waited for a DNS timeout, in milliseconds, the default is 15 seconds.

Location—User-supplied text describing the printer's location

Name—The name of the printer

Parameters—Any printer parameters

Port—The port the printer is connected to

Print Processor—The print processor; WinPrint is the default.

Printer Driver—The DLL file used to drive the printer

Priority—The printer's priority

Security—Security attributes

Separator File—The name of the job separator file

Share Name—The name used to share the printer if it is shared

SpoolDirectory—The directory used to spool, if not the default spool directory

StartTime—This data key set the earliest time the printer is available (see UntilTime). If StartTime = UntilTime = 0, the printer is always available.

Status—The current printer status

TotalBytes—The total number of bytes in the print queue

TotalJobs—The total number of jobs in the print queue

TotalPages—The total pages to be printed

txTimeout—The time in milliseconds until the printer times out, the default is 45 seconds.

UntilTime—The latest time the printer is available (see StartTime), for example, the time set in the Scheduling tab of the printer's property page

The only sub-hive, PrinterDriverData, has information about the printer's paper sources, permissions, and more. Information in PrinterDriverData is specific to each driver.

Providers   The default provider for printing in Windows NT networking is LanMan Print Services. Another provider is Microsoft Windows Network. However, specifying this provider may cause problems in some installations.

There are three data keys in the Providers hive:

EventLog—This data key is a DWORD value that specifies the event log status.

NetPopup—This data key is a DWORD value that specifies the Net Pop-up services status. It is set to 1 to display a pop-up message for remote print jobs.

Order—This data key is a REG_MULTI_SZ multiple string that specifies the order of providers. Generally, Windows NT networks should list Lan-Man Print Services first in the Order key. If you find that you are unable to browse printers, check the Order key and ensure that it contains only Lan-Man Print Services and not Microsoft Windows Network.

A sub-hive for each provider will be under the Providers hive; we will use the LanMan Print Services as an example. The following entries may be present for each provider:

DisplayName—This entry is a string that contains the name of the provider. For our example, it is "LanMan Print Services."

Name—This entry is a string that contains the name of the driver DLL. For our example, it is win32spl.dll.

LoadTrustedDrivers—This is an optional data key that is a DWORD value. If it is set to 1, drivers will not be installed from a remote print server, but may only be taken from the path specified in TrustedDriver-Path.

TrustedDriverPath—This is an optional data key that is a string containing the path to load trusted print drivers from. Both this data key and LoadTrustedDrivers = 1 must be specified to restrict the loading of drivers.

A sub-hive under the LanMan Print Services hive named Servers may exist. This sub-hive may contain the AddPrinterDrivers data key. This data key is a DWORD value that is used to specify who is allowed to add printer drivers using the Printer applet in the Control Panel. When set to 1, only administrators and print operators (if on a server) or power users (if on a workstation) may add printer drivers.

PriorityControl

The PriorityControl hive contains a single data key: Win32PrioritySeparation. It is a DWORD value containing a value between 0 and 2. The Performance tab of the System applet in the Control Panel includes a section called Application Performance. A slider control labeled "Boost" controls the value contained in in32Priority-Separation. When this control is at the left end (labeled "None"), this key is set to 0; when the control is to the right, the key is set to 2.

WARNING   Microsoft cautions that the only way to successfully set Win32PrioritySeparation is to use the System applet in the Control Panel. Do not attempt to change this key manually.

ProductOptions

ProductOptions has a single data key, which describes the type of product that is installed; Windows NT has several different versions:

ProductType—Contains a string with one of the following values:

LANMANNT—A Windows NT Advanced Server (3.1) is running, or a Windows NT 4 PDC or BDC configuration.

SERVERNT—Windows NT Server 3.5 or later is running in stand-alone (not a domain) mode.

WINNT—Windows NT Workstation is running.

SecurePipeServers

Pipes—Long, hollow objects used to transport fluid materials. Or, a virtual connection between two computers using a network. A secure pipe is a virtual pipe that has encryption and other security features to enhance the security of data being moved in the pipe.

Each item in SecurePipeServers has an entry in the form of a sub-hive, such as SecurePipeServers\winreg, and this entry will have unique entries that the pipe server uses.

Most Windows NT systems have a single entry in the registry for SecurePipe-Servers. The Windows NT installation includes entries for winreg, the remote Windows registry editing facility. The winreg sub-hive contains one data key and one sub-hive. The data key, named Description, has the value Registry Server.

The winreg\AllowedPaths sub-hive contains a single data key, Machine. Machine is A REG_MULTI_SZ string containing the registry hives that may be remotely edited using one of the registry editors. This string can be modified to add or remove hives that you wish to edit remotely. The default values in the Machine key are:

- System\CurrentControlSet\Control\ProductOptions
- System\CurrentControlSet\Control\Print\Printers
- System\CurrentControlSet\Services\Eventlog
- Software\Microsoft\Windows NT\CurrentVersion
- System\CurrentControlSet\Services\Replicator

SecurityProviders

Security and privacy are important buzzwords in cyberspace today. Governments are working hard at limiting privacy and essentially security, too. It is also the keen intent of users to keep what is private to them private from the prying eyes of their governments. This all makes security a hot, hot topic.

Windows NT includes support for security in the SecurityProviders sub-hive. SecurityProviders contains the five sub-hives, discussed next.

NOTE The abbreviation, CA, in the entries in SecurityProviders doesn't stand for California, it stands for Certificate Authority.

CertificationAuthorities The CertificationAuthorities sub-hive contains the names of a number of different organizations that issue certificates and their products. A typical installation might contain the following values:

- AT&T Certificate Services
- AT&T Directory Services
- AT&T Prototype Research CA
- GTE Cybertrust ROOT
- internetMCI Mall
- Keywitness Canada Inc.
- Thawte Premium Server CA
- Thawte Server CA
- Verisign Class 1 Public Primary CA
- Verisign Class 2 Public Primary CA
- Verisign Class 3 Public Primary CA
- Verisign Class 4 Public Primary CA
- Verisign/RSA Commercial
- Verisign/RSA Secure Server

Ciphers   A *cipher* is a code or key that is used to encrypt or encode an object. Generally, the term "ciphers" includes the methodology in addition to the actual key. The Ciphers sub-hive contains a number of cipher technologies. Some are more secure than others, though all are satisfactory for most routine work. Ciphers that may be supported in Windows NT include the following:

- DES 40/56
- DES 56/56
- NULL
- RC2 128/128
- RC2 40/128
- RC4 128/128
- RC4 40/128
- RC4 64/128
- Skipjack
- Triple DES 168/168

Hashes   *Hashes* are a form of ciphers. Typically thought of as weak encryption, hashes can serve well where small amounts of data are transmitted; some hash algorithms are quite secure. Windows NT includes the ability to support the following hashes:

- MD5
- SHA

KeyExchangeAlgorithms   *Key exchange* is the process where users are able to pass keys between themselves. An encryption algorithm, called a *public-key algorithm*, is one where the key may be sent using plain text. This is possible because the key used to encrypt the message is not the same key used to decrypt it. The encryption key, called the *public key*, is given out to everyone who is to send you encrypted messages. The decryption key, used by you to read your encrypted messages, is kept secure.

WARNING Improperly designed public-key encryption schemes have a great potential for back-door type flaws. A *back door* is a way to decrypt a message without actually having the decryption (or private) key. Many governments argue that they should have the ability to decrypt messages to promote law and order. However, that policy has yet to be shown valid.

KeyExchangeAlgorithms supported by Windows NT include the following:

- Diffie-Hellman
- Fortezza
- PKCS

Protocols   *Protocols* are the methodologies used to transmit information. Windows NT supports five protocols. The most common protocol that computer users are aware of is SSL (Secure Sockets Layer), which is used to transmit information over TCP/IP networks, such as the Internet.

Secure protocols that Windows NT may support include the following:

- Protocols\Multi-Protocol Unified Hello
- Protocols\PCT 1.0
- Protocols\SSL 2.0
- Protocols\SSL 3.0
- Protocols\TLS 1.0

ServiceGroupOrder

The ServiceGroupOrder sub-hive has a single data key named "List". The List data key includes a REG_MULTI_SZ string containing the names, in load order, for the services.

When Windows NT starts services, it will start them in the order that they are listed in ServiceGroupOrder\List. Services within each group are then started in accordance with the values contained in the CurrentControlSet\Control\ GroupOrderList hive.

Drivers are loaded into memory in the order specified in ServiceGroupOrder\List, with the default for most servers being the following:

- System Bus Extender
- SCSI miniport
- port
- Primary disk
- SCSI class
- SCSI CDROM class
- filter
- boot file system
- Base
- Pointer Port
- Keyboard Port
- Pointer Class
- Keyboard Class
- Video Init
- Video
- Video Save
- file system
- Event log
- Streams Drivers
- PNP_TDI
- NDIS
- NDISWAN
- TDI
- NetBIOSGroup
- SpoolerGroup
- NetDDEGroup

- Parallel arbitrator

- extended base

- RemoteValidation

- PCI Configuration

Notice that service groups may be different in different computers. Don't expect your system to have entries in the same order, or even to always have the same entries.

NOTE   Generally, it would not be prudent to change the load order for services. Some services expect that other services are already loaded.

ServiceProvider

The ServiceProvider sub-hive is used to work with the Winsock (Windows Sockets) RNR (Resolution and Registration) Service APIs. ServiceProvider contains sub-hives including Order and ServiceTypes. The entries in this sub-hive are pointers to other registry hives and data keys.

NOTE   Microsoft recommends that these entries not be changed manually.

The sub-hive ServiceProvider\Order contains two data keys:

> **ExcludedProviders**—This data key is a REG_MULTI_SZ string consisting of numbers indicating service providers. Most Windows NT systems do not have any entries in this list. To add an excluded provider, enter the service provider's identifier from Table 19.1.

TABLE 19.1: Service Providers and Their Identifiers

Service Provider	Identifier
NS_SAP	1
NS_NDS	2
NS_TCPIP_LOCAL	10

Continued on next page

TABLE 19.1 CONTINUED: Service Providers and Their Identifiers

Service Provider	Identifier
NS_TCPIP_HOSTS	11
NS_DNS	12
NS_NETBT	13
NS_WINS	14
NS_NBP	20
NS_MS	30
NS_STDA	31
NS_CAIRO	32
NS_X500	40
NS_NIS	41

ProviderOrder—This data key is a REG_MULTI_SZ data key containing zero, one, or more entries. The number of entries varies with the number of installed protocols. Systems might have Tcpip, NwlnkIpx, or other entries in this data key. These entries correspond to CurrentControlSet\ Services entries.

A second sub-hive under ServiceProvider is ServiceTypes. This sub-hive is used with IIS (Internet Information Server). ServiceTypes typically contains four sub-hives; there may be fewer or more, depending on what IIS components you have installed:

GOPHERSVC—The Gopher service is configured in this sub-hive. Information includes the GUID for the handler for Gopher requests and the TCP/IP port number (70 by default).

Microsoft Internet Information Server—Microsoft's IIS is capable of serving remotely as a service. That is, a user is able to remotely administer IIS.

MSFTPCVC—The FTP service is configured in this sub-hive. The information contained here includes the GUID for the handler for FTP requests and the TCP/IP port number (21 by default).

W3SVC—The Web (WWW) service is configured in this sub-hive. The information contained here includes the GUID for the handler for Web requests and the TCP/IP port number (80 by default).

Users may modify the TCP ports for these services; see the Windows NT Server Resource Kit for more information. When modifying ports, use a port number greater than 1023 to avoid conflict with any existing assigned ports.

Session Manager

Session Manager is a complex sub-hive used to manage the user's session and basic Windows NT start-up. Session Manager contains a number of data keys and sub-hives.

The data keys in Session Manager are relatively constant between different installations of Windows NT. These data keys are:

BootExecute—Specifies what programs are run at start-up. The default is autocheck autochk *. Autochk is the Auto Check Utility that is included with Windows NT.

CriticalSectionTimeout—Specifies the time, in seconds, to wait for critical sections to time out. Since Windows NT (retail product) does not wait for critical sections to time out, the default value is about 30 days. Anyone care to wait that long? Not me!

EnableMCA—MCA (Machine Check Architecture) is used in some systems. This key tells if MCA is enabled or not. The default value is set to be enabled. Some Pentium Pro processors support MCA.

EnableMCE—MCE (Machine Check Exception) is supported by some Pentium processors. Support for MCE is turned off by default.

ExcludeFromKnownDlls—Windows NT will use entries in the KnownDLLs hive to search for DLLs when loading them. ExcludeFrom-KnownDlls is used to exclude a DLL from the KnownDLLs search.

GlobalFlag—The GlobalFlag key controls various Windows NT internal operations using a bitmapped flag. Table 19.2 shows some common GlobalFlag bit values. GFLAG.EXE (see Figure 19.2) is a useful tool to set GlobalFlag. It is a component of the Windows NT Server Resource Kit Supplement 2.

FIGURE 19.2:

The GFLAGS program makes it easy to set the GlobalFlag key. Just click and select a value to be set.

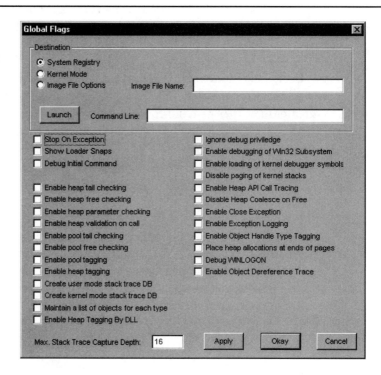

> **NOTE**
>
> To disable the OS/2 subsystem in earlier versions of Windows NT, the user could change the value contained in GlobalFlag to 20100000. However, Windows NT 4 does not support this.

TABLE 19.2: GlobalFlag Bit Values

Value (bit)	Description
0x00000001	Stop when there is an exception.
0x00000002	Show loader snaps.
0x00000004	Debug initial command.
0x00000008	Stop on hung GUI.
0x00000010	Enable heap tail check.

Continued on next page

TABLE 19.2 CONTINUED: GlobalFlag Bit Values

Value (bit)	Description
0x00000020	Enable heap free check.
0x00000040	Check heap validate parameters.
0x00000080	Validate all heap allocations.
0x00000100	Enable pool tail check.
0x00000200	Enable pool free check.
0x00000400	Set up memory tagging.
0x00000800	Enable heap tagging.
0x00001000	Create User mode stack trace DB.
0x00002000	Create Kernel mode stack trace DB.
0x00004000	Maintain a list of objects for each type.
0x00008000	Enable heap tags by DLL.
0x00010000	Ignore debug privilege.
0x00020000	Enable csrdebug.
0x00040000	Enable kernel debug symbol loading.
0x00080000	Disable page kernel stacks.
0x00100000	Enable heap call tracing.
0x00200000	Enable heap coalescing.

HeapDeCommitFreeBlockThreshold—This key has a default of zero.

HeapDeCommitTotalFreeThreshold—This key has a default of zero.

HeapSegmentCommit—This key has a default of zero.

HeapSegmentReserve—This key has a default of zero.

LicensedProcessors—This key specifies the maximum number of processors that are allowed. The standard retail version of Windows NT allows a maximum of four processors in a multiprocessor server environment and two processors in a workstation environment.

ObjectDirectories—This key contains a list of object directories to create during start-up.

ProcessorControl—This key is an undocumented DWORD variable. The default value is 0x2.

ProtectionMode—When this key's value is set to 1, security is increased on shared base objects. The default of 0 reflects a weaker security level.

NOTE   For more information on making Windows NT secure, see `http://spider.osfl .disa.mil/dii/aog twg/twg/ntsig/ntdoc diicoe dec5 DISA.htm`.

RegisteredProcessors—This key specifies the number of processors allowed. The standard retail version of Windows NT allows a maximum of four processors in a multiprocessor server environment and two processors in a workstation environment.

ResourceTimeoutCount—This key specifies the number of four-second ticks allowed before a resource will time out. Windows NT does not normally time out on resources, and the default value is 30 days.

There are also a number of sub-hives in Session Manager. These are discussed next.

AppPatches   The sub-hive AppPatches contains patches for a number of applications. Typical installations include patches for the following:

- CWD
- Myst
- PalEd40
- USA
- VB
- VB 4

DOS Devices The DOS Devices sub-hive contains symbolic names and their corresponding logical names. Most systems have the following default entries in DOS Devices:

- `advapi32 = advapi32.dll`

- `comdlg32 = comdlg32.dll`

- `crtdll = crtdll.dll`

- `DllDirectory = %SystemRoot%\System32`

- `gdi32 = gdi32.dll`

- `kernel32 = kernel32.dll`

- `lz32 = lz32.dll`

- `olecli32 = olecli32.dll`

- `olesvr32 = olesvr32.dll`

- `rpcrt4 = rpcrt4.dll`

- `shell32 = shell32.dll`

- `user32 = user32.dll`

- `version = version.dll`

Memory Management Memory Management controls the system's virtual memory, paging files, and so on.

The paging file parameters should be defined by using the System icon in the Control Panel and choosing the Virtual Memory button. The paging file parameters should be defined by using the System icon in the Control Panel and choosing the Virtual Memory button. Other memory management entries include the following:

> **ClearPageFileAtShutdown**—If set to a value of 1, the paging file's contents (not the file, just its contents) will be cleared. This option is useful for Windows NT installations that require a high degree of security. The default of 0 causes the paging file's contents to be left on the disk.

> **DisablePagingExecutive**—Setting this key to 1 will disable Windows NT's automatic paging system. The default of 0 allows the paging executive to

run normally. Do not change this option unless you understand exactly what the effects of disabling paging are.

IoPageLockLimit—This key specifies the number of bytes that may be locked for an I/O operation. The default is 0, which is equal to 512K.

LargeSystemCache—This key specifies that the system will favor the system cache working set rather than the processes working set. Server installations typically set this to 1, while workstations will use a 0 for this value.

NonPagedPoolQuota—The maximum space that may be allocated by one process in a non-paged pool.

NonPagedPoolSize—The non-paged pool size. The default value of –0 indicates a default size based on the system's physical memory size. The maximum value allowed is 80 percent of the physical memory size.

PagedPoolQuota—The maximum space that may be allocated by one process in a paged pool.

PagedPoolSize—The paged pool size. The default value of 0 specifies that the value will be 32MB. This value affects the maximum registry size.

PagingFiles—The name, initial size, and maximum size for the system paging file(s). Set this information using the Change button in the Performance tab of the System applet in the Control Panel.

SecondLevelDataCache—This key specifies the size of the second-level data cache.

SystemPages—This key specifies the number of system page table entries. The default value of 0 denotes that the default number of entries is to be used.

SubSystems   The SubSystems sub-hive contains subsystem settings established at start-up time. The following entries are found in most systems:

Debug—The debug path, if used; most installations do not have Debug set.

Kmode—The path to the Win32 Driver; the default is win32k.sys.

Optional—This entry defines optional components that are only loaded when the user runs an application that requires them. Typical values include Os2 and Posix.

Os2—This entry is the path and filename of the optional Windows NT OS/2 1.*x* emulator.

Posix—This entry is the path and filename of the optional POSIX subsystem. This is the only POSIX entry in the registry.

Required—The default entry, Debug Windows, is required.

Windows—This entry is the path and name of the executable that will be used to start the Win32 subsystem. The default value is:

```
%SystemRoot%\System32\csrss.exe ObjectDirectory=\Windows SharedSection=
1024,3072 Windows=On SubSystemType=Windows ServerDll=basesrv,1 ServerDll=
winsrv:UserServerDllInitialization,3 ServerDll=winsrv:ConServerDllIni-
tialization,2 ProfileControl=Off MaxRequestThreads=16
```

SessionManager

SessionManager is different from Session Manager with a space, discussed earlier in this chapter. SessionManager contains lists of applications that may not run correctly with Windows NT 4. There are two sub-hives in SessionManager:

CheckBadApps—This sub-hive contains applications that may be incompatible with earlier versions of Windows NT, such as Windows NT 3.51. There are only a few applications listed in this section.

CheckBadApps400—This sub-hive contains applications that may be incompatible with Windows NT 4. More applications are listed in this section.

Whenever an application is listed in one of these two sub-hives, a message will be displayed for the user. This message tells the user about the possible problems that may be encountered. The system does not prevent the user from running the application if a warning message is displayed.

Setup

The Setup hive contains three data keys:

keyboard—The default value, STANDARD (indicating a standard keyboard), is found in virtually all systems.

pointer—The default value, msser, indicates the standard Microsoft serial mouse is the default choice for setup.

video—The default value, VGA, indicates that VGA is the default video choice for setup.

SystemResources

The SystemResources sub-hive holds information about various system resources, generally related to the computer's bus architecture. SystemResources contains the three sub-hives discussed next.

AssignmentOrdering   The AssignmentOrdering sub-hive contains entries for each possible bus type. Each entry specifies either an entry (the default is PCFlat), or a REG_RESOURCE_REQUIREMENTS_LIST object. Data keys in Assignment-Ordering include the following:

Eisa—This data key contains the string PCFlat.

Isa—This data key contains the string PCFlat.

MCA—This data key contains the string PCFlat.

PCFlat—Contains a REG_RESOURCE_REQUIREMENTS_LIST object.

PCI—This data key contains a REG_RESOURCE_REQUIREMENTS_LIST object.

PCMCIA—This data key contains the string PCFlat.

BusValues   Data key entries in BusValues order each bus structure using a REG_BINARY object. This object also contains a second field, and this field's use is unknown. Table 19.3 shows each key and the two values stored in the key.

TABLE 19.3: BusValue Entries Are Named for the Bus Type and Contain Two Values in a Single REG_BINARY Object

Bus Type	Order Number	Unknown Number
Internal	0	0
Isa	1	0
Eisa	2	1

Continued on next page

TABLE 19.3 CONTINUED: BusValue Entries Are Named for the Bus Type and Contain Two Values in a Single REG_BINARY Object

Bus Type	Order Number	Unknown Number
MCA	3	1
TurboChannel	4	0
PCI	5	1
VME	6	0
NuBus	7	0
PCMCIA	8	1
CBus	9	0
MPI	10	0
MPSA	11	0

NOTE   Did you realize that there were that many different buses available for microcomputers? Actually, many of these buses are not used anymore, or they are rather uncommon.

ReservedResources   Only one entry is found in the ReservedResources sub-hive: Isa. It contains a REG_RESOURCE_LIST object listing the ISA bus's reserved resource as being bus number 0.

TimeZoneInformation

The TimeZoneInformation sub-hive contains information used to manage time, time zones, and daylight time. Each entry is filled in from the time zone table contained in the sub-hive HKEY_LOCAL_MACHINE\SOFTWARE\Microsoft\Windows NT\CurrentVersion\Time Zones.

See "CurrentVersion\Time Zones" in Chapter 18, "Introduction to HKEY_LOCAL_MACHINE\SOFTWARE," and HKEY_LOCAL_MACHINE\ SOFTWARE\Microsoft\Windows NT\CurrentVersion\Times Zones in the registry.

Data keys contained in this sub-hive include the following:

ActiveTimeBias—This data key specifies the number of minutes that local time is currently offset from GMT (UTC) time. This includes DST (daylight saving time). Divide this value by 60 to convert hours.

Bias—This data key specifies the number of minutes that local time is nominally offset from GMT (UTC) time, ignoring DST. Divide this value by 60 to convert to hours.

DaylightBias—This data key specifies the amount to change Bias to achieve ActiveTimeBias when DST is in effect.

DaylightName—This data key specifies the name of the time zone when DST is active, for example, eastern daylight time.

DaylightStart—This data key is a SYSTEMTIME structure indicating the start date for DST.

StandardBias—This data key is the amount to change Bias to achieve ActiveTimeBias when DST is not in effect. This value is typically 0.

StandardName—This data key specifies the name of the time zone when DST is not active, for example, eastern standard time.

StandardStart—This data key is a SYSTEMTIME structure indicating the end date for DST.

Update

Update contains information about how policies, which are set using the System Policy Editor, should be updated. Policies are updated to the file CONFIG.POL, and this file's path is known. When a user logs on, the user's computer policies may be automatically updated.

The Update sub-hive contains up to four data keys:

NetworkPath—This data key contains either an empty string if Update-Mode is 1, or the network path to the location of the update files if UpdateMode is 2.

UpdateMode—This data kwy contains a DWORD value indicating the update mode. There are three values allowed in UpdateMode:

0—Do not use policies for updates.

1—Automatic Policy mode is in effect when the user is validated on the domain.

2—Manual policy mode is in effect. The NetworkPath variable must be filled in when using this mode.

Verbose—This data key allows the system to display error messages if Verbose = 1. The default does not display error messages and does not have the Verbose data key.

LoadBalance—This data key allows the system to balance loads if Load-Balance = 1. The default does not display error messages and does not have the LoadBalance data key.

VirtualDeviceDrivers

Windows NT does not support VDD (virtual device drivers). The VirtualDevice-Drivers sub-hive contains any VDDs that are loaded in the VDM (Virtual DOS Machine) when it is initialized. This sub-hive is provided for IHVs (independent hardware vendors) who find it necessary to supply drivers for their hardware products.

There is a single data key in VirtualDeviceDrivers: VDD. It contains a REG_MULTI_SZ string. These strings will contain the names of any VDDs used by the VDM. By default, this key is empty because there are no VDDs for Windows NT.

NOTE   Windows NT does not support any 16-bit virtual device drivers. Applications that rely on 16-bit virtual device drivers will fail.

Windows

The Windows sub-hive contains some configuration information for Windows NT. Data keys included in this sub-hive are:

CSDVersion—The CSD (Microsoft's nomenclature for their Service Packs) status can be determined from the CSDVersion. In earlier versions of Windows NT (other than Windows NT 3.1 Advanced Server), CSDVersion was a string. However, Windows NT 4 uses a DWORD value.

Directory—The Directory key includes a REG_EXPAND_SZ string containing the value %SystemRoot%.

ErrorMode—This data key may contain a number between 0 and 2 These values have the following meanings:

0—The default mode that serializes errors and waits for a user response

1—When the value is set to 1, non-system errors are considered normal and are not reported. System errors are logged to the event log. No error message is given to the user.

2—When the value is set to 2, errors are logged to the event log and no error message is given to the user.

NoInteractiveServices—If this key is set to 1, no interactive services are allowed.

ShutdownTime—This key specifies the time of the last shutdown.

SystemDirectory—The SystemDirectory key includes a REG_EXPAND_SZ string containing the value %SystemRoot%\System32.

WOW

WOW, or Windows on Windows, is an emulator that allows 16-bit applications to run on Windows NT 4. It uses a simple emulation of the Windows 3.*x* standard mode. There are seven data keys in the WOW sub-hive:

cmdline—This sub-hive contains the command line used to start the WOW system.

size—This sub-hive contains the memory size allocated. A value of 0 specifies that the system used the default size.

Wowcmdline—This sub-hive contains the command line used to start the WOW system, including any parameters.

wowsize—This sub-hive specifies the amount of memory supplied to WOW applications. Released versions of Windows NT 4 automate this value, and changes should not be necessary. The default value is 16.

DefaultSeparateVDM—This sub-hive specifies whether WOW is to allocate a default separate VDM (Virtual DOS Machine).

LPT_timeout—This sub-hive specifies the timeout period for the printer port.

KnownDLLs—This sub-hive contains a list of DLLs that the WOW VDM will load to provide compatibility for non-Win32 applications.

Enum

The Enum hive represents the beginning of the hardware tree. Through the Enum hive, any sub-hive named Root (regardless of case) will represent devices that have been enumerated using non–Plug-and-Play services.

The Enum hive contains two sub-hives, HTREE and Root, which are discussed next.

HTREE

This sub-hive represents the hardware devices. There is a sub-hive under HTREE called ROOT, and within ROOT is a sub-hive called 0. Two data keys are contained within HTREE\ROOT\0:

FoundAtEnum—This data key is a DWORD, the default value being 1, indicating that the data key AttachedComponents lists the objects found.

AttachedComponents—This data key is a REG_MULTI_SZ string that lists all devices rooted at the top of the hardware tree. When your system is unable to recognize a specific device, check the entries in this key. If the device is not listed, this indicates that Windows NT did not recognize the device. As an example, the system described in the next Note has an old Mitsumi LU002S CD-ROM drive attached to a non-standard controller card. This device, which is unrecognized, is not usable on the system. Even though the device is enumerated (see the entry `Root\LEGACY_MITSUMI\0000`), this device has no driver for Windows NT 4.

NOTE Is there an old Mitsumi driver that works? If so, I can't find it. The funny thing is, I remember using this device during the Windows NT 4 beta with great success. Today, it just sits there, but it works fine when I dual boot to Windows 95/98.

On one system, this key contains the following entries. These entries are based on installed hardware, so your AttachedComponents entries may vary:

- `Root\LEGACY_ATAPI\0000`

- Root\LEGACY_DISK\0000
- Root\LEGACY_FASTFAT\0000
- Root\LEGACY_FLOPPY\0000
- Root\LEGACY_FS_REC\0000
- Root\LEGACY_NULL\0000
- Root\LEGACY_KSECDD\0000
- Root\LEGACY_BEEP\0000
- Root\LEGACY_MOUCLASS\0000
- Root\LEGACY_KBDCLASS\0000
- Root\LEGACY_VGASAVE\0000
- Root\LEGACY_MSFS\0000
- Root\LEGACY_NPFS\0000
- Root\LEGACY_NDIS\0000
- Root\LEGACY_PARALLEL\0000
- Root\LEGACY_PARPORT\0000
- Root\LEGACY_PARVDM\0000
- Root\LEGACY_RPCSS\0000
- Root\LEGACY_SERIAL\0000
- Root*PNP030b\1_2_22_0_32_0
- Root\MSH0001_-_MICROSOFT_SERIAL_MOUSE_WITH_WHEEL\1_2_17_0_31_0
- Root\LEGACY_NETDETECT\0000
- Root\LEGACY_SPOOLER\0000
- Root\LEGACY_TCPIP\0000
- Root\LEGACY_LANMANWORKSTATION\0000
- Root\LEGACY_RDR\0000
- Root\LEGACY_MUP\0000

- Root\LEGACY_NETBIOS\0000

- Root\LEGACY_AFD\0000

- Root\LEGACY_BROWSER\0000

- Root\LEGACY_LMHOSTS\0000

- Root\LEGACY_LANMANSERVER\0000

- Root\LEGACY_DHCP\0000

- Root\LEGACY_MESSENGER\0000

- Root\LEGACY_SRV\0000

- Root\LEGACY_NETBT\0000

- Root\LEGACY_EL90X\0000

- Root\LEGACY_NETLOGON\0000

- Root\LEGACY_ARK\0000

- Root\LEGACY_MITSUMI\0000

- Root*PNP030b\1_0_22_0_32_0

- Root\MSH0001_-_MICROSOFT_SERIAL_MOUSE_WITH_WHEEL\1_0_17_0_31_0

- Root\LEGACY_PROTECTEDSTORAGE\0000

- Root\LEGACY_SERIALKEYS\0000

- Root\LEGACY_MSSERMOU\0000

- Root\LEGACY_TAPISRV\0000

- Root\PRACTICAL_MODEM47\0000

- Root\LEGACY_EL59X\0000

Notice that not all "devices" are really hardware. Items such as virtual drivers are included in the list.

Root

The Root sub-hives represent enumerators that Windows NT uses to hold information about the device(s). Each device listed in AttachedComponents receives a sub-hive under the Root hive.

These sub-hives include information about each device. Devices that receive support from Windows NT have additional information in the form of an extra sub-hive. An example, the NIC (network interface card) in the computer is a 3Com 3C900, which is a PCI device (actually, Plug-and-Play) that Windows NT is able to support.

The sub-hive for the 3C900 is Enum\Root\LEGACY_EL90X. Where'd the EL90X come from? EL is short for EtherLink (3Com's terminology for their Ethernet cards). The 90X is the designator for the 3C900 series, which contains a number of different devices with varying speeds (10Mbps and 100Mbps) and connection form factors.

The LEGACY_EL90X sub-hive contains the following entries:

- HKEY_CURRENT_CONFIG (which is AKA [that's "also known as"])

- HKEY_LOCAL_MACHINE\SYSTEM\CurrentControlSet\Hardware Profiles\Current (which is DBA [that's "does business as"])

- HKEY_LOCAL_MACHINE\SYSTEM\CurrentControlSet\Hardware Profiles\0001

That's a mouthful, but it really says that there are three names for the same piece of information.

NOTE Changes made in the Current sub-hive will be reflected in the sub-hive of the currently used configuration and vice versa.

A decidedly "un-hardware" entry is also contained in the Hardware Profiles: Software. A single entry is found in the Software sub-hive: Internet Settings. The Internet Settings hive contains two data keys for controlling how the Internet is connected to:

EnableAutodial—This data key contains a DWORD value. If the value is 0x0, the system will not attempt to auto-dial to connect to the Internet (or other remote host). If the value is 0x1, the system will attempt to auto-dial when this is necessary to connect to the remote network.

ProxyEnable—This data key contains a DWORD value. If the value is 0x0, the system *will not* use a proxy server to connect to the Internet. If the value is 0x1, the system *will* use a proxy server to connect to the Internet.

Services

The Services hive contains information about the Windows NT services. The Services sub-hive is managed primarily from the Services applet in the Control Panel, and it describes each service completely.

A service is any Windows NT Service, such as a device driver, the file system drivers, and so on. Services are started as:

Automatic—The service will be started automatically when Windows NT starts.

Manual—The service will be started manually and not when Windows NT starts.

Disabled—The service will be disabled and cannot be started.

The Services sub-hive contains devices that are listed in the Devices applet of the Control Panel. Similar to services, a device may have a number of different start-up states:

Boot—The device will be started when the system is booted, before any other devices.

System—The device will be started when the system is booted, after boot devices.

Automatic—The device will be started when the system is booted, after boot and system devices.

Manual—The device may be started manually; the system will not attempt to start the device automatically.

Disabled—The device cannot be started by a user.

Boot—The device will be started when the system is booted.

When a service runs, it often must log on as a user. Choices for a service include logging on as the System Account or as a specific account. When logging on as a specific account, the service must be configured with the account name and password information.

WARNING   Be careful not to compromise system security by allowing a service to log on as a privileged account and interact with the desktop.

ControlSet001

ControlSet001 is the ControlSet used to boot the computer during normal operations. If ControlSet001 fails to boot for some reason, then ControlSet002 (or ControlSet003) will be used instead.

ControlSet002

Except for the contents of keys that may be different, ControlSet002 (or ControlSet003, if that is what your computer has) is identical to ControlSet001.

ControlSet003 is the backup ControlSet and is also known as the LastKnownGood ControlSet.

DISK

The DISK hive contains information about specific types of drives, such as CD-ROM drive letter mappings, for example. Information about disk configurations, such as fault tolerant configurations (consisting of mirroring, stripe sets, stripe sets with parity, and so on), is also contained in the DISK hive.

All information in the DISK hive is managed using the Disk Administrator. In fact, this hive doesn't even exist until the first time a user runs Disk Administrator. Disk Administrator may also be used to make backups of this hive. Start Disk Administrator and select Partition ➤ Configuration Save. Disk Administrator will then write the DISK hive information to a floppy disk. It will not write to any other device, such as a hard drive.

WARNING
Disk Administrator writes the entire HKEY_LOCAL_MACHINE\SYSTEM hive to a registry export file. However, reloading this file is not recommended, except by using Disk Administrator because any other program may restore hives and keys that are not up to date.

Select

The Select hive contains information about which ControlSet has been loaded by the system. The following four data keys reside in this hive:

Current—This data key defines the currently used ControlSet.

Default—This data key defines the currently used ControlSet, which is typically also the current ControlSet.

Failed—This data key lists a ControlSet that has failed when the system was attempting to start.

LastKnownGood—This data key specifies the ControlSet that will be accessed when a user requests the LastKnownGood ControlSet from Windows NT at boot time.

WARNING
When Windows NT shuts down, the current ControlSet will be copied to the LastKnownGood ControlSet. Be careful when attempting to boot the system that you do not inadvertently overwrite your LastKnownGood copy of the ControlSet with a copy that does not work correctly.

Setup

Setup contains information used by the system during the setup stage. This information is contained in a number of data keys:

SetupType—This key has a value of 0, 1, or 4. These values indicate the following:

0—Indicates that setup has completed.

1—Indicates a new full install.

4—Indicates that an upgrade is being performed.

CmdLine—This key will contain the command string to set up Windows NT. Typically, this command is `"setup -newsetup."`

SystemSetupInProgress—If the setup has not completed, the value in this key will be 0x1. Once setup has completed, SystemSetupInProgress will contain the value 0x0.

SystemPrefix—This key is a value used to determine the system type.

SystemPartition—This key is a pointer to the device that the system has been installed on. Typically, for SCSI systems, this string will be `"\\Device\\Harddisk0\\Partition1."`

OsLoaderPath—This key contains the path for the OS Loader.

NetcardDlls—This key contains the names for the drivers for the NIC.

uniqueid—This key is a unique directory name used during setup.

UpgradeInProgress—This key is only present when an upgrade is being performed (see SetupType at the beginning of this list). The only value in UpgradeInProgress will be a 0x1, and this key will be deleted as soon as the upgrade is completed.

HKEY_CURRENT_CONFIG

The HKEY_CURRENT_CONFIG hive is new to Windows NT 4. It is nothing more than an alias (or pointer) to the HKEY_LOCAL_MACHINE\System\CurrentControlSet\Hardware Profiles\Current hive. HKEY_CURRENT_CONFIG stores only items that are changed from the standard configuration contained in HKEY_LOCAL_MACHINE\System\CurrentControlSet. The most common entries found in HKEY_CURRENT_CONFIG are the entries under Services for the video display. This key was introduced in Windows 95 and Windows NT version 4.0.

The Hardware Profiles hive contains basic hardware profiles. Hardware profiles are used when a particular computer may have several different hardware configurations. HKEY_CURRENT_CONFIG will then point to the currently used hardware profile, enabling users to specify the hardware configuration at boot-up.

Typically, hardware profiles are used with portable computer components that can be swapped (such as floppy and CD-ROM drives) and removable components. For example, my notebook sports an external floppy drive and a permanent built-in CD-ROM drive. Portables with docking stations also benefit from using hardware profiles. Most docking stations have a built-in bus that allows the installation of high-performance NICs, SCSI, and IDE devices; and even ISA and PCI buses that are accessible to the user.

Most desktop users will find little need for hardware profiles. However, some of us find them helpful when using external devices on SCSI buses (items like scanners, tape drives, and so on), which may be removed or reinstalled on a frequent basis. Hardware profiles make it possible to avoid the situation where the system waits for the device or even attempts to use it.

HKEY_CURRENT_CONFIG contains two hives, Software and System, which are discussed next.

HKEY_CURRENT_CONFIG\Software

The Software hive contains some configurations that users may wish to be configured. Notice that there is no built-in methodology to edit or modify items in the Software hive—each application or system must manage these entries and provide the method for the user to modify entries.

Microsoft applications include a sub-hive named Microsoft. This sub-hive contains only one entry on most systems: Windows. The Windows sub-hive includes a sub-hive named CurrentVersion. Get the drift here? This structure HKEY_CURRENT_CONFIG\SOFTWARE\Microsoft\Windows\CurrentVersion is exactly the same structure we find in HKEY_LOCAL_MACHINE\SYSTEM\CurrentControlSet\Hardware Profiles\Current. Both of the these sub-hives have

Microsoft\Windows\CurrentVersion. However, it is possible that other applications might have sub-hives there, as well. Do not count on the Microsoft sub-hive being the only one present in HKEY_CURRENT_CONFIG\SOFTWARE. There may be others some day.

The Software hive contains a sub-hive called Internet Settings. There are two data keys in this hive:

EnableAutodial—This data key contains a DWORD value. If the value is 0x0, then the system will not attempt to auto-dial to connect to the Internet or any other remote host. If the value is 0x1, then the system will attempt auto-dial if necessary to connect to the remote network.

ProxyEnable—This data key contains a DWORD value. If the value is 0x0, then the system will not use a proxy server to connect to the Internet. If the value is 0x1, then the system will use a proxy server to connect to the Internet.

HKEY_CURRENT_CONFIG\System

The HKEY_CURRENT_CONFIG\System hive contains objects that are used to temporarily modify the CurrentControlSet. Microsoft chose to implement multiple hardware configurations this way, rather than attempting to modify the CurrentControlSet on the fly, for reliability reasons. Regardless of what happens to the system, Windows NT can be sure that CurrentControlSet is representative for all users and configurations, and that if changes must be implemented for a specific configuration, these changes will be pointed to by HKEY_CURRENT_CONFIG.

CurrentControlSet\Control

The System sub-hive contains a sub-hive called CurrentControlSet. This sub-hive matches the HKEY_LOCAL_MACHINE\System\CurrentControlSet hive in function. Again, remember: Only modifiers are present in HKEY_CURRENT_CONFIG. So, if nothing in the HKEY_LOCAL_MACHINE\System\CurrentControlSet needs to be modified, the HKEY_CURRENT_CONFIG\System\CurrentControlSet classes will be empty.

The HKEY_CURRENT_CONFIG\System\CurrentControlSet hive contains three sub-hives: Control, Enum, and Services, which are discussed next.

Control

In HKEY_LOCAL_MACHINE\System\CurrentControlSet, the Control sub-hive has a number of data keys used for booting and system initialization. Control also contains about 30 sub-hives. In HKEY_CURRENT_CONFIG, the Control sub-hive will typically be empty unless it is necessary to modify HKEY_LOCAL_MACHINE\System\CurrentControlSet\Control based on a particular configuration.

In HKEY_CURRENT_CONFIG, the Control hive could contain the following data keys:

RegistrySizeLimit—If the registry size limit has been changed from the default value of 8MB, RegistrySizeLimit will contain the maximum registry size, in bytes. Though users are only able to set the registry size limit in MB, Windows NT will store the value as a DWORD containing the maximum registry size in bytes.

SystemStartOptions—This key contains options used during start-up, passed from firmware or the start-up process (contained in BOOT.INI). Options could include debugging information (such as a debugging port and the debugging port parameters) and perhaps information on the system root directory to be used.

WaitToKillService—This key specifies the time period, in milliseconds, to wait before killing a service when Windows NT is shutting down. If this value is too small, Windows NT may kill a service before it has finished writing its data; if this value is too large, a hung service will delay Windows NT shutdown. It is best to leave the WaitToKillService value at its default value of 20000, unless you know you are having a problem.

Control could also contain any of the sub-hives found in HKEY_LOCAL_MACHINE\System\CurrentControlSet\Control.

Enum

The Enum sub-hives represent the beginning of the hardware tree. Through the Enum hive, any sub-hive named Root (regardless of case) will represent devices that have been enumerated using non–Plug-and-Play services.

Though HKEY_CURRENT_CONFIG\System\CurrentControlSet\Enum is typically empty, it could contain the two sub-hives: HTREE and Root. These sub-hives are discussed next.

HTREE   This sub-hive represents the hardware devices. There is a sub-hive under HTREE called ROOT, and within ROOT, there is a sub-hive called 0. HTREE\ROOT\0 includes any devices that may be transient, such as a device contained within a docking station.

Similar to HKEY_LOCAL_MACHINE\System\CurrentControlSet\Control\Enum, notice that not all devices are really hardware. The list includes items such as virtual drivers and so on.

Root   The Root sub-hives represent enumerators used by Windows NT to hold information about the device(s). Each device listed in AttachedComponents receives a sub-hive under the Root hive.

These sub-hives contain information about each device. Devices that receive support from Windows NT have extra information in the form of an additional sub-hive. For example, the NIC (network interface card) in the computer is a 3Com 3C900, which is a PCI device (actually Plug-and-Play) that Windows NT is able to support.

Again, because HKEY_CURRENT_CONFIG is used to modify HKEY_LOCAL_MACHINE\System\CurrentControlSet\Enum\Root, only items that must be changed on a temporary basis would be included in HKEY_CURRENT_CONFIG.

Services

The Services hive contains information about the Windows NT services. It is managed primarily from the Services applet in the Control Panel and describes each service completely.

Some services change when the hardware configuration changes. For example, every Windows NT installation will have an entry for the video system. This entry will contain information used to configure the video for each hardware configuration.

A service is any Windows NT Service, such as a device driver, the file system drivers, and so on. Services are started in one of the following modes:

Automatic—The service will be started automatically when Windows NT starts.

Manual—The service will be started manually and not when Windows NT starts.

Disabled—The service will be disabled and cannot be started.

The Services sub-hive also includes devices that are listed in the Devices applet of the Control Panel. Similar to services, a device may have a number of different start-up states:

Boot—The service will be started when the system is booted, before any other devices.

System—The service will be started when the system is booted, after boot devices.

Automatic—The service will be started when the system is booted, after boot and system devices.

Manual—The service may be started manually; the system will not attempt to start the device automatically.

Disabled—The service cannot be started by a user.

Boot—The service will be started when the system is booted.

When a service runs, it often must log on as a user. Choices for a service include logging on as the System Account or as a specific account. When logging on as a specific account, the service must be configured with the account name and password information.

WARNING   Be careful not to compromise system security by allowing a service to log on as a privileged account to interact with the desktop at the same time.

Services   Services contains sub-hives for each device that must be changed from the default configuration. Every system has at least one entry in this sub-hive for the video card. For example, consider one computer that is running Windows NT Workstation with an ARK chipset video adapter. This device's parameters are stored in a sub-hive called ark, at HKEY_CURRENT_CONFIG\ System\CurrentControlSet\Services\ark.

Your computer will have a similar sub-hive for its video card with virtually identical entries. The name will be different. For example, if you have a Matrox Millennium video card, the sub-hive's name would be mga_mil, and not ark.

For video (specifically VGA) sub-hives, typical entries include:

DefaultSettings.BitsPerPel—Indicates the number of bits per pel (pixel) that would be a number between 1 (indicating a monochrome system) and 32 (true-color systems).

DefaultSettings.Xresolution—The resolution in the X plane (horizontal). Settings might range from 640 to 1280 or more for very high-resolution systems.

DefaultSettings.Yresolution—The resolution in the Y plane (vertical), settings might range from 480 to 1024 or more for very high-resolution systems.

DefaultSettings.Vrefresh—The vertical refresh rate, which usually has a value between 20 and 100, with a typical value of about 70. This reflects the monitor's refresh rate, in Hz. If you change this value, make sure the video adapter at the specified resolution supports the value chosen. Oh, also realize that the Display Properties dialog box will probably change it back to whatever it wants.

DefaultSettings.Flags—This entry controls the specification of any device flags, as necessary.

DefaultSettings.Xpanning—If the device supports hardware panning, this specifies the default horizontal panning value.

DefaultSettings.YPanning—If the device supports hardware panning, this is the default vertical panning value.

Hints and Kinks from the Experts

In this chapter's Hints and Kinks, we cover a few hints on using the two registry editors.

Disabling Autodisconnect   Windows NT uses two different auto-disconnect parameters—one for disconnecting Remote Access Service (RAS) connections and another for disconnecting LAN connections. The RAS autodisconnect parameter is well documented in the Windows NT Server Remote Access Service manual on page 82, but the LAN version is undocumented.

You can find the LAN autodisconnect parameter in the registry at HKEY_LOCAL_MACHINE\System\CurrentControlSet\Services\LanmanServer\Parameters. Its purpose is to disconnect idle sessions after a set number of minutes. The number of minutes can be set at a command prompt using the Net Config Server command. For example, this is how you would set the autodisconnect value to 30 minutes:

Net Config Server /autodisconnect:30

The valid value range of this REG_DWORD value is –1 to 65535 minutes at the command line. To disable autodisconnect, set it to –1.

Setting autodisconnect to 0 does not turn it off and results in very fast disconnects within a few seconds of idle time. However, the RAS auto-disconnect parameter is turned off if you set it to a value of 0.

TIP   It is preferable to modify the LAN autodisconnect directly in the registry. If you modify it at the command line, Windows NT may turn off its autotuning functions.

The valid value range, if you edit the LAN autodisconnect parameter in the registry, is 0 to 4294967295 (0xffffffff). If you configure the autodisconnect option to –1 at the command prompt, autodisconnect is set to the upper value in the registry. This is approximately 8,171 years (not tested), which should be long enough to be the equivalent of turning autodisconnect off.

(Courtesy of Jerold Schulman)

Does Your CD-ROM Changer Cycle Excessively?   If your CD-ROM Changer cycles excessively, try these three simple steps:

1. Set HKEY_LOCAL_MACHINE\SYSTEM\CurrentControlSet\Services\ Cdrom\Autorun to 0.

2. Set Start Up for CD Audio in Control Panel/Devices to Manual. Click the Stop button. (This may not be required on your installation.)

3. Create a shortcut to Explorer (set to minimized) and place it in your Startup folder. Leave it minimized. It will share the CD information with all other copies of Explorer that you open and with all properly written applications.

(Courtesy of John Savill)

How Do I Get Remote Access to the NT 4 Registry?   In Windows NT 4, only members of the Administrators group have access to the registry.

You can alter this default by editing the registry at HKEY_LOCAL_MACHINE\ SYSTEM\CurrentControlSet\Control\SecurePipeServers\winreg. To change the default value, perform the following steps:

1. If the SecurePipeServers key does not exist, add it with a Class of REG_SZ2. If the winreg key does not exist, add it with a Class of REG_SZ.

2. Add value of Description as type REG_SZ and set the string to Registry Server.

3. Select the winreg key and choose Security/Permissions from the Regedt32 menu.

4. Grant the users and groups the access you desire them to have. I would grant Full Control to Administrators.

It is possible to bypass these access permissions. Some services, such as Directory Replicator and Spooler, require remote access to the Registry. You can grant access to the account that runs these services. Or you can edit the registry at

HKEY_LOCAL_MACHINE\SYSTEM\CurrentControlSet\Control\SecurePipe-Servers\winreg by following these steps:

1. Add a key of AllowedPaths with an empty Class.

2. Select HKEY_LOCAL_MACHINE\SYSTEM\CurrentControlSet\Control\SecurePipeServers\winreg\All.

3. Add a value name of Machine as type REG_MULTI_SZ with the following String values, one per line:

    System\CurrentControlSet\Control\ProductOptions

    System\CurrentControlSet\Control\Print\Printers

    System\CurrentControlSet\Services\Eventlog

    Software\Microsoft\Windows NT\CurrentVersion

    System\CurrentControlSet\Services\Replicator

If you wish, you can grant users access to listed locations in the registry by adding a value name of Users as type REG_MULTI_SZ and listing the registry locations, one per line.

(Courtesy of John Savill)

I Make Changes to HKEY_LOCAL_MACHINE, but They Are Lost on Reboot   This is because some hives in HKEY_LOCAL_MACHINE are re-created by the system at boot time. This means that any settings, such as ACLs, are lost.

(Courtesy of John Savill)

VgaSave.   What is VgaSave? And why do I have it?

VgaSave is a place where the settings for the default VGA adapter are stored when the user installs a new driver and a new VGA card, as the case may be. Windows NT copies the original settings to VgaSave and creates a new hive for the new video driver.

How Do I Set RAS to Answer after More Than One Ring?   The only way I have been able to get RAS to answer on "x" rings is to edit the registry at HKEY_LOCAL_MACHINE\System\CurrentControlSet\Control\Class. Follow these steps:

1. Locate the modem's entry, which is usually the fourth entry.

2. Double-click to expand the entry.

3. Locate the modem in question, where 0000 is the first modem.

4. Double-click and highlight the Monitor key.

5. Double-click the first entry, which should be ATS0= and change the number of rings.

You will need to stop and restart the RAS service, and a reboot may be necessary.

NOTE   This technique could probably be done in HKEY_CURRENT_CONFIG by adding the necessary entries under the HKEY_CURRENT_CONFIG\System\Current-ControlSet\Control\Class sub-hive.

(Courtesy of Jerold Schulman)

APPENDIX

APPENDIX

A

Common Hives and Keys

TABLE A.1: Some Common Registry Hives and Keys

Hive	Sub-Hive	Description
HKEY_LOCAL_MACHINE	All hives	Main system description hive. Critical to execution of Windows NT.
HKEY_LOCAL_MACHINE\HARDWARE\DESCRIPTION\	All hives	Information on installed hardware. Hive created at boot time, though some entries may be retained from previous executions.
HKEY_LOCAL_MACHINE\HARDWARE\DESCRIPTION\	System	System device information, excluding NIC (Network Interface Card) and video devices.
HKEY_LOCAL_MACHINE\HARDWARE\DESCRIPTION\	System\Central-Processor	CPU information, such as make, model, and version.
HKEY_LOCAL_MACHINE\HARDWARE\DESCRIPTION\	System\Floating-PointProcessor	Floating Point Processor data, such as make, model, and version.
HKEY_LOCAL_MACHINE\HARDWARE\DESCRIPTION\	System\Multifunc-tionAdapter\2\DiskController\0\DiskPeripheral	Installed disk controller information. Systems may have one, two, or three controllers in a typical configuration: Primary IDE, Secondary IDE, and SCSI.
HKEY_LOCAL_MACHINE\HARDWARE\DESCRIPTION\	System\Multifunc-tionAdapter\2\KeyboardController	Keyboard controller information at hardware level.
HKEY_LOCAL_MACHINE\HARDWARE\DESCRIPTION\	System\Multifunc-tionAdapter\2\ParallelController	Printer (parallel) port information.
HKEY_LOCAL_MACHINE\HARDWARE\DESCRIPTION\	System\Multifunc-tionAdapter\2\PointerController	Mouse port information.
HKEY_LOCAL_MACHINE\HARDWARE\DESCRIPTION\	System\Multifunc-tionAdapter\2\SerialController	Installed serial ports information.

Continued on next page

TABLE A.1 CONTINUED: Some Common Registry Hives and Keys

Hive	Sub-Hive	Description
HKEY_LOCAL_MACHINE\HARDWARE\DESCRIPTION\	`System\Multifunc-` `tionAdapter`	Device classes, other than network and disk, information.
HKEY_LOCAL_MACHINE\HARDWARE\DESCRIPTION\	`System\PCMCIA` `PCCARDs`	PCMCIA (PC-Card) devices information, if installed.
HKEY_LOCAL_MACHINE\HARDWARE\DEVICEMAP\	All hives	Basic device mapping and control information.
HKEY_LOCAL_MACHINE\HARDWARE\DEVICEMAP\	`KeyboardClass`	Keyboard device mapping information.
HKEY_LOCAL_MACHINE\HARDWARE\DEVICEMAP\	`KeyboardPort`	Keyboard port configuration information.
HKEY_LOCAL_MACHINE\HARDWARE\DEVICEMAP\	`PARALLEL PORTS`	Printer (parallel) port configuration information.
HKEY_LOCAL_MACHINE\HARDWARE\DEVICEMAP\	`PointerClass`	Mouse information.
HKEY_LOCAL_MACHINE\HARDWARE\DEVICEMAP\	`Scsi`	General disk interface information on IDE and SCSI devices.
HKEY_LOCAL_MACHINE\HARDWARE\DEVICEMAP\	`Scsi\Scsi Port 0`	Information on first disk drive interface adapter (though labeled as SCSI, this may be an IDE device).
HKEY_LOCAL_MACHINE\HARDWARE\DEVICEMAP\	`Scsi\Scsi Port 1`	Information on second disk drive interface adapter (though labeled as SCSI, this may be an IDE device).
HKEY_LOCAL_MACHINE\HARDWARE\DEVICEMAP\	`SERIALCOMM`	Information on serial communications device configurations.
HKEY_LOCAL_MACHINE\HARDWARE\DEVICEMAP\	`VIDEO`	Video configuration information.
HKEY_LOCAL_MACHINE\HARDWARE\RESOURCEMAP\	All hives	Information on (hardware) system mapping.

Continued on next page

TABLE A.1 CONTINUED: Some Common Registry Hives and Keys

Hive	Sub-Hive	Description
HKEY_LOCAL_MACHINE\HARDWARE\DEVICEMAP\	PointerPort	Information on port (mouse port, PS/2 mouse port, serial port, and so on) mouse (pointer) is connected to.
HKEY_LOCAL_MACHINE\HARDWARE\RESOURCEMAP\	Hardware Abstraction Layer\PC Compatible Eisa/Isa HAL	Description of system configuration to Windows NT. HALs exist for generic systems and for computers that have special hardware configurations, such as multiple processors, or special bus configurations.
HKEY_LOCAL_MACHINE\HARDWARE\RESOURCEMAP\	KeyboardPort/ PointerPort	General keyboard/mouse interface information.
HKEY_LOCAL_MACHINE\HARDWARE\RESOURCEMAP\	KeyboardPort/Pointer Port\msi8042prt	Mouse/keyboard interface information.
HKEY_LOCAL_MACHINE\HARDWARE\RESOURCEMAP\	LOADED PARALLEL DRIVER RESOURCES	Description of currently loaded printer (parallel) port driver configurations.
HKEY_LOCAL_MACHINE\HARDWARE\RESOURCEMAP\	LOADED SERIAL DRIVER RESOURCES	Description of currently loaded serial port driver configurations.
HKEY_LOCAL_MACHINE\HARDWARE\RESOURCEMAP\	OtherDrivers	General information on devices not otherwise classified.
HKEY_LOCAL_MACHINE\HARDWARE\RESOURCEMAP\	OtherDrivers\Elnk3	Description of NIC. In this example Elnk3 is 3Com 3C589 PCMCIA interface.
HKEY_LOCAL_MACHINE\HARDWARE\RESOURCEMAP\	ScsiAdapter	Information about SCSI and IDE adapters.
HKEY_LOCAL_MACHINE\HARDWARE\RESOURCEMAP\	ScsiAdapter\atapi	Description of installed IDE (ATAPI) disk interface.
HKEY_LOCAL_MACHINE\HARDWARE\RESOURCEMAP\	System Resources	General information on system resources.
HKEY_LOCAL_MACHINE\HARDWARE\RESOURCEMAP\	System Resources\ Reserved	Reserved system resources information.

Continued on next page

TABLE A.1 CONTINUED: Some Common Registry Hives and Keys

Hive	Sub-Hive	Description
HKEY_LOCAL_MACHINE\HARDWARE\RESOURCEMAP\	System Resources\ Physical Memory	System memory resources information.
HKEY_LOCAL_MACHINE\HARDWARE\RESOURCEMAP\	VIDEO	Information on video configurations supported by system.
HKEY_LOCAL_MACHINE\HARDWARE\RESOURCEMAP\	VIDEO\chips	Information on installed VGA adapter for Chips & Technology VGA system.
HKEY_LOCAL_MACHINE\HARDWARE\RESOURCEMAP\	VIDEO\VgaSave	Information on originally installed VGA video system, generally a generic VGA system.
HKEY_LOCAL_MACHINE\HARDWARE\RESOURCEMAP\	VIDEO\VgaStart	Information on VGA driver used to start the system.
HKEY_LOCAL_MACHINE\SAM\	All hives	SAM hive. Usually protected from user browsing and modification.
HKEY_LOCAL_MACHINE\SAM\	SAM\Domains\ Account\Aliases	SAM alias information.
HKEY_LOCAL_MACHINE\SAM\	SAM\Domains\ Account\Aliases\ Members	Member aliases information.
HKEY_LOCAL_MACHINE\SAM\	SAM\Domains\Account\ Aliases\Names	Domain name alias information.
HKEY_LOCAL_MACHINE\SAM\	SAM\Domains\Account\ Groups	Groups information.
HKEY_LOCAL_MACHINE\SAM\	SAM\Domains\Account\ Groups\Names	Group name information.
HKEY_LOCAL_MACHINE\SAM\	SAM\Domains\Account\ Users	Specific users information.
HKEY_LOCAL_MACHINE\SAM\	SAM\Domains\Account\ Users\Names	User name information.

Continued on next page

TABLE A.1 CONTINUED: Some Common Registry Hives and Keys

Hive	Sub-Hive	Description
HKEY_LOCAL_MACHINE\SAM\	SAM\Domains\ Account\Users\ Names\Administrator	User Administrator information
HKEY_LOCAL_MACHINE\SAM\	SAM\Domains\ Account\Users\ Names\Guest	User Guest information.
HKEY_LOCAL_MACHINE\SAM\	SAM\Domains\Built in\Aliases\Mem- bers\S-1-5-21- 1949642934-206577 2114-2122337923	Information on built-in users: Adminis-trator and Guest.
HKEY_LOCAL_MACHINE\SAM\	SAM\Domains\Built in\Aliases\Mem- bers\S-1-5-21- 1949642934-206577 2114-2122337923\ 000001F4	Information on built-in user: Administrator.
HKEY_LOCAL_MACHINE\SAM\	SAM\Domains\Built in\Aliases\Mem- bers\S-1-5-21- 1949642934-206577 2114-2122337923\ 000001F5	Built-in user information.
HKEY_LOCAL_MACHINE\SAM\	SAM\Domains\Built in\Aliases\Mem- bers\S-1-5-21- 45749729-16073390 -2133884337	Domain groups information.
HKEY_LOCAL_MACHINE\SAM\	SAM\Domains\Builtin\ Aliases\Members\S- 1-5-21-45749729- 16073390-21338843 37\00000200	Domain Admins group information.

Continued on next page

TABLE A.1 CONTINUED: Some Common Registry Hives and Keys

Hive	Sub-Hive	Description
HKEY_LOCAL_MACHINE\SAM\	SAM\Domains\Built-in\Aliases\Members\S-1-5-21-45749729- 16073390-2133884337\00000201	Domain users group information.
HKEY_LOCAL_MACHINE\SAM\	SAM\Domains\Builtin\Aliases\Members	Member alias information for user groups.
HKEY_LOCAL_MACHINE\SAM\	SAM\Domains\Builtin\Aliases\Names\Administrators	Member alias information for Administrators.
HKEY_LOCAL_MACHINE\SAM\	SAM\Domains\Builtin\Aliases\Names\Backup Operators	Member alias information for Backup Operators (users who perform system backups).
HKEY_LOCAL_MACHINE\SAM\	SAM\Domains\Builtin\Aliases\Names\Guests	Member alias information for Domain guests.
HKEY_LOCAL_MACHINE\SAM\	SAM\Domains\Builtin\Aliases\Names\Power Users	Member alias information for Power Users.
HKEY_LOCAL_MACHINE\SAM\	SAM\Domains\Builtin\Aliases\Names\Replicator	Member alias information for Replicator accounts.
HKEY_LOCAL_MACHINE\SAM\	SAM\Domains\Builtin\Aliases\Names\Users	Member alias information for Domain users.
HKEY_LOCAL_MACHINE\SAM\	SAM\RXACT	SAM RXACT hive. Typically contains nothing.

Continued on next page

TABLE A.1 CONTINUED: Some Common Registry Hives and Keys

Hive	Sub-Hive	Description
HKEY_LOCAL_MACHINE\SECURITY	All hives	Protected Windows NT security hive.
HKEY_LOCAL_MACHINE\SOFTWARE	All hives	Information about installed user and system software.
HKEY_LOCAL_MACHINE\SOFTWARE	Classes	Information about extensions and usage of file types.
HKEY_LOCAL_MACHINE\SOFTWARE	Classes*\	Information about files in general— that is, files that are not otherwise classified.
HKEY_LOCAL_MACHINE\SOFTWARE	Classes\CLSID	Information about CLSID (class ID) assignments. Almost all applications, and those that support OLE, have a CLSID.
HKEY_LOCAL_MACHINE\SOFTWARE	Classes\Interface	Information about OLE interface assignments. Almost all applications that support OLE have OLE interface.
HKEY_LOCAL_MACHINE\SOFTWARE	Description	Information about RPC objects and configurations.
HKEY_LOCAL_MACHINE\SOFTWARE	Windows NT\ CurrentVersion\	Information on currently installed version of Windows NT.
HKEY_LOCAL_MACHINE\SOFTWARE	Program Groups	Information on program groups as used by Program Manager.
HKEY_LOCAL_MACHINE\SOFTWARE	Secure	Security information.
HKEY_LOCAL_MACHINE\SOFTWARE	Windows 3.1 Migration Status	Information on migration from Windows NT 3.x to Windows NT 4.
HKEY_LOCAL_MACHINE\SYSTEM\ControlSet001\	All hives	Control sets used to manage system resources.
HKEY_LOCAL_MACHINE\SYSTEM\ControlSet003\	All hives	Backup control sets numbered 002, 003, 004, and so on.
HKEY_LOCAL_MACHINE\SYSTEM\ControlSet004\	All hives	Backup control sets are numbered 002, 003, 004, and so on.

Continued on next page

TABLE A.1 CONTINUED: Some Common Registry Hives and Keys

Hive	Sub-Hive	Description
HKEY_LOCAL_MACHINE\SYSTEM\CurrentControlSet\	All hives	Current control set mapped to set used for starting computer.
HKEY_LOCAL_MACHINE\SYSTEM\CurrentControlSet\	Control\BootVeri-ficationProgram	Program used to verify that system booted correctly.
HKEY_LOCAL_MACHINE\SYSTEM\CurrentControlSet\	Control\Class	Information about CLSID (OLE).
HKEY_LOCAL_MACHINE\SYSTEM\CurrentControlSet\	Control\Computer-Name\Active-ComputerName	Computer's current name.
HKEY_LOCAL_MACHINE\SYSTEM\CurrentControlSet\	Control\Computer-Name\ComputerName	Computer's name.
HKEY_LOCAL_MACHINE\SYSTEM\CurrentControlSet\	Control\CrashControl	Determiner of events when/if system fails.
HKEY_LOCAL_MACHINE\SYSTEM\CurrentControlSet\	Control\FileSystem	Description of system file system (FAT or NTFS).
HKEY_LOCAL_MACHINE\SYSTEM\DISK	All hives	Description of system disk.
HKEY_LOCAL_MACHINE\SYSTEM\Select	All hives	Description of control set being used.
HKEY_LOCAL_MACHINE\SYSTEM\Setup	All hives	Description of system setup state.
HKEY_LOCAL_MACHINE\SYSTEM	All hives	System description.
HKEY_USERS	All hives	General user information.
HKEY_USERS\.DEFAULT\	All hives	Default user active when no other user logged on. All information in .DEFAULT would also be found for specific users.
HKEY_USERS\.DEFAULT\	AppEvents\EventLabels	EventLabels are used to notify users (with sound) when event happens.

Continued on next page

TABLE A.1 CONTINUED: Some Common Registry Hives and Keys

Hive	Sub-Hive	Description
HKEY_USERS\.DEFAULT\	AppEvents\Schemes	Scheme used to apply which sounds are used for event.
HKEY_USERS\.DEFAULT\	AppEvents	Application events, such as startup, document open, and so on.
HKEY_USERS\.DEFAULT\	Console	System's command prompt for window(s) configuration.
HKEY_USERS\.DEFAULT\	Control Panel	System Control Panel used to configure Windows NT.
HKEY_USERS\.DEFAULT\	Control Panel\ Accessibility	Control Panel's Accessibility applet.
HKEY_USERS\.DEFAULT\	Control Panel\ Appearance	Control Panel's Appearance applet.
HKEY_USERS\.DEFAULT\	Control Panel\ Colors	Control Panel's Colors applet.
HKEY_USERS\.DEFAULT\	Control Panel\ Current	Control Panel's Current applet.
HKEY_USERS\.DEFAULT\	Control Panel\ Custom Colors	Control Panel's Custom Colors applet.
HKEY_USERS\.DEFAULT\	Control Panel\ Desktop	Control Panel's Desktop applet.
HKEY_USERS\.DEFAULT\	Control Panel\ International	Control Panel's International applet.
HKEY_USERS\.DEFAULT\	Control Panel\ IOProcs	Control Panel's IOProcs applet.
HKEY_USERS\.DEFAULT\	Control Panel\ Keyboard	Control Panel's Keyboard applet.

Continued on next page

TABLE A.1 CONTINUED: Some Common Registry Hives and Keys

Hive	Sub-Hive	Description
HKEY_USERS\.DEFAULT\	Control Panel\ MMCPL	Control Panel's MMCPL applet
HKEY_USERS\.DEFAULT\	Control Panel\ Mouse	Control Panel's Mouse applet.
HKEY_USERS\.DEFAULT\	Control Panel\ Patterns	Control Panel's Patterns applet.
HKEY_USERS\.DEFAULT\	Control Panel\ Screen Saver .3DFlyingObj	Control Panel's Screen Saver .3DFlyingObj saved configuration.
HKEY_USERS\.DEFAULT\	Control Panel\ Screen Saver .3DPipes	Control Panel's Screen Saver.3DPipes saved configuration.
HKEY_USERS\.DEFAULT\	Control Panel\ Screen Saver .Bezier	Control Panel's Screen Saver.Bezier saved configuration.
HKEY_USERS\.DEFAULT\	Control Panel\ Screen Saver .Marquee	Control Panel's Screen Saver.Marquee saved configuration.
HKEY_USERS\.DEFAULT\	Control Panel\ Screen Saver .Mystify	Control Panel's Screen Saver.Mystify saved configuration.
HKEY_USERS\.DEFAULT\	Control Panel\ Screen Saver.Stars	Control Panel's Screen Saver.Stars saved configuration.
HKEY_USERS\.DEFAULT\	Control Panel\ Sound	Control Panel's Sound applet.

Continued on next page

TABLE A.1 CONTINUED: Some Common Registry Hives and Keys

Hive	Sub-Hive	Description
HKEY_USERS\.DEFAULT\	Environment	Definition of environment variables, used with both Windows NT and command prompts.
HKEY_USERS\.DEFAULT\	Keyboard Layout	Keyboard layouts for NLS (National Language Support).
HKEY_USERS\.DEFAULT\	Software\Microsoft\Windows Help	Configuration for Windows NT help system.
HKEY_USERS\.DEFAULT\	Software\Microsoft\Windows NT\CurrentVersion	Windows NT current software configuration.
HKEY_USERS\.DEFAULT\	Software\Microsoft\Windows NT\CurrentVersion\Devices	Configuration of software drivers for hardware.
HKEY_USERS\.DEFAULT\	Software\Microsoft\Windows NT	Windows NT configuration items.
HKEY_USERS\.DEFAULT\	Software\Microsoft\Windows\CurrentVersion	Windows configuration items.
HKEY_USERS\.DEFAULT\	Software\Microsoft\Windows	General information about Windows.
HKEY_USERS\.DEFAULT\	Software\Microsoft	Information about Microsoft components and software.
HKEY_USERS\.DEFAULT\	Software	Software configuration (as compared to hardware configurations).
HKEY_USERS\.DEFAULT\	UNICODE Program Groups	Unused on most systems.
HKEY_USERS\<SID>	All hives	Information for specific user as identified by <SID>.
HKEY_USERS\<SID>	AppEvents\EventLabels\.Default	Information regarding application event labels, as in .DEFAULT.

APPENDIX

B

Registry Data Types

A data key in the registry may contain data in different formats. These types can be classed as:

Common data types—These are supported and edited by both RegEdit, RegEdt32, and most other registry tools.

Windows NT specific data types—These are supported and edited by RegEdt32 and some other registry tools.

Special and component/application specific data types—These are both supported and unsupported by registry tools, but cannot usually be edited by users, except as binary data.

Keep in mind that registry editors actually would allow editing of non-supported data types, including data types that are displayed as REG_UNKNOWN. However, editing is done in binary mode, requiring the user to have intimate knowledge of the data object.

Understanding each data type, how data is stored for each data type, and so on can be very important to a user who finds that the registry entry must be modified. The registry data types are listed in Table B.1.

TABLE B.1: Known Registry Data Types

Type	Data Type Index (if known)	Size	Short Description
REG_BINARY	3	0 or more bytes	A binary object that may contain any data
REG_COLOR_RGB	*	4 bytes	A color description
REG_DWORD	4	4 bytes	A DWORD value
REG_DWORD_BIG_ENDIAN	5	4 bytes	A value stored in reverse order of a DWORD value
REG_DWORD_LITTLE_ENDIAN	4	4 bytes	A DWORD value
REG_EXPAND_SZ	2	0 or more bytes	A string with an environment substitution placeholder
REG_FILE_NAME	*	0 or more bytes	A filename

Continued on next page

TABLE B.1 CONTINUED: Known Registry Data Types

Type	Data Type Index (if known)	Size	Short Description
REG_FILE_TIME	*	Unknown	A file time
REG_FULL_RESOURCE_DESCRIPTOR	9	Unknown	A list of hardware resources
REG_LINK	6	0 or more bytes	A Unicode string naming a symbolic link
REG_MULTI_SZ	7	0 or more bytes	A collection of strings, each separated by a null, with the final string terminated with two nulls
REG_NONE	0	Unknown	A data object with a defined type of REG_NONE for data that needn't be otherwise classified, different from REG_UNKNOWN.
REG_RESOURCE_LIST	8	Unknown	A list of resources used for a device
REG_RESOURCE_REQUIREMENTS_LIST	10	Unknown	A list of resources required by a driver
REG_SZ	1	0 or more bytes	A string terminated with a null
REG_UNKNOWN	(Undefined)	Unknown	The object's type cannot be determined because the data type index is not valid.

* These object types appear to be unsupported by Windows NT at this time.

Now, to tell the registry what type a particular object is, the registry stores a data type index value that indicates the data type of the object. For instance, a REG_SZ object would have a data type index of 1. For those objects in Table B.1 without a data type index value, Windows NT will list them as REG_UNKNOWN.

Oh, there is always the possibility that some additional data types will be added as Windows NT matures. Expect that Windows NT version 5 will change this support somewhat when it is released.

The following sections describe the compatibility of each data type. The darkened tools in each section represent compatibility.

REG_BINARY

REG_BINARY holds binary type data.

It is compatible with the following registry tool(s):

> RegEdit
>
> RegEdt32 Create
>
> RegEdt32 Edit
>
> RegEdt32 Display
>
> RegChg (RegChange)

REG_BINARY is the most basic data type used in the registry. All of the other registry data types may be expressed in REG_BINARY form, although this may be very inconvenient.

A binary object is saved in the registry as a length and a series of bytes. When a REG_BINARY object is stored in the registry, the length parameter is preserved. However, the user is unable to change the length parameter except by changing the object's actual size.

REG_COLOR_RGB

REG_COLOR_RGB holds color definition.

It is compatible with the following registry tool(s):

> RegEdit
>
> RegEdt32 Create
>
> RegEdt32 Edit

RegEdt32 Display

RegChg (RegChange)

REG_COLOR_RGB holds an RGB color index, which may be displayed by RegEdt32. None of the registry tools are able to create a REG_COLOR_RGB data object, and it cannot be determined whether either Windows NT or any component supports this object type.

It is possible that this object type will be supported in future versions of Windows NT. However, there is currently no support for the REG_COLOR_RGB object.

REG_DWORD

REG_DWORD holds a 32-bit number (that's 4 bytes folks, no more, no fewer) expressed in either decimal or hexadecimal.

REG_DWORD is compatible with the following registry tool(s):

RegEdit

RegEdt32 Create

RegEdt32 Edit

RegEdt32 Display

RegChg (RegChange)

Like REG_BINARY, the REG_DWORD type is a basic data type for registry data keys.

REG_DWORD_BIG_ENDIAN

REG_DWORD_BIG_ENDIAN holds a DWORD value.

REG_DWORD_BIG_ENDIAN is compatible with the following registry tool(s):

RegEdit

RegEdt32 Create

RegEdt32 Edit

RegEdt32 Display

RegChg (RegChange)

Different computers store numbers in memory in different orders. Two orders are used: big endian and little endian. The Intel processor stores numbers in little endian format.

In the big endian format, the 4 bytes of a DWORD value are stored with the highest order byte at the highest address, and the lowest order byte at the lowest address. See Table B.2 for an example of how the value 0x12345678 (in decimal that's 305419896) would be stored at memory address 0x5.

T A B L E B . 2 : A DWORD Value Stored in Big Endian Format

Address	Value
0x5	12
0x6	34
0x7	56
0x8	78

REG_DWORD_LITTLE_ENDIAN

REG_DWORD_LITTLE_ENDIAN holds a DWORD value.

REG_DWORD_LITTLE_ENDIAN is compatible with the following registry tool(s):

RegEdit

RegEdt32 Create

RegEdt32 Edit

RegEdt32 Display

RegChg (RegChange)

Different computers store numbers in memory in different orders. Two orders are used: big endian and little endian. The Intel processor stores numbers in little endian format.

In the little endian format, the 4 bytes of a DWORD value are stored with the highest order byte at the lowest address, and the lowest order byte is stored at the highest address. Table B.3 shows an example of the value 0x12345678 (in decimal that's 305419896) stored at memory address 0x5.

TABLE B.3: A DWORD Value Stored in Little Endian Format

Address	Value
0x5	78
0x6	56
0x7	34
0x8	12

Both Windows NT and Windows 95/98 run on computers that store numbers in little endian format. Some operating systems are designed for big endian computers. When an operating system is designed for a different endian than what the hardware supports, the operating system will convert as necessary.

NOTE It is generally unnecessary for users to consider endian issues. The only time that endian format becomes important is when data is transferred between two dissimilar computer systems using raw binary transfer methods. Since virtually all transfer methods (including data transfers over the Internet) do not use raw binary transfers, users needn't consider this issue.

In all cases, the Windows NT registry treats REG_DWORD_LITTLE_EDIAN as a REG_DWORD type. There is no real difference between these two types in the Windows NT registry.

REG_EXPAND_SZ

The REG_EXPAND_SZ data object contains a single string terminated with a null; a null is a character whose value is zero.

The REG_EXPAND_SZ data object is compatible with the following registry tool(s):

RegEdit

RegEdt32 Create

RegEdt32 Edit

RegEdt32 Display

RegChg (RegChange)

This string may contain one or more unexpanded environment variables.

There are many examples of REG_EXPAND_SZ in the registry, most of which are references to files accessed from the environment variables %SystemRoot%, %SystemDrive%, and %Path%.

Environment variables will only be substituted when surrounded with percent (%) signs. In a command prompt window, type the command **SET**, and a list of all the current environment variables will be displayed. These environment variables (with surrounding percent signs) may be used from command prompts or in batch files. In the next example, lines that I typed are in bold and lines starting with REM are comments:

```
Windows NT Version 4.0  18:05:31 C:\TEMP
REM-display the contents of the environment variable SystemRoot
Windows NT Version 4.0  18:05:32 C:\TEMP
set systemroot
SystemRoot=C:\WINNT40

Windows NT Version 4.0  18:05:34 C:\TEMP
REM-Use the environment variable SystemRoot
Windows NT Version 4.0  18:05:35 C:\TEMP
dir %SystemRoot%\*.bat
 Volume in drive C is (c) - Boot drive
 Volume Serial Number is CC56-5631
```

```
Directory of C:\WINNT40

02/10/98  03:55p                    46              PB.BAT
              1 File(s)            46 bytes
                         152,050,688 bytes free

Windows NT Version 4.0  18:05:40 C:\TEMP
```

REG_FILE_NAME

The REG_FILE_NAME object type is not currently used (or supported) other than in RegEdt32 display mode.

The REG_FILE_NAME object type is compatible with the following registry tool(s):

> RegEdit
>
> RegEdt32 Create
>
> RegEdt32 Edit
>
> **RegEdt32 Display**
>
> RegChg (RegChange)

None of the registry tools are able to create a REG_FILE_NAME data object and it cannot be determined whether either Windows NT or any component supports this object type.

It is possible that this object type will be supported in future versions of Windows NT. However, there is currently no support for the REG_FILE_NAME object.

REG_FILE_TIME

The REG_FILE_TIME object type is not currently used (or supported) other than in RegEdt32 display mode.

The REG_FILE_TIME object type is compatible with the following registry tool(s):

RegEdit

RegEdt32 Create

RegEdt32 Edit

RegEdt32 Display

RegChg (RegChange)

None of the registry tools are able to create a REG_FILE_TIME data object, and it cannot be determined whether either Windows NT or any component supports this object type.

It is possible that this object type will be supported in future versions of Windows NT. However, there is currently no support for the REG_FILE_TIME object.

REG_FULL_RESOURCE_DESCRIPTOR

The REG_FULL_RESOURCE_DESCRIPTOR object contains a list of hardware resources that a physical device is using.

The REG_FULL_RESOURCE_DESCRIPTOR object is compatible with the following registry tool(s):

RegEdit

RegEdt32 Create

RegEdt32 Edit

RegEdt32 Display

RegChg (RegChange)

This information is detected and written into the HKEY_LOCAL_MACHINE\Hardware\Description tree by the system at boot-up time.

Generally, it would be very unwise to edit a REG_FULL_RESOURCE_DESCRIPTOR object. RegChg allows the creation of a REG_FULL_RESOURCE_DESCRIPTOR object if an edit becomes necessary.

REG_LINK

REG_LINK is a Unicode string naming a symbolic link.

REG_LINK is compatible with the following registry tool(s):

RegEdit

RegEdt32 Create

RegEdt32 Edit

RegEdt32 Display

RegChg (RegChange)

This type is irrelevant to device and intermediate drivers and should be of no interest to anyone except programmers.

REG_MULTI_SZ

REG_MULTI_SZ object consists of one or more strings.

REG_MULTI_SZ object is compatible with the following registry tool(s):

RegEdit

RegEdt32 Create

RegEdt32 Edit

RegEdt32 Display

RegChg (RegChange)

Each string is separated from the next by a null. The final string is terminated by a double null. For strings that are Unicode (all strings in the Windows NT registry are Unicode), the null shall be the same width as a Unicode character. For example (\0 indicates a null character):

```
String one\0
String two\0
```

```
String three\0

Last string\0\0
```

> **NOTE**   What the heck is a null? A *null character* has a numeric value of zero, irrespective of the character's width.

REG_NONE

REG_NONE is data with no particular type.

REG_NONE is compatible with the following registry tool(s):

RegEdit

RegEdt32 Create

RegEdt32 Edit

RegEdt32 Display

RegChg (RegChange)

Notice that this type is different from REG_UNKNOWN. REG_NONE is data that is stored in binary format, with 0 or more bytes of information. Generally, REG_NONE objects are created by default, although some components and applications may create a REG_NONE object intentionally.

REG_RESOURCE_LIST

A REG_RESOURCE_LIST object describes information about resources used by a specific device.

A REG_RESOURCE_LIST object is compatible with the following registry tool(s):

RegEdit

RegEdt32 Create

RegEdt32 Edit

RegEdt32 Display

RegChg (RegChange)

A REG_RESOURCE_LIST object describes information about resources used by a specific device. Found primarily in HKEY_LOCAL_MACHINE\Hardware\Resourcemap, there are entries for each device installed in the system. REG_RESOURCE_LIST information is organized under the bus structure:

- CBus
- Eisa
- Internal
- Isa
- MicroChannel
- MPIBus
- MPSABus
- NuBus
- PCIBus
- PCMCIABus
- TurboChannel
- VMEBus

Information stored in REG_RESOURCE_LIST may include:

- DeviceSpecificData DataSize
- DeviceSpecificData Reserved1
- DeviceSpecificData Reserved2
- Dma Channel
- Dma Port
- Dma Reserved1
- Interrupt Affinity

- Interrupt Level

- Interrupt Vector

- Memory Length

- Memory PhysicalAddress

- Memory Start

- Port Length

- Port PhysicalAddress

- Port Start

REG_RESOURCE_REQUIREMENTS_LIST

REG_RESOURCE_REQUIREMENTS_LIST objects contain a list of hardware resources that a device driver would require.

REG_RESOURCE_REQUIREMENTS_LIST objects are compatible with the following registry tool(s):

RegEdit

RegEdt32 Create

RegEdt32 Edit

XRegEdt32 Display

RegChg (RegChange)

This list of hardware resources is used to update the HKEY_LOCAL_MACHINE\Hardware\Resourcemap sub-hive.

REG_SZ

REG_SZ contains a single string terminated with a null.

REG_SZ is compatible with the following registry tool(s):

RegEdit

RegEdt32 Create

RegEdt32 Edit

RegEdt32 Display

RegChg (RegChange)

The REG_SZ string will be in Unicode for Windows NT installations.

REG_UNKNOWN

The REG_UNKNOWN object type is used whenever an invalid or undefined registry data index type is found.

The REG_UNKNOWN object type is compatible with the following registry tool(s):

RegEdit

RegEdt32 Create

RegEdt32 Edit

RegEdt32 Display

RegChg (RegChange)

Both system components and system applications are allowed to write their own types of data into the registry. And none of the registry tools, such as the registry editors, will know about these data types. Whenever a registry tool encounters a data type that it does not know about, the tool will display the data in binary format and flag it as REG_UNKNOWN type.

APPENDIX

C

Where Can I Get More Help?

Maybe this book didn't have enough information for you, or more likely, you need some very specialized help. There are lots of sources of assistance. Many are free, and some are costly; but generally, we get what we pay for in life. As a rule, personalized, hand-holding assistance can be expensive—consultants typically cost between $80 and $350 an hour, and usually charge for travel time and other expenses.

User groups, and other self-help sources are cheaper, but you may not profit from assistance that is quickly shot out to you in an e-mail. You must determine if this will work for you.

The Web

There are many sites on the Internet's Web (WWW or World Wide Web) that offer some assistance to users of Windows NT. No site is specific to the registry, though many of these sites offer either a section for the registry or a general area that may be helpful to everyone who has a registry problem.

The site at `http://www.jsiinc.com/reghack.htm` is run by Jerold Schulman (JSI, Inc.). It is jam packed with helpful tips and ideas. The registry section that Jerold has set up includes almost 500 different registry-related tips and techniques.

The site at `http://www.ntfaq.com` is run by John Savill (SavillTech Ltd.). It has a number of very interesting features including answers to over 800 common questions, a Java and CGI search engine with a single-file version that can be downloaded, and a help file version that can be used locally.

The site at `http://www.bhs.com` is run by Beverly Hills Software. It is one of the premier sites for users of Windows NT. A close alliance with Microsoft has allowed BHS to remain in the forefront of Windows NT support and technology.

The site at `http://backoffice.microsoft.com` is Microsoft's entry into both Windows NT and the other members of the Microsoft BackOffice family. BackOffice is Microsoft's offering for advanced users.

It is possible to contact Microsoft's technical people by using Microsoft's Web sites at `http://www.microsoft.com/support/` and `http://backoffice.microsoft.com/bbs/newsgroups.asp`. The second URL allows access to the newsgroups described in the section "Newsgroups," later in this appendix.

Companies and Magazines

Many companies offer support, training, and other services. These companies are usually a combination of consultants and resellers. To find larger support companies, peruse magazines, such as *PC Magazine*, *InfoWorld*, and *PC Week*.

Consultants

Independent consultants are found in virtually all locations. They are sometimes difficult to find, and most consultants don't advertise. Consultants are usually one and two person outfits, and they are typically expensive.

Similar to the procedure with stores (discussed next), always check references, if possible. Check the consultant's areas of expertise. A consultant who is respected in the field and writes articles and books is probably qualified.

Ask the consultant if he or she is using tools, such as Microsoft TechNet and MSDN. If not, the consultant is probably going to spend a lot of time reinventing the wheel by trying to solve problems that were solved and documented long ago.

Consultants' rates vary, with most requiring either a minimum charge of one to two hours, and/or a charge for travel time. Most consultants do not have a storefront, so walk-in business is not the norm. Hourly rates vary from a low of about $100 to a high of almost $350. Generally, the higher-priced service people are going to solve the problem more quickly than the lower-priced ones.

Stores

Many companies offer services to users of Microsoft Windows NT. Start with local, non-chain computer stores. Most chain stores do not specialize in offering service, while non-chain stores usually excel in this type of service. Ask for references. Some businesses are not nearly as good as they seem.

Rates vary, with most requiring either a minimum charge of one to two hours and/or a charge for travel time. Consider bringing in the computer if possible, to save on the cost of repair. Hourly rates vary from a low of about $50 to a high of almost $200. Generally the higher-priced organizations will solve the problem quicker than the lower-priced ones.

NOTE   No one has solved the problem of paying for incompetence. You hire someone to do a job and may actually end up paying for his or her learning experience. To avoid paying for work that is not solving the problem, be sure to check references, if possible.

User Groups

User groups are a two-way street: If you get assistance from the group, you should support them, as well. Most user groups are either not funded or very limited financially—don't ask them to call you back long distance.

Table C.1 is a listing of some Windows NT user's groups. Please either check the group's Web page or e-mail the contact at the address given for more information about such points as the group's meeting place, date, and time. Some user groups don't hold regular meetings, but there may be other assistance the group can provide.

Sizes of groups range from small (perhaps fewer than 20 members), to medium (about 20 to 100 members), to large (generally more than 100 members).

No user group in your area? Start one! Most newspapers will provide free publicity. Meetings can usually be arranged at local libraries, schools, or at your business. You will meet new people, make friends, and become very popular. Oh, and if you didn't guess, starting a user group will take some time and effort—but it's worth it!

TABLE C.1: Some Windows NT User Groups around the World

Users Group Name	Url/Web page address	City/State/Country	Group Size	Contact
Birmingham Windows NT Users Group	None	Birmingham, Alabama	Small	Mike Chilson mchilson@bwntug.org
Huntsville NT Users Group - HUNTUG	http://www.mbsinc.com/huntug	Huntsville, Alabama	Medium	Dan Wygant huntug@mbsinc.com
Anchorage Windows NT Users Group	http://www.rmm.com/awntug/	Anchorage, Alaska	Unknown	Jon Dawson jdawson@anc.ak.net
Interior Alaska Windows NT Users Group	http://www.iawntug.org/	Fairbanks, Alaska	Small	Roger M. Marty marty@rmm.com
Windows NT Group (Argentina)	http://mspro.smart.com.ar	Capital Federal, Argentina	Medium	Ricardo Fig RFig@smart.com.ar
NT Users Group	None	San Miguel, Argentina	Unknown	Angulo ANGULOA@TELEFONICA.COM.AR
Phoenix PCUG NT SIG	None	Phoenix, Arizona	Unknown	Ray Moore nt-sig@phoenixpcug.org
Brisbane NT Users Group	http://www.ozemail.com.au/~dkowald/bntug.htm	Brisbane, Australia	Unknown	Derek Kowald dkowald@ozemail.com.au
Queensland NT Users Group	http://www.qntug.asn.au/	Brisbane, Australia	Medium	David Steadson davids@ambience.com
Microsoft Systems Users Group	http://www.adfa.oz.au/~rjn/msug/	Canberra, Australia	Medium	Neil Pinkerton neil.pinkerton@cao.mts.dec.com

Continued on next page

TABLE C.1 CONTINUED: Some Windows NT User Groups around the World

Users Group Name	Url/Web page address	City/State/Country	Group Size	Contact
Melbourne NT Users Group	http://www.co.rmit.edu.au/ausnt	Melbourne, Australia	Small	Mark A. Gregory m.gregory@rmit.edu.au
Perth NT Users Group	None	Perth, Australia	Small	Kevin Merritt kevinm@acslink.aone.net.au
Suntug NT Users Group	None	Sunshine Coast, Australia	Unknown	Peter Williams peter@beachaccess.com.au
Sydney NT Users Group	None	Sydney, Australia	Unknown	J. Noiles killara@hotmail.com
NT Users in Vienna	None	Vienna, Austria	Unknown	Gerhard Wenk wenk@vienna.at
Windows NT Users group of Austria	http://www.wug.or.at	Vienna, Austria	Medium	Sepp Reichholf josef.reichholf@reichholf.co.at
WUG-Oesterreich	http://www.wug.or.at	Vienna, Austria	Medium	Windows User Group Oesterreich josef.reichholf@reichholf.co.at
MBS	None	Belgium	Small	Gonzalez Jose jgon@usa.net
BeNTUG - Belgian NT Users Group	http://www.bentug.org	Brussels, Belgium	Medium	Bentug Info info@bentug.org
NTX - Belgian Windows NT Corporate Account Group	http://www.econ.kuleuven.ac.be/ntx	Leuven, Belgium	Medium	Wim Van Holder Wim.VanHolder@econ.kuleuven.ac.be

Continued on next page

TABLE C.1 CONTINUED: Some Windows NT User Groups around the World

Users Group Name	Url/Web page address	City/State/Country	Group Size	Contact
DIN NT Users Group	None	Curitiba, Brazil	Small	Wallace A.B.S. Macedo wallace@furukawa.com.br
Exchange	None	Rio de Janeiro, Brazil	Unknown	Roberto Boclin boclin@unikey.com.br
NT Users Group Brazil - NT.br	None	Rio de Janeiro, Brazil	Unknown	Paul Smith psmith@centroin.com.br
NT Services	None	Sao Paulo, Brazil	Unknown	Ana analucia@opus.com.br
Fresno PC Users Group	None	Fresno, California	Large	Susy Ball Or George Simpson susyball@aol.com or georgesi@cybergate.com
jk	None	Los Angles, California	Medium	La User's Group bla@aol.com
Los Angeles Windows NT Users Group	http://www.lantug.org	Los Angeles, California	Large	Jerry Boshear info@lantug.org
Riverside NT Users Group	None	Riverside, California	Unknown	Chris Navigato chris@navigato.com
Sacramento NT Users Group	None	Sacramento, California	Unknown	Steven W. Linthicum slinthi@ns.net
San Diego County Windows NT Users Group	http://www.sdwntug.org	San Diego, California	Unknown	Chris Dickey webmaster@sdwntug.org
Northern California Windows NT Users Group	http://www.actioninc.com/winntug.htm	San Francisco, California	Unknown	Check With The Group's Web Page
NT Engineering Assoc. (NTEA)	http://www.wntea.org	San Jose, California	Large	Michael Masterson mmasterson@taos.com

Continued on next page

TABLE C.1 CONTINUED: Some Windows NT User Groups around the World

Users Group Name	Url/Web page address	City/State/Country	Group Size	Contact
Southern California Exchange Users Group	None	Santa Monica, California	Medium	Ivan K. Nikkhoo `ivann@vertexsystems.com`
Edmonton Windows NT/BackOffice User Group	`http://www.tnc.com/mug`	Edmonton, Alberta, Canada	Medium	Leigh Anne Chisholm `lachisho@tnc.com`
csp	None	Kishibeu, Yukon Territory, Canada	Small	Timur Fbucashvili `tt97702@usm.md`
Quebec Windows NT Users Group	None	Montreal, Quebec, Canada	Unknown	Maxime Bombardier `maxime@4dm.com`
NT Networking and MCSE Forum	`http://move.to/mcse_mtl`	Montreal, Quebec, Canada	Small	Florian Hehlen `fh@binex.com`
Vancouver Island NT Users Group	`http://www.vintug.bc.ca`	Victoria British Columbia, Canada	Large	Guy Gondor `webmaster@vintug.bc.ca`
Vancouver NT Users Group (VANTUG)	`http://www.vantug.com`	Vancouver British Columbia, Canada	Large	Nancy Pearce `nancy@steeves.bc.ca`
Windows NT Group - La Serena, Chile	None	La Serena, Chile	Small	Pablo Pea, `win-nt` `@mercury.andesnet.cl`
Download Center	None	Nj, China	Unknown	Ghost `Heaven_ghost@163.net`
NT-Colombia-Cali	None	Cali, Colombia	Small	Guillermo Matiz `gmatizo@col2.telecom` `.com.co`

Continued on next page

TABLE C.1 CONTINUED: Some Windows NT User Groups around the World

Users Group Name	Url/Web page address	City/State/Country	Group Size	Contact
GUNTCOL	None	Cartagena de Indias, Santafé de Bogotá, Colombia	Unknown	Tomas Mac Master ima@axisgate.com
Rocky Mountain Windows NT Users Group	http://www.rmwntug.org	Denver, Colorado	Unknown	Dennis Martin 76314.1441@compuserve.com
Northern Colorado Windows NT Users Group	None	Fort Collins, Colorado	Unknown	Eric Leftwich ncwntug@ataman.com
Connecticut Area NT Users Group	None	Farmington, Connecticut	Medium	Art Alexander Arthur_Alexander@msn.com
Windows NT Group Consults	None	Costa Rica	Unknown	Alejandro Esquivel Rodriguez aesquiv@irazu.una.ac.cr
Zagreb Windows NT Users Group	http://winnt.zv.hr	Zagreb, Croatia (Hrvatska)	Medium	Andrej Skendrovic askendrovic@zv.hr
Association of Windows NT Systems Professionals (NT*Pro)	http://www.ntpro.org	Washington, DC	Large	Charles Kelly ckelly@msn.com
S.Florida NT group	None	Ft. Lauderdale, Florida	Unknown	Gabriel B.H. Polmar mongo@netrox.net
Jacksonville BackOffice Users Group	http://www.jbug.com	Jacksonville, Florida	Unknown	Kevin Haynes jbug@tech-point.com
Jacksonville BackOffice Users Group	None	Jacksonville, Florida	Small	James Farhat jbug@tech-point.com
NW Florida NT Users Group	None	Panama City, Florida	Small	Jeff Bankston jeff@mail.bciassoc.com

Continued on next page

TABLE C.1 CONTINUED: Some Windows NT User Groups around the World

Users Group Name	Url/Web page address	City/State/Country	Group Size	Contact
Atlanta BackOffice Users Group	None	Atlanta, Georgia	Large	Lisa Thomassie mind_share@msn.com
Looking for One	None	Atlanta, Georgia	Unknown	Donameche Miller Donameche@Tsi.Tsifax.Com
Manu	None	Essen, Germany	Unknown	Lars Hasshoff lhasshof@manu.com
NT Guatemala Users Group	None	Guatemala City, Guatemala	Small	Jose A. Chajon viacomp@guate.net
Big Island NT	http://bintug.org	Kamuela, Hawaii	Small	Matthew Pearce sysop@bintug.org
Boise NT Users Group (BNTUG)	http://www.bntug.com (under development)	Boise, Idaho	Small	Kelly Householder kellyh@primenet.com
Windows NT Users Group of the Chicago Computer Society	http://billslater.com/ntsig.htm	Chicago, Illinois	Small	Bill Slater slater@xsite.net
infosys nt group	None	Bangalore, India	Unknown	Krishnakumar krishnakumarc@inf.com
NT Developers Group, INDIA	None	Bangalore, India	Small	Nilendu Pal nilendu@wipinfo.soft.net
Trigent-systems	None	Bangalore, India	Small	Saravana Bhavan saravana_bk@trigent.com
Migration from Novell Netware to Windows NT	None	Bombay, India	Medium	Manoj Rakheja manoj.rakheja@owenscorning.com

Continued on next page

TABLE C.1 CONTINUED: Some Windows NT User Groups around the World

Users Group Name	Url/Web page address	City/State/Country	Group Size	Contact
KPMF NT Users Group	None	Chennai, India	Small	Solomon Sagayaraj solomonj@hotmail.com
NTGROUP	None	Chennai, India	Small	M.Subramonian MSM24@HOTMAIL.COM
Welcome Group	None	Chennai, India	Unknown	Santhosh santhosh@pentafour.com
Mavericks	None	Madras, India	Small	Ramesh Venkatraman tnvlramesh@hotmail.com
HAWKS	None	New Delhi, India	Small	Himanshu Sharma himanshu @rsysi.stpn.soft.net
Aroostook NT Users Group	http://www.aroostook.org	Huntington Indiana	Unknown	Jerry Curtis winnt_users @aroostook.org
Windows NT Users Group of Indianapolis	http://www.wintugi.org	Indianapolis, Indiana	Medium	Peter Vanvleet vanvleetp@juno.com
gba c-250	None	Bandung, Indonesia	Unknown	Ipoel ikocel@rocketmail.com
NT Blom Indonesia	None	Kemang Raya 24 Jakarta 12730, Indonesia	Unknown	Muhammad Abduh ma@blom.co.id
MS Israel	None	Tel Aviv, Israel	Medium	Cohen Gal root@widecom.sys.co.il
Windows NT Italian Users Group WNTIUG	None	Potenza, Italy	Medium	Enrico Fasulo webmaster@powernet.it
WIN NT - BHS Gruppo Italia - Discussione	None	Rome, Italy	Unknown	Davide Rossi rossi@ancitel.it

Continued on next page

TABLE C.1 CONTINUED: Some Windows NT User Groups around the World

Users Group Name	Url/Web page address	City/State/Country	Group Size	Contact
Windows NT Users Group of Indianapolis	`http://www.wintugi.org`	Indianapolis, Indiana	Medium	Peter Vanvleet `vanvleetp@juno.com`
ClieNT & Servers	None	Ames, Iowa	Unknown	Rick Gammon `bulldog@netins.net`
Iowa NT Users Group	`http://nt-resources.idesignworks.com`	Cedar Rapids, Iowa	Medium	Don Howard `DonHoward@earthlink.net`
IOWA Windows NT Users Group	None	Iowa City, Iowa	Unknown	Alex Postnikov `apostnik@blue.weeg.uiowa.edu`
MS Israel	None	Tel Aviv, Israel	Medium	Cohen Gal `root@widecom.sys.co.il`
Japan Windows NT Users Group	`http://www.jwntug.or.jp/`	Tokyo, Japan	Large	Ryoji Kaneko `rkaneko@jwntug.or.jp`
Tokyo English NT Users Group	`http://www.tentug.org`	Tokyo, Japan	Unknown	Administrator `admin@tentug.org`
Kansas City Windows NT Users Group	None	Kansas City, Kansas	Unknown	Steve Rodgers `srodgers@kumc.edu`
Northeast Kansas Windows NT Users Group	None	Unknown, somewhere in Kansas	Unknown	Lad `lad@tinman.dot.state.ks.us`
JPA Communications	None	Elizabethtown, Kentucky	Small	June Mizoguchi `jpa@ekx.infi.net`
NT Bluegrass Users Group (NTBUG)	`http://www.rmm.com/ntbug/`	Lexington, Kentucky	Unknown	Richard K. Marshall `rkm@mis.net`

Continued on next page

TABLE C.1 CONTINUED: Some Windows NT User Groups around the World

Users Group Name	Url/Web page address	City/State/Country	Group Size	Contact
NT-ISP-Support	None	Lexington, Kentucky	Unknown	Lee Murphy web@chapel1.com
LitNT	None	Kaunas, Lithuania	Small	Ricardas Baltaduonis baltad@soften.ktu.lt
Louisiana WinNT Users Group	None	Monroe, Louisiana	Small	Richard Driggers richard@lawinntug.org
NT Users Group	None	Unknown, somewhere in Louisiana	Unknown	Laird Goolsby laird@addtech.com
NT4U	http://www.info-trek.com/nt4uhome.htm	Kuala Lumpur, Malaysia	Unknown	Noel Teng nt4u@lycosemail.com
PowerNT	None	Kuala Lumpur, Malaysia	Large	Ahmad Ridzuan Mohd Noor ridzuan.mn@feldaprodata.com.my
Baltimore Windows NT Users Group (BUGME)	http://www.techarchitects.com/bugme	Baltimore, Maryland	Small	Jack Bauer jackb@techarchitects.com
New England Computer Society Windows 95/NT Users Group	None	Springfield, Massachusetts	Small	Rene M. Laviolette rene@costimator.com
NENTUG	http://www.nentug.org.	Waltham, Massachusetts	Medium	Mike Eisenberg mikeei@micrsoft.com
BWUG - Boston Windows Users Group	http://www.bwug.org	Waltham, Massachusetts	Medium	Steve Allen sallen@world.std.com
WinTech Group	http://www.webss.com	Boston/Waltham Massachusetts	Small	Len Segal lsegal@fc1.net

Continued on next page

TABLE C.1 CONTINUED: Some Windows NT User Groups around the World

Users Group Name	Url/Web page address	City/State/Country	Group Size	Contact
GUNT - Grupo de Usarios de NT	None	Celaya, Mexico	Unknown	German Rodriguez soporte@mail.mindvox.ciateq.mx
West Michigan NT Users Group (WMNTUG)	http://www.wmntug.org	Grand Rapids, Michigan	Medium	Brett R. Mello bmello@perrigo.com
Great Lakes Windows NT Users Group	http://www.ntexperts.com/greatlakes	Southfield, Michigan	Large	Tim Rothe GreatLakes@NTug.com
Michigan Windows NT Users Group	None	Southfield, Michigan	Unknown	Donald Barry dbarry@wisne.com
Minneapolis Windows NT Users Group	http://mnnt1.hep.umn.edu/ntug/ntug.cgi	Minneapolis, Minnesota	Small	Henley Quadling bleimeyer.paul@mayo.edu
Minnesota Windows NT/BackOffice User's Group	http://www.mnwinnt.org	Twin Cities, Minnesota	Large	Paul Bleimeyer paulb@mayo.edu
Windows NT Users Group of St. Louis (WNTUG-STL)	http://www.directpt.com/wntug-stl	St. Louis, Missouri	Large	Bryan Muehlberger bryan@directpoint.net
csp	None	Kishibeu, Moldova	Small	Timur Fbucashvili tt97702@usm.md
Windows NT The Netherlands (TADIS)	None	Leusden, Netherlands	Small	A.P. Meeuwsen tadis@Compuserve.com
Las Vegas Windows NT Users Group	http://www.lv.vitrex.com/lvwntug/default.htm	Las Vegas, Nevada	Medium	Kenneth Pribble ken.pribble@vitrex.com

Continued on next page

TABLE C.1 CONTINUED: Some Windows NT User Groups around the World

Users Group Name	Url/Web page address	City/State/Country	Group Size	Contact
NT Support	None	Las Vegas, Nevada	Unknown	Nigel Sampson Nigel@therio.net
New Jersey Windows NT Users Group	http://www.njwindows.org	Edison, New Jersey	Medium	David J. Straley djs@sandyhook.com
The Mad Scientist Club	None	Warren, New Jersey	Small	Frank A. Del Buono delbuono@hiserv-na.com
New Jersey PC Users Group - NT-SIG	http://www.njpcug.org	Wyckoff, New Jersey	Medium	Terry P. Gustafson terryg@warwick.net
Developer' SIG	None	Unknown, somewhere in New Jersey	Unknown	Djs@Cnj.Digex.Net djs@cnj.digex.net
Monkeys	None	Albuquerque, New Mexico	Small	Pedro Morales Pmorales@bernco.gov
Albuquerque WindowsNT Users Group	http://mack.rt66.com/jheald/ntuser.htm	Albuquerque, New Mexico	Small	Jerry Heald jheald@RT66.com
Capital District NT/Backoffice Users Group	None	Albany, New York	Small	Cindy Hermann hermann@taconic.net
Westchester County NT Users Group	None	Elmsford, New York	Unknown	Dinesh Ganesh sherrydin@yahoo.com
New York Developers SIG Only	http://budman.cmd1.noaa.gov/rmwntug/user_groups/nyntsig3.htm	New York, New York	Unknown	Check With The Group's Web Page
New York Windows NT Users Group	None	New York, New York	Large	Bill Zack wzack@compuserve.com

Continued on next page

TABLE C.1 CONTINUED: Some Windows NT User Groups around the World

Users Group Name	Url/Web page address	City/State/Country	Group Size	Contact
New York City NT Developers SIG	None	New York, New York	Unknown	Lee_T@Access.Digex.Net lee_t@access.digex.net
New York City Windows NT Users Group	None	New York, New York	Large	John Rhodes JRhodes@bbn.com
Rochester/Monroe County Library Users Group	None	Rochester, New York	Small	David Deaugustine davidd@mcls.rochester.lib.ny.us
SI NT Admin	None	Staten Island, New York	Unknown	Craig Caggiano crc61@bigfoot.com
Long Island NT Users Group	None	Uniondale, New York	Unknown	Gerald Shamberger Gerald.Shamberger@uscoopers.com
NZNTUG	None	New Zealand	Unknown	Nathan Mercer nathan@MCS.co.nz
Taranaki NT Users Group	None	New Plymouth, New Zealand	Unknown	Chris Sharpe chris.sharpe@computerland.co.nz
NCNT	None	Charlotte, North Carolina	Unknown	Stephen Carabetta vianet@ix.netcom.com
Piedmont Triad NT Users Group	http://www.ptntug.org	Greensboro, North Carolina	Medium	Dr. Bill Bailey baileyb@ptntug.org
TNTUG - Triangle NT Users Group	None	Raleigh, North Carolina	Large	John Mcmains tntug@networks.com

Continued on next page

TABLE C.1 CONTINUED : Some Windows NT User Groups around the World

Users Group Name	Url/Web page address	City/State/Country	Group Size	Contact
Red River Windows NT Users Group	None	Grand Forks, North Dakota	Medium	Roy Beard rbeard@plains.nodak.edu
MANUS - Microsoft Advanced Network Users Society	None	Norway	Large	Kay Seljeseth Kay.Seljeseth@Cinet.No
BACUP - Backoffice Atlantic Canada Users Platform	http://www.bacup.com	Nova Scotia	Medium	John Gauthier gauthier.john@mit-it.com
COUNT, Central Ohio Users NT	None	Columbus, Ohio	Medium	Ed Zirkle Zirkle.5@osu.edu
Dayton NT Users Group (DAYNTUG)	None	Dayton, Ohio	Medium	Chris T Haaker chris.haaker@stdreg.com
NT in Manufacturing Automation Users	None	Findlay, Ohio	Unknown	Bill Wagner BillW@FESTech.com
Philadelphia Back Office Users Group (PBOG)	None	Philadelphia, Pennsylvania	Medium	Bill Wolff; Mike Ward bill@wolffdata.com, Mike_Ward@on1c.com
Pittsburgh Area Windows NT Users Group(PAWNTUG)	http://www.pghnt.org	Pittsburgh, Pennsylvania	Medium	Robert Smith Jr., Avram Cheaney info@pghnt.org
Print & Publishing in Poland	http://arra.com.pl	Kalisz, Poland	Medium	Roman Lewicki Webmaster@arra.com.pl
Media Print & Publishing in Poland - Inwestycje, Marketin, Media	http://www.arra.com.pl	Kalisz, Poland	Small	Roman Lewicki Webmaster@arra.com.pl

Continued on next page

TABLE C.1 CONTINUED: Some Windows NT User Groups around the World

Users Group Name	Url/Web page address	City/State/Country	Group Size	Contact
Polish users of Windows NT 4.0 Server	None	Poznan, Poland	Medium	Tomasz Waslowicz tomaszwa@free.polbox.pl
Windows NT Group - Portugal (WNTGP)	None	Portugal	Unknown	Luis Centeio luisc@poboxes.com
PRUNT (Puerto Rico NT Users Group)	None	Toa Alta, Puerto Rico	Unknown	Richard Arroyo rarroyo@prtc.net
Rhode Island NT Users Group	None	Coventry, Rhode Island	Unknown	Ernie Quaglieri celebty@concentric.net
SneNUG Southern New England Network Users Group	None	East Providence, Rhode Island	Large	Bill Dwyer bill1d@loa.com
Russian Windows NT Users Group	None	Moscow, Russian Federation	Unknown	Konstantin Gusev gusevk@quarta.com
Cape Microsoft Users Group	None	Cape Town, South Africa	Unknown	Gordon Thelander enigmax@iafrica.com
Grupo de Usarios de NT Espanoles	None	Valencia, Spain	Unknown	Isaac Jaramillo ijs@mx3.redestb.es
NT Anvndargruppen	None	Stockholm, Sweden	Unknown	Friberg iir@iir.telegate.se
NT Syria by CompuCrest	None	Damascus, Syria	Small	A. Aziz maziz@usa.net
CERN Windows NT Users Group	None	Geneva, Switzerland	Unknown	Alberto AIMAR alberto.aimar@cern.ch
Chattanooga-River Valley NT Users Group	None	Chattanooga, Tennessee	Unknown	James james@press.southern.edu

Continued on next page

TABLE C.1 CONTINUED: Some Windows NT User Groups around the World

Users Group Name	Url/Web page address	City/State/Country	Group Size	Contact
NT4_Users Group	None	Martin, Tennessee	Large	J. Garner jgarner@utm.edu
Microsoft Networking SIG	http://budman.cmd1.noaa.gov/rmntug/user_groups/d1sugan.htm	In Tennessee, see their Web page	Unknown	Deborah deborah@microsoft.com
Capital Area NT Users Group	None	Austin, Texas	Unknown	Perry Stokes stokes@jump.net
DFW NT Users Group	None	Dallas/Ft. Worth, Texas	Unknown	Ralph Shumway rshumway@swbell.net
Dallas BackOffice Users Group (DeBUG)	http://www.debug.org/	Dallas, Texas	Medium	Mark Saum info@debug.org
North Texas NT Users Group (NTsquared)	None	Dallas, Texas	Large	Charles Reiss charlier@unicomp.net
The El Paso & Las Cruces Windows NT User Group	None	El Paso, Texas	Medium	Shane A. Weddle swedd1e@world1net.att.net
Fort Worth NT Users Group	None	Fort Worth, Texas	Unknown	Paul Knox paulk@netaci.com
Houston Area NT Users Group	None	Houston, Texas	Unknown	Arthur Kettelhut atkette@ix.netcom.com
Houston Microsoft Users Group	None	Houston, Texas	Medium	Alisa Wanger alisaw@infotecweb.com
NT TECH PARTY	None	Houston, Texas	Unknown	Hiphop hiphop1uva@hotmail.com
Plano BackOffice Users Group (PBUG)	None	Plano, Texas	Medium	Marcia Loughry mloughry@cyberramp.net

Continued on next page

TABLE C.1 CONTINUED: Some Windows NT User Groups around the World

Users Group Name	Url/Web page address	City/State/Country	Group Size	Contact
Alamo PC Organzation Windows NT SIG	None	San Antonio, Texas	Medium	Larry Lentz `Larry@LentzComputer.com`
Rio Grande Valley Area IT Group	None	Weslaco, Texas	Unknown	Cindy Barber `cabarber@usa.net`
ThaiNTprimer	None	Bangkok, Thailand	Unknown	Siramet `siramet@yth.co.th`
Turkey NT Users Group	None	Istanbul, Turkey	Small	Ozan Zkara `OZAN.OZKARA@USA.NET`
Wyndows NT GRUBU	None	Istanbul, Turkey	Small	Harun Aksoz `harunaksoz@hotmail.com.tr`
TURKWNT	`http://www.turkwnt.org`	Izmir, Turkey	Medium	E.Onder Kokturk `kokturk@bornova.ege.edu.tr`
Emirates NT Users Group	None	Dubai, United Arab Emirates	Small	Rizwan Ahmed Khan `rizwan@emirates.net.ae`
Microsoft Windows NT & BackOffice Forum	None	London, United Kingdom	Large	Tony Larks `tony_larks@research-group.co.uk`
The Microsoft Windows (NT) & BackOffice Forum (UK)	`http://www.research-group.co.uk`	London, United Kingdom	Large	Simon Moores `smoores@softech.co.uk`
Wasatch Windows NT Users Group	`http://www.wwntug.org`	Salt Lake, Utah	Medium	Steve Adams `sadams@acs.utah.edu`
Vermont NT Users Group (VTNTUG)	None	Burlington, Vermont	Medium	Michael Gambler `mgambler@sover.net`

Continued on next page

TABLE C.1 CONTINUED: Some Windows NT User Groups around the World

Users Group Name	Url/Web page address	City/State/Country	Group Size	Contact
Central Virginia NT Users Group	`http://www.harbour.net/ntgroup/`	Richmond, Virginia	Small	Anthony S. Harbour, Med `aharbour@harbour.net`
BackOffice Professionals Association	None	Seattle, Washington	Large	Marjorie James `backoffice@ariscorp.com`
Pacific NorthWest NT Users/Small Business Group	`http://www.ntug.org`	Tacoma, Washington	Small	Chris Melton `info@ntug.org`
Wisconsin Nt Users Group	None	Brookfield, Wisconsin	Medium	Bob Escher `bescher@wintug.org`
NT User Group	None	Belgrade, Yugoslavia	Large	Milan Zivkovic `zivkovic@internetplus.ch`
BackOffice Users Group	`http://www.elcoma.ch/bousgroup/?`	Belgrade, Yugoslavia	Large	Milan Zivkovic `mzivkovic@elcoma.ch`
Swiss NT Users Group	None	Unknown, e-mail contact for information	Unknown	Deffer@Eunet.Ch `deffer@eunet.ch`
German NT Users Group	None	Unknown, e-mail contact for information	Unknown	Paulette Feller `pfeler@skd.de`
French Windows NT Users Group (FWNTUG)	`http://www.fwntug.org/`	Unknown, see Web page for information.	Large	Anthony Moillic `AMoillic@fwntug.org`
IRELAND	None	Unknown, e-mail contact for information.	Unknown	John Doherty `doherty_mj@hotmail.com`

Virtual Support Groups

There are a number of groups that are dedicated to assisting users of Microsoft products; ClubWin is an important one of these. This group is part of Microsoft's marketing arm. It is comprised of volunteer, non-Microsoft users who have demonstrated a great deal of skill in their fields.

I am a member of ClubWin. The group is an excellent source of help and information.

ClubWin

We are a self-organized group of individual computer professionals and advanced users from the U.S., Canada, and Europe who have hundreds of thousands of hours of experience with Microsoft Windows 95. The group is made up of hardware, software, applications, networking, and support professionals who have a commitment to assisting others and providing information and support for others using Windows 95. We have joined forces to cover major online services (such as MSN, CompuServe, America Online, Prodigy, and so on) and the World Wide Web. The ClubWin designation on a Web page, in a tagline or signature, designates a person who has made a commitment to our organization.

The ClubWin Web page is located at `http://www.clubwin.com`.

> **NOTE** ClubIE recently merged with ClubWin.

Training for Registry Use

There are several companies that offer training on registry-related maintenance. Contact Data-Tech Institute at `http://www.datatech.com` for more information on their courses.

Another source of training is to check with your local college or university. For example, Boston University offers a number of excellent training courses for Windows professionals, mostly in the Boston, Massachusetts area.

Generally, conferences offer some useful training opportunities. Most conferences are advertised using direct mail.

Other Internet Information Sources

The Internet offers many areas of support and assistance, including newsgroups and chat (IRC) groups. Both of these resources can be unexpected sources of valuable advice and information.

Newsgroups

Other sources of information on the Internet include virtual newsgroups, or simply newsgroups.

The `msnews.microsoft.com` site has all of the Microsoft supported newsgroups. There are over 700 different groups on this news server, and between 40 and 50 groups are dedicated to various versions of Windows NT. As well, there are a number of programming groups oriented toward Windows NT platforms from which valuable information may be gleaned.

If you are unfamiliar with using newsgroups, you need to have a newsgroup reader. There are many free, or low cost, newsreaders. For example, Microsoft's Outlook Express has a built-in newsreader. Also Forté offers a product called FreeAgent; see their licensing agreement to know if you qualify for a free version. You can contact Forté at `http://www.forteinc.com/agent/`.

There are well established protocols for posting in a newsgroup. It is generally best if you simply read messages for a few days to get the feel of things. This is called *lurking*. Then you will have a feel for how questions are asked. Follow these simple guidelines when posting:

- Don't post "off topic" messages. If you are in the Windows NT Setup group, don't post a message about Exchange.

- Never, ever post a "get rich quick" message.

- Make the title of your message or topic informative and catchy. You want the right people to read your question. Don't title your message "Help Me!" Say something like, "System Hangs with BSD after Installing ASDF App."

- Though your message will contain your e-mail address (and you should include your name and e-mail in the message), don't expect anyone to e-mail you a solution. They will post the reply in the newsgroup, so check there. It is considered bad form to ask for e-mail replies.

- To avoid getting SPAM (unsolicited, mass e-mail marking messages), it is considered acceptable to subtly change your e-mail address, both in the program and in the message signature. Many users add something to their e-mail address that is somewhat obvious in that it doesn't belong there; for example `phipson@nospam.acm.org`, would be altered by someone by deleting the "nospam." part of the address.

- Last, but certainly not least, check the newsgroup's previous messages before posting your problem. It is quite possible that someone else has had the same problem recently and you can benefit from responses to that person. People get tired of answering the same question over and over again.

Chat

Chat (IRC) is a well used part of the Internet. Chat sessions can sometimes be useful, especially if you get onto the right chat server. The best chat server for Windows NT users is accessed infrequently, but it can be helpful. Figure C.1 lists the chats that were available to users early one Saturday morning. There were only 11 users online with this server, guaranteeing good performance.

OK, this is secret, very hidden, never discussed, information: The URL for Microsoft's BackOffice chat server is `chat.backoffice.microsoft.com`. Got that? Virtually no one knows about this chat server.

One interesting thing about chat servers is that if there is not a chat covering the topic you are interested in, you can start your own chat session. Microsoft also offers an ActiveX control to access chat groups. It is available at the Microsoft BackOffice Web site. The best chat client is Microsoft's Comic Chat. Go to Microsoft's Web site at `http://www.microsoft.com/ie/chat/chat21overview.htm` and download Comic Chat.

> **NOTE** Like those classy Comic Chat characters? If so, you can actually create a personalized character for your identity. Use the Comic Chat Character editor, which is available at the same Web address as Comic Chat.

FIGURE C.1:

Chat Room List: This shows
how little used the
Microsoft BackOffice Chat
server really is.

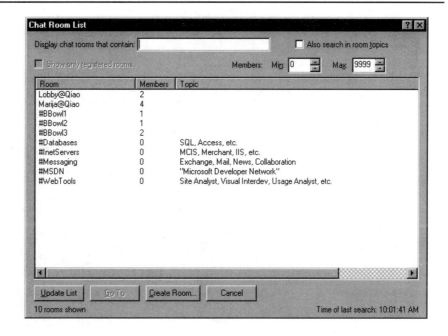

APPENDIX

D

Performance Counters and Descriptions

Table D.1 shows the performance monitor counters for a typical Windows NT Server installation that includes Microsoft IIS (Internet Information Server). These entries are saved in two registry data keys—one key for the counter name, the other for the help description. All performance counters are arranged in a hierarchical manner. Refer to Figure D.1 for an example of the first few entries shown in Table D.1.

FIGURE D.1:

Add to Chart: The Add to Chart dialog box allows the Performance Monitor to add a counter for display.

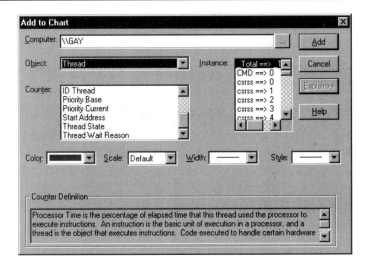

Let me begin by explaining the columns in Table D.1. The first column in Table D.1 is the index number for the counter name and the second column is the counter name itself. The counter names are stored in the REG_MULTI_SZ data key at HKEY_LOCAL_MACHINE\SOFTWARE\Microsoft\Windows NT\CurrentVersion\Perflib\009\Counter.

The third column is the counter description. The counter descriptions are stored in the REG_MULTI_SZ data key at HKEY_LOCAL_MACHINE\SOFTWARE\Microsoft\Windows NT\CurrentVersion\Perflib\009\Help.

All of the counter descriptions are taken directly from the registry, so your counter descriptions should match those listed in this appendix. Each description also has an index. The description index is typically one more than the index for the counter name. For example, to derive the counter description for counter 16 (File Read Bytes/sec), add 1 to the counter name index (16 + 1), which results in the description having an index of 17.

NOTE What's that hive named 009 there for? This information is language specific; the names for the performance counters and their descriptions are based on a language. If your installation is not US English (language ID 009), it is possible that your registry will have a different sub-hive here with counters and descriptions in your language.

See Chapter 9, "Programming and the Registry—A Developer's Paradise?" for more on using these counters, and for information on adding custom counters for your applications and systems. All of the object and counter index numbers mean little at this stage. The (hidden) registry hive HKEY_PERFORMANCE_DATA contains the necessary information to allow an application to successfully interact with and display performance data.

NOTE I've noticed that RegEdit has some difficulty with these sub-hives. I suggest using RegEdt32 to edit and view these items.

TABLE D.1: Registry Performance Counters on a Windows NT Server with IIS Installed

Index	Counter or Object Name	Description or Help Text
2	System	The *System object type* includes those counters that apply to all processors on the computer collectively. These counters represent the activity of all processors on the computer.
4	Memory	The *Memory object type* includes those counters that describe the behavior of both real and virtual memory on the computer. Real memory is allocated in units of pages. Virtual memory may exceed real memory in size, causing page traffic as virtual pages are moved between disk and real memory.
6	% Processor Time	*% Processor Time* is expressed as a percentage of the elapsed time that a processor is busy executing a non-Idle thread. It can be viewed as the fraction of the time spent doing useful work. Each processor is assigned an Idle thread in the Idle process, which consumes those unproductive processor cycles not used by any other threads.
8	% Total DPC Time	*% Total DPC Time* is the sum of % DPC Time of all processors divided by the number of processors in the system. (See % DPC Time for details.)
10	File Read Operations/sec	*File Read Operations/sec* is an aggregate of all the file system read operations on the computer.
12	File Write Operations/sec	*File Write Operations/sec* is an aggregate of all the file system write operations on the computer.
14	File Control Operations/sec	*File Control Operations/sec* is an aggregate of all file system operations that are neither reads nor writes. These operations usually include file system control requests or requests for information about device characteristics or status.

TABLE D.1 CONTINUED: Registry Performance Counters on a Windows NT Server with IIS Installed

Index	Counter or Object Name	Description or Help Text
16	File Read Bytes/sec	*File Read Bytes/sec* is an aggregate of the bytes transferred for all the file system read operations on the computer.
18	File Write Bytes/sec	*File Write Bytes/sec* is an aggregate of the bytes transferred for all the file system write operations on the computer.
20	File Control Bytes/sec	*File Control Bytes/sec* is an aggregate of bytes transferred for all file system operations that are neither reads nor writes. These operations usually include file system control requests or requests for information about device characteristics or status.
24	Available Bytes	*Available Bytes* displays the size of the virtual memory currently on the Zeroed, Free, and Standby lists. Zeroed and Free memory is ready for use, with Zeroed memory cleared to zeros. *Standby memory* is memory removed from a process's Working Set, but still available. Notice that this is an instantaneous count, not an average over the time interval.
26	Committed Bytes	*Committed Bytes* displays the size of virtual memory (in bytes) that has been Committed (as opposed to simply reserved). Committed memory must have backing, for example, disk storage available, or must be assured never to need disk storage because main memory is large enough to hold it. Notice that this is an instantaneous count, not an average over the time interval.
28	Page Faults/sec	*Page Faults/sec* is a count of the Page Faults in the processor. A page fault occurs when a process refers to a virtual memory page that is not in its Working Set in main memory. A Page Fault will not cause the page to be fetched from disk if that page is on the standby list already in main memory, or if it is in use by another process with which the page is shared.
30	Commit Limit	*Commit Limit* is the size (in bytes) of virtual memory that can be committed without having to extend the paging file(s). If the paging file(s) can be extended, this is a soft limit.
32	Write Copies/sec	*Write Copies/sec* is the number of page faults that have been satisfied by making a copy of a page when an attempt to write to the page is made. This is an economical way of sharing data since the copy of the page is only made on an attempt to write to the page; otherwise, the page is shared.
34	Transition Faults/sec	*Transition Faults/sec* is the number of page faults resolved by recovering pages that were in transition, that is, being written to disk at the time of the page fault. The pages were recovered without additional disk activity.
36	Cache Faults/sec	*Cache Faults* occur whenever the Cache Manager does not find a file's page in the immediate Cache and must ask the memory manager to locate the page elsewhere in memory or on the disk so that it can be loaded into the immediate Cache.
38	Demand Zero Faults/sec	*Demand Zero Faults* are the number of page faults for pages that must be filled with zeros before the fault is satisfied. If the Zeroed list is not empty, the fault can be resolved by removing a page from the Zeroed list.
40	Pages/sec	*Pages/sec* is the number of pages read from the disk or written to the disk to resolve memory references to pages that were not in memory at the time of the reference. This is the sum of Pages Input/sec and Pages Output/sec. This counter includes paging traffic on behalf of the system Cache to access file data for applications. This value also includes the pages to/from non-cached mapped memory files. This is the primary counter to observe if you are concerned about excessive memory pressure (that is, thrashing) and the excessive paging that may result.

TABLE D.1 CONTINUED: Registry Performance Counters on a Windows NT Server with IIS Installed

Index	Counter or Object Name	Description or Help Text
42	Page Reads/sec	*Page Reads/sec* is the number of times the disk was read to retrieve pages of virtual memory necessary to resolve page faults. Multiple pages can be read during a disk read operation.
44	Processor Queue Length	*Processor Queue Length* is the instantaneous length of the processor queue in units of threads. This counter is always 0, unless you are also monitoring a thread counter. All processors use a single queue in which threads wait for processor cycles. This length does not include the threads that are currently executing. A sustained processor queue length greater than two generally indicates processor congestion. This is an instantaneous count, not an average over the time interval.
46	Thread State	*Thread State* is the current state of the thread. It is 0 for Initialized, 1 for Ready, 2 for Running, 3 for Standby, 4 for Terminated, 5 for Wait, 6 for Transition, and 7 for Unknown. A Running thread is using a processor; a Standby thread is about to use one. A Ready thread wants to use a processor, but is waiting for a processor because none are free. A thread in Transition is waiting for a resource in order to execute, such as waiting for its execution stack to be paged in from disk. A Waiting thread has no use for the processor because it is waiting for a peripheral operation to complete or a resource to become free.
48	Pages Output/sec	*Pages Output/sec* is a count of the number of pages that are written to disk because the pages have been modified in main memory.
50	Page Writes/sec	*Page Writes/sec* is a count of the number of times pages have been written to the disk because they were changed since last retrieved. Each such write operation may transfer a number of pages.
52	Browser	Browser statistics are stored in the Browser group.
54	Announcements Server/sec	*Announcements Server/sec* is the rate that the servers in this domain have announced themselves to this server.
56	Pool Paged Bytes	*Pool Paged Bytes* is the number of bytes in the Paged Pool, a system memory area where space is acquired by operating system components as they accomplish their appointed tasks. Paged Pool pages can be paged out to the paging file when not accessed by the system for sustained periods of time.
58	Pool Nonpaged Bytes	*Pool Nonpaged Bytes* is the number of bytes in the Nonpaged Pool, a system memory area where space is acquired by operating system components as they accomplish their appointed tasks. Nonpaged Pool pages cannot be paged out to the paging file, but instead remain in main memory as long as they are allocated.
60	Pool Paged Allocs	*Pool Paged Allocs* is the number of calls to allocate space in the system Paged Pool. Paged Pool is a system memory area where space is acquired by operating system components as they accomplish their appointed tasks. Paged Pool pages can be paged out to the paging file when not accessed by the system for sustained periods of time.
62	*Pool Paged Resident Byte*	*Pool Paged Resident Bytes* is the size of paged Pool resident in core memory. This is the actual cost of the paged Pool allocation, since this is actively in use and using real physical memory.

TABLE D.1 CONTINUED: Registry Performance Counters on a Windows NT Server with IIS Installed

Index	Counter or Object Name	Description or Help Text
64	Pool Nonpaged Allocs	*Pool Nonpaged Allocs* is the number of calls to allocate space in the system Nonpaged Pool. Nonpaged Pool is a system memory area where space is acquired by operating system components as they accomplish their appointed tasks. Nonpaged Pool pages cannot be paged out to the paging file, but instead remain in main memory as long as they are allocated.
66	Pool Paged Resident Bytes	*Pool Paged Resident Bytes* is the size of paged pool resident in core memory. This is the actual cost of the paged pool.
68	System Code Total Bytes	*System Code Total Bytes* is the number of bytes of pageable pages in ntoskrnl.exe, hal.dll, and the boot drivers and file systems loaded by ntldr/osloader.
70	System Code Resident Bytes	*System Code Resident Bytes* is the number of bytes of System Code Total Bytes currently resident in core memory. This is the code working set of the pageable executive. In addition to this, there is another ~300k bytes of nonpaged kernel code.
72	System Driver Total Bytes	*System Driver Total Bytes* is the number of bytes of pageable pages in all other loaded device drivers.
74	System Driver Resident Bytes	*System Driver Resident Bytes* is the number of bytes of System Driver Total Bytes currently resident in core memory. This number is the code working set of the pageable drivers. In addition to this, there is another 700K bytes of nonpaged driver code.
76	System Cache Resident Bytes	*System Cache Resident Bytes* is the number of bytes currently resident in the global disk cache.
78	Announcements Domain/sec	*Announcements Domain/sec* is the rate that a Domain has announced itself to the network.
80	Election Packets/sec	*Election Packets/sec* is the rate of browser election packets that have been received by this workstation.
82	Mailslot Writes/sec	*Mailslot Writes/sec* is the rate of mailslot messages that have been successfully received.
84	Server List Requests/sec	*Server List Requests/sec* is the rate of requests to retrieve a list of browser servers that have been processed by this workstation.
86	Cache	The *Cache object type* manages memory for rapid access to files. Files on Windows NT are cached in main memory in units of pages. Main memory not being used in the working sets of processes is available to the Cache for this purpose. The Cache preserves file pages in memory for as long as possible to permit access to the data through the file system without having to access the disk.
88	Data Maps/sec	*Data Maps/sec* is the frequency that a file system, such as NTFS or HPFS, maps a page of a file into the Cache to read the page.
90	Sync Data Maps/sec	*Sync Data Maps/sec* counts the frequency that a file system, such as NTFS or HPFS, maps a page of a file into the Cache to read the page and wishes to wait for the Cache to retrieve the page if it is not in main memory.
92	Async Data Maps/sec	*Async Data Maps/sec* is the frequency that an application using a file system, such as NTFS or HPFS, maps a page of a file into the Cache to read the page and does not wish to wait for the Cache to retrieve the page if it is not in main memory.

TABLE D.1 CONTINUED: Registry Performance Counters on a Windows NT Server with IIS Installed

Index	Counter or Object Name	Description or Help Text
94	Data Map Hits %	*Data Map Hits* % is the percentage of Data Maps in the Cache that could be resolved without having to retrieve a page from the disk, i.e. the page was already in physical memory.
96	Data Map Pins/sec	*Data Map Pins/sec* is the frequency of Data Maps in the Cache that resulted in pinning a page in main memory, an action usually preparatory to writing to the file on disk. While pinned, a page's physical address in main memory and virtual address in the Cache will not be altered.
98	Pin Reads/sec	*Pin Reads/sec* is the frequency of reading data into the Cache preparatory to writing the data back to disk. Pages read in this fashion are pinned in memory at the completion of the read. While pinned, a page's physical address in the Cache will not be altered.
100	Sync Pin Reads/sec	*Sync Pin Reads/sec* is the frequency of reading data into the Cache preparatory to writing the data back to disk. Pages read in this fashion are pinned in memory at the completion of the read. The file system will not regain control until the page is pinned in the Cache, in particular, if the disk must be accessed to retrieve the page. While pinned, a page's physical address in the Cache will not be altered.
102	Async Pin Reads/sec	*Async Pin Reads/sec* is the frequency of reading data into the Cache, preparatory to writing the data back to disk. Pages read in this fashion are pinned in memory at the completion of the read. The file system will regain control immediately even if the disk must be accessed to retrieve the page. While pinned, a page's physical address will not be altered.
104	Pin Read Hits %	*Pin Read Hits* % is the percentage of Cache Pin Read requests that hit the Cache, that is, they did not require a disk read in order to provide access to the page in the Cache. While pinned, a page's physical address in the Cache will not be altered. The LAN Redirector uses this method for retrieving Cache information, as does the LAN Server for small transfers. This is usually the method used by the disk file systems as well.
106	Copy Reads/sec	*Copy Reads/sec* is the frequency of reads from Cache pages that involve a memory copy of the data from the Cache to the application's buffer. The LAN Redirector uses this method for retrieving Cache information, as does the LAN Server for small transfers. This is a method used by the disk file systems as well.
108	Sync Copy Reads/sec	*Sync Copy Reads/sec* is the frequency of reads from Cache pages that involve a memory copy of the data from the Cache to the application's buffer. The file system will not regain control until the copy operation is complete, even if the disk must be accessed to retrieve the page.
110	Async Copy Reads/sec	*Async Copy Reads/sec* is the frequency of reads from Cache pages that involve a memory copy of the data from the Cache to the application's buffer. The application will regain control immediately even if the disk must be accessed to retrieve the page.
112	Copy Read Hits %	*Copy Read Hits* % is the percentage of Cache Copy Read requests that hit the Cache, that is, that did not require a disk read in order to provide access to the page in the Cache. A Copy Read is a file read operation that is satisfied by a memory copy from a Cache page to the application's buffer. The LAN Redirector uses this method for retrieving Cache information, as does the LAN Server for small transfers. This is a method used by the disk file systems as well.

TABLE D.1 CONTINUED: Registry Performance Counters on a Windows NT Server with IIS Installed

Index	Counter or Object Name	Description or Help Text
114	MDL Reads/sec	*MDL Reads/sec* is the frequency of reads from Cache pages that use a Memory Descriptor List (MDL) to access the data. The MDL contains the physical address of each page involved in the transfer, and thus can employ a hardware Direct Memory Access (DMA) device to effect the copy. The LAN Server uses this method for large transfers out of the server.
116	Sync MDL Reads/sec	*Sync MDL Reads/sec* is the frequency of reads from Cache pages that use a Memory Descriptor List (MDL) to access the pages. The MDL contains the physical address of each page in the transfer, thus permitting Direct Memory Access (DMA) of the pages. If the accessed page(s) are not in main memory, the caller will wait for the pages to fault in from the disk.
118	Async MDL Reads/sec	*Async MDL Reads/sec* is the frequency of reads from Cache pages using a Memory Descriptor List (MDL) to access the pages. The MDL contains the physical address of each page in the transfer, thus permitting Direct Memory Access (DMA) of the pages. If the accessed page(s) are not in main memory, the calling application program will not wait for the pages to fault in from disk.
120	MDL Read Hits %	*MDL Read Hits %* is the percentage of Cache Memory Descriptor List (MDL) Read requests that hit the Cache, that is, that did not require disk accesses in order to provide memory access to the page(s) in the Cache.
122	Read Aheads/sec	*Read Aheads/sec* is the frequency of Cache reads where the Cache detects sequential access to a file. The read aheads permit the data to be transferred in larger blocks than those being requested by the application, reducing the overhead per access.
124	Fast Reads/sec	*Fast Reads/sec* is the frequency of reads from Cache pages that bypass the installed file system and retrieve the data directly from the Cache. Normally, file I/O requests invoke the appropriate file system to retrieve data from a file, but this path permits direct retrieval of Cache data without file system involvement if the data is in the Cache. Even if the data is not in the Cache, one invocation of the file system is avoided.
126	Sync Fast Reads/sec	*Sync Fast Reads/sec* is the frequency of reads from Cache pages that bypass the installed file system and retrieve the data directly from the Cache. Normally, file I/O requests invoke the appropriate file system to retrieve data from a file, but this path permits direct retrieval of Cache data without file system involvement if the data is in the Cache. Even if the data is not in the Cache, one invocation of the file system is avoided. If the data is not in the Cache, the request (application program call) will wait until the data has been retrieved from disk.
128	Async Fast Reads/sec	*Async Fast Reads/sec* is the frequency of reads from Cache pages that bypass the installed file system and retrieve the data directly from the Cache. Normally, file I/O requests will invoke the appropriate file system to retrieve data from a file, but this path permits direct retrieval of Cache data without file system involvement if the data is in the Cache. Even if the data is not in the Cache, one invocation of the file system is avoided. If the data is not in the Cache, the request (application program call) will not wait until the data has been retrieved from disk, but will get control immediately.
130	Fast Read Resource Misses/sec	*Fast Read Resource Misses/sec* is the frequency of Cache misses necessitated by the lack of available resources to satisfy the request.

TABLE D.1 CONTINUED: Registry Performance Counters on a Windows NT Server with IIS Installed

Index	Counter or Object Name	Description or Help Text
132	Fast Read Not Possibles/sec	*Fast Read Not Possibles/sec* is the frequency of attempts by an Application Program Interface (API) function call to bypass the file system to get at Cache data, that could not be honored without invoking the file system after all.
134	Lazy Write Flushes/sec	*Lazy Write Flushes/sec* is the frequency the Cache's Lazy Write thread has written to disk. Lazy Writing is the process of updating the disk after the page has been changed in memory, so the application making the change to the file does not have to wait for the disk write to complete before proceeding. More than one page can be transferred on each write operation.
136	Lazy Write Pages/sec	*Lazy Write Pages/sec* is the frequency the Cache's Lazy Write thread has written to disk. Lazy Writing is the process of updating the disk after the page has been changed in memory, so the application making the change to the file does not have to wait for the disk write to complete before proceeding. More than one page can be transferred on a single disk write operation.
138	Data Flushes/sec	*Data Flushes/sec* is the frequency the Cache has flushed its contents to disk as the result of a request to flush or to satisfy a write-through file write request. More than one page can be transferred on each flush operation.
140	Data Flush Pages/sec	*Data Flush Pages/sec* is the number of pages the Cache has flushed to disk as a result of a request to flush or to satisfy a write-through file write request. More than one page can be transferred on each flush operation.
142	% User Time	*% User Time* is the percentage of processor time spent in User Mode in non-Idle threads. All application code and subsystem code execute in User Mode. The graphics engine, graphics device drivers, printer device drivers, and the window manager also execute in User Mode. Code executing in User Mode cannot damage the integrity of the Windows NT Executive, Kernel, and device drivers. Unlike some early operating systems, Windows NT uses process boundaries for subsystem protection in addition to the traditional protection of User and Privileged modes. These subsystem processes provide additional protection. Therefore, some work done by Windows NT on behalf of your application may appear in other subsystem processes in addition to the Privileged Time in your process.
144	% Privileged Time	*% Privileged Time* is the percentage of processor time spent in Privileged Mode in non-Idle threads. The Windows NT service layer, the Executive routines, and the Windows NT Kernel execute in Privileged Mode. Device drivers for most devices other than graphics adapters and printers also execute in Privileged Mode. Unlike some early operating systems, Windows NT uses process boundaries for subsystem protection in addition to the traditional protection of User and Privileged modes. These subsystem processes provide additional protection. Therefore, some work done by Windows NT on behalf of your application may appear in other subsystem processes in addition to the Privileged Time in your process.
146	Context Switches/sec	*Context Switches/sec* is the rate of switches from one thread to another. Thread switches can occur either inside of a single process or across processes. A thread switch may be caused either by one thread asking another for information, or by a thread being preempted by another, higher priority thread becoming ready to run. Unlike some early operating systems, Windows NT uses process boundaries for subsystem protection in addition to the traditional protection of User and Privileged modes. These subsystem processes provide additional protection. Therefore, some work done by Windows NT on behalf of an application may appear in other subsystem processes in addition to the Privileged Time in the application. Switching to the subsystem process causes one Context Switch in the application thread. Switching back causes another Context Switch in the subsystem thread.

TABLE D.1 CONTINUED: Registry Performance Counters on a Windows NT Server with IIS Installed

Index	Counter or Object Name	Description or Help Text
148	Interrupts/sec	*Interrupts/sec* is the number of device interrupts the processor is experiencing. A device interrupts the processor when it has completed a task or when it otherwise requires attention. Normal thread execution is suspended during interrupts. An interrupt may cause the processor to switch to another, higher priority thread. Clock interrupts are frequent, and periodic, and create a background of interrupt activity.
150	System Calls/sec	*Systems Calls/sec* is the frequency of calls to Windows NT system service routines. These routines perform all of the basic scheduling and synchronization of activities on the computer, and provide access to non-graphical devices, memory management, and name space management.
152	Level 1 TLB Fills/sec	*Level 1 TLB Fills/sec* is the frequency of faults that occur when reference is made to memory whose Page Table Entry (PTE) is not in the Translation Lookaside Buffer (TLB). On some computers this fault is handled by software loading the PTE into the TLB, and this counter is incremented.
154	Level 2 TLB Fills/sec	*Level 2 TLB Fills/sec* is the frequency of faults that occur when reference is made to memory whose Page Table Entry (PTE) is not in the Translation Lookaside Buffer (TLB), nor is the page containing the PTE. On some computers, this fault is handled by software loading the PTE into the TLB, and this counter is incremented.
156	Enumerations Server/sec	*Enumerations Server/sec* is the rate of Server browse requests that have been processed by this workstation.
158	Enumerations Domain/sec	*Enumerations Domain/sec* is the rate of Domain browse requests that have been processed by this workstation.
160	Enumerations Other/sec	*Enumerations Other/sec* is the rate of browse requests processed by this workstation that were not domain or server browse requests.
162	Missed Server Announcements	*Missed Server Announcements* is the number of server announcements that have been missed due to configuration or allocation limits
164	Missed Mailslot Datagrams	*Missed Mailslot Datagrams* is the number of Mailslot Datagrams that have been discarded due to configuration or allocation limits.
166	Missed Server List Requests	*Missed Server List Requests* is the number of requests to retrieve a list of browser servers that were received by this workstation, but could not be processed.
168	Server Announce Allocations Failed/sec	*Server Announce Allocations Failed/sec* is the rate of server (or domain) announcements that have failed due to lack of memory.
170	Mailslot Allocations Failed	*Mailslot Allocations Failed* is the number of times the datagram receiver has failed to allocate a buffer to hold a user mailslot write.
172	Virtual Bytes Peak	*Virtual Bytes Peak* is the maximum number of bytes of virtual address space the process has used at any one time. Use of virtual address space does not necessarily imply corresponding use of either disk or main memory pages. Virtual space, however, is finite, and by using too much, the process may limit its ability to load libraries.
174	Virtual Bytes	*Virtual Bytes* is the current size, in bytes, of the virtual address space the process is using. Use of virtual address space does not necessarily imply corresponding use of either disk or main memory pages. Virtual space is, however, finite; and by using too much, the process may limit its ability to load libraries.

TABLE D.1 CONTINUED: Registry Performance Counters on a Windows NT Server with IIS Installed

Index	Counter or Object Name	Description or Help Text
176	*Page Faults/sec*	*Page Faults/sec* is the rate of Page Faults by the threads executing in this process. A page fault occurs when a thread refers to a virtual memory page that is not in its working set in main memory. This will not cause the page to be fetched from disk if it is on the standby list and hence, already in main memory; or if it is in use by another process with which the page is shared.
178	Working Set Peak	*Working Set Peak* is the maximum number of bytes in the Working Set of this process at any point in time. The Working Set is the set of memory pages touched recently by the threads in the process. If free memory in the computer is above a threshold, pages are left in the Working Set of a process even if they are not in use. When free memory falls below a threshold, pages are trimmed from Working Sets. If they are needed, they will then be soft-faulted back into the Working Set before they leave main memory.
180	Working Set	*Working Set* is the current number of bytes in the Working Set of this process. The Working Set is the set of memory pages touched recently by the threads in the process. If free memory in the computer is above a threshold, pages are left in the Working Set of a process, even if they are not in use. When free memory falls below a threshold, pages are trimmed from Working Sets. If they are needed, they will then be soft-faulted back into the Working Set before they leave main memory.
182	Page File Bytes Peak	*Page File Bytes Peak* is the maximum number of bytes this process has used in the paging file(s). Paging files are used to store pages of memory used by the process that are not contained in other files. Paging files are shared by all processes, and lack of space in paging files can prevent other processes from allocating memory.
184	Page File Bytes	*Page File Bytes* is the current number of bytes this process has used in the paging file(s). Paging files are used to store pages of memory used by the process that are not contained in other files. Paging files are shared by all processes, and lack of space in paging files can prevent other processes from allocating memory.
186	Private Bytes	*Private Bytes* is the current number of bytes this process has allocated that cannot be shared with other processes.
188	Announcements Total/sec	*Announcements Total/sec* is the sum of Announcements Server/sec and Announcements Domain/sec.
190	Enumerations Total/sec	*Enumerations Total/sec* is the rate of browse requests that have been processed by this workstation. This is the sum of Enumerations Server, Enumerations Domain, and Enumerations Other.
192	User Time	*User Time* is the percentage of elapsed time that this thread has spent executing code in User Mode. Applications execute in User Mode, as do subsystems like the window manager and the graphics engine. Code executing in User Mode cannot damage the integrity of the Windows NT Executive, Kernel, and device drivers. Unlike some early operating systems, Windows NT uses process boundaries for subsystem protection in addition to the traditional protection of User and Privileged modes. These subsystem processes provide additional protection. Therefore, some work done by Windows NT on behalf of your application may appear in other subsystem processes in addition to the Privileged Time in your process.

TABLE D.1 CONTINUED: Registry Performance Counters on a Windows NT Server with IIS Installed

Index	Counter or Object Name	Description or Help Text
194	Privileged Time	*Privileged Time* is the percentage of elapsed time that this thread has spent executing code in Privileged Mode. When a Windows NT system service is called, the service will often run in Privileged Mode in order to gain access to system-private data. Such data is protected from access by threads executing in User Mode. Calls to the system may be explicit, or they may be implicit, such as when a page fault or an interrupt occurs. Unlike some early operating systems, Windows NT uses process boundaries for subsystem protection in addition to the traditional protection of User and Privileged modes. These subsystem processes provide additional protection. Therefore, some work done by Windows NT on behalf of your application may appear in other subsystem processes in addition to the Privileged Time in your process.
196	Context Switches/sec	*Context Switches/sec* is the rate of switches from one thread to another. Thread switches can occur either inside of a single process or across processes. A thread switch may be caused either by one thread asking another for information, or by a thread being preempted by another, higher priority thread becoming ready to run. Unlike some early operating systems, Windows NT uses process boundaries for subsystem protection in addition to the traditional protection of User and Privileged modes. These subsystem processes provide additional protection. Therefore, some work done by Windows NT on behalf of an application may appear in other subsystem processes in addition to the Privileged Time in the application. Switching to the subsystem process causes one Context Switch in the application thread. Switching back causes another Context Switch in the subsystem thread.
198	Current Disk Queue Length	*Current Disk Queue Length* is the number of requests outstanding on the disk at the time the performance data is collected. It includes requests in service at the time of the snapshot. This is an instantaneous length, not an average over the time interval. Multi-spindle disk devices can have multiple requests active at one time, but other concurrent requests are awaiting service. This counter may reflect a transitory high or low queue length, but if there is a sustained load on the disk drive, it is likely that this will be consistently high. Requests are experiencing delays proportional to the length of this queue minus the number of spindles on the disks. This difference should average less than two for good performance.
200	% Disk Time	*% Disk Time* is the percentage of elapsed time that the selected disk drive is busy servicing read or write requests.
202	% Disk Read Time	*% Disk Read Time* is the percentage of elapsed time that the selected disk drive is busy servicing read requests.
204	% Disk Write Time	*% Disk Write Time* is the percentage of elapsed time that the selected disk drive is busy servicing write requests.
206	Avg. Disk sec/Transfer	*Avg. Disk sec/Transfer* is the time in seconds of the average disk transfer.
208	Avg. Disk sec/Read	*Avg. Disk sec/Read* is the average time in seconds of a read of data from the disk.
210	Avg. Disk sec/Write	*Avg. Disk sec/Write* is the average time in seconds of a write of data to the disk.
212	Disk Transfers/sec	*Disk Transfers/sec* is the rate of read and write operations on the disk.
214	Disk Reads/sec	*Disk Reads/sec* is the rate of read operations on the disk.
216	Disk Writes/sec	*Disk Writes/sec* is the rate of write operations on the disk.

TABLE D.1 CONTINUED: Registry Performance Counters on a Windows NT Server with IIS Installed

Index	Counter or Object Name	Description or Help Text
218	Disk Bytes/sec	*Disk Bytes/sec* is the rate bytes are transferred to or from the disk during write or read operations.
220	Disk Read Bytes/sec	*Disk Read Bytes/sec* is the rate bytes are transferred from the disk during read operations.
222	Disk Write Bytes/sec	*Disk Write Bytes* is the rate bytes are transferred to the disk during write operations.
224	Avg. Disk Bytes/Transfer	*Avg. Disk Bytes/Transfer* is the average number of bytes transferred to or from the disk during write or read operations.
226	Avg. Disk Bytes/Read	*Avg. Disk Bytes/Read* is the average number of bytes transferred from the disk during read operations.
228	Avg. Disk Bytes/Write	*Avg. Disk Bytes/Write* is the average number of bytes transferred to the disk during write operations.
230	Process	The *Process object type* is created when a program is run. All the threads in a process share the same address space and have access to the same data.
232	Thread	The *Thread object type* is the basic object that executes instructions in a processor. Every running process has at least one thread.
234	PhysicalDisk	A *PhysicalDisk object type* is a hard or fixed disk drive. It will contain 1 or more logical partitions. Disks are used to store file, program, and paging data. The disk is read to retrieve these items, and written to record changes to them.
236	LogicalDisk	A *LogicalDisk object type* is a partition on a hard or fixed disk drive and is assigned a drive letter, such as C. Disks can be partitioned into distinct sections where they can store file, program, and page data. The disk is read to retrieve these items, and written to record changes to them.
238	Processor	The *Processor object type* includes as instances all processors on the computer. A processor is the part in the computer that performs arithmetic and logical computations, and initiates operations on peripherals. It executes (i.e., runs) programs on the computer.
240	% Total Processor Time	The *% Total Processor Time* is the average percentage of time that all the processors on the system are busy executing non-Idle threads. On a multi-processor system, if all processors are always busy, this is 100%. If all processors are 50% busy, this is 50%; and if 1/4th of the processors are 100% busy, this is 25%. It can be viewed as the fraction of the time spent doing useful work. Each processor is assigned an Idle thread in the Idle process, which consumes those unproductive processor cycles not used by any other threads.
242	% Total User Time	The *% Total User Time* is the average percentage of time spent in User mode by all processors. On a multi-processor system, if all processors are always in User mode, this is 100%; if all processors are 50% in User mode, this is 50%; and if 1/4th of the processors are in User mode, this is 25%. Applications execute in User Mode, as do subsystems like the window manager and the graphics engine. Code executing in User Mode cannot damage the integrity of the Windows NT Executive, Kernel, and device drivers. Unlike some early operating systems, Windows NT uses process boundaries for subsystem protection in addition to the traditional protection of User and Privileged modes. These subsystem processes provide additional protection. Therefore, some work done by Windows NT on behalf of an application may appear in other subsystem processes in addition to the Privileged Time in the application process.

TABLE D.1 CONTINUED: Registry Performance Counters on a Windows NT Server with IIS Installed

Index	Counter or Object Name	Description or Help Text
244	% Total Privileged Time	The *% Total Privileged Time* is the average percentage of time spent in Privileged mode by all processors. On a multi-processor system, if all processors are always in Privileged mode, this is 100%; and if 1/4th of the processors are in Privileged mode, this is 25%. When a Windows NT system service is called, the service will often run in Privileged Mode in order to gain access to system-private data. Such data is protected from access by threads executing in User Mode. Calls to the system may be explicit, or they may be implicit, such as when a page fault or an interrupt occurs. Unlike some early operating systems, Windows NT uses process boundaries for subsystem protection in addition to the traditional protection of User and Privileged modes. These subsystem processes provide additional protection. Therefore, some work done by Windows NT on behalf of an application may appear in other subsystem processes in addition to the Privileged Time in the application process.
246	Total Interrupts/sec	*Total Interrupts/sec* is the rate the computer is receiving and servicing hardware interrupts. Some devices that may generate interrupts are the system timer, the mouse, data communication lines, network interface cards, and other peripheral devices. This counter provides an indication of how busy these devices are on a computer-wide basis. See also Interrupts/sec.
248	Processes	*Processes* is the number of processes in the computer at the time of data collection. Notice that this is an instantaneous count, not an average over the time interval. Each process represents the running of a program.
250	Threads	*Threads* is the number of threads in the computer at the time of data collection. Notice that this is an instantaneous count, not an average over the time interval. A thread is the basic executable entity that can execute instructions in a processor.
252	Events	*Events* is the number of events in the computer at the time of data collection. Notice that this is an instantaneous count, not an average over the time interval. An event is used when two or more threads wish to synchronize execution.
254	Semaphores	*Semaphores* is the number of semaphores in the computer at the time of data collection. Notice that this is an instantaneous count, not an average over the time interval. Threads use semaphores to obtain exclusive access to data structures that they share with other threads.
256	Mutexes	*Mutexes* counts the number of mutexes in the computer at the time of data collection. This is an instantaneous count, not an average over the time interval. Mutexes are used by threads to assure only one thread is executing some section of code.
258	Sections	*Sections* is the number of sections in the computer at the time of data collection. Notice that this is an instantaneous count, not an average over the time interval. A section is a portion of virtual memory created by a process for a storing data. A process may share sections with other processes.
260	Objects	The *Objects object type* is a meta-object that contains information about the objects in existence on the computer. This information can be used to detect the unnecessary consumption of computer resources. Each object requires memory to store basic information about the object.
262	Redirector	The *Redirector* is the object that manages network connections to other computers that originate from your own computer.
264	Bytes Received/sec	*Bytes Received/sec* is the rate of bytes coming into the Redirector from the network. It includes all application data, as well as network protocol information (such as packet headers).

TABLE D.1 CONTINUED: Registry Performance Counters on a Windows NT Server with IIS Installed

Index	Counter or Object Name	Description or Help Text
266	Packets Received/sec	*Packets Received/sec* is the rate that the Redirector is receiving packets (also called SMBs or Server Message Blocks). Network transmissions are divided into packets. The average number of bytes received in a packet can be obtained by dividing Bytes Received/sec by this counter. Some packets received may not contain incoming data, for example, an acknowledgment to a write made by the Redirector would count as an incoming packet.
268	Read Bytes Paging/sec	*Read Bytes Paging/sec* is the rate that the Redirector is attempting to read bytes in response to page faults. Page faults are caused by loading of modules (such as programs and libraries) by a miss in the Cache (see Read Bytes Cache/sec), or by files directly mapped into the address space of applications (a high-performance feature of Windows NT).
270	Read Bytes Non-Paging/sec	*Read Bytes Non-Paging/sec* are those bytes read by the Redirector in response to normal file requests by an application when they are redirected to come from another computer. In addition to file requests, this counter includes other methods of reading across the network, such as Named Pipes and Transactions. This counter does not count network protocol information, just application data.
272	Read Bytes Cache/sec	*Read Bytes Cache/sec* is the rate that applications on your computer are accessing the Cache using the Redirector. Some of these data requests may be satisfied by merely retrieving the data from the system Cache on your own computer if it happened to be used recently, and there was room to keep it in the Cache. Requests that miss the Cache will cause a page fault (see Read Bytes Paging/sec).
274	Read Bytes Network/sec	*Read Bytes Network/sec* is the rate that applications are reading data across the network. For one reason or another the data was not in the system Cache, and these bytes actually came across the network. Dividing this number by Bytes Received/sec will indicate the "efficiency" of data coming in from the network, since all of these bytes are real application data (see Bytes Received/sec).
276	Bytes Transmitted/sec	*Bytes Transmitted/sec* is the rate that bytes are leaving the Redirector to the network. It includes all application data as well as network protocol information, such as packet headers and the like.
278	Packets Transmitted/sec	*Packets Transmitted/sec* is the rate that the Redirector is sending packets, also called SMBs or Server Message Blocks. Network transmissions are divided into packets. The average number of bytes transmitted in a packet can be obtained by dividing Bytes Transmitted/sec by this counter.
280	Write Bytes Paging/sec	*Write Bytes Paging/sec* is the rate that the Redirector is attempting to write bytes changed in the pages being used by applications. The program data changed by modules, such as programs and libraries, that were loaded over the network are "paged out" when no longer needed. Other output pages come from the Cache (see Write Bytes Cache/sec).
282	Write Bytes Non-Paging/sec	*Write Bytes Non-Paging/sec* is the rate of the bytes that are written by the Redirector in response to normal file outputs by an application when they are redirected to go to another computer. In addition to file requests, this counter includes other methods of writing across the network such as Named Pipes and Transactions. This counter does not count network protocol information, just application data.

TABLE D.1 CONTINUED: Registry Performance Counters on a Windows NT Server with IIS Installed

Index	Counter or Object Name	Description or Help Text
284	Write Bytes Cache/sec	*Write Bytes Cache/sec* is the rate that applications on your computer are writing to the Cache using the Redirector. The data may not leave your computer immediately, but may be retained in the Cache for further modification before being written to the network. This saves network traffic. Each write of a byte into the Cache is counted here.
286	Write Bytes Network/sec	*Write Bytes Network/sec* is the rate that your applications are writing data across the network. Either the system Cache was bypassed, as for Named Pipes or Transactions, or else the Cache wrote the bytes to make room for other data. Dividing this counter by Bytes Transmitted/sec will indicate the "efficiency" of data written to the network, since all of these bytes are real application data (see Transmitted Bytes/sec).
288	Read Operations/sec	*Read Operations/sec* is the rate the server is performing file read operations for the clients on this CPU. This value is a measure of how busy the Server is. This value will always be 0 in the Blocking Queue instance.
290	Read Operations Random/sec	*Read Operations Random/sec* counts the rate that, on a file-by-file basis, reads are made that are not sequential. If a read is made using a particular file handle and then is followed by another read that is not immediately the contiguous next byte, this counter is incremented by one.
292	Read Packets/sec	*Read Packets/sec* is the rate that read packets are being placed on the network. Each time a single packet is sent with a request to read data remotely, this counter is incremented by one.
294	Reads Large/sec	*Reads Large/sec* is the rate that reads over two times the server's negotiated buffer size are made by applications. Too many of these could place a strain on server resources. This counter is incremented once for each read. It does not count packets.
296	Read Packets Small/sec	*Read Packets Small/sec* is the rate that reads less than one-fourth of the server's negotiated buffer size are made by applications. Too many of these could indicate a waste of buffers on the server. This counter is incremented once for each read. It does not count packets.
298	Write Operations/sec	*Write Operations/sec* is the rate the server is performing file write operations for the clients on this CPU. This value is a measure of how busy the Server is. This value will always be 0 in the Blocking Queue instance.
300	Write Operations Random/sec	*Write Operations Random/sec* is the rate that, on a file-by-file basis, writes are made that are not sequential. If a write is made using a particular file handle, and then is followed by another write that is not immediately the next contiguous byte, this counter is incremented by one.
302	Write Packets/sec	*Write Packets/sec* is the rate that writes are being sent to the network. Each time a single packet is sent with a request to write remote data, this counter is incremented by one.
304	Writes Large/sec	*Writes Large/sec* is the rate that writes are made by applications that are over two times the server's negotiated buffer size. Too many of these could place a strain on server resources. This counter is incremented once for each write: It counts writes, not packets.
306	Write Packets Small/sec	*Write Packets Small/sec* is the rate that writes are made by applications that are less than one-fourth of the server's negotiated buffer size. Too many of these could indicate a waste of buffers on the server. This counter is incremented once for each write: It counts writes, not packets!

TABLE D.1 CONTINUED: Registry Performance Counters on a Windows NT Server with IIS Installed

Index	Counter or Object Name	Description or Help Text
308	Reads Denied/sec	*Reads Denied/sec* is the rate that the server is unable to accommodate requests for Raw Reads. When a read is much larger than the server's negotiated buffer size, the Redirector requests a Raw Read that, if granted, would permit the transfer of the data without lots of protocol overhead on each packet. To accomplish this, the server must lock out other requests, so the request is denied if the server is really busy.
310	Writes Denied/sec	*Writes Denied/sec* is the rate that the server is unable to accommodate requests for Raw Writes. When a write is much larger than the server's negotiated buffer size, the Redirector requests a Raw Write that, if granted, would permit the transfer of the data without lots of protocol overhead on each packet. To accomplish this the server must lock out other requests, so the request is denied if the server is really busy.
312	Network Errors/sec	*Network Errors/sec* counts serious unexpected errors that generally indicate the Redirector and one or more Servers are having serious communication difficulties. For example, an SMB (Server Manager Block) protocol error will generate a Network Error. These result in an entry in the system Event Log, so look there for details.
314	Server Sessions	The *Server Sessions object* counts the total number of security objects the Redirector has managed. For example, a Logon to a server followed by a network access to the same server will establish one connection, but two sessions.
316	Server Reconnects	*Server Reconnects* counts the number of times your Redirector has had to reconnect to a server in order to complete a new active request. You can be disconnected by the Server if you remain inactive for too long. Locally, even if all your remote files are closed, the Redirector will keep your connections intact for (nominally) ten minutes. Such inactive connections are called Dormant Connections. Reconnecting is expensive in time.
318	Connects Core	*Connects Core* counts the number of connections you have to servers running the original MS-Net SMB protocol, including MS-Net itself and Xenix and Vax's.
320	Connects Lan Manager 2.0	*Connects Lan Manager 2.0* counts connections to Lan Manager 2.0 servers, including LMX servers.
322	Connects Lan Manager 2.1	*Connects Lan Manager 2.1* counts connections to Lan Manager 2.1 servers, including LMX servers.
324	Connects Windows NT	*Connects Windows NT* counts the connections to Windows NT computers. Good choice!
326	Server Disconnects	*Server Disconnects* counts the number of times a Server has disconnected your Redirector. See also Server Reconnects.
328	Server Sessions Hung	*Server Sessions Hung* counts the number of active sessions that are timed out and unable to proceed due to a lack of response from the remote server.
330	Server	*Server help* is the process that interfaces the services from the local computer to the network services.
336	Thread Wait Reason	*Thread Wait Reason* is only applicable when the thread is in the Wait state (see Thread State.) It is 0 or 7 when the thread is waiting for the Executive, 1 or 8 for a Free Page, 2 or 9 for a Page In, 3 or 10 for a Pool Allocation, 4 or 11 for an Execution Delay, 5 or 12 for a Suspended condition, 6 or 13 for a User Request, 14 for an Event Pair High, 15 for an Event Pair Low, 16 for an LPC Receive, 17 for an LPC Reply, 18 for Virtual Memory, 19 for a Page Out, 20 and higher are not assigned at the time of this writing. Event Pairs are used to communicate with protected subsystems (see Context Switches).

TABLE D.1 CONTINUED: Registry Performance Counters on a Windows NT Server with IIS Installed

Index	Counter or Object Name	Description or Help Text
338	% DPC Time	% *DPC Time* is the percentage of elapsed time that the Processor spent in Deferred Procedure Calls. When a hardware device interrupts the Processor, the Interrupt Handler may elect to execute the majority of its work in a DPC. DPCs run at lower priority than Interrupts, and so permit Interrupts to occur while DPC are being executed. Deferred Procedure Calls are executed in Privileged Mode, so this is a component of Processor: % Privileged Time. This counter can help determine the source of excessive time being spent in Privileged Mode.
340	Sessions Timed Out	*Sessions Timed Out* is the number of sessions that have been closed due to their idle time exceeding the autodisconnect parameter for the server. Shows whether the autodisconnect setting is helping to conserve resources.
342	Sessions Errored Out	*Sessions Errored Out* is the number of sessions that have been closed due to unexpected error conditions. Indicates how frequently network problems are causing dropped sessions on the server.
344	Sessions Logged Off	*Sessions Logged Off* is the number of sessions that have terminated normally. Useful in interpreting the Sessions Timed Out and Sessions Errored Out statistics—allows percentage calculations.
346	Sessions Forced Off	*Sessions Forced Off* is the number of sessions that have been forced to logoff. Can indicate how many sessions were forced to logoff due to logon time constraints.
348	Errors Logon	*Errors Logon* is the number of failed logon attempts to the server. Can indicate whether password guessing programs are being used to crack the security on the server.
350	Errors Access Permissions	*Errors Access Permissions* is the number of times opens on behalf of clients have failed with STATUS_ACCESS_DENIED. Can indicate whether somebody is randomly attempting to access files in hopes of getting at something that was not properly protected.
352	Errors Granted Access	*Errors Granted Access* is the number of times accesses to files opened successfully were denied. Can indicate attempts to access files without proper access authorization.
354	Errors System	*Errors System* is the number of times an internal Server Error was detected. Unexpected errors usually indicate a problem with the Server.
356	Blocking Requests Rejected	*Blocking Requests Rejected* is the number of times the server has rejected blocking SMBs due to insufficient count of free work items. Indicates whether the maxworkitem or minfreeworkitems server parameters may need tuning.
358	Work Item Shortages	*Work Item Shortages* is the number of times STATUS_DATA_NOT_ACCEPTED was returned at receive indication time. This occurs when no work item is available or can be allocated to service the incoming request. Indicates whether the initworkitems or maxworkitems parameters may need tuning.
360	Files Opened Total	*Files Opened Total* is the number of successful open attempts performed by the server on behalf of clients. Useful in determining the amount of file I/O, determining overhead for path-based operations, determining the effectiveness of oplocks.
362	Files Open	*Files Open* is the number of files currently opened in the server. Indicates current server activity.

TABLE D.1 CONTINUED: Registry Performance Counters on a Windows NT Server with IIS Installed

Index	Counter or Object Name	Description or Help Text
366	File Directory Searches	*File Directory Searches* is the number of searches for files currently active in the server. Indicates current server activity.
370	Pool Nonpaged Failures	*Pool Nonpaged Failures* is the number of times allocations from a nonpaged pool have failed. Indicates that the computer's physical memory is too small.
372	Pool Nonpaged Peak	*Pool Nonpaged Peak* is the maximum number of bytes of nonpaged pool the server has had in use at any one point. Indicates how much physical memory the computer should have.
376	Pool Paged Failures	*Pool Paged Failures* is the number of times allocations from a paged pool have failed. Indicates that the computer's physical memory of pagefile are too small.
378	Pool Paged Peak	*Pool Paged Peak* is the maximum number of bytes of paged pool the server has had allocated. Indicates the proper sizes of the Page File(s) and physical memory.
384	Mailslot Receives Failed	*Mailslot Receives Failed* indicates the number of mailslot messages that couldn't be received due to transport failures.
386	Mailslot Writes Failed	*Mailslot Writes Failed* is the total number of mailslot messages that have been successfully received, but that were unable to be written to the mailslot.
388	Bytes Total/sec	*Bytes Total/sec* is the rate the Redirector is processing data bytes. This includes all application and file data in addition to protocol information, such as packet headers.
390	File Data Operations/sec	*File Data Operations/sec* is the rate the Redirector is processing data operations. One operation includes (hopefully) many bytes. We say hopefully here because each operation has overhead. You can determine the efficiency of this path by dividing the Bytes/sec by this counter to determine the average number of bytes transferred/operation.
392	Current Commands	*Current Commands* counts the number of requests to the Redirector that are currently queued for service. If this number is much larger than the number of network adapter cards installed in the computer, the network(s) and/or the server(s) being accessed are seriously bottlenecked.
396	% Interrupt Time	*% Interrupt Time* is the percentage of elapsed time that the Processor spent handling hardware Interrupts. When a hardware device interrupts the Processor, the Interrupt Handler will execute to handle the condition, usually by signaling I/O completion and possibly issuing another pending I/O request. Some of this work may be done in a Deferred Procedure Call (see % DPC Time). However, time spent in DPCs is not counted as time in Interrupts. Interrupts are executed in Privileged Mode, so this is a component of Processor: % Privileged Time. This counter can help determine the source of excessive time being spent in Privileged Mode.
398	NWLink NetBIOS	The *NWLink NetBIOS* protocol layer handles the interface to applications communicating over the IPX transport.
400	Packets/sec	*Packets/sec* is the rate the Redirector is processing data packets. One packet includes (hopefully) many bytes. We say hopefully here because each packet has protocol overhead. You can determine the efficiency of this path by dividing the Bytes/sec by this counter to determine the average number of bytes transferred/packet. You can also divide this counter by Operations/sec to determine the average number of packets per operation, another measure of efficiency.

TABLE D.1 CONTINUED: Registry Performance Counters on a Windows NT Server with IIS Installed

Index	Counter or Object Name	Description or Help Text
404	Context Blocks Queued/sec	*Context Blocks Queued/sec* is the rate that work context blocks had to be placed on the server's FSP queue to await server action.
406	File Data Operations/sec	*File Data Operations/sec* is the rate that the computer is issuing Read and Write operations to file system devices. It does not include File Control Operations.
408	% Free Space	*% Free Space* is the ratio of the free space available on the logical disk unit to the total usable space provided by the selected logical disk drive.
410	Free Megabytes	*Free Megabytes* displays the unallocated space on the disk drive in megabytes. One megabyte = 1,048,576 bytes.
412	Connections Open	*Connections Open* is the number of connections currently open for this protocol. This counter shows the current count only and does not accumulate over time.
414	Connections No Retries	*Connections No Retries* is the total count of connections that were successfully made on the first try. This number is an accumulator and shows a running total.
416	Connections With Retries	*Connections With Retries* is the total count of connections that were made after retrying the attempt. A retry occurs when the first connection attempt failed. This number is an accumulator and shows a running total.
418	Disconnects Local	*Disconnects Local* is the number of session disconnections that were initiated by the local computer. This number is an accumulator and shows a running total.
420	Disconnects Remote	*Disconnects Remote* is the number of session disconnections that were initiated by the remote computer. This number is an accumulator and shows a running total.
422	Failures Link	*Failures Link* is the number of connections that were dropped due to a link failure. This number is an accumulator and shows a running total.
424	Failures Adapter	*Failures Adapter* is the number of connections that were dropped due to an adapter failure. This number is an accumulator and shows a running total.
426	Connection Session Timeouts	*Connection Session Timeouts* is the number of connections that were dropped due to a session timeout. This number is an accumulator and shows a running total.
428	Connections Canceled	*Connections Canceled* is the number of connections that were canceled. This number is an accumulator and shows a running total.
430	Failures Resource Remote	*Failures Resource Remote* is the number of connections that failed because of resource problems or shortages on the remote computer. This number is an accumulator and shows a running total.
432	Failures Resource Local	*Failures Resource Local* is the number of connections that failed because of resource problems or shortages on the local computer. This number is an accumulator and shows a running total.
434	Failures Not Found	*Failures Not Found* is the number of connection attempts that failed because the remote computer could not be found. This number is an accumulator and shows a running total.
436	Failures No Listen	*Failures No Listen* is the number of connections that were rejected because the remote computer was not listening for connection requests.
438	Datagrams/sec	*Datagrams/sec* is the rate that datagrams are processed by the computer. This counter displays the sum of datagrams sent and datagrams received. A datagram is a connectionless packet whose delivery to a remote is not guaranteed.

TABLE D.1 CONTINUED: Registry Performance Counters on a Windows NT Server with IIS Installed

Index	Counter or Object Name	Description or Help Text
440	Datagram Bytes/sec	*Datagram Bytes/sec* is the rate that datagram bytes are processed by the computer. This counter is the sum of datagram bytes that are sent as well as received. A datagram is a connectionless packet whose delivery to a remote is not guaranteed.
442	Datagrams Sent/sec	*Datagrams Sent/sec* is the rate that datagrams are sent from the computer. A datagram is a connectionless packet whose delivery to a remote computer is not guaranteed.
444	Datagram Bytes Sent/sec	*Datagram Bytes Sent/sec* is the rate that datagram bytes are sent from the computer. A datagram is a connectionless packet whose delivery to a remote computer is not guaranteed.
446	Datagrams Received/sec	*Datagrams Received/sec* is the rate that datagrams are received by the computer. A datagram is a connectionless packet whose delivery to a remote computer is not guaranteed.
448	Datagram Bytes Received/sec	*Datagram Bytes Received/sec* is the rate that datagram bytes are received by the computer. A datagram is a connectionless packet whose delivery to a remote computer is not guaranteed.
450	Packets/sec	Packets/sec is the rate that packets are processed by the computer. This count is the sum of Packets Sent and Packets Received per second. This counter includes all packets processed: control, as well as data packets.
452	Packets Sent/sec	*Packets Sent/sec* is the rate that packets are sent by the computer. This counter counts all packets sent by the computer, i.e. control, as well as data packets.
454	Packets Received/sec	Packets Received/sec is the rate that packets are received by the computer. This counter counts all packets processed: control as well as data packets.
456	Frames/sec	*Frames/sec* is the rate that data frames (or packets) are processed by the computer. This counter is the sum of data frames sent and data frames received. This counter only counts those frames (packets) that carry data.
458	Frame Bytes/sec	*Frame Bytes/sec* is the rate that data bytes are processed by the computer. This counter is the sum of data frame bytes sent and received. This counter only counts the byte in frames (packets) that carry data.
460	Frames Sent/sec	*Frames Sent/sec* is the rate that data frames are sent by the computer. This counter only counts the frames (packets) that carry data.
462	Frame Bytes Sent/sec	*Frame Bytes Sent/sec* is the rate that data bytes are sent by the computer. This counter only counts the bytes in frames (packets) that carry data.
464	Frames Received/sec	*Frames Received/sec* is the rate that data frames are received by the computer. This counter only counts the frames (packets) that carry data.
466	Frame Bytes Received/sec	*Frame Bytes Received/sec* is the rate that data bytes are received by the computer. This counter only counts the frames (packets) that carry data.
468	Frames Re-Sent/sec	*Frames Re-Sent/sec* is the rate that data frames (packets) are re-sent by the computer. This counter only counts the frames or packets that carry data.
470	Frame Bytes Re-Sent/sec	*Frame Bytes Re-Sent/sec* is the rate that data bytes are re-sent by the computer. This counter only counts the bytes in frames that carry data.

TABLE D.1 CONTINUED: Registry Performance Counters on a Windows NT Server with IIS Installed

Index	Counter or Object Name	Description or Help Text
472	Frames Rejected/sec	*Frames Rejected/sec* is the rate that data frames are rejected. This counter only counts the frames (packets) that carry data.
474	Frame Bytes Rejected/sec	*Frame Bytes Rejected/sec* is the rate that data bytes are rejected. This counter only counts the bytes in data frames (packets) that carry data.
476	Expirations Response	*Expirations Response* is the count of T1 timer expirations.
478	Expirations Ack	*Expirations Ack* is the count of T2 timer expirations.
480	Window Send Maximum	*Window Send Maximum* is the maximum number of bytes of data that will be sent before waiting for an acknowledgment from the remote computer.
482	Window Send Average	*Window Send Average* is the running average number of data bytes that were sent before waiting for an acknowledgment from the remote computer.
484	Piggyback Ack Queued/sec	*Piggyback Ack Queued/sec* is the rate that piggybacked acknowledgments are queued. Piggyback acknowledgments are acknowledgments to received packets that are to be included in the next outgoing packet to the remote computer.
486	Piggyback Ack Timeouts	*Piggyback Ack Timeouts* is the number of times that a piggyback acknowledgment could not be sent because there was no outgoing packet to the remote on which to piggyback. A piggyback ack is an acknowledgment to a received packet that is sent along in an outgoing data packet to the remote computer. If no outgoing packet is sent within the timeout period, an ack packet is sent and this counter is incremented.
488	NWLink IPX	The *NWLink IPX* transport handles datagram transmission to and from computers using the IPX protocol.
490	NWLink SPX	The *NWLink SPX* transport handles data transmission and session connections for computers using the SPX protocol.
492	NetBEUI	The *NetBEUI protocol* handles data transmission for that network activity that follows the NetBIOS End User Interface standard.
494	NetBEUI Resource	The *NetBEUI Resource object* tracks the use of resources (i.e., buffers) by the NetBEUI protocol.
496	Used Maximum	*Used Maximum* is the maximum number of NetBEUI resources (buffers) in use at any point in time. This value is useful in sizing the maximum resources provided. The number in parentheses following the resource name is used to identify the resource in Event Log messages.
498	Used Average	*Used Average* is the current number of resources (buffers) in use at this time. The number in parentheses following the resource name is used to identify the resource in Event Log messages.
500	Times Exhausted	*Times Exhausted* is the number of times all the resources (buffers) were in use. The number in parentheses following the resource name is used to identify the resource in Event Log messages.
502	NBT Connection	The *NBT Connection object type* includes those counters that describe the rates that bytes are received and sent over a single NBT connection connecting the local computer with some remote computer. The connection is identified by the name of the remote computer.

TABLE D.1 CONTINUED: Registry Performance Counters on a Windows NT Server with IIS Installed

Index	Counter or Object Name	Description or Help Text
504	*Bytes Received/sec*	*Bytes Received/sec* is the rate that bytes are received by the local computer over an NBT connection to some remote computer. All the bytes received by the local computer over the particular NBT connection are counted.
506	Bytes Sent/sec	*Bytes Sent/sec* is the rate that bytes are sent by the local computer over an NBT connection to some remote computer. All the bytes sent by the local computer over the particular NBT connection are counted.
508	Total Bytes/sec	*Total Bytes/sec* is the rate that bytes are sent or received by the local computer over an NBT connection to some remote computer. All the bytes sent or received by the local computer over the particular NBT connection are counted.
510	Network Interface	The *Network Interface object type* includes those counters that describe the rates that bytes and packets are received and sent over a Network TCP/IP connection. It also describes various error counts for the same connection.
512	Bytes Total/sec	*Bytes Total/sec* is the rate that bytes are sent and received on the interface, including framing characters.
514	Packets/sec	*Packets/sec* is the rate that packets are sent and received on the network interface.
516	Packets Received/sec	*Packets Received/sec* is the rate that packets are received on the network interface.
518	Packets Sent/sec	*Packets Sent/sec* is the rate that packets are sent on the network interface.
520	Current Bandwidth	*Current Bandwidth* is an estimate of the interface's current bandwidth in bits per second (bps). For interfaces that do not vary in bandwidth or for those where no accurate estimation can be made, this value is the nominal bandwidth.
522	Bytes Received/sec	*Bytes Received/sec* is the rate that bytes are received on the interface, including framing characters.
524	Packets Received Unicast/sec	*Packets Received Unicast/sec* is the rate that (subnet) unicast packets are delivered to a higher-layer protocol.
526	Packets Received Non-Unicast/sec	*Packets Received Non-Unicast/sec* is the rate that non-unicast (i.e., subnet broadcast or subnet multicast) packets are delivered to a higher-layer protocol.
528	Packets Received Discarded	*Packets Received Discarded* is the number of inbound packets that were chosen to be discarded even though no errors had been detected to prevent their being deliverable to a higher-layer protocol. One possible reason for discarding such a packet could be to free up buffer space.
530	Packets Received Errors	*Packets Received Errors* is the number of inbound packets that contained errors preventing them from being deliverable to a higher-layer protocol.
532	Packets Received Unknown	*Packets Received Unknown* is the number of packets received via the interface that were discarded because of an unknown or unsupported protocol.
534	*Bytes Sent/sec*	*Bytes Sent/sec* is the rate that bytes are sent on the interface, including framing characters.
536	Packets Sent Unicast/sec	*Packets Sent Unicast/sec* is the rate that packets are requested to be transmitted to subnet-unicast addresses by higher-level protocols. The rate includes the packets that were discarded or not sent.

TABLE D.1 CONTINUED: Registry Performance Counters on a Windows NT Server with IIS Installed

Index	Counter or Object Name	Description or Help Text
538	Packets Sent Non-Unicast/sec	*Packets Sent Non-Unicast/sec* is the rate that packets are requested to be transmitted to non-unicast (for example, subnet broadcast or subnet multicast) addresses by higher-level protocols. The rate includes the packets that were discarded or not sent.
540	Packets Outbound Discarded	*Packets Outbound Discarded* is the number of outbound packets that were chosen to be discarded even though no errors had been detected to prevent their being transmitted. One possible reason for discarding such a packet could be to free up buffer space.
542	Packets Outbound Errors	*Packets Outbound Errors* is the number of outbound packets that could not be transmitted because of errors.
544	Output Queue Length	*Output Queue Length* is the length of the output packet queue (in packets.) If this is longer than 2, delays are being experienced and the bottleneck should be found and eliminated if possible. Since the requests are queued by NDIS in this implementations, this will always be 0.
546	IP	The *IP object type* includes those counters that describe the rates that IP datagrams are received and sent by a certain computer using the IP protocol. It also describes various error counts for the IP protocol.
548	*Datagrams/sec*	*Datagrams/sec* is the rate that IP datagrams are received from or sent to the interfaces, including those in error. Any forwarded datagrams are not included in this rate.
550	*Datagrams Received/sec*	*Datagrams Received/sec* is the rate that IP datagrams are received from the interfaces, including those in error.
552	Datagrams Received Header Errors	*Datagrams Received Header Errors* is the number of input datagrams discarded due to errors in their IP headers, including bad checksums, version number mismatch, other format errors, time-to-live exceeded, errors discovered in processing their IP options, etc.
554	Datagrams Received Address Errors	*Datagrams Received Address Errors* is the number of input datagrams discarded because the IP address in their IP header's destination field was not a valid address to be received at this entity. This count includes invalid addresses (e.g., 0.0. 0.0) and addresses of unsupported Classes (e.g., Class E). For entities that are not IP Gateways and, therefore, do not forward datagrams, this counter includes datagrams discarded because the destination address was not a local address.
556	Datagrams Forwarded/sec	*Datagrams Forwarded/sec* is the rate of input datagrams for which this entity was not their final IP destination, as a result of which, an attempt was made to find a route to forward them to that final destination. In entities that do not act as IP Gateways, this rate will include only those packets that were Source-Routed via this entity, and the Source-Route option processing was successful.
558	Datagrams Received Unknown Protocol	*Datagrams Received Unknown Protocol* is the number of locally-addressed datagrams received successfully but discarded because of an unknown or unsupported protocol.
560	Datagrams Received Discarded	*Datagrams Received Discarded* is the number of input IP datagrams for which no problems were encountered to prevent their continued processing, but which were discarded (e.g., for lack of buffer space). This counter does not include any datagrams discarded while awaiting re-assembly.

TABLE D.1 CONTINUED: Registry Performance Counters on a Windows NT Server with IIS Installed

Index	Counter or Object Name	Description or Help Text
562	Datagrams Received Delivered/sec	*Datagrams Received Delivered/sec* is the rate that input datagrams are successfully delivered to IP user-protocols (including ICMP).
564	Datagrams Sent/sec	*Datagrams Sent/sec* is the rate that IP datagrams are supplied to IP for transmission by local IP user-protocols (including ICMP). This counter does not include any datagrams counted in Datagrams Forwarded.
566	Datagrams Outbound Discarded	*Datagrams Outbound Discarded* is the number of output IP datagrams for which no problems were encountered to prevent their transmission to their destination, but which were discarded (e.g., for lack of buffer space.) This counter would include datagrams counted in Datagrams Forwarded if any such packets met this (discretionary) discard criterion.
568	Datagrams Outbound No Route	*Datagrams Outbound No Route* is the number of IP datagrams discarded because no route could be found to transmit them to their destination. This counter includes any packets counted in Datagrams Forwarded that meet this "no route" criterion.
570	Fragments Received/sec	*Fragments Received/sec* is the rate that IP fragments that need to be re-assembled at this entity are received.
572	Fragments Re-assembled/sec	*Fragments Re-assembled/sec* is the rate that IP fragments are successfully re-assembled.
574	Fragment Re-assembly Failures	*Fragment Re-assembly Failures* is the number of failures detected by the IP re-assembly algorithm (for whatever reason: timed out, errors, etc.). This is not necessarily a count of discarded IP fragments since some algorithms (notably RFC 815) can lose track of the number of fragments by combining them as they are received.
576	Fragmented Datagrams/sec	*Fragmented Datagrams/sec* is the rate that datagrams are successfully fragmented at this entity.
578	Fragmentation Failures	*Fragmentation Failures* is the number of IP datagrams that have been discarded because they needed to be fragmented at this entity but could not be, e.g., because their 'Don't Fragment' flag was set.
580	Fragments Created/sec	*Fragments Created/sec* is the rate that IP datagram fragments have been generated as a result of fragmentation at this entity.
582	ICMP	The *ICMP object type* includes those counters that describe the rates that ICMP Messages are received and sent by a certain entity using the ICMP protocol. It also describes various error counts for the ICMP protocol.
584	Messages/sec	*Messages/sec* is the total rate that ICMP messages are received and sent by the entity. The rate includes those messages received or sent in error.
586	Messages Received/sec	*Messages Received/sec* is the rate that ICMP messages are received by the entity. The rate includes those messages received in error.
588	Messages Received Errors	*Messages Received Errors* is the number of ICMP messages that the entity received but determined as having errors (bad ICMP checksums, bad length, etc.).
590	Received DestUnreachable	*ReceivedDestUnreachable* is the number of ICMP Destination Unreachable messages received.
592	Received Time Exceeded	*Received Time Exceeded* is the number of ICMP Time Exceeded messages received.

TABLE D.1 CONTINUED: Registry Performance Counters on a Windows NT Server with IIS Installed

Index	Counter or Object Name	Description or Help Text
594	Received Parameter Problem	*Received Parameter Problem* is the number of ICMP Parameter Problem messages received.
596	Received Source Quench	*Received Source Quench* is the number of ICMP Source Quench messages received.
598	Received Redirect/sec	*Received Redirect/sec* is the rate of ICMP Redirect messages received.
600	Received Echo/sec	*Received Echo/sec* is the rate of ICMP Echo messages received.
602	Received Echo Reply/sec	*Received Echo Reply/sec* is the rate of ICMP Echo Reply messages received.
604	Received Timestamp/sec	*Received Timestamp/sec* is the rate of ICMP Timestamp (request) messages received.
606	Received Timestamp Reply/sec	*Received Timestamp Reply/sec* is the rate of ICMP Timestamp Reply messages received.
608	Received Address Mask	*Received Address Mask* is the number of ICMP Address Mask Request messages received.
610	Received Address Mask Reply	*Received Address Mask Reply* is the number of ICMP Address Mask Reply messages received.
612	Messages Sent/sec	*Messages Sent/sec* is the rate that ICMP messages are attempted to be sent by the entity. The rate includes those messages sent in error.
614	Messages Outbound Errors	*Messages Outbound Errors* is the number of ICMP messages that this entity did not send due to problems discovered within ICMP, such as lack of buffers. This value should not include errors discovered outside the ICMP layer, such as the inability of IP to route the resultant datagram. In some implementations there may be no types of error that contribute to this counter's value.
616	Sent Destination Unreachable	*Sent Destination Unreachable* is the number of ICMP Destination Unreachable messages sent.
618	Sent Time Exceeded	*Sent Time Exceeded* is the number of ICMP Time Exceeded messages sent.
620	Sent Parameter Problem	*Sent Parameter Problem* is the number of ICMP Parameter Problem messages sent.
622	Sent Source Quench	*Sent Source Quench* is the number of ICMP Source Quench messages sent.
624	Sent Redirect/sec	*Sent Redirect/sec* is the rate of ICMP Redirect messages sent.
626	Sent Echo/sec	*Sent Echo/sec* is the rate of ICMP Echo messages sent.
628	Sent Echo Reply/sec	*Sent Echo Reply/sec* is the rate of ICMP Echo Reply messages sent.
630	Sent Timestamp/sec	*Sent Timestamp/sec* is the rate of ICMP Timestamp (request) messages sent.
632	Sent Timestamp Reply/sec	*Sent Timestamp Reply/sec* is the rate of ICMP Timestamp Reply messages sent.
634	Sent Address Mask	*Sent Address Mask* is the number of ICMP Address Mask Request messages sent.
636	Sent Address Mask Reply	*Sent Address Mask Reply* is the number of ICMP Address Mask Reply messages sent.
638	TCP	The *TCP object type* includes those counters that describe the rates that TCP Segments are received and sent by a certain entity using the TCP protocol. In addition, it describes the number of TCP connections that are in each of the possible TCP connection states.

TABLE D.1 CONTINUED: Registry Performance Counters on a Windows NT Server with IIS Installed

Index	Counter or Object Name	Description or Help Text
640	Segments/sec	*Segments/sec* is the rate that TCP segments are sent or received using the TCP protocol.
642	Connections Established	*Connections Established* is the number of TCP connections for which the current state is either ESTABLISHED or CLOSE-WAIT.
644	Connections Active	*Connections Active* is the number of times TCP connections have made a direct transition to the SYN-SENT state from the CLOSED state.
646	Connections Passive	*Connections Passive* is the number of times TCP connections have made a direct transition to the SYN-RCVD state from the LISTEN state.
648	Connection Failures	*Connection Failures* is the number of times TCP connections have made a direct transition to the CLOSED state from the SYN-SENT state or the SYN-RCVD state, plus the number of times TCP connections have made a direct transition to the LISTEN state from the SYN-RCVD state.
650	Connections Reset	*Connections Reset* is the number of times TCP connections have made a direct transition to the CLOSED state from either the ESTABLISHED state or the CLOSE-WAIT state.
652	Segments Received/sec	*Segments Received/sec* is the rate that segments are received, including those received in error. This count includes segments received on currently established connections.
654	Segments Sent/sec	*Segments Sent/sec* is the rate that segments are sent, including those on current connections, but excluding those containing only retransmitted bytes.
656	Segments Retransmitted/sec	*Segments Retransmitted/sec* is the rate that segments are retransmitted, that is, segments transmitted containing one or more previously transmitted bytes.
658	UDP	The *UDP object type* includes those counters that describe the rates that UDP datagrams are received and sent by a certain entity using the UDP protocol. It also describes various error counts for the UDP protocol.
660	% Total DPC Time	*% Total DPC Time* is the sum of % DPC Time of all processors divided by the number of processors in the system. (See % DPC Time for detail.)
662	% Total Interrupt Time	*% Total Interrupt Time* is the sum of % Interrupt Time of all processors divided by the number of processors in the system. (See Processor: % Interrupt Time for detail.)
664	Datagrams No Port/sec	*Datagrams No Port/sec* is the rate of received UDP datagrams for which there was no application at the destination port.
666	Datagrams Received Errors	*Datagrams Received Errors* is the number of received UDP datagrams that could not be delivered for reasons other than the lack of an application at the destination port.
668	Datagrams Sent/sec	*Datagrams Sent/sec* is the rate that UDP datagrams are sent from the entity.
670	Disk Storage Unit	*Disk Storage Unit* maintains disk storage device statistics from the foreign computer.
672	Allocation Failures	*Allocation Failures* is the number of allocation failures reported by the disk storage device.
674	System Up Time	*System Up Time* is the Total Time (in seconds) that the computer has been operational since it was last started.

TABLE D.1 CONTINUED: Registry Performance Counters on a Windows NT Server with IIS Installed

Index	Counter or Object Name	Description or Help Text
676	System Handle Count	*System Handle Count* is the current number of system handles in use.
678	Free System Page Table Entries	Free System Page Table Entries is the number of Page Table Entries not currently in use by the system.
680	Thread Count	*Thread Count* is the number of threads currently active in this process. An instruction is the basic unit of execution in a processor, and a thread is the object that executes instructions. Every running process has at least one thread.
682	Priority Base	*Priority Base* is the current base priority of this process. Threads within a process can raise and lower their own base priority relative to the process's base priority.
684	Elapsed Time	*Elapsed Time* is the total elapsed time (in seconds) this process has been running.
686	Alignment Fixups/sec	*Alignment Fixups/sec* is the rate of alignment faults fixed by the system.
688	Exception Dispatches/sec	*Exception Dispatches/sec* is the rate of exceptions dispatched by the system.
690	Floating Emulations/sec	*Floating Emulations/sec* is the rate of floating emulations performed by the system.
692	Logon/sec	*Logon/sec* is the rate of all server logons.
694	Priority Current	*Priority Current* is the current dynamic priority of this thread. The system may raise the thread's dynamic priority above the base priority if the thread is handling user input, or lower it towards the base priority if the thread becomes compute bound.
696	% DPC Time	*% DPC Time* is the current base priority of this thread. The system may raise the thread's dynamic priority above the base priority if the thread is handling user input, or lower it towards the base priority if the thread becomes compute bound.
698	% Interrupt Time	*% Interrupt Time* is the total elapsed time (in seconds) this thread has been running.
700	Paging File	*Paging File* displays information about the system's Page File(s).
702	% Usage	*% Usage* is the amount of the Page File instance in use in percent. See also Process: Page File Bytes.
704	% Usage Peak	% Usage Peak is the peak usage of the Page File instance in percent. See also Process: Page File Bytes Peak.
706	Start Address	*Start Address* is the starting virtual address for this thread.
708	User PC	*User PC* is the Current User Program Counter for this thread.
710	Mapped Space No Access	*Mapped Space No Access* is virtual memory that has been mapped to a specific virtual address (or range of virtual addresses) in the process's virtual address space. *No Access protection* prevents a process from writing to or reading from these pages and will generate an access violation if either is attempted.
712	Mapped Space Read Only	*Mapped Space Read Only* is virtual memory that has been mapped to a specific virtual address (or range of virtual addresses) in the process's virtual address space. *Read Only protection* prevents the contents of these pages from being modified. Any attempts to write or modify these pages will generate an access violation.
714	Mapped Space Read/Write	Mapped Space Read/Write is virtual memory that has been mapped to a specific virtual address (or range of virtual addresses) in the process's virtual address space. *Read/Write protection* allows a process to read, modify, and write to these pages.

TABLE D.1 CONTINUED: Registry Performance Counters on a Windows NT Server with IIS Installed

Index	Counter or Object Name	Description or Help Text
716	Mapped Space Write Copy	*Mapped Space Write Copy* is virtual memory that has been mapped to a specific virtual address (or range of virtual addresses) in the process's virtual address space. *Write Copy* protection is used when memory is shared for reading but not for writing. When processes are reading this memory, they can share the same memory, however, when a sharing process wants to have write access to this shared memory, a copy of that memory is made.
718	Mapped Space Executable	*Mapped Space Executable* is virtual memory that has been mapped to a specific virtual address (or range of virtual addresses) in the process's virtual address space. *Executable memory* is memory that can be executed by programs, but may not be read or written. This type of protection is not supported by all processor types.
720	Mapped Space Exec Read Only	*Mapped Space Exec Read Only* is virtual memory that has been mapped to a specific virtual address (or range of virtual addresses) in the process's virtual address space. *Execute/Read Only* memory is memory that can be executed as well as read.
722	Mapped Space Exec Read/Write	*Mapped Space Exec Read/Write* is virtual memory that has been mapped to a specific virtual address (or range of virtual addresses) in the process's virtual address space. *Execute/Read/Write memory* is memory that can be executed by programs as well as read and modified.
724	Mapped Space Exec Write Copy	*Mapped Space Exec Write Copy* is virtual memory that has been mapped to a specific virtual address (or range of virtual addresses) in the process's virtual address space. *Execute Write Copy* is memory that can be executed by programs as well as read and written. This type of protection is used when memory needs to be shared between processes. If the sharing processes only read the memory, then they will all use the same memory. If a sharing process desires write access, then a copy of this memory will be made for that process.
726	Reserved Space No Access	*Reserved Space* is virtual memory that has been reserved for future use by a process, but has not been mapped or committed. *No Access protection* prevents a process from writing to or reading from these pages and will generate an access violation if either is attempted.
728	Reserved Space Read Only	*Reserved Space* is virtual memory that has been reserved for future use by a process, but has not been mapped or committed. *Read Only* protection prevents the contents of these pages from being modified. Any attempts to write or modify these pages will generate an access violation.
730	Reserved Space Read/Write	*Reserved Space* is virtual memory that has been reserved for future use by a process, but has not been mapped or committed. *Read/Write protection* allows a process to read, modify, and write to these pages.
732	Reserved Space Write Copy	*Reserved Space* is virtual memory that has been reserved for future use by a process, but has not been mapped or committed. *Write Copy protection* is used when memory is shared for reading but not for writing. When processes are reading this memory, they can share the same memory, however, when a sharing process wants to have read/write access to this shared memory, a copy of that memory is made.
734	Reserved Space Executable	*Reserved Space* is virtual memory that has been reserved for future use by a process, but has not been mapped or committed. *Executable memory* is memory that can be executed by programs, but may not be read or written. This type of protection is not supported by all processor types.

TABLE D.1 CONTINUED: Registry Performance Counters on a Windows NT Server with IIS Installed

Index	Counter or Object Name	Description or Help Text
736	Reserved Space ExecRead Only	*Reserved Space* is virtual memory that has been reserved for future use by a process, but has not been mapped or committed. *Execute/Read Only memory* is memory that can be executed as well as read.
738	Reserved Space ExecRead/Write	*Reserved Space* is virtual memory that has been reserved for future use by a process, but has not been mapped or committed. *Execute/Read/Write memory* is memory that can be executed by programs as well as read and modified.
740	Image	The *Image object type* displays information about the virtual address usage of the images being executed by a process on the computer.
742	Reserved Space Exec Write Copy	*Reserved Space* is virtual memory that has been reserved for future use by a process, but has not been mapped or committed. *Exec Write Copy* is memory that can be executed by programs as well as read and written. This type of protection is used when memory needs to be shared between processes. If the sharing processes only read the memory, they will all use the same memory. If a sharing process desires write access, a copy of this memory will be made for that process.
744	Unassigned Space No Access	*Unassigned Space* is mapped and committed virtual memory in use by the process that is not attributable to any particular image being executed by that process. *No Access protection* prevents a process from writing to or reading from these pages and will generate an access violation if either is attempted.
746	Unassigned Space Read Only	*Unassigned Space* is mapped and committed virtual memory in use by the process that is not attributable to any particular image being executed by that process. *Read Only protection* prevents the contents of these pages from being modified. Any attempts to write or modify these pages will generate an access violation.
748	Unassigned Space Read/Write	*Unassigned Space* is mapped and committed virtual memory in use by the process that is not attributable to any particular image being executed by that process. *Read/Write protection* allows a process to read, modify, and write to these pages.
750	Unassigned Space Write Copy	*Unassigned Space* is mapped and committed virtual memory in use by the process that is not attributable to any particular image being executed by that process. *Write Copy protection* is used when memory is shared for reading but not for writing. When processes are reading this memory, they can share the same memory; however, when a sharing process wants to have read/write access to this shared memory, a copy of that memory is made for writing to.
752	Unassigned Space Executable	*Unassigned Space* is mapped and committed virtual memory in use by the process that is not attributable to any particular image being executed by that process. *Executable memory* is memory that can be executed by programs, but may not be read or written. This type of protection is not supported by all processor types.
754	Unassigned Space ExecRead Only	*Unassigned Space* is mapped and committed virtual memory in use by the process that is not attributable to any particular image being executed by that process. *Execute/Read Only memory* is memory that can be executed as well as read.
756	Unassigned Space ExecuRead/Write	*Unassigned Space* is mapped and committed virtual memory in use by the process that is not attributable to any particular image being executed by that process. *Execute/Read/Write memory* is memory that can be executed by programs as well as read and written.

TABLE D.1 CONTINUED: Registry Performance Counters on a Windows NT Server with IIS Installed

Index	Counter or Object Name	Description or Help Text
758	Unassigned Space Exec Write Copy	*Unassigned Space* is mapped and committed virtual memory in use by the process that is not attributable to any particular image being executed by that process. *Execute Write Copy* is memory that can be executed by programs as well as read and written. This type of protection is used when memory needs to be shared between processes. If the sharing processes only read the memory, then they will all use the same memory. If a sharing process desires write access, a copy of this memory will be made for that process.
760	Image Space No Access	*Image Space* is the virtual address space in use by the images being executed by the process. This is the sum of all the address space with this protection allocated by images run by the selected process. *No Access protection* prevents a process from writing to or reading from these pages and will generate an access violation if either is attempted.
762	Image Space Read Only	*Image Space* is the virtual address space in use by the images being executed by the process. This is the sum of all the address space with this protection allocated by images run by the selected process. *Read Only protection* prevents the contents of these pages from being modified. Any attempts to write or modify these pages will generate an access violation.
764	Image Space Read/Write	*Image Space* is the virtual address space in use by the images being executed by the process. This is the sum of all the address space with this protection allocated by images run by the selected process. *Read/Write protection* allows a process to read, modify, and write to these pages.
766	Image Space Write Copy	*Image Space* is the virtual address space in use by the images being executed by the process. This is the sum of all the address space with this protection allocated by images run by the selected process *Write Copy protection* is used when memory is shared for reading but not for writing. When processes are reading this memory, they can share the same memory; however, when a sharing process wants to have read/write access to this shared memory, a copy of that memory is made for writing to.
768	Image Space Executable	*Image Space* is the virtual address space in use by the images being executed by the process. This is the sum of all the address space with this protection allocated by images run by the selected process. *Executable memory* is memory that can be executed by programs, but may not be read or written. This type of protection is not supported by all processor types.
770	Image Space Exec Read Only	*Image Space* is the virtual address space in use by the images being executed by the process. This is the sum of all the address space with this protection allocated by images run by the selected process. *Execute/Read Only memory* is memory that can be executed as well as read.
772	Image Space Exec Read/Write	*Image Space* is the virtual address space in use by the images being executed by the process. This is the sum of all the address space with this protection allocated by images run by the selected process. *Execute/Read/Write memory* is memory that can be executed by programs as well as read, and written, and modified.
774	Image Space Exec Write Copy	*Image Space* is the virtual address space in use by the images being executed by the process. This is the sum of all the address space with this protection allocated by images run by the selected process. *Execute Write Copy* is memory that can be executed by programs as well as read and written. This type of protection is used when memory needs to be shared between processes. If the sharing processes only read the memory, they will all use the same memory. If a sharing process desires write access, a copy of this memory will be made for that process.

T A B L E D . 1 C O N T I N U E D : Registry Performance Counters on a Windows NT Server with IIS Installed

Index	Counter or Object Name	Description or Help Text
776	Bytes Image Reserved	*Bytes Image Reserved* is the sum of all virtual memory reserved by images run within this process.
778	Bytes Image Free	*Bytes Image Free* is the amount of virtual address space that is not in use or reserved by images within this process.
780	Bytes Reserved	*Bytes Reserved* is the total amount of virtual memory reserved for future use by this process.
782	Bytes Free	*Bytes Free* is the total unused virtual address space of this process.
784	ID Process	*ID Process* is the unique identifier of this process. ID Process numbers are reused, so they only identify a process for the lifetime of that process.
786	Process Address Space	The *Process Address Space object type* displays details about the virtual memory usage and allocation of the selected process.
788	No Access	*No Access protection* prevents a process from writing or reading these pages and will generate an access violation if either is attempted.
790	Read Only	*Read Only protection* prevents the contents of these pages from being modified. Any attempts to write or modify these pages will generate an access violation.
792	Read/Write	*Read/Write protection* allows a process to read, modify and write to these pages.
794	Write Copy	*Write Copy protection* is used when memory is shared for reading but not for writing. When processes are reading this memory, they can share the same memory; however, when a sharing process wants to have read/write access to this shared memory, a copy of that memory is made for writing to.
796	Executable	*Executable memory* is memory that can be executed by programs, but may not be read or written. This type of protection is not supported by all processor types.
798	ExecRead Only	*Execute/Read Only memory* is memory that can be executed as well as read.
800	ExecRead/Write	*Execute/Read/Write memory* is memory that can be executed by programs as well as read and written.
802	Exec Write Copy	*Exec Write Copy* is memory that can be executed by programs as well as read and written. This type of protection is used when memory needs to be shared between processes. If the sharing processes only read the memory, they will all use the same memory. If a sharing process desires write access, a copy of this memory will be made for that process.
804	ID Thread	*ID Thread* is the unique identifier of this thread. ID Thread numbers are reused, so they only identify a thread for the lifetime of that thread.
810	Mailslot Opens Failed/sec	*Mailslot Opens Failed/sec* indicates the rate of mailslot messages received by this workstation that were to be delivered to mailslots that are not present on this workstation.
812	Duplicate Master Announcements	*Duplicate Master Announcements* indicates the number of times that the master browser has detected another master browser on the same domain.
814	Illegal Datagrams/sec	*Illegal Datagrams/sec* is the rate of incorrectly formatted datagrams that have been received by the workstation.

TABLE D.1 CONTINUED: Registry Performance Counters on a Windows NT Server with IIS Installed

Index	Counter or Object Name	Description or Help Text
816	Thread Details	The *Thread Details object* contains the thread counters that are time consuming to collect.
818	Cache Bytes	*Cache Bytes* measures the number of bytes currently in use by the system Cache. The system Cache is used to buffer data retrieved from disk or LAN. The system Cache uses memory not in use by active processes in the computer.
820	Cache Bytes Peak	*Cache Bytes Peak* measures the maximum number of bytes used by the system Cache. The system Cache is used to buffer data retrieved from disk or LAN. The system Cache uses memory not in use by active processes in the computer.
822	Pages Input/sec	*Pages Input/sec* is the number of pages read from the disk to resolve memory references to pages that were not in memory at the time of the reference. This counter includes paging traffic on behalf of the system Cache to access file data for applications. This is an important counter to observe if you are concerned about excessive memory pressure (that is, thrashing) and the excessive paging that may result.
824	FTP Server	The *FTP Server object type* includes counters specific to the FTP Server service.
826	Bytes Sent/sec	*Bytes Sent/sec* is the rate that data bytes are sent by the FTP Server.
828	Bytes Received/sec	*Bytes Received/sec* is the rate that data bytes are received by the FTP Server.
830	Bytes Total/sec	*Bytes Total/sec* is the sum of Bytes Sent/sec and Bytes Received/sec. This is the total rate of bytes transferred by the FTP Server.
832	Files Sent	*Files Sent* is the total number of files sent by the FTP Server.
834	Files Received	*Files Received* is the total number of files received by the FTP Server.
836	Files Total	*Files Total* is the sum of Files Sent and Files Received. This is the total number of files transferred by the FTP Server.
838	Current Anonymous Users	*Current Anonymous Users* is the number of anonymous users currently connected to the FTP Server.
840	Current NonAnonymous Users	*Current NonAnonymous Users* is the number of nonanonymous users currently connected to the FTP Server.
842	Total Anonymous Users	*Total Anonymous Users* is the total number of anonymous users that have ever connected to the FTP Server.
844	Total NonAnonymous Users	*Total NonAnonymous Users* is the total number of nonanonymous users that have ever connected to the FTP Server.
846	Maximum Anonymous Users	*Maximum Anonymous Users* is the maximum number of anonymous users simultaneously connected to the FTP Server.
848	Maximum NonAnonymous Users	*Maximum NonAnonymous Users* is the maximum number of nonanonymous users simultaneously connected to the FTP Server.
850	Current Connections	*Current Connections* is the current number of connections to the FTP Server.
852	Maximum Connections	*Maximum Connections* is the maximum number of simultaneous connections to the FTP Server.
854	Connection Attempts	*Connection Attempts* is the number of connection attempts that have been made to the FTP Server.

TABLE D.1 CONTINUED: Registry Performance Counters on a Windows NT Server with IIS Installed

Index	Counter or Object Name	Description or Help Text
856	Logon Attempts	*Logon Attempts* is the number of logon attempts that have been made by the FTP Server.
870	RAS Port	The *RAS Port object type* handles individual ports of the RAS device on your system.
872	Bytes Transmitted	*Bytes Transmitted* is the number of bytes transmitted total for this connection.
874	Bytes Received	*Bytes Received* is the number of bytes received total for this connection.
876	Frames Transmitted	*Frames Transmitted* is the number of data frames transmitted total for this connection.
878	Frames Received	*Frames Received* is the number of data frames received total for this connection.
880	Percent Compression Out	*Percent Compression Out* is the compression ratio for bytes being transmitted.
882	Percent Compression In	*Percent Compression In* is the compression ratio for bytes being received.
884	CRC Errors	*CRC Errors* is the total number of CRC Errors for this connection. CRC Errors occur when the frame received contains erroneous data.
886	Timeout Errors	*Timeout Errors* is the total number of Timeout Errors for this connection. Timeout Errors occur when an expected object is not received in time.
888	Serial Overrun Errors	*Serial Overrun Errors* is the total number of Serial Overrun Errors for this connection. Serial Overrun Errors occur when the hardware cannot handle the rate at which data is received.
890	Alignment Errors	*Alignment Errors* is the total number of Alignment Errors for this connection. Alignment Errors occur when a byte received is different from the byte expected.
892	Buffer Overrun Errors	*Buffer Overrun Errors* is the total number of Buffer Overrun Errors for this connection. Buffer Overrun Errors occurs when the software cannot handle the rate at which data is received.
894	Total Errors	*Total Errors* is the total number of CRC, Timeout, Serial Overrun, Alignment, and Buffer Overrun Errors for this connection.
896	Bytes Transmitted/Sec	*Bytes Transmitted/Sec* is the number of bytes transmitted per second.
898	Bytes Received/Sec	*Bytes Received/Sec* is the number of bytes received per second.
900	Frames Transmitted/Sec	*Frames Transmitted/Sec* is the number of frames transmitted per second.
902	Frames Received/Sec	*Frames Received/Sec* is the number of frames received per second.
904	Total Errors/Sec	*Total Errors/Sec* is the total number of CRC, Timeout, Serial Overrun, Alignment, and Buffer Overrun Errors per second.
906	RAS Total	The *RAS Total object type* handles all combined ports of the RAS device on your system.
908	Total Connections	*Total Connections* is the total number of Remote Access connections.
920	WINS Server	The *WINS Server object type* includes counters specific to the WINS Server service.
922	Unique Registrations/sec	*Unique Registrations/sec* is the rate at which unique registrations are received by the WINS server.
924	Group Registrations/sec	*Group Registrations/sec* is the rate at which group registrations are received by the WINS server.

TABLE D.1 CONTINUED: Registry Performance Counters on a Windows NT Server with IIS Installed

Index	Counter or Object Name	Description or Help Text
926	Total Number of Registrations/sec	*Total Number of Registrations/sec* is the sum of the Unique and Group registrations per sec. This is the total rate at which registrations are received by the WINS server.
928	Unique Renewals/sec	*Unique Renewals/sec* is the rate at which unique renewals are received by the WINS server.
930	Group Renewals/sec	*Group Renewals/sec* is the rate at which group renewals are received by the WINS server.
932	Total Number of Renewals/sec	*Renewals/sec* is the sum of the Unique and Group renewals per sec. This is the total rate at which renewals are received by the WINS server.
934	Releases/sec	The total number of *Releases/sec* is the rate at which releases are received by the WINS server.
936	Queries/sec	*Queries/sec* is the rate at which queries are received by the WINS server.
938	Unique Conflicts/sec	*Unique Conflicts/sec* is the rate at which unique registrations/renewals received by the WINS server resulted in conflicts with records in the database.
940	Group Conflicts/sec	*Group Conflicts/sec* is the rate at which group registration received by the WINS server resulted in conflicts with records in the database.
942	Total Number of Conflicts/sec	*Total Number of Conflicts/sec* is the sum of the Unique and Group conflicts per sec. This is the total rate at which conflicts were seen by the WINS server.
944	Successful Releases/sec	*Successful Releases/sec* is the total number of Successful Releases/sec.
946	Failed Releases/sec	*Failed Releases/sec* is the total number of Failed Releases/sec.
948	Successful Queries/sec	*Successful Queries/sec* is the total number of Successful Queries/sec.
950	Failed Queries/sec	Failed Queries/sec is the Total Number of Failed Queries/sec.
952	Handle Count	*Handle Count* is the total number of handles currently open by this process. This number is the sum of the handles currently open by each thread in this process.
1000	MacFile Server	*MacFile Server* is the Services for Macintosh AFP File Server.
1002	Max Paged Memory	*Max Paged Memory* is the maximum amount of paged memory resources used by the MacFile Server.
1004	Current Paged Memory	*Current Paged Memory* is the current amount of paged memory resources used by the MacFile Server.
1006	Max NonPaged Memory	*Max NonPaged Memory* is the maximum amount of nonpaged memory resources used by the MacFile Server.
1008	Current NonPaged memory	*Current NonPaged memory* is the current amount of nonpaged memory resources used by the MacFile Server.
1010	Current Sessions	*Current Sessions* is the number of sessions currently connected to the MacFile server. Indicates current server activity.
1012	Maximum Sessions	*Maximum Sessions* is the maximum number of sessions connected at one time to the MacFile server. Indicates usage level of server.
1014	Current Files Open	*Current Files Open* is the number of internal files currently open in the MacFile server. This count does not include files opened on behalf of Macintosh clients.

TABLE D.1 CONTINUED: Registry Performance Counters on a Windows NT Server with IIS Installed

Index	Counter or Object Name	Description or Help Text
1016	Maximum Files Open	*Maximum Files Open* is the maximum number of internal files open at one time in the MacFile server. This count does not include files opened on behalf of Macintosh clients.
1018	Failed Logons	*Failed Logons* is the number of failed logon attempts to the MacFile server. Can indicate whether password guessing programs are being used to crack the security on the server.
1020	Data Read/sec	*Data Read/sec* is the number of bytes read from disk per second.
1022	Data Written/sec	*Data Written/sec* is the number of bytes written to disk per second.
1024	Data Received/sec	*Data Received/sec* is the number of bytes received from the network per second. Indicates how busy the server is.
1026	Data Transmitted/sec	*Data Transmitted/sec* is the number of bytes sent on the network per second. Indicates how busy the server is.
1028	Current Queue Length	*Current Queue Length* is the number of outstanding work items waiting to be processed.
1030	Maximum Queue Length	*Maximum Queue Length* is the maximum number of outstanding work items waiting at one time.
1032	Current Threads	*Current Threads* is the current number of threads used by MacFile server. Indicates how busy the server is.
1034	Maximum Threads	*Maximum Threads* is the maximum number of threads used by MacFile server. Indicates peak usage level of the server.
1050	AppleTalk	*AppleTalk* is the AppleTalk Protocol.
1052	Packets In/sec	*Packets In/sec* is the Number of packets received per second by AppleTalk on this port.
1054	Packets Out/sec	*Packets Out/sec* is the Number of packets sent per second by AppleTalk on this port.
1056	Bytes In/sec	*Bytes In/sec* is the Number of bytes received per second by AppleTalk on this port.
1058	Bytes Out/sec	*Bytes Out/sec* is the Number of bytes sent per second by AppleTalk on this port.
1060	Average Time/DDP Packet	*Average Time/DDP Packet* is the Average time in milliseconds to process a DDP packet on this port.
1062	DDP Packets/sec	*DDP Packets/sec* is the Number of DDP packets per second received by AppleTalk on this port.
1064	Average Time/AARP Packet	*Average Time/AARP Packet* is the Average time in milliseconds to process an AARP packet on this port.
1066	AARP Packets/sec	*AARP Packets/sec* is the Number of AARP packets per second received by AppleTalk on this port.
1068	Average Time/ATP Packet	*Average Time/ATP Packet* is the Average time in milliseconds to process an ATP packet on this port.
1070	ATP Packets/sec	*ATP Packets/sec* is the Number of ATP packets per second received by AppleTalk on this port.

TABLE D.1 CONTINUED: Registry Performance Counters on a Windows NT Server with IIS Installed

Index	Counter or Object Name	Description or Help Text
1072	Average Time/NBP Packet	*Average Time/NBP Packet* is the Average time in milliseconds to process an NBP packet on this port.
1074	NBP Packets/sec	*NBP Packets/sec* is the Number of NBP packets per second received by AppleTalk on this port.
1076	Average Time/ZIP Packet	*Average Time/ZIP Packet* is the Average time in milliseconds to process a ZIP packet on this port.
1078	ZIP Packets/sec	*ZIP Packets/sec* is the Number of ZIP packets per second received by AppleTalk on this port.
1080	Average Time/RTMP Packet	*Average Time/RTMP Packet* is the average time in milliseconds to process an RTMP packet on this port.
1082	RTMP Packets/sec	*RTMP Packets/sec* is the number of RTMP packets per second received by AppleTalk on this port.
1084	ATP Retries Local	*ATP Retries Local* is the number of ATP requests retransmitted on this port.
1086	ATP Response Timouts	*ATP Response Timouts* is the number of ATP release timers that have expired on this port.
1088	ATP XO Response/sec	*ATP XO Response/sec* is the number of ATP Exactly-once transaction responses per second on this port.
1090	ATP ALO Response/sec	*ATP ALO Response/sec* is the Number of ATP At-least-once transaction responses per second on this port.
1092	ATP Recvd Release/sec	*ATP Recvd Release/sec* is the Number of ATP transaction release packets per second received on this port.
1094	Current NonPaged Pool	*Current NonPaged Pool* is the current amount of nonpaged memory resources used by AppleTalk.
1096	Packets Routed In/Sec	*Packets Routed In/Sec* is the number of packets routed in on this port.
1098	Packets dropped	*Packets dropped* is the number of packets dropped due to resource limitations on this port.
1100	ATP Retries Remote	*ATP Retries Remote* is the number of ATP requests retransmitted to this port.
1102	Packets Routed Out/sec	*Packets Routed Out/sec* is the number of packets routed out on this port.
1110	Network Segment	*Network Segment* provides network statistics for the local network segment via the Network Monitor Service.
1112	Total frames received/second	*Total frames received/second* is the total number of frames received per second on this network segment.
1114	Total bytes received/second	*Total bytes received/second* is the number of bytes received per second on this network segment.
1116	Broadcast frames received/second	*Broadcast frames received/second* is the number of Broadcast frames received per second on this network segment.
1118	Multicast frames received/second	*Multicast frames received/second* is the number of Multicast frames received per second on this network segment.

TABLE D.1 CONTINUED: Registry Performance Counters on a Windows NT Server with IIS Installed

Index	Counter or Object Name	Description or Help Text
1120	% Network utilization	*% Network utilization* is the percentage of network bandwidth in use on this network segment.
1124	% Broadcast Frames	*% Broadcast Frames* is the percentage of network bandwidth that is made up of broadcast traffic on this network segment.
1126	% Multicast Frames	*% Multicast Frames* is the percentage of network bandwidth that is made up of multicast traffic on this network segment.
1150	Telephony	*Telephony* is the telephony system.
1152	Lines	*Lines* is the number of telephone lines serviced by this computer.
1154	Telephone Devices	*Telephone Devices* is the number of telephone devices serviced by this computer.
1156	Active Lines	*Active Lines* is the number of telephone lines serviced by this computer that are currently active.
1158	Active Telephones	*Active Telephones* is the number of telephone devices that are currently being monitored.
1160	Outgoing Calls/sec	*Outgoing Calls/sec* is the rate of outgoing calls made by this computer.
1162	Incoming Calls/sec	*Incoming Calls/sec* is the rate of incoming calls answered by this computer.
1164	Client Apps	*Client Apps* is the number of applications that are currently using telephony services.
1166	Current Outgoing Calls	*Current Outgoing Calls* is the Current outgoing calls being serviced by this computer.
1168	Current Incoming Calls	*Current Incoming Calls* is the Current incoming calls being serviced by this computer.
1228	Gateway Service For NetWare	*Gateway Service For NetWare* is the Gateway Service for NetWare object type.
1230	Client Service For NetWare	*Client Service For NetWare* is the Client Service for NetWare object type.
1232	Packet Burst Read NCP Count/sec	*Packet Burst Read NCP Count/sec* is the rate of NetWare Core Protocol requests for Packet Burst Read. Packet Burst is a windowing protocol that improves performance.
1234	Packet Burst Read Timeouts/sec	*Packet Burst Read Timeouts/sec* is the rate the NetWare Service needs to retransmit a Burst Read Request because the NetWare server took too long to respond.
1236	Packet Burst Write NCP Count/sec	*Packet Burst Write NCP Count/sec* is the rate of NetWare Core Protocol requests for Packet Burst Write. Packet Burst is a windowing protocol that improves performance.
1238	Packet Burst Write Timeouts/sec	*Packet Burst Write Timeouts/sec* is the rate the NetWare Service needs to retransmit a Burst Write Request because the NetWare server took too long to respond.
1240	Packet Burst IO/sec	*Packet Burst IO/sec* is the sum of Packet Burst Read NCPs/sec and Packet Burst Write NCPs/sec.
1242	Connect NetWare 2.x	*Connect NetWare 2.x* counts connections to NetWare 2.x servers.
1244	Connect NetWare 3.x	*Connect NetWare 3.x* counts connections to NetWare 3.x servers.
1246	Connect NetWare 4.x	*Connect NetWare 4.x* counts connections to NetWare 4.x servers.
1260	Logon Total	*Logon Total* includes all interactive logons, network logons, service logons, successful logon, and failed logons since the machine is last rebooted.

TABLE D.1 CONTINUED: Registry Performance Counters on a Windows NT Server with IIS Installed

Index	Counter or Object Name	Description or Help Text
1300	Server Work Queues	*Server Work Queues* explain text.
1302	Queue Length	*Queue Length* is the current length of the server work queue for this CPU. A sustained queue length greater than four may indicate processor congestion. This is an instantaneous count, not an average over time.
1304	Active Threads	*Active Threads* is the number of threads currently working on a request from the server client for this CPU. The system keeps this number as low as possible to minimize unnecessary context switching. This is an instantaneous count for the CPU, not an average over time.
1306	Available Threads	*Available Threads* is the number of server threads on this CPU not currently working on requests from a client. The server dynamically adjusts the number of threads to maximize server performance.
1308	Available Work Items	*Available Work Items* represents a request from a client, represented in the server as a 'work item,' and the server maintains a pool of available work items per CPU to speed processing. This is the instantaneous number of available work items for this CPU. A sustained near-zero value indicates the need to increase the MinFreeWorkItems registry value for the Server service. This value will always be 0 in the Blocking Queue instance.
1310	Borrowed Work Items	*Borrowed Work Items* represents a request from a client, represented in the server as a 'work item,' and the server maintains a pool of available work items per CPU to speed processing. When a CPU runs out of work items, it borrows a free work item from another CPU. An increasing value of this running counter may indicate the need to increase the 'MaxWorkItems' or 'MinFreeWorkItems' registry values for the Server service. This value will always be 0 in the Blocking Queue instance.
1312	Work Item Shortages	*Work Item Shortages* represents a request from a client, represented in the server as a 'work item,' and the server maintains a pool of available work items per CPU to speed processing. A sustained value greater than zero indicates the need to increase the 'MaxWorkItems' registry value for the Server service. This value will always be 0 in the Blocking Queue instance.
1314	Current Clients	*Current Clients* is the instantaneous count of the clients being serviced by this CPU. The server actively balances the client load across all of the CPUs in the system. This value will always be 0 in the Blocking Queue instance.
1320	Bytes Transferred/sec	*Bytes Transferred/sec* is the rate at which the Server is sending and receiving bytes with the network clients on this CPU. This value is a measure of how busy the Server is.
1324	Read Bytes/sec	*Read Bytes/sec* is the rate the server is reading data from files for the clients on this CPU. This value is a measure of how busy the Server is.
1328	Write Bytes/sec	*Write Bytes/sec* is the rate the server is writing data to files for the clients on this CPU. This value is a measure of how busy the Server is.
1332	Total Operations/sec	*Total Operations/sec* is the rate the Server is performing file read and file write operations for the clients on this CPU. This value is a measure of how busy the Server is. This value will always be 0 in the Blocking Queue instance.
1334	DPCs Queued/sec	*DPCs Queued/sec* is the rate DPC objects are queued to this processor's DPC queue.

TABLE D.1 CONTINUED: Registry Performance Counters on a Windows NT Server with IIS Installed

Index	Counter or Object Name	Description or Help Text
1336	DPC Rate	*DPC Rate* is the average rate DPC objects are queued to this processor's DPC queue per clock tick.
1338	DPC Bypasses/sec	*DPC Bypasses/sec* is the rate Dispatch interrupts were short-circuited.
1340	APC Bypasses/sec	*APC Bypasses/sec* is the rate kernel APC interrupts were short-circuited.
1342	Total DPCs Queued/sec	*Total DPCs Queued/sec* is the rate DPC objects are queued to all processors' DPC queues.
1344	Total DPC Rate	*Total DPC Rate* is the average rate DPC objects are queued to all processors' DPC queue per clock tick.
1346	Total DPC Bypasses/sec	*Total DPC Bypasses/sec* is the overall rate Dispatch interrupts were short-circuited across all processors.
1348	Total APC Bypasses/sec	*Total APC Bypasses/sec* is the overall rate kernel APC interrupts were short-circuited across all processors.
1350	% Registry Quota In Use	*% Registry Quota In Use* indicates the percentage of the Total Registry Quota Allowed currently in use by the system.
1400	Avg. Disk Queue Length	*Avg. Disk Queue Length* is the average number of both read and write requests that were queued for the selected disk during the sample interval.
1402	Avg. Disk Read Queue Length	*Avg. Disk Read Queue Length* is the average number of read requests that were queued for the selected disk during the sample interval.
1404	Avg. Disk Write Queue Length	*Avg. Disk Write Queue Length* is the average number of write requests that were queued for the selected disk during the sample interval.
1406	% Committed Bytes In Use	*% Committed Bytes In Use* is the ratio of the Committed Bytes to the Commit Limit. This represents the amount of available virtual memory in use. Note that the Commit Limit may change if the paging file is extended. This is an instantaneous value, not an average.
1846	End Marker	*End marker* is the end marker.
1848	Internet Information Services Global	The Cache Summary for HTTP, FTP, & Gopher type contains the additive memory cache counters from the Microsoft HTTP, FTP and Gopher Services.
1850	Cache Size	*Cache Size* is the configured maximum size of the shared HTTP, FTP & Gopher memory cache.
1852	Cache Used	*Cache Used* is the total number of bytes currently containing cached data in the shared memory cache. This includes directory listings, file handle tracking, and service specific objects.
1854	Cached File Handles	*Cached File Handles* is the number of open file handles cached by all of the Internet Information Services.
1856	Directory Listings	*Directory Listings* is the number of cached directory listings cached by all of the Internet Information Services.
1858	Objects	*Objects* is the number of cached objects cached by all of the Internet Information Services. The objects include file handle tracking objects, directory listing objects, and service specific objects.

TABLE D.1 CONTINUED: Registry Performance Counters on a Windows NT Server with IIS Installed

Index	Counter or Object Name	Description or Help Text
1860	Cache Flushes	*Cache Flushes* is the number of times a portion of the memory cache has been expired due to file or directory changes in an Internet Information Services directory tree.
1862	Cache Hits	*Cache Hits* is the total number of times a file open, directory listing, or service specific objects request was found in the cache.
1864	Cache Misses	*Cache Misses* is the total number of times a file open, directory listing, or service specific objects request was not found in the cache.
1866	Cache Hits %	*Cache Hits %* is the ratio of cache hits to all cache requests.
1870	Total Allowed Async I/O Requests	*Total Allowed Async I/O Requests* are the async I/O requests allowed by Bandwidth Throttler.
1872	Total Blocked Async I/O Requests	*Total Blocked Async I/O Requests* are the total async I/O requests blocked by Bandwidth Throttler.
1874	Total Rejected Async I/O Requests	*Total Rejected Async I/O Requests* are the total async I/O requests rejected by Bandwidth Throttler.
1876	Current Blocked Async I/O Requests	*Current Blocked Async I/O Requests* are the current async I/O requests blocked by Bandwidth Throttler.
1878	Measured Async I/O Bandwidth usage/	*Measured Async I/O Bandwidth usage/* is the measured bandwidth of async I/O averaged over a minute.
1880	HTTP Service	The HTTP Service object type includes counters specific to the HTTP Server service.
1882	Bytes Sent/sec	*Bytes Sent/sec* is the rate that data bytes are sent by the HTTP Server.
1884	Bytes Received/sec	*Bytes Received/sec* is the rate that data bytes are received by the HTTP Server.
1886	Bytes Total/sec	*Bytes Total/sec* is the sum of Bytes Sent/sec and Bytes Received/sec. This is the total rate of bytes transferred by the HTTP Server.
1888	Files Sent	*Files Sent* is the total number of files sent by the HTTP Server.
1890	Files Received	*Files Received* is the total number of files received by the HTTP Server.
1892	Files Total	*Files Total* is the sum of Files Sent and Files Received. This is the total number of files transferred by the HTTP Server.
1894	Current Anonymous Users	*Current Anonymous Users* is the number of anonymous users currently connected to the HTTP Server.
1896	Current NonAnonymous Users	*Current NonAnonymous Users* is the number of nonanonymous users currently connected to the HTTP Server.
1898	Total Anonymous Users	*Total Anonymous Users* is the total number of anonymous users that have ever connected to the HTTP Server.
1900	Total NonAnonymous Users	*Total NonAnonymous Users* is the total number of nonanonymous users that have ever connected to the HTTP Server.
1902	Maximum Anonymous Users	*Maximum Anonymous Users* is the maximum number of anonymous users simultaneously connected to the HTTP Server.

TABLE D.1 CONTINUED: Registry Performance Counters on a Windows NT Server with IIS Installed

Index	Counter or Object Name	Description or Help Text
1904	Maximum NonAnonymous Users	*Maximum NonAnonymous Users* is the maximum number of nonanonymous users simultaneously connected to the HTTP Server.
1906	Current Connections	*Current Connections* is the current number of connections to the HTTP Server.
1908	Maximum Connections	*Maximum Connections* is the maximum number of simultaneous connections to the HTTP Server.
1910	Connection Attempts	*Connection Attempts* is the number of connection attempts that have been made to the HTTP Server.
1912	Logon Attempts	*Logon Attempts* is the number of logon attempts that have been made by the HTTP Server.
1914	Get Requests	*Get Requests* is the number of HTTP requests using the GET method. Get requests are generally used for basic file retrievals or image maps, though they can be used with forms.
1916	Post Requests	*Post Requests* is the number of HTTP requests using the POST method. Post requests are generally used for forms or gateway requests.
1918	Head Requests	*Head Requests* is the number of HTTP requests using the HEAD method. Head requests generally indicate that a client is querying the state of a document they already have open, to see if it needs to be refreshed.
1920	Other Request Methods	*Other Request Methods* is the number of HTTP requests that are not GET, POST or HEAD methods. These may include PUT, DELETE, LINK or other methods supported by gateway applications.
1922	CGI Requests	*CGI Requests* are custom common gateway interface executables (.exe) the administrator can install to add forms processing or other dynamic data sources.
1924	ISAPI Extension Requests	*ISAPI Extension Requests* are custom gateway Dynamic Link Libraries (.dlls) the administrator can install to add forms processing or other dynamic data sources.
1926	Not Found Errors	*Not Found Errors* is the number of requests that couldn't be satisfied by the server because the requested document could not be found. These are generally reported as an HTTP 404 error code to the client.
1928	Current CGI Requests	*Current CGI Requests* is the current number of CGI requests that are simultaneously being processed by the HTTP Server. This includes WAIS index queries.
1930	Current ISAPI Extension Requests	*Current ISAPI Extension Requests* is the current number of Extension requests that are simultaneously being processed by the HTTP Server.
1932	Maximum CGI Requests	*Maximum CGI Requests* is the maximum number of CGI requests that have been simultaneously processed by the HTTP Server. This includes WAIS index queries.
1934	Maximum ISAPI Extension Requests	*Maximum ISAPI Extension Requests* is the maximum number of Extension requests that have been simultaneously processed by the HTTP Server.
1936	Connections/sec	*Connections/sec* is the number of HTTP requests being handled per second.
1938	Gopher Service	The *Gopher Server object type* includes counters specific to the Gopher Server service.
1940	Bytes Sent/sec	*Bytes Sent/sec* is the rate that data bytes are sent by the Gopher Server.

TABLE D.1 CONTINUED: Registry Performance Counters on a Windows NT Server with IIS Installed

Index	Counter or Object Name	Description or Help Text
1942	Bytes Received/sec	*Bytes Received/sec* is the rate that data bytes are received by the Gopher Server.
1944	Bytes Total/sec	*Bytes Total/sec* is the sum of Bytes Sent/sec and Bytes Received/sec. This is the total rate of bytes transferred by the Gopher Server.
1946	Files Sent	*Files Sent* is the total number of files sent by the Gopher Server.
1948	Directory Listings Sent	*Directory Listings Sent* is the total number of directory listings sent by the Gopher Server.
1950	Searches Sent	*Searches Sent* is the total number of searches performed by the Gopher Server.
1952	Current Anonymous Users	*Current Anonymous Users* is the number of anonymous users currently connected to the Gopher Server.
1954	Current NonAnonymous Users	*Current NonAnonymous Users* is the number of nonanonymous users currently connected to the Gopher Server.
1956	Total Anonymous Users	*Total Anonymous Users* is the total number of anonymous users that have ever connected to the Gopher Server.
1958	Total NonAnonymous Users	*Total NonAnonymous Users* is the total number of nonanonymous users that have ever connected to the Gopher Server.
1960	Maximum Anonymous Users	*Maximum Anonymous Users* is the maximum number of anonymous users simultaneously connected to the Gopher Server.
1962	Maximum NonAnonymous Users	*Maximum NonAnonymous Users* is the maximum number of nonanonymous users simultaneously connected to the Gopher Server.
1964	Current Connections	*Current Connections* is the current number of connections to the Gopher Server.
1966	Maximum Connections	*Maximum Connections* is the maximum number of simultaneous connections to the Gopher Server.
1968	Connection Attempts	*Connection Attempts* is the number of connection attempts that have been made to the Gopher Server.
1970	Logon Attempts	*Logon Attempts* is the number of logon attempts that have been made by the Gopher Server.
1972	Aborted Connections	*Aborted Connections* is the total number of connections aborted due to error or over the limit requests made to the Gopher Server.
1974	Connections in Error	*Connections in Error* is the number of connections that had errors when processed by the Gopher Server.
1976	Gopher Plus Requests	*Gopher Plus Requests* is the number of Gopher Plus requests received by Gopher Server.
1978	FTP Service	The *FTP Server object type* includes counters specific to the FTP Server service.
1980	Bytes Sent/sec	*Bytes Sent/sec* is the rate that data bytes are sent by the FTP Server.
1982	Bytes Received/sec	*Bytes Received/sec* is the rate that data bytes are received by the FTP Server.
1984	Bytes Total/sec	*Bytes Total/sec* is the sum of Bytes Sent/sec and Bytes Received/sec. This is the total rate of bytes transferred by the FTP Server.

TABLE D.1 CONTINUED: Registry Performance Counters on a Windows NT Server with IIS Installed

Index	Counter or Object Name	Description or Help Text
1986	Files Sent	*Files Sent* is the total number of files sent by the FTP Server.
1988	Files Received	*Files Received* is the total number of files received by the FTP Server.
1990	Files Total	*Files Total* is the sum of Files Sent and Files Received. This is the total number of files transferred by the FTP Server.
1992	Current Anonymous Users	*Current Anonymous Users* is the number of anonymous users currently connected to the FTP Server.
1994	Current NonAnonymous Users	*Current NonAnonymous Users* is the number of nonanonymous users currently connected to the FTP Server.
1996	Total Anonymous Users	*Total Anonymous Users* is the total number of anonymous users that have ever connected to the FTP Server.
1998	Total NonAnonymous Users	*Total NonAnonymous Users* is the total number of nonanonymous users that have ever connected to the FTP Server.
2000	Maximum Anonymous Users	*Maximum Anonymous Users* is the maximum number of anonymous users simultaneously connected to the FTP Server.
2002	Maximum NonAnonymous Users	*Maximum NonAnonymous Users* is the maximum number of nonanonymous users simultaneously connected to the FTP Server.
2004	Current Connections	*Current Connections* is the current number of connections to the FTP Server.
2006	Maximum Connections	*Maximum Connections* is the maximum number of simultaneous connections to the FTP Server.
2008	Connection Attempts	*Connection Attempts* is the number of connection attempts that have been made to the FTP Server.
2010	Logon Attempts	*Logon Attempts* is the number of logon attempts that have been made by the FTP Server.

INDEX

Note to the Reader: Throughout this index **boldfaced** page numbers indicate primary discussions of a topic. *Italicized* page numbers indicate illustrations.

B

C

D

G

H

I

J

K

L

M

N

0

P

S

T

X

Y

Z

A Quick Reference to Essential Registry Keys

Hive	Sub-Hive	Description
HKEY_LOCAL_MACHINE	All hives	This is the main system description hive. This hive is critical to the execution of Windows NT.
HKEY_LOCAL_MACHINE\HARDWARE\DESCRIPTION\	All hives	Contains information about the hardware installed in the computer. Much of this hive is created at boot time, though some entries may be retained from previous executions.
HKEY_LOCAL_MACHINE\HARDWARE\DESCRIPTION\	System	Contains all system device information, excluding NIC and video devices.
HKEY_LOCAL_MACHINE\HARDWARE\DESCRIPTION\	System\Central-Processor	Information about the actual CPU, such as make, model, and version information
HKEY_LOCAL_MACHINE\HARDWARE\DEVICEMAP\	All hives	Contains basic device mapping and control information.
HKEY_LOCAL_MACHINE\HARDWARE\DEVICEMAP\	KeyboardClass	Contains keyboard device mapping.
HKEY_LOCAL_MACHINE\HARDWARE\DEVICEMAP\	KeyboardPort	Contains information about the keyboard port configuration.
HKEY_LOCAL_MACHINE\HARDWARE\DEVICEMAP\	PARALLEL PORTS	Contains information about the printer (parallel) port configuration.
HKEY_LOCAL_MACHINE\HARDWARE\DEVICEMAP\	PointerClass	Contains information about the mouse.
HKEY_LOCAL_MACHINE\HARDWARE\DEVICEMAP\	PointerPort	Contains information on what port (mouse port, PS/2 mouse port, serial port, and so on) that the mouse (pointer) is connected to.
HKEY_LOCAL_MACHINE\HARDWARE\DEVICEMAP\	Scsi	Contains general disk interface information for both IDE and SCSI devices.
HKEY_LOCAL_MACHINE\HARDWARE\DEVICEMAP\	SERIALCOMM	Contains Serial communications device configurations.
HKEY_LOCAL_MACHINE\HARDWARE\DEVICEMAP\	VIDEO	Contains video configuration information.
HKEY_LOCAL_MACHINE\HARDWARE\RESOURCEMAP\	All hives	Contains information about how resources (hardware) are mapped in the system.